Praise for the previous edition of *R in Action*

"Essential to anyone doing data analysis with R, whether in industry or academia."
—Cristofer Weber, NeoGrid

"A go-to reference for general R and many statistics questions."
—George Gaines, KYOS Systems Inc.

"Accessible language, realistic examples, and clear code."
—Samuel D. McQuillin, University of Houston

"Offers a gentle learning curve to those starting out with R for the first time."
—Indrajit Sen Gupta, Mu Sigma Business Solutions

R in Action, Third Edition

R in Action, Third Edition

R in Action, Third Edition
DATA ANALYSIS AND GRAPHICS WITH R AND TIDYVERSE

ROBERT I. KABACOFF

MANNING
SHELTER ISLAND

For online information and ordering of this and other Manning books, please visit
www.manning.com. The publisher offers discounts on this book when ordered in quantity.
For more information, please contact

> Special Sales Department
> Manning Publications Co.
> 20 Baldwin Road
> PO Box 761
> Shelter Island, NY 11964
> Email: orders@manning.com

Manning Publications Co.
20 Baldwin Road
PO Box 761
Shelter Island, NY 11964

Development editor:	Karen Miller
Technical development editor:	Mike Shepard
Review editor:	Aleksandar Dragosavljević
Production editor:	Deirdre S. Hiam
Copy editor:	Suzanne G. Fox
Proofreader:	Katie Tennant
Technical proofreader:	Ninoslav Cerkez
Typesetter and cover designer:	Marija Tudor

ISBN 9781617296055
Printed in the United States of America

brief contents

brief contents

contents

22 *Creating a package* 543

preface

What is the use of a book without pictures or conversations?

—Alice, *Alice's Adventures in Wonderland*

It's wondrous, with treasures to satiate desires both subtle and gross; but it's not for the timid.

—Q, "Q Who?" *Star Trek: The Next Generation*

When I began writing this book, I spent quite a bit of time searching for a good quote to start things off. I ended up with two. R is a wonderfully flexible platform and language for exploring, visualizing, and understanding data. I chose the quote from *Alice's Adventures in Wonderland* to capture the flavor of statistical analysis today—an interactive process of exploration, visualization, and interpretation.

The second quote reflects the generally held notion that R is difficult to learn. What I hope to show you is that it doesn't have to be. R is broad and powerful, with so many analytic and graphic functions available (more than 50,000 at last count) that it easily intimidates both novice and experienced users alike. But there is rhyme and reason to the apparent madness. With guidelines and instructions, you can navigate the tremendous resources available, selecting the tools you need to accomplish your work with style, elegance, efficiency—and more than a little coolness.

I first encountered R several years ago when I was applying for a new statistical consulting position. The prospective employer asked in the pre-interview material if I was conversant in R. Following the standard advice of recruiters, I immediately said yes and set off to learn it. I was an experienced statistician and researcher, had 25 years of experience as an SAS and SPSS programmer, and was fluent in a half-dozen programming languages. How hard could it be? Famous last words.

As I tried to learn the language (as fast as possible, with an interview looming), I found either tomes on the underlying structure of the language or dense treatises on specific advanced statistical methods, written by and for subject-matter experts. The online help was written in a Spartan style that was more reference than tutorial. Every time I thought I had a handle on the overall organization and capabilities of R, I found something new that made me feel ignorant and small.

To make sense of it all, I approached R as a data scientist. I thought about what it takes to successfully process, analyze, and understand data, including

- Accessing the data (getting the data into the application from multiple sources)
- Cleaning the data (coding missing data, fixing or deleting miscoded data, transforming variables into more useful formats)
- Annotating the data (to remember what each piece represents)
- Summarizing the data (getting descriptive statistics to help characterize the data)
- Visualizing the data (because a picture really is worth a thousand words)
- Modeling the data (uncovering relationships and testing hypotheses)
- Preparing the results (creating publication-quality tables and graphs)

Then I tried to understand how I could use R to accomplish each of these tasks. Because I learn best by teaching, I eventually created a website (www.statmethods.net) to document what I had learned.

Then, about a year later, Marjan Bace, Manning's publisher, called and asked if I would like to write a book on R. I had already written 50 journal articles, 4 technical manuals, numerous book chapters, and a book on research methodology, so how hard could it be? At the risk of sounding repetitive—famous last words.

The first edition came out in 2011, and the second edition came out in 2015. I started working on the third edition two-and-a-half years ago. Describing R has always been a moving target, but the last few years have seen a revolution of sorts. It's been driven by the growth of big data, the broad adoption of tidyverse (tidyverse.org) software, the rapid development of new predictive analytic and machine learning approaches, and the development of new and more powerful data visualization technologies. I wanted the third edition to do justice to these important changes.

The book you're holding is the one that I wished I had so many years ago. I have tried to provide you with a guide to R that will allow you to quickly access the power of this great open source endeavor, without all the frustration and angst. I hope you enjoy it.

P.S. I was offered the job but didn't take it. But learning R has taken my career in directions that I could never have anticipated. Life can be funny.

acknowledgments

Many people worked hard to make this a better book. They include the following:

- Marjan Bace, Manning's publisher, who asked me to write this book in the first place.

- Sebastian Stirling, Jennifer Stout, and Karen Miller, development editors on the first, second, and third editions, respectively. Each spent many hours helping me organize the material, clarify concepts, and generally make the text more interesting.

- Mike Shepard, technical proofreader, who helped uncover areas of confusion and provided an independent and expert eye for testing code. I came to rely on his careful reviews and considered judgment.

- Aleks Dragosavljevic, my review editor, who helped obtain reviewers and coordinate the review process.

- Deirdre Hiam, who helped shepherd this book through the production process, and her team of Suzanne G. Fox, my copy editor, and Katie Tennant, my proofreader.

- The peer reviewers who spent hours of their own time carefully reading through the material, finding typos, and making valuable substantive suggestions: Alain Lompo, Alessandro Puzielli, Arav Agarwal, Ashley Paul Eatly, Clemens Baader, Daniel C Daugherty, Daniel Kenney-Jung, Erico Lendzian, James Frohnhofer, Jean-François Morin, Jenice Tom, Jim Frohnhofer, Kay Engelhardt, Kelvin Meeks, Krishna Shrestha, Luis Felipe Medeiro Alves, Mario Giesel, Martin Perry, Nick Drozd, Nicole Koenigstein, Robert Samohyl, Tiklu Ganguly, Tom Jeffries, Ulrich Gauger, Vishal Singh.

- The many Manning Early Access Program (MEAP) participants who bought the book before it was finished, asked great questions, pointed out errors, and made helpful suggestions.

Each contributor has made this a better and more comprehensive book.

I would also like to acknowledge the many software authors who have contributed to making R such a powerful data analytic platform. They include not only the core developers, but also the selfless individuals who have created and maintain contributed packages, extending R's capabilities greatly. Appendix E provides a list of the authors of contributed packages described in this book. In particular, I would like to mention John Fox, Hadley Wickham, Frank E. Harrell, Jr., Deepayan Sarkar, and William Revelle, whose works I greatly admire. I have tried to represent their contributions accurately, and I remain solely responsible for any errors or distortions inadvertently included in this book.

I really should have started this book by thanking my wife and partner, Carol Lynn. Although she has no intrinsic interest in statistics or programming, she read each chapter multiple times and made countless corrections and suggestions. No greater love has any person than to read multivariate statistics for another. Just as important, she suffered the long nights and weekends that I spent writing this book with grace, support, and affection. There is no logical explanation why I should be this lucky.

There are two other people I would like to thank. One is my father, whose love of science was inspiring and who gave me an appreciation of the value of data. I miss him dearly. The other is Gary K. Burger, my mentor in graduate school. Gary got me interested in a career in statistics and teaching when I thought I wanted to be a clinician. This is all his fault.

about this book

If you picked up this book, you probably have some data that you need to collect, summarize, transform, explore, model, visualize, or present. If so, then R is for you. R has become the worldwide language for statistics, predictive analytics, and data visualization. It offers the widest range of methodologies for understanding data currently available, from the most basic to the most complex and bleeding edge.

As an open source project, it's freely available for a range of platforms, including Windows, macOS, and Linux. It's under constant development, with new procedures added daily. Furthermore, R is supported by a large and diverse community of data scientists and programmers who gladly offer their help and advice to users.

Although R is probably best known for its ability to create beautiful and sophisticated graphs, it can handle just about any statistical problem. The base installation provides hundreds of data management, statistical, and graphical functions right out of the box. But some of its most powerful features come from the thousands of extensions (packages) provided by contributing authors.

This breadth comes at a price. It can be hard for new users to get a handle on what R is and what it can do. Even the most experienced R user can be surprised to learn about features they were unaware of.

R in Action, Third Edition, provides you with a guided introduction to R, a 2,000-foot view of the platform and its capabilities. It will introduce you to the most important functions in the base installation and more than 70 of the most useful contributed packages. Throughout the book, the goal is practical application—how you can make sense of your data and communicate that understanding to others. When you finish, you should have a good grasp of how R works, what it can do, and where you can go to learn more. You'll be able to apply a variety of techniques for visualizing data, and you'll have the skills to tackle both basic and advanced data analytic problems.

What's new in the third edition

There are numerous changes in the third edition, including extensive coverage of tidyverse approaches to data management and analysis. Here are some of the more notable changes.

Chapter 2 (creating a dataset) now includes coverage of the readr, readxl, and haven packages for importing data. There is also a new section on tibbles, a modern update to the data frame.

Chapters 3 (basic data management) and 5 (advanced data management) include coverage of the dplyr and tidyr packages for data management, transformation, and summarization.

Chapters 4 (getting started with graphs), 6 (basic graphs), 11 (intermediate graphs) and 19 (advanced graphs) are new and provide extensive coverage of ggplot2 and its extensions.

Chapter 16 (cluster analysis) offers improved graphics and a new section on evaluating the clusterability of data.

Chapter 17 (classification) has a new section on the use of break-down and Shapley values plots for understanding black box models.

Chapter 18 (advanced methods for missing data) has been expanded, with new sections on k-nearest neighbor and random forest approaches to missing values imputation.

Chapter 20 (advanced programming) has new sections on nonstandard evaluation and visual debugging.

Chapter 21 (creating dynamic reports) has expanded coverage of R Markdown and new sections on parameterized reports and common coding errors.

Chapter 22 (creating a package) has been completely rewritten to incorporate the use of new tools for streamlined package creation. There are also new sections on how to share and promote your packages through CRAN, GitHub, and software-generated websites.

Appendix A (graphical user interfaces) has been updated to reflect rapid changes in this area.

Appendix B (customizing the startup environment) has been revised to include new methods of customization and greater sensitivity to potential side effects on reproducible research.

Appendix F (working with large datasets) has coverage of new packages for larger-than-RAM datasets, analytic methods for terabyte-size problems, and the incorporation of R with cloud services.

There are new sections on the use of RStudio for programming, debugging, report writing, and package creation scattered throughout the book. Finally, numerous updates and corrections have been made throughout the text.

Who should read this book

R in Action, Third Edition, should appeal to anyone who deals with data. No background in statistical programming or the R language is assumed. Although the book is accessible to novices, there should be enough new and practical material to satisfy even experienced R mavens.

Users without a statistical background who want to use R to manipulate, summarize, and graph data should find chapters 1–6, 11, and 19 easily accessible. Chapters 7 and 10 assume a one-semester course in statistics; and readers of chapters 8, 9, and 12–18 will benefit from two semesters of statistics. Chapters 20–22 offer a deeper dive into the R language and have no statistical prerequisites. I've tried to write each chapter in such a way that both beginning and expert data analysts will find something interesting and useful.

How this book is organized: A road map

This book is designed to give you a guided tour of the R platform with a focus on those methods most immediately applicable for manipulating, visualizing, and understanding data. The book has 22 chapters and is divided into 5 parts: "Getting Started," "Basic Methods," "Intermediate Methods," "Advanced Methods," and "Expanding Your Skills." Additional topics are covered in seven appendices.

Chapter 1 begins with an introduction to R and the features that make it so useful as a data analysis platform. The chapter covers how to obtain the program and how to enhance the basic installation with extensions that are available online. The remainder of the chapter is spent exploring the user interface and learning how to run your first programs.

Chapter 2 covers the many methods available for getting data into R. The first half of the chapter introduces the data structures R uses to hold data. The second half discusses methods for importing data into R from the keyboard, text files, web pages, spreadsheets, statistical packages, and databases.

Chapter 3 covers basic data management, including sorting, merging, and subsetting datasets, and transforming, recoding, and deleting variables.

Chapter 4 introduces you to data visualization through the grammar of graphics. We review methods of creating graphs, modifying them, and saving them in a variety of formats.

Building on the material in chapter 3, chapter 5 covers the use of functions (mathematical, statistical, character) and control structures (looping, conditional execution) for data management. We then discuss how to write your own R functions and how to reshape and aggregate data in various ways.

Chapter 6 demonstrates methods for creating common univariate graphs, such as bar plots, pie charts, histograms, density plots, box plots, treemaps, and dot plots. Each is useful for understanding the distribution of a single variable.

Chapter 7 starts by showing how to summarize data, including the use of descriptive statistics and cross-tabulations. We then look at basic methods for understanding relationships between two variables, including correlations, t-tests, chi-square tests, and nonparametric methods.

Chapter 8 introduces regression methods for modeling the relationship between a numeric outcome variable and a set of one or more numeric predictor variables.

Methods for fitting these models, evaluating their appropriateness, and interpreting their meaning are discussed in detail.

Chapter 9 considers the analysis of basic experimental designs through the analysis of variance and its variants. Here, we're usually interested in how treatment combinations or conditions affect a numerical outcome. Methods for assessing the appropriateness of the analyses and visualizing the results are also covered.

Chapter 10 provides a detailed treatment of power analysis. Starting with a discussion of hypothesis testing, the chapter focuses on how to determine the sample size necessary to detect a treatment effect of a given size with a given degree of confidence. This can help you plan experimental and quasi-experimental studies that are likely to yield useful results.

Chapter 11 expands on the material in chapter 6, covering the creation of graphs that help you visualize relationships among two or more variables. These include various types of 2D and 3D scatter plots, scatter plot matrices, line plots, correlograms, and mosaic plots.

Chapter 12 presents analytic methods that work well in cases where data are sampled from unknown or mixed distributions, where sample sizes are small, where outliers are a problem, or where devising an appropriate test based on a theoretical distribution is too complex and mathematically intractable. They include both resampling and bootstrapping approaches—computer-intensive methods that are easily implemented in R.

Chapter 13 expands on the regression methods in chapter 8 to cover data that are not normally distributed. The chapter starts with a discussion of generalized linear models and then focuses on cases in which you're trying to predict an outcome variable that is either categorical (logistic regression) or a count (Poisson regression).

One of the challenges of multivariate data problems is simplification. Chapter 14 describes methods of transforming a large number of correlated variables into a smaller set of uncorrelated variables (principal component analysis), as well as methods for uncovering the latent structure underlying a given set of variables (factor analysis). The many steps involved in an appropriate analysis are covered in detail.

Chapter 15 describes methods for creating, manipulating, and modeling time series data. It covers visualizing and decomposing time series data as well as exponential and ARIMA approaches to forecasting future values.

Chapter 16 illustrates methods of clustering observations into naturally occurring groups. The chapter begins with a discussion of the common steps in a comprehensive cluster analysis, followed by a presentation of hierarchical clustering and partitioning methods. Several methods for determining the proper number of clusters are presented.

Chapter 17 presents popular supervised machine learning methods for classifying observations into groups. Decision trees, random forests, and support vector machines are considered in turn. You'll also learn about methods for evaluating the accuracy of each approach. New methods for understanding the results are presented.

In keeping with my attempt to present practical methods for analyzing data, chapter 18 considers modern approaches to the ubiquitous problem of missing data values. R supports a number of elegant approaches for analyzing datasets that are incomplete. Several of the best are described here, along with guidance for which ones to use when and which ones to avoid.

Chapter 19 wraps up the discussion of graphs with a deep dive into customizing the axes, color scheme, fonts, legend, annotations, and plot area. You'll learn how to combine several graphs into a single plot. Finally, you'll learn how to turn a static graph into an interactive web-based visualization.

Chapter 20 covers advanced programming techniques. You'll learn about object-oriented programming techniques and debugging approaches. The chapter also presents tips for efficient programming. This chapter will be particularly helpful if you're seeking a greater understanding of how R works, and it's a prerequisite for chapter 22.

Chapter 21 describes several methods for creating attractive reports from within R. You'll learn how to generate web pages, reports, articles, and even books from your R code. The resulting documents can include your code, tables of results, graphs, and commentary.

Finally, chapter 22 provides a step-by-step guide to creating R packages. This will allow you to create more sophisticated programs, document them efficiently, and share them with others. Methods for sharing and promoting your packages are discussed in detail.

The afterword points you to many of the best internet sites for learning more about R, joining the R community, getting questions answered, and staying current with this rapidly changing product.

Last, but not least, the seven appendices (A through G) extend the text's coverage to include such useful topics as R graphic user interfaces, customizing and upgrading an R installation, exporting data to other applications, using R for matrix algebra (à la MATLAB), and working with very large datasets.

We also offer a bonus chapter that is available online only on the publisher's website at https://www.manning.com/books/r-in-action-third-edition. Online chapter 23 covers the `lattice` package, an alternative approach to data visualization in R.

Advice for data miners

Data mining is a field of analytics concerned with discovering patterns in large datasets. Many data mining specialists are turning to R for its cutting-edge analytical capabilities. If you're a data miner making the transition to R and want to access the language as quickly as possible, I recommend the following reading sequence: chapter 1 (introduction), chapter 2 (data structures and those portions of importing data that are relevant to your setting), chapter 4 (basic data management), chapter 7 (descriptive statistics), chapter 8 (sections 1, 2, and 6, regression), chapter 13 (section 2, logistic regression), chapter 16 (clustering), chapter 17 (classification), and appendix F (working with large datasets). Then review the other chapters as needed.

About the code

To make this book as broadly applicable as possible, I've chosen examples from a range of disciplines, including psychology, sociology, medicine, biology, business, and engineering. None of these examples requires specialized knowledge of that field.

The datasets used in these examples were selected because they pose interesting questions and because they're small. This allows you to focus on the techniques described and quickly understand the processes involved. When you're learning new methods, smaller is better. The datasets are provided with the base installation of R or available through add-on packages that are available online.

The following typographical conventions are used throughout this book:

- A monospaced font is used for code listings that should be typed as is.
- A monospaced font is also used within the general text to denote code words or previously defined objects.
- *Italics* within code listings indicate placeholders. You should replace them with appropriate text and values for the problem at hand. For example, *path_to _my_file* would be replaced with the actual path to a file on your computer.
- R is an interactive language that indicates readiness for the next line of user input with a prompt (> by default). Many of the listings in this book capture interactive sessions. When you see code lines that start with >, don't type the prompt.
- Code annotations are used in place of inline comments (a common convention in Manning books). Additionally, some annotations appear with numbered bullets like ❶ that refer to explanations appearing later in the text.
- To save room or make text more legible, the output from interactive sessions may include additional whitespace or omit text that is extraneous to the point under discussion.

You can get executable snippets of code from the liveBook (online) version of this book at https://livebook.manning.com/book/r-in-action-third-edition. The complete code for the examples in the book is available for download from the Manning website at https://www.manning.com/books/r-in-action-third-edition and from GitHub at www .github.com/rkabacoff/RiA3. To get the most out of this book, I recommend that you try the examples as you read them.

Finally, a common maxim states that if you ask two statisticians how to analyze a dataset, you'll get three answers. The flip side of this assertion is that each answer will move you closer to an understanding of the data. I make no claim that a given analysis is the best or only approach to a given problem. Using the skills taught in this text, I invite you to play with the data and see what you can learn. R is interactive, and the best way to learn is to experiment.

liveBook discussion forum

Purchase of *R in Action, Third Edition,* includes free access to liveBook, Manning's online reading platform. Using liveBook's exclusive discussion features, you can attach comments to the book globally or to specific sections or paragraphs. It's a snap to make notes for yourself, ask and answer technical questions, and receive help from the author and other users. To access the forum, go to https://livebook.manning.com/book/r-in -action-third-edition/discussion. You can also learn more about Manning's forums and the rules of conduct at https://livebook.manning.com/discussion.

Manning's commitment to our readers is to provide a venue in which a meaningful dialogue between individual readers and between readers and the author can take place. It is not a commitment to any specific amount of participation on the part of the author, whose contribution to the forum remains voluntary (and unpaid). We suggest you try asking the author some challenging questions, lest his interest stray. The forum and the archives of previous discussions will be accessible from the publisher's website as long as the book is in print.

about the author

DR. ROBERT KABACOFF is a professor of quantitative analytics at Wesleyan University and a seasoned data scientist with more than 30 years of experience providing statistical programming and data analytic support in business, health care, and government settings. He has taught both undergraduate and graduate courses in data analysis and statistical programming and manages the Quick-R website at statmethods.net and the Data Visualization with R website at rkabacoff.github.io/datavis.

about the cover illustration

The figure on the cover of *R in Action, Third Edition,* is "A man from Zadar," taken from an album of Croatian traditional costumes from the mid-nineteenth century by Nikola Arsenovic.

In those days, it was easy to identify where people lived and what their trade or station in life was just by their dress. Manning celebrates the inventiveness and initiative of the computer business with book covers based on the rich diversity of regional culture centuries ago, brought back to life by pictures from collections such as this one.

Part 1

Getting started

Welcome to *R in Action*! R is one of the most popular platforms for data analysis and visualization currently available. It's free, open source software, available for Windows, macOS, and Linux operating systems. This book will provide you with the skills you need to master this comprehensive software and apply it effectively to your own data.

The book is divided into four sections. Part 1 covers the basics of installing the software, learning to navigate the interface, importing data, and massaging it into a useful format for further analysis.

Chapter 1 is all about becoming familiar with the R environment. The chapter begins with an overview of R and the features that make it such a powerful platform for modern data analysis. After briefly describing how to obtain and install the software, the chapter explores the user interface through a series of simple examples. Next, you'll learn how to enhance the functionality of the basic installation with extensions (called *contributed packages*) that can be freely downloaded from online repositories. The chapter ends with an example that allows you to test your new skills.

Once you're familiar with the R interface, the next challenge is to get your data into the program. In our information-rich world, data can come from many sources and in many formats. Chapter 2 covers the wide variety of methods available for importing data into R. The first half of the chapter introduces the data structures R uses to hold data and describes how to input data manually. The second half discusses methods for importing data from text files, web pages, spreadsheets, statistical packages, and databases.

Data rarely comes in a readily usable format. You often must spend significant time combining data from different sources, cleaning up messy data (miscoded data, mismatched data, missing data), and creating new variables (combined variables, transformed variables, recoded variables) before your questions can be addressed. Chapter 3 covers basic data management tasks in R, including sorting, merging, and subsetting datasets and transforming, recoding, and deleting variables.

Many users approach R for the first time because of its powerful graphics capabilities. Chapter 4 provides an overview of the *grammar of graphics* package ggplot2. You'll start by building a simple graph and then add features one at a time, until you've created a comprehensive data visualization. You'll also learn how to perform basic plot customizations and save your work in various image formats.

Chapter 5 builds on the material in chapter 3. It covers the use of numeric (arithmetic, trigonometric, and statistical) and character functions (string subsetting, concatenation, and substitution) in data management. A comprehensive example is used throughout this section to illustrate many of the functions. Next, control structures (looping, conditional execution) are discussed, and you'll learn how to write your own R functions. Writing custom functions allows you to extend R's capabilities by encapsulating many programming steps into a single, flexible function call. Finally, powerful methods for reorganizing (reshaping) and aggregating data are discussed. Reshaping and aggregation are often useful in preparing data for further analyses.

After having completed part 1, you'll be thoroughly familiar with programming in the R environment. You'll have the skills you need to enter or access your data, clean it up, and prepare it for further analyses. You'll also have gained experience in creating, customizing, and saving a variety of graphs.

Introduction to R 1

This chapter covers

- Installing R and RStudio
- Understanding the R language
- Running programs

In recent years, how we analyze data has changed dramatically. With the advent of personal computers and the internet, the sheer volume of data we have available has grown enormously. Companies have terabytes of data about the consumers they interact with, and governmental, academic, and private research institutions have extensive archival and survey data on every manner of research topic. Gleaning information (let alone wisdom) from these massive stores of data has become an industry in itself. At the same time, presenting the information in easily accessible and digestible ways has become increasingly challenging.

The science of data analysis (statistics, psychometrics, econometrics, and machine learning) has kept pace with this explosion of data. Before personal computers and the internet, academic researchers developed new statistical methods that they published as theoretical papers in professional journals. It could take years for programmers to adapt these methods and incorporate them into the statistical packages that were widely available to data analysts. Now new methodologies are appearing *daily*. Statistical researchers publish new and improved methods, along with the code to produce them, on easily accessible websites.

The advent of personal computers had another effect on the way we analyze data. When data analysis was carried out on mainframe computers, computer time was precious and difficult to come by. Analysts carefully set up a computer run with all the parameters and options they thought would be needed. The resulting output of the procedure could be dozens or hundreds of pages long. The analyst sifted through this output, extracting useful material and discarding the rest. Many popular statistical packages (such as SAS and SPSS) were originally developed during this period and still follow this approach to some degree.

With the cheap and easy access afforded by personal computers, the paradigm of modern data analysis has shifted. Rather than setting up a complete data analysis all at once, the process has become highly interactive, with the output from each stage serving as the input for the next stage. Figure 1.1 shows a typical analysis. At any point, the cycles may include transforming the data, imputing missing values, adding or deleting variables, fitting statistical models, and looping back through the whole process again. The process stops when the analyst believes they understand the data intimately and have answered all the relevant questions that can be answered.

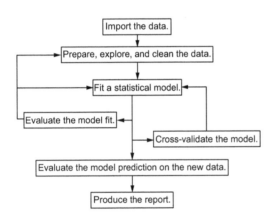

Figure 1.1 Steps in a typical data analysis

The advent of personal computers (and especially the availability of high-resolution monitors) has also affected how results are understood and presented. A picture really can be worth a thousand words, and human beings are adept at extracting useful information from visual presentations. Modern data analysis increasingly relies on graphical presentations to uncover meaning and convey results.

Data analysts now need to access data from a wide range of sources (database management systems, text files, statistical packages, spreadsheets, and web pages), merge the pieces of data together, clean and annotate them, analyze them with the latest methods, present the findings in meaningful and graphically appealing ways, and incorporate the results into attractive reports that can be distributed to stakeholders and the public. As you'll see in this chapter, R is a comprehensive software package that's ideally suited to achieve these goals.

1.1 Why use R?

R is a language and environment for statistical computing and graphics, similar to the S language originally developed at Bell Labs. It's an open source solution to data analysis that's supported by a large and active worldwide research community. But many popular statistical and graphing packages are available (such as Microsoft Excel, SAS, IBM SPSS, Stata, and Minitab). Why turn to R?

R has many features to recommend it:

- Most commercial statistical software platforms cost thousands, if not tens of thousands, of dollars. R is free! If you're a teacher or a student, the benefits are obvious.

- R is a comprehensive statistical platform that offers all manner of data analytic techniques. Just about any type of data analysis can be done in R.

- R contains advanced statistical routines that are not yet available in other packages. In fact, new methods become available for download on a weekly basis. If you're a SAS user, imagine getting a new SAS PROC every few days.

- R has state-of-the-art graphics capabilities. If you want to visualize complex data, R has the most comprehensive and powerful feature set.

- R is a powerful platform for interactive data analysis and exploration. From its inception, it was designed to support the approach outlined in figure 1.1. For example, the results of any analytic step can easily be saved, manipulated, and used as input for additional analyses.

- Getting data into a usable form from multiple sources can be challenging. R can easily import data from a wide variety of sources, including text files, database-management systems, statistical packages, and specialized data stores. It can write data out to these systems as well. R can also access data directly from web pages, social media sites, and a wide range of online data services.

- R provides an unparalleled platform for programming new statistical methods in an easy, straightforward manner. It's easily extensible and provides a natural language for quickly programming recently published methods.

- R functionality can be integrated into applications written in other languages, including C++, Java, Python, PHP, Pentaho, SAS, and SPSS. This allows you to continue working in a language that you are familiar with while adding R's capabilities to your applications.

- R runs on a wide array of platforms, including Windows, Unix, and macOS. It's likely to run on any computer you may have. (I've even come across guides for installing R on an iPhone, which is impressive, but probably not a good idea.)

- If you don't want to learn a new language, a variety of graphic user interfaces (GUIs) are available, offering the power of R through menus and dialogs.

You can see an example of R's graphic capabilities in figure 1.2. This graph describes the relationships between years of experience and wages for men in women in six industries, collected from the US Current Population Survey in 1985. Technically, it's

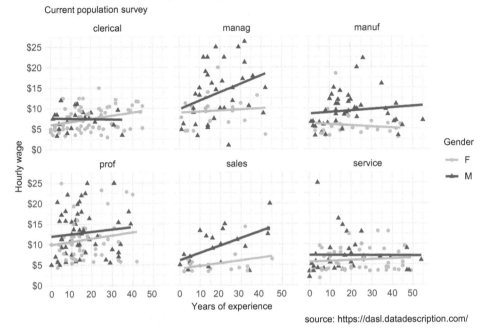

Relationship between wages and experience

Figure 1.2   **Relationships between wages and years of experience for men and women in six industries. Graphs like this can be created easily with a few lines of code in R (graph created with** `mosaicData` **package).**

a matrix of scatterplots with gender displayed by color and symbol. Trends are described using linear regression lines. If these terms *scatterplot* and *regression lines* are unfamiliar to you, don't worry. We'll cover them in later chapters.

Some of the more interesting findings from this graph are

- The relationship between experience and wages varies by both gender and industry.
- In the service industry, wages do not appear to go up with experience for either men or women.
- In management positions, wages tend to go up with experience for men, but not for women.

Are these differences real, or can they be explained as chance sampling variation? We'll discuss this further in chapter 8. The important point is that R allows you to create elegant, informative, highly customized graphs in a simple and straightforward fashion. Creating similar plots in other statistical languages would be difficult, time-consuming, or impossible.

Unfortunately, R can have a steep learning curve. Because it can do so much, documentation and help files are voluminous. Additionally, because much of the functionality comes from optional modules created by independent contributors, this documentation can be scattered and difficult to locate. In fact, getting a handle on all that R can do is challenging.

The goal of this book is to make access to R quick and easy. We'll tour the many features of R, covering enough material to get you started on your data, with pointers on where to go when you need to learn more. Let's begin by installing the program.

1.2 Obtaining and installing R

R is freely available from the Comprehensive R Archive Network (CRAN) at https://cran.r-project.org. Precompiled binaries are available for Linux, macOS, and Windows. Follow the directions for installing the base product on the platform of your choice. Later, we'll talk about adding functionality through optional modules called packages (also available from CRAN).

1.3 Working with R

R is a case-sensitive, interpreted language. You can enter commands one at a time at the command prompt (>) or run a set of commands from a source file. There are a wide variety of data types, including vectors, matrices, data frames (similar to datasets), and lists (collections of objects). I'll discuss each of these data types in chapter 2.

Most functionality is provided through built-in and user-created functions and the creation and manipulation of objects. An *object* is basically anything that can be assigned a value. For R, that is just about everything (data, functions, graphs, analytic results, and more). Every object has a *class attribute* (basically one or more associated text descriptors) that tells R how to print, plot, summarize, or in some other way manipulate the object.

All objects are kept in memory during an interactive session. Basic functions are available by default. Other functions are contained in packages that can be attached to a current session as needed.

Statements consist of functions and assignments. R uses the symbol <- for assignments, rather than the typical = sign. For example, the statement

```
x <- rnorm(5)
```

creates a vector object named x that contains five random deviates from a standard normal distribution.

> **NOTE** R allows the = sign to be used for object assignments. That said, you won't find many programs written that way because it's not standard syntax, it won't work in some situations, and R programmers will make fun of you. You can also reverse the assignment direction. For instance, rnorm(5) -> x is equivalent to the previous statement. Again, doing so is uncommon and isn't recommended in this book.

Comments are preceded by the # symbol. The R interpreter ignores any text appearing after the #. An example program is given in section 1.3.1.

1.3.1   *Getting started*

The first step in using R is, of course, installing it. Instructions are provided on CRAN. Once R is installed, start it up. If you're using Windows, launch R from the Start menu. On a Mac, double-click the R icon in the Applications folder. For Linux, type R at the command prompt of a terminal window. Any of these will start the R interface (see figure 1.3 for an example).

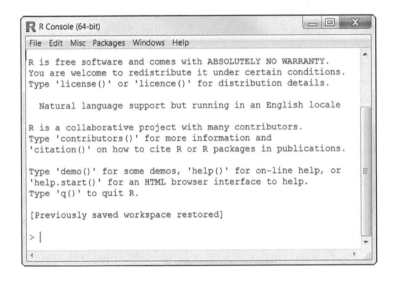

Figure 1.3
Example of the R interface on Windows

To get a feel for the interface, let's work through a simple example. Say you're studying physical development, and you've collected the ages and weights of 10 infants in their first year of life (see table 1.1). You're interested in the distribution of the weights and their relationship to age.

Listing 1.1 shows the analysis. Age and weight data are entered as vectors using the function c(), which combines its arguments into a vector or list. The mean and standard deviation of the weights, along with the correlation between age and weight, are provided by the functions mean(), sd(), and cor(), respectively. Finally, age is plotted against weight using the plot() function, allowing you to visually inspect the trend. The q() function ends the session and lets you quit.

Table 1.1   The ages and weights of 10 infants

Age (mo.)	Weight (kg.)
01	4.4
03	5.3
05	7.2
02	5.2
11	8.5
09	7.3
03	6.0
09	10.4
12	10.2
03	6.1

Note: These are fictional data.

Listing 1.1   A sample R session

```
> age <- c(1,3,5,2,11,9,3,9,12,3)
> weight <- c(4.4,5.3,7.2,5.2,8.5,7.3,6.0,10.4,10.2,6.1)
> mean(weight)
[1] 7.06
> sd(weight)
[1] 2.077498
> cor(age,weight)
[1] 0.9075655
> plot(age,weight)
```

You can see from listing 1.1 that the mean weight for these 10 infants is 7.06 kilograms, that the standard deviation is 2.08 kilograms, and that there is strong linear relationship between age in months and weight in kilograms (correlation = 0.91). The relationship can also be seen in the scatter plot in figure 1.4. Not surprisingly, as infants get older, they tend to weigh more.

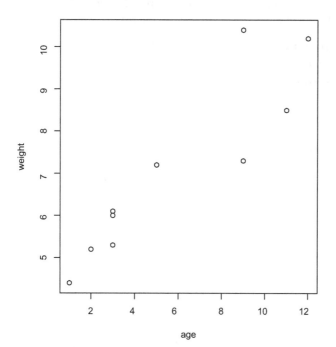

Figure 1.4   Scatter plot of infant weight (kg.) by age (mo.)

The scatter plot in figure 1.4 is informative, but somewhat utilitarian and unattractive. In later chapters, you'll see how to create more attractive and sophisticated graphs.

TIP   To get a sense of what R can do graphically, take a look at the graphs described in Data Visualization with R (http://rkabacoff.github.io/datavis) and The Top 50 ggplot2 Visualizations – The Master List (http://r-statistics .co/Top50-Ggplot2-Visualizations-MasterList-R-Code.html).

1.3.2 Using RStudio

The standard interface to R is very basic, offering little more than a command prompt for entering lines of code. For real-life projects, you'll want a more comprehensive tool for writing code and viewing output. Several such tools, called Integrated Development Environments (IDEs), have been developed for R, including Eclipse with StatET, Visual Studio for R, and RStudio Desktop.

RStudio Desktop (https://www.rstudio.com) is by far the most popular choice. It provides a multiwindow, multitabbed environment with tools for importing data, writing clean code, debugging errors, visualizing output, and writing reports.

RStudio is freely available as an open source product and is easily installed on Windows, Mac, and Linux. Since RStudio is an interface to R, be sure to install R before installing RStudio Desktop.

> **TIP** You can customize the RStudio interface by selecting the Tools> Global Options ... from the menu bar. On the General tab, I recommend unchecking Restore .RData into Workspace at Startup and selecting Never for Save Workspace to .RData on Exit. This will ensure a clean startup each time you run RStudio.

Let's rerun the code from listing 1.1 using RStudio. If you're using Windows, launch RStudio from the Start menu. On a Mac, double-click the RStudio icon in the Applications folder. For Linux, type `rstudio` at the command prompt of a terminal window. The same interface will appear on all three platforms (see figure 1.5).

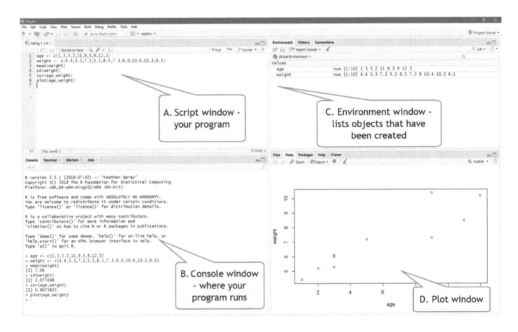

Figure 1.5 RStudio Desktop

SCRIPT WINDOW

From the File menu, select New File > R Script. A new script window will open in the upper left-hand corner of the screen (figure 1.5 A). Type the code from listing 1.1. into this window.

As you type, the editor offers syntax highlighting and code completion (see figure 1.6). For example, as you type `plot` a pop-up window will appear with all functions that start with the letters that you've typed so far. You can use the up and down arrow keys to select a function from the list and press Tab to select it. Within functions (parentheses), press Tab to see function options. Within quote marks, press Tab to complete file paths.

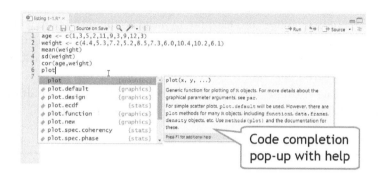

Figure 1.6
Script window

To execute code, highlight/select it and click the Run button or press Ctrl+Enter. Pressing Ctrl+Shift+Enter will run the entire script.

To save the script, press the Save icon or select File > Save from the menu bar. Select a name and location from the dialog box that opens. By convention, script files end with a .R extension. The name of the script file will appear in the window tab in a red starred format if the current version has not been saved.

CONSOLE WINDOW

Code runs in the console window (figure 1.5 B). This is basically the same console you would see if you were using the basic R interface. You can submit code from a script window with a Run command or enter interactive commands directly in this window at the command prompt (>).

If the command prompt changes to a plus (+) sign, the interpreter is waiting for a complete statement. This will often happen if the statement is too long for one line or if there are mismatched parentheses in the code. You can get back to the command prompt by pressing the Esc key.

Additionally, pressing the up and down arrow keys will cycle through past commands. You can edit a command and resubmit it with the Enter key. Clicking on the broom icon clears text from the window.

ENVIRONMENT AND HISTORY WINDOWS

Any objects that were created (in this example, `age` and `weight`) will appear in the Environment window (see figure 1.5 C). A record of executed commands will be saved in the History window (the tab to the right of Environment).

PLOT WINDOW

Any plots that are created from the script will appear in the plot window (figure 1.5 D). The toolbar for this window allows you to cycle through the graphs that have been created. In addition, you can open a zoom window to see the graph at different sizes, export the graphs in several formats, and delete one or all the graphs you've created so far.

1.3.3 Getting help

R provides extensive help facilities, and learning to navigate them will help you significantly in your programming efforts. The built-in help system provides details, references, and examples of any function contained in a currently installed package. You can obtain help by executing any of functions listed in table 1.2.

Help is also available through the RStudio interface. In the script window, place the cursor on a function name and press F1 to bring up the help window.

Table 1.2   R help functions

Function	Action
`help.start()`	General help
`help("foo")` or `?foo`	Help on function `foo`
`help(package ="foo")`	Help on a package named `foo`
`help.search("foo")` or `??foo`	Searches the help system for instances of the string `foo`
`example("foo")`	Examples of function `foo` (quotation marks optional)
`data()`	Lists all available example datasets contained in currently loaded packages
`vignette()`	Lists all available vignettes for currently installed packages
`vignette("foo")`	Displays specific vignettes for topic `foo`

The function `help.start()` opens a browser window with access to introductory and advanced manuals, FAQs, and reference materials. Alternatively, choose Help > R Help from the menu. The vignettes returned by the `vignette()` function are practical introductory articles provided in PDF or HTML format. Not all packages have vignettes.

All help files have a similar format (see figure 1.7). The help page has a title and brief description, followed by the function's syntax and options. Computational details are provided in the Details section. The See Also section describes and links to

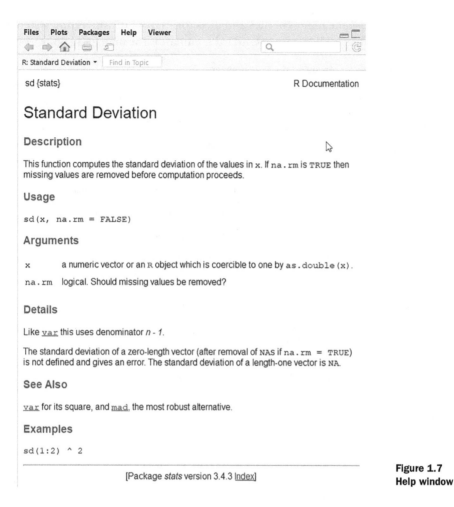

Figure 1.7
Help window

related functions. The help page almost always ends with examples illustrating typical uses of the function.

As you can see, learning to navigate R's extensive help facilities will definitely aid your programming efforts. It's a rare session that I don't use ? to look up the features (such as options or return values) of some function.

1.3.4 *The workspace*

The workspace is your current R working environment and includes any user-defined objects (vectors, matrices, functions, data frames, and lists). The current working directory is the directory from which R will read files and to which it will save results by default. You can identify the current working directory by using the getwd() function. You can set the current working directory by using the setwd() function. If you need to input a file that isn't in the current working directory, use the full pathname in the call. Always enclose the names of files and directories from the operating system in quotation marks. Table 1.3 lists some standard commands for managing your workspace.

Table 1.3   Functions for managing the R workspace

Function	Action
getwd()	Lists the current working directory
setwd("*mydirectory*")	Changes the current working directory to *mydirectory*
ls()	Lists the objects in the current workspace
rm(*objectlist*)	Removes (deletes) one or more objects
help(*options*)	Provides information about available options
options()	Lets you view or set current options
save.image("*myfile*")	Saves the workspace to *myfile* (default = .RData)
save(*objectlist*, file="*myfile*")	Saves specific objects to a file
load("*myfile*")	Loads a workspace into the current session

To see these commands in action, look at the following listing.

Listing 1.2   An example of commands used to manage the R workspace

```
setwd("C:/myprojects/project1")
options()
options(digits=3)
```

First, the current working directory is set to C:/myprojects/project1. The current option settings are then displayed, and numbers are formatted to print with three digits after the decimal place.

Note the forward slashes in the pathname of the setwd() command. R treats the backslash (\) as an escape character. Even when you're using R on a Windows platform, use forward slashes in pathnames. Also note that the setwd() function won't create a directory that doesn't exist. If necessary, you can use the dir.create() function to create a directory and then use setwd() to change to its location.

1.3.5   *Projects*

It's a good idea to keep your projects in separate directories. RStudio provides a simple mechanism for this. Choose File > New Project … and specify either New Directory to start a project in a brand-new working directory or Existing Directory to associate a project with an existing working directory. All your program files, command history, report output, graphs, and data will be saved in the project directory. You can easily switch between projects using the Project drop-down menu in the upper-right portion of the RStudio application.

It is easy to become overwhelmed with project files. I recommend creating several subfolders within the main project folder. I usually create a *data* folder to contain raw data files, an *img* folder for image files and graphical output, a *docs* folder for project documentation, and a *reports* folder for reports. I keep the R scripts and a README file in the main directory. If there is an order to the R scripts, I number them (e.g., 01_import_data.R, 02_clean_data.R, etc.). The README is a text file containing information such as author, date, stakeholders and their contact information, and the purpose of the project. Six months from now, this will remind me of what I did and why I did it.

1.4 Packages

R comes with extensive capabilities right out of the box, but some of its most exciting features are available as optional modules that you can download and install. There are more than 10,000 user-contributed modules, called *packages*, that you can download from http://cran.r-project.org/web/packages. They provide a tremendous range of new capabilities, from the analysis of geospatial data to protein mass spectra processing to the analysis of psychological tests! You'll use many of these optional packages in this book.

One set of packages, collectively called the *tidyverse*, deserves particular attention. This is a relatively new collection that offers a streamlined, consistent, and intuitive approach to data manipulation and analysis. The advantages offered by tidyverse packages (with names like *tidyr*, *dplyr*, *lubridate*, *stringr*, and *ggplot2*) are changing the way data scientists write code in R, and we will be employing these packages often. In fact, the opportunity to describe how to use these packages for data analysis and visualization was a major motivation for writing a third edition of this book.

1.4.1 What are packages?

Packages are collections of R functions, data, and compiled code in a well-defined format. The directory where packages are stored on your computer is called the *library*. The function .libPaths() shows you where your library is located, and the function library() shows you what packages you've saved in your library.

R comes with a standard set of packages (including base, datasets, utils, gr-Devices, graphics, stats, and methods). They provide a wide range of functions and datasets that are available by default. Other packages are available for download and installation. Once installed, they must be loaded into the session to be used. The command search() tells you which packages are loaded and ready to use.

1.4.2 Installing a package

Several R functions let you manipulate packages. To install a package for the first time, use the install.packages() command. For example, the gclus package contains functions for creating enhanced scatter plots. You can download and install the package with the command install.packages("gclus").

You only need to install a package once. But like any software, packages are often updated by their authors. Use the command `update.packages()` to update any packages that you've installed. To see details on your packages, you can use the `installed.packages()` command. It lists the packages you have, along with their version numbers, dependencies, and other information.

You can also install and update packages using the RStudio interface. Select the Packages tab (from the window on the lower right). Enter the name (or partial name) in the search box in the upper right of that tabbed window. Place a check mark next to the package(s) you want to install and click the Install button. Alternatively, click the Update button to update a package that's already installed.

1.4.3   *Loading a package*

Installing a package downloads it from a CRAN mirror site and places it in your library. To use it in an R session, you need to load the package using the `library()` command. For example, to use the package `gclus`, issue the command `library(gclus)`.

Of course, you must have installed a package before you can load it. You'll only have to load the package once in a given session. If you like, you can customize your startup environment to automatically load the packages you use most often. Appendix B explains how to customize your startup.

1.4.4   *Learning about a package*

When you load a package, a new set of functions and datasets becomes available. Small illustrative datasets are provided along with sample code, allowing you to try out the new functionalities. The help system contains a description of each function (along with examples) and information about each dataset included. Entering `help(package="package_name")` provides a brief description of the package and an index of the functions and datasets that are included. Using `help()` with any of these function or dataset names provides further details. The same information can be downloaded as a PDF manual from CRAN. To get help on a package using the RStudio interface, click on the Packages tab (the lower-right window), enter the name of the package in the search window, and click on the name of the package.

Common mistakes in R programming

Both beginning and experienced R programmers frequently make some common mistakes. If your program generates an error, be sure to check for the following:

- *Using the wrong case*—`help()`, `Help()`, and `HELP()` are three different functions (only the first will work).
- *Forgetting to use quotation marks when they're needed*—`install.packages("gclus")` works, whereas `install.packages(gclus)` generates an error.

- *Forgetting to include the parentheses in a function call*—For example, `help()` works, but `help` doesn't. Even if there are no options, you still need the `()`.
- *Using the \ in a pathname on Windows*—R sees the backslash character as an escape character. `setwd("c:\mydata")` generates an error. Use `setwd("c:/mydata")` or `setwd("c:\\mydata")` instead.
- *Using a function from a package that's not loaded*—The function `order.clusters()` is contained in the `gclus` package. If you try to use it before loading the package, you'll get an error.

The error messages in R can be cryptic, but if you're careful about following these points, you should avoid seeing many of them.

1.5 *Using output as input: Reusing results*

One of the most useful design features of R is that the output of analyses can easily be saved and used as input to additional analyses. Let's walk through an example, using one of the datasets that comes preinstalled with R. If you don't understand the statistics involved, don't worry. We're focusing on the general principle here.

R comes with many built-in datasets that can be used to practice data analyses. One such dataset, called `mtcars`, contains information about 32 automobiles collected from *Motor Trend* magazine road tests. Suppose we're interested in describing the relationship between a car's fuel efficiency and weight.

First, we could run a simple linear regression predicting miles per gallon (`mpg`) from car weight (`wt`). This is accomplished with the following function call:

```
lm(mpg~wt, data=mtcars)
```

The results are displayed on the screen, and no information is saved.

Alternatively, run the regression, but store the results in an object:

```
lmfit <- lm(mpg~wt, data=mtcars)
```

The assignment creates a list object called `lmfit` that contains extensive information from the analysis (including the predicted values, residuals, regression coefficients, and more). Although no output is sent to the screen, the results can be both displayed and manipulated further.

Typing `summary(lmfit)` displays a summary of the results, and `plot(lmfit)` produces diagnostic plots. The statement `cook<-cooks.distance(lmfit)` generates and stores influence statistics, and `plot(cook)` graphs them. To predict miles per gallon from car weight in a new set of data, you'd use `predict(lmfit, mynewdata)`.

To see what a function returns, look at the Value section of the R help page for that function. Here you'd look at `help(lm)` or `?lm`. This tells you what's saved when you assign the results of that function to an object.

1.6   *Working with large datasets*

Programmers frequently ask me if R can handle large data problems. Typically, they work with massive amounts of data gathered from web research, climatology, or genetics. Because R holds objects in memory, you're generally limited by the amount of RAM available. For example, on my nine-year-old Windows PC with 2 GB of RAM, I can easily handle datasets with 10 million elements (100 variables by 100,000 observations). On an iMac with 4 GB of RAM, I can usually handle 100 million elements without difficulty.

But there are two issues to consider: the size of the dataset and the statistical methods that will be applied. R can handle data analysis problems in the gigabyte to terabyte range, but specialized procedures are required. Appendix F discusses the management and analysis of very large datasets.

1.7   *Working through an example*

We'll finish this chapter with an example that ties together many of these ideas. Here's the task:

1   Open the general help and look at the Introduction to R section.
2   Install the `vcd` package (a package for visualizing categorical data that you'll be using in chapter 11).
3   List the functions and datasets available in this package.
4   Load the package and read the description of the dataset `Arthritis`.
5   Print out the `Arthritis` dataset (entering the name of an object will list it).
6   Run the example that comes with the `Arthritis` dataset. Don't worry if you don't understand the results; it basically shows that arthritis patients receiving treatment improved much more than patients receiving a placebo.

The code required is provided in the following listing, with a sample of the results displayed in figure 1.8. As this short exercise demonstrates, you can accomplish a great deal with a small amount of code.

Listing 1.3   Working with a new package

```
help.start()
install.packages("vcd")
help(package="vcd")
library(vcd)
help(Arthritis)
Arthritis
example(Arthritis)
```

In this chapter, we looked at some of the strengths that make R an attractive option for students, researchers, statisticians, and data analysts who are trying to understand the meaning of their data. We walked through the program's installation and talked about how to enhance R's capabilities by downloading additional packages. We explored the basic interface and produced a few simple graphs. Because R can be a

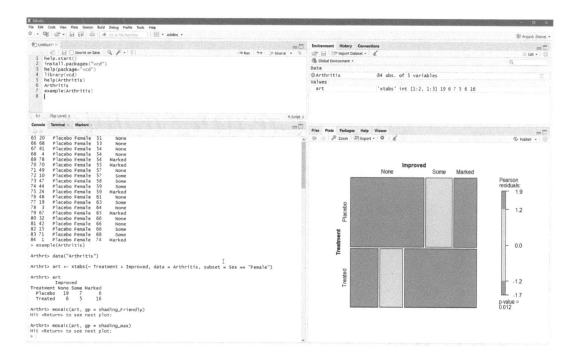

Figure 1.8 RStudio window when executing the code in listing 1.3

complex program, we spent some time looking at how to access the extensive help that's available. Hopefully you're getting a sense of how powerful this freely available software can be.

Now that you have R and RStudio up and running, it's time to add your data to the mix. In the next chapter, we'll look at the types of data R can handle and how to import them into R from text files, other programs, and database management systems.

Summary

- R provides a comprehensive, highly interactive environment for analyzing and visualizing data.

- RStudio is an integrated development environment that makes programming in R easier and more productive.

- Packages are freely available add-on modules that greatly extend the power of the R platform.

- R has an extensive help system, and learning how to use it will greatly facilitate your ability to program effectively.

Creating a dataset

2

This chapter covers

- Exploring R data structures
- Using data entry
- Importing data
- Annotating datasets

The first step in any data analysis is creating a dataset containing the information to be studied in a format that meets your needs. In R, this task involves

- Selecting a data structure to hold your data
- Entering or importing your data into the data structure

Sections 2.1 and 2.2 of this chapter describe the wealth of structures that R can use to hold data. In particular, section 2.2 describes vectors, factors, matrices, data frames, lists, and tibbles. Familiarizing yourself with these structures (and the notation used to access elements within them) will help you tremendously in understanding how R works. You might want to take your time working through this section.

Section 2.3 covers the many methods for importing data into R. Data can be entered manually or imported from an external source. These data sources can include text files, spreadsheets, statistical packages, and database-management systems. For example, the data that I work with typically comes as comma-delimited text files or Excel spreadsheets. On occasion, though, I receive data as SAS and SPSS datasets or through connections to SQL databases. It's likely that you'll only have to use one or two of the methods described in this section, so feel free to choose those that fit your situation.

Once a dataset is created, you'll typically annotate it, adding descriptive labels for variables and variable codes. Section 2.4 of this chapter looks at annotating datasets, while section 2.5 reviews some useful functions for working with datasets. Let's start with the basics.

2.1 Understanding datasets

A dataset is usually a rectangular array of data with rows representing observations and columns representing variables. Table 2.1 provides an example of a hypothetical patient dataset.

Table 2.1 A patient dataset

PatientID	AdmDate	Age	Diabetes	Status
1	10/15/2018	25	Type1	Poor
2	11/01/2018	34	Type2	Improved
3	10/21/2018	28	Type1	Excellent
4	10/28/2018	52	Type1	Poor

Different traditions have different names for the rows and columns of a dataset. Statisticians refer to them as observations and variables, database analysts call them records and fields, and those from the data mining and machine learning disciplines call them examples and attributes. I use the terms *observations* and *variables* throughout this book.

You can distinguish between the structure of the dataset (in this case, a rectangular array) and the contents or data types included. In the dataset shown in table 2.1, `PatientID` is a row or case identifier, `AdmDate` is a date variable, `Age` is a continuous (quantitative) variable, `Diabetes` is a nominal variable, and `Status` is an ordinal variable. Both nominal and ordinal variables are categorical, but the categories in an ordinal variable have a natural ordering.

R contains a wide variety of structures for holding data, including scalars, vectors, arrays, data frames, and lists. Table 2.1 corresponds to a data frame in R. This diversity of structures provides the R language with a great deal of flexibility in dealing with data.

The data types that R can handle include numeric, character, logical (`TRUE`/`FALSE`), complex (imaginary numbers), and raw (bytes). In R, `PatientID`, `AdmDate`, and `Age` are numeric variables, whereas `Diabetes` and `Status` are character variables. Additionally, you need to tell R that `PatientID` is a case identifier, that `Adm-Date` contains dates, and that `Diabetes` and `Status` are nominal and ordinal variables, respectively. R refers to case identifiers as `rownames` and categorical variables (nominal, ordinal) as `factors`. We'll cover each of these in the next section. You'll learn about dates in chapter 3.

2.2   Data structures

R has a wide variety of objects for holding data, including scalars, vectors, matrices, arrays, data frames, and lists. They differ in terms of the type of data they can hold, how they're created, their structural complexity, and the notation used to identify and access individual elements. Figure 2.1 shows a diagram of these data structures. Let's look at each structure in turn, starting with vectors.

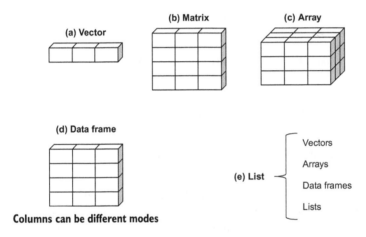

Figure 2.1   R data structures

Some definitions

Several terms are idiosyncratic to R and thus confusing to new users.

In R, an *object* is anything that can be assigned to a variable. This includes constants, data structures, functions, and even graphs. An object has a *mode* (which describes how the object is stored) and a *class* (which tells generic functions like `print` how to handle it).

A *data frame* is a structure in R that holds data and is similar to the datasets found in standard statistical packages (for example, SAS, SPSS, and Stata). The columns are variables, and the rows are observations. You can have variables of different types (for example, numeric or character) in the same data frame. Data frames are the main structures you use to store datasets.

> *Factors* are nominal or ordinal variables. They're stored and treated specially in R. You'll learn about factors in section 2.2.5.
>
> Most other terms used in R should be familiar to you and follow the terminology used in statistics and computing in general.

2.2.1 Vectors

Vectors are one-dimensional arrays that can hold numeric data, character data, or logical data. The combine function c() is used to form the vector. Here are examples of each type of vector:

```
a <- c(1, 2, 5, 3, 6, -2, 4)
b <- c("one", "two", "three")
c <- c(TRUE, TRUE, TRUE, FALSE, TRUE, FALSE)
```

Here, a is a numeric vector, b is a character vector, and c is a logical vector. Note that the data in a vector must be of only one type or mode (numeric, character, or logical). You can't mix modes in the same vector.

> **NOTE** *Scalars* are one-element vectors. Examples include f <- 3, g <- "US", and h <- TRUE. They're used to hold constants.

You can refer to elements of a vector using a numeric vector of positions within square brackets. Unlike programming languages such as C++, Java, and Python, R position indices start with 1 rather than 0. For example, a[c(1, 3)] refers to the first and third elements of vector a. Here are additional examples:

```
> a <- c("k", "j", "h", "a", "c", "m")
> a[3]
[1] "h"
> a[c(1, 3, 5)]
[1] "k" "h" "c"
> a[2:6]
[1]  "j" "h" "a" "c" "m"
```

The colon operator used in the last statement generates a sequence of numbers. For example, a <- c(2:6) is equivalent to a <- c(2, 3, 4, 5, 6).

2.2.2 Matrices

A *matrix* is a two-dimensional array in which each element has the same mode (numeric, character, or logical). Matrices are created with the matrix function. The general format is

```
myymatrix <- matrix(vector, nrow=number_of_rows, ncol=number_of_columns,
                byrow=logical_value, dimnames=list(
                char_vector_rownames, char_vector_colnames))
```

where vector contains the elements for the matrix, nrow and ncol specify the row and column dimensions, and dimnames contains optional row and column labels stored in character vectors. The option `byrow` indicates whether the matrix should be filled in by row (`byrow=TRUE`) or by column (`byrow=FALSE`). The default is by column. The following listing demonstrates the `matrix` function.

Listing 2.1 Creating matrices

```
> y <- matrix(1:20, nrow=5, ncol=4)        ❶ Creates a 5 × 4 matrix
> y
      [,1] [,2] [,3] [,4]
[1,]    1    6   11   16
[2,]    2    7   12   17
[3,]    3    8   13   18
[4,]    4    9   14   19
[5,]    5   10   15   20
> cells    <- c(1,26,24,68)
> rnames   <- c("R1", "R2")
> cnames   <- c("C1", "C2")
> mymatrix <- matrix(cells, nrow=2, ncol=2, byrow=TRUE,     ❷ 2 × 2 matrix filled
               dimnames=list(rnames, cnames))                  by rows
> mymatrix
   C1 C2
R1  1 26
R2 24 68
> mymatrix <- matrix(cells, nrow=2, ncol=2, byrow=FALSE,
               dimnames=list(rnames, cnames))               ❸ 2 × 2 matrix filled
> mymatrix                                                     by columns
   C1 C2
R1  1 24
R2 26 68
```

First, you create a 5 × 4 matrix ❶. Then you create a 2 × 2 matrix with labels and fill the matrix by rows ❷. Finally, you create a 2 × 2 matrix and fill the matrix by columns ❸.

You can identify rows, columns, or elements of a matrix by using subscripts and brackets. X[i,] refers to the *i*th row of matrix X, X[,j] refers to the *j*th column, and X[i, j] refers to the *ij*th element, respectively. The subscripts *i* and *j* can be numeric vectors to select multiple rows or columns, as shown in the following listing.

Listing 2.2 Using matrix subscripts

```
> x <- matrix(1:10, nrow=2)
> x
      [,1] [,2] [,3] [,4] [,5]
[1,]    1    3    5    7    9
[2,]    2    4    6    8   10
> x[2,]
  [1]  2  4  6  8 10
> x[,2]
[1] 3 4
> x[1,4]
[1] 7
> x[1, c(4,5)]
[1] 7 9
```

First, you create a 2 x 5 matrix containing the numbers 1 to 10. By default, the matrix is filled by column. Then the elements in the second row are selected, followed by the elements in the second column. Next, the element in the first row and fourth column is selected. Finally, the elements in the first row and the fourth and fifth columns are selected.

Matrices are two-dimensional and, like vectors, can contain only one data type. When there are more than two dimensions, you use arrays (see section 2.2.3). When there are multiple modes of data, you use data frames (see section 2.2.4).

2.2.3 Arrays

Arrays are similar to matrices but can have more than two dimensions. They're created with an array function of the following form:

```
myarray <- array(vector, dimensions, dimnames)
```

where *vector* contains the data for the array, *dimensions* is a numeric vector giving the maximal index for each dimension, and *dimnames* is an optional list of dimension labels. The following listing gives an example of creating a three-dimensional ($2 \times 3 \times 4$) array of numbers.

> **Listing 2.3 Creating an array**

```
> dim1 <- c("A1", "A2")
> dim2 <- c("B1", "B2", "B3")
> dim3 <- c("C1", "C2", "C3", "C4")
> z <- array(1:24, c(2, 3, 4), dimnames=list(dim1, dim2, dim3))
> z
, , C1
    B1 B2 B3
A1   1  3  5
A2   2  4  6

, , C2
    B1 B2 B3
A1   7  9 11
A2   8 10 12

, , C3
    B1 B2 B3
A1  13 15 17
A2  14 16 18

, , C4
    B1 B2 B3
A1  19 21 23
A2  20 22 24
```

As you can see, arrays are a natural extension of matrices. They can be useful in creating functions that perform statistical calculations. Like matrices, they must be of a single mode. Identifying elements follows what you've seen for matrices. In the previous example, the z[1,2,3] element is 15.

2.2.4 *Data frames*

A *data frame* is more general than a matrix in that different columns can contain different modes of data (numeric, character, and so on). It's similar to the dataset you'd typically see in SAS, SPSS, and Stata. Data frames are the most common data structure you'll deal with in R.

The patient dataset in table 2.1 consists of numeric and character data. Because there are multiple modes of data, you can't contain the data in a matrix. In this case, a data frame is the structure of choice.

A data frame is created with the data.frame() function:

```
mydata <- data.frame(col1, col2, col3,...)
```

where *col1*, *col2*, *col3*, and so on are column vectors of any type (such as character, numeric, or logical). Names for each column can be provided with the names function. The following listing makes this clear.

Listing 2.4 Creating a data frame

```
> patientID <- c(1, 2, 3, 4)
> age <- c(25, 34, 28, 52)
> diabetes <- c("Type1", "Type2", "Type1", "Type1")
> status <- c("Poor", "Improved", "Excellent", "Poor")
> patientdata <- data.frame(patientID, age, diabetes, status)
> patientdata
  patientID age diabetes    status
1         1  25    Type1      Poor
2         2  34    Type2  Improved
3         3  28    Type1 Excellent
4         4  52    Type1      Poor
```

Each column must have only one mode (e.g., numeric, character, logical), but you can put columns of different modes together to form the data frame. Because data frames are close to what analysts typically think of as datasets, we'll use the terms *columns* and *variables* interchangeably when discussing data frames.

There are several ways to identify the elements of a data frame. You can use the subscript notation you used before (for example, with matrices), or you can specify column names. Using the patientdata data frame created earlier, the following listing demonstrates these approaches.

Listing 2.5 Specifying elements of a data frame

```
> patientdata[1:2]
  patientID age
1         1  25
2         2  34
3         3  28
4         4  52
```

```
> patientdata[c("diabetes", "status")]
  diabetes    status
1    Type1      Poor
2    Type2  Improved
3    Type1 Excellent
4    Type1      Poor
 > patientdata$age
[1] 25 34 28 52
```

> **Indicates the age variable in the patient data frame**

The $ notation in the third example is new. It's used to indicate a particular variable from a given data frame. For example, if you want to cross-tabulate diabetes type by status, you can use the following code:

```
> table(patientdata$diabetes, patientdata$status)

        Excellent Improved Poor
  Type1         1        0    2
  Type2         0        1    0
```

It can get tiresome typing `patientdata$` at the beginning of every variable name, but shortcuts are available. For example, the `with()` function can simplify your code.

USING WITH

Consider the built-in data frame `mtcars`, which contains fuel efficiency data on 32 automobiles. The code

```
summary(mtcars$mpg)
plot(mtcars$mpg, mtcars$disp)
plot(mtcars$mpg, mtcars$wt)
```

provides a summary of the miles per gallon (mpg) variable, along with plots of mpg versus engine displacement and car weight. You can write this code mode concisely as

```
with(mtcars, {
  summary(mpg)
  plot(mpg, disp)
  plot(mpg, wt)
})
```

The statements within the {} brackets are evaluated with reference to the `mtcars` data frame. If there's only one statement (for example, `summary(mpg)`), the {} brackets are optional.

The limitation of the `with()` function is that assignments exist only within the function brackets. Consider

```
> with(mtcars, {
   stats <- summary(mpg)
   stats
  })
   Min. 1st Qu. Median    Mean 3rd Qu.    Max.
  10.40   15.43  19.20   20.09   22.80   33.90
> stats
Error: object 'stats' not found
```

If you need to create objects that will exist outside of the with() construct, use the special assignment operator (<<-) instead of the standard one (<-). It saves the object to the global environment outside of the with() call. This can be demonstrated with the following code:

```
> with(mtcars, {
    nokeepstats <- summary(mpg)
    keepstats <<- summary(mpg)
})
> nokeepstats
Error: object 'nokeepstats' not found
> keepstats
   Min. 1st Qu. Median   Mean 3rd Qu.   Max.
  10.40   15.43  19.20  20.09   22.80  33.90
```

CASE IDENTIFIERS

In the patient data example, patientID is used to identify observations in the dataset. In R, case identifiers can be specified with a rowname option in the data .frame() function. For example, the statement

```
patientdata <- data.frame(patientID, age, diabetes,
                          status, row.names=patientID)
```

specifies patientID as the variable to use in labeling cases on various printouts and graphs R produces.

2.2.5   *Factors*

As you've seen, variables can be described as nominal, ordinal, or continuous. Nominal variables are categorical, without an implied order. Diabetes (Type1, Type2) is an example of a nominal variable. Even if Type1 is coded as a 1 and Type2 is coded as a 2 in the data, no order is implied. Ordinal variables imply order, but not amount. Status (poor, improved, excellent) is a good example of an ordinal variable. You know that a patient with a poor status isn't doing as well as a patient with an improved status, but not by how much. Continuous variables can take on any value within some range, and both order and amount are implied. Age in years is a continuous variable and can take on values such as 14.5 or 22.8 and any value in between. You know that someone who is 15 is 1 year older than someone who is 14.

Categorical (nominal) and ordered categorical (ordinal) variables in R are called *factors*. Factors are crucial in R because they determine how data is analyzed and presented visually. You'll see examples of this throughout the book.

The function factor() stores the categorical values as a vector of integers in the range $[1... k]$ (where k is the number of unique values in the nominal variable) and an internal vector of character strings (the original values) mapped to these integers.

For example, assume that you have this vector:

```
diabetes <- c("Type1", "Type2", "Type1", "Type1")
```

The statement `diabetes <- factor(diabetes)` stores this vector as (1, 2, 1, 1) and associates it with 1=Type1 and 2=Type2 internally (the assignment is alphabetical). Any analyses performed on the vector `diabetes` will treat the variable as nominal and select the statistical methods that are appropriate for this level of measurement.

For vectors representing ordinal variables, you add the parameter `ordered=TRUE` to the `factor()` function. Given the vector

```
status <- c("Poor", "Improved", "Excellent", "Poor")
```

the statement `status <- factor(status, ordered=TRUE)` will encode the vector as (3, 2, 1, 3) and associate these values internally as 1=Excellent, 2=Improved, and 3=Poor. Additionally, any analyses performed on this vector will treat the variable as ordinal and select the statistical methods appropriately.

By default, factor levels for character vectors are created in alphabetical order. This worked for the `status` factor, because the order "Excellent," "Improved," "Poor" made sense. There would have been a problem if "Poor" had been coded as "Ailing" instead, because the order would have been "Ailing," "Excellent," "Improved." A similar problem would exist if the desired order was "Poor," "Improved," "Excellent". For ordered factors, the alphabetical default is rarely sufficient.

You can override the default by specifying a levels option. For example,

```
status <- factor(status, order=TRUE,
            levels=c("Poor", "Improved", "Excellent"))
```

assigns the levels as 1=Poor, 2=Improved, and 3=Excellent. Be sure the specified levels match your actual data values. Any data values not in the list will be set to `missing`.

Numeric variables can be coded as factors using the `levels` and `labels` options. If sex was coded as 1 for male and 2 for female in the original data, then

```
sex <- factor(sex, levels=c(1, 2), labels=c("Male", "Female"))
```

would convert the variable to an unordered factor. Note that the order of the labels must match the order of the levels. In this example, sex would be treated as categorical, the labels `"Male"` and `"Female"` would appear in the output instead of 1 and 2, and any sex value that wasn't initially coded as a 1 or 2 would be set to `missing`.

The following listing demonstrates how specifying factors and ordered factors impacts data analyses.

Listing 2.6   Using factors

```
> patientID <- c(1, 2, 3, 4)          ❶ Enters data as vectors
> age <- c(25, 34, 28, 52)
> diabetes <- c("Type1", "Type2", "Type1", "Type1")
> status <- c("Poor", "Improved", "Excellent", "Poor")
> diabetes <- factor(diabetes)
> status <- factor(status, order=TRUE)
> patientdata <- data.frame(patientID, age, diabetes, status)    ❷ Displays the
> str(patientdata)                                                  object structure
```

```
'data.frame':   4 obs. of  4 variables:
 $ patientID: num  1 2 3 4
 $ age      : num  25 34 28 52
 $ diabetes : Factor w/ 2 levels "Type1","Type2": 1 2 1 1
 $ status   : Ord.factor w/ 3 levels "Excellent"<"Improved"<..: 3 2 1 3
> summary(patientdata)
   patientID          age          diabetes        status
 Min.   :1.00    Min.   :25.00    Type1:3    Excellent:1
 1st Qu.:1.75    1st Qu.:27.25    Type2:1    Improved :1
 Median :2.50    Median :31.00               Poor     :2
 Mean   :2.50    Mean   :34.75
 3rd Qu.:3.25    3rd Qu.:38.50
 Max.   :4.00    Max.   :52.00
```

❸ **Displays the object summary**

First, you enter the data as vectors ❶. Then you specify that `diabetes` is a factor and `status` is an ordered factor. Finally, you combine the data into a data frame. The function `str(object)` provides information about an object in R (the data frame, in this case) ❷. The output indicates that `diabetes` is a factor and `status` is an ordered factor, along with how they're coded internally. Note that the `summary()` function treats the variables differently ❸. It provides the minimum, maximum, mean, and quartiles for the continuous variable `age` and frequency counts for the categorical variables `diabetes` and `status`.

2.2.6 *Lists*

Lists are the most complex of the R data types. Basically, a list is an ordered collection of objects (components). A list allows you to gather a variety of (possibly unrelated) objects under one name. For example, a list may contain a combination of vectors, matrices, data frames, and even other lists. You create a list using the `list()` function:

```
mylist <- list(object1, object2, ...)
```

where the objects are any of the structures seen so far. Optionally, you can name the objects in a list:

```
mylist <- list(name1=object1, name2=object2, ...)
```

The following listing shows an example.

Listing 2.7 Creating a list

```
> g <- "My First List"
> h <- c(25, 26, 18, 39)
> j <- matrix(1:10, nrow=5)
> k <- c("one", "two", "three")
> mylist <- list(title=g, ages=h, j, k)     ← Creates a list
> mylist                                     ← Prints the entire list
$title
[1] "My First List"

$ages
[1] 25 26 18 39
```

```
[[3]]
     [,1] [,2]
[1,]    1    6
[2,]    2    7
[3,]    3    8
[4,]    4    9
[5,]    5   10

[[4]]
[1] "one"     "two"     "three"
```

Prints the second
component

```
> mylist[[2]]
[1] 25 26 18 39
> mylist[["ages"]]
[[1] 25 26 18 39
```

In this example, you create a list with four components: a string, a numeric vector, a matrix, and a character vector. You can combine any number of objects and save them as a list.

You can also specify elements of the list by indicating a component number or a name within double brackets. In this example, `mylist[[2]]` and `mylist[["ages"]]` both refer to the same four-element numeric vector. For named components, `mylist$ages` would also work. Lists are important R structures for two reasons. First, they allow you to organize and recall disparate information in a simple way. Second, the results of many R functions return lists. It's up to the analyst to pull out the components that are needed. You'll see numerous examples of functions that return lists in later chapters.

2.2.7 *Tibbles*

Before moving on, it is worth mentioning tibbles, which are data frames that have specialized behaviors that are designed to make them more useful. They're created using either the `tibble()` or `as_tibble()` function from the `tibble` package. To install the `tibble` package, use `install.packages("tibble")`. Some of their attractive features are described below.

Tibbles print in a more compact format than standard data frames. Additionally, variable labels describe the data type of each column:

```
library(tibble)
mtcars <- as_tibble(mtcars)
mtcars

# A tibble: 32 x 11
    mpg   cyl  disp    hp  drat    wt  qsec    vs    am  gear  carb
  * <dbl> <dbl> <dbl> <dbl> <dbl> <dbl> <dbl> <dbl> <dbl> <dbl> <dbl>
  1 21       6  160   110  3.9   2.62  16.5     0     1     4     4
  2 21       6  160   110  3.9   2.88  17.0     0     1     4     4
  3 22.8     4  108    93  3.85  2.32  18.6     1     1     4     1
  4 21.4     6  258   110  3.08  3.22  19.4     1     0     3     1
  5 18.7     8  360   175  3.15  3.44  17.0     0     0     3     2
  6 18.1     6  225   105  2.76  3.46  20.2     1     0     3     1
```

```
 7   14.3    8   360    245   3.21   3.57   15.8      0      0      3      4
 8   24.4    4   147.    62   3.69   3.19   20        1      0      4      2
 9   22.8    4   141.    95   3.92   3.15   22.9      1      0      4      2
10   19.2    6   168.   123   3.92   3.44   18.3      1      0      4      4
# ... with 22 more rows
```

Tibbles never convert character variables to factors. In older versions of R (prior to R 4.0), functions such as `read.table()`, `data.frame()` and `as.data.frame()` convert character data to factors by default. You would have to add the option `strings-AsFactors = FALSE` to these functions to suppress this behavior.

Tibbles never change the names of variables. If the dataset being imported has a variable called `Last Address`, base R functions would convert the name to `Last.Address`, since R variable names don't use spaces. Tibbles would keep the name as is and use backticks (e.g., `` `Last Address` ``) to make the variable name syntactically correct.

Subsetting a tibble always returns a tibble. For example, subsetting the `mtcars` data frame using `mtcars[, "mpg"]` would return a vector, rather than a one-column data frame. R automatically simplifies the results. To get a one-column data frame, you would have to include the `drop = FALSE` option (`mtcars[, "mpg", drop = FALSE]`). In contrast, if `mtcars` is a tibble, then `mtcars[, "mpg"]` would return a one-column tibble. The results are not simplified, allowing you to easily predict what the results of a subsetting operation will return.

Finally, tibbles don't support row names. The function `rownames_to_column()` can be used to convert the row names in a data frame to a variable in a tibble.

Tibbles are important because many popular packages, such as `readr`, `tidyr`, `dplyr`, and `purr`, save data frames as tibbles. Although tibbles have been designed to be "a modern take on data frames," note that they can be used interchangeably with data frames. Any function that requires a data frame can take a tibble and vice versa. To learn more, see https://r4ds.had.co.nz/tibbles.html.

A note for programmers

Experienced programmers typically find several aspects of the R language unusual. Here are some features of the language you should be aware of:

- The period (.) has no special significance in object names. The dollar sign ($) has a somewhat analogous meaning to the period in other object-oriented languages and can be used to identify the parts of a data frame or list. For example, `A$x` refers to variable `x` in data frame `A`.
- R doesn't provide multiline or block comments. You must start each line of a multiline comment with #. For debugging purposes, you can also surround code that you want the interpreter to ignore with the statement `if (FALSE) { ... }`. Changing the `FALSE` to `TRUE` allows the code to be executed.
- Assigning a value to a nonexistent element of a vector, matrix, array, or list expands that structure to accommodate the new value. For example, consider the following:

```
> x <- c(8, 6, 4)
> x[7] <- 10
> x
[1]  8  6  4 NA NA NA 10
```

The vector x has expanded from 3 to 7 elements through the assignment.
x <- x[1:3] would shrink it back to 7 elements.

- R doesn't have scalar values. Scalars are represented as one-element vectors.
- Indices in R start at 1, not at 0. In the vector earlier, x[1] is 8.
- Variables can't be declared. They come into existence on first assignment.

To learn more, see John Cook's excellent blog post, "R Language for Programmers" (http://mng.bz/6NwQ). Programmers looking for stylistic guidance may also want to check out Hadley Wickham's *The Tidyverse Style Guide* (https://style.tidyverse.org/).

2.3 Data input

Now that you have data structures, you need to put some data in them. As a data analyst, you're typically faced with data that comes from a variety of sources and in a variety of formats. Your task is to import the data into your tools, analyze the data, and report on the results. R provides a wide range of tools for importing data. The definitive guide for importing data in R is the *R Data Import/Export* manual available at http://mng.bz/urwn.

As you can see in figure 2.2, R can import data from the keyboard, from text files, from Microsoft Excel and Access, from popular statistical packages, from a variety of relational database management systems, from specialty databases, and from websites and online services. Because you never know where your data will come from, we'll cover each of them here. You only need to read about the ones you're going to be using.

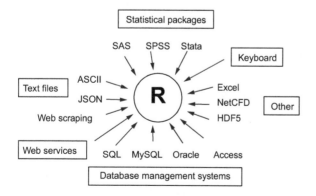

Figure 2.2 **Sources of data that can be imported into R**

2.3.1   *Entering data from the keyboard*

Perhaps the simplest way to enter data is from the keyboard. There are two common methods: entering data through R's built-in text editor and embedding data directly into your code. We'll consider the editor first.

The edit() function in R invokes a text editor that lets you enter data manually. Here are the steps:

1. Create an empty data frame (or matrix) with the variable names and modes you want to have in the final dataset.
2. Invoke the text editor on this data object, enter your data, and save the results to the data object.

The following example creates a data frame named mydata with three variables: age (numeric), gender (character), and weight (numeric). You then invoke the text editor, add your data, and save the results:

```
mydata <- data.frame(age=numeric(0), gender=character(0),
                     weight=numeric(0))
mydata <- edit(mydata)
```

Assignments like age=numeric(0) create a variable of a specific mode, but without actual data. Note that the result of the editing is assigned back to the object itself. The edit() function operates on a copy of the object. If you don't assign it a destination, all of your edits will be lost.

Figure 2.3 shows the results of invoking the edit() function on a Windows platform. In this figure, I've added some data. If you click a column title, the editor gives you the option of changing the variable name and type (numeric or character). You

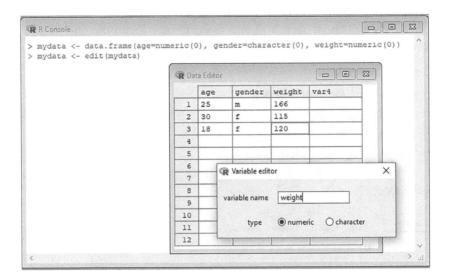

Figure 2.3   Entering data via the built-in editor on a Windows platform

can add variables by clicking the titles of unused columns. When the text editor is closed, the results are saved to the object assigned (mydata, in this case). Invoking mydata <- edit(mydata) again allows you to edit the data you've entered and to add new data. A shortcut for mydata <- edit(mydata) is fix(mydata).

Alternatively, you can embed the data directly in your program. For example, the following code creates the same data frame as that created with the edit() function:

```
mydatatxt <- "
age gender weight
25 m 166
30 f 115
18 f 120
"
mydata <- read.table(header=TRUE, text=mydatatxt)
```

A character string is created containing the raw data, and the read.table() function is used to process the string and return a data frame. The read.table() function is described more fully in the next section.

Keyboard data entry can be convenient when you're working with small datasets. For larger datasets, you'll want to use the methods described next for importing data from existing text files, Excel spreadsheets, statistical packages, or database-management systems.

2.3.2 Importing data from a delimited text file

You can import data from delimited text files using read.table(), a function that reads a file in table format and saves it as a data frame. Each row of the table appears as one line in the file. The syntax is

```
mydataframe <- read.table(file, options)
```

where *file* is a delimited ASCII file and the *options* are parameters controlling how data is processed. Table 2.2 lists the most common options.

Table 2.2 read.table() options

Option	Description
header	A logical value indicating whether the file contains the variable names in the first line.
sep	The delimiter separating data values. The default is sep="", which denotes one or more spaces, tabs, new lines, or carriage returns. Use sep="," to read comma-delimited files, and sep="\t" to read tab-delimited files.
row.names	An optional parameter specifying one or more variables to represent row identifiers.
col.names	If the first row of the data file doesn't contain variable names (header=FALSE), you can use col.names to specify a character vector containing the variable names. If header=FALSE and the col.names option is omitted, variables will be named V1, V2, and so on.

Table 2.2 `read.table()` options *(continued)*

Option	Description
na.strings	An optional character vector indicating missing-values codes. For example, `na.strings=c("-9", "?")` converts each `-9` and `?` value to `NA` as the data is read.
colClasses	An optional vector of classes to be assigned to the columns. For example, `colClasses=c("numeric", "numeric", "character", "NULL", "numeric")` reads the first two columns as numeric, reads the third column as character, skips the fourth column, and reads the fifth column as numeric. If there are more than five columns in the data, the values in `colClasses` are recycled. When you're reading large text files, including the `colClasses` option can speed up processing considerably.
quote	Character(s) used to delimit strings that contain special characters. By default, this is either double (") or single (') quotes.
skip	The number of lines in the data file to skip before beginning to read the data. This option is useful for skipping header comments in the file.
stringsAsFactors	A logical value indicating whether character variables should be converted to factors. Before R 4.0, the default was `TRUE`. For more recent versions, the default is now `FALSE` unless it's overridden by `colClasses`. When you're processing large text files, setting `stringsAsFactors=FALSE` can speed up processing.
text	A character string specifying a text string to process. If `text` is specified, leave `file` blank. Section 2.3.1 gives an example.

Consider a text file named studentgrades.csv containing students' grades in math, science, and social studies. Each line of the file represents a student. The first line contains the variable names, separated with commas. Each subsequent line contains a student's information, also separated with commas. The first few lines of the file are as follows:

```
StudentID,First,Last,Math,Science,Social Studies
011,Bob,Smith,90,80,67
012,Jane,Weary,75,,80
010,Dan,"Thornton, III",65,75,70
040,Mary,"O'Leary",90,95,92
```

The file can be imported into a data frame using the following code:

```
grades <- read.table("studentgrades.csv", header=TRUE,
    row.names="StudentID", sep=",")
```

The results are

```
> grades

   First          Last Math Science Social.Studies
11   Bob         Smith   90      80             67
12  Jane         Weary   75      NA             80
10   Dan Thornton, III   65      75             70
40  Mary       O'Leary   90      95             92
```

```
> str(grades)

'data.frame':   4 obs. of  5 variables:
 $ First        : chr  "Bob" "Jane" "Dan" "Mary"
 $ Last         : chr  "Smith" "Weary" "Thornton, III" "O'Leary"
 $ Math         : int  90 75 65 90
 $ Science      : int  80 NA 75 95
 $ Social.Studies: int  67 80 70 92
```

There are several interesting things to note about how the data is imported. The variable name `Social Studies` is automatically renamed to follow R conventions. The `StudentID` column is now the row name, no longer has a label, and has lost its leading zero. The missing science grade for Jane is correctly read as missing. I had to put quotation marks around Dan's last name to escape the comma between `Thornton` and `III`. Otherwise, R would have seen seven values on that line rather than six. I also had to put quotation marks around `O'Leary`. Otherwise, R would have read the single quote as a string delimiter, which isn't what I want.

The stringsAsFactors option

In the functions `read.table()`, `data.frame()`, and `as.data.frame()`, the `stringsAsFactors` option controls whether character variables are automatically converted to factors. Prior to R version 4.0.0, the default was `TRUE`. Starting with R 4.0.0, the default is `FALSE`. If you are using an older version of R, the variables `First` and `Last` in the previous example are now factors rather than character variables.

Converting character variables to factors may not always be desirable. For example, there would be little reason to convert a character variable containing a respondent's comments into a factor. Additionally, you may want to manipulate or mine the text in a variable, and this is hard to do once it has been converted to a factor.

You can suppress this behavior in several ways. Including the option `stringsAsFactors=FALSE` turns off this behavior for all character variables. Alternatively, you can use the `colClasses` option to specify a class (for example, logical, numeric, character, or factor) for each column.

Let's import the same data while specifying the class for each variable:

```
grades <- read.table("studentgrades.csv", header=TRUE,
           row.names="StudentID", sep=",",
           colClasses=c("character", "character", "character",
                        "numeric", "numeric", "numeric"))
> grades

     First           Last Math Science Social.Studies
011    Bob          Smith   90      80             67
012   Jane          Weary   75      NA             80
010    Dan  Thornton, III   65      75             70
040   Mary        O'Leary   90      95             92

> str(grades)
```

```
'data.frame':   4 obs. of  5 variables:
 $ First        : chr  "Bob" "Jane" "Dan" "Mary"
 $ Last         : chr  "Smith" "Weary" "Thornton, III" "O'Leary"
 $ Math         : num  90 75 65 90
 $ Science      : num  80 NA 75 95
 $ Social.Studies: num  67 80 70 92
```

Now the row names retain their leading zero, and `First` and `Last` are not factors (even in earlier versions of R). Additionally, the grades are stored as real values rather than integers.

The `read.table()` function has many options for fine-tuning data imports. See `help(read.table)` for details.

Importing data via connections

Many of the examples in this chapter import data from files that exist on your computer. R provides several mechanisms for accessing data via connections as well. For example, the functions `file()`, `gzfile()`, `bzfile()`, `xzfile()`, `unz()`, and `url()` can be used in place of the filename. The `file()` function allows you to access files, the clipboard, and C-level standard input. The `gzfile()`, `bzfile()`, `xzfile()`, and `unz()` functions let you read compressed files.

The `url()` function lets you access internet files through a complete URL that includes http://, ftp://, or file://. For HTTP and FTP, proxies can be specified. For convenience, complete URLs (surrounded by double quotation marks) can usually be used directly in place of filenames as well. See `help(file)` for details.

Base R also provides the functions `read.csv()` and `read.delim()` for importing rectangular text files. These are simply wrapper functions that call `read.table()` with specific defaults. For example, `read.csv()` calls `read.table()` with header =TRUE, and sep="," while `read.delim()` calls `read.table()` with header=TRUE and sep="\t". Details are provided in the `read.table()` help.

The `readr` package provides a powerful alternative to base R functions for reading rectangular text files. The primary function is `read_delim()` with helper functions `read_csv()` and `read_tsv()` for reading comma-delimited and tab-delimited files, respectively. After installing the package, the previous data could have been read using this code:

```
library(readr)
grades <- read_csv("studentgrades.csv")
```

The package also provides for importing fixed-width files (where data appears in specific columns), tabular files (where columns are separated by whitespace), and web log files.

Functions in the `readr` package provide a number of advantages over those in base R. First and foremost, they are *significantly* faster. This can be a tremendous advantage when reading large data files. Additionally, they are very good at guessing the correct data type of each column (numeric, character, date, and date-time). Finally, unlike base R functions prior to R 4.0.0, they won't convert character data to factors by default. Functions in the readr package return data as tibbles (data frames with some specialized features). To learn more, see https://readr.tidyverse.org.

2.3.3 Importing data from Excel

The best way to read an Excel file is to export it to a comma-delimited file from Excel and import it into R using the method described earlier. Alternatively, you can import Excel worksheets directly using the readxl package. Be sure to download and install it before you first use it.

The readxl package can be used to read both .xls and .xlsx versions of Excel files. The read_excel() function imports a worksheet into a data frame as a tibble. The simplest format is read_excel(file, n), where file is the path to an Excel workbook, n is the number of the worksheet to be imported, and the first line of the worksheet contains the variable names. For example, on a Windows platform, the code

```
library(readxl)
workbook <- "c:/myworkbook.xlsx"
mydataframe <- read_xlsx(workbook, 1)
```

imports the first worksheet from the workbook myworkbook.xlsx stored on the C: drive and saves it as the data frame mydataframe.

The read_excel() function has options that allow you to specify a specific cell range (e.g., range = "Mysheet!B2:G14"), along with the class of each column (col_types). See help(read_excel) for details.

Other packages that can help you work with Excel files include xlsx, XLConnect, and openxlsx. The xlsx and XLConnect packages depend on Java, while openxlsx doesn't. Unlike readxl, these packages can do more than import worksheets—they can also create and manipulate Excel files. Programmers who need to develop an interface between R and Excel should check out one or more of these packages.

2.3.4 Importing data from JSON

Increasingly, data are provided in JSON (JavaScript Object Notation) format. R has several packages for working with JSON. For example, the jsonlite package allows you to read, write, and manipulate JSON objects. Data can be imported from JSON files directly into R data frames. Coverage of JSON is beyond the scope of this text; if you're interested, see the jsonlite vignettes (https://cran.r-project.org/web/packages/jsonlite/).

2.3.5 Importing data from the web

Data can be obtained from the web via *web scraping* or by using *application programming interfaces* (APIs). Web scraping is used to extract the information embedded in specific web pages, whereas APIs allow you to interact with web services and online data stores.

Typically, web scraping is used to extract data from a web page and save it into an R structure for further analysis. For example, the text on a web page can be downloaded into an R character vector using the readLines() function and manipulated with functions such as grep() and gsub(). The rvest package provides functions that can simplify extracting data from web pages. It was inspired by the Python library Beautiful Soup. The RCurl and XML packages can also be used to extract information. For more information, including examples, see "Examples of Web Scraping with R" on the website *ProgrammingR* (www.programmingr.com).

APIs specify how software components should interact with each other. Several R packages use this approach to extract data from web-accessible resources. These include data sources in biology, medicine, earth sciences, physical science, economics and business, finance, literature, marketing, news, and sports.

For example, if you're interested in social media, you can access Twitter data via twitteR, Facebook data via Rfacebook, and Flickr data via Rflickr. Other packages allow you to access popular web services provide by Google, Amazon, Dropbox, Salesforce, and others. For a comprehensive list of R packages that can help you access web-based resources, see the CRAN Task View on "Web Technologies and Services" (http://mng.bz/370r).

2.3.6   *Importing data from SPSS*

IBM SPSS datasets can be imported into R via the read_spss() function in the haven package. First, download and install the package:

```
install.packages("haven")
```

Then use the following code to import the data:

```
library(haven)
mydataframe <- read_spss("mydata.sav")
```

The imported dataset is a data frame (as a tibble), and variables containing imported SPSS value labels are assigned the class labelled. You can convert these labeled variables to R factors using the following code:

```
labelled_vars <- names(mydataframe)[sapply(mydataframe, is.labelled)]
for (vars in labelled_vars){
  mydataframe[[vars]] = as_factor(mydataframe[[vars]])
}
```

The haven package has additional functions for reading SPSS files in compressed (.zsav) or transport (.por) format.

2.3.7   *Importing data from SAS*

SAS datasets can be imported using read_sas() in the haven package. After installing the package, import that data using

```
library(haven)
mydataframe <- read_sas("mydata.sas7bdat")
```

If the user also has a catalogue of variable formats, they can be imported and applied to the data as well using

```
mydataframe <- read_sas("mydata.sas7bdat",
                        catalog_file = "mydata.sas7bcat")
```

In either case, the result is a data frame saved as a tibble.

Alternatively, there is a commercial product named Stat/Transfer (described in section 2.3.10) that does an excellent job of saving SAS datasets (including any existing variable formats) as R data frames.

2.3.8 Importing data from Stata

Importing data from Stata to R is straightforward. Again, use the haven package:

```
library(haven)
mydataframe <- read_dta("mydata.dta")
```

Here, `mydata.dta` is the Stata dataset, and `mydataframe` is the resulting R data frame, saved as a tibble.

2.3.9 Accessing database management systems

R can interface with a wide variety of relational database management systems (DBMSs), including Microsoft SQL Server, Microsoft Access, MySQL, Oracle, PostgreSQL, DB2, Sybase, Teradata, and SQLite. Some packages provide access through native database drivers, whereas others offer access via ODBC or JDBC. Using R to access data stored in external DBMSs can be an efficient way to analyze large datasets (see appendix F) and takes advantage of the power of both SQL and R.

THE ODBC INTERFACE

Perhaps the most popular method of accessing a DBMS in R is through the RODBC package, which allows R to connect to any DBMS that has an ODBC driver. This includes all the DBMSs listed earlier.

The first step is to install and configure the appropriate ODBC driver for your platform and database (these drivers aren't part of R). If the requisite drivers aren't already installed on your machine, an internet search should provide you with options ("Setting up ODBC Drivers" at https://db.rstudio.com/best-practices/drivers/ is a good place to start).

Once the drivers are installed and configured for the database(s) of your choice, install the RODBC package. You can do so with the `install.packages("RODBC")` command. Table 2.3 lists the primary functions included with RODBC.

Table 2.3 RODBC functions

Function	Description
odbcConnect(*dsn*,uid="",pwd="")	Opens a connection to an ODBC database
sqlFetch(*channel,sqltable*)	Reads a table from an ODBC database into a data frame
sqlQuery(*channel,query*)	Submits a query to an ODBC database and returns the results

Table 2.3 RODBC functions *(continued)*

Function	Description
sqlSave(*channel*,*mydf*,tablename = *sqltable*,append=FALSE)	Writes or updates (append=TRUE) a data frame to a table in the ODBC database
sqlDrop(*channel*,*sqltable*)	Removes a table from the ODBC database
close(*channel*)	Closes the connection

The RODBC package allows two-way communication between R and an ODBC-connected SQL database. This means you can not only read data from a connected database into R, but you can also use R to alter the contents of the database itself. Assume that you want to import two tables (Crime and Punishment) from a DBMS into two R data frames called crimedat and pundat, respectively. You can accomplish this with code similar to this:

```
library(RODBC)
myconn <-odbcConnect("mydsn", uid="Rob", pwd="aardvark")
crimedat <- sqlFetch(myconn, Crime)
pundat <- sqlQuery(myconn, "select * from Punishment")
close(myconn)
```

Here, you load the RODBC package and open a connection to the ODBC database through a registered data source name (mydsn) with a security UID (rob) and password (aardvark). The connection string is passed to sqlFetch, which copies the table Crime into the R data frame crimedat. You then run the SQL select statement against the table Punishment and save the results to the data frame pundat. Finally, you close the connection.

The sqlQuery() function is powerful because any valid SQL statement can be inserted. This flexibility allows you to select specific variables, subset the data, create new variables, and recode and rename existing variables.

DBI-RELATED PACKAGES

The DBI package provides a general and consistent client-side interface to DBMS. Building on this framework, the RJDBC package provides access to DBMS via a JDBC driver. Be sure to install the necessary JDBC drivers for your platform and database. Other useful DBI-based packages include RMySQL, ROracle, RPostgreSQL, and RSQLite. These packages provide native database drivers for their respective databases but may not be available on all platforms. Check the documentation on CRAN (https://cran.r-project.org) for details.

2.3.10 *Importing data via Stat/Transfer*

Before we end our discussion of importing data, it's worth mentioning a commercial product that can make the task significantly easier. Stat/Transfer (https://www.stattransfer.com) is a standalone application that can transfer data among 34 data formats, including R (see figure 2.4).

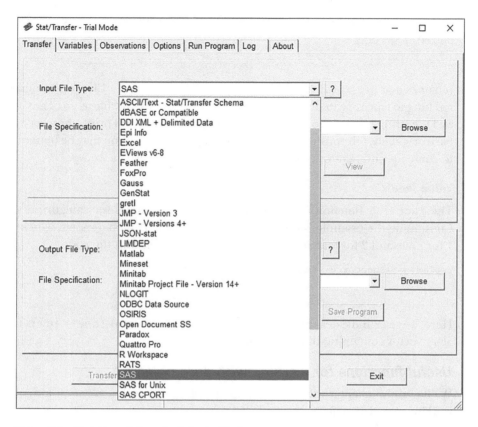

Figure 2.4 Stat/Transfer's main dialog in Windows

Stat/Transfer is available for Windows, Mac, and Unix platforms. It supports the latest versions of the statistical packages we've discussed so far, as well as ODBC-accessed DBMSs such as Oracle, Sybase, Informix, and DB/2.

2.4   Annotating datasets

Data analysts typically annotate datasets to make the results easier to interpret. Annotating generally includes adding descriptive labels to variable names and value labels to the codes used for categorical variables. For example, for the variable age, you might want to attach the more descriptive label "Age at hospitalization (in years)." For the variable gender, coded 1 or 2, you might want to associate the labels "male" and "female."

2.4.1   Variable labels

Unfortunately, R's ability to handle variable labels is limited. One approach is to use the variable label as the variable's name and then refer to the variable by its position index. Consider the earlier example, where you have a data frame containing patient data. The second column, age, contains the ages at which individuals were first hospitalized. The code

```
names(patientdata)[2] <- "Age at hospitalization (in years)"
```

renames age to `"Age at hospitalization (in years)"`. Clearly this new name is too long to type repeatedly. Instead, you can refer to this variable as `patientdata[2]`, and the string `"Age at hospitalization (in years)"` will print wherever age would have originally. Obviously, this isn't an ideal approach, and you may be better off trying to come up with better variable names (for example, `admissionAge`).

2.4.2 Value labels

The `factor()` function can be used to create value labels for categorical variables. Continuing the example, suppose you have a variable named `gender`, which is coded 1 for male and 2 for female. You can create value labels with the code

```
patientdata$gender <- factor(patientdata$gender,
                    levels = c(1,2),
                    labels = c("male", "female"))
```

Here, `levels` indicates the actual values of the variable, and `labels` refers to a character vector containing the desired labels.

2.5 Useful functions for working with data objects

We'll end this chapter with a brief summary of functions that are useful when you are working with data objects (see table 2.4).

Table 2.4   Functions for working with data objects

Function	Purpose
length(*object*)	Gives the number of elements/components
dim(*object*)	Gives the dimensions of an object
str(*object*)	Gives the structure of an object.
class(*object*)	Gives the class of an object
mode(*object*)	Determines how an object is stored
names(*object*)	Gives the names of components in an object
c(*object, object,...*)	Combines objects into a vector.
cbind(*object, object, ...*)	Combines objects as columns
rbind(*object, object,...*)	Combines objects as rows
object	Prints an object
head(*object*)	Lists the first part of an object
tail(*object*)	Lists the last part of an object

Table 2.4 Functions for working with data objects *(continued)*

Function	Purpose
`ls()`	Lists current objects
`rm(`*object, object,* `...)`	Deletes one or more objects. The statement `rm(list = ls())` removes most objects from the working environment.
newobject `<- edit(`*object*`)`	Edits `object` and saves it as `newobject`
`fix(`*object*`)`	Edits an object in place

We've already discussed most of these functions. `head()` and `tail()` are useful for quickly scanning large datasets. For example, `head(patientdata)` lists the first six rows of the data frame, whereas `tail(patientdata)` lists the last six. We'll cover functions such as `length()`, `cbind()`, and `rbind()` in the next chapter; they're gathered here as a reference.

As you've seen, R offers a wealth of functions for accessing external data. Appendix C covers exporting data from R to other formats, and appendix F covers methods of working with large datasets (in the gigabyte-to-terabyte range).

Once you import your datasets into R, it's likely that you'll have to manipulate them into a more conducive format. In chapter 3, we'll explore ways to create new variables, transform and recode existing variables, merge datasets, and select observations.

Summary

- R provides various objects for holding data, including vectors, matrices, data frames, and lists.
- You can import data into R data frames from external sources, including text files, Excel worksheets, web APIs, statistical packages, and databases.
- There are extensive functions for describing, modifying, and combining data structures.

Basic data management

This chapter covers

- Manipulating dates and missing values
- Understanding data type conversions
- Creating and recoding variables
- Sorting, merging, and subsetting datasets
- Selecting and dropping variables

In chapter 2, we covered various methods for importing data into R. Unfortunately, getting your data in the rectangular arrangement of a matrix or data frame is only the first step in preparing it for analysis. To paraphrase Captain Kirk in the *Star Trek* episode "A Taste of Armageddon" (and proving my geekiness once and for all), "Data is a messy business—a very, very messy business." In my own work, as much as 60% of any data analysis project is spent cleaning and organizing the data. I'll go out on a limb and say that the same is probably true for most real-world data analysts. Let's take a look at an example.

3.1 A working example

One of the topics that I study in my current job is how men and women differ in the ways they lead their organizations. Typical questions might be

- Do men and women in management positions differ in the degree to which they defer to superiors?
- Does this vary from country to country, or are these gender differences universal?

One way to address these questions is to have bosses in multiple countries rate their managers on deferential behavior, using questions like the following.

This manager asks my opinion before making personnel decisions.				
1	2	3	4	5
strongly disagree	disagree	neither agree nor disagree	agree	strongly agree

The resulting data might resemble that in table 3.1. Each row represents the ratings given to a manager by their boss.

Table 3.1 **Gender differences in leadership behavior**

Manager	Date	Country	Gender	Age	q1	q2	q3	q4	q5
1	10/24/14	US	M	32	5	4	5	5	5
2	10/28/14	US	F	45	3	5	2	5	5
3	10/01/14	US	F	25	3	5	5	5	2
4	10/12/14	US	M	39	3	3	4		
5	05/01/14	US	F	99	2	2	1	2	1

Here, each manager is rated by their boss on five statements (q1 to q5) related to deference to authority. For example, manager 1 is a 32-year-old male working in the US and is rated as deferential by his boss, whereas manager 5 is a female of unknown age (99 probably indicates that the information is missing) working in the UK and is rated low on deferential behavior. The Date column captures when the ratings were made.

Although a dataset might have dozens of variables and thousands of observations, I've included only 10 columns and 5 rows to simplify the examples. Additionally, I've limited the number of items pertaining to the managers' deferential behavior to 5. In a real-world study, you'd probably use 10 to 20 such items to improve the reliability and validity of the results. You can create a data frame containing the data in table 3.1 using the following code.

Listing 3.1   Creating the leadership data frame

```
leadership <- data.frame(
    manager = c(1, 2, 3, 4, 5),
    date    = c("10/24/08", "10/28/08", "10/1/08", "10/12/08", "5/1/09"),
    country = c("US", "US", "UK", "UK", "UK"),
    gender  = c("M", "F", "F", "M", "F"),
    age     = c(32, 45, 25, 39, 99),
    q1      = c(5, 3, 3, 3, 2),
    q2      = c(4, 5, 5, 3, 2),
    q3      = c(5, 2, 5, 4, 1),
    q4      = c(5, 5, 5, NA, 2),
    q5      = c(5, 5, 2, NA, 1)
)
```

To address the questions of interest, you must first deal with several data management issues. Here's a partial list:

- The five ratings (q1 to q5) need to be combined, yielding a single mean deferential score from each manager.

- In surveys, respondents often skip questions. For example, the boss rating manager 4 skipped questions 4 and 5. You need a method of handling incomplete data. You also need to recode values like 99 for age to *missing*.

- There may be hundreds of variables in a dataset, but you may only be interested in a few. To simplify matters, you'll want to create a new dataset with only the variables of interest.

- Past research suggests that leadership behavior may change as a function of the manager's age. To examine this, you may want to recode the current values of age into a new categorical age grouping (for example, young, middle-aged, elderly).

- Leadership behavior may change over time. You might want to focus on deferential behavior during the recent global financial crisis. To do so, you may want to limit the study to data gathered during a specific period of time (say, January 1, 2009, to December 31, 2009).

We'll work through each of these issues in this chapter, as well as other basic data management tasks such as combining and sorting datasets. Then, in chapter 5, we'll look at some advanced topics.

3.2   *Creating new variables*

In a typical research project, you'll need to create new variables and transform existing ones. This is accomplished with statements of the form:

```
variable <- expression
```

A wide array of operators and functions can be included in the `expression` portion of the statement. Table 3.2 lists R's arithmetic operators.

Table 3.2 Arithmetic operators

Operator	Description
+	Addition
–	Subtraction
*	Multiplication
/	Division
^ or **	Exponentiation
x%%y	Modulus (x mod y): for example, 5%%2 is 1
x%/%y	Integer division: for example, 5%/%2 is 2

Given the data frame `leadership`, say you want to create a new variable `total_score` that adds the variables q1 to q5 and a new variable called `mean_score` that averages these variables. If you use the code

```
total_score  <-  q1 + q2 + q3 + q4 + q5
mean_score <- (q1 + q2 + q3 + q4 + q5)/5
```

you'll get an error, because R doesn't know that q1, q2, q3, q4, and q5 are from the data frame `leadership`. If you use this code instead

```
total_score  <-  leadership$q1 + leadership$q2 + leadership$q3 +
                 leadership$q4 + leadership$q5
mean_score <- (leadership$q1 + leadership$q2 + leadership$q3 +
                 leadership$q4 + leadership$q5)/5
```

the statements will succeed, but you'll end up with a data frame (`leadership`) and two separate vectors (`total_score` and `mean_score`). This probably isn't the result you want. Ultimately, you want to incorporate new variables into the original data frame. The following listing provides two separate ways to accomplish this goal. The one you choose is up to you; the results will be the same.

Listing 3.2 Creating new variables

```
leadership$total_score  <-  leadership$q1 + leadership$q2 + leadership$q3 +
                 leadership$q4 + leadership$q5
leadership$mean_score <- (leadership$q1 + leadership$q2 + leadership$q3 +
                 leadership$q4 + leadership$q5)/5

leadership <- transform(leadership,
               total_score  =  q1 + q2 + q3 + q4 + q5,
               mean_score = (q1 + q2 + q3 + q4 + q5)/5)
```

Personally, I prefer the second method, exemplified by the use of the `transform()` function. It simplifies the inclusion of as many new variables as you want and saves the results to the data frame.

3.3   *Recoding variables*

Recoding involves creating new values of a variable conditional on the existing values of the same and/or other variables. For example, you may want to

- Change a continuous variable into a set of categories
- Replace miscoded values with correct values
- Create a pass/fail variable based on a set of cutoff scores

To recode data, you can use one or more of R's logical operators (see table 3.3). Logical operators are expressions that return TRUE or FALSE.

Table 3.3   Logical operators

Operator	Description
<	Less than
<=	Less than or equal to
>	Greater than
>=	Greater than or equal to
==	Exactly equal to
!=	Not equal to
!x	Not x
x | y	x or y
x & y	x and y
isTRUE(x)	Tests whether x is TRUE

Let's say you want to recode the ages of the managers in the leadership dataset from the continuous variable age to the categorical variable agecat (Young, Middle Aged, Elder). First, you must recode the value 99 for age to indicate that the value is missing using code such as

```
leadership$age[leadership$age  == 99]      <- NA
```

The statement variable[condition] <- expression will only make the assignment when condition is TRUE.

Once missing values for age have been specified, you can then use the following code to create the agecat variable:

```
leadership$agecat[leadership$age  > 75]    <- "Elder"
leadership$agecat[leadership$age >= 55 &
              leadership$age <= 75]    <- "Middle Aged"
leadership$agecat[leadership$age  < 55]    <- "Young"
```

You include the data frame names in leadership$agecat to ensure that the new variable is saved back to the data frame. (I defined middle-aged as 55 to 75 so I won't feel so old.) Note that if you hadn't recoded 99 as *missing* for age first, manager 5 would've erroneously been given the value "Elder" for `agecat`.

This code can be written more compactly as

```
leadership <- within(leadership, {
                  agecat <- NA
                  agecat[age > 75]                <- "Elder"
                  agecat[age >= 55 & age <= 75] <- "Middle Aged"
                  agecat[age < 55]                <- "Young" })
```

The `within()` function is similar to the `with()` function (section 2.2.4), but it allows you to modify the data frame. First, the variable `agecat` is created and set to missing for each row of the data frame. Then, the remaining statements within the braces are executed in order. Remember that `agecat` is a character variable; you're likely to want to turn it into an ordered factor, as explained in section 2.2.5.

Several packages offer useful recoding functions; in particular, the `car` package's `recode()` function recodes numeric and character vectors and factors very simply. The package `doBy` offers `recodeVar()`, another popular function. Finally, R ships with `cut()`, which allows you to divide the range of a numeric variable into intervals, returning a factor.

3.4 Renaming variables

If you're not happy with your variable names, you can change them interactively or programmatically. Let's say you want to change the variable `manager` to `managerID` and `date` to `testDate`. You can use the following statement to invoke an interactive editor:

```
fix(leadership)
```

Then you click the variable names and rename them in the dialogs that are presented (see figure 3.1).

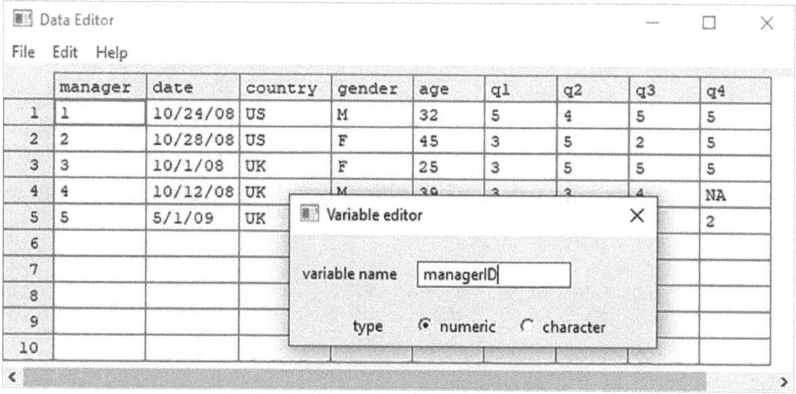

Figure 3.1 Renaming variables interactively using the `fix()` function

Programmatically, you can rename variables via the names() function. For example, the statement

```
names(leadership)[2] <- "testDate"
```

renames date to testDate as demonstrated in the following code:

```
> names(leadership)
 [1] "manager" "date"     "country" "gender"  "age"      "q1"       "q2"
 [8] "q3"      "q4"       "q5"
> names(leadership)[2] <- "testDate"
> leadership
  manager testDate country gender age q1 q2 q3 q4 q5
1       1 10/24/08      US      M  32  5  4  5  5  5
2       2 10/28/08      US      F  45  3  5  2  5  5
3       3  10/1/08      UK      F  25  3  5  5  5  2
4       4 10/12/08      UK      M  39  3  3  4 NA NA
5       5   5/1/09      UK      F  99  2  2  1  2  1
```

In a similar fashion, the statement

```
names(leadership)[6:10] <- c("item1", "item2", "item3", "item4", "item5")
```

renames q1 through q5 to item1 through item5.

3.5 *Missing values*

In a project of any size, data is likely to be incomplete because of missed questions, faulty equipment, or improperly coded data. In R, missing values are represented by the symbol NA (not available). Unlike programs such as SAS, R uses the same missing-value symbol for character and numeric data.

R provides a number of functions for identifying observations that contain missing values. The function is.na() allows you to test for the presence of missing values. Assume that you have this vector:

```
y <- c(1, 2, 3, NA)
```

Then the following function returns c(FALSE, FALSE, FALSE, TRUE):

```
is.na(y)
```

Notice how the is.na() function works on an object. It returns an object of the same size, with the entries replaced by TRUE if the element is a missing value or FALSE if the element isn't a missing value. The following listing applies this to the leadership example.

Listing 3.3 Applying the is.na() function

```
> is.na(leadership[,6:10])
        q1    q2    q3    q4    q5
[1,] FALSE FALSE FALSE FALSE FALSE
[2,] FALSE FALSE FALSE FALSE FALSE
```

```
[3,] FALSE FALSE FALSE FALSE FALSE
[4,] FALSE FALSE FALSE  TRUE  TRUE
[5,] FALSE FALSE FALSE FALSE FALSE
```

Here, `leadership[,6:10]` limits the data frame to columns 6 to 10, and `is.na()` identifies which values are missing.

You need to keep two important things in mind when you're working with missing values in R. First, missing values are considered noncomparable, even to themselves. This means you can't use comparison operators to test for the presence of missing values. For example, the logical test `myvar == NA` is never `TRUE`. Instead, you have to use missing-value functions like `is.na()` to identify the missing values in R data objects.

Second, R doesn't represent infinite or impossible values as missing values. Again, this is different than the way other programs like SAS handle such data. Positive and negative infinity are represented by the symbols `Inf` and `-Inf`, respectively. Thus, `5/0` returns `Inf`. Impossible values (for example, `sin(Inf)`) are represented by the symbol `NaN` (not a number). To identify these values, you need to use `is.infinite()` or `is.nan()`.

3.5.1 Recoding values to missing

As we saw in section 3.3, you can use assignments to recode values to *missing*. In the leadership example, missing age values are coded as 99. Before analyzing this dataset, you must let R know that the value 99 means *missing* in this case—otherwise, the mean age for this sample of bosses will be way off. You can accomplish this by recoding the variable:

```
leadership$age[leadership$age == 99] <- NA
```

Any value of age that's equal to 99 is changed to NA. Be sure that any missing data is properly coded as missing before you analyze the data, or the results will be meaningless.

3.5.2 Excluding missing values from analyses

Once you've identified missing values, you need to eliminate them in some way before analyzing your data further. The reason is that arithmetic expressions and functions that contain missing values yield missing values. For example, consider this code:

```
x <- c(1, 2, NA, 3)
y <- x[1] + x[2] + x[3] + x[4]
z <- sum(x)
```

Both y and z will be NA (missing) because the third element of x is missing.

Luckily, most numeric functions have an `na.rm=TRUE` option that removes missing values prior to calculations and applies the function to the remaining values:

```
x <- c(1, 2, NA, 3)
y <- sum(x, na.rm=TRUE)
```

Here, y is equal to 6.

When using a function with incomplete data, be sure to check how that function handles missing data by looking at its online help (for example, `help(sum)`). The `sum()` function is only one of many functions we'll consider in chapter 5. Functions allow you to transform data with flexibility and ease.

You can remove any observation with missing data by using the `na.omit()` function, which deletes any rows with missing data. Let's apply this to the leadership dataset in the following listing.

Listing 3.4 Using `na.omit()` to delete incomplete observations

```
> leadership
  manager     date country gender age q1 q2 q3 q4 q5
1       1 10/24/08      US      M  32  5  4  5  5  5
2       2 10/28/08      US      F  40  3  5  2  5  5
3       3 10/01/08      UK      F  25  3  5  5  5  2
4       4 10/12/08      UK      M  39  3  3  4 NA NA
5       5 05/01/09      UK      F  NA  2  2  1  2  1

> newdata <- na.omit(leadership)
> newdata
  manager     date country gender age q1 q2 q3 q4 q5
1       1 10/24/08      US      M  32  5  4  5  5  5
2       2 10/28/08      US      F  40  3  5  2  5  5
3       3 10/01/08      UK      F  25  3  5  5  5  2
```

Data frame with missing data

Data frame with complete cases only

Any rows containing missing data are deleted from leadership before the results are saved to `newdata`.

Deleting all observations with missing data (called *listwise deletion*) is one of several methods of handling incomplete datasets. If only a few values are missing or they're concentrated in a small number of observations, listwise deletion can provide a good solution to the missing-values problem. But if missing values are spread throughout the data or a great deal of data are missing in a small number of variables, listwise deletion can exclude a substantial percentage of your data. We'll explore several more sophisticated methods of dealing with missing values in chapter 18. Next, let's look at dates.

3.6 *Date values*

Dates are typically entered into R as character strings and then translated into date variables that are stored numerically. The function `as.Date()` is used to make this translation. The syntax is `as.Date(x, "input_format")`, where x is the character data and `input_format` gives the appropriate format for reading the date (see table 3.4).

Table 3.4 Date formats

Symbol	Meaning	Example
%d	Day as a number (0–31)	01–31
%a	Abbreviated weekday	Mon
%A	Unabbreviated weekday	Monday

Table 3.4 Date formats *(continued)*

Symbol	Meaning	Example
%m	Month (01–12)	01–12
%b	Abbreviated month	Jan
%B	Unabbreviated month	January
%y	Two-digit year	07
%Y	Four-digit year	2007

The default format for inputting dates is yyyy-mm-dd. The statement

```
mydates <- as.Date(c("2007-06-22", "2004-02-13"))
```

converts the character data to dates using this default format. In contrast,

```
strDates <- c("01/05/1965", "08/16/1975")
dates <- as.Date(strDates, "%m/%d/%Y")
```

reads the data using a mm/dd/yyyy format.

In the leadership dataset, date is coded as a character variable in mm/dd/yy format. Therefore

```
myformat <- "%m/%d/%y"
leadership$date <- as.Date(leadership$date, myformat)
```

uses the specified format to read the character variable and replace it in the data frame as a date variable. Once the variable is in date format, you can analyze and plot the dates using the wide range of analytic techniques covered in later chapters.

Two functions are especially useful for time-stamping data. Sys.Date() returns today's date, and date() returns the current date and time. As I write this, it's July 7, 2021, at 6:43 p.m. Executing those functions produces

```
> Sys.Date()
[1] "2021-07-20"
> date()
[1] "Tue Jul 20 18:43:40 2021"
```

You can use the format(x, format="output_format") function to output dates in a specified format and to extract portions of dates:

```
> today <- Sys.Date()
> format(today, format="%B %d %Y")
[1] "July 20 2021"
> format(today, format="%A")
[1] "Tuesday"
```

The format() function takes an argument (a date, in this case) and applies an output format (in this case, assembled from the symbols in table 3.4). The important result here is that there are only two more days until the weekend!

When R stores dates internally, they're represented as the number of days since January 1, 1970, with negative values for earlier dates. That means you can perform arithmetic operations on them. For example,

```
> startdate <- as.Date("2020-02-13")
> enddate  <- as.Date("2021-01-22")
> days     <- enddate - startdate
> days
Time difference of 344 days
```

displays the number of days between February 13, 2020, and January 22, 2021.

Finally, you can also use the function difftime() to calculate a time interval and express it as seconds, minutes, hours, days, or weeks. Let's assume that I was born on October 12, 1956. How old am I?:

```
> today <- Sys.Date()
> dob   <- as.Date("1956-10-12")
> difftime(today, dob, units="weeks")
Time difference of 3380 weeks
```

Apparently, I am 3,380 weeks old. Who knew? Extra credit: On which day of the week was I born?

3.6.1 *Converting dates to character variables*

You can also convert date variables to character variables. Date values can be converted to character values using the as.character() function:

```
strDates <- as.character(dates)
```

The conversion allows you to apply a range of character functions to the data values (subsetting, replacement, concatenation, and so on). We'll cover character functions in detail in section 5.2.4.

3.6.2 *Going further*

To learn more about converting character data to dates, look at help(as.Date) and help(strftime). To learn more about formatting dates and times, see help(ISO-datetime). The lubridate package contains a number of functions that simplify working with dates, including functions to identify and parse date-time data, extract date-time components (for example, years, months, days, hours, and minutes), and perform arithmetic calculations on date-times. If you need to do complex calculations with dates, the timeDate package can also help. It provides a myriad of functions for dealing with dates, can handle multiple time zones at once, and provides sophisticated calendar manipulations that recognize business days, weekends, and holidays.

3.7 *Type conversions*

We just discussed how to convert character data to date values and vice versa. R provides a set of functions to identify an object's data type and convert it to a different data type.

Type conversions in R work similarly to those in other statistical programming languages. For example, adding a character string to a numeric vector converts all the elements in the vector to character values. You can use the functions listed in table 3.5 to test for a data type and convert it to a given type.

Functions of the form `is.data-type()` return TRUE or FALSE, whereas `as.datatype()` converts the argument to that type. The following listing provides an example.

Table 3.5 Type-conversion functions

Test	Convert
is.numeric()	as.numeric()
is.character()	as.character()
is.vector()	as.vector()
is.matrix()	as.matrix()
is.data.frame()	as.data.frame()
is.factor()	as.factor()
is.logical()	as.logical()

Listing 3.5   Converting from one data type to another

```
> a <- c(1,2,3)
> a
[1] 1 2 3
> is.numeric(a)
[1] TRUE
> is.vector(a)
[1] TRUE
> a <- as.character(a)
> a
[1] "1" "2" "3"
> is.numeric(a)
[1] FALSE
> is.vector(a)
[1] TRUE
> is.character(a)
[1] TRUE
```

When combined with the flow controls (such as `if-then`) that we'll discuss in chapter 5, the `is.datatype()` function can be a powerful tool, allowing you to handle data in different ways depending on its type. Additionally, some R functions require data of a specific type (character or numeric, matrix or data frame), and `as.data-type()` lets you transform your data into the format required prior to analyses.

3.8   Sorting data

Sometimes, viewing a dataset in a sorted order can tell you quite a bit about the data. For example, which managers are most deferential? To sort a data frame in R, you use the `order()` function. By default, the sorting order is ascending. Prepend the sorting variable with a minus sign to indicate descending order. The following examples illustrate sorting with the leadership data frame.

The statement

```
newdata <- leadership[order(leadership$age),]
```

creates a new dataset containing rows sorted from youngest manager to oldest manager. The statement

```
newdata <- leadership[order(leadership$gender, leadership$age),]
```

sorts the rows into female followed by male and youngest to oldest within each gender. Finally,

```
newdata <-leadership[order(leadership$gender, -leadership$age),]
```

sorts the rows by gender, and then from oldest to youngest manager within each gender.

3.9   *Merging datasets*

If your data exists in multiple locations, you'll need to combine it before moving forward. This section shows you how to add columns (variables) and rows (observations) to a data frame.

3.9.1   *Adding columns to a data frame*

To merge two data frames (datasets) horizontally, you use the merge() function. In most cases, two data frames are joined by one or more common key variables (that is, an inner join). For example,

```
total <- merge(dataframeA, dataframeB, by="ID")
```

merges dataframeA and dataframeB by ID. Similarly,

```
total <- merge(dataframeA, dataframeB, by=c("ID","Country"))
```

merges the two data frames by ID and Country. Horizontal joins like this are typically used to add variables to a data frame.

> **Horizontal concatenation with cbind()**
>
> If you're joining two matrices or data frames horizontally and don't need to specify a common key, you can use the cbind() function:
>
> ```
> total <- cbind(A, B)
> ```
>
> This function horizontally concatenates objects A and B. For the function to work properly, each object must have the same number of rows and must be sorted in the same order.

3.9.2   *Adding rows to a data frame*

To join two data frames (datasets) vertically, use the rbind() function:

```
total <- rbind(dataframeA, dataframeB)
```

The two data frames must have the same variables, but they don't have to be in the same order. If dataframeA has variables that dataframeB doesn't, then before joining them, do one of the following:

- Delete the extra variables in `dataframeA`.
- Create the additional variables in `dataframeB` and set them to `NA` (missing).

Vertical concatenation is typically used to add observations to a data frame.

3.10 *Subsetting datasets*

R has powerful indexing features for accessing the elements of an object. These features can be used to select and exclude variables, observations, or both. The following sections demonstrate several methods for keeping or deleting variables and observations.

3.10.1 *Selecting variables*

It's common to create a new dataset from a limited number of variables chosen from a larger dataset. Chapter 2 showed that the elements of a data frame are accessed using the notation `dataframe[row indices, column indices]`. You can use this to select variables. For example,

```
newdata <- leadership[, c(6:10)]
```

selects variables q1, q2, q3, q4, and q5 from the leadership data frame and saves them to the data frame `newdata`. Leaving the row indices blank (`,`) selects all the rows by default.

The statements

```
vars <- c("q1", "q2", "q3", "q4", "q5")
newdata <-leadership[, vars]
```

accomplish the same variable selection. Here, variable names (in quotes) are entered as column indices, thereby selecting the same columns.

If only one set of indices is provided for a data frame, R assumes that you are subsetting the columns. In the following statement, the comma is assumed

```
newdata <- leadership[vars]
```

and subsets the same set of variables.

Finally, you could use

```
myvars <- paste("q", 1:5, sep="")
newdata <- leadership[myvars]
```

This example uses the `paste()` function to create the same character vector as in the previous example. The `paste()` function will be covered in chapter 5.

3.10.2 *Dropping variables*

There are many reasons to exclude variables. For example, if a variable has many missing values, you may want to drop it prior to further analyses. Let's look at some methods of excluding variables.

You can exclude variables q3 and q4 with these statements:

```
myvars <- names(leadership) %in% c("q3", "q4")
newdata <- leadership[!myvars]
```

To understand why this works, you need to break it down:

1 `names(leadership)` produces a character vector containing the variable names:

   ```
   c("managerID","testDate","country","gender","age","q1","q2","q3","q4","q5")
   ```

2 `names(leadership) %in% c("q3", "q4")` returns a logical vector with TRUE for each element in `names(leadership)` that matches q3 or q4 and FALSE otherwise:

   ```
   c(FALSE, FALSE, FALSE, FALSE, FALSE, FALSE, FALSE, TRUE, TRUE, FALSE)
   ```

3 The not (`!`) operator reverses the logical values:

   ```
   c(TRUE, TRUE, TRUE, TRUE, TRUE, TRUE, TRUE, FALSE, FALSE, TRUE)
   ```

4 `leadership[c(TRUE, TRUE, TRUE, TRUE, TRUE, TRUE, TRUE, FALSE, FALSE, TRUE)]` selects columns with TRUE logical values, so q3 and q4 are excluded.

Knowing that q3 and q4 are the eighth and ninth variables, you can exclude them with the following statement:

```
newdata <- leadership[c(-8,-9)]
```

This works because prepending a column index with a minus sign (-) excludes that column.

Finally, the same deletion can be accomplished via

```
leadership$q3 <- leadership$q4 <- NULL
```

Here you set columns q3 and q4 to undefined (NULL). Note that NULL isn't the same as NA (missing).

Dropping variables is the converse of keeping variables. The choice depends on which is easier to code. If there are many variables to drop, it may be easier to keep the ones that remain, or vice versa.

3.10.3 *Selecting observations*

Selecting or excluding observations (rows) is typically a key aspect of successful data preparation and analysis. Several examples are given in the following listing.

Listing 3.6   Selecting observations

```
newdata <- leadership[1:3,]
```
Asks for rows 1 through 3 (the first three observations)

```
newdata <- leadership[leadership$gender=="M" &
                      leadership$age > 30,]
```
❶ Selects all men over 30

Each of these examples provides the row indices and leaves the column indices blank (therefore choosing all columns). Let's break down the line of code at ❶ to understand it:

1 The logical comparison `leadership$gender=="M"` produces the vector `c(TRUE, FALSE, FALSE, TRUE, FALSE)`.

2 The logical comparison `leadership$age > 30` produces the vector `c(TRUE, TRUE, FALSE, TRUE, TRUE)`.

3 The logical comparison `c(TRUE, FALSE, FALSE, TRUE, FALSE) & c(TRUE, TRUE, FALSE, TRUE, TRUE)` produces the vector `c(TRUE, FALSE, FALSE, TRUE, FALSE)`.

4 `leadership[c(TRUE, FALSE, FALSE, TRUE, FALSE),]` selects the first and fourth observations from the data frame (when the row index is `TRUE`, the row is included; when it's `FALSE`, the row is excluded). This meets the selection criteria (men over 30).

At the beginning of this chapter, I suggested that you might want to limit your analyses to observations collected between January 1, 2009, and December 31, 2009. How can you do this? Here's one solution:

```
leadership$date <- as.Date(leadership$date, "%m/%d/%y")    ◁─── Converts the date values read
                                                                in originally as character
startdate <- as.Date("2009-01-01")    ◁─── Creates starting date    values to date values using
enddate   <- as.Date("2009-12-31")    ◁─── Creates ending date      the format mm/dd/yy

newdata <- leadership[which(leadership$date >= startdate &
        leadership$date <= enddate),]
```

Selects cases meeting your desired criteria, as in the previous example

Note that the default for the `as.Date()` function is yyyy-mm-dd, so you don't have to supply it here.

3.10.4 *The subset() function*

The examples in the previous two sections are important because they help describe the ways in which logical vectors and comparison operators are interpreted in R. Understanding how these examples work will help you interpret R code in general. Now that you've done things the hard way, let's look at a shortcut.

The `subset()` function is probably the easiest way to select variables and observations. Here are two examples:

```
newdata <- subset(leadership, age >= 35 | age < 23,
            select=c(q1, q2, q3, q4))
```

Selects all rows that have a value of age greater than or equal to 35 or less than 23. Keeps variables ql through q4.

```
newdata <- subset(leadership, gender=="M" & age > 25,
            select=gender:q4)
```

Selects all men over the age of 25, and keeps variables gender through q4 (gender, q4, and all columns between them).

You saw the colon operator used to generate a sequence of numbers in chapter 2. In the subset function, `from:to` returns all variables in a data frame between the `from` variable and the `to` variable, inclusive.

3.10.5 *Random samples*

Sampling from larger datasets is common in data mining and machine learning. For example, you may want to select two random samples, creating a predictive model from one and validating its effectiveness on the other. The `sample()` function enables you to take a random sample (with or without replacement) of size n from a dataset.

You could take a random sample of size 3 from the leadership dataset using the following statement:

```
mysample <- leadership[sample(1:nrow(leadership), 3, replace=FALSE),]
```

The first argument to `sample()` is a vector of elements to choose from. Here, the vector is 1 to the number of observations in the data frame. The second argument is the number of elements to be selected, and the third argument indicates sampling without replacement. `sample()` returns the randomly sampled elements, which are then used to select rows from the data frame.

R has extensive facilities for sampling, including drawing and calibrating survey samples (see the `sampling` package) and analyzing complex survey data (see the `survey` package). Other methods that rely on sampling, including bootstrapping and resampling statistics, are described in chapter 12.

3.11 *Using dplyr to manipulate data frames*

So far, we've manipulated R data frames using base R functions. The `dplyr` package provides a series of shortcuts that allow you to complete the same data management tasks in a streamlined fashion. It is rapidly becoming one of the most popular R packages for data management.

3.11.1 *Basic dplyr functions*

The `dplyr` package provides a set of functions that can be used to select variables and observations, transform variables, rename variables, and sort rows. Table 3.6 lists the relevant functions.

Table 3.6 `dplyr` functions for manipulating data frames

Function	Use
`select()`	Select variables/columns
`filter()`	Select observations/rows
`mutate()`	Transform or recode variables
`rename()`	Rename variables/columns
`recode()`	Recode variable values
`arrange()`	Order rows by variable values

Let's return to the data frame created in table 3.1 and reproduced in table 3.7 for convenience.

Table 3.7 Gender differences in leadership behavior

Manager	Date	Country	Gender	Age	q1	q2	q3	q4	q5
1	10/24/14	US	M	32	5	4	5	5	5
2	10/28/14	US	F	45	3	5	2	5	5
3	10/01/14	UK	F	25	3	5	5	5	2
4	10/12/14	UK	M	39	3	3	4		
5	05/01/14	UK	F	99	2	2	1	2	1

This time, we'll use `dplyr` functions to manipulate the dataset. The code is provided in listing 3.7. Since `dplyr` is not part of base R, install it (`install.packages("dplyr")`) first.

Listing 3.7 Listing 3.7 Manipulating data with `dplyr`

```
leadership <- data.frame(
   manager = c(1, 2, 3, 4, 5),
   date    = c("10/24/08", "10/28/08", "10/1/08", "10/12/08", "5/1/09"),
   country = c("US", "US", "UK", "UK", "UK"),
   gender  = c("M", "F", "F", "M", "F"),
   age     = c(32, 45, 25, 39, 99),
   q1      = c(5, 3, 3, 3, 2),
   q2      = c(4, 5, 5, 3, 2),
   q3      = c(5, 2, 5, 4, 1),
   q4      = c(5, 5, 5, NA, 2),
   q5      = c(5, 5, 2, NA, 1)
   )
library(dplyr)          ←┘  Load the dplyr
                            package.

leadership <- mutate(leadership,
                 total_score = q1 + q2 + q3 + q4 + q5,       Create two
                 mean_score = total_score / 5)               summary variables.

leadership$gender <- recode(leadership$gender,        Recode M and F to
                 "M" = "male", "F" = "female")        male and female.

leadership <- rename(leadership, ID = "manager", sex = "gender")   ←┘   Rename the manager
                                                                        and gender variables.

leadership <- arrange(leadership, sex, total_score)   ←┘  Sort the data by sex and
                                                          then total score within sex.

leadership_ratings <- select(leadership, ID, mean_score)   ←┐  Create a new data
                                                               frame containing
                                                               the rating variables.
```

```
leadership_men_high <- filter(leadership,
                              sex == "male" & total_score > 10)
```

**Create a new data frame containing
males with total scores above 10.**

First, the `dplyr` package is loaded. Then `mutate()` function is used to create a total score and mean score. The format is

```
dataframe <- mutate(dataframe,
                    newvar1 = expression,
                    newvar2 = expression, ...).
```

The new variables are added to the data frame.

Next, the `recode()` function is used to modify the values of the `gender` variable. The format is

```
vector <- recode(vector,
                 oldvalue1 = newvalue2,
                 oldvalue2 = newvalue2, ...).
```

Vector values that are not given new values are left unchanged. For example,

```
x <- c("a", "b", "c")
x <- recode(x, "a" = "apple", "b" = "banana")
x
[1] "apple" "banana" "c"
```

For numeric values, use backticks to quote the original values:

```
> y <- c(1, 2, 3)
> y <- recode(y, `1` = 10, `2` = 15)
> y
[1] 10 15 3
```

Next, use the `rename()` function to change the variable names. The format is

```
dataframe <- rename(dataframe,
                    newname1 = "oldname1",
                    newname2 = "oldname2", ...).
```

The data are then sorted using the `arrange()` function. First, the rows are sorted in ascending order by `sex` (females followed by males). Next, the rows are sorted in ascending order by `total_score` (low scores to high scores) separately within each sex group. The `desc()` function is used to reverse the order of the sorting. For example,

```
leadership <- arrange(leadership, sex, desc(total_score))
```

would sort the data in ascending order by `sex` and in descending order (high to low `total_scores`) within each sex.

The `select` statement is used to select or exclude variables. In this case, the variables `ID` and `mean_score` are selected.

The format for the `select()` function is

```
dataframe <- select(dataframe, variablelist1, variablelist2, ...)
```

Variable lists are typically variable names without quotes. The colon operator (:) can be used to select a range of variables. Additionally, functions can be used to select variables containing specific text strings. For example, the statement

```
leadership_subset <- select(leadership,
                            ID, country:age, starts_with("q"))
```

would select the variables `ID`, `country`, `sex`, `age`, `q1`, `q2`, `q3`, `q4` and `q5`. See `help(select_helpers)` for a list of functions that can be used to aid in the selection of variables.

A minus sign (-) is used to exclude variables. The statement

```
leadership_subset <- select(leadership, -sex, -age)
```

would include all variables *except* `sex` and `age`.

Finally, the `filter()` function is used to select the observations or rows in a data frame meeting a given set of criteria. Here, men with total scores greater than 10 are retained. The format is

```
dataframe <- filter(dataframe, expression)
```

and rows are retained if the expression is `TRUE`. Any of the logical operators in table 3.3 can be used, and parentheses can be used to clarify the precedence of these operators. For example,

```
extreme_men <- filter(leadership,
                      sex == "male" &
                      (mean_score < 2 | mean_score > 4))
```

would create a data frame containing all male managers with mean scores below 2 or above 4.

3.11.2 *Using pipe operators to chain statements*

The `dplyr` package allows you to write code in a compact format using the pipe operator (`%>%`) provided by the `magrittr` package. Consider the following three statements:

```
high_potentials <- filter(leadership, total_score > 10)
high_potentials <- select(high_potential, ID, country, mean_score)
high_potentials <- arrange(high_potential, country, mean_score)
```

These statements can be rewritten as a single statement using the pipe operator:

```
high_potentials <- filter(leadership, total_score > 10) %>%
   select(ID, country, mean_score) %>%
   arrange(country, mean_score)
```

The `%>%` operator (pronounced THEN) passes the result on the left-hand side to the first parameter of the function on the right-hand side. A statement rewritten this way is often easier to read.

Although we have covered basic `dplyr` functions, the package also contains functions for summarizing, combining, and restructuring data. These additional functions will be discussed in chapter 5.

3.12 *Using SQL statements to manipulate data frames*

Until now, you've been using R statements and functions to manipulate data. But many data analysts come to R well versed in Structured Query Language (SQL). It would be a shame to lose all that accumulated knowledge. Therefore, before we end, let me briefly mention the `sqldf` package. (If you're unfamiliar with SQL, please feel free to skip this section.)

After downloading and installing the package (`install.packages("sqldf")`), you can use the `sqldf()` function to apply SQL `SELECT` statements to data frames. Two examples are given in the following listing.

> **Listing 3.8   Using SQL statements to manipulate data frames**

Selects all variables (columns) from data frame mtcars, keeps only automobiles (rows) with one carburetor (carb), sorts in ascending order by mpg, and saves the results as the data frame newdf. The option row.names=TRUE carries the row names from the original data frame over to the new one.

```
> library(sqldf)
> newdf <- sqldf("select * from mtcars where carb=1 order by mpg",
                 row.names=TRUE)
> newdf
                   mpg cyl  disp  hp drat   wt qsec vs am gear carb
Valiant           18.1   6 225.0 105 2.76 3.46 20.2  1  0    3    1
Hornet 4 Drive    21.4   6 258.0 110 3.08 3.21 19.4  1  0    3    1
Toyota Corona     21.5   4 120.1  97 3.70 2.46 20.0  1  0    3    1
Datsun 710        22.8   4 108.0  93 3.85 2.32 18.6  1  1    4    1
Fiat X1-9         27.3   4  79.0  66 4.08 1.94 18.9  1  1    4    1
Fiat 128          32.4   4  78.7  66 4.08 2.20 19.5  1  1    4    1
Toyota Corolla    33.9   4  71.1  65 4.22 1.83 19.9  1  1    4    1

> sqldf("select avg(mpg) as avg_mpg, avg(disp) as avg_disp, gear
              from mtcars where cyl in (4, 6) group by gear")
  avg_mpg avg_disp gear
1    20.3      201    3
2    24.5      123    4
3    25.4      120    5
```

Prints the mean mpg and disp within each level of gear for automobiles with four or six cylinders (cyl)

Experienced SQL users will find the `sqldf` package a useful adjunct to data management in R. See the project home page (https://github.com/ggrothendieck/sqldf) for more details.

Summary

- Creating new variables and recoding existing variables are important parts of data management.
- Functions allow you to store and manipulate missing and date values.
- Variables can be converted from one type (e.g., numeric) to another (e.g., character).
- Based on a set of criteria, you can retain (or delete) observations and variables.
- It is possible to merge datasets horizontally (adding variables) or vertically (adding observations).

Getting started with graphs

4

On many occasions, I've presented clients with carefully crafted statistical results in the form of numbers and text, only to have their eyes glaze over while the chirping of crickets permeated the room. Yet those same clients had enthusiastic "Ah-ha!" moments when I presented the same information to them in the form of graphs. Often, I can see patterns in data or detect anomalies in data values by looking at graphs—patterns or anomalies that I completely missed when conducting more formal statistical analyses.

Human beings are remarkably adept at discerning relationships from visual representations. A well-crafted graph can help you make meaningful comparisons among thousands of pieces of information, extracting patterns not easily found through other methods. This is one reason why advances in the field of statistical graphics have had such a major impact on data analysis. Data analysts need to *look* at their data, and this an area in which R shines.

The R language has grown organically over the years through the contributions of many independent software developers. This has led to the creation of four distinct approaches to graph creation in R—base, `lattice`, `ggplot2`, and `grid` graphics. In this chapter, and throughout the majority of the remaining chapters, we'll focus on `ggplot2`, the most powerful and popular approach currently available in R.

The `ggplot2` package, written by Hadley Wickham (2009a), provides a system for creating graphs based on the grammar of graphics described by Wilkinson (2005) and expanded by Wickham (2009b). The `ggplot2` package aims to provide a comprehensive, grammar-based system for generating graphs in a unified and coherent manner, allowing users to create new and innovative data visualizations.

This chapter will walk you through the major concepts and functions used to create `ggplot2` graphs by using visualizations to address the following questions:

- What is the relationship between a worker's past experience and their salary?
- How can we summarize this relationship simply?
- Is this relationship different for men and women?
- Does it matter what industry the worker is in?

We'll start with a simple scatterplot displaying the relationship between workers' experience and wages. Then in each section, we'll add new features until we've produced a single publication quality plot that addresses these questions. At each step, we'll gain greater insight into the questions.

To answer these questions, we'll use the `CPS85` data frame contained in the `mosaicData` package. The data frame contains a random sample of 534 individuals selected from the 1985 *Current Population Survey* and includes information about their wages, demographics, and work experience. Be sure to install both the `mosaicData` and `ggplot2` packages before continuing (`install.packages(c("mosaicData", "ggplot2"))`).

4.1 Creating a graph with ggplot2

The `ggplot2` package uses a series of functions to build up a graph in layers. We'll build a complex graph by starting with a simple graph and adding elements one at a time. By default, `ggplot2` graphs appear on a grey background with white reference lines.

4.1.1 ggplot

The first function in building a graph is the `ggplot()` function. It specifies the following:

- The data frame containing the data to be plotted.
- The mapping of the variables to visual properties of the graph. The mappings are placed in an `aes()` function (which stands for aesthetics or "something you can see").

The following code produces the graph in figure 4.1:

```
library(ggplot2)
library(mosaicData)
ggplot(data = CPS85, mapping = aes(x = exper, y = wage))
```

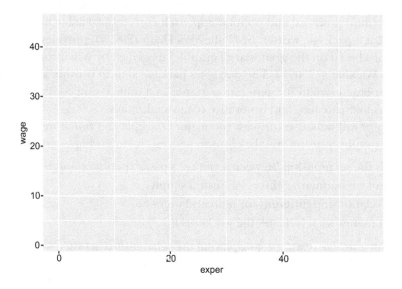

Figure 4.1   Mapping worker experience and wages to the *x*- and *y*-axes

Why is the graph empty? We specified that the `exper` variable should be mapped to the *x*-axis and that the `wage` variable should be mapped to the *y*-axis, but we haven't yet specified *what* we wanted placed on the graph. In this case, we'll want points to represent each participant.

4.1.2   Geoms

Geoms are the geometric objects (points, lines, bars, and shaded regions) that can be placed on a graph. They are added using functions whose names begin with `geom_`. Currently, 37 different geoms are available, and the list is growing. Table 4.1 describes the more common geoms, along with frequently used options for each.

Table 4.1   Geom functions

Function	Adds	Options
`geom_bar()`	Bar chart	`color, fill, alpha`
`geom_boxplot()`	Box plot	`color, fill, alpha, notch, width`
`geom_density()`	Density plot	`color, fill, alpha, linetype`

Table 4.1 Geom functions *(continued)*

Function	Adds	Options
geom_histogram()	Histogram	color, fill, alpha, linetype, binwidth
geom_hline()	Horizontal lines	color, alpha, linetype, size
geom_jitter()	Jittered points	color, size, alpha, shape
geom_line()	Line graph	colorvalpha, linetype, size
geom_point()	Scatterplot	color, alpha, shape, size
geom_rug()	Rug plot	color, side
geom_smooth()	Fitted line	method, formula, color, fill, linetype, size
geom_text()	Text annotations	Many; see the help for this function
geom_violin()	Violin plot	color, fill, alpha, linetype
geom_vline()	Vertical lines	color, alpha, linetype, size

We'll add points using the geom_point() function, creating a scatterplot. In ggplot2 graphs, functions are chained together using the + sign to build a final plot:

```
library(ggplot2)
library(mosaicData)
ggplot(data = CPS85, mapping = aes(x = exper, y = wage)) +
  geom_point()
```

Figure 4.2 shows the results.

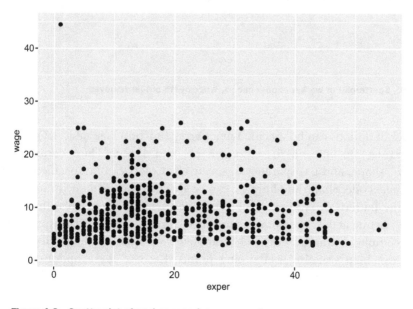

Figure 4.2 Scatterplot of worker experience vs. wages

It appears that as experience goes up, wages go up, but the relationship is weak. The graph also indicates that there is an outlier. One individual has a wage much higher than the rest. We'll delete this case and reproduce the plot:

```
CPS85 <- CPS85[CPS85$wage < 40, ]
ggplot(data = CPS85, mapping = aes(x = exper, y = wage)) +
  geom_point()
```

Figure 4.3 displays the new graph.

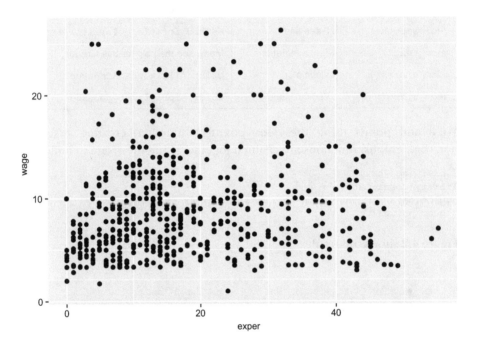

Figure 4.3 Scatterplot of worker experience vs. wages with outlier removed

A number of options can be specified in a geom_ function (see table 4.1). Options for geom_point() include color, size, shape, and alpha. These control the point color, size, shape, and transparency, respectively. Colors can be specified by name or hexadecimal code. Shape and linetype can be specified by the name or number representing the pattern or symbol, respectively. Point size is specified with positive real numbers starting at 0. Large numbers produce larger point sizes. Transparency ranges from 0 (completely transparent) to 1 (completely opaque). Adding a degree of transparency can help visualize overlapping points. Each of these options is described more fully in chapter 19.

Let's make the points in figure 4.3 larger, semitransparent, and blue. We'll also change the gray background to white using a theme (themes are described in section 4.1.7 and chapter 19). The following code produces the graph in figure 4.4:

```
ggplot(data = CPS85, mapping = aes(x = exper, y = wage)) +
  geom_point(color = "cornflowerblue", alpha = .7, size = 1.5) +
  theme_bw()
```

I might argue that the chart is more attractive (at least if you have color output), but it doesn't add to our insights. It would be helpful if the graph had a line summarizing the trend between experience and wages.

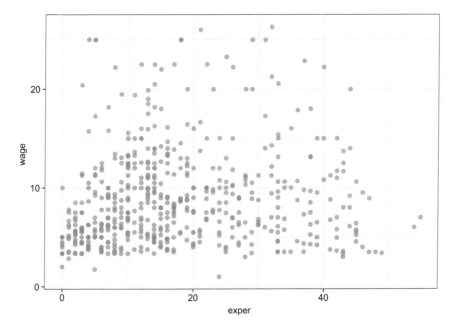

Figure 4.4   Scatterplot of worker experience vs. wages with outlier removed with modified point color, transparency, and point size. The bw theme (dark on light) has been applied.

We can add this line with the geom_smooth() function. Options control the type of line (linear, quadratic, nonparametric), the thickness of the line, the line's color, and the presence or absence of a confidence interval. Each of these is discussed in chapter 11. Here we request a linear regression (method = lm) line (where lm stands for linear model):

```
ggplot(data = CPS85, mapping = aes(x = exper, y = wage)) +
  geom_point(color = "cornflowerblue", alpha = .7, size = 1.5) +
  geom_smooth(method = "lm") +
  theme_bw()
```

The results are shown in figure 4.5.

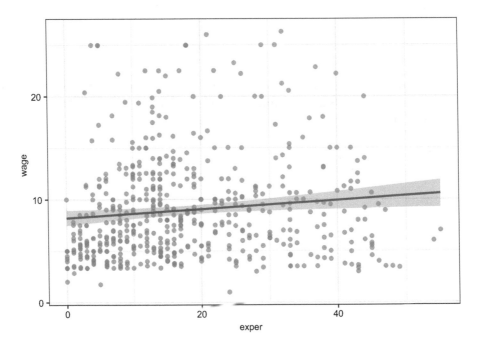

Figure 4.5   Scatterplot of worker experience vs. wages with a line of best fit

We can see from this line that, on average, wages appear to increase to a moderate degree with experience. This chapter uses only two geoms. In future chapters, we'll use others to create a wide variety of graph types, including bar charts, histograms, box plots, density plots, and others.

4.1.3   Grouping

In the previous section, we set graph characteristics such as color and transparency to a *constant* value. However, we can also map variables values to the color, shape, size, transparency, line style, and other visual characteristics of geometric objects. This allows groups of observations to be superimposed in a single graph (a process called *grouping*).

Let's add sex to the plot and represent it by color, shape, and linetype:

```
ggplot(data = CPS85,
       mapping = aes(x = exper, y = wage,
                     color = sex, shape = sex, linetype = sex)) +
  geom_point(alpha = .7, size = 1.5) +
  geom_smooth(method = "lm", se = FALSE, size = 1.5) +
  theme_bw()
```

By default, the first group (female) is represented by pink-filled circles and a solid pink line, while the second group (male) is represent by teal-filled triangles and a dashed teal line. Figure 4.6 shows the new graph.

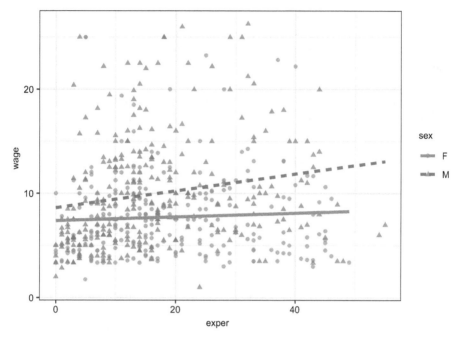

Figure 4.6   Scatterplot of worker experience vs. wages with points colored by sex and separate line of best fit for men and women

Note that the color=sex, shape=sex, and linetype=sex options are placed in the aes() function because we are mapping a variable to an aesthetic. The geom_smooth option (se = FALSE) was added to suppresses the confidence intervals, making the graph less busy and easier to read. The size = 1.5 option makes the line a bit thicker.

Simplifying graphs

In general, our goal is to create graphs that are as simple as possible while conveying the information accurately. In the graphs in this chapter, I would probably map gender to color alone. Adding mappings to shape and line type makes the graphs unnecessarily busy. I've added them here to create graphs that are more easily readable in both color (e-book) and the greyscale (print) formats of this book.

It now appears that men tend to make more money than women (higher line). Additionally, there may be a stronger relationship between experience and wages for men than for women (steeper line).

4.1.4 Scales

As we've seen, the aes() function is used to map variables to the visual characteristics of a plot. Scales specify how each of these mappings occurs. For example, ggplot2 automatically creates plot axes with tick marks, tick mark labels, and axis labels. Often they look fine, but occasionally, you'll want to take greater control over their appearance. Colors that represent groups are chosen automatically, but you may want to select a different set of colors based on your tastes or a publication's requirements.

Scale functions (which start with scale_) allow you to modify default scaling. Table 4.2 lists some common scaling functions.

Table 4.2 Some common scale functions

Function	Description
scale_x_continuous(), scale_y_continuous()	Scales the x and y axes for quantitative variables. Options include breaks for specifying tick marks, labels for specifying tick mark labels, and limits to control the range of the values displayed.
scale_x_discrete(), scale_y_discrete()	Same as above for axes representing categorical variables.
scale_color_manual()	Specifies the colors used to represent the levels of a categorical variable. The values option specifies the colors. A table of colors can be found at www.stat.columbia.edu/~tzheng/files/Rcolor.pdf.

In the next plot, we'll change the *x*- and *y*-axis scaling and the colors representing males and females. The *x*-axis representing exper will range from 0 to 60 by 10, and the *y*-axis representing wage will range from 0 to 30 by 5. Females will be coded with an off-red color, and males will be coded with an off-blue color. The following code produces the graph in figure 4.7:

```
ggplot(data = CPS85,
       mapping = aes(x = exper, y = wage,
                     color = sex, shape=sex, linetype=sex)) +
   geom_point(alpha = .7, size = 3) +
   geom_smooth(method = "lm", se = FALSE, size = 1.5) +
   scale_x_continuous(breaks = seq(0, 60, 10)) +
   scale_y_continuous(breaks = seq(0, 30, 5)) +
   scale_color_manual(values = c("indianred3", "cornflowerblue")) +
 theme_bw()
```

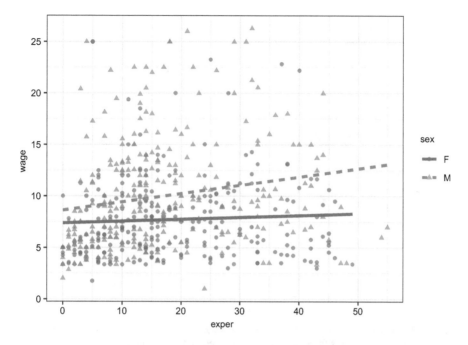

Figure 4.7 Scatterplot of worker experience vs. wages with custom *x*- and *y*-axes and custom color mappings for sex

Breaks are defined by a vector of values. Here, the seq() function provides a shortcut. For example, seq(0, 60, 10) generates a numeric vector starting with 0, ending with 60, and incrementing by 10.

The numbers on the *x*- and *y*-axes are better, and the colors are more attractive (IMHO). However, wages are in dollars. We can change the labels on the *y*-axis to represent dollars using the scales package, which provides label formatting for dollars, euros, percentages, and more.

Install the scales package (install.packages("scales")), and then run the following code:

```
ggplot(data = CPS85,
       mapping = aes(x = exper, y = wage,
                             color = sex, shape=sex, linetype=sex)) +
    geom_point(alpha = .7, size = 3) +
    geom_smooth(method = "lm", se = FALSE, size = 1.5) +
    scale_x_continuous(breaks = seq(0, 60, 10)) +
    scale_y_continuous(breaks = seq(0, 30, 5),
                       label = scales::dollar) +
    scale_color_manual(values = c("indianred3", "cornflowerblue")) +
  theme_bw()
```

Figure 4.8 provides the results.

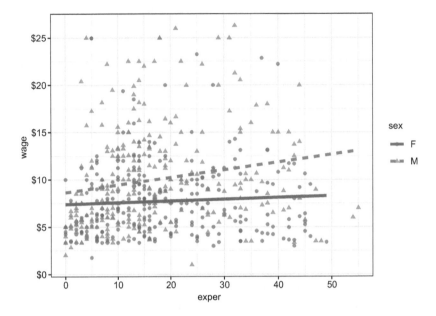

Figure 4.8 Scatterplot of worker experience vs. wages with custom *x*- and *y*-axes and custom color mappings for sex. Wages are printed in dollar format.

We are definitely getting there. The next question is whether the relationship between experience, wages, and sex is the same for each job sector. Let's repeat this graph once for each job sector to explore this.

4.1.5 *Facets*

Sometimes relationships are clearer if groups appear in side-by-side graphs rather than overlapping in a single graph. Facets reproduce a graph for each level of a given variable (or combination of variables). You can create faceted graphs using the `facet_wrap()` and `facet_grid()` functions. The syntax is given in table 4.3, where var, rowvar, and colvar are factors.

Table 4.3 `ggplot2` facet functions

Syntax	Results
`facet_wrap(~var, ncol=n)`	Separate plots for each level of var arranged into *n* columns
`facet_wrap(~var, nrow=n)`	Separate plots for each level of var arranged into *n* rows
`facet_grid(rowvar~colvar)`	Separate plots for each combination of rowvar and colvar, where rowvar represents rows and colvar represents columns
`facet_grid(rowvar~.)`	Separate plots for each level of rowvar, arranged as a single column
`facet_grid(.~colvar)`	Separate plots for each level of colvar, arranged as a single row

Here, facets will be defined by the eight levels of the sector variable. Since each facet will be smaller than a one-panel graph alone, we'll omit `size=3` from `geom_point()` and `size=1.5` from `geom_smooth()`. This will reduce the point and line sizes compared with the previous graphs and looks better in a faceted graph. The following code produces figure 4.9:

```
ggplot(data = CPS85,
       mapping = aes(x = exper, y = wage,
                     color = sex, shape = sex, linetype = sex)) +
  geom_point(alpha = .7) +
  geom_smooth(method = "lm", se = FALSE) +
  scale_x_continuous(breaks = seq(0, 60, 10)) +
  scale_y_continuous(breaks = seq(0, 30, 5),
                     label = scales::dollar) +
  scale_color_manual(values = c("indianred3", "cornflowerblue")) +
  facet_wrap(~sector) +
  theme_bw()
```

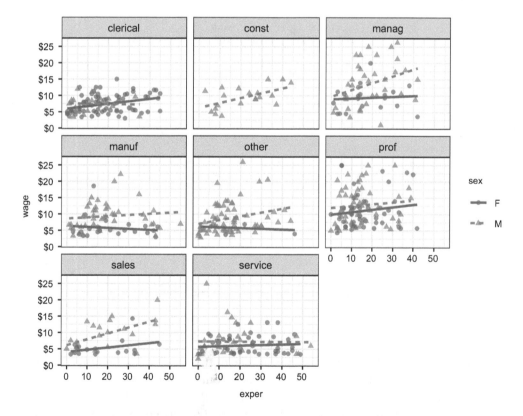

Figure 4.9 Scatterplot of worker experience vs. wages with custom x- and y-axes and custom color mappings for sex. Separate graphs (facets) are provided for each of eight job sectors.

It appears that the differences between men and women depend on the job sector under consideration. For example, there is a strong positive relationship between experience and wages for male managers, but not for female managers. To a lesser extent, this is also true for sales workers. There appears to be no relationship between experience and wages for either male and female service workers. In either case, males make slightly more. Wages go up with experience for female clerical workers, but they may go down for male clerical workers (the relationship may not be significant here). We have gained a great deal of insight into the relationship between wages and experience at this point.

4.1.6　Labels

Graphs should be easy to interpret, and informative labels are a key element in achieving this goal. The `labs()` function provides customized labels for the axes and legends. Additionally, a custom title, subtitle, and caption can be added. Let's modify each in the following code:

```
ggplot(data = CPS85,
       mapping = aes(x = exper, y = wage,
                 color = sex, shape=sex, linetype=sex)) +
    geom_point(alpha = .7) +
    geom_smooth(method = "lm", se = FALSE) +
    scale_x_continuous(breaks = seq(0, 60, 10)) +
    scale_y_continuous(breaks = seq(0, 30, 5),
                       label = scales::dollar) +
    scale_color_manual(values = c("indianred3",
                                  "cornflowerblue")) +
    facet_wrap(~sector) +
    labs(title = "Relationship between wages and experience",
        subtitle = "Current Population Survey",
        caption = "source: http://mosaic-web.org/",
        x = " Years of Experience",
        y = "Hourly Wage",
        color = "Gender", shape = "Gender", linetype = "Gender") +
    theme_bw()
```

Figure 4.10 shows the graph.

Now a viewer doesn't need to guess what the labels `expr` and `wage` mean or where the data comes from.

4.1.7　Themes

Finally, we can fine-tune the appearance of the graph using themes. Theme functions (which start with `theme_`) control background colors, fonts, grid lines, legend placement, and other non-data-related features of the graph. Let's use a cleaner theme. Starting with figure 4.4, we used a theme that produced a white background and light

Relationship between wages and experience

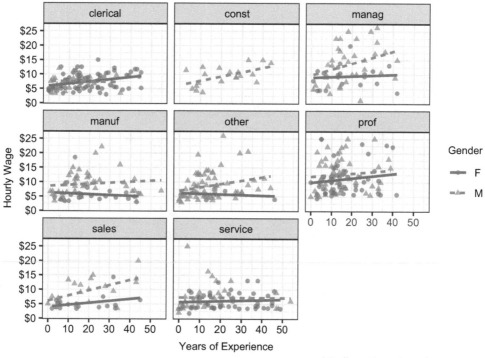

Figure 4.10 Scatterplot of worker experience vs. wages with separate graphs (facets) for each of eight job sectors and custom titles and labels

grey reference lines. Let's try a different theme—one that is more minimalistic. The following code produces the graph in figure 4.11:

```
ggplot(data = CPS85,
       mapping = aes(x = exper, y = wage,
                     color = sex, shape=sex, linetype=sex)) +
    geom_point(alpha = .7) +
    geom_smooth(method = "lm", se = FALSE) +
    scale_x_continuous(breaks = seq(0, 60, 10)) +
    scale_y_continuous(breaks = seq(0, 30, 5),
                       label = scales::dollar) +
    scale_color_manual(values = c("indianred3",
                                  "cornflowerblue")) +
    facet_wrap(~sector) +
    labs(title = "Relationship between wages and experience",
       subtitle = "Current Population Survey",
       caption = "source: http://mosaic-web.org/",
       x = " Years of Experience",
```

```
        y = "Hourly Wage",
        color = "Gender", shape = "Gender", linetype = "Gender") +
theme_minimal()
```

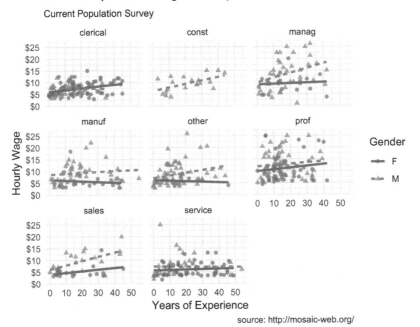

Figure 4.11 Scatterplot of worker experience vs. wages with separate graphs (facets) for each of eight job sectors, custom titles and labels, and a cleaner theme

This is our finished graph, ready for publication. Of course, these findings are tentative. They are based on a limited sample size and don't involve statistical testing to assess whether differences may be due to chance variation. Appropriate tests for this type of data will be described in chapter 8. Themes are described more fully in chapter 19.

4.2   *ggplot2 details*

Before finishing this chapter, there are three important topics to consider: the placement of the aes() function, the treatment of ggplot2 graphs as R objects, and various methods to save your graphs for use in reports and web pages.

4.2.1   *Placing the data and mapping options*

Plots created with ggplot2 always start with the ggplot function. In the previous examples, the data= and mapping= options were placed in this function. In this case, they apply to each geom function that follows.

You can also place these options directly within a geom. In that case, they only apply to that *specific* geom. Consider the following graph:

```
ggplot(CPS85, aes(x = exper, y = wage, color = sex)) +
        geom_point(alpha = .7, size = 1.5) +
        geom_smooth(method = "lm", se = FALSE, size = 1)  +
        scale_color_manual(values = c("lightblue", "midnightblue")) +
        theme_bw()
```

Figure 4.12 shows the resulting plot.

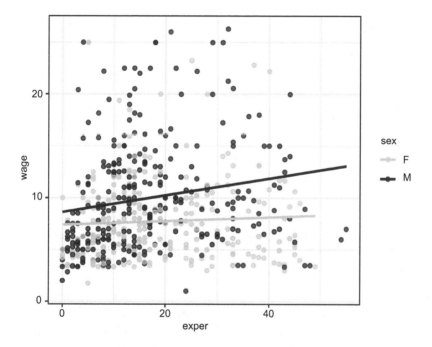

Figure 4.12 Scatterplot of experience and wage by sex, where `aes(color=sex)` is placed in the `ggplot()` function. The mapping is applied to both `geom_point()` and `geom_smooth()`, producing separate point colors for males and females, along with separate lines of best fit.

Since the mapping of `sex` to color appears in the `ggplot()` function, it applies to both `geom_point` and `geom_smooth`. The color of the point indicates the sex, and a separate colored-trend line is produced for men and women. Compare this to

```
ggplot(CPS85,    aes(x = exper, y = wage)) +
        geom_point(aes(color = sex), alpha = .7, size = 1.5) +
        geom_smooth(method = "lm", se = FALSE, size = 1) +
        scale_color_manual(values = c("lightblue", "midnightblue")) +
        theme_bw()
```

Figure 4.13 shows the resulting graph.

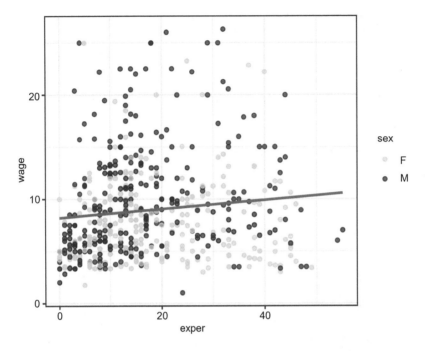

Figure 4.13 Scatterplot of experience and wage by sex, where `aes(color=sex)` **is placed in the** `geom_point()` **function. The mapping is applied to point color, producing separate point colors for men and women, but a single line of best fit for all workers.**

Since the sex-to-color mapping only appears in the `geom_point()` function, it is only used there. A single trend line is created for all observations.

Most of the examples in this book place the data and mapping options in the `ggplot` function. Additionally, the phrases `data=` and `mapping=` are omitted since the first option always refers to data and the second option always refers to mapping.

4.2.2 Graphs as objects

A `ggplot2` graph can be saved as a named R object (a list), manipulated further, and then printed or saved to disk. Consider the code in the following listing.

Listing 4.1 Using a `ggplot2` graph as an object

```
data(CPS85 , package = "mosaicData")       Prepare data.
CPS85 <- CPS85[CPS85$wage < 40,]

myplot <- ggplot(data = CPS85,              Create a scatterplot
        aes(x = exper, y = wage)) +         and save it as myplot.
    geom_point()
```

```
myplot              ←— Display myplot.

myplot2 <- myplot + geom_point(size = 3, color = "blue")
myplot2                                                        Make the points
                                                               larger and blue, save
myplot + geom_smooth(method = "lm") +    Display myplot with a    it as myplot2, and
   labs(title = "Mildly interesting graph")  best fit line and a title.  display the graph.
```

First, the data is imported and outliers are removed. Then, a simple scatter plot of experience versus wages is created and saved as myplot. Next, the plot is printed. The plot is then modified by changing the point size and color, saved as myplot2, and printed. Finally, the original plot is given a line of best fit and title and printed. Note that these changes are not saved.

The ability to save graphs as objects allows you to continue to work with and modify them. This can be a real time saver (and help you avoid carpal tunnel syndrome). It is also handy when saving graphs programmatically, as we'll see in the next section.

4.2.3 Saving graphs

You can save the graphs created by ggplot2 via the RStudio GUI or through your code. To save a graph using the RStudio menus, go to the Plots tab and choose Export (see figure 4.14).

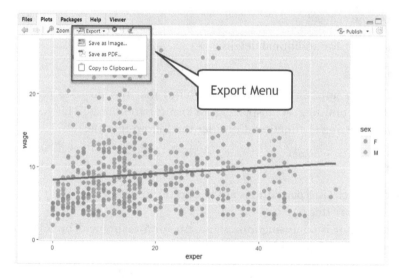

Figure 4.14 Saving a graph using the RStudio interface

Graphs can be saved via code using the ggsave() function. You can specify the plot to save, its size and format, and where to save it. Consider this example:

```
ggsave(file="mygraph.png", plot=myplot, width=5, height=4)
```

This saves `myplot` as a 5" × 4" PNG file named mygraph.png in the current working directory. You can save the graph in a different format by changing the file extension. Table 4.4 lists descriptions of the most common formats.

The PDF, SVG, and WMF formats are vectorial formats—they resize without fuzziness or pixilation. The other formats are bitmaps—they will pixelate when resized. This is especially noticeable when small images are enlarged. The

Table 4.4 Image file formats

Extension	Format
pdf	Portable Document Format
jpeg	JPEG
tiff	Tagged Image File Format
png	Portable Network Graphics
svg	Scalable Vector Graphics
wmf	Windows Metafile

PNG format is popular for images destined for web pages. The JPEG and TIF formats are usually reserved for photographs.

The WMF format is usually recommended for graphs that will appear in Microsoft Word or PowerPoint documents. MS Office does not support PDF or SVG files, and the WMF format will rescale well. However, WMF files will lose any transparency settings that have been set.

If you omit the `plot=` option, the most recently created graph is saved. The following code is valid and saves the graph to disk as a PDF document:

```
ggplot(data=mtcars, aes(x=mpg)) + geom_histogram()
ggsave(file="mygraph.pdf")
```

See `help(ggsave)` for additional details.

4.2.4 *Common mistakes*

After working with `ggplot2` for years, I've found that two mistakes are frequently made. The first is omitting or misplacing a closing parenthesis. This happens most often following the `aes()` function. Consider the following code:

```
ggplot(CPS85, aes(x = exper, y = wage, color = sex) +
  geom_point()
```

Note the lack of a closing parenthesis at the end of the first line. I can't tell you how many times I've done this.

The second error is confusing an assignment for a mapping. The following code produces the graph in figure 4.15:

```
ggplot(CPS85, aes(x = exper, y = wage, color = "blue")) +
  geom_point()
```

The `aes()` function is used to map *variables* to the visual characteristics of the graph. Assigning constant values is done outside the `aes()` function. The correct code would be

```
ggplot(CPS85, aes(x = exper, y = wage) +
  geom_point(color = "blue")
```

The points are red (not blue), and there is a strange legend. What happened?

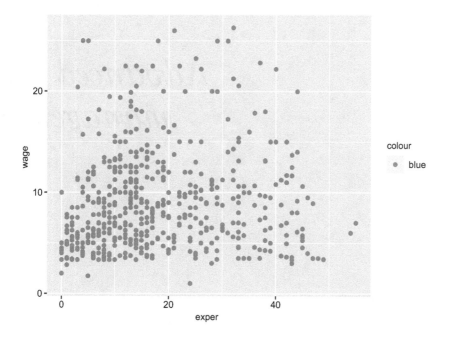

Figure 4.15 Placing an assignment statement in the `aes()` function

Summary

- The `ggplot2` package provides a language and grammar for creating comprehensive visualizations of data.
- Scatterplots describe the relationship between two quantitative variables.
- Trend lines can be added to a scatterplot to summarize the relationship.
- You can use color, shape, and size to represent groups of observations.
- Facets are useful for plotting the data for more than one group.
- You can customize graphs with scales, labels, and themes.
- Graphs can be saved in many formats.

Advanced data
management

This chapter covers

- Using mathematical and statistical functions
- Utilizing character functions
- Looping and conditional execution
- Writing your own functions
- Aggregating and reshaping data

In chapter 3, we reviewed the basic techniques used for managing datasets in R. In this chapter, we'll focus on advanced topics. The chapter is divided into three basic parts. In the first part, we'll take a whirlwind tour of R's many functions for mathematical, statistical, and character manipulation. To give this section relevance, we begin with a data management problem that can be solved using these functions. After covering the functions themselves, we'll look at one possible solution to the data management problem.

Next, we'll cover how to write your own functions to accomplish data management and analysis tasks. First, we'll explore ways of controlling program flow, including looping and conditional statement execution. Then we'll investigate the structure of user-written functions and how to invoke them once they have been created.

Then, we'll look at ways of aggregating and summarizing data, along with methods of reshaping and restructuring datasets. When aggregating data, you can specify the use of any appropriate built-in or user-written function to accomplish the summarization, so the topics you learn in the first two parts of the chapter will really benefit you.

5.1 A data management challenge

To begin our discussion of numerical and character functions, let's consider a data management problem. A group of students have taken exams in math, science, and English. You want to combine these scores to determine a single performance indicator for each student. Additionally, you want to assign an A to the top 20% of students, a B to the next 20%, and so on. Finally, you want to sort the students alphabetically. Table 5.1 presents the data.

Table 5.1 Student exam data

Student	Math	Science	English
John Davis	502	95	25
Angela Williams	600	99	22
Bullwinkle Moose	412	80	18
David Jones	358	82	15
Janice Markhammer	495	75	20
Cheryl Cushing	512	85	28
Reuven Ytzrhak	410	80	15
Greg Knox	625	95	30
Joel England	573	89	27
Mary Rayburn	522	86	18

When you look at this dataset, several obstacles are immediately evident. First, scores on the three exams aren't comparable. They have widely different means and standard deviations, so averaging them doesn't make sense. You must transform the exam scores into comparable units before combining them. Second, you'll need a method of determining a student's percentile rank on this score to assign a grade. Third, there's a single field for names, complicating the task of sorting students. You'll need to split their names into first name and last name to sort them properly.

Each of these tasks can be accomplished through the judicious use of R's numerical and character functions. After working through the functions described in the next section, we'll consider a possible solution to this data management challenge.

5.2   *Numerical and character functions*

In this section, we'll review functions in R that can be used as the basic building blocks for manipulating data. They can be divided into numerical (mathematical, statistical, probability) and character functions. After I review each type, I'll show you how to apply functions to the columns (variables) and rows (observations) of matrices and data frames (see section 5.2.6).

5.2.1   *Mathematical functions*

Table 5.2 lists common mathematical functions along with short examples.

Table 5.2   **Mathematical functions**

Function	Description
abs(x)	Absolute value abs(-4) returns 4.
sqrt(x)	Square root sqrt(25) returns 5. This is the same as 25^(0.5).
ceiling(x)	Smallest integer not less than x ceiling(3.475) returns 4.
floor(x)	Largest integer not greater than x floor(3.475) returns 3.
trunc(x)	Integer formed by truncating values in x toward 0 trunc(5.99) returns 5.
round(x, digits=n)	Rounds x to the specified number of decimal places round(3.475, digits=2) returns 3.48.
signif(x, digits=n)	Rounds x to the specified number of significant digits signif(3.475, digits=2) returns 3.5.
cos(x), sin(x), tan(x)	Cosine, sine, and tangent cos(2) returns -0.416.
acos(x), asin(x), atan(x)	Arc-cosine, arc-sine, and arc-tangent acos(-0.416) returns 2.
cosh(x), sinh(x), tanh(x)	Hyperbolic cosine, sine, and tangent sinh(2) returns 3.627.
acosh(x), asinh(x), atanh(x)	Hyperbolic arc-cosine, arc-sine, and arc-tangent asinh(3.627) returns 2.
log(x,base=n) log(x) log10(x)	Logarithm of x to the base n For convenience: • log(x) is the natural logarithm. • log10(x) is the common logarithm. • log(10) returns 2.3026. • log10(10) returns 1.
exp(x)	Exponential function exp(2.3026) returns 10.

Data transformation is one of the primary uses for these functions. For example, you often transform positively skewed variables such as income to a log scale before further analyses. Mathematical functions are also used as components in formulas, in plotting functions (for example, x versus sin(x)), and in formatting numerical values prior to printing.

The examples in table 5.2 apply mathematical functions to *scalars* (individual numbers). When these functions are applied to numeric vectors, matrices, or data frames, they operate on each individual value; for example: sqrt(c(4, 16, 25)) returns c(2, 4, 5).

5.2.2 *Statistical functions*

Table 5.3 presents common statistical functions. Many of these functions have optional parameters that affect the outcome. For example,

```
y <- mean(x)
```

provides the arithmetic mean of the elements in object x, and

```
z <- mean(x, trim = 0.05, na.rm=TRUE)
```

provides the trimmed mean, dropping the highest and lowest 5% of scores and any missing values. Use the help() function to learn more about each function and its arguments.

Table 5.3 Statistical functions

Function	Description
mean(x)	Mean mean(c(1,2,3,4)) returns 2.5.
median(x)	Median median(c(1,2,3,4)) returns 2.5.
sd(x)	Standard deviation sd(c(1,2,3,4)) returns 1.29.
var(x)	Variance var(c(1,2,3,4)) returns 1.67.
mad(x)	Median absolute deviation mad(c(1,2,3,4)) returns 1.48.
quantile(x, probs)	Quantiles where x is the numeric vector, where quantiles are desired and probs is a numeric vector with probabilities in [0,1] # 30th and 84th percentiles of x y <- quantile(x, c(.3,.84))
range(x)	Range x <- c(1,2,3,4) range(x) returns c(1,4). diff(range(x)) returns 3.

Table 5.3   Statistical functions *(continued)*

Function	Description
sum(x)	Sum sum(c(1,2,3,4)) returns 10.
diff(x, lag=n)	Lagged differences, with lag indicating which lag to use. The default lag is 1. x<- c(1, 5, 23, 29) diff(x) returns c(4, 18, 6).
min(x)	Minimum min(c(1,2,3,4)) returns 1.
max(x)	Maximum max(c(1,2,3,4)) returns 4.
scale(x, center=TRUE, scale=TRUE)	Column center (center=TRUE) or standardize (center=TRUE, scale=TRUE) data object x. An example is given in listing 5.6.

To see these functions in action, look at the next listing. This example demonstrates two ways to calculate the mean and standard deviation of a vector of numbers.

Listing 5.1   Calculating the mean and standard deviation

```
> x <- c(1,2,3,4,5,6,7,8)

> mean(x)
[1] 4.5                        Short way
> sd(x)
[1] 2.449490

> n <- length(x)
> meanx <- sum(x)/n
> css <- sum((x - meanx)^2)
> sdx <- sqrt(css / (n-1))      Long way
> meanx
[1] 4.5
> sdx
[1] 2.449490
```

It's instructive to view how the corrected sum of squares (css) is calculated in the second approach:

1   x equals c(1, 2, 3, 4, 5, 6, 7, 8), and mean x equals 4.5 (length(x) returns the number of elements in x).

2   (x – meanx) subtracts 4.5 from each element of x, resulting in c(-3.5, -2.5, -1.5, -0.5, 0.5, 1.5, 2.5, 3.5)

3   (x – meanx)^2 squares each element of (x - meanx), resulting in

    c(12.25, 6.25, 2.25, 0.25, 0.25, 2.25, 6.25, 12.25)

4   sum((x - meanx)^2) sums each of the elements of (x - meanx)^2, resulting in 42.

Writing formulas in R has much in common with matrix-manipulation languages such as MATLAB (we'll look more specifically at solving matrix algebra problems in appendix D).

> ### Standardizing data
>
> By default, the `scale()` function standardizes the specified columns of a matrix or data frame to a mean of 0 and a standard deviation of 1:
>
> ```
> newdata <- scale(mydata)
> ```
>
> To standardize each column to an arbitrary mean and standard deviation, you can use code similar to the following:
>
> ```
> newdata <- scale(mydata)*SD + M
> ```
>
> where M is the desired mean and SD is the desired standard deviation. Using the `scale()` function on non-numeric columns produces an error. To standardize a specific column rather than an entire matrix or data frame, you can use code such as this:
>
> ```
> newdata <- transform(mydata, myvar = scale(myvar)*10+50)
> ```
>
> This code standardizes the variable `myvar` to a mean of 50 and standard deviation of 10. You'll use the `scale()` function in the solution to the data management challenge in section 5.3.

5.2.3 Probability functions

You may wonder why probability functions aren't listed with the statistical functions (that was really bothering you, wasn't it?). Although probability functions are statistical by definition, they're unique enough to deserve their own section. Probability functions are often used to generate simulated data with known characteristics and to calculate probability values within user-written statistical functions.

In R, probability functions take the form

```
[dpqr]distribution_abbreviation()
```

where the first letter refers to the aspect of the *distribution* returned:

   d = Density
   p = Distribution function
   q = Quantile function
   r = Random generation (random deviates)

Table 5.4 lists the common probability functions.

Table 5.4 Probability distributions

Distribution	Abbreviation	Distribution	Abbreviation
Beta	`beta`	Logistic	`logis`
Binomial	`binom`	Multinomial	`multinom`

Table 5.4 Probability distributions (continued)

Distribution	Abbreviation	Distribution	Abbreviation
Cauchy	`cauchy`	Negative binomial	`nbinom`
Chi-squared (noncentral)	`chisq`	Normal	`norm`
Exponential	`exp`	Poisson	`pois`
F	`f`	Wilcoxon signed rank	`signrank`
Gamma	`gamma`	T	`t`
Geometric	`geom`	Uniform	`unif`
Hypergeometric	`hyper`	Weibull	`weibull`
Lognormal	`lnorm`	Wilcoxon rank sum	`wilcox`

To see how these work, let's look at functions related to the normal distribution. If you don't specify a mean and a standard deviation, the standard normal distribution is assumed (mean=0, sd=1). Table 5.5 gives examples of the density (dnorm), distribution (pnorm), quantile (qnorm), and random deviate generation (rnorm) functions.

Table 5.5 Normal distribution functions

Problem	Solution

Plot the standard normal curve on the interval [-3,3] (see figure below).	```library(ggplot2)```
	```x <- seq(from = -3, to = 3, by = 0.1)```
	```y = dnorm(x)```
	```data <- data.frame(x = x, y=y)```
	```ggplot(data, aes(x, y)) +```
	``` geom_line() +```
	``` labs(x = "Normal Deviate",```
	``` y = "Density") +```
	``` scale_x_continuous(```
	``` breaks = seq(-3, 3, 1))```

What is the area under the standard normal curve to the left of z=1.96?	`pnorm(1.96)` equals `0.975`.
What is the value of the 90th percentile of a normal distribution with a mean of 500 and a standard deviation of 100?	`qnorm(.9, mean=500, sd=100)` equals `628.16`.
Generate 50 random normal deviates with a mean of 50 and a standard deviation of 10.	`rnorm(50, mean=50, sd=10)`

Each time you generate pseudo-random deviates, a different seed, and therefore different results, are produced. To make your results reproducible, you can specify the seed explicitly using the set.seed() function. An example is given in the next listing. Here, the runif() function is used to generate pseudo-random numbers from a uniform distribution on the interval 0 to 1.

Listing 5.2 Generating pseudo-random numbers from a uniform distribution

```
> runif(5)
[1] 0.8725344 0.3962501 0.6826534 0.3667821 0.9255909
> runif(5)
[1] 0.4273903 0.2641101 0.3550058 0.3233044 0.6584988
> set.seed(1234)
> runif(5)
[1] 0.1137034 0.6222994 0.6092747 0.6233794 0.8609154
> set.seed(1234)
> runif(5)
[1] 0.1137034 0.6222994 0.6092747 0.6233794 0.8609154
```

By setting the seed manually, you're able to reproduce your results. This ability can be helpful in creating examples you can access in the future and share with others.

GENERATING MULTIVARIATE NORMAL DATA

In simulation research and Monte Carlo studies, you often want to draw data from a multivariate normal distribution with a given mean vector and covariance matrix. The draw.d.variate.normal() function in the MultiRNG package makes this easy. After installing and loading the package, the function call is

```
draw.d.variate.normal(n, nvar, mean, sigma)
```

where n is the desired sample size, nvar is the number of variables, mean is the vector of means, and sigma is the variance-covariance (or correlation) matrix. Listing 5.3 samples 500 observations from a three-variable multivariate normal distribution for which the following are true:

Mean vector	230.7	146.7	3.6
Covariance matrix	15360.8	6721.2	-47.1
	6721.2	4700.9	-16.5
	-47.1	-16.5	0.3

Listing 5.3 Generating data from a multivariate normal distribution

```
> install.packages("MultiRNG")
> library(MultiRNG)
> options(digits=3)
> set.seed(1234)
```
Sets the random number seed

```
> mean <- c(230.7, 146.7, 3.6)                                    Specifies the mean
> sigma <- matrix(c(15360.8, 6721.2, -47.1,                       vector and
                    6721.2, 4700.9, -16.5,                        covariance matrix
                    -47.1,   -16.5,    0.3), nrow=3, ncol=3)

> mydata <- draw.d.variate.normal(500, 3, mean, sigma)
> mydata <- as.data.frame(mydata)                                 Generates data
> names(mydata) <- c("y","x1","x2")

> dim(mydata)
[1] 500  3                           Views the results
> head(mydata, n=10)
        y    x1   x2
1    81.1 122.6 3.69
2   265.1 110.4 3.49
3   365.1 235.3 2.67
4   -60.0  14.9 4.72
5   283.9 244.8 3.88
6   293.4 163.9 2.66
7   159.5  51.5 4.03
8   163.0 137.7 3.77
9   160.7 131.0 3.59
10  120.4  97.7 4.11
```

In listing 5.3, you set a random number seed so you can reproduce the results at a later time. You specify the desired mean vector and variance-covariance matrix and generate 500 pseudo-random observations. For convenience, the results are converted from a matrix to a data frame, and the variables are given names. Finally, you confirm that you have 500 observations and 3 variables, and you print out the first 10 observations. Note that because a correlation matrix is also a covariance matrix, you could have specified the correlation structure directly.

The `MultiRNG` package allows you to generate random data from 10 other multivariate distributions, including multivariate versions of the T, uniform, Bernoulli, hypergeometric, beta, multinomial, Laplace, and Wishart distributions.

The probability functions in R allow you to generate simulated data, sampled from distributions with known characteristics. Statistical methods that rely on simulated data have grown exponentially in recent years, and you'll see several examples of these in later chapters.

5.2.4   Character functions

Whereas mathematical and statistical functions operate on numerical data, character functions extract information from textual data or reformat textual data for printing and reporting. For example, you may want to concatenate a person's first name and last name, ensuring that the first letter of each is capitalized. Or you may want to count the instances of obscenities in open-ended feedback. Table 5.6 lists some of the most useful character functions.

Table 5.6 Character functions

Function	Description
`nchar(x)`	Counts the number of characters of *x*. `x <- c("ab", "cde", "fghij")` `length(x)` returns 3 (see table 5.7). `nchar(x[3])` returns 5.
`substr(x, start, stop)`	Extracts or replaces substrings in a character vector. `x <- "abcdef"` `substr(x, 2, 4)` returns bcd. `substr(x, 2, 4) <- "22222"` (x is now "a222ef").
`grep(pattern, x, ignore.case=FALSE, fixed=FALSE)`	Searches for *pattern* in *x*. If `fixed=FALSE`, then *pattern* is a regular expression. If `fixed=TRUE`, then *pattern* is a text string. Returns the matching indices. `grep("A", c("b","A","ac", "Aw"), fixed=TRUE)` returns `c(2, 4)`.
`sub(pattern, replacement, x, ignore.case=FALSE, fixed=FALSE)`	Finds *pattern* in *x* and substitutes the *replacement* text. If `fixed=FALSE`, then *pattern* is a regular expression. If `fixed=TRUE`, then *pattern* is a text string. `sub("\\s",".","Hello There")` returns Hello.There. Note that `"\s"` is a regular expression for finding whitespace; use `"\\s"` instead, because `"\"` is R's escape character (see section 1.3.4).
`strsplit(x, split, fixed=FALSE)`	Splits the elements of character vector *x* at *split*. If `fixed=FALSE`, then *pattern* is a regular expression. If `fixed=TRUE`, then *pattern* is a text string. `y <- strsplit("abc", "")` returns a one-component, three-element list containing `"a" "b" "c"` `unlist(y)[2]` and `sapply(y, "[", 2)` both return "b".
`paste(..., sep="")`	Concatenates strings after using the *sep* string to separate them. `paste("x", 1:3, sep="")` returns `c("x1", "x2", "x3")`. `paste("x",1:3,sep="M")` returns `c("xM1","xM2" "xM3")`. `paste("Today is", date())` returns `Today is Thu Jul 22 10:36:14 2021`
`toupper(x)`	Uppercase. `toupper("abc")` returns "ABC".
`tolower(x)`	Lowercase. `tolower("ABC")` returns "abc".

Note that the functions `grep()`, `sub()`, and `strsplit()` can search for a text string (`fixed=TRUE`) or a regular expression (`fixed=FALSE`); `FALSE` is the default. Regular expressions provide a clear and concise syntax for matching a pattern of text. For example, the regular expression

`^[hc]?at`

matches any string that starts with zero or one occurrences of *h* or *c*, followed by *at*. The expression therefore matches *hat*, *cat*, and *at*, but not *bat*. To learn more, see the *regular expression* entry in Wikipedia. Helpful tutorials include Ryans Regular Expression Tutorial (https://ryanstutorials.net/regular-expressions-tutorial/) and an engaging interactive tutorial from RegexOne (https://regexone.com).

5.2.5 *Other useful functions*

The functions in table 5.7 are also quite useful for data management and manipulation, but they don't fit cleanly into the other categories.

Table 5.7 **Other useful functions**

Function	Description
length(*x*)	Returns the length of object *x*. x <- c(2, 5, 6, 9) length(x) returns 4.
seq(*from*, *to*, *by*)	Generates a sequence. indices <- seq(1,10,2) indices is c(1, 3, 5, 7, 9).
rep(*x*, *n*)	Repeats *x* *n* times. y <- rep(1:3, 2) y is c(1, 2, 3, 1, 2, 3).
cut(*x*, *n*)	Divides the continuous variable *x* into a factor with *n* levels. To create an ordered factor, include the option ordered_result = TRUE.
cat(... , file = "myfile", append = FALSE)	Concatenates the objects in ... and outputs them to the screen or to a file (if one is declared). name <- c("Jane") cat("Hello" , name, "\n")

The last example in the table demonstrates the use of escape characters in printing. Use \n for new lines, \t for tabs, \' for a single quote, \b for backspace, and so forth (type ?Quotes for more information). For example, the code

```
name <- "Bob"
cat( "Hello", name, "\b.\n", "Isn\'t R", "\t", "GREAT?\n")
```

produces

```
Hello Bob.
 Isn't R        GREAT?
```

Note that the second line is indented one space. When cat concatenates objects for output, it separates each by a space. That's why you include the backspace (\b) escape character before the period. Otherwise, it would produce "Hello Bob".

How you apply the functions covered so far to numbers, strings, and vectors is intuitive and straightforward, but how do you apply them to matrices and data frames? That's the subject of the next section.

5.2.6 *Applying functions to matrices and data frames*

One of the interesting features of R functions is that they can be applied to a variety of
data objects (scalars, vectors, matrices, arrays, and data frames). The following listing
provides an example.

Listing 5.4 Applying functions to data objects

```
> a <- 5
> sqrt(a)
[1] 2.236068
> b <- c(1.243, 5.654, 2.99)
> round(b)
[1] 1 6 3
> c <- matrix(runif(12), nrow=3)
> c
        [,1]  [,2]  [,3]  [,4]
[1,] 0.4205 0.355 0.699 0.323
[2,] 0.0270 0.601 0.181 0.926
[3,] 0.6682 0.319 0.599 0.215
> log(c)
         [,1]   [,2]   [,3]   [,4]
[1,] -0.866 -1.036 -0.358 -1.130
[2,] -3.614 -0.508 -1.711 -0.077
[3,] -0.403 -1.144 -0.513 -1.538
> mean(c)
[1] 0.444
```

Notice that the mean of matrix c in listing 5.4 results in a scalar (0.444). The mean()
function takes the average of all 12 elements in the matrix. But what if you want the
three row means or the four column means?

R provides a function, apply(), that allows you to apply an arbitrary function to
any dimension of a matrix, array, or data frame. The format for the apply() function is

```
apply(x, MARGIN, FUN, ...)
```

where x is the data object, MARGIN is the dimension index, FUN is a function you specify, and ... are any parameters you want to pass to FUN. In a matrix or data frame,
MARGIN=1 indicates rows and MARGIN=2 indicates columns. Look at the following
examples.

Listing 5.5 Applying a function to the rows (columns) of a matrix

```
> mydata <- matrix(rnorm(30), nrow=6)         ◄────┐  Generates
> mydata                                           ❶  data
          [,1]    [,2]    [,3]   [,4]   [,5]
[1,]  0.71298  1.368 -0.8320 -1.234 -0.790
[2,] -0.15096 -1.149 -1.0001 -0.725  0.506
[3,] -1.77770  0.519 -0.6675  0.721 -1.350
[4,] -0.00132 -0.308  0.9117 -1.391  1.558
[5,] -0.00543  0.378 -0.0906 -1.485 -0.350
[6,] -0.52178 -0.539 -1.7347  2.050  1.569
```

Calculates the column means ③

```
> apply(mydata, 1, mean)
[1] -0.155 -0.504 -0.511  0.154 -0.310  0.165
> apply(mydata, 2, mean)
[1] -0.2907  0.0449 -0.5688 -0.3442  0.1906
> apply(mydata, 2, mean, trim=0.2)
[1] -0.1699  0.0127 -0.6475 -0.6575  0.2312
```

Calculates the row means ②

Calculates the trimmed column means ④

You start by generating a 6 × 5 matrix containing random normal variates ①. Then you calculate the six row means ② and five column means ③. Finally, you calculate the trimmed column means (in this case, means based on the middle 60% of the data, with the bottom 20% and top 20% of the values discarded) ④.

Because FUN can be any R function, including a function that you write yourself (see section 5.4), apply() is a powerful mechanism. Whereas apply() applies a function over the margins of an array, lapply() and sapply() apply a function over a list. You'll see an example of sapply() (which is a user-friendly version of lapply()) in the next section.

You now have all the tools you need to solve the data challenge presented in section 5.1, so let's give it a try.

5.2.7 *A solution for the data management challenge*

Your challenge from section 5.1 is to combine subject test scores into a single performance indicator for each student, grade each student from A to F based on their relative standing (top 20%, next 20%, and so on), and sort the roster by last name followed by first name. The following listing gives a solution.

Listing 5.6 A solution to the learning example

```
> options(digits=2)          <─── Step 1

> Student <- c("John Davis", "Angela Williams", "Bullwinkle Moose",
               "David Jones", "Janice Markhammer", "Cheryl Cushing",
               "Reuven Ytzrhak", "Greg Knox", "Joel England",
               "Mary Rayburn")
> Math <- c(502, 600, 412, 358, 495, 512, 410, 625, 573, 522)
> Science <- c(95, 99, 80, 82, 75, 85, 80, 95, 89, 86)
> English <- c(25, 22, 18, 15, 20, 28, 15, 30, 27, 18)
> roster <- data.frame(Student, Math, Science, English,
                       stringsAsFactors=FALSE)
```

Step 2 →
```
> z <- scale(roster[,2:4])
```
Step 3
```
> score <- apply(z, 1, mean)
> roster <- cbind(roster, score)
```
Obtains the performance scores

Step 4 →
```
> y <- quantile(score, c(.8,.6,.4,.2))
```
Step 5
```
> roster$grade <- NA
> roster$grade[score >= y[1]] <- "A"
> roster$grade[score < y[1] & score >= y[2]] <- "B"
> roster$grade[score < y[2] & score >= y[3]] <- "C"
> roster$grade[score < y[3] & score >= y[4]] <- "D"
> roster$grade[score < y[4]] <- "F"
```
Grades the students

Step 6 ⟶
Step 7

```
> name <- strsplit((roster$Student), " ")
> Lastname <- sapply(name, "[", 2)
> Firstname <- sapply(name, "[", 1)
> roster <- cbind(Firstname,Lastname, roster[,-1])
```

Extracts the last and first names

Step 8 ⟶

```
> roster <- roster[order(Lastname,Firstname),]
```

Sorts by last and first names

```
> roster
   Firstname   Lastname Math Science English score grade
6     Cheryl    Cushing  512      85      28  0.35     C
1       John      Davis  502      95      25  0.56     B
9       Joel    England  573      89      27  0.70     B
4      David      Jones  358      82      15 -1.16     F
8       Greg       Knox  625      95      30  1.34     A
5     Janice Markhammer  495      75      20 -0.63     D
3  Bullwinkle     Moose  412      80      18 -0.86     D
10      Mary    Rayburn  522      86      18 -0.18     C
2     Angela   Williams  600      99      22  0.92     A
7     Reuven    Ytzrhak  410      80      15 -1.05     F
```

The code is dense, so let's walk through the solution step by step.

1 The original student roster is given. options(digits=2) limits the number of digits printed after the decimal place and makes the printouts easier to read:

```
> options(digits=2)
> roster
             Student Math Science English
1        John Davis  502      95      25
2    Angela Williams  600      99      22
3  Bullwinkle Moose  412      80      18
4       David Jones  358      82      15
5   Janice Markhammer  495      75      20
6    Cheryl Cushing  512      85      28
7    Reuven Ytzrhak  410      80      15
8         Greg Knox  625      95      30
9      Joel England  573      89      27
10     Mary Rayburn  522      86      18
```

2 Because the math, science, and English tests are reported on different scales (with widely differing means and standard deviations), you need to make them comparable before combining them. One way to do this is to standardize the variables so that each test is reported in standard deviation units rather than in their original scales. You can do this with the scale() function:

```
> z <- scale(roster[,2:4])
> z
       Math Science English
[1,]  0.013   1.078   0.587
[2,]  1.143   1.591   0.037
[3,] -1.026  -0.847  -0.697
[4,] -1.649  -0.590  -1.247
[5,] -0.068  -1.489  -0.330
[6,]  0.128  -0.205   1.137
```

```
 [7,] -1.049  -0.847   -1.247
 [8,]  1.432   1.078    1.504
 [9,]  0.832   0.308    0.954
[10,]  0.243  -0.077   -0.697
```

3 You can then get a performance score for each student by calculating the row means using the mean() function and adding them to the roster using the cbind() function:

```
> score <- apply(z, 1, mean)
> roster <- cbind(roster, score)
> roster
            Student Math Science English score
1        John Davis  502      95      25  0.56
2   Angela Williams  600      99      22  0.92
3   Bullwinkle Moose 412      80      18 -0.86
4        David Jones  358      82      15 -1.16
5  Janice Markhammer  495      75      20 -0.63
6    Cheryl Cushing  512      85      28  0.35
7    Reuven Ytzrhak  410      80      15 -1.05
8         Greg Knox  625      95      30  1.34
9      Joel England  573      89      27  0.70
10     Mary Rayburn  522      86      18 -0.18
```

4 The quantile() function gives you the percentile rank of each student's performance score. You see that the cutoff for an A is 0.74, for a B is 0.44, and so on:

```
> y <- quantile(roster$score, c(.8,.6,.4,.2))
> y
  80%   60%   40%   20%
 0.74  0.44 -0.36 -0.89
```

5 Using logical operators, you can recode students' percentile ranks into a new categorical grade variable. This code creates the variable grade in the roster data frame:

```
> roster$grade <- NA
> roster$grade[score >= y[1]] <- "A"
> roster$grade[score < y[1] & score >= y[2]] <- "B"
> roster$grade[score < y[2] & score >= y[3]] <- "C"
> roster$grade[score < y[3] & score >= y[4]] <- "D"
> roster$grade[score < y[4]] <- "F"
> roster
            Student Math Science English score grade
1        John Davis  502      95      25  0.56     B
2   Angela Williams  600      99      22  0.92     A
3   Bullwinkle Moose 412      80      18 -0.86     D
4        David Jones  358      82      15 -1.16     F
5  Janice Markhammer  495      75      20 -0.63     D
6    Cheryl Cushing  512      85      28  0.35     C
7    Reuven Ytzrhak  410      80      15 -1.05     F
8         Greg Knox  625      95      30  1.34     A
9      Joel England  573      89      27  0.70     B
10     Mary Rayburn  522      86      18 -0.18     C
```

6 You use the `strsplit()` function to break the student names into first name and last name at the space character. Applying `strsplit()` to a vector of strings returns a list:

```
> name <- strsplit((roster$Student), " ")
> name

[[1]]
[1] "John"  "Davis"

[[2]]
[1] "Angela"   "Williams"

[[3]]
[1] "Bullwinkle" "Moose"

[[4]]
[1] "David" "Jones"

[[5]]
[1] "Janice"      "Markhammer"

[[6]]
[1] "Cheryl"  "Cushing"

[[7]]
[1] "Reuven"  "Ytzrhak"

[[8]]
[1] "Greg" "Knox"

[[9]]
[1] "Joel"     "England"

[[10]]
[1] "Mary"     "Rayburn"
```

7 You use the `sapply()` function to take the first element of each component and put it in a `Firstname` vector, and the second element of each component and put it in a `Lastname` vector. `"["` is a function that extracts part of an object—here the first or second component of the list name. You use `cbind()` to add these elements to the roster. Because you no longer need the `student` variable, you drop it (with the `-1` in the roster index):

```
> Firstname <- sapply(name, "[", 1)
> Lastname <- sapply(name, "[", 2)
> roster <- cbind(Firstname, Lastname, roster[,-1])
> roster
    Firstname    Lastname Math Science English score grade
1        John       Davis  502      95      25  0.56     B
2      Angela    Williams  600      99      22  0.92     A
3  Bullwinkle       Moose  412      80      18 -0.86     D
4       David       Jones  358      82      15 -1.16     F
```

```
5       Janice Markhammer   495      75       20 -0.63     D
6       Cheryl   Cushing   512      85       28  0.35     C
7       Reuven   Ytzrhak   410      80       15 -1.05     F
8        Greg      Knox    625      95       30  1.34     A
9        Joel    England   573      89       27  0.70     B
10       Mary    Rayburn   522      86       18 -0.18     C
```

8 Finally, you sort the dataset by first and last name using the `order()` function:

```
> roster[order(Lastname,Firstname),]
     Firstname    Lastname Math Science English score grade
6       Cheryl     Cushing  512      85      28  0.35     C
1         John      Davis   502      95      25  0.56     B
9         Joel    England   573      89      27  0.70     B
4        David      Jones   358      82      15 -1.16     F
8         Greg       Knox   625      95      30  1.34     A
5       Janice Markhammer   495      75      20 -0.63     D
3    Bullwinkle     Moose   412      80      18 -0.86     D
10        Mary    Rayburn   522      86      18 -0.18     C
2        Angela   Williams  600      99      22  0.92     A
7       Reuven    Ytzrhak   410      80      15 -1.05     F
```

Voilà! Piece of cake!

There are many other ways to accomplish these tasks, but this code helps capture the flavor of these functions. Now it's time to look at control structures and user-written functions.

5.3   Control flow

In the normal course of events, the statements in an R program are executed sequentially from the top of the program to the bottom. But there are times that you'll want to execute some statements repetitively while executing other statements only if certain conditions are met. This is where control-flow constructs come in.

R has the standard control structures you'd expect to see in a modern programming language. First, we'll go through the constructs used for conditional execution, followed by the constructs used for looping.

For the syntax examples throughout this section, keep the following in mind:

- `statement` is a single R statement or a compound statement (a group of R statements enclosed in curly braces {} and separated by semicolons).
- `cond` is an expression that resolves to TRUE or FALSE.
- `expr` is a statement that evaluates to a number or character string.
- `seq` is a sequence of numbers or character strings.

After we discuss control-flow constructs, you'll learn how to write your own functions.

5.3.1   Repetition and looping

Looping constructs repetitively execute a statement or series of statements until a condition isn't true. These include the `for` and `while` structures.

FOR

The for loop executes a statement repetitively for each value in the vector seq. The syntax is

```
for (var in seq) statement
```

In this example,

```
for (i in 1:10)  print("Hello")
```

the word *Hello* is printed 10 times.

WHILE

A while loop executes a statement repetitively until the condition is no longer true. The syntax is

```
while (cond) statement
```

In a second example, the code

```
i <- 10
while (i > 0) {print("Hello"); i <- i - 1}
```

once again prints the word *Hello* 10 times. Make sure the statements inside the brackets modify the while condition so that sooner or later, it's no longer true—otherwise, the loop will never end! In the previous example, the statement

```
i <- i - 1
```

subtracts 1 from object i on each loop, so that after the tenth loop, it's no longer larger than 0. If you instead added 1 on each loop, R would never stop saying *Hello*. This is why while loops can be more dangerous than other looping constructs.

Looping in R can be inefficient and time consuming when you're processing the rows or columns of large datasets. Whenever possible, it's better to use R's built-in numerical and character functions in conjunction with the apply family of functions.

5.3.2 *Conditional execution*

In conditional execution, a statement or statements are executed only if a specified condition is met. These constructs include if-else, ifelse, and switch.

IF-ELSE

The if-else control structure executes a statement if a given condition is true. Optionally, a different statement is executed if the condition is false. The syntax is

```
if (cond) statement
if (cond) statement1 else statement2
```

Here are some examples:

```
if (is.character(grade)) grade <- as.factor(grade)
if (!is.factor(grade)) grade <- as.factor(grade) else print("Grade already
    is a factor")
```

In the first instance, if `grade` is a character vector, it's converted into a factor. In the second instance, one of two statements is executed. If grade isn't a factor (note the ! symbol), it's turned into one. If it's a factor, then the message is printed.

IFELSE

The `ifelse` construct is a compact and vectorized version of the `if-else` construct. The syntax is

```
ifelse(cond, statement1, statement2)
```

The first statement is executed if `cond` is `TRUE`. If `cond` is `FALSE`, the second statement is executed. Here are some examples:

```
ifelse(score > 0.5, print("Passed"), print("Failed"))
outcome <- ifelse (score > 0.5, "Passed", "Failed")
```

Use `ifelse` when you want to take a binary action or when you want to input and output vectors from the construct.

SWITCH

`switch` chooses statements based on the value of an expression. The syntax is

```
switch(expr, ...)
```

where . . . represents statements tied to the possible outcome values of `expr`. It's easiest to understand how `switch` works by looking at the example in the following listing.

Listing 5.7   A `switch` example

```
> feelings <- c("sad", "afraid")
> for (i in feelings)
    print(
      switch(i,
        happy  = "I am glad you are happy",
        afraid = "There is nothing to fear",
        sad    = "Cheer up",
        angry  = "Calm down now"
      )
    )

[1] "Cheer up"
[1] "There is nothing to fear"
```

This is a silly example, but it shows the main features. You'll learn how to use `switch` in user-written functions in the next section.

5.4   *User-written functions*

One of R's greatest strengths is the user's ability to add functions. In fact, many of R's functions are functions of existing functions. The structure of a function looks like this:

```
myfunction <- function(arg1, arg2, ... ){
  statements
```

```
    return(object)
}
```

Objects in the function are local to the function. The object returned can be any data type, from scalar to list. Let's look at an example.

Say you'd like to have a function that calculates the central tendency and spread of data objects. The function should give you a choice between parametric (mean and standard deviation) and nonparametric (median and median absolute deviation) statistics. The results should be returned as a named list. Additionally, the user should have the choice of automatically printing the results or not. Unless otherwise specified, the function's default behavior should be to calculate parametric statistics and not print the results. One solution is given in the following listing.

Listing 5.8 `mystats()`**: a user-written function for summary statistics**

```
mystats <- function(x, parametric=TRUE, print=FALSE) {
  if (parametric) {
    center <- mean(x); spread <- sd(x)
  } else {
    center <- median(x); spread <- mad(x)
  }
  if (print & parametric) {
    cat("Mean=", center, "\n", "SD=", spread, "\n")
  } else if (print & !parametric) {
    cat("Median=", center, "\n", "MAD=", spread, "\n")
  }
  result <- list(center=center, spread=spread)
  return(result)
}
```

To see this function in action, first generate some data (a random sample of size 500 from a normal distribution):

```
set.seed(1234)
x <- rnorm(500)
```

After executing the statement

```
y <- mystats(x)
```

y$center contains the mean (0.00184), and y$spread contains the standard deviation (1.03). No output is produced. If you execute the statement

```
y <- mystats(x, parametric=FALSE, print=TRUE)
```

y$center contains the median (–0.0207), and y$spread contains the median absolute deviation (1.001). In addition, the following output is produced:

```
Median= -0.0207
MAD= 1
```

Next, let's look at a user-written function that uses the `switch` construct. This function gives the user a choice regarding the format of today's date. Values that are assigned to parameters in the function declaration are taken as defaults. In the `mydate()` function, `long` is the default format for dates if `type` isn't specified:

```
mydate <- function(type="long") {
  switch(type,
    long =  format(Sys.time(), "%A %B %d %Y"),
    short = format(Sys.time(), "%m-%d-%y"),
    cat(type, "is not a recognized type\n")
    )
}
```

Here's the function in action:

```
> mydate("long")
[1] "Saturday July 24 2021"
> mydate("short")
[1] "07-24-21"
> mydate()
[1] "Saturday July 24 2021"
> mydate("medium")
medium is not a recognized type
```

Note that the `cat()` function is executed only if the entered type doesn't match `"long"` or `"short"`. It's usually a good idea to have an expression that catches user-supplied arguments that have been entered incorrectly.

Several functions can help add error trapping and correction to your functions. You can use the function `warning()` to generate a warning message, `message()` to generate a diagnostic message, and `stop()` to stop execution of the current expression and carry out an error action. I will discuss error trapping and debugging more fully in section 20.6.

After creating your own functions, you may want to make them available in every session. Appendix B describes how to customize the R environment so that user-written functions are loaded automatically at startup. We'll look at additional examples of user-written functions in later chapters.

You can accomplish a great deal using the basic techniques provided in this section. Control flow and other programming topics are covered in greater detail in chapter 20. Creating a package is covered in chapter 22. If you'd like to explore the subtleties of function writing, or you want to write professional-level code that you can distribute to others, I recommend reading these two chapters and then reviewing three excellent books listed in the References section: Venables and Ripley (2000), Chambers (2008), and Wickham (2019). Together, they provide a significant level of detail and breadth of examples.

Now that we've covered user-written functions, we'll end this chapter with a discussion of data aggregation and reshaping.

5.5 Reshaping data

When you *reshape* data, you alter the structure (rows and columns) determining how the data is organized. The three most common reshaping tasks are (1) transposing a dataset; (2) converting a wide dataset to a long dataset; and (3) converting a long dataset to a wide dataset. Each is described in the following sections.

5.5.1 Transposing

Transposing (reversing rows and columns) is perhaps the simplest method of reshaping a dataset. Use the `t()` function to transpose a matrix or a data frame. In the latter case, the data frame is converted to a matrix first, and row names become variable (column) names.

We'll illustrate transposing using the `mtcars` data frame that's included with the base installation of R. This dataset, extracted from *Motor Trend* magazine (1974), describes the design and performance characteristics (number of cylinders, displacement, horsepower, mpg, and so on) for 34 automobiles. To learn more about the dataset, see `help(mtcars)`.

The following listing shows an example of the transpose operation. A subset of the dataset in used to conserve space on the page.

Listing 5.9 Transposing a dataset

```
> cars <- mtcars[1:5,1:4]
> cars
                   mpg cyl disp  hp
Mazda RX4         21.0   6  160 110
Mazda RX4 Wag     21.0   6  160 110
Datsun 710        22.8   4  108  93
Hornet 4 Drive    21.4   6  258 110
Hornet Sportabout 18.7   8  360 175
> t(cars)
     Mazda RX4 Mazda RX4 Wag Datsun 710 Hornet 4 Drive Hornet Sportabout
mpg         21            21       22.8           21.4              18.7
cyl          6             6        4.0            6.0               8.0
disp       160           160      108.0          258.0             360.0
hp         110           110       93.0          110.0             175.0
```

The `t()` function always returns a matrix. Since a matrix can only have one type (numeric, character, or logical), the transpose operation works best when all the variables in the original dataset are numeric or logical. If there are any character variables in the dataset, the *entire* dataset will be converted to character values in the resulting transpose.

5.5.2 Converting from wide to long dataset formats

A rectangular dataset is typically in either wide or long format. In *wide format*, each row represents a unique *observation*. Table 5.8 shows an example. The table contains the life expectancy estimates for four countries in 1990, 2000, and 2010. It is part of a much larger dataset obtained from Our World in Data (https://ourworldindata.org/ life-expectancy). Note that each row represents the data gathered on a country.

Table 5.8   Life expectancy by year and country—wide format

ID	Country	LExp1990	LExp2000	LExp2010
AU	Australia	76.9	79.6	82.0
CN	China	69.3	72.0	75.2
PRK	North Korea	69.9	65.3	69.6

In *long format*, each row represents a unique *measurement*. Table 5.9 shows an example with the same data in long format.

Table 5.9   Life expectancy by year and country—long format

ID	Country	Variable	LifeExp
AU	Australia	LExp1990	76.9
CN	China	LExp1990	69.3
PRK	North Korea	LExp1990	69.9
AU	Australia	LExp2000	79.6
CN	China	LExp2000	72.0
PRK	North Korea	LExp2000	65.3
AU	Australia	LExp2010	82.0
CN	China	LExp2010	75.2
PRK	North Korea	LExp2010	69.6

Different types of data analysis can require different data formats. For example, if you want to identify countries that have similar life expectancy trends over time, you could use cluster analysis (chapter 16). Cluster analysis requires data that is in wide format. On the other hand, you may want to predict life expectancy from country and year using multiple regression (chapter 8). In this case, the data would have to be in long format.

While most R functions expect wide format data frames, some require the data to be in a long format. Fortunately, the `tidyr` package provides functions that can easily convert data frames from one format to the other. Use `install.packages("tidyr")` to install the package before continuing.

The `gather()` function in the `tidyr` package converts a wide format data frame to a long format data frame. The syntax is

```
longdata <- gather(widedata, key, value, variable list)
```

where

- `widedata` is the data frame to be converted.
- `key` specifies the name to be used for the variable column (Variable in this example).
- `value` specifies the name to be used for the value column (LifeExp in this example).
- `variable list` specifies the variables to be stacked (LExp1990, LExp2000, LExp2010 in this example).

The following listing shows an example.

Listing 5.10 Converting a wide format data frame to a long format

```
> library(tidyr)

> data_wide <- data.frame(ID = c("AU", "CN", "PRK"),
                     Country = c("Australia", "China", "North Korea"),
                     LExp1990 = c(76.9, 69.3, 69.9),
                     LExp2000 = c(79.6, 72.0, 65.3),
                     LExp2010 = c(82.0, 75.2, 69.6))
> data_wide
   ID      Country LExp1990 LExp2000 LExp2010
1  AU    Australia     76.9     79.6     82.0
2  CN        China     69.3     72.0     75.2
3 PRK North Korea     69.9     65.3     69.6

> data_long <- gather(data_wide, key="Variable", value="Life_Exp",
                  c(LExp1990, LExp2000, LExp2010))
> data_long
   ID      Country Variable Life_Exp
1  AU    Australia LExp1990     76.9
2  CN        China LExp1990     69.3
3 PRK North Korea LExp1990     69.9
4  AU    Australia LExp2000     79.6
5  CN        China LExp2000     72.0
6 PRK North Korea LExp2000     65.3
7  AU    Australia LExp2010     82.0
8  CN        China LExp2010     75.2
9 PRK North Korea LExp2010     69.6
```

The `spread()` function in the `tidyr` package converts a long format data frame to a wide format data frame. The format is

```
widedata <- spread(longdata, key, value)
```

where

- `longdata` is the data frame to be converted.
- `key` is the column containing the variable names.
- `value` is the column containing the variable values.

Continuing the example, the code in the following listing is used to convert the long format data frame back to a wide format.

Listing 5.11   Converting a long format data frame to a wide format

```
> data_wide <- spread(data_long, key=Variable, value=Life_Exp)
> data_wide
   ID      Country LExp1990 LExp2000 LExp2010
1  AU     Australia     76.9     79.6     82.0
2  CN         China     69.3     72.0     75.2
3 PRK North Korea       69.9     65.3     69.6
```

To learn more about the long and wide data formats, see Simon Ejdemyr's excellent tutorial (https://sejdemyr.github.io/r-tutorials/basics/wide-and-long/).

5.6 *Aggregating data*

When you aggregate data, you replace groups of observations with summary statistics based on those observations. Data aggregation can be a precursor to statistical analyses or a method of summarizing data for presentation in tables or graphs.

It's relatively easy to collapse data in R using one or more by variables and a defined function. In base R, the `aggregate()` is typically used. The format is

```
aggregate(x, by, FUN)
```

where x is the data object to be collapsed, by is a list of variables that will be crossed to form the new observations, and FUN is a function used to calculate the summary statistics that will make up the new observation values. The by variables must be enclosed in a list (even if there's only one).

As an example, let's aggregate the `mtcars` data by number of cylinders and gears, returning means for each of the numeric variables.

Listing 5.12   Aggregating data with the `aggregate()` function

```
> options(digits=3)
> aggdata <-aggregate(mtcars,
                  by=list(mtcars$cyl,mtcars$gear),
                  FUN=mean, na.rm=TRUE)
> aggdata
  Group.1 Group.2  mpg cyl disp  hp drat   wt qsec  vs   am gear carb
1       4       3 21.5   4  120  97 3.70 2.46 20.0 1.0 0.00    3 1.00
2       6       3 19.8   6  242 108 2.92 3.34 19.8 1.0 0.00    3 1.00
3       8       3 15.1   8  358 194 3.12 4.10 17.1 0.0 0.00    3 3.08
4       4       4 26.9   4  103  76 4.11 2.38 19.6 1.0 0.75    4 1.50
5       6       4 19.8   6  164 116 3.91 3.09 17.7 0.5 0.50    4 4.00
6       4       5 28.2   4  108 102 4.10 1.83 16.8 0.5 1.00    5 2.00
7       6       5 19.7   6  145 175 3.62 2.77 15.5 0.0 1.00    5 6.00
8       8       5 15.4   8  326 300 3.88 3.37 14.6 0.0 1.00    5 6.00
```

In these results, `Group.1` represents the number of cylinders (4, 6, or 8), and `Group.2` represents the number of gears (3, 4, or 5). For example, cars with 4 cylinders and

3 gears have a mean of 21.5 miles per gallon (mpg). Here we used the mean function, but any function in R or any user-defined function that computes summary statistics can be used.

There are two limitations to this code. First, Group.1 and Group.2 are terribly uninformative variable names. Second, the original cyl and gear variables are included in the aggregated data frame. These columns are now redundant.

You can declare custom names for the grouping variables from within the list. For instance, by=list(Cylinders=cyl, Gears=gear will replace Group.1 and Group.2 with Cylinders and Gears. The redundant columns can be dropped from the input data frame using bracket notation (mtcars[-c(2, 10)]). The following listing shows an improved version.

Listing 5.13 Improved code for aggregating data with `aggregate()`

```
> aggdata <-aggregate(mtcars[-c(2, 10)],
          by=list(Cylinders=mtcars$cyl, Gears=mtcars$gear),
          FUN=mean, na.rm=TRUE)
> aggdata
  Cylinders Gears  mpg disp  hp drat   wt qsec  vs   am carb
1         4     3 21.5  120  97 3.70 2.46 20.0 1.0 0.00 1.00
2         6     3 19.8  242 108 2.92 3.34 19.8 1.0 0.00 1.00
3         8     3 15.1  358 194 3.12 4.10 17.1 0.0 0.00 3.08
4         4     4 26.9  103  76 4.11 2.38 19.6 1.0 0.75 1.50
5         6     4 19.8  164 116 3.91 3.09 17.7 0.5 0.50 4.00
6         4     5 28.2  108 102 4.10 1.83 16.8 0.5 1.00 2.00
7         6     5 19.7  145 175 3.62 2.77 15.5 0.0 1.00 6.00
8         8     5 15.4  326 300 3.88 3.37 14.6 0.0 1.00 6.00
```

The dplyr package provides a more natural method of aggregating data. Consider the code in the next listing.

Listing 5.14 Aggregating data with the `dplyr` **package**

```
> mtcars %>%
    group_by(cyl, gear) %>%
    summarise_all(list(mean), na.rm=TRUE)

# A tibble: 8 x 11
# Groups:   cyl [3]
    cyl  gear   mpg  disp    hp  drat    wt  qsec    vs    am  carb
  <dbl> <dbl> <dbl> <dbl> <dbl> <dbl> <dbl> <dbl> <dbl> <dbl> <dbl>
1     4     3  21.5  120.   97   3.7   2.46  20.0   1     0    1
2     4     4  26.9  103.   76   4.11  2.38  19.6   1     0.75 1.5
3     4     5  28.2  108.  102   4.1   1.83  16.8   0.5   1    2
4     6     3  19.8  242.  108.  2.92  3.34  19.8   1     0    1
5     6     4  19.8  164.  116.  3.91  3.09  17.7   0.5   0.5  4
6     6     5  19.7  145   175   3.62  2.77  15.5   0     1    6
7     8     3  15.0  358.  194.  3.12  4.10  17.1   0     0    3.08
8     8     5  15.4  326   300.  3.88  3.37  14.6   0     1    6
```

The grouping variables retain their names and are not duplicated in the data. We'll expand on `dplyr`'s powerful summarization capabilities when discussing summary statistics in chapter 7.

Now that you've gathered the tools you need to get your data into shape (no pun intended), you're ready to bid part 1 goodbye and enter the exciting world of data analysis! In upcoming chapters, we'll begin to explore the many statistical and graphical methods available for turning data into information.

Summary

- Base R contains hundreds of mathematical, statistical, and probability functions that are useful for manipulating data. They can be applied to a wide range of data objects, including vectors, matrices, and data frames.
- Functions for conditional execution and looping allow you to execute some statements repetitively and execute other statements only when certain conditions are met.
- You can easily write your own functions, vastly increasing the power of your programs.
- Data often have to be aggregated and/or restructured before further analyses are possible.

Part 2

Basic methods

In part 1, we explored the R environment and discussed how to input data from various sources, combine and transform it, and prepare it for further analyses. Once your data has been inputted and cleaned up, the next step is typically to explore the variables one at a time. This provides you with information about the distribution of each variable, which is useful in understanding the characteristics of the sample, identifying unexpected or problematic values, and selecting appropriate statistical methods. Next, variables are typically studied two at a time. This can help you to uncover basic relationships among variables and is a useful first step in developing more complex models.

Part 2 focuses on graphical and statistical techniques for obtaining basic information about data. Chapter 6 describes methods for visualizing the distribution of individual variables. For categorical variables, this includes bar plots, pie charts, and the newer tree maps. For numeric variables, this includes histograms, density plots, box plots, dot plots, and the less-well-known violin plot. Each type of graph is useful for understanding the distribution of a single variable.

Chapter 7 describes statistical methods for summarizing individual variables and bivariate relationships. The chapter starts by covering descriptive statistics for numerical data based on the dataset as a whole and on subgroups of interest. Next, the use of frequency tables and cross-tabulations for summarizing categorical data is described. The chapter ends by discussing basic inferential methods for understanding relationships between two variables at a time, including bivariate correlations, chi-square tests, t-tests, and nonparametric methods.

When you have finished this part of the book, you'll be able to use basic graphical and statistical methods available in R to describe your data, explore group differences, and identify significant relationships among variables.

Basic graphs

Whenever we analyze data, the first thing we should do is *look* at it. For each variable, what are the most common values? How much variability is present? Are there any unusual observations? R provides a wealth of functions for visualizing data. In this chapter, we'll look at graphs that help you understand a single categorical or continuous variable. This topic includes

- Visualizing the distribution of a variable
- Comparing the distribution of a variable across two or more groups

In both cases, the variable can be continuous (for example, car mileage as miles per gallon) or categorical (for example, treatment outcome as none, some, or marked). In later chapters, we'll explore graphs that display more complex relationships among variables.

The following sections explore the use of bar charts, pie charts, tree maps, histograms, kernel density plots, box plots, violin plots, and dot plots. Some of these may

117

be familiar to you, whereas others (such as tree charts or violin plots) may be new. The goal, as always, is to understand your data better and to communicate this understanding to others. Let's start with bar charts.

6.1   Bar charts

A bar plot displays the distribution (frequency) of a categorical variable through vertical or horizontal bars. Using the `ggplot2` package, we can create a bar chart using the code

```
ggplot(data, aes(x=catvar) + geom_bar()
```

where `data` is a data frame and `catvar` is a categorical variable.

In the following examples, you'll plot the outcome of a study investigating a new treatment for rheumatoid arthritis. The data is contained in the `Arthritis` data frame distributed with the `vcd` package. This package isn't included in the default R installation, so install it before first use (`install.packages("vcd")`). Note that the `vcd` package isn't needed to create bar charts. You're installing it to gain access to the `Arthritis` dataset.

6.1.1   Simple bar charts

In the Arthritis study, the variable `Improved` records the patient outcomes for individuals receiving a placebo or drug:

```
> data(Arthritis, package="vcd")
> table(Arthritis$Improved)

  None   Some Marked
    42     14     28
```

Here, you see that 28 patients showed marked improvement, 14 showed some improvement, and 42 showed no improvement. We'll discuss the use of the `table()` function to obtain cell counts more fully in chapter 7.

You can graph these counts using a vertical or horizontal bar chart. The following listing shows the code, and figure 6. 1 displays the resulting graphs.

Listing 6.1   Simple bar charts

```
library(ggplot2)
ggplot(Arthritis, aes(x=Improved)) + geom_bar() +
  labs(title="Simple Bar chart",                     Simple bar chart
      x="Improvement",
      y="Frequency")

ggplot(Arthritis, aes(x=Improved)) + geom_bar() +
  labs(title="Horizontal Bar chart",                 Horizontal bar chart
      x="Improvement",
      y="Frequency") +
  coord_flip()
```

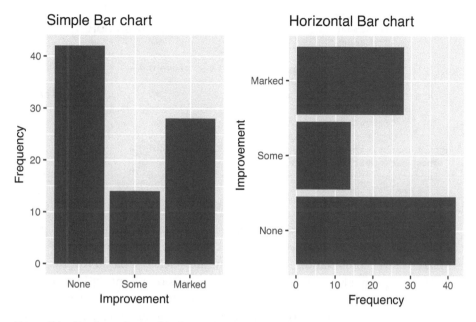

Figure 6.1 Simple vertical and horizontal bar charts

What happens if you have long labels? In section 6.1.4, you'll see how to tweak labels so they don't overlap.

6.1.2 Stacked, grouped, and filled bar charts

The central question in the Arthritis study is, "How does the level of improvement vary between the placebo and treated conditions?" The `table()` function can used to generate a cross-tabulation of the variables:

```
> table(Arthritis$Improved, Arthritis$Treatment)

        Treatment
Improved Placebo Treated
  None        29      13
  Some         7       7
  Marked       7      21
```

While the tabulation is helpful, the results are easier to grasp with a bar chart. The relationship between two categorical variables can be plotted using *stacked*, *grouped*, or *filled* bar charts. The next listing provides the code, and figure 6.2 displays the graph.

Listing 6.2 Stacked, grouped, and filled bar charts

```
library(ggplot2)
ggplot(Arthritis, aes(x=Treatment, fill=Improved)) +          Stacked bar chart
  geom_bar(position = "stack") +
```

```
labs(title="Stacked Bar chart",
     x="Treatment",
     y="Frequency")
```
Stacked bar chart

```
ggplot(Arthritis, aes(x=Treatment, fill=Improved)) +
  geom_bar(position = "dodge") +
  labs(title="Grouped Bar chart",
       x="Treatment",
       y="Frequency")
```
Grouped bar chart

```
ggplot(Arthritis, aes(x=Treatment, fill=Improved)) +
  geom_bar(position = "fill") +
  labs(title="Filled Bar chart",
       x="Treatment",
       y="Proportion")
```
Filled bar chart

In the stacked bar chart, each segment represents the frequency or proportion of cases within a given Treatment (Placebo, Treated) and Improvement (None, Some, Marked) level combination. The segments are stacked separately for each Treatment level. The grouped bar chart places the segments representing Improvement side by side within each Treatment level. The filled bar chart is a stacked bar chart rescaled so that the height of each bar is 1 and the segment heights represent proportions.

Filled bar charts are particularly useful for comparing the proportions of one categorical variable over the levels of another categorical variable. For example, the filled bar chart in figure 6.2 clearly displays the larger percentage of treated patients with marked improvement compared with patients receiving a placebo.

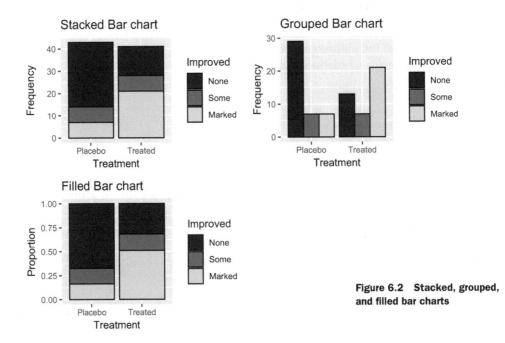

Figure 6.2   Stacked, grouped, and filled bar charts

6.1.3 Mean bar charts

Bar plots needn't be based on counts or frequencies. You can create bar charts that represent means, medians, percentages, standard deviations, and so forth by summarizing the data with an appropriate statistic and passing the results to ggplot2.

In the following graph, we'll plot the mean illiteracy rate for regions of the United States in 1970. The built-in R dataset state.x77 has the illiteracy rates by state, and the dataset state.region has the region names for each state. The following listing provides the code needed to create the graph in figure 6.3.

Listing 6.3   Bar chart for sorted mean values

```
> states <- data.frame(state.region, state.x77)
> library(dplyr)
> plotdata <- states %>%
    group_by(state.region) %>%
    summarize(mean = mean(Illiteracy))        ❶ Generates means
  plotdata                                      by region

# A tibble: 4 x 2
  state.region    mean
  <fct>           <dbl>
1 Northeast       1
2 South           1.74
3 North Central   0.7
4 West            1.02

> ggplot(plotdata, aes(x=reorder(state.region, mean), y=mean)) +
    geom_bar(stat="identity") +
    labs(x="Region",                           ❷ Plots means
        y="",                                    in a sorted
        title = "Mean Illiteracy Rate")          bar chart
```

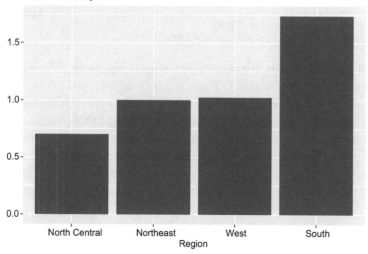

Figure 6.3   Bar chart of mean illiteracy rates for US regions sorted by rate

First, the mean illiteracy rate is calculated for each region ❶. Next, the means are sorted in ascending order and plotted as bars ❷. Normally, the geom_bar() function calculates and plots cell counts, but adding the stat="identity" option forces the function to plot the numbers provided (means, in this case). The reorder() function is used to order the bars by increasing mean illiteracy.

When plotting summary statistics such as means, it's good practice to indicate the variability of the estimates involved. One measure of variability is the standard error of the statistic—an estimate of the expected variation of the statistic across hypothetical repeated samples. The following plot (figure 6.4) adds error bars using the standard error of the mean.

Listing 6.4   Bar chart of mean values with error bars

```
> plotdata <- states %>%
    group_by(state.region) %>%                          ❶ Generates means and
    summarize(n=n(),                                        standard errors by region
              mean = mean(Illiteracy),
              se = sd(Illiteracy)/sqrt(n))

> plotdata

# A tibble: 4 x 4
  state.region       n   mean      se
  <fct>          <int> <dbl>   <dbl>
1 Northeast          9  1     0.0928
2 South             16  1.74  0.138
3 North Central     12  0.7   0.0408
4 West              13  1.02  0.169

> ggplot(plotdata, aes(x=reorder(state.region, mean), y=mean)) +     ❷ Plots means in a sorted bar chart
    geom_bar(stat="identity", fill="skyblue") +
    geom_errorbar(aes(ymin=mean-se, ymax=mean+se), width=0.2) +      ❸ Adds error bars
    labs(x="Region",
         y="",
         title = "Mean Illiteracy Rate",
         subtitle = "with standard error bars")
```

The means and standard errors are calculated for each region ❶. The bars are then plotted in order of increasing illiteracy. The color is changed from a default dark grey to a lighter shade (sky blue) so that error bars that will be added in the next step will stand out ❷. Finally, the error bars are plotted ❸. The width option in the geom_errorbar() function controls the horizontal width of the error bars and is purely aesthetic—it has no statistical meaning. In addition to displaying the mean illiteracy rates, we can see that the mean for the North Central region is the most reliable (least variability) and the mean for the West region is least reliable (largest variability).

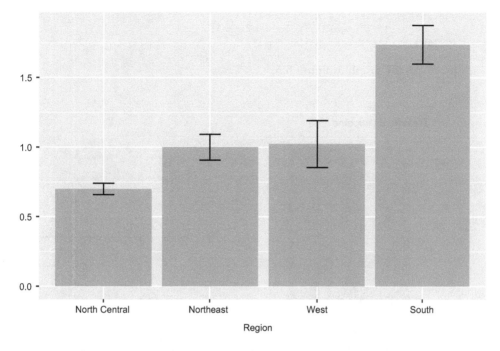

**Mean Illiteracy Rate
with standard error bars**

Figure 6.4 Bar chart of mean illiteracy rates for US regions sorted by rate. The standard error of the mean has been added to each bar.

6.1.4 *Tweaking bar charts*

There are several ways to tweak the appearance of a bar chart. The most common are customizing the bar colors and labels. We'll look at each in turn.

BAR CHART COLORS

Custom colors can be selected for the bar areas and borders. In the `geom_bar()` function, the option `fill="color"` assigns a color for the area, while `color ="color"` assigns a color for the border.

Fill vs. color

In general, `ggplot2` uses *fill* to specify the color of geometric objects that have area (such as bars, pie slices, boxes) and *color* when referring to the color of geometric objects without area (such as lines, points, and borders).

For example, the code

```
data(Arthritis, package="vcd")
ggplot(Arthritis, aes(x=Improved)) +
   geom_bar(fill="gold", color="black") +
   labs(title="Treatment Outcome")
```

produces the graph in figure 6.5.

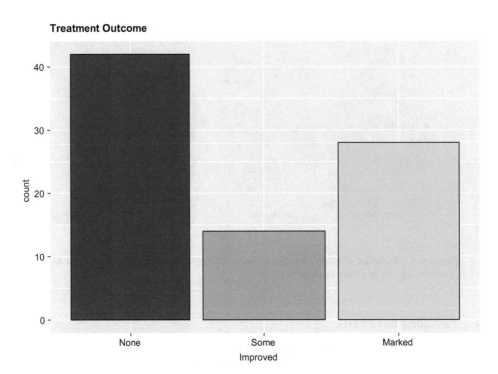

Figure 6.5   Bar chart with custom fill and border colors

In the previous example, single colors were assigned. Colors can also be mapped to the levels of a categorical variable. For example, the code

```
ggplot(Arthritis, aes(x=Treatment, fill=Improved)) +
  geom_bar(position = "stack", color="black") +
  scale_fill_manual(values=c("red", "grey", "gold")) +
  labs(title="Stacked Bar chart",
       x="Treatment",
       y="Frequency")
```

produces the graph in figure 6.6.

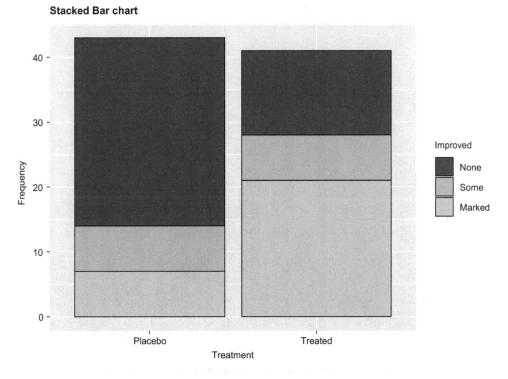

Figure 6.6 Stacked bar chart with custom fill colors mapped to Improvement

Here, bar fill colors are mapped to the levels of the variable `Improved`. The `scale_fill_manual()` function specifies red for `None`, grey for `Some`, and gold for `Marked` improvement. Color names can be obtained from http://www.stat.columbia.edu/~tzheng/files/Rcolor.pdf. Chapter 19 discusses other methods of selecting colors.

BAR CHART LABELS

When there are many bars or long labels, bar chart labels tend to overlap and become unreadable. Consider the following example. The dataset `mpg` in the `ggplot2` package describes fuel economy data for 38 popular car models in 1999 and 2008. Each model has several configurations (transmission type, number of cylinders, etc.). Let's say that we want a count of how many instances of each model are in the dataset. The code

```
ggplot(mpg, aes(x=model)) +
  geom_bar() +
  labs(title="Car models in the mpg dataset",
      y="Frequency", x="")
```

produces the graph in figure 6.7.

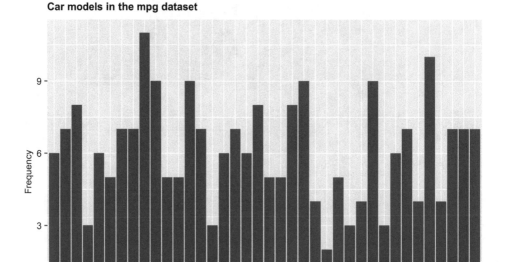

Figure 6.7   Bar chart with overlapping labels

Even with my glasses (or a glass of wine), I can't read this. Two simple tweaks will make the labels readable. First, we can plot the data as a horizontal bar chart (figure 6.8):

```
ggplot(mpg, aes(x=model)) +
  geom_bar() +
  labs(title="Car models in the mpg dataset",
       y="Frequency", x="") +
  coord_flip()
```

Second, we can angle the label text and use a smaller font (figure 6.9):

```
ggplot(mpg, aes(x=model)) +
  geom_bar() +
  labs(title="Model names in the mpg dataset",
       y="Frequency", x="") +
  theme(axis.text.x = element_text(angle = 45, hjust = 1, size=8))
```

Car models in the mpg dataset

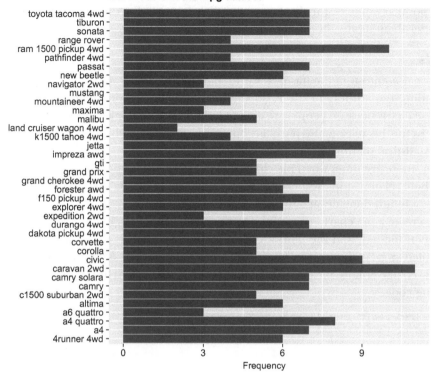

**Figure 6.8
A horizontal bar
chart avoids
label overlap.**

Model names in the mpg dataset

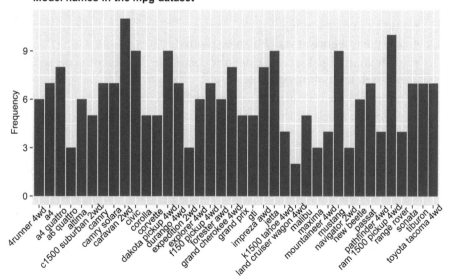

Figure 6.9   Bar chart with angled labels and a smaller label font

Chapter 19 discusses the theme() function more fully. In addition to bar charts, pie charts are popular vehicles for displaying the distribution of a categorical variable. We'll consider them next.

6.2   *Pie charts*

Pie charts are ubiquitous in the business world, but they're denigrated by most statisticians, including the authors of the R documentation. They recommend bar or dot plots over pie charts because people are able to judge length more accurately than volume. Perhaps for this reason, the pie chart options in R are severely limited compared with other statistical platforms.

However, there are times when pie charts can be useful. In particular, they can capture part-whole relationships well. For example, a pie chart can be used to display the percentage of tenured faculty at a university who are female.

You can create a pie chart in base R using the pie() function, but as I've said, the functionality is limited, and the plots are unattractive. To address this, I've created a package called ggpie that allows you to create a wide variety of pie charts using ggplot2 (no flame emails, please!). You can install it from my GitHub repository with the following code:

```
if (!require(remotes)) install.packages("remotes")
remotes::install_github("rkabacoff/ggpie")
```

The basic syntax is

```
ggpie(data, x, by, offset, percent, legend, title)
```

where

- data is a data frame.
- x is the categorical variable to be plotted.
- by is an optional second categorical variable. If present, a pie will be produced for each level of this variable.
- offset is the distance of the pie slice labels from the origin. A value of 0.5 will place the labels in the center of the slices, and a value greater than 1.0 will place them outside the slice.
- percent is logical. If FALSE, percentage printing is suppressed.
- legend is logical. If FALSE, the legend is omitted, and each pie slice is labeled.
- title is an option title.

Additional options (described on the ggpie website) allow you to customize the pie chart's appearance. Let's create a pie chart displaying the distribution of car classes in the mpg data frame:

```
library(ggplot2)
library(ggpie)
ggpie(mpg, class)
```

Figure 6.10 shows the results. From the graph, we see that 26% percent of cars are SUVS, while only 2% are two-seaters.

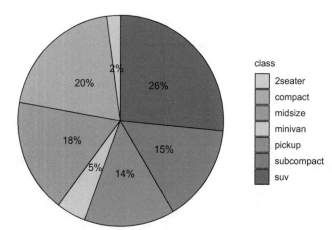

Figure 6.10 **Pie chart displaying the percentage of each car class in the** mpg **data frame**

In the next version (figure 6.11), the legend is removed, and each pie slice is labeled. In addition, the labels are placed outside the pie area, and a title is added:

```
ggpie(mpg, class, legend=FALSE, offset=1.3,
        title="Automobiles by Car Class")
```

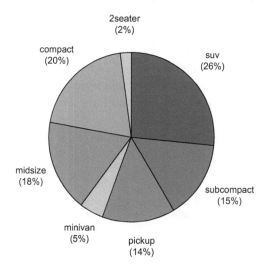

Figure 6.11 **Pie chart with labels displayed outside the pie**

In the final example (figure 6.12), the distribution of car class is displayed by year.

```
ggpie(mpg, class, year,
      legend=FALSE, offset=1.3, title="Car Class by Year")
```

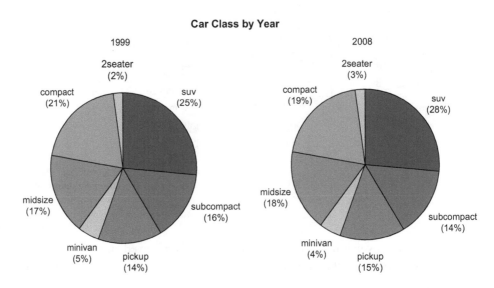

Figure 6.12   Pie charts displaying the distribution of car classes by year

Between 1999 and 2008, the distribution of car classes appears to have remained rather constant. The `ggpie` package can create more complex and customized pie charts. See the documentation (https://rkabacoff.github.io/ggpie) for details.

6.3   *Tree maps*

An alternative to a pie chart is a tree map, which displays the distribution of a categorical variable using rectangles that are proportional to variable levels. We'll create tree maps using the `treemapify` package. Be sure to install it before proceeding (`install.packages("treemapify")`).

We'll start by creating a tree map displaying the distribution of car manufacturers in the `mpg` data frame. The following listing shows the code, and figure 6.13 shows the resulting graph.

Listing 6.5   Simple tree map

```
library(ggplot2)
library(dplyr)
library(treemapify)

plotdata <- mpg %>% count(manufacturer)
```
 **Summarizes
the data**

```
ggplot(plotdata,
       aes(fill = manufacturer,
           area = n,
           label = manufacturer)) +
geom_treemap() +
geom_treemap_text() +
theme(legend.position = "none")
```

❷ Creates the
tree map

First, we calculate the frequency counts for each level of the `manufacturer` variable ❶. This information is passed to `ggplot2` to create the graph ❷. In the `aes()` function, `fill` refers to the categorical variable, `area` is the count for each level, and `label` is the option variable used to label the cells. The `geom_treemap()` function creates the tree map, and the `geom_treemap_text()` function adds the labels to each cell. The `theme()` function is used to suppress the legend, which is redundant here because each cell is labeled.

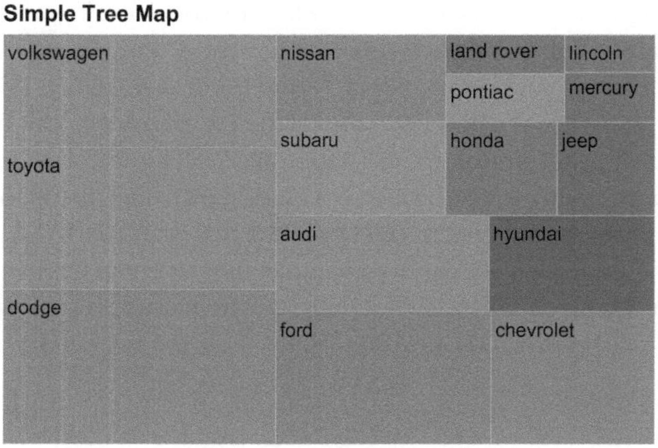

Simple Tree Map

Figure 6.13 Tree map displaying the distribution of car manufacturers in the `mpg` dataset. Rectangle size is proportional to the number of cars from each manufacturer.

As you can see, a tree map can be used to visualize a categorical variable with *many* levels (unlike a pie chart). In the next example, a second variable is added—drivetrain. The number of cars by manufacturer is plotted for front-wheel, rear-wheel, and four-wheel drives. The next listing provides the code, and figure 6.14 shows the plot.

Listing 6.6 Tree map with subgrouping

```
library(ggplot2)
library(dplyr)
library(treemapify)
plotdata <- mpg %>%                                ❶ Computes cell
  count(manufacturer, drv)                           counts
  plotdata$drv <- factor(plotdata$drv,
                  levels=c("4", "f", "r"),
                  labels=c("4-wheel", "front-wheel", "rear"))
```

❶ Computes cell
counts

❷ Provides better
labels for
drivetrains

```
ggplot(plotdata,
       aes(fill = manufacturer,
           area = n,
           label = manufacturer,
           subgroup=drv)) +
  geom_treemap() +
  geom_treemap_subgroup_border() +
  geom_treemap_subgroup_text(
    place = "middle",
    colour = "black",
    alpha = 0.5,
    grow = FALSE) +
  geom_treemap_text(colour = "white",
                    place = "centre",
                    grow=FALSE) +
  theme(legend.position = "none")
```

❸ Creates
tree map

First, the frequencies for each manufacturer-drivetrain combination are calculated ❶. Next, better labels are provided for the `drivetrain` variable ❷. The new data frame is passed to `ggplot2` to produce the tree map ❸. The subgroup option in the `aes()` function creates separate subplots for each `drivetrain` type. The `geom_treemap_border()` and `geom_treemap_subgroup_text()` add borders and labels for the subgroups, respectively. Options in each function control their appearance. The subgroup text is centered and given some transparency (`alpha=0.5`). The text font remains a constant size, rather than growing to fill the area (`grow=FALSE`). The tree map cell text is printed in a white font, centered in each cell, and does not grow to fill the boxes.

From the graph in figure 6.14, it is clear, for example, that Hyundai has front-wheel-drive cars, but not rear-wheel- or four-wheel-drive cars. The manufacturers with rear-wheel-drive cars are primarily Ford and Chevrolet. Many of the four-wheel-drive cars are made by Dodge.

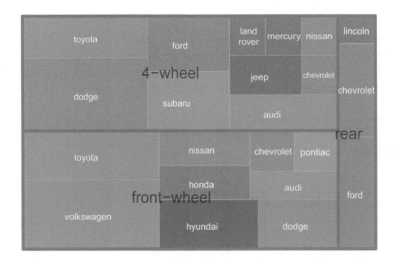

Figure 6.14 Tree map with car manufacturers by drive-train type

Now that we've covered pie charts and tree maps, let's move on to histograms. Unlike bar charts, pie charts, and tree maps, histograms describe the distribution of a continuous variable.

6.4   *Histograms*

Histograms display the distribution of a continuous variable by dividing the range of scores into a specified number of bins on the *x*-axis and displaying the frequency of scores in each bin on the *y*-axis. You can create histograms using

```
ggplot(data, aes(x = contvar)) + geom_histogram()
```

where data is a data frame and contvar is a continuous variable. Using the mpg datasets in the ggplot package, we'll examine the distribution of city miles per gallon (cty) for 117 automobile configurations in 2008. The following listing creates four variations of a histogram, and figure 6.15 shows the resulting graphs.

Listing 6.7   Histograms

```
library(ggplot2)
library(scales)

data(mpg)
cars2008 <- mpg[mpg$year == 2008, ]

ggplot(cars2008, aes(x=cty)) +                          ❶ Simple histogram
    geom_histogram() +
    labs(title="Default histogram")

ggplot(cars2008, aes(x=hwy)) +
    geom_histogram(bins=20, color="white", fill="steelblue") +     ❷ Colored histogram
    labs(title="Colored histogram with 20 bins",                       with 20 bins
        x="City Miles Per Gallon",
        y="Frequency")


ggplot(cars2008, aes(x=hwy, y=..density..)) +
    geom_histogram(bins=20, color="white", fill="steelblue") +
    scale_y_continuous(labels=scales::percent) +            ❸ Histogram with
  labs(title="Histogram with percentages",                     percentages
        y= "Percent".
        x="City Miles Per Gallon")

ggplot(cars2008, aes(x=cty, y=..density..)) +
    geom_histogram(bins=20, color="white", fill="steelblue") +
    scale_y_continuous(labels=scales::percent) +
    geom_density(color="red", size=1) +                     ❹ Histogram with
    labs(title="Histogram with density curve",                  density curve
        y="Percent" ,
        x="Highway Miles Per Gallon")
```

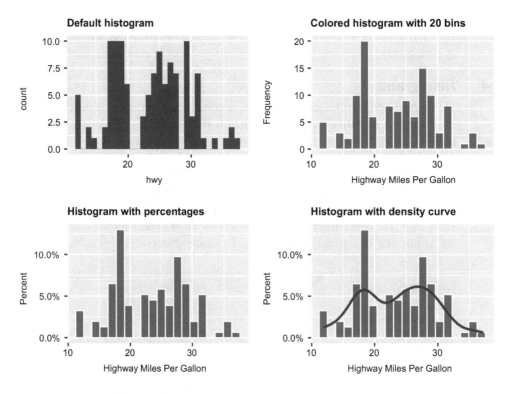

Figure 6.15 Histogram examples

The first histogram ❶ demonstrates the default plot when no options are specified. In this case, 30 bins are created. For the second histogram ❷, 20 bins, a steel-blue fill, and a white border color are specified. In addition, more informative labels have been added. The number of bins can strongly influence the appearance of the histogram. It is a good idea to experiment with the bins value until you find one that captures the distribution well. With 20 bins, it appears that there are two peaks to the distribution—one around 13 mpg and one around 20.5 mpg.

The third histogram ❸ plots the data as percentages rather than frequencies. This is accomplished by assigning the built-in variable ..density.. to the y-axis. The scales package is used to format the y-axis as percentages. Be sure to install the package (install.packages("scales")) before running this part of the code.

The fourth histogram ❹ is similar to the previous plot but adds a density curve. The density curve is a kernel density estimate and is described in the next section. It provides a smoother description of the distribution of scores. The geom_density() function is used to plot the kernel curve in a red color and a width that's slightly larger than the default thickness for lines. The density curve also suggests a bimodal distribution (two peaks).

6.5   *Kernel density plots*

In the previous section, you saw a kernel density plot superimposed on a histogram. Technically, kernel density estimation is a nonparametric method for estimating the probability density function of a random variable. Basically, we're trying to draw a smoothed histogram, where the area under the curve equals 1. Although the mathematics are beyond the scope of this text, density plots can be an effective way to view the distribution of a continuous variable. The format for a density plot is

```
ggplot(data, aes(x = contvar)) + geom_density()
```

where `data` is a data frame and `contvar` is a continuous variable. Again, let's plot the distribution of city miles per gallon (`cty`) for cars in 2008. The next listing gives three kernel density examples, and figure 6.16 shows the results.

Listing 6.8   Kernel density plots

```
library(ggplot2)
data(mpg)
cars2008 <- mpg[mpg$year == 2008, ]

ggplot(cars2008, aes(x=cty)) +                        ❶ Default density plot
    geom_density() +
    labs(title="Default kernel density plot")

ggplot(cars2008, aes(x=cty)) +
    geom_density(fill="red") +                        ❷ Filled density plot
    labs(title="Filled kernel density plot",
        x="City Miles Per Gallon)

> bw.nrd0(cars2008$cty)        ❸ Prints default
1.408                             bandwidth

ggplot(cars2008, aes(x=cty)) +
    geom_density(fill="red", bw=.5) +                 ❹ Density plot with
    labs(title="Kernel density plot with bw=0.5",        smaller bandwidth
        x="City Miles Per Gallon")
```

The default kernel density plot is given first ❶. In the second example, the area under the curve is fill with red. The smoothness of the curve is control with a bandwidth parameter, which is calculated from the data being plotted ❷. The code `bw.nrd0(cars2008$cty)` displays this value (`1.408`) ❸. Using a larger bandwidth will give a smoother curve with fewer details. A smaller value will give a more jagged curve. The third example uses a smaller bandwidth (`bw=.5`), allowing us to see more detail ❹. As with the `bins` parameter for histograms, it is a good idea to try several bandwidth values to see which value helps you visualize the data most effectively.

Kernel density plots can be used to compare groups. This is a highly underutilized approach, probably due to a general lack of easily accessible software. Fortunately, the `ggplot2` package fills this gap nicely.

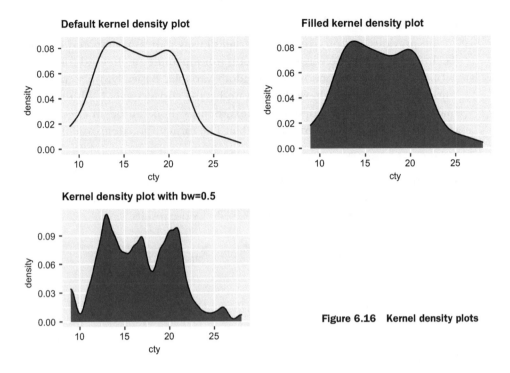

Figure 6.16   Kernel density plots

For this example, we'll compare the 2008 city gas mileage estimates for four-, six-, and eight-cylinder cars. There are only a handful of cars with 5 cylinders, so we will drop them from the analyses. The next listing presents the code. Figures 6.17 and 6.18 show the resulting graphs.

Listing 6.9   Comparative kernel density plots

```
data(mpg, package="ggplot2")
cars2008 <- mpg[mpg$year == 2008 & mpg$cyl != 5,]      ❶ Prepares the data
cars2008$Cylinders <- factor(cars2008$cyl)

ggplot(cars2008, aes(x=cty, color=Cylinders, linetype=Cylinders)) +    ❷ Plots the
    geom_density(size=1)   +                                              density
    labs(title="Fuel Efficiecy by Number of Cylinders",                  curves
        x = "City Miles per Gallon")

ggplot(cars2008, aes(x=cty, fill=Cylinders)) +
    geom_density(alpha=.4) +                             ❸ Plots the filled
    labs(title="Fuel Efficiecy by Number of Cylinders",   density curves
        x = "City Miles per Gallon")
```

First, a fresh copy of the data is loaded, and 2008 data for cars with four, six, or eight cylinders is retained ❶. The number of cylinders (cyl) is saved as a categorical factor (Cylinders). The transformation is required because ggplot2 expects the grouping variable to be categorical (and cyl is stored as a continuous variable).

A kernel density curve is plotted for each level of the Cylinders variable ❷. Both the color (red, green, blue) and line type (solid, dotted, dashed) are mapped to the number of cylinders. Finally, the same plot is produced with filled curves ❸. Transparency is added (alpha=0.4), since the filled curves overlap, and we want to be able to see each one.

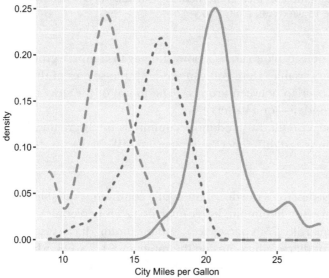

Figure 6.17
Kernel density curves of city mpg by number of cylinders

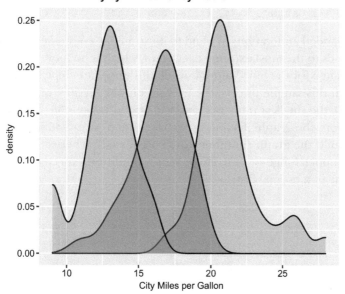

Figure 6.18 **Filled kernel density curves of city mpg by number of cylinders**

Printing in greyscale

By default, ggplot2 selects colors that may be difficult to distinguish when printed in greyscale. This is the case for figure 6.18 in the hard copy version of this book. When greyscale figures are required, you can add the `scale_fill_grey()` and `scale_color_grey()` functions to your code. This will produce a color scheme that works well when it's printed in black and white. Alternatively, you can select colors using the `bpy.colors()` function in the sp package. This will choose a blue-pink-yellow color scheme that also prints well on both color and black/white printers. However, you have to like blue, pink, and yellow!

Overlapping kernel density plots can be a powerful way to compare groups of observations on an outcome variable. Here you can see both the shapes of the distributions and the amount of overlap between groups. (The moral of the story is that my next car will have four cylinders—or a battery.)

Box plots are also a wonderful (and more commonly used) graphical approach to visualizing distributions and differences among groups. We'll discuss them next.

6.6   *Box plots*

A *box-and-whiskers plot* describes the distribution of a continuous variable by plotting its five-number summary: the minimum, lower quartile (25th percentile), median (50th percentile), upper quartile (75th percentile), and maximum. It can also display observations that may be outliers (values outside the range of $\pm 1.5 \times QR$, where IQR is the interquartile range defined as the upper quartile minus the lower quartile). For example, the following code produces the plot shown in figure 6.19:

```
ggplot(mtcars, aes(x="", y=mpg)) +
  geom_boxplot() +
  labs(y = "Miles Per Gallon", x="", title="Box Plot")
```

In figure 6.19, I've added annotations by hand to illustrate the components. By default, each whisker extends to the most extreme data point, which is no more than 1.5 times the interquartile range for the box. Values outside this range are depicted as dots.

For example, in this sample of cars, the median mpg is 17, 50% of the scores fall between 14 and 19, the smallest value is 9, and the largest value is 35. How did I read this so precisely from the graph? Issuing `boxplot.stats(mtcars$mpg)` prints the statistics used to build the graph (in other words, I cheated). There are four outliers (greater than the upper hinge of 26). These values would be expected to occur less than 1% of the time in a normal distribution.

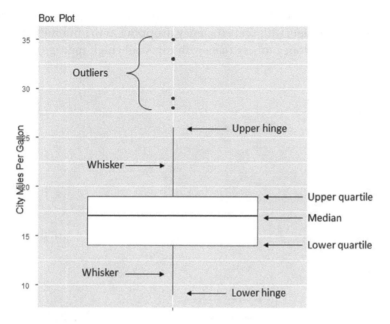

Figure 6.19 Box plot with annotations added by hand

6.6.1 *Using parallel box plots to compare groups*

Box plots are a useful method of comparing the distribution of a quantitative variable across the levels of a categorical variable. Once again, let's compare city gas mileage for four-, six-, and eight-cylinder cars, but this time, we'll use both 1999 and 2008 data. Since there are only a few five-cylinder cars, we will delete them. We'll also convert year and cyl from continuous numeric variables into categorical (grouping) factors:

```
library(ggplot2)
cars <- mpg[mpg$cyl != 5, ]
cars$Cylinders <- factor(cars$cyl)
cars$Year <- factor(cars$year)
```

The code

```
ggplot(cars, aes(x=Cylinders, y=cty)) +
  geom_boxplot() +
  labs(x="Number of Cylinders",
       y="Miles Per Gallon",
       title="Car Mileage Data")
```

produces the graph in figure 6.20. You can see that there's a good separation of groups based on gas mileage, with fuel efficiency dropping as the number of cylinders increases. There are also four outliers (cars with unusually high mileage) in the four-cylinder group.

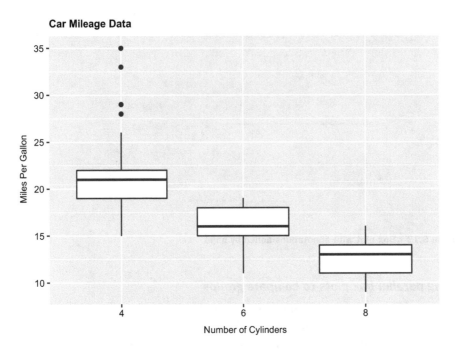

Figure 6.20 Box plots of car mileage vs. number of cylinders

Box plots are very versatile. By adding notch=TRUE, you get *notched* box plots. If two boxes' notches don't overlap, there's strong evidence that their medians differ (Chambers et al., 1983, p. 62). The following code creates notched box plots for the mileage example:

```
ggplot(cars, aes(x=Cylinders, y=cty)) +
  geom_boxplot(notch=TRUE,
               fill="steelblue",
               varwidth=TRUE) +
  labs(x="Number of Cylinders",
       y="Miles Per Gallon",
       title="Car Mileage Data")
```

The fill option fills the box plots with a dark color. In a standard box plot, the box width has no meaning. Adding varwidth=TRUE draws box widths proportional to the square roots of the number of observations in each group.

You can see in figure 6.21 that the median car mileage for four-, six-, and eight-cylinder cars differs. Mileage clearly decreases with number of cylinders. Additionally, there are fewer eight-cylinder cars, than four- or six-cylinder cars (although the difference is subtle).

Finally, you can produce box plots for more than one grouping factor. The following code provides box plots for city miles per gallon versus the number of cylinders by year (see figure 6.21). The `scale_fill_manual()` function has been added to customize the fill colors:

```
ggplot(cars, aes(x=Cylinders, y=cty, fill=Year)) +
  geom_boxplot() +
  labs(x="Number of Cylinders",
       y="Miles Per Gallon",
       title="City Mileage by # Cylinders and Year") +
  scale_fill_manual(values=c("gold", "green"))
```

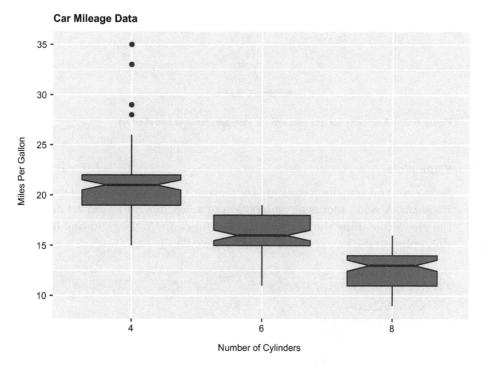

Figure 6.21 Notched box plots for car mileage vs. number of cylinders

As figure 6.22 shows, it's again clear that median mileage decreases with number of cylinders. Additionally, for each group, mileage has increased between 1999 and 2008.

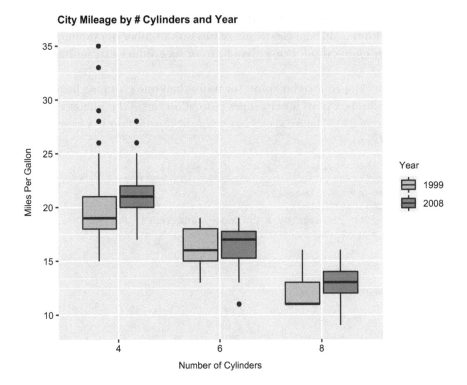

Figure 6.22   Box plots for car mileage vs. year and number of cylinders

6.6.2   *Violin plots*

Before we end our discussion of box plots, it's worth examining a variation called a *violin plot*. A violin plot is a combination of a box plot and a kernel density plot. You can create one using the geom_violin() function. In the following listing, we'll add violin plots to the box plots, shown in figure 6.23.

Listing 6.10   Violin plots

```
library(ggplot2)
cars <- mpg[mpg$cyl != 5, ]
cars$Cylinders <- factor(cars$cyl)

ggplot(cars, aes(x=Cylinders, y=cty)) +
  geom_boxplot(width=0.2,
               fill-"green") +
  geom_violin(fill="gold",
              alpha=0.3) +
  labs(x="Number of Cylinders",
       y="City Miles Per Gallon",
       title="Violin Plots of Miles Per Gallon")
```

The width of the box plots is set to 0.2 so they will fit inside the violin plots. The violin plots are set with a transparency level of 0.3 so the box plots are still visible.

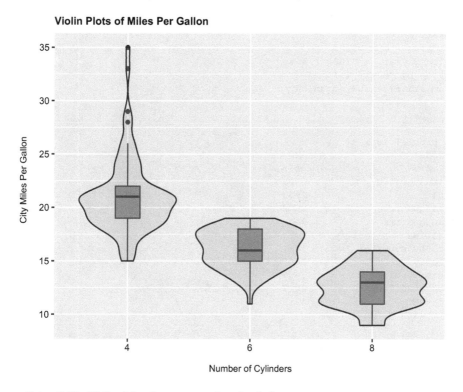

Violin Plots of Miles Per Gallon

Figure 6.23 **Violin plots of mpg vs. number of cylinders**

Violin plots are basically kernel density plots superimposed in a mirror-image fashion over box plots. The middle lines are the medians, the black boxes range from the lower to the upper quartile, and the thin black lines represent the whiskers. Dots are outliers. The outer shape provides the kernel density plot. Here we can see that the distribution of gas mileage for eight-cylinder cars may be bimodal—a fact that is obscured by using box plots alone. Violin plots haven't really caught on yet. Again, this may be due to a lack of easily accessible software; time will tell.

We'll end this chapter with a look at dot plots. Unlike the graphs you've seen previously, dot plots plot every value for a variable.

6.7 Dot plots

Dot plots provide a method of plotting a large number of labeled values on a simple horizontal scale. You create them with the dotchart() function, using the format

```
ggplot(data, aes(x=contvar, y=catvar)) + geom_point()
```

where data is a data frame, contvar is a continuous variable, and catvar is a categorical variable. Here's an example using the highway gas mileage for the 2008 automobiles in the mpg dataset. Highway gas mileage is averaged by car model:

```
library(ggplot2)
library(dplyr)
plotdata <- mpg %>%
  filter(year == "2008") %>%
  group_by(model) %>%
  summarize(meanHwy=mean(hwy))

> plotdata

# A tibble: 38 x 2
    model               meanHwy
    <chr>                 <dbl>
 1 4runner 4wd            18.5
 2 a4                     29.3
 3 a4 quattro             26.2
 4 a6 quattro             24
 5 altima                 29
 6 c1500 suburban 2wd     18
 7 camry                  30
 8 camry solara           29.7
 9 caravan 2wd            22.2
10 civic                  33.8
# ... with 28 more rows


ggplot(plotdata, aes(x=meanHwy, y=model)) +
  geom_point() +
  labs(x="Miles Per Gallon",
       y="",
       title="Gas Mileage for Car Models")
```

The resulting plot is shown in figure 6.24.

This graph allows you to see the mpg for each car model on the same horizontal axis. Dot plots typically become most useful when they're sorted. The following code sorts the cars from lowest to highest mileage:

```
ggplot(plotdata, aes(x=meanHwy, y=reorder(model, meanHwy))) +
  geom_point() +
  labs(x="Miles Per Gallon",
       y="",
       title="Gas Mileage for Car Models")
```

The resulting graph is given in figure 6.25. To plot in descending order, use reorder (model, -meanHwy).

You can gain significant insight from the dot plot in this example because each point is labeled, the value of each point is inherently meaningful, and the points are arranged in a manner that promotes comparisons. But as the number of data points increases, the utility of the dot plot decreases.

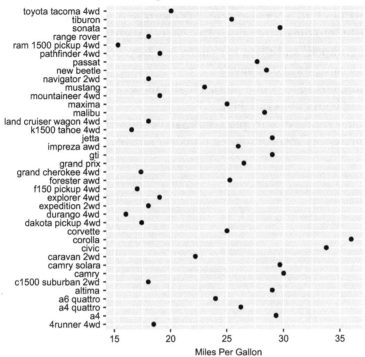

**Figure 6.24
Dot plot of mpg
for each car
model**

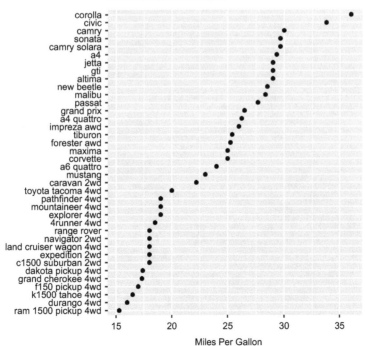

**Figure 6.25   Dot
plot of mpg for car
models sorted by
mileage**

Summary

- Bar charts (and, to a lesser extent, pie charts and tree maps) can be used to gain insight into the distribution of a categorical variable.
- Stacked, grouped, and filled bar charts can help you understand how groups differ on a categorical outcome.
- Histograms, box plots, violin plots, and dot plots can help you visualize the distribution of continuous variables.
- Overlapping kernel density plots and parallel box plots can help you visualize group differences on a continuous outcome variable.

Basic statistics 7

This chapter covers

- Descriptive statistics
- Frequency and contingency tables
- Correlations and covariances
- T-tests
- Nonparametric statistics

In previous chapters, you learned how to import data into R and use a variety of functions to organize and transform the data into a useful format. We then reviewed basic methods for visualizing data.

Once your data is properly organized and you've begun to explore it visually, the next step is typically to describe the distribution of each variable numerically, followed by an exploration of the relationships among selected variables, two at a time. The goal is to answer questions like these:

- What kind of mileage are cars getting these days? Specifically, what's the distribution of miles per gallon (mean, standard deviation, median, range, and so on) in a survey of automobile makes and models?

- After a new drug trial, what's the outcome (no improvement, some improvement, marked improvement) for drug versus placebo groups? Does the gender of the participants have an impact on the outcome?
- What's the correlation between income and life expectancy? Is it significantly different from zero?
- Are you more likely to receive imprisonment for a crime in different regions of the United States? Are the differences between regions statistically significant?

In this chapter, we'll review R functions for generating basic descriptive and inferential statistics. First, we'll look at measures of location and scale for quantitative variables. Then, you'll learn how to generate frequency and contingency tables (and associated chi-square tests) for categorical variables. Next, we'll examine the various forms of correlation coefficients available for continuous and ordinal variables. Finally, we'll turn to the study of group differences through parametric (t-tests) and nonparametric (Mann–Whitney U test, Kruskal–Wallis test) methods. Although our focus is on numerical results, we'll refer to graphical methods for visualizing these results throughout.

The statistical methods covered in this chapter are typically taught in a first-year undergraduate statistics course. If these methodologies are unfamiliar to you, two excellent references are McCall (2000) and Kirk (2008). Alternatively, many informative online resources are available (such as Wikipedia) for each of the topics covered.

7.1   Descriptive statistics

In this section, we'll look at measures of central tendency, variability, and distribution shape for continuous variables. For illustrative purposes, we'll use several of the variables from the Motor Trend Car Road Tests (`mtcars`) dataset you first saw in chapter 1. Our focus will be on miles per gallon (`mpg`), horsepower (`hp`), and weight (`wt`):

```
> myvars <- c("mpg", "hp", "wt")
> head(mtcars[myvars])
                   mpg  hp   wt
Mazda RX4         21.0  110  2.62
Mazda RX4 Wag     21.0  110  2.88
Datsun 710        22.8   93  2.32
Hornet 4 Drive    21.4  110  3.21
Hornet Sportabout 18.7  175  3.44
Valiant           18.1  105  3.46
```

First, we'll look at descriptive statistics for all 32 cars. Then, we'll examine descriptive statistics by transmission type (`am`) and engine cylinder configuration (`vs`). The former is coded 0=automatic, 1=manual, and the latter is coded 0=V-shape and 1=straight.

7.1.1   A menagerie of methods

When it comes to calculating descriptive statistics, R has an embarrassment of riches. Let's start with functions that are included in the base installation. Then we'll look at extensions that are available through the use of user-contributed packages.

In the base installation, you can use the `summary()` function to obtain descriptive statistics. An example is presented in the following listing.

Listing 7.1 **Descriptive statistics via** `summary()`

```
> myvars <- c("mpg", "hp", "wt")
> summary(mtcars[myvars])
      mpg              hp              wt
 Min.   :10.4    Min.   : 52.0    Min.   :1.51
 1st Qu.:15.4    1st Qu.: 96.5    1st Qu.:2.58
 Median :19.2    Median :123.0    Median :3.33
 Mean   :20.1    Mean   :146.7    Mean   :3.22
 3rd Qu.:22.8    3rd Qu.:180.0    3rd Qu.:3.61
 Max.   :33.9    Max.   :335.0    Max.   :5.42
```

The `summary()` function provides the minimum, maximum, quartiles, and mean for numerical variables and frequencies for factors and logical vectors. You can use the `apply()` and `sapply()` functions from chapter 5 to provide any descriptive statistics you choose. The `apply()` function is used with matrices, and the `sapply()` function is used with data frames. The format for the for the `sapply()` function is

```
sapply(x, FUN, options)
```

where *x* is the data frame and *FUN* is an arbitrary function. If *options* are present, they're passed to *FUN*. Typical functions that you can plug in here are `mean()`, `sd()`, `var()`, `min()`, `max()`, `median()`, `length()`, `range()`, and `quantile()`. The function `fivenum()` returns Tukey's five-number summary (minimum, lower-hinge, median, upper-hinge, and maximum).

Surprisingly, the base installation doesn't provide functions for skew and kurtosis, but you can add your own. The example in the next listing provides several descriptive statistics, including skew and kurtosis.

Listing 7.2 **Descriptive statistics via** `sapply()`

```
> mystats <- function(x, na.omit=FALSE){
               if (na.omit)
                   x <- x[!is.na(x)]
               m <- mean(x)
               n <- length(x)
               s <- sd(x)
               skew <- sum((x-m)^3/s^3)/n
               kurt <- sum((x-m)^4/s^4)/n - 3
               return(c(n=n, mean=m, stdev=s,
                   skew=skew, kurtosis=kurt))
           }

> myvars <- c("mpg", "hp", "wt")
> sapply(mtcars[myvars], mystats)
           mpg       hp       wt
n       32.000   32.000   32.0000
mean    20.091  146.688    3.2172
```

```
stdev       6.027   68.563   0.9785
skew        0.611    0.726   0.4231
kurtosis   -0.373   -0.136  -0.0227
```

For cars in this sample, the mean mpg is 20.1, with a standard deviation of 6.0. The distribution is skewed to the right (+0.61) and is somewhat flatter than a normal distribution (−0.37). This is most evident if you graph the data. Note that if you wanted to omit missing values, you could use `sapply(mtcars[myvars], mystats, na.omit =TRUE)`.

7.1.2   *Even more methods*

Several user-contributed packages offer functions for descriptive statistics, including `Hmisc`, `pastecs`, `psych`, `skimr`, and `summytools`. Due to space limitations, we'll only demonstrate the first three, but you can generate useful summaries with any of the five. Because these packages aren't included in the base distribution, you'll need to install them on first use (see section 1.4).

The `describe()` function in the `Hmisc` package returns the number of variables and observations, the number of missing and unique values, the mean, quantiles, and the five highest and lowest values. The following listing provides an example.

Listing 7.3   Descriptive statistics via `describe()` in the `Hmisc` package

```
> library(Hmisc)
> myvars <- c("mpg", "hp", "wt")
> describe(mtcars[myvars])

 3 Variables      32 Observations
---------------------------------------------------------------------------
mpg
n missing  unique  Mean    .05    .10    .25    .50    .75    .90    .95
32       0      25  20.09  12.00  14.34  15.43  19.20  22.80  30.09  31.30

lowest : 10.4 13.3 14.3 14.7 15.0, highest: 26.0 27.3 30.4 32.4 33.9
---------------------------------------------------------------------------
hp
n missing  unique  Mean    .05     .10    .2     .50     .75     .90      .95
32       0      22  146.7  63.65  66.00  96.50 123.00 180.00 243.50 253.55

lowest :  52  62  65  66  91, highest: 215 230 245 264 335
---------------------------------------------------------------------------
wt
n missing  unique  Mean    .05    .10    .25    .50    .75    .90    .95
32       0      29  3.217  1.736  1.956  2.581  3.325  3.610  4.048 5.293

lowest : 1.513 1.615 1.835 1.935 2.140, highest: 3.845 4.070 5.250 5.345
       5.424
---------------------------------------------------------------------------
```

The `pastecs` package includes a function named `stat.desc()` that provides a wide range of descriptive statistics. The format is

```
stat.desc(x, basic=TRUE, desc=TRUE, norm=FALSE, p=0.95)
```

where *x* is a data frame or time series. If `basic=TRUE` (the default), the number of values, null values, missing values, minimum, maximum, range, and sum are provided. If `desc=TRUE` (also the default), the median, mean, standard error of the mean, 95% confidence interval for the mean, variance, standard deviation, and coefficient of variation are also provided. Finally, if `norm=TRUE` (not the default), normal distribution statistics are returned, including skewness and kurtosis (and their statistical significance) and the Shapiro–Wilk test of normality. A p-value option is used to calculate the confidence interval for the mean (.95 by default). The next listing gives an example.

Listing 7.4 Descriptive statistics via `stat.desc()` in the `pastecs` package

```
> library(pastecs)
> myvars <- c("mpg", "hp", "wt")
> stat.desc(mtcars[myvars])
                  mpg        hp       wt
nbr.val         32.00    32.000   32.000
nbr.null         0.00     0.000    0.000
nbr.na           0.00     0.000    0.000
min             10.40    52.000    1.513
max             33.90   335.000    5.424
range           23.50   283.000    3.911
sum            642.90  4694.000  102.952
median          19.20   123.000    3.325
mean            20.09   146.688    3.217
SE.mean          1.07    12.120    0.173
CI.mean.0.95     2.17    24.720    0.353
var             36.32  4700.867    0.957
std.dev          6.03    68.563    0.978
coef.var         0.30     0.467    0.304
```

As if this isn't enough, the `psych` package also has a function called `describe()` that provides the number of nonmissing observations, mean, standard deviation, median, trimmed mean, median absolute deviation, minimum, maximum, range, skew, kurtosis, and standard error of the mean. You can see an example in the following listing.

Listing 7.5 Descriptive statistics via `describe()` in the `psych` package

```
> library(psych)
Attaching package: 'psych'
        The following object(s) are masked from package:Hmisc :
          describe
> myvars <- c("mpg", "hp", "wt")
> describe(mtcars[myvars])
     var  n    mean     sd median trimmed   mad   min    max
mpg    1 32   20.09   6.03  19.20   19.70  5.41 10.40  33.90
hp     2 32  146.69  68.56 123.00  141.19 77.10 52.00 335.00
wt     3 32    3.22   0.98   3.33    3.15  0.77  1.51   5.42
     range skew kurtosis    se
mpg  23.50 0.61    -0.37  1.07
hp  283.00 0.73    -0.14 12.12
wt    3.91 0.42    -0.02  0.17
```

I told you that it was an embarrassment of riches!

> **NOTE** In the previous examples, the packages psych and Hmisc both pro-
> vide a function named describe(). How does R know which one to use?
> Simply put, the package last loaded takes precedence, as shown in listing 7.5.
> Here, psych is loaded after Hmisc, and a message is printed indicating that
> the describe() function in Hmisc is masked by the function in psych.
> When you type in the describe() function and R searches for it, R comes to
> the psych package first and executes it. If you want the Hmisc version
> instead, you can type Hmisc::describe(mt). The function is still there. You
> have to give R more information to find it.

Now that you know how to generate descriptive statistics for the data as a whole, let's
review how to obtain statistics for subgroups of the data.

7.1.3   *Descriptive statistics by group*

When comparing groups of individuals or observations, the focus is usually on the
descriptive statistics of each group rather than the total sample. Group statistics can
be generated using base R's by() function. The format is

```
by(data, INDICES, FUN)
```

where *data* is a data frame or matrix, *INDICES* is a factor or list of factors that defines
the groups, and *FUN* is an arbitrary function that operates on all the columns of a data
frame. The next listing provides an example.

Listing 7.6   Descriptive statistics by group using by()

```
> dstats <- function(x)sapply(x, mystats)
> myvars <- c("mpg", "hp", "wt")
> by(mtcars[myvars], mtcars$am, dstats)

mtcars$am: 0
              mpg       hp       wt
n          19.000   19.0000   19.000
mean       17.147  160.2632    3.769
stdev       3.834   53.9082    0.777
skew        0.014   -0.0142    0.976
kurtosis   -0.803   -1.2097    0.142
------------------------------------------
mtcars$am: 1
              mpg       hp       wt
n          13.0000   13.000   13.000
mean       24.3923  126.846    2.411
stdev       6.1665   84.062    0.617
skew        0.0526    1.360    0.210
kurtosis   -1.4554    0.563   -1.174
```

In this case, dstats() applies the mystats() function from listing 7.2 to each column of the data frame. Placing it in the by() function gives you summary statistics for
each level of am.

In the next example (listing 7.7), summary statistics are generated for two by variables (am and vs), and the results for each group are printed with custom labels. Additionally, missing values are omitted before calculating statistics.

Listing 7.7 Descriptive statistics for groups defined by multiple variables

```
> dstats <- function(x)sapply(x, mystats, na.omit=TRUE)
> myvars <- c("mpg", "hp", "wt")
> by(mtcars[myvars],
      list(Transmission=mtcars$am,
           Engine=mtcars$vs),
      FUN=dstats)


Transmission: 0
Engine: 0
                 mpg          hp           wt
n         12.0000000  12.0000000  12.0000000
mean      15.0500000 194.1666667   4.1040833
stdev      2.7743959  33.3598379   0.7683069
skew      -0.2843325   0.2785849   0.8542070
kurtosis  -0.9635443  -1.4385375  -1.1433587
-----------------------------------------------------------------
Transmission: 1
Engine: 0
                 mpg          hp           wt
n          5.0000000   6.0000000   6.00000000
mean      19.5000000 180.8333333   2.85750000
stdev      4.4294469  98.8158219   0.48672117
skew       0.3135121   0.4842372   0.01270294
kurtosis  -1.7595065  -1.7270981  -1.40961807
-----------------------------------------------------------------
Transmission: 0
Engine: 1
                 mpg          hp           wt
n          7.0000000   7.0000000   7.0000000
mean      20.7428571 102.1428571   3.1942857
stdev      2.4710707  20.9318622   0.3477598
skew       0.1014749  -0.7248459  -1.1532766
kurtosis  -1.7480372  -0.7805708  -0.1170979
-----------------------------------------------------------------
Transmission: 1
Engine: 1
                 mpg          hp           wt
n          7.0000000   7.0000000   7.0000000
mean      28.3714286  80.5714286   2.0282857
stdev      4.7577005  24.1444068   0.4400840
skew      -0.3474537   0.2609545   0.4009511
kurtosis  -1.7290639  -1.9077611  -1.3677833
```

Although the previous examples used the mystats() function, you could have used the describe() function from the Hmisc and psych packages or the stat.desc() function from the pastecs package. In fact, the by() function provides a general mechanism for repeating *any* analysis by subgroups.

7.1.4   *Summarizing data interactively with dplyr*

So far, we've focused on methods that generate a comprehensive set of descriptive statistics for a given data frame. However, in interactive, exploratory data analyses, our goal is to answer targeted questions. In this case, we'll want to obtain a limited number of statistics on specific groups of observations.

The dplyr package, introduced in section 3.11, provides us with tools to quickly and flexibly accomplish this. The summarize() and summarize_all() functions can be used to calculate any statistic, and the group_by() function can be used to specify the groups on which to calculate those statistics.

As a demonstration, let's ask and answer a set of questions using the Salaries data frame in the carData package. The dataset contains 2008–2009 nine-month salaries in US dollars (salary) for 397 faculty members at a university in the United States. The data were collected as part of ongoing efforts to monitor salary differences between male and female faculty.

Before continuing, be sure that the carData and dplyr packages are installed (install.packages(c("carData", "dplyr")). Then load the packages

```
library(dplyr)
library(carData)
```

We're now ready to interrogate the data.

What is the median salary and salary range for the 397 professors?

```
> Salaries %>%
    summarize(med = median(salary),
              min = min(salary),
              max = max(salary))
     med    min     max
1 107300 57800 231545
```

The Salaries dataset is passed to the summarize() function, which calculates the median, minimum, and maximum value for salary and returns the result as a one-row tibble (data frame). The median nine-month salary is $107,300, and at least one person was making more than $230,000. Clearly, I need to ask for a raise.

What is the faculty count, median salary, and salary range by sex and rank?

```
> Salaries %>%
    group_by(rank, sex) %>%
    summarize(n = length(salary),
              med = median(salary),
              min = min(salary),
              max = max(salary))
```

rank	sex	n	med	min	max
<fct>	<fct>	<int>	<dbl>	<int>	<int>
1 AsstProf	Female	11	77000	63100	97032
2 AsstProf	Male	56	80182	63900	95079
3 AssocProf	Female	10	90556.	62884	109650
4 AssocProf	Male	54	95626.	70000	126431

```
5 Prof     Female     18 120258. 90450 161101
6 Prof     Male      248 123996  57800 231545
```

When categorical variables are specified in a by_group() statement, the summa-rize() function generates a row of statistics for each combination of their levels. Women have a lower median salary than men within each faculty rank. In addition, there is a very large number of male full professors at this university.

What are the mean years of service and years since PhD for faculty by sex and rank?

```
> Salaries %>%
    group_by(rank, sex) %>%
    select(yrs.service, yrs.since.phd) %>%
    summarize_all(mean)

  rank       sex     yrs.service yrs.since.phd
  <fct>      <fct>        <dbl>         <dbl>
1 AsstProf   Female        2.55          5.64
2 AsstProf   Male          2.34          5
3 AssocProf  Female       11.5          15.5
4 AssocProf  Male         12.0          15.4
5 Prof       Female       17.1          23.7
6 Prof       Male         23.2          28.6
```

The summarize_all() function calculates a summary statistic for each nongrouping variable (yrs.service and yrs.since.phd). If you want more than one statistic for each variable, provide them in a list. For example, summarize_all(list (mean=mean, std=sd)) would calculate the mean and standard deviation for each variable. Men and women have comparable experience histories at the assistant and associate professor levels. However, female full professors have fewer years of experience than their male counterparts.

One advantage of the dplyr approach is that results are returned as tibbles (data frames). This allows you to analyze these summary results further, plot them, and reformat them for printing. It also provides an easy mechanism for aggregating data.

In general, data analysts have their own preferences for which descriptive statistics to display and how they like to see them formatted. This is probably why there are many variations available. Choose the one that works best for you, or create your own!

7.1.5 *Visualizing results*

Numerical summaries of a distribution's characteristics are important, but they're no substitute for a visual representation. For quantitative variables, you have histograms (section 6.4), density plots (section 6.5), box plots (section 6.6), and dot plots (section 6.7). They can provide insights that are easily missed by reliance on a small set of descriptive statistics.

The functions considered so far provide summaries of quantitative variables. The functions in the next section allow you to examine the distributions of categorical variables.

7.2   *Frequency and contingency tables*

In this section, we'll look at frequency and contingency tables from categorical variables along with tests of independence, measures of association, and methods for graphically displaying results. We'll be using functions in the basic installation, along with functions from the vcd and gmodels packages. In the following examples, assume that A, B, and C represent categorical variables.

The data for this section come from the Arthritis dataset included with the vcd package. The data are from Koch and Edward (1988) and represents a double-blind clinical trial of new treatments for rheumatoid arthritis. Here are the first few observations:

```
> library(vcd)
> head(Arthritis)
  ID Treatment  Sex Age Improved
1 57   Treated Male  27     Some
2 46   Treated Male  29     None
3 77   Treated Male  30     None
4 17   Treated Male  32   Marked
5 36   Treated Male  46   Marked
6 23   Treated Male  58   Marked
```

Treatment (Placebo, Treated), Sex (Male, Female), and Improved (None, Some, Marked) are all categorical factors. In the next section, you'll create frequency and contingency tables (cross-classifications) from the data.

7.2.1   *Generating frequency tables*

R provides several methods for creating frequency and contingency tables. The most important functions are listed in table 7.1.

Table 7.1   Functions for creating and manipulating contingency tables

Function	Description
table(*var1, var2, ..., varN*)	Creates an N-way contingency table from N categorical variables (factors)
xtabs(*formula, data*)	Creates an N-way contingency table based on a formula and a matrix or data frame
prop.table(*table, margins*)	Expresses table entries as fractions of the marginal table defined by the margins
margin.table(*table, margins*)	Computes the sum of table entries for a marginal table defined by the margins
addmargins(*table, margins*)	Puts summary margins (sums by default) on a table
ftable(*table*)	Creates a compact, "flat" contingency table

In the next sections, we'll use each of these functions to explore categorical variables. We'll begin with simple frequencies, followed by two-way contingency tables, and end with multiway contingency tables. The first step is to create a table using either the table() or xtabs() function and then manipulate it using the other functions.

ONE-WAY TABLES

You can generate simple frequency counts using the table() function. Here's an example:

```
> mytable <- with(Arthritis, table(Improved))
> mytable
Improved
  None  Some  Marked
    42    14      28
```

You can turn these frequencies into proportions with prop.table()

```
> prop.table(mytable)
Improved
  None   Some  Marked
 0.500  0.167   0.333
```

or into percentages using prop.table()*100:

```
> prop.table(mytable)*100
Improved
  None  Some  Marked
  50.0  16.7    33.3
```

Here you can see that 50% of study participants had some or marked improvement (16.7 + 33.3).

TWO-WAY TABLES

For two-way tables, the format for the table() function is

```
mytable <- table(A, B)
```

where *A* is the row variable and *B* is the column variable. Alternatively, the xtabs() function allows you to create a contingency table using formula-style input. The format is

```
mytable <- xtabs(~ A + B, data=mydata)
```

where *mydata* is a matrix or data frame. In general, the variables to be cross-classified appear on the right of the formula (that is, to the right of the ~), separated by + signs. If a variable is included on the left side of the formula, it's assumed to be a vector of frequencies (useful if the data have already been tabulated).

For the Arthritis data, you have

```
> mytable <- xtabs(~ Treatment + Improved, data=Arthritis)
> mytable
          Improved
Treatment  None  Some  Marked
  Placebo    29     7       7
  Treated    13     7      21
```

You can generate marginal frequencies and proportions using the `margin.table()` and `prop.table()` functions, respectively. For row sums and row proportions, you have

```
> margin.table(mytable, 1)
Treatment
Placebo Treated
    43      41
> prop.table(mytable, 1)
          Improved
Treatment   None   Some    Marked
  Placebo  0.674  0.163    0.163
  Treated  0.317  0.171    0.512
```

The index (1) refers to the first variable in the `xtabs()` statement—the row variable. The proportions in each row add up to 1. Looking at the table, you can see that 51% of treated individuals had marked improvement, compared to 16% of those receiving a placebo.

For column sums and column proportions, you have

```
> margin.table(mytable, 2)
Improved
  None   Some   Marked
   42     14      28
> prop.table(mytable, 2)
          Improved
Treatment   None   Some    Marked
  Placebo  0.690  0.500    0.250
  Treated  0.310  0.500    0.750
```

Here, the index (2) refers to the second variable in the `xtabs()` statement—i.e., the columns. The proportions in each column add up to 1.

Cell proportions are obtained with this statement:

```
> prop.table(mytable)
          Improved
Treatment   None    Some    Marked
  Placebo  0.3452  0.0833   0.0833
  Treated  0.1548  0.0833   0.2500
```

The sum of all the cell proportions adds up to 1.

You can use the `addmargins()` function to add marginal sums to these tables. For example, the following code adds a `Sum` row and column:

```
> addmargins(mytable)
                Improved
Treatment   None    Some    Marked    Sum
  Placebo    29       7        7       43
  Treated    13       7       21       41
  Sum        42      14       28       84
> addmargins(prop.table(mytable))
                Improved
Treatment   None    Some    Marked    Sum
  Placebo  0.3452  0.0833   0.0833   0.5119
  Treated  0.1548  0.0833   0.2500   0.4881
  Sum      0.5000  0.1667   0.3333   1.0000
```

When using addmargins(), the default is to create sum margins for all variables in a table. In contrast, the following code adds a Sum column alone:

```
> addmargins(prop.table(mytable, 1), 2)
             Improved
Treatment   None    Some   Marked    Sum
   Placebo  0.674   0.163   0.163   1.000
   Treated  0.317   0.171   0.512   1.000
```

Similarly, this code adds a Sum row:

```
> addmargins(prop.table(mytable, 2), 1)
            Improved
Treatment   None    Some   Marked
   Placebo  0.690   0.500   0.250
   Treated  0.310   0.500   0.750
   Sum      1.000   1.000   1.000
```

In the table, you see that 25% of those patients with marked improvement received a placebo.

> **NOTE** The table() function ignores missing values (NAs) by default. To include NA as a valid category in the frequency counts, include the table option useNA="ifany".

A third method for creating two-way tables is the CrossTable() function in the gmodels package. The CrossTable() function produces two-way tables modeled after PROC FREQ in SAS or CROSSTABS in SPSS. The following listing shows an example.

Listing 7.8 Two-way table using CrossTable

```
> library(gmodels)
> CrossTable(Arthritis$Treatment, Arthritis$Improved)

   Cell Contents
|-------------------------|
|                       N |
| Chi-square contribution |
|           N / Row Total |
|           N / Col Total |
|         N / Table Total |
|-------------------------|

Total Observations in Table:   84

                     | Arthritis$Improved
Arthritis$Treatment  |    None  |    Some  |   Marked  | Row Total |
---------------------|----------|----------|-----------|-----------|
            Placebo  |     29   |      7   |       7   |      43   |
                     |   2.616  |   0.004  |    3.752  |           |
                     |   0.674  |   0.163  |    0.163  |    0.512  |
                     |   0.690  |   0.500  |    0.250  |           |
                     |   0.345  |   0.083  |    0.083  |           |
---------------------|----------|----------|-----------|-----------|
```

```
      Treated |        13 |         7 |        21 |        41 |
              |     2.744 |     0.004 |     3.935 |           |
              |     0.317 |     0.171 |     0.512 |     0.488 |
              |     0.310 |     0.500 |     0.750 |           |
              |     0.155 |     0.083 |     0.250 |           |
--------------------|-----------|-----------|-----------|-----------|
  Column Total |        42 |        14 |        28 |        84 |
              |     0.500 |     0.167 |     0.333 |           |
--------------------|-----------|-----------|-----------|-----------|
```

The `CrossTable()` function has options to report percentages (row, column, and cell); specify decimal places; produce chi-square, Fisher, and McNemar tests of independence; report expected and residual values (Pearson, standardized, and adjusted standardized); include missing values as valid; annotate with row and column titles; and format as SAS- or SPSS-style output. See `help(CrossTable)` for details.

If you have more than two categorical variables, you're dealing with multidimensional tables. We'll consider these next.

MULTIDIMENSIONAL TABLES

Both `table()` and `xtabs()` can be used to generate multidimensional tables based on three or more categorical variables. The `margin.table()`, `prop.table()`, and `addmargins()` functions extend naturally to more than two dimensions. Additionally, the `ftable()` function can be used to print multidimensional tables in a compact and attractive manner. An example is given in the next listing.

Listing 7.9   Three-way contingency table

```
> mytable <- xtabs(~ Treatment+Sex+Improved, data=Arthritis)    ◁─┐  Cell
> mytable                                                        ❶  frequencies
, , Improved = None

         Sex
Treatment Female  Male
  Placebo     19    10
  Treated      6     7

, , Improved = Some

         Sex
Treatment Female  Male
  Placebo      7     0
  Treated      5     2

, , Improved = Marked

         Sex
Treatment Female  Male
  Placebo      6     1
  Treated     16     5

> ftable(mytable)
```

```
                    Sex Female Male
Treatment Improved
Placebo   None           19   10
          Some            7    0
          Marked          6    1
Treated   None            6    7
          Some            5    2
          Marked         16    5

> margin.table(mytable, 1)

Treatment
Placebo Treated
    43      41
> margin.table(mytable, 2)
Sex
Female   Male
    59     25
> margin.table(mytable, 3)
Improved
 None   Some Marked
   42     14     28
> margin.table(mytable, c(1, 3))
          Improved
Treatment None Some Marked
  Placebo   29    7      7
  Treated   13    7     21
 > ftable(prop.table(mytable, c(1, 2)))
                Improved  None   Some  Marked
Treatment Sex
Placebo   Female          0.594 0.219  0.188
          Male            0.909 0.000  0.091
Treated   Female          0.222 0.185  0.593
          Male            0.500 0.143  0.357

> ftable(addmargins(prop.table(mytable, c(1, 2)), 3))
                Improved  None   Some  Marked    Sum
Treatment Sex
Placebo   Female          0.594 0.219  0.188  1.000
          Male            0.909 0.000  0.091  1.000
Treated   Female          0.222 0.185  0.593  1.000
          Male            0.500 0.143  0.357  1.000
```

❶

❷ Marginal frequencies

❸ Treatment × Improved marginal frequencies

❹ Improved proportions for Treatment × Sex

The code at ❶ produces cell frequencies for the three-way classification. The code also demonstrates how the `ftable()` function can be used to print a more compact and attractive version of the table.

The code at ❷ produces the marginal frequencies for `Treatment`, `Sex`, and `Improved`. Because you created the table with the formula `~Treatment+Sex + Improved`, `Treatment` is referred to by index 1, `Sex` is referred to by index 2, and `Improved` is referred to by index 3.

The code at ❸ produces the marginal frequencies for the `Treatment x Improved` classification, summed over `Sex`. ❹ provides the proportion of patients with None, Some, and Marked improvement for each `Treatment x Sex` combination.

Here you see that 36% of treated males had marked improvement compared to 59% of treated females. In general, the proportions will add to 1 over the indices not included in the prop.table() call (the third index, or Improved in this case). You can see this in the last example, where you add a sum margin over the third index.

If you want percentages instead of proportions, you can multiply the resulting table by 100. For example, this statement

```
ftable(addmargins(prop.table(mytable, c(1, 2)), 3)) * 100
```

produces this table:

```
                   Sex Female   Male    Sum
Treatment Improved
Placebo   None           65.5   34.5  100.0
          Some          100.0    0.0  100.0
          Marked         85.7   14.3  100.0
Treated   None           46.2   53.8  100.0
          Some           71.4   28.6  100.0
          Marked         76.2   23.8  100.0
```

Contingency tables tell you the frequency or proportions of cases for each combination of the variables that make up the table, but you're probably also interested in whether the variables in the table are related or independent. Tests of independence are covered in the next section.

7.2.2 Tests of independence

R provides several methods of testing the independence of categorical variables. The three tests described in this section are the chi-square test of independence, the Fisher exact test, and the Cochran-Mantel–Haenszel test.

CHI-SQUARE TEST OF INDEPENDENCE

You can apply the function chisq.test() to a two-way table to produce a chi-square test of independence of the row and column variables. See the next listing for an example.

Listing 7.10   Chi-square test of independence

```
> library(vcd)
> mytable <- xtabs(~Treatment+Improved, data=Arthritis)
> chisq.test(mytable)
        Pearson's Chi-squared test
data:  mytable
 X-squared = 13.1, df = 2, p-value = 0.001463          ◄─┐  ❶ Treatment and Improved
                                                              aren't independent.
> mytable <- xtabs(~Improved+Sex, data=Arthritis)
> chisq.test(mytable)
        Pearson's Chi-squared test
data:  mytable                                               ❷ Gender and Improved
 X-squared = 4.84, df = 2, p-value = 0.0889           ◄─┘     are independent.

Warning message:
In chisq.test(mytable) : Chi-squared approximation may be incorrect
```

From the results, there appears to be a relationship between treatment received and level of improvement (p < .01). But there doesn't appear to be a relationship ❷ between patient sex and improvement (p > .05). The p-values are the probability of obtaining the sampled results, assuming independence of the row and column variables in the population. Because the probability is small for ❶, you reject the hypothesis that treatment type and outcome are independent. Because the probability for ❷ isn't small, it's not unreasonable to assume that outcome and gender are independent. The warning message in listing 7.10 is produced because one of the six cells in the table (male, some improvement) has an expected value less than 5, which may invalidate the chi-square approximation.

FISHER'S EXACT TEST

You can produce a Fisher's exact test via the `fisher.test()` function. Fisher's exact test evaluates the null hypothesis of independence of rows and columns in a contingency table with fixed marginals. The format is `fisher.test(mytable)`, where `mytable` is a two-way table. Here's an example:

```
> mytable <- xtabs(~Treatment+Improved, data=Arthritis)
> fisher.test(mytable)
        Fisher's Exact Test for Count Data
data:  mytable
p-value = 0.001393
alternative hypothesis: two.sided
```

In contrast to many statistical packages, the `fisher.test()` function can be applied to any two-way table with two or more rows and columns, not just a 2 × 2 independence table.

COCHRAN–MANTEL–HAENSZEL TEST

The `mantelhaen.test()` function provides a Cochran–Mantel–Haenszel chi-square test of the null hypothesis that two nominal variables are conditionally independent in each stratum of a third variable. The following code tests the hypothesis that the `Treatment` and `Improved` variables are independent within each level for `Sex`. The test assumes that there's no three-way (`Treatment × Improved × Sex`) interaction:

```
> mytable <- xtabs(~Treatment+Improved+Sex, data=Arthritis)
> mantelhaen.test(mytable)
        Cochran-Mantel-Haenszel test
data:  mytable
Cochran-Mantel-Haenszel M^2 = 14.6, df = 2, p-value = 0.0006647
```

The results suggest that the treatment received and the improvement reported aren't independent within each level of `Sex` (that is, treated individuals improved more than those receiving placebos when controlling for sex).

7.2.3 *Measures of association*

The significance tests in the previous section evaluate whether sufficient evidence exists to reject a null hypothesis of independence between variables. If you can reject the null hypothesis, your interest turns naturally to measures of association to gauge the strength of the relationships present. The `assocstats()` function in the `vcd` package can be used to calculate the phi coefficient, contingency coefficient, and Cramér's V for a two-way table. An example is given in the following listing.

Listing 7.11 Measures of association for a two-way table

```
> library(vcd)
> mytable <- xtabs(~Treatment+Improved, data=Arthritis)
> assocstats(mytable)
                    X^2 df  P(> X^2)
Likelihood Ratio 13.530  2 0.0011536
Pearson          13.055  2 0.0014626

Phi-Coefficient   : 0.394
Contingency Coeff.: 0.367
Cramer's V        : 0.394
```

In general, larger magnitudes indicate stronger associations. The `vcd` package also provides a `kappa()` function that can calculate Cohen's kappa and weighted kappa for a confusion matrix (for example, the degree of agreement between two judges classifying a set of objects into categories).

7.2.4 Visualizing results

R has mechanisms for visually exploring the relationships among categorical variables that go well beyond those found in most other statistical platforms. You typically use bar charts to visualize frequencies in one dimension (see section 6.1). The `vcd` package has excellent functions for visualizing relationships among categorical variables in multidimensional datasets using mosaic and association plots (see section 11.4). Finally, correspondence-analysis functions in the `ca` package allow you to visually explore relationships between rows and columns in contingency tables using various geometric representations (Nenadić and Greenacre, 2007).

This ends the discussion of contingency tables until we take up more advanced topics in chapters 11 and 19. Next, let's look at various types of correlation coefficients.

7.3 Correlations

Correlation coefficients are used to describe relationships among quantitative variables. The sign (plus or minus) indicates the direction of the relationship (positive or inverse), and the magnitude indicates the strength of the relationship (ranging from 0 for no relationship to 1 for a perfectly predictable relationship).

In this section, we'll look at a variety of correlation coefficients, as well as tests of significance. We'll use the `state.x77` dataset available in the base R installation. It provides data on the population, income, illiteracy rate, life expectancy, murder rate, and high school graduation rate for the 50 US states in 1977. There are also temperature and land-area measures, but we'll drop them to save space. Use `help(state .x77)` to learn more about the file. In addition to the base installation, we'll be using the `psych` and `ggm` packages.

7.3.1 *Types of correlations*

R can produce a variety of correlation coefficients, including Pearson, Spearman, Kendall, partial, polychoric, and polyserial. Let's look at each in turn.

PEARSON, SPEARMAN, AND KENDALL CORRELATIONS

The Pearson product-moment correlation assesses the degree of linear relationship between two quantitative variables. Spearman's rank-order correlation coefficient assesses the degree of relationship between two rank-ordered variables. Kendall's tau is also a nonparametric measure of rank correlation.

The `cor()` function produces all three correlation coefficients, whereas the `cov()` function provides covariances. There are many options, but a simplified format for producing correlations is

```
cor(x, use= , method= )
```

The options are described in table 7.2.

Table 7.2 `cor/cov` **options**

Option	Description
x	Matrix or data frame.
use	Specifies the handling of missing data. The options are `all.obs` (assumes no missing data—missing data will produce an error), `everything` (any correlation involving a case with missing values will be set to `missing`), `complete.obs` (listwise deletion), and `pairwise.complete.obs` (pairwise deletion).
method	Specifies the type of correlation. The options are `pearson`, `spearman`, and `kendall`.

The default options are `use="everything"` and `method="pearson"`. You can see an example in the following listing.

Listing 7.12 Covariances and correlations

```
> states<- state.x77[,1:6]
> cov(states)
           Population Income Illiteracy Life Exp  Murder  HS Grad
Population   19931684 571230    292.868 -407.842 5663.52 -3551.51
Income         571230 377573   -163.702  280.663 -521.89  3076.77
Illiteracy        293   -164      0.372   -0.482    1.58    -3.24
Life Exp         -408    281     -0.482    1.802   -3.87     6.31
Murder           5664   -522      1.582   -3.869   13.63   -14.55
HS Grad         -3552   3077     -3.235    6.313  -14.55    65.24

> cor(states)
           Population  Income Illiteracy Life Exp  Murder  HS Grad
Population     1.0000  0.208      0.108   -0.068   0.344  -0.0985
Income         0.2082  1.000     -0.437    0.340  -0.230   0.6199
Illiteracy     0.1076 -0.437      1.000   -0.588   0.703  -0.6572
Life Exp      -0.0681  0.340     -0.588    1.000  -0.781   0.5822
Murder         0.3436 -0.230      0.703   -0.781   1.000  -0.4880
```

```
HS Grad         -0.0985  0.620      -0.657     0.582 -0.488  1.0000
> cor(states, method="spearman")
          Population Income Illiteracy Life Exp Murder HS Grad
Population     1.000  0.125      0.313   -0.104  0.346  -0.383
Income         0.125  1.000     -0.315    0.324 -0.217   0.510
Illiteracy     0.313 -0.315      1.000   -0.555  0.672  -0.655
Life Exp      -0.104  0.324     -0.555    1.000 -0.780   0.524
Murder         0.346 -0.217      0.672   -0.780  1.000  -0.437
HS Grad       -0.383  0.510     -0.655    0.524 -0.437   1.000
```

The first call produces the variances and covariances, the second provides Pearson product-moment correlation coefficients, and the third produces Spearman rank-order correlation coefficients. You can see, for example, that a strong positive correlation exists between income and high school graduation rate and that a strong negative correlation exists between illiteracy rates and life expectancy.

Notice that you get square matrices by default (all variables crossed with all other variables). You can also produce nonsquare matrices, as shown in the following example:

```
> x <- states[,c("Population", "Income", "Illiteracy", "HS Grad")]
> y <- states[,c("Life Exp", "Murder")]
> cor(x,y)
          Life Exp Murder
Population  -0.068  0.344
Income       0.340 -0.230
Illiteracy  -0.588  0.703
HS Grad      0.582 -0.488
```

This version of the function is particularly useful when you're interested in the relationships between one set of variables and another. Notice that the results don't tell you if the correlations differ significantly from 0 (that is, whether there's sufficient evidence based on the sample data to conclude that the population correlations differ from 0). For that, you need tests of significance (described in section 7.3.2).

PARTIAL CORRELATIONS

A *partial* correlation is a correlation between two quantitative variables, controlling for one or more other quantitative variables. You can use the pcor() function in the ggm package to provide partial correlation coefficients. The ggm package isn't installed by default, so be sure to install it on first use. The format is

pcor(*u*, *S*)

where *u* is a vector of numbers, with the first two numbers being the indices of the variables to be correlated, and the remaining numbers being the indices of the conditioning variables (that is, the variables being partialed out). *S* is the covariance matrix among the variables. An example will help clarify this:

```
> library(ggm)
> colnames(states)
[1] "Population" "Income" "Illiteracy" "Life Exp" "Murder" "HS Grad"
> pcor(c(1,5,2,3,6), cov(states))
[1] 0.346
```

In this case, 0.346 is the correlation between population (variable 1) and murder rate (variable 5), controlling for the influence of income, illiteracy rate, and high school graduation rate (variables 2, 3, and 6, respectively). The use of partial correlations is common in the social sciences.

OTHER TYPES OF CORRELATIONS

The hetcor() function in the polycor package can compute a heterogeneous correlation matrix containing Pearson product-moment correlations between numeric variables, polyserial correlations between numeric and ordinal variables, polychoric correlations between ordinal variables, and tetrachoric correlations between two dichotomous variables. Polyserial, polychoric, and tetrachoric correlations assume that the ordinal or dichotomous variables are derived from underlying normal distributions. See the documentation that accompanies this package for more information.

7.3.2 *Testing correlations for significance*

Once you've generated correlation coefficients, how do you test them for statistical significance? The typical null hypothesis is no relationship (that is, the correlation in the population is 0). You can use the cor.test() function to test an individual Pearson, Spearman, and Kendall correlation coefficient. A simplified format is

```
cor.test(x, y, alternative = , method = )
```

where *x* and *y* are the variables to be correlated, alternative specifies a two-tailed or one-tailed test ("two.side", "less", or "greater"), and method specifies the type of correlation ("pearson", "kendall", or "spearman") to compute. Use alternative="less" when the research hypothesis is that the population correlation is less than 0. Use alternative="greater" when the research hypothesis is that the population correlation is greater than 0. By default, alternative="two.side" (the population correlation isn't equal to 0) is assumed. See the following listing for an example.

Listing 7.13 Testing a correlation coefficient for significance

```
> cor.test(states[,3], states[,5])

        Pearson's product-moment correlation

data:  states[, 3] and states[, 5]
t = 6.85, df = 48, p-value = 1.258e-08
alternative hypothesis: true correlation is not equal to 0
95 percent confidence interval:
 0.528 0.821
sample estimates:
  cor
0.703
```

This code tests the null hypothesis that the Pearson correlation between life expectancy and murder rate is 0. Assuming that the population correlation is 0, you'd expect to see a sample correlation as large as 0.703 less than 1 time out of 10 million (that is, p=1.258e-08). Given how unlikely this is, you reject the null hypothesis in favor of the research hypothesis that the population correlation between life expectancy and murder rate is *not* 0.

Unfortunately, you can test only one correlation at a time using cor.test(). Luckily, the corr.test() function provided in the psych package allows you to go further. The corr.test() function produces correlations and significance levels for matrices of Pearson, Spearman, and Kendall correlations. An example is given in the following listing.

Listing 7.14 Correlation matrix and tests of significance via corr.test()

```
> library(psych)
> corr.test(states, use="complete")

Call:corr.test(x = states, use = "complete")
Correlation matrix
           Population Income Illiteracy Life Exp Murder HS Grad
Population      1.00   0.21       0.11    -0.07   0.34   -0.10
Income         0.21   1.00      -0.44     0.34  -0.23    0.62
Illiteracy     0.11  -0.44       1.00    -0.59   0.70   -0.66
Life Exp      -0.07   0.34      -0.59     1.00  -0.78    0.58
Murder         0.34  -0.23       0.70    -0.78   1.00   -0.49
HS Grad       -0.10   0.62      -0.66     0.58  -0.49    1.00

Sample Size
[1] 50

Probability value
           Population Income Illiteracy Life Exp Murder HS Grad
Population      0.00   0.15       0.46     0.64   0.01    0.5
Income         0.15   0.00       0.00     0.02   0.11    0.0
Illiteracy     0.46   0.00       0.00     0.00   0.00    0.0
Life Exp       0.64   0.02       0.00     0.00   0.00    0.0
Murder         0.01   0.11       0.00     0.00   0.00    0.0
HS Grad        0.50   0.00       0.00     0.00   0.00    0.0
```

The use= options can be "pairwise" or "complete" (for pairwise or listwise deletion of missing values, respectively). The method= option is "pearson" (the default), "spearman", or "kendall". Here you see that the correlation between illiteracy and life expectancy (–0.59) is significantly different from zero (p=0.00) and suggests that as the illiteracy rate goes up, life expectancy tends to go down. However, the correlation between population size and high school graduation rate (–0.10) is not significantly different from 0 (p=0.5).

OTHER TESTS OF SIGNIFICANCE

In section 7.4.1, we looked at partial correlations. The pcor.test() function in the psych package can be used to test the conditional independence of two variables controlling for one or more additional variables, assuming multivariate normality. The format is

```
pcor.test(r, q, n)
```

where r is the partial correlation produced by the pcor() function, q is the number of variables being controlled, and n is the sample size.

Before leaving this topic, I should mention that the r.test() function in the psych package also provides a number of useful significance tests. The function can be used to test the following:

- The significance of a correlation coefficient
- The difference between two independent correlations
- The difference between two dependent correlations sharing a single variable
- The difference between two dependent correlations based on completely different variables

See help(r.test) for details.

7.3.3 *Visualizing correlations*

The bivariate relationships underlying correlations can be visualized through scatter plots and scatter plot matrices, whereas correlograms provide a unique and powerful method for comparing a large number of correlation coefficients in a meaningful way. Chapter 11 covers both.

7.4 *T-tests*

The most common activity in research is the comparison of two groups. Do patients receiving a new drug show greater improvement than patients using an existing medication? Does one manufacturing process produce fewer defects than another? Which of two teaching methods is most cost effective? If your outcome variable is categorical, you can use the methods described in section 7.3. Here, we'll focus on group comparisons in which the outcome variable is continuous and assumed to be distributed normally.

For this illustration, we'll use the UScrime dataset distributed with the MASS package. It contains information about the effect of punishment regimes on crime rates in 47 US states in 1960. The outcome variables of interest will be Prob (the probability of imprisonment), U1 (the unemployment rate for urban males ages 14–24), and U2 (the unemployment rate for urban males ages 35–39). The categorical variable So (an indicator variable for Southern states) will serve as the grouping variable. The data have been rescaled by the original authors. (I considered naming this section "Crime and Punishment in the Old South," but cooler heads prevailed.)

7.4.1 *Independent t-test*

Are you more likely to be imprisoned if you commit a crime in the South? The comparison of interest is Southern versus non-Southern states, and the dependent variable is the probability of incarceration. A two-group independent t-test can be used to test the hypothesis that the two population means are equal. Here, you assume that the two groups are independent and that the data is sampled from normal populations. The format is either

```
t.test(y ~ x, data)
```

where *y* is numeric and *x* is a dichotomous variable, or

```
t.test(y1, y2)
```

where *y1* and *y2* are numeric vectors (the outcome variable for each group). The optional *data* argument refers to a matrix or data frame containing the variables. In contrast to most statistical packages, the default test assumes unequal variance and applies the Welsh degrees-of-freedom modification. You can add a var.equal=TRUE option to specify equal variances and a pooled variance estimate. By default, a two-tailed alternative is assumed (that is, the means differ, but the direction isn't specified). You can add the option alternative="less" or alternative="greater" to specify a directional test.

The following code compares Southern (group 1) and non-Southern (group 0) states on the probability of imprisonment using a two-tailed test without the assumption of equal variances:

```
> library(MASS)
> t.test(Prob ~ So, data=UScrime)

        Welch Two Sample t-test

data:  Prob by So
t = -3.8954, df = 24.925, p-value = 0.0006506
alternative hypothesis: true difference in means is not equal to 0
95 percent confidence interval:
 -0.03852569 -0.01187439
sample estimates:
mean in group 0 mean in group 1
     0.03851265      0.06371269
```

You can reject the hypothesis that Southern states and non-Southern states have equal probabilities of imprisonment (p < .001).

NOTE   Because the outcome variable is a proportion, you might try to transform it to normality before carrying out the t-test. In the current case, all reasonable transformations of the outcome variable (Y/1-Y, log(Y/1-Y), arcsin(Y), and arcsin(sqrt(Y))) would lead to the same conclusions. Chapter 8 covers transformations in detail.

7.4.2   *Dependent t-test*

As a second example, you might ask if the unemployment rate for younger males (14–24) is greater than for older males (35–39). In this case, the two groups aren't independent. You wouldn't expect the unemployment rate for younger and older males in Alabama to be unrelated. When observations in the two groups are related, you have a dependent-groups design. Pre-post or repeated-measures designs also produce dependent groups.

A dependent t-test assumes that the difference between groups is normally distributed. In this case, the format is

```
t.test(y1, y2, paired=TRUE)
```

where *y1* and *y2* are the numeric vectors for the two dependent groups. The results are as follows:

```
> library(MASS)
> sapply(UScrime[c("U1","U2")], function(x)(c(mean=mean(x),sd=sd(x))))
        U1    U2
mean 95.5 33.98
sd   18.0  8.45

> with(UScrime, t.test(U1, U2, paired=TRUE))

        Paired t-test

data:  U1 and U2
t = 32.4066, df = 46, p-value < 2.2e-16
alternative hypothesis: true difference in means is not equal to 0
95 percent confidence interval:
 57.67003 65.30870
sample estimates:
mean of the differences
               61.48936
```

The mean difference (61.5) is large enough to warrant rejection of the hypothesis that the mean unemployment rate for older and younger males is the same. Younger males have a higher rate. In fact, the probability of obtaining a sample difference this large if the population means are equal is less than 0.00000000000000022 (that is, 2.2e–16).

7.4.3 When there are more than two groups

What do you do if you want to compare more than two groups? If you can assume that the data are independently sampled from normal populations, you can use analysis of variance (ANOVA). ANOVA is a comprehensive methodology that covers many experimental and quasi-experimental designs. As such, it has earned its own chapter. Feel free to abandon this section and jump to chapter 9 at any time.

7.5 Nonparametric tests of group differences

If you're unable to meet the parametric assumptions of a t-test or ANOVA, you can turn to nonparametric approaches. For example, if the outcome variables are severely skewed or ordinal in nature, you may wish to use the techniques in this section.

7.5.1 Comparing two groups

If the two groups are independent, you can use the Wilcoxon rank-sum test (more popularly known as the Mann–Whitney U test) to assess whether the observations are sampled from the same probability distribution (that is, whether the probability of obtaining higher scores is greater in one population than the other). The format is either

```
wilcox.test(y ~ x, data)
```

where *y* is numeric and *x* is a dichotomous variable, or

```
wilcox.test(y1, y2)
```

where *y1* and *y2* are the outcome variables for each group. The optional *data* argument refers to a matrix or data frame containing the variables. The default is a two-tailed test. You can add the option exact to produce an exact test, and -alternative="less" or alternative="greater" to specify a directional test.

If you apply the Mann–Whitney U test to the question of incarceration rates from the previous section, you'll get these results:

```
> with(UScrime, by(Prob, So, median))

So: 0
[1] 0.0382
--------------------
So: 1
[1] 0.0556

> wilcox.test(Prob ~ So, data=UScrime)

        Wilcoxon rank sum test

data:  Prob by So
W = 81, p-value = 8.488e-05
alternative hypothesis: true location shift is not equal to 0
```

Again, you can reject the hypothesis that incarceration rates are the same in Southern and non-Southern states ($p < .001$).

The Wilcoxon signed rank test provides a nonparametric alternative to the dependent sample t-test. It's appropriate in situations when the groups are paired and the assumption of normality is unwarranted. The format is identical to the Mann–Whitney U test, but you add the paired=TRUE option. Let's apply it to the unemployment question from the previous section:

```
> sapply(UScrime[c("U1","U2")], median)
U1 U2
92 34

> with(UScrime, wilcox.test(U1, U2, paired=TRUE))

        Wilcoxon signed rank test with continuity correction

data:  U1 and U2
V = 1128, p-value = 2.464e-09
alternative hypothesis: true location shift is not equal to 0
```

Again, you reach the same conclusion as you reached with the paired t-test.

In this case, the parametric t-tests and their nonparametric equivalents reach the same conclusions. When the assumptions for the t-tests are reasonable, the parametric tests are more powerful (more likely to find a difference if it exists). The nonparametric tests are more appropriate when the assumptions are grossly unreasonable (for example, rank-ordered data).

7.5.2 Comparing more than two groups

When you're comparing more than two groups, you must turn to other methods. Consider the `state.x77` dataset from section 7.3. It contains population, income, illiteracy rate, life expectancy, murder rate, and high school graduation rate data for US states. What if you want to compare the illiteracy rates in four regions of the country (Northeast, South, North Central, and West)? This is called a *one-way design*, and there are both parametric and nonparametric approaches for addressing the question.

If you can't meet the assumptions of ANOVA designs, you can use nonparametric methods to evaluate group differences. If the groups are independent, a Kruskal–Wallis test is a useful approach. If the groups are dependent (for example, repeated measures or randomized block design), the Friedman test is more appropriate.

The format for the Kruskal–Wallis test is

```
kruskal.test(y ~ A, data)
```

where *y* is a numeric outcome variable and *A* is a grouping variable with two or more levels (if there are two levels, it's equivalent to the Mann–Whitney U test). For the Friedman test, the format is

```
friedman.test(y ~ A | B, data)
```

where *y* is the numeric outcome variable, *A* is a grouping variable, and *B* is a blocking variable that identifies matched observations. In both cases, *data* is an option argument specifying a matrix or data frame containing the variables.

Let's apply the Kruskal–Wallis test to the illiteracy question. First, you'll have to add the region designations to the dataset. These are contained in the dataset `state.region` distributed with the base installation of R:

```
states <- data.frame(state.region, state.x77)
```

Now you can apply the test:

```
> kruskal.test(Illiteracy ~ state.region, data=states)
        Kruskal-Wallis rank sum test
data:  states$Illiteracy by states$state.region
Kruskal-Wallis chi-squared = 22.7, df = 3, p-value = 4.726e-05
```

The significance test suggests that the illiteracy rate isn't the same in each of the four regions of the country ($p < .001$).

Although you can reject the null hypothesis of no difference, the test doesn't tell you *which* regions differ significantly from each other. To answer this question, you could compare groups two at a time using the Wilcoxon test. A more elegant approach is to apply a multiple-comparisons procedure that computes all pairwise comparisons while controlling the Type I error rate (the probability of finding a difference that isn't there). I have created a function called wmc() that can be used for this purpose. It compares groups two at a time using the Wilcoxon test and adjusts the probability values using the p.adj() function.

To be honest, I'm stretching the definition of *basic* in the chapter title quite a bit, but because the function fits well here, I hope you'll bear with me. You can download a text file containing wmc() from https://rkabacoff.com/RiA/wmc.R. The following listing uses this function to compare the illiteracy rates in the four US regions.

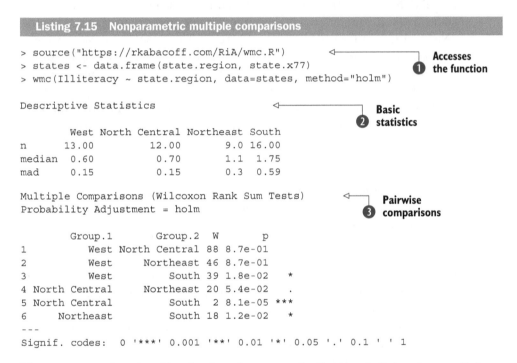

> **Listing 7.15   Nonparametric multiple comparisons**

```
> source("https://rkabacoff.com/RiA/wmc.R")          ◄──────────  ❶ Accesses
> states <- data.frame(state.region, state.x77)                      the function
> wmc(Illiteracy ~ state.region, data=states, method="holm")


Descriptive Statistics                        ◄──────────  ❷ Basic
                                                              statistics
          West North Central Northeast South
n        13.00        12.00       9.0 16.00
median    0.60         0.70       1.1  1.75
mad       0.15         0.15       0.3  0.59


Multiple Comparisons (Wilcoxon Rank Sum Tests)    ◄─────  ❸ Pairwise
Probability Adjustment = holm                                comparisons

          Group.1       Group.2  W        p
1           West North Central 88 8.7e-01
2           West     Northeast 46 8.7e-01
3           West         South 39 1.8e-02    *
4 North Central     Northeast 20 5.4e-02    .
5 North Central         South  2 8.1e-05 ***
6     Northeast         South 18 1.2e-02    *
---
Signif. codes:  0 '***' 0.001 '**' 0.01 '*' 0.05 '.' 0.1 ' ' 1
```

The source() function downloads and executes the R script defining the wmc() function ❶. The function's format is wmc(y ~ A, *data*, *method*), where y is a numeric outcome variable, A is a grouping variable, *data* is the data frame containing these variables, and *method* is the approach used to limit Type I errors. Listing 7.15 uses an adjustment method developed by Holm (1979) that provides strong control of the family-wise error rate (the probability of making one or more Type I errors in a set of comparisons). See help(p.adjust) for a description of the other methods available.

The wmc() function first provides the sample sizes, medians, and median absolute deviations for each group ❷. The West has the lowest illiteracy rate, and the South has the highest. The function then generates six statistical comparisons (West versus North Central, West versus Northeast, West versus South, North Central versus Northeast, North Central versus South, and Northeast versus South) ❸. You can see from the two-sided p-values (p) that the South differs significantly from the other three regions and that the other three regions don't differ from each other at a p < .05 level.

7.6 *Visualizing group differences*

In sections 7.4 and 7.5, we looked at statistical methods for comparing groups. Examining group differences visually is also a crucial part of a comprehensive data analysis strategy. It allows you to assess the magnitude of the differences, identify any distributional characteristics that influence the results (such as skew, bimodality, or outliers), and evaluate the appropriateness of the test assumptions. R provides a wide range of graphical methods for comparing groups, including box plots (simple, notched, and violin), covered in section 6.6; overlapping kernel density plots, covered in section 6.5; and graphical methods for visualizing outcomes in an ANOVA framework, discussed in chapter 9.

Summary

- Descriptive statistics can describe the distribution of a quantitative variable numerically. Many packages in R provide descriptive statistics for data frames. The choice among packages is primarily a matter of personal preference.
- Frequency tables and cross-tabulations summarize the distributions of categorical variables.
- The t-tests and the Mann-Whitney U test can be used to compare two groups on a quantitative outcome.
- A chi-square test can be used to evaluate the association between two categorical variables. The correlation coefficient is used to evaluate the association between two quantitative variables.
- Data visualizations should usually accompany numeric summaries and statistical tests. Otherwise, you might miss important features of the data.

Part 3

Intermediate methods

Whereas part 2 of this book covered basic graphical and statistical methods, part 3 discusses intermediate methods. In chapter 8, we move from describing the relationship between two variables to using regression models to model the relationship between a numerical outcome variable and a set of numeric and/or categorical predictor variables. Modeling data is typically a complex, multistep, interactive process. Chapter 8 provides step-by-step coverage of the methods available for fitting linear models, evaluating their appropriateness, and interpreting their meaning.

Chapter 9 considers the analysis of basic experimental and quasi-experimental designs through the analysis of variance and its variants. Here we're interested in how treatment combinations or conditions affect a numerical outcome variable. The chapter introduces the functions in R that are used to perform an analysis of variance, analysis of covariance, repeated measures analysis of variance, multifactor analysis of variance, and multivariate analysis of variance. It also discusses methods for assessing the appropriateness of these analyses and visualizing the results.

In designing experimental and quasi-experimental studies, it's important to determine whether the sample size is adequate for detecting the effects of interest (power analysis). Otherwise, why conduct the study? Chapter 10 provides a detailed treatment of power analysis. Starting with a discussion of hypothesis testing, the presentation focuses on how to use R functions to determine the sample size necessary to detect a treatment effect of a given size with a given degree of confidence. This can help you to plan studies that are likely to yield useful results.

Chapter 11 expands on the material in chapter 6 by covering the creation of graphs that help you visualize relationships among two or more variables. This includes the various types of 2D and 3D scatter plots, scatter plot matrices, line plots, and bubble plots. It also introduces the very useful, but less well-known, corrgrams and mosaic plots.

The linear models described in chapters 8 and 9 assume that the outcome or response variable is not only numeric, but also randomly sampled from a normal distribution. In some situations, this distributional assumption is untenable. Chapter 12 presents analytic methods that work well in cases when data are sampled from unknown or mixed distributions, when sample sizes are small, when outliers are a problem, or when devising an appropriate test based on a theoretical distribution is mathematically intractable. They include both resampling and bootstrapping approaches—computer-intensive methods that are powerfully implemented in R. The methods described in this chapter will allow you to devise hypothesis tests for data that don't fit traditional parametric assumptions.

After completing part 3, you'll have the tools to analyze most common data analytic problems you'll encounter in practice. You'll also be able to create some gorgeous graphs!

Regression

In many ways, regression analysis lives at the heart of statistics. It's a broad term for a set of methodologies used to predict a response variable (also called a dependent, criterion, or outcome variable) from one or more predictor variables (also called independent or explanatory variables). In general, regression analysis can be used to identify the explanatory variables that are related to a response variable, to describe the form of the relationships involved, and to provide an equation for predicting the response variable from the explanatory variables.

For example, an exercise physiologist might use regression analysis to develop an equation for predicting the expected number of calories a person will burn while exercising on a treadmill. The response variable is the number of calories burned (calculated from the amount of oxygen consumed), and the predictor variables might include duration of exercise (minutes), percentage of time spent at

179

their target heart rate, average speed (mph), age (years), gender, and body mass index (BMI).

From a theoretical point of view, the analysis will help answer such questions as these:

- What's the relationship between exercise duration and calories burned? Is it linear or curvilinear? For example, does exercise have less impact on the number of calories burned after a certain point?
- How does effort (the percentage of time at the target heart rate, the average walking speed) factor in?
- Are these relationships the same for young and old, male and female, heavy and slim?

From a practical point of view, the analysis will help answer such questions as these:

- How many calories can a 30-year-old man with a BMI of 28.7 expect to burn if he walks for 45 minutes at an average speed of 4 miles per hour and stays within his target heart rate 80% of the time?
- What's the minimum number of variables you need to collect to accurately predict the number of calories a person will burn while walking?
- How accurate will your prediction tend to be?

Because regression analysis plays such a central role in modern statistics, we'll cover it in some depth in this chapter. First, we'll look at how to fit and interpret regression models. Next, we'll review a set of techniques for identifying potential problems with these models and how to deal with them. Third, we'll explore the issue of variable selection. Of all the potential predictor variables available, how do you decide which ones to include in your final model? Fourth, we'll address the question of generalizability. How well will your model work when you apply it in the real world? Finally, we'll consider relative importance. Of all the predictors in your model, which is the most important, the second most important, and the least important?

As you can see, we're covering a lot of ground. Effective regression analysis is an interactive, holistic process with many steps, and it involves more than a little skill. Rather than break it up into multiple chapters, I've opted to present this topic in a single chapter to capture this flavor. As a result, this will be the longest and most involved chapter in the book. Stick with it to the end, and you'll have all the tools you need to tackle a wide variety of research questions. I promise!

8.1 The many faces of regression

The term *regression* can be confusing because there are so many specialized varieties (see table 8.1). In addition, R has powerful and comprehensive features for fitting regression models, and the abundance of options can be confusing. For example, in 2005, Vito Ricci created a list of more than 205 functions in R that are used to generate regression analyses (http://mng.bz/NJhu).

Table 8.1 Varieties of regression analysis

Type of regression	Typical use
Simple linear	Predicting a quantitative response variable from a quantitative explanatory variable
Polynomial	Predicting a quantitative response variable from a quantitative explanatory variable, where the relationship is modeled as an *nth* order polynomial
Multiple linear	Predicting a quantitative response variable from two or more explanatory variables
Multilevel	Predicting a response variable from data that have a hierarchical structure (for example, students within classrooms within schools). Also called hierarchical, nested, or mixed models.
Multivariate	Predicting more than one response variable from one or more explanatory variables
Logistic	Predicting a categorical response variable from one or more explanatory variables
Poisson	Predicting a response variable representing counts from one or more explanatory variables
Cox proportional hazards	Predicting time to an event (death, failure, relapse) from one or more explanatory variables
Time-series	Modeling time-series data with correlated errors
Nonlinear	Predicting a quantitative response variable from one or more explanatory variables, where the form of the model is nonlinear
Nonparametric	Predicting a quantitative response variable from one or more explanatory variables, where the form of the model is derived from the data and not specified a priori
Robust	Predicting a quantitative response variable from one or more explanatory variables using an approach that's resistant to the effect of influential observations

In this chapter, we'll focus on regression methods that fall under the rubric of ordinary least squares (OLS) regression, including simple linear regression, polynomial regression, and multiple linear regression. Chapter 13 will cover other types of regression models, including logistic regression and Poisson regression.

8.1.1 Scenarios for using OLS regression

In OLS regression, a quantitative dependent variable is predicted from a weighted sum of predictor variables, where the weights are parameters estimated from the data. Let's take a look at a concrete example (no pun intended), loosely adapted from Fwa (2006).

An engineer wants to identify the most important factors related to bridge deterioration (such as age, traffic volume, bridge design, construction materials and methods, construction quality, and weather conditions) and determine the mathematical form of these relationships. She collects data on each of these variables from a representative sample of bridges and models the data using OLS regression.

The approach is highly interactive. She fits a series of models, checks their compliance with underlying statistical assumptions, explores any unexpected or aberrant findings, and finally chooses the "best" model from among many possible models. If successful, the results will help her to

- Focus on important variables by determining which of the many collected variables are useful in predicting bridge deterioration, along with their relative importance.
- Look for bridges that are likely to be in trouble by providing an equation that can be used to predict bridge deterioration for new cases (where the values of the predictor variables are known, but the degree of bridge deterioration isn't).
- Take advantage of serendipity by identifying unusual bridges. If she finds that some bridges deteriorate much faster or slower than predicted by the model, a study of these outliers may yield important findings that could help her understand the mechanisms involved in bridge deterioration.

Bridges may hold no interest for you. I'm a clinical psychologist and statistician, and I know next to nothing about civil engineering. But the general principles apply to an amazingly wide selection of problems in the physical, biological, and social sciences. Each of the following questions could also be addressed using an OLS approach:

- What's the relationship between surface stream salinity and paved road surface area (Montgomery, 2007)?
- What aspects of a user's experience contribute to the overuse of massively multiplayer online role-playing games (MMORPGs) (Hsu, Wen, and Wu, 2009)?
- Which qualities of an educational environment are most strongly related to higher student achievement scores?
- What's the form of the relationship between blood pressure, salt intake, and age? Is it the same for men and women?
- What's the impact of stadiums and professional sports on metropolitan area development (Baade and Dye, 1990)?
- What factors account for interstate differences in the price of beer (Culbertson and Bradford, 1991)? (That one got your attention!)

Our primary limitation is our ability to formulate an interesting question, devise a useful response variable to measure, and gather appropriate data.

8.1.2   *What you need to know*

For the remainder of this chapter, I'll describe how to use R functions to fit OLS regression models, evaluate the fit, test assumptions, and select among competing models. I assume you've had exposure to least squares regression as typically taught in a second-semester undergraduate statistics course. But I've made efforts to keep the mathematical notation to a minimum and focus on practical rather than theoretical issues. Several excellent texts cover the statistical material outlined in this chapter. My favorites are John Fox's *Applied Regression Analysis and Generalized Linear Models* (2008) (for theory) and *An R and S-Plus Companion to Applied Regression* (2002) (for application). They both served as major sources for this chapter. Licht (1995) provides a good nontechnical overview.

8.2 OLS regression

For most of this chapter, we'll be predicting the response variable from a set of predictor variables (also called *regressing* the response variable on the predictor variables—hence the name) using OLS. OLS regression fits models of the form where n is the number of observations and k is the number of predictor variables. (Although I've tried to keep equations out of these discussions, this is one of the few places where it simplifies things.) In this equation:

$$\hat{Y}_i = \hat{\beta}_0 + \hat{\beta}_1 X_{1i} + \ldots + \hat{\beta}_k X_{1k} \quad i = 1 \ldots n$$

- $\hat{Y}_i$ is the predicted value of the dependent variable for observation i (specifically, it's the estimated mean of the Y distribution, conditional on the set of predictor values).
- X_{ij} is the jth predictor value for the ith observation.
- $\hat{\beta}_0$ is the intercept (the predicted value of Y when all the predictor variables equal zero).
- $\hat{\beta}_j$ is the regression coefficient for the jth predictor (slope representing the change in Y for a unit change in X_j).

Our goal is to select model parameters (intercept and slopes) that minimize the difference between actual response values and those predicted by the model. Specifically, model parameters are selected to minimize the sum of squared residuals:

$$\sum_{i=1}^{n}(Y_i - \hat{Y}_i)^2 = \sum_{i=1}^{n}(Y_i - \hat{\beta}_0 + \hat{\beta}_1 X_{1i} + \ldots + \hat{\beta}_k X_{1k})^2 = \sum_{i=1}^{n}\varepsilon_i^2$$

To properly interpret the coefficients of the OLS model, you must satisfy a number of statistical assumptions:

- *Normality*—For fixed values of the independent variables, the dependent variable is normally distributed.
- *Independence*—The Y_i values are independent of each other.
- *Linearity*—The dependent variable is linearly related to the independent variables.

- *Homoscedasticity*—The variance of the dependent variable doesn't vary with the levels of the independent variables. (I could call this constant variance, but saying homoscedasticity makes me feel smarter.)

If you violate these assumptions, your statistical significance tests and confidence intervals may not be accurate. Note that OLS regression also assumes that the independent variables are fixed and measured without error, but this assumption is typically relaxed in practice.

8.2.1   *Fitting regression models with lm()*

In R, the basic function for fitting a linear model is `lm()`. The format is

```
myfit <- lm(formula, data)
```

where *formula* describes the model to be fit and *data* is the data frame containing the data to be used in fitting the model. The resulting object (`myfit`, in this case) is a list that contains extensive information about the fitted model. The formula is typically written as

```
Y ~ X1 + X2 + ... + Xk
```

where the ~ separates the response variable on the left from the predictor variables on the right, and the predictor variables are separated by + signs. Other symbols can be used to modify the formula in various ways (see table 8.2).

Table 8.2   Symbols commonly used in R formulas

Symbol	Usage
~	Separates response variables on the left from the explanatory variables on the right. For example, a prediction of y from x, z, and w would be coded y ~ x + z + w.
+	Separates predictor variables
:	Denotes an interaction between predictor variables. A prediction of y from x, z, and the interaction between x and z would be coded y ~ x + z + x:z.
*	A shortcut for denoting all possible interactions. The code y ~ x * z * w expands to y ~ x + z + w + x:z + x:w + z:w + x:z:w.
^	Denotes interactions up to a specified degree. The code y ~ (x + z + w) ^2 expands to y ~ x + z + w + x:z + x:w + z:w.
.	A placeholder for all other variables in the data frame except the dependent variable. For example, if a data frame contained the variables x, y, z, and w, then the code y ~. would expand to y ~ x + z + w.
-	A minus sign removes a variable from the equation. For example, y ~ (x + z + w) ^2 – x:w expands to y ~ x + z + w + x:z + z:w.
-1	Suppresses the intercept. For example, the formula y ~ x -1 fits a regression of y on x and forces the line through the origin at x=0.

Table 8.2 Symbols commonly used in R formulas *(continued)*

Symbol	Usage
I()	Elements within the parentheses are interpreted arithmetically. For example, y ~ x + (z + w)^2 expands to y ~ x + z + w + z:w. In contrast, the code y ~ x + I((z + w)^2) expands to y ~ x + h, where h is a new variable created by squaring the sum of z and w.
function	Mathematical functions can be used in formulas. For example, log(y) ~ x + z + w predicts log(y) from x, z, and w.

In addition to lm(), table 8.3 lists several functions that are useful when generating a simple or multiple regression analysis. Each of these functions is applied to the object returned by lm() to generate additional information based on that fitted model.

Table 8.3 Other functions that are useful when fitting linear models

Function	Action
summary()	Displays detailed results for the fitted model
coefficients()	Lists the model parameters (intercept and slopes) for the fitted model
confint()	Provides confidence intervals for the model parameters (95% by default)
fitted()	Lists the predicted values in a fitted model
residuals()	Lists the residual values in a fitted model
anova()	Generates an ANOVA table for a fitted model or an ANOVA table comparing two or more fitted models
vcov()	Lists the covariance matrix for model parameters
AIC()	Prints Akaike's Information Criterion
plot()	Generates diagnostic plots for evaluating the fit of a model
predict()	Uses a fitted model to predict response values for a new dataset

When the regression model contains one dependent variable and one independent variable, the approach is called *simple linear regression*. When there's one predictor variable but powers of the variable are included (for example, X, X^2, X^3), it's called *polynomial regression*. When there's more than one predictor variable, it's called *multiple linear regression*. We'll start with an example of simple linear regression, progress to examples of polynomial and multiple linear regression, and end with an example of multiple regression that includes an interaction among the predictors.

8.2.2 Simple linear regression

Let's look at the functions in table 8.3 through a simple regression example. The dataset women in the base installation provides the height and weight for a set of 15 women ages 30 to 39. Suppose you want to predict weight from height. Having an equation for predicting weight from height can help you identify overweight or underweight individuals. The following listing provides the analysis, and figure 8.1 shows the resulting graph.

Listing 8.1 Simple linear regression

```
> fit <- lm(weight ~ height, data=women)
> summary(fit)

Call:
lm(formula=weight ~ height, data=women)

Residuals:
   Min    1Q Median    3Q    Max
-1.733 -1.133 -0.383  0.742  3.117

Coefficients:
            Estimate Std. Error t value Pr(>|t|)
(Intercept) -87.5167     5.9369   -14.7  1.7e-09 ***
height        3.4500     0.0911    37.9  1.1e-14 ***
---
Signif. codes:  0 '***' 0.001 '**' 0.01 '*' 0.05 '.' 0.1 ' ' 1

Residual standard error: 1.53 on 13 degrees of freedom
Multiple R-squared: 0.991,      Adjusted R-squared: 0.99
F-statistic: 1.43e+03 on 1 and 13 DF,  p-value: 1.09e-14

> women$weight

 [1] 115 117 120 123 126 129 132 135 139 142 146 150 154 159 164

> fitted(fit)

      1       2       3       4       5       6       7       8       9
 112.58 116.03 119.48 122.93 126.38 129.83 133.28 136.73 140.18
     10      11      12      13      14      15
 143.63 147.08 150.53 153.98 157.43 160.88

> residuals(fit)

    1     2     3     4     5     6     7     8     9    10    11
 2.42  0.97  0.52  0.07 -0.38 -0.83 -1.28 -1.73 -1.18 -1.63 -1.08
   12    13    14    15
-0.53  0.02  1.57  3.12

> plot(women$height,women$weight,
       xlab="Height (in inches)",
       ylab="Weight (in pounds)")
> abline(fit)
```

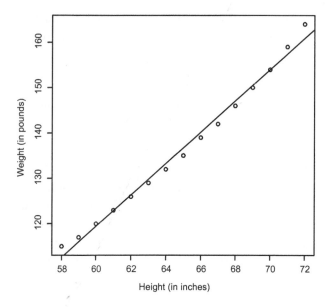

Figure 8.1 Scatter plot with regression line for weight predicted from height

From the output, you see that the prediction equation is

$$weight = -87.52 + 3.45 \times height$$

Because a height of 0 is impossible, you wouldn't try to give a physical interpretation to the intercept. It merely becomes an adjustment constant. From the `Pr(>|t|)` column, you see that the regression coefficient (3.45) is significantly different from zero ($p < 0.001$) and indicates that there's an expected increase of 3.45 pounds of weight for every 1 inch increase in height. The multiple R-squared (0.991) indicates that the model accounts for 99.1% of the variance in weights. The multiple R-squared is also the squared correlation between the actual and predicted value (that is, $R^2 = r_{\hat{y}y}$). The residual standard error (1.53 pounds) can be thought of as the average error in predicting weight from height using this model. The F-statistic tests whether the predictor variables, taken together, predict the response variable above chance levels. Because there's only one predictor variable in simple regression, in this example, the F-test is equivalent to the t-test for the regression coefficient for height.

For demonstration purposes, we've printed out the actual, predicted, and residual values. Evidently, the largest residuals occur for low and high heights, which can also be seen in the plot (figure 8.1).

The plot suggests that you might be able to improve on the prediction by using a line with one bend. For example, a model of the form

$$\hat{Y}_i = \hat{\beta}_0 + \hat{\beta}_1 X + \hat{\beta}_2 X^2$$

may provide a better fit to the data. Polynomial regression allows you to predict a response variable from an explanatory variable, where the form of the relationship is an nth-degree polynomial.

8.2.3   *Polynomial regression*

The plot in figure 8.1 suggests that you might be able to improve your prediction using a regression with a quadratic term (that is, X^2). You can fit a quadratic equation using the statement

```
fit2 <- lm(weight ~ height + I(height^2), data=women)
```

The new term `I(height^2)` requires explanation. `height^2` adds a height-squared term to the prediction equation. The `I()` function treats the contents within the parentheses as an R expression. You need this because the `^` operator has a special meaning in formulas that you don't want to invoke here (see table 8.2).

The following listing shows the results of fitting the quadratic equation.

Listing 8.2   Polynomial regression

```
> fit2 <- lm(weight ~ height + I(height^2), data=women)
> summary(fit2)

Call:
lm(formula=weight ~ height + I(height^2), data=women)

Residuals:
    Min      1Q  Median      3Q     Max
-0.5094 -0.2961 -0.0094  0.2862  0.5971

Coefficients:
             Estimate Std. Error t value Pr(>|t|)
(Intercept) 261.87818   25.19677   10.39  2.4e-07 ***
height        -7.34832    0.77769   -9.45  6.6e-07 ***
I(height^2)    0.08306    0.00598   13.89  9.3e-09 ***
---
Signif. codes:  0 '***' 0.001 '**' 0.01 '*' 0.05 '.' 0.1 ' ' 1

Residual standard error: 0.384 on 12 degrees of freedom
Multiple R-squared: 0.999,       Adjusted R-squared: 0.999
F-statistic: 1.14e+04 on 2 and 12 DF,  p-value: <2e-16

> plot(women$height,women$weight,
       xlab="Height (in inches)",
       ylab="Weight (in lbs)")
> lines(women$height,fitted(fit2))
```

From this new analysis, the prediction equation is

$$weight = 261.88 - 7.35 \times height + 0.083 \times height^2$$

and both regression coefficients are significant at the $p < 0.0001$ level. The amount of variance accounted for has increased to 99.9%. The significance of the squared term (t = 13.89, p < .001) suggests that inclusion of the quadratic term improves the model fit. If you look at the plot of `fit2` (figure 8.2), you can see that the curve does indeed provide a better fit.

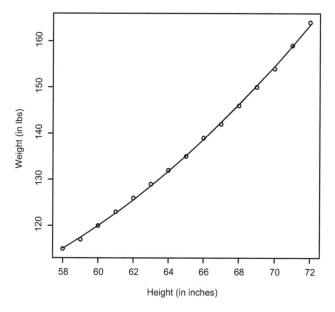

Figure 8.2 Quadratic regression for weight predicted by height

Linear vs. nonlinear models

Note that this polynomial equation still fits under the rubric of linear regression. It's linear because the equation involves a weighted sum of predictor variables (height and height-squared in this case). Even a model such as

$$\hat{Y}_i = \hat{\beta}_0 \times \log(X_1) + \hat{\beta}_2 \times \sin X_2$$

would be considered a linear model (in terms of the parameters) and fit with the formula

$$Y \sim \log(X1) + \sin(X2)$$

In contrast, here's an example of a truly nonlinear model:

$$\hat{Y}_i = \hat{\beta}_0 + \hat{\beta}_1 e^{X/\hat{\beta}_2}$$

Nonlinear models of this form can be fit with the `nls()` function.

In general, an *n*th-degree polynomial produces a curve with *n* - 1 bends. To fit a cubic polynomial, you'd use

```
fit3 <- lm(weight ~ height + I(height^2) +I(height^3), data=women)
```

Although higher polynomials are possible, I've rarely found that terms higher than cubic are necessary.

8.2.4 *Multiple linear regression*

When there's more than one predictor variable, simple linear regression becomes multiple linear regression, and the analysis grows more involved. Technically, polynomial regression is a special case of multiple regression. Quadratic regression has two predictors (X and X^2), and cubic regression has three predictors (X, X^2, and X^3). Let's look at a more general example.

We'll use the `state.x77` dataset in the base package for this example. Suppose you want to explore the relationship between a state's murder rate and other characteristics of the state, including population, illiteracy rate, average income, and frost levels (mean the number of days below freezing).

Because the `lm()` function requires a data frame (and the `state.x77` dataset is contained in a matrix), you can simplify your life with the following code:

```
states <- as.data.frame(state.x77[,c("Murder", "Population",
                  "Illiteracy", "Income", "Frost")])
```

This code creates a data frame called `states` that contains the variables you're interested in. You'll use this new data frame for the remainder of the chapter.

A good first step in multiple regression is to examine the relationships among the variables two at a time. The bivariate correlations are provided by the `cor()` function, and scatter plots are generated from the `scatterplotMatrix()` function in the `car` package (see the following listing and figure 8.3).

Listing 8.3 Examining bivariate relationships

```
> states <- as.data.frame(state.x77[,c("Murder", "Population",
                  "Illiteracy", "Income", "Frost")])

> cor(states)
           Murder Population Illiteracy Income Frost
Murder       1.00       0.34       0.70  -0.23 -0.54
Population   0.34       1.00       0.11   0.21 -0.33
Illiteracy   0.70       0.11       1.00  -0.44 -0.67
Income      -0.23       0.21      -0.44   1.00  0.23
Frost       -0.54      -0.33      -0.67   0.23  1.00

> library(car)
> scatterplotMatrix(states, smooth=FALSE, main="Scatter Plot Matrix")
```

By default, the `scatterplotMatrix()` function provides scatter plots of the variables with each other in the off-diagonals and superimposes smoothed (loess) and linear fit lines on these plots. The principal diagonal contains density and rug plots for each variable. The smoothed lines are suppressed with the argument `smooth=FALSE`.

You can see that the murder rate may be bimodal and that each of the predictor variables is skewed to some extent. Murder rates rise with population and illiteracy,

Scatter Plot Matrix

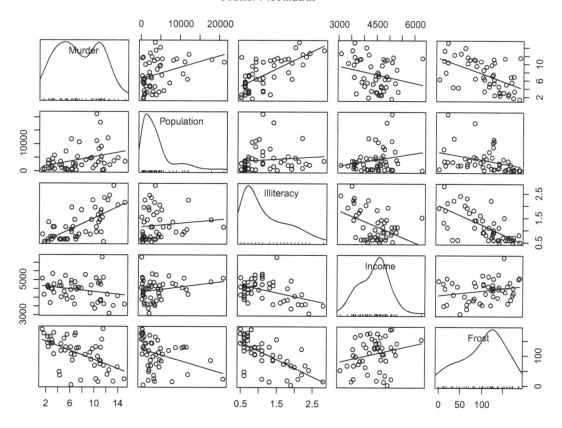

Figure 8.3 Scatter plot matrix of dependent and independent variables for the states data, including linear and smoothed fits, and marginal distributions (kernel density plots and rug plots)

and they fall with higher income levels and frost. At the same time, colder states have lower illiteracy rates, lower population, and higher incomes.

Now let's fit the multiple regression model with the lm() function.

Listing 8.4 Multiple linear regression

```
> states <- as.data.frame(state.x77[,c("Murder", "Population",
                         "Illiteracy", "Income", "Frost")])

> fit <- lm(Murder ~ Population + Illiteracy + Income + Frost,
            data=states)
> summary(fit)

Call:
lm(formula=Murder ~ Population + Illiteracy + Income + Frost,
   data=states)
```

```
Residuals:
    Min      1Q  Median      3Q     Max
-4.7960 -1.6495 -0.0811  1.4815  7.6210

Coefficients:
            Estimate Std. Error t value Pr(>|t|)
(Intercept) 1.23e+00   3.87e+00    0.32    0.751
Population  2.24e-04   9.05e-05    2.47    0.017 *
Illiteracy  4.14e+00   8.74e-01    4.74  2.2e-05 ***
Income      6.44e-05   6.84e-04    0.09    0.925
Frost       5.81e-04   1.01e-02    0.06    0.954
---
Signif. codes:  0 '***' 0.001 '**' 0.01 '*' 0.05 '.v 0.1 'v' 1

Residual standard error: 2.5 on 45 degrees of freedom
Multiple R-squared: 0.567,     Adjusted R-squared: 0.528
F-statistic: 14.7 on 4 and 45 DF,  p-value: 9.13e-08
```

When there's more than one predictor variable, the regression coefficients indicate the increase in the dependent variable for a unit change in a predictor variable, holding all other predictor variables constant. For example, the regression coefficient for Illiteracy is 4.14, suggesting that an increase of 1% in illiteracy is associated with a 4.14% increase in the murder rate, controlling for population, income, and temperature. The coefficient is significantly different from zero at the $p < .0001$ level. On the other hand, the coefficient for Frost isn't significantly different from zero ($p = 0.954$), suggesting that Frost and Murder aren't linearly related when controlling for the other predictor variables. Taken together, the predictor variables account for 57% of the variance in murder rates across states.

Up to this point, we've assumed that the predictor variables don't interact. In the next section, we'll consider a case in which they do.

8.2.5 *Multiple linear regression with interactions*

Some of the most interesting research findings are those involving interactions among predictor variables. Consider the automobile data in the mtcars data frame. Let's say that you're interested in the impact of automobile weight and horsepower on mileage. You could fit a regression model that includes both predictors, along with their interaction, as shown in the next listing.

Listing 8.5 Multiple linear regression with a significant interaction term

```
> fit <- lm(mpg ~ hp + wt + hp:wt, data=mtcars)
> summary(fit)

Call:
lm(formula=mpg ~ hp + wt + hp:wt, data=mtcars)

Residuals:
   Min     1Q Median     3Q    Max
-3.063 -1.649 -0.736  1.421  4.551
```

```
Coefficients:
            Estimate Std. Error t value Pr(>|t|)
(Intercept) 49.80842    3.60516   13.82  5.0e-14 ***
hp          -0.12010    0.02470   -4.86  4.0e-05 ***
wt          -8.21662    1.26971   -6.47  5.2e-07 ***
hp:wt        0.02785    0.00742    3.75  0.00081 ***
---
Signif. codes:  0 '***' 0.001 '**' 0.01 '*' 0.05 '.' 0.1 ' ' 1

Residual standard error: 2.1 on 28 degrees of freedom
Multiple R-squared: 0.885,      Adjusted R-squared: 0.872
F-statistic: 71.7 on 3 and 28 DF,  p-value: 2.98e-13
```

You can see from the Pr(>|t|) column that the interaction between horsepower and car weight is significant. What does this mean? A significant interaction between two predictor variables tells you that the relationship between one predictor and the response variable depends on the level of the other predictor. Here it means the relationship between miles per gallon and horsepower varies by car weight.

The model for predicting mpg is mpg = 49.81 − 0.12 × hp − 8.22 × wt + 0.03 × hp × wt. To interpret the interaction, you can plug in various values of wt and simplify the equation. For example, you can try the mean of wt (3.2) and one standard deviation below and above the mean (2.2 and 4.2, respectively). For wt=2.2, the equation simplifies to mpg = 49.81 − 0.12 × hp − 8.22 × (2.2) + 0.03 × hp × (2.2) = 31.41 − 0.06 × hp. For wt=3.2, this becomes mpg = 23.37 − 0.03 × hp. Finally, for wt=4.2 the equation becomes mpg = 15.33 − 0.003 × hp. You see that as weight increases (2.2, 3.2, 4.2), the expected change in mpg from a unit increase in hp decreases (0.06, 0.03, 0.003).

You can visualize interactions using the effect() function in the effects package. The format is

```
plot(effect(term, mod,, xlevels), multiline=TRUE)
```

where *term* is the quoted model term to plot, *mod* is the fitted model returned by lm(), and *xlevels* is a list specifying the variables to be set to constant values and the values to employ. The multiline=TRUE option superimposes the lines being plotted, and the lines option specifies the line type for each line (where 1 = solid, 2 = dashed, and 3 = dotted, etc.). For the previous model, this becomes

```
library(effects)
plot(effect("hp:wt", fit,, list(wt=c(2.2,3.2,4.2))),
    lines=c(1,2,3), multiline=TRUE)
```

Figure 8.4 displays the resulting graph.

You can see from this graph that as the weight of the car increases, the relationship between horsepower and miles per gallon weakens. For wt=4.2, the line is almost horizontal, indicating that as hp increases, mpg doesn't change.

Unfortunately, fitting the model is only the first step in the analysis. Once you fit a regression model, you need to evaluate whether you've met the statistical assumptions underlying your approach before you can have confidence in the inferences you draw. This is the topic of the next section.

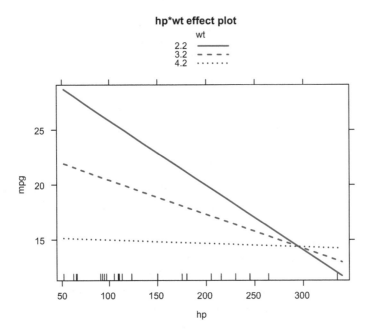

Figure 8.4   Interaction plot for `hp*wt`. This plot displays the relationship between `mpg` and `hp` at three values of `wt`.

8.3   *Regression diagnostics*

In the previous section, you used the `lm()` function to fit an OLS regression model and the `summary()` function to obtain the model parameters and summary statistics. Unfortunately, nothing in this printout tells you whether the model you've fit is appropriate. Your confidence in inferences about regression parameters depends on the degree to which you've met the statistical assumptions of the OLS model. Although the `summary()` function in listing 8.4 describes the model, it provides no information concerning the degree to which you've satisfied the statistical assumptions underlying the model.

Why is this important? Irregularities in the data or misspecifications of the relationships between the predictors and the response variable can lead you to settle on a model that's wildly inaccurate. On the one hand, you may conclude that a predictor and a response variable are unrelated when, in fact, they are. On the other hand, you may conclude that a predictor and a response variable are related when, in fact, they aren't. You may also end up with a model that makes poor predictions when applied in real-world settings, with significant and unnecessary error.

Let's look at the output from the `confint()` function applied to the `states` multiple regression problem in section 8.2.4:

```
> states <- as.data.frame(state.x77[,c("Murder", "Population",
                      "Illiteracy", "Income", "Frost")])
```

```
> fit <- lm(Murder ~ Population + Illiteracy + Income + Frost, data=states)
> confint(fit)
                  2.5 %    97.5 %
(Intercept) -6.55e+00 9.021318
Population   4.14e-05 0.000406
Illiteracy   2.38e+00 5.903874
Income      -1.31e-03 0.001441
Frost       -1.97e-02 0.020830
```

The results suggest that you can be 95% confident that the interval [2.38, 5.90] contains the true change in murder rate for a 1% change in illiteracy rate. Additionally, because the confidence interval for Frost contains 0, you can conclude that a change in temperature is unrelated to murder rate, holding the other variables constant. But your faith in these results is only as strong as the evidence you have that your data satisfies the statistical assumptions underlying the model.

A set of techniques called *regression diagnostics* provides the necessary tools for evaluating the appropriateness of the regression model and can help you to uncover and correct problems. We'll start with a standard approach that uses functions that come with R's base installation. Then we'll look at newer, improved methods available through the car package.

8.3.1 A typical approach

R's base installation provides numerous methods for evaluating the statistical assumptions in a regression analysis. The most common approach is to apply the plot() function to the object returned by lm(). Doing so produces four graphs that are useful for evaluating the model fit. Applying this approach to the simple linear regression example

```
fit <- lm(weight ~ height, data=women)
par(mfrow=c(2,2))
plot(fit)
par(mfrow=c(1,1))
```

produces the graphs shown in figure 8.5. The par(mfrow=c(2,2)) statement is used to combine the four plots produced by the plot() function into one large two-by-two graph. The second par() function returns you to single graphs.

To understand these graphs, consider the assumptions of OLS regression:

- *Normality*—If the dependent variable is normally distributed for a fixed set of predictor values, then the residual values should be normally distributed with a mean of 0. The normal Q-Q plot (upper right) is a probability plot of the standardized residuals against the values that would be expected under normality. If you've met the normality assumption, the points on this graph should fall on the straight 45-degree line. Because they don't, you've clearly violated the normality assumption.

- *Independence*—You can't tell if the dependent variable values are independent of these plots. You have to use your understanding of how the data was collected.

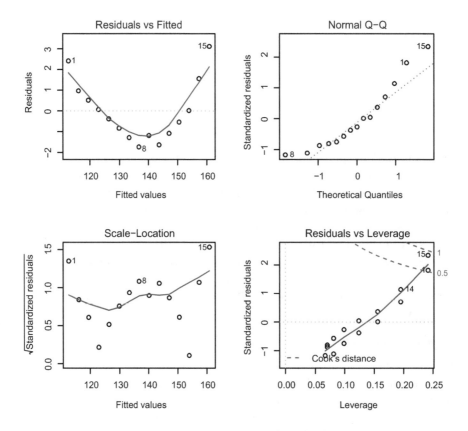

Figure 8.5   Diagnostic plots for the regression of weight on height

There's no a priori reason to believe that one woman's weight influences another woman's weight. If you found out that the data were sampled from families, you might have to adjust your assumption of independence.

- *Linearity*—If the dependent variable is linearly related to the independent variables, there should be no systematic relationship between the residuals and the predicted (that is, fitted) values. In other words, the model should capture all the systematic variance present in the data, leaving nothing but random noise. In the residuals-versus-fitted graph (upper left), you see clear evidence of a curved relationship, which suggests that you may want to add a quadratic term to the regression.

- *Homoscedasticity*—If you've met the constant variance assumption, the points in the scale-location graph (bottom left) should be a random band around a horizontal line. You seem to meet this assumption.

Finally, the residuals-versus-leverage graph (bottom right) provides information about individual observations that you may wish to attend to. The graph identifies outliers, high-leverage points, and influential observations. Specifically,

- An outlier is an observation that isn't predicted well by the fitted regression model (that is, has a large positive or negative residual).
- An observation with a high leverage value has an unusual combination of predictor values. That is, it's an outlier in the predictor space. The dependent variable value isn't used to calculate an observation's leverage.
- An influential observation is an observation that has a disproportionate impact on the determination of the model parameters. Influential observations are identified using a statistic called Cook's distance, or Cook's D.

To be honest, I find the residuals-versus-leverage plot difficult to read and not useful. You'll see better representations of this information in later sections.

Although these standard diagnostic plots are helpful, better tools are now available in R, and I recommend their use over the `plot(fit)` approach.

8.3.2 An enhanced approach

The `car` package provides a number of functions that significantly enhance your ability to fit and evaluate regression models (see table 8.4).

Table 8.4 Useful functions for regression diagnostics (`car` package)

Function	Purpose
`qqPlot()`	Quantile comparisons plot
`durbinWatsonTest()`	Durbin–Watson test for autocorrelated errors
`crPlots()`	Component plus residual plots
`ncvTest()`	Score test for nonconstant error variance
`spreadLevelPlot()`	Spread-level plots
`outlierTest()`	Bonferroni outlier test
`avPlots()`	Added variable plots
`influencePlot()`	Regression influence plots
`vif()`	Variance inflation factors

Let's look at each in turn by applying them to our multiple regression example.

NORMALITY

The `qqPlot()` function provides a more accurate method of assessing the normality assumption than that provided by the `plot()` function in the base package. It plots the studentized residuals (also called *studentized deleted residuals* or *jackknifed residuals*) against a *t* distribution with $n - p - 1$ degrees of freedom, where n is the sample size and p is the number of regression parameters (including the intercept). The code follows:

```
library(car)
states <- as.data.frame(state.x77[,c("Murder", "Population",
                        "Illiteracy", "Income", "Frost")])
```

```
fit <- lm(Murder ~ Population + Illiteracy + Income + Frost, data=states)
qqPlot(fit, labels=row.names(states), id=list(method="identify"),
       simulate=TRUE, main="Q-Q Plot")
```

The qqPlot() function generates the probability plot displayed in figure 8.6. The option id=list(method="identify") makes the plot interactive—after the graph is drawn, mouse clicks on points in the graph will label them with values specified in the labels option of the function. Pressing the Esc key or the Finish button in the upper-right corner of the graph turns off this interactive mode. Here, I identified Nevada. When simulate=TRUE, a 95% confidence envelope is produced using a parametric bootstrap. (Bootstrap methods are considered in chapter 12.)

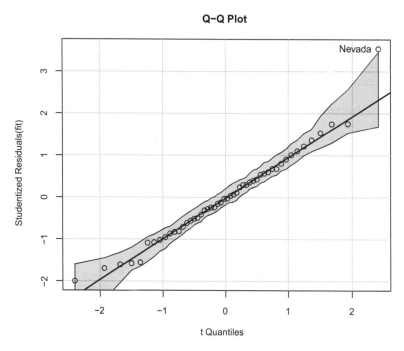

Figure 8.6 Q-Q plot for studentized residuals

With the exception of Nevada, all the points fall close to the line and are within the confidence envelope, suggesting that you've met the normality assumption fairly well. But you should definitely look at Nevada. It has a large positive residual (actual minus predicted), indicating that the model underestimates the murder rate in this state. Specifically,

```
> states["Nevada",]

       Murder Population Illiteracy Income Frost
Nevada   11.5        590        0.5   5149   188
```

```
> fitted(fit)["Nevada"]

  Nevada
3.878958

> residuals(fit)["Nevada"]

  Nevada
7.621042

> rstudent(fit)["Nevada"]

  Nevada
3.542929
```

Here you see that the murder rate is 11.5%, but the model predicts a 3.9% murder rate. The question you need to ask is, "Why does Nevada have a higher murder rate than predicted from population, income, illiteracy, and temperature?" Anyone (who hasn't seen *Casino*) want to guess?

INDEPENDENCE OF ERRORS

As noted earlier, the best way to assess whether the dependent variable values (and thus the residuals) are independent is from your knowledge of how the data were collected. For example, time-series data often display autocorrelation—observations collected closer in time are more correlated with each other than with observations distant in time. The car package provides a function for the Durbin–Watson test to detect such serially correlated errors. You can apply the Durbin–Watson test to the multiple regression problem with the following code:

```
> durbinWatsonTest(fit)
 lag Autocorrelation D-W Statistic p-value
   1          -0.201          2.32    0.282
 Alternative hypothesis: rho != 0
```

The nonsignificant p-value (p = 0.282) suggests a lack of autocorrelation and, conversely, an independence of errors. The lag value (1 in this case) indicates that each observation is being compared with the one next to it in the dataset. Although appropriate for time-dependent data, the test is less applicable for data that isn't clustered in this fashion. Note that the durbinWatsonTest() function uses bootstrapping (see chapter 12) to derive p-values. Unless you add the option simulate=FALSE, you'll get a slightly different value each time you run the test.

LINEARITY

You can look for evidence of nonlinearity in the relationship between the dependent variable and the independent variables by using component-plus-residual plots (also known as *partial residual plots*). The plot is produced by the crPlots() function in the car package. You're looking for any systematic departure from the linear model that you've specified.

To create a component-plus-residual plot for variable k, you plot the points

$$\varepsilon_i + \hat{\beta}_k \times X_{ik} \text{ vs. } X_{ik}$$

where the residuals are based on the full model (containing all the predictors), and $i = 1 \dots n$. The straight line in each graph is given by $\hat{\beta}_k \times X_{ik}$ vs. X_{ik}. A loess line (a smoothed nonparametric fit line) is also provided for each plot. Chapter 11 describes loess lines. The code to produce these plots is as follows:

```
> library(car)
> crPlots(fit)
```

Figure 8.7 provides the resulting plots. Nonlinearity in any of these plots suggests that you may not have adequately modeled the functional form of that predictor in the regression. If so, you may need to add curvilinear components such as polynomial terms, transform one or more variables (for example, use `log(X)` instead of `X`), or abandon linear regression in favor of some other regression variant. Transformations are discussed later in this chapter.

The component-plus-residual plots confirm that you've met the linearity assumption. The form of the linear model seems to be appropriate for this dataset.

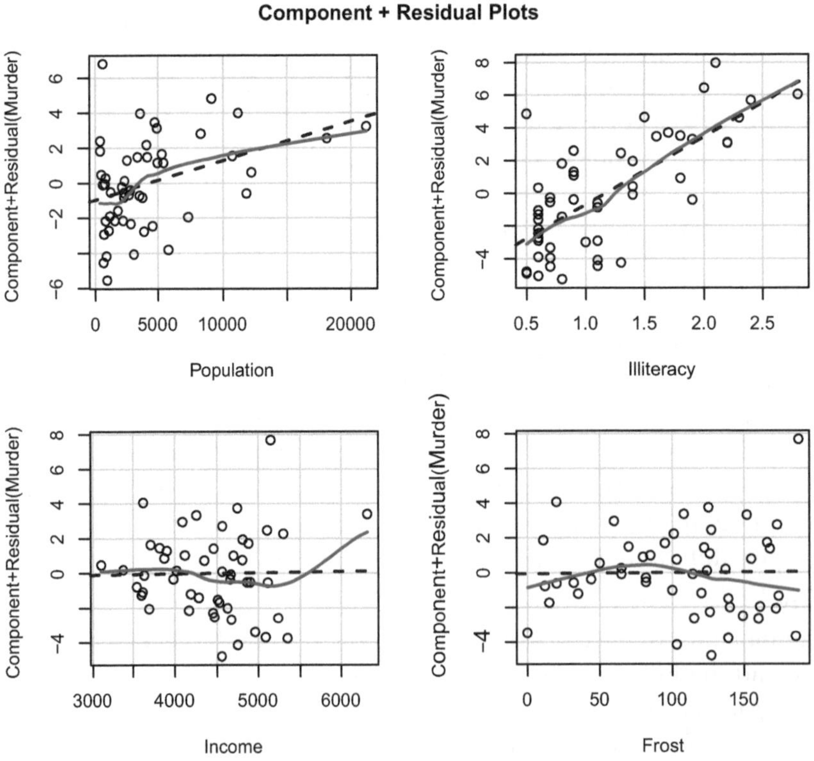

Component + Residual Plots

Figure 8.7 Component-plus-residual plots for the regression of murder rate on state characteristics

HOMOSCEDASTICITY

The car package also provides two useful functions for identifying nonconstant error variance. The ncvTest() function produces a score test of the hypothesis of constant error variance against the alternative that the error variance changes with the level of the fitted values. A significant result suggests heteroscedasticity (nonconstant error variance).

The spreadLevelPlot() function creates a scatter plot of the absolute standardized residuals versus the fitted values and superimposes a line of best fit. Both functions are demonstrated in the next listing.

Listing 8.6 Assessing homoscedasticity

```
> library(car)
> ncvTest(fit)

Non-constant Variance Score Test
Variance formula: ~ fitted.values
Chisquare=1.7      Df=1        p=0.19

> spreadLevelPlot(fit)

Suggested power transformation:  1.2
```

The score test is nonsignificant (p = 0.19), suggesting that you've met the constant variance assumption. You can also see this in the spread-level plot (figure 8.8). The points form a random horizontal band around a horizontal line of best fit. If you'd

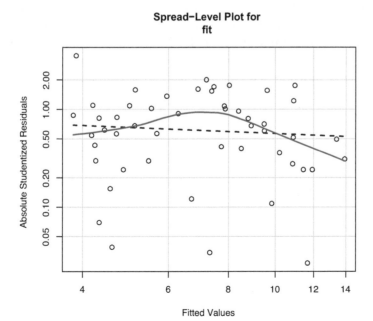

Figure 8.8 Spread-level plot for assessing constant error variance

violated the assumption, you'd expect to see a nonhorizontal line. The suggested power transformation in listing 8.6 is the suggested power p (Y^p) that would stabilize the nonconstant error variance. For example, if the plot showed a nonhorizontal trend and the suggested power transformation was 0.5, then using $\sqrt{Y}$ rather than Y in the regression equation might lead to a model that satisfied homoscedasticity. If the suggested power was 0, you'd use a log transformation. In the current example, there's no evidence of heteroscedasticity, and the suggested power is close to 1 (no transformation required).

8.3.3　*Multicollinearity*

Before leaving this section on regression diagnostics, let's focus on a problem that's not directly related to statistical assumptions but is important in helping you interpret multiple regression results. Imagine you're conducting a study of grip strength. Your independent variables include date of birth (DOB) and age. You regress grip strength on DOB and age and find a significant overall F-test at p < .001. But when you look at the individual regression coefficients for DOB and age, you find that they're both nonsignificant (that is, there's no evidence that either is related to grip strength). What happened?

The problem is that DOB and age are perfectly correlated within rounding error. A regression coefficient measures the impact of one predictor variable on the response variable, holding all other predictor variables constant. This amounts to looking at the relationship of grip strength and age, holding age constant. The problem is called multicollinearity. It leads to large confidence intervals for model parameters and makes the interpretation of individual coefficients difficult.

Multicollinearity can be detected using a statistic called the variance inflation factor (VIF). For any predictor variable, the square root of the VIF indicates the degree to which the confidence interval for that variable's regression parameter is expanded relative to a model with uncorrelated predictors (hence the name). VIF values are provided by the vif() function in the car package. As a general rule, a VIF > 10 indicates a multicollinearity problem. The following listing provides the code. The results indicate that multicollinearity isn't a problem with these predictor variables.

Listing 8.7　Evaluating multicollinearity

```
> library(car)
> vif(fit)

Population Illiteracy     Income        Frost
       1.2        2.2        1.3          2.1

> vif(fit) > 10 # problem?

Population Illiteracy     Income        Frost
     FALSE      FALSE      FALSE        FALSE
```

8.4 Unusual observations

A comprehensive regression analysis will also include a screening for unusual observations—outliers, high-leverage observations, and influential observations. These data points warrant further investigation, either because they're different from other observations in some way or because they exert a disproportionate amount of influence on the results. Let's look at each in turn.

8.4.1 Outliers

Outliers are observations that aren't predicted well by the model. They have unusually large positive or negative residuals ($Y_i - \hat{Y}_i$). Positive residuals indicate that the model is underestimating the response value, whereas negative residuals indicate an overestimation.

You've already seen one way to identify outliers. Points in the Q-Q plot of figure 8.6 that lie outside the confidence band are considered outliers. A rough rule of thumb is that standardized residuals that are larger than 2 or less than –2 are worth attention.

The `car` package also provides a statistical test for outliers. The `outlierTest()` function reports the Bonferroni adjusted p-value for the largest absolute studentized residual:

```
> library(car)
> outlierTest(fit)
      rstudent unadjusted p-value Bonferroni p
Nevada     3.5            0.00095        0.048
```

Here, you see that Nevada is identified as an outlier (p = 0.048). Note that this function tests the single largest (positive or negative) residual for significance as an outlier. If it isn't significant, there are no outliers in the dataset. If it's significant, you must delete it and rerun the test to see if others are present.

8.4.2 High-leverage points

Observations that have high leverage are outliers with regard to the other predictors. In other words, they have an unusual combination of predictor values. The response value isn't involved in determining leverage.

Observations with high leverage are identified through the *hat statistic*. For a given dataset, the average hat value is p/n, where p is the number of parameters estimated in the model (including the intercept) and n is the sample size. Roughly speaking, an observation with a hat value greater than two or three times the average hat value should be examined. The code that follows plots the `hat` values:

```
hat.plot <- function(fit) {
            p <- length(coefficients(fit))
            n <- length(fitted(fit))
            plot(hatvalues(fit), main="Index Plot of Hat Values")
            abline(h=c(2,3)*p/n, col="red", lty=2)
            identify(1:n, hatvalues(fit), names(hatvalues(fit)))
         }
hat.plot(fit)
```

Figure 8.9 shows the resulting graph.

Horizontal lines are drawn at two and three times the average hat value. The locator function places the graph in interactive mode. Clicking points of interest labels them until the user presses Esc or the Finish button in the upper-right corner of the graph.

Index Plot of Hat Values

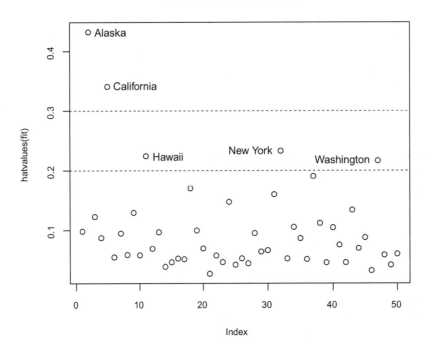

Figure 8.9 Index plot of hat values for assessing observations with high leverage

Here you see that Alaska and California are particularly unusual when it comes to their predictor values. Alaska has a much higher income than other states, while having a lower population and temperature. California has a much higher population than other states, while having a higher income and higher temperature. These states are atypical compared with the other 48 observations.

High-leverage observations may or may not be influential observations. That will depend on whether they're also outliers.

8.4.3 *Influential observations*

Influential observations have a disproportionate impact on the values of the model parameters. Imagine finding that your model changes dramatically with the removal of a single observation. It's this concern that leads you to examine your data for influential points.

There are two methods for identifying influential observations: Cook's distance (or D statistic) and added variable plots. Roughly speaking, Cook's D values greater than $4/(n - k - 1)$, where n is the sample size and k is the number of predictor variables, indicate influential observations. You can create a Cook's D plot (figure 8.10) with the following code:

```
cutoff <- 4/(nrow(states)-length(fit$coefficients)-2)
plot(fit, which=4, cook.levels=cutoff)
abline(h=cutoff, lty=2, col="red")
```

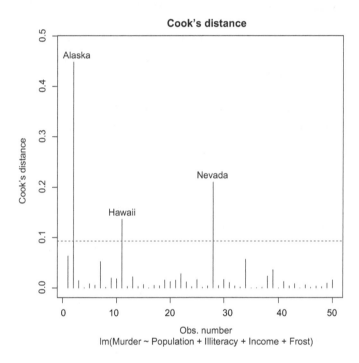

Figure 8.10 Cook's D plot for identifying influential observations

The graph identifies Alaska, Hawaii, and Nevada as influential observations. Deleting these states will have a notable impact on the values of the intercept and slopes in the regression model. Note that although it's useful to cast a wide net when searching for influential observations, I tend to find a cutoff of 1 more generally useful than $4/(n - k - 1)$. Given a criterion of D = 1, none of the observations in the dataset would appear to be influential.

Cook's D plots can help identify influential observations, but they don't provide information about how these observations affect the model. Added-variable plots can help in this regard. For one response variable and k predictor variables, you'd create k added-variable plots as follows.

For each predictor *Xk*, plot the residuals from regressing the response variable on the other *k* – 1 predictors versus the residuals from regressing *Xk* on the other *k* – 1 predictors. Added-variable plots can be created using the `avPlots()` function in the `car` package:

```
library(car)
avPlots(fit, ask=FALSE, d=list(method="identify"))
```

Figure 8.11 provides the resulting graphs. The graphs are produced one at a time, and users can click points to identify them. Press Esc or the Finish button on the upper-right corner of the graph to move to the next plot. Here, I've identified Alaska in the bottom-left plot.

The straight line in each plot is the actual regression coefficient for that predictor variable. You can see the impact of influential observations by imagining how the line would change if the point representing that observation was deleted. For example, look at the graph of Murder | Others versus Income | Others in the lower-left corner. You can see that eliminating the point labeled Alaska would move the line in a negative direction. In fact, deleting Alaska changes the regression coefficient for Income from positive (.00006) to negative (–.00085).

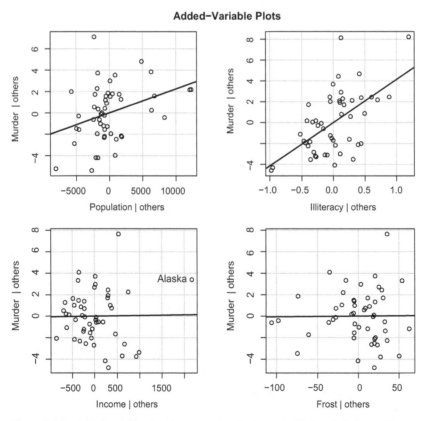

Figure 8.11   Added-variable plots for assessing the impact of influential observations

You can combine the information from outlier, leverage, and influence plots into one highly informative plot using the `influencePlot()` function from the `car` package:

```
library(car)
influencePlot(fit, id="noteworthy", main="Influence Plot",
              sub="Circle size is proportional to Cook's distance")
```

The resulting plot (figure 8.12) identifies observations that are particularly noteworthy. In particular, it shows that Nevada and Rhode Island are outliers, California, and Hawaii have high leverage, and Nevada and Alaska are influential observations.

Replacing `id="noteworthy"` with `id=list(method="identify")` allows you to identify points interactively with mouse clicks (ending with ESC or pressing the Finish button).

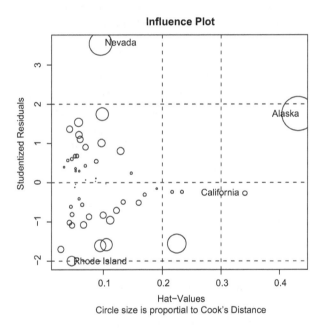

Figure 8.12 Influence plot. States above +2 or below −2 on the vertical axis are considered outliers. States above 0.2 or 0.3 on the horizontal axis have high leverage (unusual combinations of predictor values). Circle size is proportional to influence. Observations depicted by large circles may have disproportionate influence on the parameter estimates of the model.

8.5 Corrective measures

Having spent the last 16 pages learning about regression diagnostics, you may ask, "What do you do if you identify problems?" There are four approaches to dealing with violations of regression assumptions:

- Deleting observations
- Transforming variables
- Adding or deleting variables
- Using another regression approach

Let's look at each in turn.

8.5.1   Deleting observations

Deleting outliers can often improve a dataset's fit to the normality assumption. Influential observations are often deleted as well, because they have an inordinate impact on the results. The largest outlier or influential observation is deleted, and the model is refit. If there are still outliers or influential observations, the process is repeated until an acceptable fit is obtained.

Again, I urge caution when considering the deletion of observations. Sometimes you can determine that the observation is an outlier because of data errors in recording, or because a protocol wasn't followed, or because a test subject misunderstood instructions. In these cases, deleting the offending observation seems perfectly reasonable.

In other cases, the unusual observation may be the most interesting thing about the data you've collected. Uncovering why an observation differs from the rest can add great insight to the topic at hand and to other topics you might not have thought of. Some of our greatest advances have come from the serendipity of noticing that something doesn't fit our preconceptions (pardon the hyperbole).

8.5.2   Transforming variables

When models don't meet the normality, linearity, or homoscedasticity assumptions, transforming one or more variables can often improve or correct the situation. Transformations typically involve replacing a variable Y with Y^λ. Table 8.5 gives common values of λ and their interpretations. If Y is a proportion, a logit transformation [$\log^e$ (Y/1-Y)] is often used. When Y is highly skewed, a log transformation is often helpful.

Table 8.5 Common transformations

λ	-2	-1	-0.5	0	0.5	1	2
Transformation	$1/Y^2$	$1/Y$	$1/\sqrt{Y}$	log(Y)	$\sqrt{Y}$	None	Y^2

When the model violates the normality assumption, you typically attempt a transformation of the response variable. You can use the `powerTransform()` function in the car package to generate a maximum-likelihood estimation of the power λ most likely to normalize the variable X^λ. The resulting transformation is called a Box–Cox transformation. In the next listing, this is applied to the `states` data.

Listing 8.8 Box–Cox transformation to normality

```
> library(car)
> summary(powerTransform(states$Murder))
bcPower Transformation to Normality

              Est.Power Std.Err.  Wald Lower Bound Wald Upper Bound
states$Murder       0.6     0.26            0.088              1.1
```

```
Likelihood ratio tests about transformation parameters
                    LRT df  pval
LR test, lambda=(0) 5.7  1 0.017
LR test, lambda=(1) 2.1  1 0.145
```

The results suggest that you can normalize the variable `Murder` by replacing it with `Murder0.6`. Because 0.6 is close to 0.5, you could try a square-root transformation to improve the model's fit to normality. But in this case, the hypothesis that $\lambda = 1$ can't be rejected (p = 0.145), so there's no strong evidence that a transformation is needed in this case. This is consistent with the results of the Q-Q plot in figure 8.9.

Interpreting a log transformation

Log transformations are often used to make highly skewed distributions less skewed. For example, the variable `income` is often right skewed, with more individuals at the lower end of the scale and a few individuals with very high incomes. How do we interpret regression coefficients when the response variable has been log transformed?

We normally interpret the regression coefficient for X as the expected change in Y for a unit change in X. Consider the model $Y = 3 + 0.6X$. We would predict a 0.6 increase in Y for a one-unit increase in X. Similarly, a 10-unit change in X would be associated with a 0.6(10) or 6-point change in Y.

However, if the model is $\log_e(Y) = 3 + 0.6X$, then a one unit change in X multiplies the expected value of Y by $e^{0.6} = 1.06$. Thus, a one-unit increase in X would predict a 6% increase in Y. A 10-unit increase in X would multiply the expected valued of Y by $e^{0.6(10)} = 1.82$. Thus, a 10-unit increase in X would predict an 82% increase in Y.

To learn more about interpreting log transformations in linear regression, see Kenneth Benoit's excellent guide (https://kenbenoit.net/assets/courses/ME104/logmodels2.pdf).

When the assumption of linearity is violated, a transformation of the predictor variables can often help. The `boxTidwell()` function in the `car` package can be used to generate maximum-likelihood estimates of predictor powers that can improve linearity. An example of applying the Box–Tidwell transformations to a model that predicts state murder rates from their population and illiteracy rates follows:

```
> library(car)
> boxTidwell(Murder~Population+Illiteracy,data=states)

            MLE of lambda Score Statistic (z) Pr(>|z|)
Population        0.86939            -0.3228   0.7468
Illiteracy        1.35812             0.6194   0.5357
```

The results suggest trying the transformations $Population^{0.87}$ and $Population^{1.36}$ to achieve greater linearity. But the score tests for `Population` (p = .75) and `Illiteracy` (p = .54) suggest that neither variable needs to be transformed. Again, these results are consistent with the component-plus-residual plots in figure 8.7.

Finally, transformations of the response variable can help in situations of hetero-scedasticity (nonconstant error variance). You saw in listing 8.8 that the `spreadLevel Plot()` function in the `car` package offers a power transformation for improving homoscedasticity. Again, in the case of the `states` example, the constant error-variance assumption is met, and no transformation is necessary.

> ### A caution concerning transformations
>
> There's an old joke in statistics: if you can't prove A, prove B and pretend it was A. (For statisticians, that's pretty funny.) The relevance here is that if you transform your variables, your interpretations must be based on the transformed variables, not the original variables. If the transformation makes sense, such as the log of income or the inverse of distance, the interpretation is easier. But how do you interpret the relationship between the frequency of suicidal ideation and the cube root of depression? If a transformation doesn't make sense, you should avoid it.

8.5.3 Adding or deleting variables

Changing the variables in a model will impact the fit of the model. Sometimes, adding an important variable will correct many of the problems that we've discussed. Deleting a troublesome variable can do the same thing.

Deleting variables is particularly important for dealing with multicollinearity. If your only goal is to make predictions, then multicollinearity isn't a problem. But if you want to make interpretations about individual predictor variables, then you must deal with it. The most common approach is to delete one of the variables involved in the multicollinearity (that is, one of the variables with a VIF > 10). An alternative is to use lasso or ridge regression, variants of multiple regression designed to deal with multi-collinearity situations.

8.5.4 Trying a different approach

As you've just seen, one approach to dealing with multicollinearity is to fit a different type of model (ridge or lasso regression, in this case). If there are outliers and/or influential observations, you can fit a robust regression, model rather than an OLS regression. If you've violated the normality assumption, you can fit a nonparametric regression model. If there's significant nonlinearity, you can try a nonlinear regression model. If you've violated the assumptions of independence of errors, you can fit a model that specifically takes the error structure into account, such as time-series models or multilevel regression models. Finally, you can turn to generalized linear models to fit a wide range of models in situations where the assumptions of OLS regression don't hold.

We'll discuss some of these alternative approaches in chapter 13. The decision of when to try to improve the fit of an OLS regression model and when to try a different approach is complex. It's typically based on knowledge of the subject matter and an assessment of which approach will provide the best result.

Speaking of best results, let's turn now to the problem of deciding which predictor variables to include in a regression model.

8.6 Selecting the "best" regression model

When developing a regression equation, you're implicitly faced with a selection of many possible models. Should you include all the variables under study, or drop ones that don't make a significant contribution to prediction? Should you add polynomial and/or interaction terms to improve the fit? The selection of a final regression model always involves a compromise between predictive accuracy (a model that fits the data as well as possible) and parsimony (a simple and replicable model). All things being equal, if you have two models with approximately equal predictive accuracy, you favor the simpler one. This section describes methods for choosing among competing models. The word "best" is in quotation marks because there's no single criterion you can use to make the decision. The final decision requires judgment on the part of the investigator. (Think of it as job security.)

8.6.1 Comparing models

You can compare the fit of two nested models using the `anova()` function in the base installation. A nested model is one whose terms are completely included in the other model. In the `states` multiple regression model, you found that the regression coefficients for `Income` and `Frost` were nonsignificant. You can test whether a model without these two variables predicts as well as one that includes them (see the following listing).

Listing 8.9 Comparing nested models using the `anova()` function

```
> states <- as.data.frame(state.x77[,c("Murder", "Population",
                         "Illiteracy", "Income", "Frost")])
> fit1 <- lm(Murder ~ Population + Illiteracy + Income + Frost,
          data=states)
> fit2 <- lm(Murder ~ Population + Illiteracy, data=states)
> anova(fit2, fit1)

Analysis of Variance Table

Model 1: Murder ~ Population + Illiteracy
Model 2: Murder ~ Population + Illiteracy + Income + Frost
  Res.Df    RSS  Df   Sum of Sq     F Pr(>F)
1     47 289.246
2     45 289.167   2     0.079 0.0061   0.994
```

Here, model 1 is nested within model 2. The `anova()` function provides a simultaneous test that `Income` and `Frost` add to linear prediction above and beyond `Population` and `Illiteracy`. Because the test is nonsignificant (p = .994), you conclude that they don't add to the linear prediction, and you're justified in dropping them from your model.

The Akaike Information Criterion (AIC) provides another method for comparing models. The index takes into account a model's statistical fit and the number of parameters needed to achieve this fit. Models with smaller AIC values—indicating adequate fit with fewer parameters—are preferred. The criterion is provided by the AIC() function (see the following listing).

Listing 8.10 Comparing models with the AIC

```
> fit1 <- lm(Murder ~ Population + Illiteracy + Income + Frost,
        data=states)
> fit2 <- lm(Murder ~ Population + Illiteracy, data=states)
> AIC(fit1,fit2)

     df      AIC
fit1  6 241.6429
fit2  4 237.6565
```

The AIC values suggest that the model without Income and Frost is the better model. Note that although the ANOVA approach requires nested models, the AIC approach doesn't.

Comparing two models is relatively straightforward, but what do you do when there are 4, or 10, or 100 possible models to consider? That's the topic of the next section.

8.6.2 *Variable selection*

Two popular approaches to selecting a final set of predictor variables from a larger pool of candidate variables are stepwise methods and all-subsets regression.

STEPWISE REGRESSION

In stepwise selection, variables are added to or deleted from a model one at a time until some stopping criterion is reached. For example, in *forward stepwise* regression, you add predictor variables to the model one at a time, stopping when the addition of variables would no longer improve the model. In *backward stepwise* regression, you start with a model that includes all predictor variables, and then you delete them one at a time until removing variables would degrade the quality of the model. In *stepwise stepwise* regression (usually called stepwise to avoid sounding silly), you combine the forward and backward *stepwise* approaches. Variables are entered one at a time, but at each step, the variables in the model are reevaluated, and those that don't contribute to the model are deleted. A predictor variable may be added to, and deleted from, a model several times before a final solution is reached.

The implementation of stepwise regression methods varies by the criteria used to enter or remove variables. The step() function in base R performs stepwise model selection (forward, backward, or stepwise) using an AIC criterion. The next listing applies backward stepwise regression to the multiple regression problem.

Listing 8.11 Backward stepwise regression

```
> states <- as.data.frame(state.x77[,c("Murder", "Population",
                        "Illiteracy", "Income", "Frost")])

> fit <- lm(Murder ~ Population + Illiteracy + Income + Frost,
        data=states)
> step(fit, direction="backward")

Start:  AIC=97.75
Murder ~ Population + Illiteracy + Income + Frost

             Df Sum of Sq    RSS     AIC
- Frost       1     0.021 289.19  95.753
- Income      1     0.057 289.22  95.759
<none>                    289.17  97.749
- Population  1    39.238 328.41 102.111
- Illiteracy  1   144.264 433.43 115.986

Step:  AIC=95.75
Murder ~ Population + Illiteracy + Income

             Df Sum of Sq    RSS     AIC
- Income      1     0.057 289.25  93.763
<none>                    289.19  95.753
- Population  1    43.658 332.85 100.783
- Illiteracy  1   236.196 525.38 123.605

Step:  AIC=93.76
Murder ~ Population + Illiteracy

             Df Sum of Sq    RSS     AIC
<none>                    289.25  93.763
- Population  1    48.517 337.76  99.516
- Illiteracy  1   299.646 588.89 127.311

Call:
lm(formula = Murder ~ Population + Illiteracy, data = states)

Coefficients:
(Intercept)   Population   Illiteracy
  1.6515497    0.0002242    4.0807366
```

You start with all four predictors in the model. For each step, the AIC column provides the model AIC resulting from the deletion of the variable listed in that row. The AIC value for <none> is the model AIC if no variables are removed. In the first step, Frost is removed, decreasing the AIC from 97.75 to 95.75. In the second step, Income is removed, decreasing the AIC to 93.76. Deleting any more variables would increase the AIC, so the process stops.

Stepwise regression is controversial. Although it may find a good model, there's no guarantee that it will find the "best" model because not every possible model is evaluated. An approach that attempts to overcome this limitation is all subsets regression.

ALL SUBSETS REGRESSION

In all subsets regression, every possible model is inspected. The analyst can choose to have all possible results displayed or ask for the nbest models of each subset size (one predictor, two predictors, and so on). For example, if nbest=2, the two best one-predictor models are displayed, followed by the two best two-predictor models, followed by the two best three-predictor models, up to a model with all predictors.

All subsets regression is performed using the regsubsets() function from the leaps package. You can choose the R-squared, Adjusted R-squared, or Mallows Cp statistic as your criterion for reporting "best" models.

As you've seen, R-squared is the amount of variance accounted for in the response variable by the predictors variables. Adjusted R-squared is similar but takes into account the number of parameters in the model. R-squared always increases with the addition of predictors. When the number of predictors is large compared to the sample size, this can lead to significant overfitting. The adjusted R-squared is an attempt to provide a more honest estimate of the population R-squared—one that's less likely to take advantage of chance variation in the data.

In the following listing, we'll apply all subsets regression to the states data. The leaps package presents the results in a plot, but I've found that many people are confused by this graph. The code below presents the same results in the form of a table, which I believe will be easier to understand.

Listing 8.12 All subsets regression

```
library(leaps)
states <- as.data.frame(state.x77[,c("Murder", "Population",
                    "Illiteracy", "Income", "Frost")])

leaps <-regsubsets(Murder ~ Population + Illiteracy + Income +
                Frost, data=states, nbest=4)

subsTable <- function(obj, scale){
  x <- summary(leaps)
  m <- cbind(round(x[[scale]],3), x$which[,-1])
  colnames(m)[1] <- scale
  m[order(m[,1]), ]
}

subsTable(leaps, scale="adjr2)
```

	adjr2	Population	Illiteracy	Income	Frost
1	0.033	0	0	1	0
1	0.100	1	0	0	0
1	0.276	0	0	0	1
2	0.292	1	0	0	1
3	0.309	1	0	1	1
3	0.476	0	1	1	1
2	0.480	0	1	1	0

2	0.481	0	1	0	1
1	0.484	0	1	0	0
4	0.528	1	1	1	1
3	0.539	1	1	1	0
3	0.539	1	1	0	1
2	0.548	1	1	0	0

Each line of the table represents a model. The first column indicates the number of predictors in the model. The second column is the scale (adjusted R-squared in this case) used to describe each model's fit, and rows are sorted by this scale. (Note: Other scale values can be used in place of `adjr2`. See `?regsubsets` for a list of options.) The ones and zeros in the row indicate which variables are included or excluded from the model.

For example, a model based on the single predictor `Income` has an adjusted R-square of 0.033. A model with the predictors `Population`, `Illiteracy`, and `Income` has an adjusted R-square of 0.539. In contrast, a model using the predictors `Population` and `Illiteracy` alone has an adjusted R-square of 0.548. Here you see that a model with fewer predictors actually has a larger adjusted R-square (something that can't happen with an unadjusted R-square). The table suggests that the two-predictor model (`Population` and `Illiteracy`) is the best.

In most instances, all subsets regression is preferable to stepwise regression because more models are considered. But when the number of predictors is large, the procedure can require significant computing time. In general, automated variable-selection methods should be seen as an aid rather than a directing force in model selection. A well-fitting model that doesn't make sense doesn't help you. Ultimately, it's your knowledge of the subject matter that should guide you.

8.7 Taking the analysis further

We'll end our discussion of regression by considering methods for assessing model generalizability and predictor relative importance.

8.7.1 Cross-validation

In the previous section, we examined methods for selecting the variables to include in a regression equation. When description is your primary goal, the selection and interpretation of a regression model signal the end of your labor. But when your goal is prediction, you can justifiably ask, "How well will this equation perform in the real world?"

By definition, regression techniques obtain model parameters that are optimal for a given set of data. In OLS regression, the model parameters are selected to minimize the sum of squared errors of prediction (residuals) and, conversely, maximize the amount of variance accounted for in the response variable (R-squared). Because the equation has been optimized for the given set of data, it's unlikely perform as well with a new set of data.

We began this chapter with an example involving a research physiologist who wanted to predict the number of calories an individual will burn from the duration and intensity of their exercise, age, gender, and BMI. If you fit an OLS regression equation to this data, you'll obtain model parameters that uniquely maximize the

R-squared for this particular set of observations. But our researcher wants to use this equation to predict the calories burned by individuals in general, not only those in the original study. You know that the equation won't perform as well with a new sample of observations, but how much will you lose? Cross-validation is a useful method for evaluating the generalizability of a regression equation.

In cross-validation, a portion of the data is selected as the training sample, and a portion is selected as the holdout sample. A regression equation is developed on the training sample and then applied to the holdout sample. Because the holdout sample wasn't involved in the selection of the model parameters, the performance on this sample is a more accurate estimate of the operating characteristics of the model with new data.

In k-fold cross-validation, the sample is divided into k subsamples. Each of the k subsamples serves as a holdout group, and the combined observations from the remaining $k - 1$ subsamples serve as the training group. The performance for the k prediction equations applied to the k holdout samples is recorded and then averaged. (When k equals n, the total number of observations, this approach is called *jackknifing*.)

You can perform k-fold cross-validation using the `crossval()` function in the `bootstrap` package. The following listing provides a function (called `shrinkage()`) for cross-validating a model's R-square statistic using k-fold cross-validation.

Listing 8.13　Function for k-fold cross-validated R-square

```
shrinkage <- function(fit, k=10, seed=1){
  require(bootstrap)

  theta.fit <- function(x,y){lsfit(x,y)}
  theta.predict <- function(fit,x){cbind(1,x)%*%fit$coef}

  x <- fit$model[,2:ncol(fit$model)]
  y <- fit$model[,1]

  set.seed(seed)
  results <- crossval(x, y, theta.fit, theta.predict, ngroup=k)
  r2    <- cor(y, fit$fitted.values)^2
  r2cv  <- cor(y, results$cv.fit)^2
  cat("Original R-square =", r2, "\n")
  cat(k, "Fold Cross-Validated R-square =", r2cv, "\n")
}
```

Using this listing, you define your functions, create a matrix of predictor and predicted values, get the raw R-squared and residual standard error, and get the cross-validated R-squared and residual standard error. (Chapter 12 covers bootstrapping in detail.)

The `shrinkage()` function is then used to perform a 10-fold cross-validation with the `states` data, using a model with all four predictor variables:

```
> states <- as.data.frame(state.x77[,c("Murder", "Population",
        "Illiteracy", "Income", "Frost")])
> fit <- lm(Murder ~ Population + Income + Illiteracy + Frost, data=states)
> shrinkage(fit)
```

```
Original R-square = 0.567
10 Fold Cross-Validated R-square = 0.356
```

You can see that the R-square based on the sample (0.567) is overly optimistic. A better estimate of the amount of variance in murder rates that this model will account for with new data is the cross-validated R-square (0.356). (Note that observations are assigned to the *k* groups randomly, so a random number seed is provided to make the results reproducible.)

You could use cross-validation in variable selection by choosing a model that demonstrates better generalizability. For example, a model with two predictors (Population and `Illiteracy`) shows less R-square shrinkage than the full model:

```
> fit2 <- lm(Murder ~ Population + Illiteracy,data=states)
> shrinkage(fit2)

Original R-square = 0.567
10 Fold Cross-Validated R-square = 0.515
```

This may make the two-predictor model a more attractive alternative.

All other things being equal, a regression equation that's based on a larger training sample and one that's more representative of the population of interest will cross-validate better. You'll get less R-squared shrinkage and make more accurate predictions.

8.7.2 *Relative importance*

Up to this point in the chapter, we've been asking, "Which variables are useful for predicting the outcome?" But often your real interest is, "Which variables are most important in predicting the outcome?" You implicitly want to rank-order the predictors in terms of relative importance. There may be practical grounds for asking the second question. For example, if you could rank-order leadership practices by their relative importance for organizational success, you could help managers focus on the behaviors they most need to develop.

If predictor variables were uncorrelated, this would be simple. You would rank-order the predictor variables by their correlation with the response variable. In most cases, though, the predictors are correlated with each other, and this complicates the task significantly.

Many attempts have been made to develop a means for assessing the relative importance of predictors. The simplest is to compare standardized regression coefficients, which describe the expected change in the response variable (expressed in standard deviation units) for a standard deviation change in a predictor variable, holding the other predictor variables constant. You can obtain the standardized regression coefficients in R by standardizing each of the variables in your dataset to a mean of 0 and standard deviation of 1 using the `scale()` function, before submitting the dataset to a regression analysis. (Note that because the `scale()` function returns a matrix and the `lm()` function requires a data frame, you convert between the two in an intermediate step.) The code and results for the multiple regression problem are shown here:

```
> states <- as.data.frame(state.x77[,c("Murder", "Population",
                        "Illiteracy", "Income", "Frost")])
> zstates <- as.data.frame(scale(states))
> zfit <- lm(Murder~Population + Income + Illiteracy + Frost, data=zstates)
> coef(zfit)


(Intercept)   Population       Income   Illiteracy         Frost
 -9.406e-17    2.705e-01    1.072e-02     6.840e-01     8.185e-03
```

Here you see that a one-standard-deviation increase in illiteracy rate yields a 0.68 standard deviation increase in murder rate when controlling for population, income, and temperature. Using standardized regression coefficients as your guide, Illiteracy is the most important predictor and Frost is the least.

Many other attempts have been made at quantifying relative importance, which can be thought of as the contribution each predictor makes to R-square, both alone and in combination with other predictors. Several possible approaches to relative importance are captured in the relaimpo package written by Ulrike Grömping (http://mng.bz/KDYF).

A new method called *relative weights* shows significant promise. The method closely approximates the average increase in R-square obtained by adding a predictor variable across all possible submodels (Johnson, 2004; Johnson and LeBreton, 2004; LeBreton and Tonidandel, 2008). A function for generating relative weights is provided in the next listing.

Listing 8.14   relweights() for calculating relative importance of predictors

```
relweights <- function(fit,...){
  R <- cor(fit$model)
  nvar <- ncol(R)
  rxx <- R[2:nvar, 2:nvar]
  rxy <- R[2:nvar, 1]
  svd <- eigen(rxx)
  evec <- svd$vectors
  ev <- svd$values
  delta <- diag(sqrt(ev))
  lambda <- evec %*% delta %*% t(evec)
  lambdasq <- lambda ^ 2
  beta <- solve(lambda) %*% rxy
  rsquare <- colSums(beta ^ 2)
  rawwgt <- lambdasq %*% beta ^ 2
  import <- (rawwgt / rsquare) * 100
  import <- as.data.frame(import)
  row.names(import) <- names(fit$model[2:nvar])
  names(import) <- "Weights"
  import <- import[order(import),1, drop=FALSE]
  dotchart(import$Weights, labels=row.names(import),
    xlab="% of R-Square", pch=19,
```

```
        main="Relative Importance of Predictor Variables",
        sub=paste("Total R-Square=", round(rsquare, digits=3)),
        ...)
return(import)
}
```

NOTE The code in listing 8.16 is adapted from an SPSS program Dr. Johnson has generously provided. See Johnson, 2000, for an explanation of how the relative weights are derived.

In the next listing, the `relweights()` function is applied to the `states` data with murder rate predicted by the population, illiteracy, income, and temperature.

```
> states <- as.data.frame(state.x77[,c("Murder", "Population",
        "Illiteracy", "Income", "Frost")])
> fit <- lm(Murder ~ Population + Illiteracy + Income + Frost, data=states)
> relweights(fit, col="blue")

            Weights
Income         5.49
Population    14.72
Frost         20.79
Illiteracy    59.00
```

You can see from the resulting plot (figure 8.13) that the total amount of variance accounted for by the model (R-square = 0.567) has been divided among the predictor variables. `Illiteracy` accounts for 59% of the R-square, `Frost` accounts for 20.79%, and so forth. Based on the method of relative weights, `Illiteracy` has the greatest relative importance, followed by `Frost`, `Population`, and `Income`, in that order.

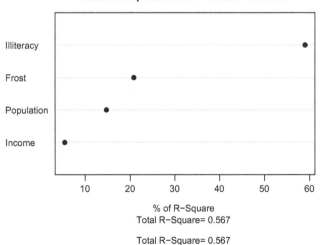

Relative Importance of Predictor Variables

% of R-Square
Total R-Square= 0.567

Total R-Square= 0.567

Figure 8.13 Dot chart of relative weights for the `states` multiple regression problem. Larger weights indicate relatively more important predictors. For example, `Illiteracy` accounts for 59% of the total explained variance (0.567), whereas `Income` only accounts for 5.49%. Thus, `Illiteracy` has greater relative importance than `Income` in this model.

Relative importance measures (and, in particular, the method of relative weights) have wide applicability. They come much closer to our intuitive conception of relative importance than standardized regression coefficients do, and I expect to see their use increase dramatically in coming years.

Summary

- Regression analysis is a highly interactive and iterative approach that involves fitting models, assessing their fit to statistical assumptions, modifying both the data and the models, and refitting to arrive at a final result.
- Regression diagnostics are used to assess the data's fit to statistical assumptions and select methods for modifying the model or the data to meet these assumptions more closely.
- Numerous methods are available for selecting the variables to include in a final regression model, including the use of significance tests, fit statistics, and automated solutions such as stepwise and all subsets regression.
- Cross-validation can be used to evaluate a predictive model's likely performance on new samples of data.
- The method of relative weights can be used to address the thorny problem of variable importance: identifying which variables are the most important for predicting an outcome.

Analysis of variance

This chapter covers
- Using R to model basic experimental designs
- Fitting and interpreting ANOVA type models
- Evaluating model assumptions

In chapter 8, we looked at regression models for predicting a quantitative response variable from quantitative predictor variables, but there's no reason why we couldn't have included nominal or ordinal factors as predictors as well. When factors are included as explanatory variables, our focus usually shifts from prediction to understanding group differences, and the methodology is referred to as *analysis of variance (ANOVA)*. ANOVA methodology is used to analyze a wide variety of experimental and quasi-experimental designs. This chapter provides an overview of R functions for analyzing common research designs.

First, we'll look at design terminology, followed by a general discussion of R's approach to fitting ANOVA models. Then, we'll explore several examples that illustrate the analysis of common designs. Along the way, you'll treat anxiety disorders, lower blood cholesterol levels, help pregnant mice have fat babies, ensure that pigs grow long in the tooth, facilitate breathing in plants, and learn which grocery shelves to avoid.

In addition to the base installation, you'll be using the `car`, `rrcov`, `multcomp`, `effects`, `MASS`, `dplyr`, `ggplot2`, and `mvoutlier` packages in the examples. Be sure to install them before trying out the sample code.

9.1 A crash course on terminology

Experimental design in general, and analysis of variance in particular, have their own language. Before discussing the analysis of these designs, we'll quickly review some important terms. We'll use a series of increasingly complex study designs to introduce the most significant concepts.

Say you're interested in studying the treatment of anxiety. Two popular therapies for anxiety are cognitive behavior therapy (CBT) and eye-movement desensitization and reprocessing (EMDR). You recruit 10 anxious individuals and randomly assign half of them to receive five weeks of CBT and half to receive five weeks of EMDR. At the conclusion of therapy, each patient is asked to complete the State-Trait Anxiety Inventory (STAI), a self-report measure of anxiety. Figure 9.1A outlines the design.

(A) One-way between-groups ANOVA

Treatment	
CBT	EMDR
s1	s6
s2	s7
s3	s8
s4	s9
s5	s10

(B) One-way within-groups ANOVA

Patient	Time	
	5 weeks	6 months
s1		
s2		
s3		
s4		
s5		
s6		
s7		
s8		
s9		
s10		

		Patient	Time	
			5 weeks	6 months
Therapy	CBT	s1		
		s2		
		s3		
		s4		
		s5		
	EMDR	s6		
		s7		
		s8		
		s9		
		s10		

(C) Two-way factorial ANOVA with one between-groups and one within-groups factor

Figure 9.1 Three analysis of variance (ANOVA) designs

In this design, Treatment is a *between-groups* factor with two levels (CBT, EMDR). It's called a between-groups factor because patients are assigned to one and only one group. No patient receives both CBT and EMDR. The *s* characters represent the subjects (patients). STAI is the *dependent variable*, and Treatment is the *independent variable*. Because there is an equal number of observations in each treatment condition, you have a *balanced design*. When the sample sizes are unequal across the cells of a design, you have an *unbalanced design*.

The statistical design in figure 9.1A is called a *one-way ANOVA* because there's a single classification variable. Specifically, it's a one-way between-groups ANOVA. Effects in ANOVA designs are primarily evaluated through F-tests. If the F-test for Treatment is significant, you can conclude that the mean STAI scores for two therapies differed after five weeks of treatment.

If you were interested in the effect of CBT on anxiety over time, you could place all 10 patients in the CBT group and assess them at the conclusion of therapy and again six months later. Figure 9.1B shows this design.

Time is a *within-groups* factor with two levels (five weeks, six months). It's called a within-groups factor because each patient is measured under both levels. The statistical design is a *one-way within-groups ANOVA*. Because each subject is measured more than once, the design is also called a *repeated measures ANOVA*. If the F-test for Time is significant, you can conclude that patients' mean STAI scores changed between five weeks and six months.

If you were interested in both treatment differences *and* change over time, you could combine the first two study designs and randomly assign five patients to CBT and five patients to EMDR and assess their STAI results at the end of therapy (five weeks) and at six months (see figure 9.1C).

By including both Therapy and Time as factors, you're able to examine the impact of Therapy (averaged across time), Time (averaged across therapy type), and the interaction of Therapy and Time. The first two are called the *main effects*, whereas the interaction is (not surprisingly) called an *interaction effect*.

When you cross two or more factors, as is done here, you have a *factorial ANOVA* design. Crossing two factors produces a two-way ANOVA, crossing three factors produces a three-way ANOVA, and so forth. When a factorial design includes both between-groups and within-groups factors, it's also called a *mixed-model ANOVA*. The current design is a two-way mixed-model factorial ANOVA (phew!).

In this case, you'll have three F-tests: one for Therapy, one for Time, and one for the Therapy × Time interaction. A significant result for Therapy indicates that CBT and EMDR differ in their impact on anxiety. A significant result for Time indicates that anxiety changed from week five to the six-month follow-up. A significant Therapy × Time interaction indicates that the two treatments for anxiety had a differential impact over time (that is, the change in anxiety from five weeks to six months was different for the two treatments).

Now let's extend the design a bit. It's known that depression can have an impact on therapy, and that depression and anxiety often co-occur. Even though subjects were randomly assigned to treatment conditions, it's possible that the two therapy groups differed in patient depression levels at the initiation of the study. Any post-therapy differences might then be due to the preexisting depression differences and not to your experimental manipulation. Because depression could also explain the group differences on the dependent variable, it's a *confounding* factor. And because you're not interested in depression, it's called a *nuisance* variable.

If you recorded depression levels using a self-report depression measure such as the Beck Depression Inventory (BDI) when patients were recruited, you could statistically adjust for any treatment group differences in depression before assessing the impact of therapy type. In this case, BDI would be called a *covariate*, and the design would be called an *analysis of covariance (ANCOVA)*.

Finally, you've recorded a single dependent variable in this study (the STAI). You could increase the validity of this study by including additional measures of anxiety (such as family ratings, therapist ratings, and a measure assessing the impact of anxiety on their daily functioning). When there are more than one dependent variable, the design is called a *multivariate analysis of variance (MANOVA)*. If there are covariates present, it's called a *multivariate analysis of covariance (MANCOVA)*.

Now that you have the basic terminology under your belt, you're ready to amaze your friends, dazzle new acquaintances, and learn how to fit ANOVA/ANCOVA/MANOVA models with R.

9.2   *Fitting ANOVA models*

Although ANOVA and regression methodologies developed separately, functionally they're both special cases of the general linear model. You could analyze ANOVA models using the same `lm()` function used for regression in chapter 8. But you'll primarily use the `aov()` function in this chapter. The results of `lm()` and `aov()` are equivalent, but the `aov()` function presents these results in a format that's more familiar to ANOVA methodologists. For completeness, I'll provide an example using `lm()` at the end of this chapter.

9.2.1   *The aov() function*

The syntax of the `aov()` function is `aov(formula, data=dataframe)`. Table 9.1 describes special symbols that can be used in the formulas. In this table, `y` is the dependent variable and the letters `A`, `B`, and `C` represent factors.

Table 9.1   Special symbols used in R formulas

Symbol	Usage
~	Separates response variables on the left from the explanatory variables on the right. For example, a prediction of `y` from `A`, `B`, and `C` would be coded `y ~ A + B + C`
:	Denotes an interaction between variables. A prediction of `y` from `A`, `B`, and the interaction between `A` and `B` would be coded `y ~ A + B + A:B`

Table 9.1 Special symbols used in R formulas (*continued*)

Symbol	Usage
*	Denotes the complete crossing of variables. The code `y ~ A*B*C` expands to `y ~ A + B + C + A:B + A:C + B:C + A:B:C`
^	Denotes crossing to a specified degree. The code `y ~ (A+B+C)^2` expands to `y ~ A + B + C + A:B + A:C + A:B`
.	Denotes all remaining variables. The code `y ~ .` expands to `y ~ A + B + C`

Table 9.2 provides formulas for several common research designs. In this table, lowercase letters are quantitative variables, uppercase letters are grouping factors, and `Subject` is a unique identifier variable for subjects.

Table 9.2 Formulas for common research designs

Design	Formula
One-way ANOVA	`y ~ A`
One-way ANCOVA with one covariate	`y ~ x + A`
Two-way factorial ANOVA	`y ~ A * B`
Two-way factorial ANCOVA with two covariates	`y ~ x1 + x2 + A * B`
Randomized block	`y ~ B + A` (where B is a blocking factor)
One-way within-groups ANOVA	`y ~ A + Error(Subject/A)`
Repeated measures ANOVA with one within-groups factor (`W`) and one between-groups factor (`B`)	`y ~ B * W + Error(Subject/W)`

We'll explore in-depth examples of several of these designs later in this chapter.

9.2.2 *The order of formula terms*

The order in which the effects appear in a formula matters when (a) there's more than one factor and the design is unbalanced or (b) covariates are present. When either of these two conditions is present, the variables on the right side of the equation will be correlated with each other. In this case, there's no unambiguous way to divide up their impact on the dependent variable. For example, in a two-way ANOVA with unequal numbers of observations in the treatment combinations, the model `y ~ A*B` *will not* produce the same results as the model `y ~ B*A`.

By default, R employs the Type I (sequential) approach to calculating ANOVA effects (see the sidebar "Order counts!"). The first model can be written as `y ~ A + B + A:B`. The resulting R ANOVA table will assess

- The impact of `A` on `y`
- The impact of `B` on `y`, controlling for `A`
- The interaction of `A` and `B`, controlling for the `A` and `B` main effects

Order counts!

When independent variables are correlated with each other or with covariates, there's no unambiguous method for assessing the independent contributions of these variables to the dependent variable. Consider an unbalanced two-way factorial design with factors A and B and dependent variable y. There are three effects in this design: the A and B main effects and the A × B interaction. Assuming that you're modeling the data using the formula Y ~ A + B + A:B, there are three typical approaches for partitioning the variance in y among the effects on the right side of this equation.

TYPE I (SEQUENTIAL)

Effects are adjusted for those that appear earlier in the formula. A is unadjusted. B is adjusted for A. The A:B interaction is adjusted for A and B.

TYPE II (HIERARCHICAL)

Effects are adjusted for other effects at the same or lower level. A is adjusted for B. B is adjusted for A. The A:B interaction is adjusted for both A and B.

TYPE III (MARGINAL)

Each effect is adjusted for every other effect in the model. A is adjusted for B and A:B. B is adjusted for A and A:B. The A:B interaction is adjusted for A and B.

R employs the Type I approach by default. Other programs such as SAS and SPSS employ the Type III approach by default.

The greater the imbalance in sample sizes, the greater the impact that the order of the terms will have on the results. In general, more fundamental effects should be listed earlier in the formula. In particular, covariates should be listed first, followed by main effects, followed by two-way interactions, followed by three-way interactions, and so on. For main effects, more fundamental variables should be listed first. Thus, gender would be listed before treatment. Here's the bottom line: when the research design isn't orthogonal (that is, when the factors and/or covariates are correlated), be careful when specifying the order of effects.

Before moving on to specific examples, note that the Anova() function in the car package (not to be confused with the standard anova() function) provides the option of using the Type II or Type III approach, rather than the Type I approach used by the aov() function. You may want to use the Anova() function if you're concerned about matching your results to those provided by other packages such as SAS and SPSS. See help(Anova, package="car") for details.

9.3 *One-way ANOVA*

In a one-way ANOVA, you're interested in comparing the dependent variable means of two or more groups defined by a categorical grouping factor. This example comes from the cholesterol dataset in the multcomp package, taken from Westfall, Tobias, Rom, and Hochberg (1999). Fifty patients received one of five cholesterol-reducing drug regimens (trt). Three of the treatment conditions involved the same drug administered as 20 mg once per day (1time), 10 mg twice per day (2times), or 5 mg four times per day (4times). The two remaining conditions (drugD and drugE) represented competing drugs. Which drug regimen produced the greatest cholesterol reduction (response)? The following listing provides the analysis.

Listing 9.1 One-way ANOVA

```
> library(dplyr)
> data(cholesterol, package="multcomp")
> plotdata <- cholesterol %>%
    group_by(trt) %>%
    summarize(n = n(),
              mean = mean(response),
              sd = sd(response),
              ci = qt(0.975, df = n - 1) * sd / sqrt(n))
> plotdata

  trt       n   mean    sd    ci
  <fct>  <int> <dbl> <dbl> <dbl>
1 1time     10  5.78  2.88  2.06
2 2times    10  9.22  3.48  2.49
3 4times    10 12.4   2.92  2.09
4 drugD     10 15.4   3.45  2.47
5 drugE     10 20.9   3.35  2.39

> fit <- aov(response ~ trt, data=cholesterol)

> summary(fit)

            Df Sum Sq  Mean Sq  F value     Pr(>F)
trt          4   1351      338     32.4   9.8e-13  ***
Residuals   45    469       10
---
Signif. codes:  0 '***' 0.001 '**' 0.01 '*' 0.05 '.' 0.1 ' ' 1

> library(ggplot2)
> ggplot(plotdata,
      aes(x = trt, y = mean, group = 1)) +
    geom_point(size = 3, color="red") +
    geom_line(linetype="dashed", color="darkgrey") +
    geom_errorbar(aes(ymin = mean - ci,
                      ymax = mean + ci),
                  width = .1) +
    theme_bw() +
    labs(x="Treatment",
        y="Response",
        title="Mean Plot with 95% Confidence Interval")
```

① Group sample sizes, means, standard deviations, and 95% confidence intervals

② Tests for group differences (ANOVA)

③ Plots group means and confidence intervals

Looking at the output, you can see that 10 patients received each of the drug regimens **①**. From the means, it appears that drugE produced the greatest cholesterol reduction, whereas 1time produced the least **②**. Standard deviations were relatively constant across the five groups, ranging from 2.88 to 3.48. We assume that each treatment group in our study is a sample from a larger potential population of patients who could receive the treatment. For each treatment, the sample mean +/− ci gives us an interval that we are 95% confident includes the true population means. The ANOVA F-test for treatment (`trt`) is significant (p < .0001), providing evidence that the five treatments aren't all equally effective ❷.

The `ggplot2` functions are used to create a graph of group means and their confidence intervals ❸ A plot of the treatment means, with 95% confidence limits, is provided in figure 9.2 and allows you to clearly see these treatment differences.

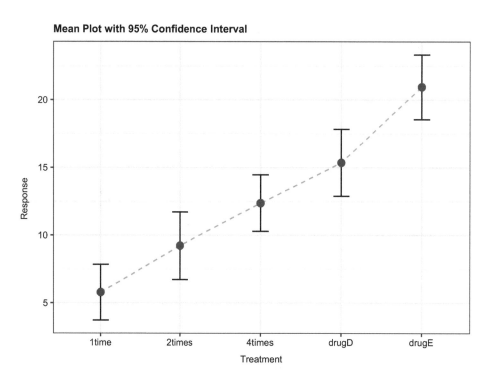

Figure 9.2   Treatment group means with 95% confidence intervals for five cholesterol-reducing drug regimens

By including the confidence intervals in figure 9.2, we show the degree of certainty (or uncertainty) in our estimates of the population means.

9.3.1   *Multiple comparisons*

The ANOVA F-test for treatment tells you that the five drug regimens aren't equally effective, but it doesn't tell you *which* treatments differ from one another. You can use a multiple comparison procedure to answer this question. For example, the

TukeyHSD() function provides a test of all pairwise differences between group means, as shown in the next listing.

Listing 9.2 Tukey HSD pairwise group comparisons

```
> pairwise <- TukeyHSD(fit)          ◄──┐  Calculates pairwise
> pairwise                              ❶  comparisons

Fit: aov(formula = response ~ trt)

$trt
                diff    lwr    upr p adj
2times-1time    3.44 -0.658   7.54 0.138
4times-1time    6.59  2.492 10.69 0.000
drugD-1time     9.58  5.478 13.68 0.000
drugE-1time    15.17 11.064 19.27 0.000
4times-2times   3.15 -0.951   7.25 0.205
drugD-2times    6.14  2.035 10.24 0.001
drugE-2times   11.72  7.621 15.82 0.000
drugD-4times    2.99 -1.115   7.09 0.251
drugE-4times    8.57  4.471 12.67 0.000
drugE-drugD     5.59  1.485   9.69 0.003

> plotdata <- as.data.frame(pairwise[[1]])      ❷  Creates a dataset
> plotdata$conditions <- row.names(plotdata)        of the results

> library(ggplot2)
> ggplot(data=plotdata, aes(x=conditions, y=diff)) +
   geom_point(size=3, color="red") +
   geom_errorbar(aes(ymin=lwr, ymax=upr, width=.2)) +
   geom_hline(yintercept=0, color="red", linetype="dashed") +    ❸  Plots the
     labs(y="Difference in mean levels", x="",                       results
       title="95% family-wise confidence level") +
   theme_bw() +
   coord_flip()
```

For example, the mean cholesterol reductions for 1time and 2times aren't significantly different from each other (p = 0.138), whereas the difference between 1time and 4times is significantly different (p < .001).

Figure 9.3 plots the pairwise comparisons. In this graph, confidence intervals that include 0 indicate treatments that aren't significantly different (p > 0.5). Here, we can see that the largest mean difference is between drugE and 1time and that the difference is significant (the confidence interval does not include 0).

Before moving on, I should point out that we could have created the graphs in figure 9.3 using base graphics. In this case, the code would simply be plot(pairwise). The advantage of the ggplot2 approach is that it creates a more attractive plot and allows you to fully customize the graph to meet your needs.

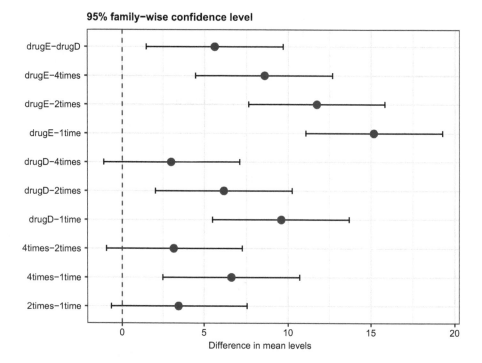

Figure 9.3   Plot of Tukey HSD pairwise mean comparisons

The glht() function in the multcomp package provides a much more comprehensive set of methods for multiple mean comparisons that you can use for both linear models (such as those described in this chapter) and generalized linear models (covered in chapter 13). The following code reproduces the Tukey HSD test, along with a different graphical representation of the results (figure 9.4):

```
> tuk <- glht(fit, linfct=mcp(trt="Tukey"))
> summary(tuk)

        Simultaneous Tests for General Linear Hypotheses

Multiple Comparisons of Means: Tukey Contrasts


Fit: aov(formula = response ~ trt, data = cholesterol)

Linear Hypotheses:
                    Estimate Std. Error t value Pr(>|t|)
2times - 1time == 0    3.443      1.443   2.385  0.13812
4times - 1time == 0    6.593      1.443   4.568  < 0.001 ***
drugD  - 1time == 0    9.579      1.443   6.637  < 0.001 ***
drugE  - 1time == 0   15.166      1.443  10.507  < 0.001 ***
4times - 2times == 0   3.150      1.443   2.182  0.20504
drugD  - 2times == 0   6.136      1.443   4.251  < 0.001 ***
```

```
drugE - 2times == 0     11.723      1.443   8.122  < 0.001 ***
drugD - 4times == 0      2.986      1.443   2.069  0.25120
drugE - 4times == 0      8.573      1.443   5.939  < 0.001 ***
drugE - drugD == 0       5.586      1.443   3.870  0.00308 **
---
Signif. codes:  0 '***' 0.001 '**' 0.01 '*' 0.05 '.' 0.1 ' ' 1
(Adjusted p values reported -- single-step method)

> labels1 <- cld(tuk, level=.05)$mcletters$Letters
> labels2 <- paste(names(labels1), "\n", labels1)
> ggplot(data=fit$model, aes(x=trt, y=response)) +
    scale_x_discrete(breaks=names(labels1), labels=labels2) +
    geom_boxplot(fill="lightgrey") +
    theme_bw() +
    labs(x="Treatment",
         title="Distribution of Response Scores by Treatment",
         subtitle="Groups without overlapping letters differ significantly
         (p < .05)")
```

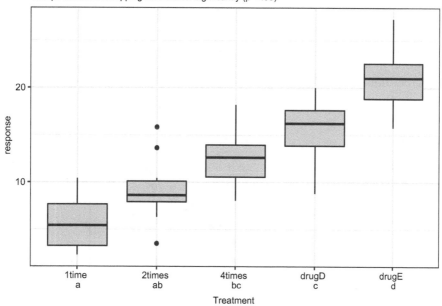

Figure 9.4   Tukey HSD tests provided by the `multcomp` package

The `level` option in the `cld()` function provides the significance level to use (0.05, or 95% confidence in this case).

Groups (represented by box plots) that have the same letter don't have significantly different means. You can see that `1time` and `2times` aren't significantly different (they both have the letter a) and that `2times` and `4times` aren't significantly different (they both have the letter b), but `1time` and `4times` are different (they don't share a letter). Personally, I find figure 9.4 easier to read than figure 9.3. It also has the advantage of providing information on the distribution of scores within each group.

From these results, you can see that taking the cholesterol-lowering drug in 5-mg doses four times a day was better than taking a 20-mg dose once per day. The competitor `drugD` wasn't superior to this four-times-per-day regimen. But competitor `drugE` was superior to both `drugD` and all three dosage strategies for the focus drug.

Multiple comparisons methodology is a complex and rapidly changing area of study. To learn more, see Bretz, Hothorn, and Westfall (2010).

9.3.2 *Assessing test assumptions*

As you saw in the previous chapter, confidence in results depends on the degree to which your data satisfies the assumptions underlying the statistical tests. In a one-way ANOVA, the dependent variable is assumed to be normally distributed and have equal variance in each group. You can use a Q-Q plot to assess the normality assumption:

```
> library(car)
> fit <- aov(response ~ trt, data=cholesterol)
> qqPlot(fit, simulate=TRUE, main="Q-Q Plot")
```

Figure 9.5 provides the graph. By default, the two observations with the highest standardized residuals are identified by data frame row number. The data falls within the 95% confidence envelope, suggesting that the normality assumption has been met fairly well.

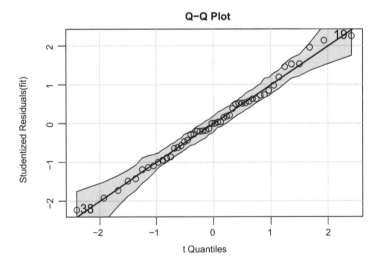

Figure 9.5 Test of the normality for the studentized residuals. Residuals are the actual minus the predicted outcomes, and studentized residuals are these residuals divided by estimates of their standard deviations. If the studentized residuals are normally distributed, they should cluster around the line.

R provides several tests for the equality (homogeneity) of variances. For example, you can perform Bartlett's test with this code:

```
> bartlett.test(response ~ trt, data=cholesterol)

        Bartlett test of homogeneity of variances

data:  response by trt
Bartlett's K-squared = 0.5797, df = 4, p-value = 0.9653
```

Bartlett's test indicates that the variances in the five groups don't differ significantly ($p = 0.97$). Other possible tests include the Fligner–Killeen test (provided by the `fligner.test()` function) and the Brown–Forsythe test (provided by the `hov()` function in the HH package). Although not shown, the other two tests reach the same conclusion.

Finally, analysis of variance methodologies can be sensitive to the presence of outliers. You can test for outliers using the `outlierTest()` function in the car package:

```
> library(car)
> outlierTest(fit)

No Studentized residuals with Bonferroni  p < 0.05
Largest |rstudent|:
   rstudent unadjusted p-value Bonferroni p
19 2.251149          0.029422           NA
```

From the output, you can see that there's no indication of outliers in the cholesterol data (NA occurs when $p > 1$). Taking the Q-Q plot, Bartlett's test, and outlier test together, the data appear to fit the ANOVA model quite well. This, in turn, adds to your confidence in the results.

9.4 One-way ANCOVA

A one-way analysis of covariance (ANCOVA) extends the one-way ANOVA to include one or more quantitative covariates. This example comes from the `litter` dataset in the `multcomp` package (see Westfall et al., 1999). Pregnant mice were divided into four treatment groups; each group received a different dose of a drug (0, 5, 50, or 500). The mean post-birth weight for each litter was the dependent variable, and gestation time was included as a covariate. The following listing gives the analysis.

Listing 9.3   One-way ANCOVA

```
> library(multcomp)
> library(dplyr)
> litter %>%
    group_by(dose) %>%
    summarise(n=n(), mean=mean(gesttime), sd=sd(gesttime))

  dose      n  mean     sd
  <fct> <int> <dbl>  <dbl>
1 0        20  22.1  0.438
2 5        19  22.2  0.451
3 50       18  21.9  0.404
4 500      17  22.2  0.431
```

```
> fit <- aov(weight ~ gesttime + dose, data=litter)
> summary(fit)
            Df Sum Sq Mean Sq F value  Pr(>F)
gesttime     1  134.3  134.30   8.049 0.00597 **
dose         3  137.1   45.71   2.739 0.04988 *
Residuals   69 1151.3   16.69
---
Signif. codes:  0 '***' 0.001 '**' 0.01 '*' 0.05 '.' 0.1 ' ' 1
```

From the summarise() function, you can see that there is an unequal number of litters at each dosage level, with 20 litters at zero dosage (no drug) and 17 litters at dosage 500. Based on the group means, the *no-drug* group had the highest mean litter weight (32.3). The ANCOVA F-tests indicate that (a) gestation time was related to birth weight, and (b) drug dosage was related to birth weight after controlling for gestation time. The mean birth weight isn't the same for each of the drug dosages after controlling for gestation time.

Because you're using a covariate, you may want to obtain adjusted group means—that is, the group means obtained after partialing out the effects of the covariate. You can use the effect() function in the effects library to calculate adjusted means:

```
> library(effects)
> effect("dose", fit)

 dose effect
dose
   0    5   50  500
32.4 28.9 30.6 29.3
```

These are the mean litter weights for each treatment dose after statistically adjusting for initial differences in gestation time. In this case, the adjusted means differ quite a bit from the unadjusted means produced by the summarise() function. The effects package provides a powerful method of obtaining adjusted means for complex research designs and presenting them visually. See the package documentation on CRAN for more details.

As with the one-way ANOVA example in the last section, the F-test for dose indicates that the treatments don't have the same mean birth weight, but it doesn't tell you which means differ from one another. Again, you can use the multiple comparison procedures provided by the multcomp package to compute all pairwise mean comparisons. Additionally, the multcomp package can be used to test specific user-defined hypotheses about the means.

Suppose you're interested in whether the no-drug condition differs from the three-drug condition. The code in the following listing can be used to test this hypothesis.

Listing 9.4   Multiple comparisons employing user-supplied contrasts

```
> library(multcomp)
> contrast <- rbind("no drug vs. drug" = c(3, -1, -1, -1))
> summary(glht(fit, linfct=mcp(dose=contrast)))
```

```
Multiple Comparisons of Means: User-defined Contrasts

Fit: aov(formula = weight ~ gesttime + dose)

Linear Hypotheses:
                      Estimate Std. Error t value Pr(>|t|)
no drug vs. drug == 0    8.284      3.209   2.581   0.0120 *
---
Signif. codes:  0 '***' 0.001 '**' 0.01 '*' 0.05 '.' 0.1 ' ' 1
```

The contrast `c(3, -1, -1, -1)` specifies a comparison of the first group with the average of the other three. Specifically, the hypothesis being tested is

$$3 \times \mu_0 - 1 \times \mu_5 - 1 \times \mu_{50} - 1 \times \mu_{500} = 0$$

or

$$\mu_0 = \frac{\mu_5 + \mu_{50} + \mu_{500}}{3}$$

where μ_n is the mean litter weight for dose n. The hypothesis is tested with a t-statistic (2.581 in this case), which is significant at the $p < .05$ level. Therefore, you can conclude that the no-drug group has a higher birth weight than the drug conditions. Other contrasts can be added to the `rbind()` function (see `help(glht)` for details).

9.4.1 Assessing test assumptions

ANCOVA designs make the same normality and homogeneity of variance assumptions described for ANOVA designs, and you can test these assumptions using the same procedures described in section 9.3.2. In addition, standard ANCOVA designs assume homogeneity of regression slopes. In this case, it's assumed that the regression slope for predicting birth weight from gestation time is the same in each of the four treatment groups. A test for the homogeneity of regression slopes can be obtained by including a gestation × dose interaction term in your ANCOVA model. A significant interaction would imply that the relationship between gestation and birth weight depends on the level of the dose variable. The code and results are provided in the following listing.

Listing 9.5 Testing for homogeneity of regression slopes

```
> library(multcomp)
> fit2 <- aov(weight ~ gesttime*dose, data=litter)
> summary(fit2)
              Df Sum Sq Mean Sq F value Pr(>F)
gesttime       1    134     134    8.29 0.0054 **
dose           3    137      46    2.82 0.0456 *
gesttime:dose  3     82      27    1.68 0.1789
Residuals     66   1069      16
---
Signif. codes:  0 '***' 0.001 '**' 0.01 '*' 0.05 '.' 0.1 ' ' 1
```

The interaction is nonsignificant, supporting the assumption of equality of slopes. If the assumption is untenable, you could try transforming the covariate or dependent variable, using a model that accounts for separate slopes, or employing a nonparametric ANCOVA method that doesn't require homogeneity of regression slopes. See the `sm.ancova()` function in the `sm` package for an example of the latter.

9.4.2 Visualizing the results

We can use `ggplot2` to visualize of the relationship between the dependent variable, the covariate, and the factor. For example,

```
pred <- predict(fit)
library(ggplot2)
ggplot(data = cbind(litter, pred),
        aes(gesttime, weight)) + geom_point() +
    facet_wrap(~ dose, nrow=1) + geom_line(aes(y=pred)) +
    labs(title="ANCOVA for weight by gesttime and dose") +
    theme_bw() +
    theme(axis.text.x = element_text(angle=45, hjust=1),
        legend.position="none")
```

produces the plot shown in figure 9.6.

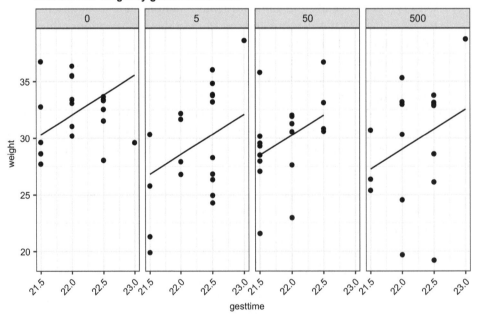

Figure 9.6 Plot of the relationship between gestation time and birth weight for each of four drug treatment groups

Here you can see that the regression lines for predicting birth weight from gestation time are parallel in each group but have different intercepts. As gestation time increases, birth weight increases. Additionally, you can see that the zero-dose group has the largest intercept, and the five-dose group has the lowest intercept. The lines are parallel because they've been specified to be. If you used the code

```
ggplot(data = litter, aes(gesttime, weight)) +
    geom_point() + geom_smooth(method="lm", se=FALSE) +
    facet_wrap(~ dose, nrow=1)
```

instead, you'd generate a plot that allows both the slopes and intercepts to vary by group. This approach is useful for visualizing the case where the homogeneity of regression slopes doesn't hold.

9.5 *Two-way factorial ANOVA*

In a two-way factorial ANOVA, subjects are assigned to groups that are formed from the cross-classification of two factors. This example uses the ToothGrowth dataset in the base installation to demonstrate a two-way between-groups ANOVA. Sixty guinea pigs are randomly assigned to receive one of three levels of ascorbic acid (0.5, 1, or 2 mg) and one of two delivery methods (orange juice or vitamin C), under the restriction that each treatment combination has 10 guinea pigs. The dependent variable is tooth length. The following listing shows the code for the analysis.

Listing 9.6 Two-way ANOVA

```
> library(dplyr)
> data(ToothGrowth)                                    ❶ Prepares
> ToothGrowth$dose <- factor(ToothGrowth$dose)            data
> stats <- ToothGrowth %>%
    group_by(supp, dose) %>%                           ❷ Calculates
    summarise(n=n(), mean=mean(len), sd=sd(len),         summary statistics
            ci = qt(0.975, df = n - 1) * sd / sqrt(n))
> stats

# A tibble: 6 x 6
# Groups:   supp [2]
  supp  dose      n  mean    sd    ci
  <fct> <fct> <int> <dbl> <dbl> <dbl>
1 OJ    0.5      10 13.2   4.46  3.19
2 OJ    1        10 22.7   3.91  2.80
3 OJ    2        10 26.1   2.66  1.90
4 VC    0.5      10  7.98  2.75  1.96
5 VC    1        10 16.8   2.52  1.80
6 VC    2        10 26.1   4.80  3.43
                                                       ❸ Fits two-way
> fit <- aov(len ~ supp*dose, data=ToothGrowth)          ANOVA model
> summary(fit)

            Df Sum Sq Mean Sq F value   Pr(>F)
supp         1  205.4   205.4  15.572 0.000231 ***
```

```
dose         2 2426.4  1213.2  92.000  < 2e-16 ***
supp:dose    2  108.3    54.2   4.107 0.021860 *
Residuals   54  712.1    13.2
---
Signif. codes:  0 '***' 0.001 '**' 0.01 '*' 0.05 '.' 0.1 ' ' 1
```

First, the dose variable is converted to a factor so the aov() function will treat it as a grouping variable rather than a numeric covariate ❶. Next, summary statistics (*n*, mean, standard deviation, and confidence interval for the mean) are calculated for each combination of treatments ❷. The sample sizes indicate that you have a balanced design (equal sample sizes in each cell of the design. The two-way ANOVA model is fitted to the data ❸, and the summary() function indicates that both main effects (supp and dose) and the interaction between these factors are significant.

You can visualize the results in several ways, including the interaction.plot() function in base R, the plotmeans() function in the gplots package, and the interaction2wt() function in the HH package. In the code following figure 9.7, we'll use ggplot2 to plot the means and 95% confidence intervals for the means for this two-way ANOVA. One advantage of using ggplot2 is that we can customize the graph to suit our research and aesthetic needs. Figure 9.7. presents the resulting graph.

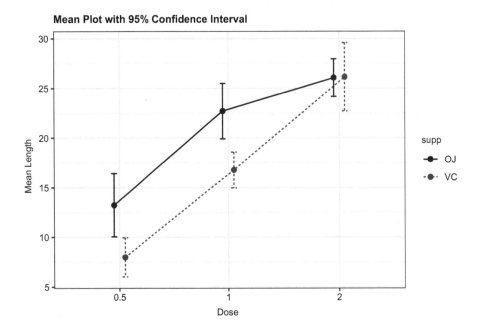

Figure 9.7   Interaction between dose and delivery mechanism on tooth growth. The plot of means was created using the ggplot2 code.

```
library(ggplot2)
pd <- position_dodge(0.2)
ggplot(data=stats,
       aes(x = dose, y = mean,
           group=supp,
           color=supp,
           linetype=supp)) +
  geom_point(size = 2,
             position=pd) +
  geom_line(position=pd) +
  geom_errorbar(aes(ymin = mean - ci, ymax = mean + ci),
                width = .1,
                position=pd) +
  theme_bw() +
  scale_color_manual(values=c("blue", "red")) +
  labs(x="Dose",
       y="Mean Length",
       title="Mean Plot with 95% Confidence Interval")
```

The graph indicates that tooth growth increases with the dose of ascorbic acid for both orange juice and vitamin C. For the 0.5 and 1 mg doses, orange juice produced more tooth growth than vitamin C. For 2 mg of ascorbic acid, both delivery methods produced identical growth.

Although I don't cover the tests of model assumptions and mean comparison procedures, they're a natural extension of the methods you've seen so far. Additionally, the design is balanced, so you don't have to worry about the order of effects.

9.6 Repeated measures ANOVA

In repeated measures ANOVA, subjects are measured more than once. This section focuses on a repeated measures ANOVA with one within-groups and one between-groups factor (a common design). We'll take our example from the field of physiological ecology. Physiological ecologists study how the physiological and biochemical processes of living systems respond to variations in environmental factors (a crucial area of study given the realities of global warming). The CO2 dataset included in the base installation contains the results of a study of cold tolerance in northern and southern plants of the grass species *Echinochloa crus-galli* (Potvin, Lechowicz, and Tardif, 1990). The photosynthetic rates of chilled plants were compared with the photosynthetic rates of nonchilled plants at several ambient CO_2 concentrations. Half the plants were from Quebec, and half were from Mississippi.

In this example, we'll focus on chilled plants. The dependent variable is carbon dioxide uptake (uptake) in ml/L, and the independent variables are Type (Quebec versus Mississippi) and ambient CO_2 concentration (conc) with seven levels (ranging from 95 to 1000 umol/m^2 sec). Type is a between-groups factor, and conc is a within-groups factor. Type is already stored as a factor, but you'll need to convert conc to a factor before continuing. The analysis is presented in the next listing.

Listing 9.7   Repeated measures ANOVA with a between- and a within-groups factor

```
> data(CO2)
> CO2$conc <- factor(CO2$conc)
> w1b1 <- subset(CO2, Treatment=='chilled')
> fit <- aov(uptake ~ conc*Type + Error(Plant/(conc)), w1b1)
> summary(fit)

Error: Plant
          Df Sum Sq Mean Sq F value Pr(>F)
Type       1   2667    2667    60.4 0.0015 **
Residuals  4    177      44
---
Signif. codes:  0 '***' 0.001 '**' 0.01 '*' 0.05 '.' 0.1 ' ' 1

Error: Plant:conc
           Df Sum Sq Mean Sq F value  Pr(>F)
conc        6   1472   245.4    52.5 1.3e-12 ***
conc:Type   6    429    71.5    15.3 3.7e-07 ***
Residuals  24    112     4.7
---
Signif. codes:  0 '***' 0.001 '**' 0.01 '*' 0.05 '.' 0.1 ' ' 1

> library(dplyr)
> stats <- CO2 %>%
    group_by(conc, Type) %>%
    summarise(mean_conc = mean(uptake))

> library(ggplot2)
> ggplot(data=stats, aes(x=conc, y=mean_conc,
          group=Type, color=Type, linetype=Type)) +
    geom_point(size=2) +
    geom_line(size=1) +
    theme_bw() + theme(legend.position="top") +
    labs(x="Concentration", y="Mean Uptake",
        title="Interaction Plot for Plant Type and Concentration")
```

The ANOVA table indicates that the `Type` and concentration main effects and the `Type` × concentration interaction are all significant at the 0.01 level. Figure 9.8 shows a plot of the interaction. In this case, I've left out confidence intervals to keep the graph from becoming too busy.

To demonstrate a different presentation of the interaction, the `geom_boxplot()` function is used to plot the same data. Figure 9.9 provides the results:

```
library(ggplot2)
ggplot(data=CO2, aes(x=conc, y=uptake, fill=Type)) +
  geom_boxplot() +
  theme_bw() + theme(legend.position="top") +
  scale_fill_manual(values=c("aliceblue", "deepskyblue"))+
  labs(x="Concentration", y="Uptake",
      title="Chilled Quebec and Mississippi Plants")
```

Interaction Plot for Plant Type and Concentration

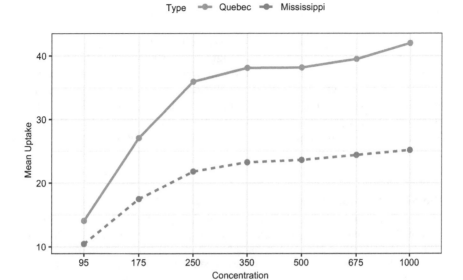

Figure 9.8   Interaction of ambient CO_2 concentration and plant type on CO_2 uptake

Chilled Quebec and Mississippi Plants

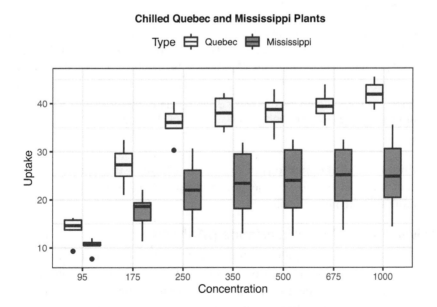

Figure 9.9   Interaction of ambient CO_2 concentration and plant type on CO_2 uptake

From either graph, you can see that there's a greater carbon dioxide uptake in plants from Quebec compared to Mississippi. The difference is more pronounced at higher ambient CO_2 concentrations.

> **NOTE** Datasets are typically in *wide format*, where columns are variables and rows are observations, and there's a single row for each subject. The `litter` data frame from section 9.4 is a good example. When dealing with repeated measures designs, you typically need the data in *long format* before fitting models. In long format, each measurement of the dependent variable is placed in its own row. The `CO2` dataset follows this form. Luckily, the `tidyr` package described in chapter 5 (section 5.5.2) can easily reorganize your data into the required format.

The many approaches to mixed-model designs

The CO_2 example in this section was analyzed using a traditional repeated measures ANOVA. The approach assumes that the covariance matrix for any within-groups factor follows a specified form known as *sphericity*. Specifically, it assumes that the variances of the differences between any two levels of the within-groups factor are equal. In real-world data, it's unlikely that this assumption will be met. This has led to a number of alternative approaches, including the following:

- Using the `lmer()` function in the `lme4` package to fit linear mixed models (Bates, 2005)
- Using the `Anova()` function in the `car` package to adjust traditional test statistics to account for lack of sphericity (for example, the Geisser–Greenhouse correction)
- Using the `gls()` function in the `nlme` package to fit generalized least squares models with specified variance-covariance structures (UCLA, 2009)
- Using multivariate analysis of variance to model repeated measured data (Hand, 1987)

Coverage of these approaches is beyond the scope of this text. If you're interested in learning more, check out Pinheiro and Bates (2000) and Zuur et al. (2009).

Up to this point, all the methods in this chapter have assumed that there's a single dependent variable. In the next section, we'll briefly consider designs that include more than one outcome variable.

9.7   *Multivariate analysis of variance (MANOVA)*

If there's more than one dependent (outcome) variable, you can test them simultaneously using a multivariate analysis of variance (MANOVA). The following example is based on the `UScereal` dataset in the `MASS` package. The dataset comes from Venables and Ripley (1999). In this example, you're interested in whether the calories, fat, and sugar content of US cereals vary by store shelf, where 1 is the bottom shelf, 2 is the middle shelf, and 3 is the top shelf. `Calories`, `fat`, and `sugars` are the dependent variables, and `shelf` is the independent variable, with three levels (1, 2, and 3). The following listing presents the analysis.

Listing 9.8 One-way MANOVA

```
> data(UScereal, package="MASS")
> shelf <- factor(UScereal$shelf)
> shelf <- factor(shelf)
> y <- cbind(UScereal$calories, UScereal$fat, UScereal$sugars)
> colnames(y) <- c("calories", "fat", "sugars")
> aggregate(y, by=list(shelf=shelf), FUN=mean)

  shelf calories  fat sugars
1     1      119 0.662    6.3
2     2      130 1.341   12.5
3     3      180 1.945   10.9

> cov(y)

         calories   fat sugars
calories   3895.2 60.67 180.38
fat          60.7  2.71   4.00
sugars      180.4  4.00  34.05

> fit <- manova(y ~ shelf)
> summary(fit)

          Df Pillai approx F num Df den Df Pr(>F)
shelf      2  0.402     5.12      6    122  1e-04 ***
Residuals 62
---
Signif. codes:  0 '***' 0.001 '**' 0.01 '*' 0.05 '.' 0.1 ' ' 1

> summary.aov(fit)
```
← ❶ **Prints univariate results**

```
Response calories :
          Df Sum Sq Mean Sq F value   Pr(>F)
shelf      2  50435   25218    7.86  0.00091 ***
Residuals 62 198860    3207
---
Signif. codes:  0 '***' 0.001 '**' 0.01 '*' 0.05 '.' 0.1 ' ' 1

 Response fat :
          Df Sum Sq Mean Sq F value Pr(>F)
shelf      2   18.4    9.22    3.68  0.031 *
Residuals 62  155.2    2.50
---
Signif. codes:  0 '***' 0.001 '**' 0.01 '*' 0.05 '.' 0.1 ' ' 1

 Response sugars :
          Df Sum Sq Mean Sq F value Pr(>F)
shelf      2    381     191    6.58 0.0026 **
Residuals 62   1798      29
---
Signif. codes:  0 '***' 0.001 '**' 0.01 '*' 0.05 '.' 0.1 ' ' 1
```

First, the shelf variable is converted to a factor so that it can represent a grouping variable in the analyses. Next, the cbind() function is used to form a matrix of the three dependent variables (calories, fat, and sugars). The aggregate() function provides the shelf means, and the cov() function provides the variance and the covariances across cereals.

The manova() function provides the multivariate test of group differences. The significant F-value indicates that the three groups differ on the set of nutritional measures. Note that the shelf variable was converted to a factor so it can represent a grouping variable.

Because the multivariate test is significant, you can use the summary.aov() function to obtain the univariate one-way ANOVAs ❶. Here, you see that the three groups differ on each nutritional measure considered separately. Finally, you can use a mean comparison procedure (such as TukeyHSD) to determine which shelves differ from each other for each of the three dependent variables (omitted here to save space).

9.7.1   Assessing test assumptions

The two assumptions underlying a one-way MANOVA are multivariate normality and homogeneity of variance-covariance matrices. The first assumption states that the vector of dependent variables jointly follows a multivariate normal distribution. You can use a Q-Q plot to assess this assumption (see the sidebar "A theory interlude" for a statistical explanation of how this works).

> **A theory interlude**
>
> If you have p × 1 multivariate normal random vector x with mean μ and covariance matrix Σ, then the squared Mahalanobis distance between x and μ is chi-square distributed with p degrees of freedom. The Q-Q plot graphs the quantiles of the chi-square distribution for the sample against the Mahalanobis D-squared values. To the degree that the points fall along a line with slope 1 and intercept 0, there's evidence that the data is multivariate normal.

The code is shown in the next listing, and the resulting graph is displayed in figure 9.10.

Listing 9.9   Assessing multivariate normality

```
> center <- colMeans(y)
> n <- nrow(y)
> p <- ncol(y)
> cov <- cov(y)
> d <- mahalanobis(y,center,cov)
> coord <- qqplot(qchisq(ppoints(n),df=p),
    d, main="Q-Q Plot Assessing Multivariate Normality",
    ylab="Mahalanobis D2")
> abline(a=0,b=1)
```

```
> identify(coord$x, coord$y, labels=row.names(UScereal))
```

If the data follows a multivariate normal distribution, then points will fall on the line. The `identify()` function allows you to interactively identify points in the graph. Click on each point of interest and then press ESC or the Finish button. Here, the dataset appears to violate multivariate normality, primarily due to the observations for Wheaties Honey Gold and Wheaties. You may want to delete these two cases and rerun the analyses.

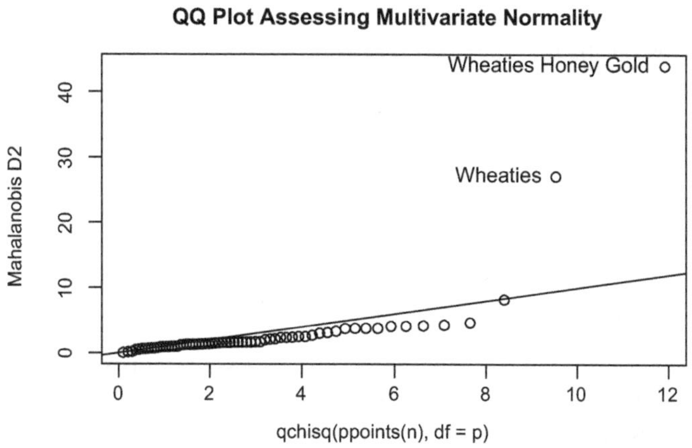

Figure 9.10   A Q-Q plot for assessing multivariate normality

The homogeneity of variance-covariance matrices assumption requires that the covariance matrix for each group is equal. The assumption is usually evaluated with a Box's M test. R doesn't include a function for Box's M, but an internet search will provide the appropriate code. Unfortunately, the test is sensitive to violations of normality, leading to rejection in most typical cases. This means that we don't yet have a good working method for evaluating this important assumption (but see Anderson (2006) and Silva et al. (2008) for interesting alternative approaches not yet available in R).

Finally, you can test for multivariate outliers using the `aq.plot()` function in the mvoutlier package. The code in this case looks like this:

```
library(mvoutlier)
outliers <- aq.plot(y)
outliers
```

Try it, and see what you get!

9.7.2   *Robust MANOVA*

If the assumptions of multivariate normality or homogeneity of variance-covariance matrices are untenable, or if you're concerned about multivariate outliers, you may want to consider using a robust or nonparametric version of the MANOVA test instead. The `Wilks.test()` function in the `rrcov` package provides a robust version of the one-way MANOVA. The `adonis()` function in the `vegan` package can provide the equivalent of a nonparametric MANOVA. The following listing applies `Wilks.test()` to the example.

Listing 9.10 Robust one-way MANOVA

```
> library(rrcov)
> Wilks.test(y,shelf,method="mcd")

        Robust One-way MANOVA (Bartlett Chi2)

data:  x
Wilks' Lambda = 0.511, Chi2-Value = 23.96, DF = 4.98, p-value =
0.0002167
sample estimates:
  calories   fat   sugars
1      120  0.701    5.66
2      128  1.185   12.54
3      161  1.652   10.35
```

From the results, you can see that using a robust test that's insensitive to both outliers and violations of MANOVA assumptions still indicates that the cereals on the top, middle, and bottom store shelves differ in their nutritional profiles.

9.8   *ANOVA as regression*

In section 9.2, we noted that ANOVA and regression are both special cases of the same general linear model. As such, the designs in this chapter could have been analyzed using the `lm()` function. But to understand the output, you need to understand how R deals with categorical variables when fitting models.

Consider the one-way ANOVA problem in section 9.3, which compares the impact of five cholesterol-reducing drug regimens (`trt`):

```
> library(multcomp)
> levels(cholesterol$trt)

[1] "1time"  "2times"  "4times"  "drugD"   "drugE"
```

First, let's fit the model using the `aov()` function:

```
> fit.aov <- aov(response ~ trt, data=cholesterol)
> summary(fit.aov)

            Df   Sum Sq  Mean Sq  F value    Pr(>F)
trt          4  1351.37   337.84   32.433  9.819e-13 ***
Residuals   45   468.75    10.42
```

Now, let's fit the same model using `lm()`. In this case, you get the results shown in the next listing.

Listing 9.11 A regression approach to the ANOVA problem in section 9.3

```
> fit.lm <- lm(response ~ trt, data=cholesterol)
> summary(fit.lm)

Coefficients:
            Estimate Std. Error t value   Pr(>|t|)
(Intercept)    5.782      1.021   5.665   9.78e-07 ***
trt2times      3.443      1.443   2.385    0.0213 *
trt4times      6.593      1.443   4.568   3.82e-05 ***
trtdrugD       9.579      1.443   6.637   3.53e-08 ***
trtdrugE      15.166      1.443  10.507   1.08e-13 ***

Residual standard error: 3.227 on 45 degrees of freedom
Multiple R-squared: 0.7425,     Adjusted R-squared: 0.7196
F-statistic: 32.43 on 4 and 45 DF,   p-value: 9.819e-13
```

What are you looking at? Because linear models require numeric predictors, when the lm() function encounters a factor, it replaces that factor with a set of numeric variables representing contrasts among the levels. If the factor has k levels, $k - 1$ contrast variables are created. R provides five built-in methods for creating these contrast variables (see table 9.3). You can also create your own (we won't cover that here). By default, treatment contrasts are used for unordered factors, and orthogonal polynomials are used for ordered factors.

Table 9.3 Built-in contrasts

Contrast	Description
contr.helmert	Contrasts the second level with the first, the third level with the average of the first two, the fourth level with the average of the first three, and so on.
contr.poly	Contrasts are used for trend analysis (linear, quadratic, cubic, and so on) based on orthogonal polynomials. Used for ordered factors with equally spaced levels.
contr.sum	Contrasts are constrained to sum to zero. Also called *deviation contrasts*, they compare the mean of each level to the overall mean across levels.
contr.treatment	Contrasts each level with the baseline level (first level by default). Also called *dummy coding*.
contr.SAS	Similar to contr.treatment, but the baseline level is the last level. This produces coefficients similar to contrasts used in most SAS procedures.

With treatment contrasts, the first level of the factor becomes the reference group, and each subsequent level is compared with it. You can see the coding scheme via the contrasts() function:

```
> contrasts(cholesterol$trt)
        2times  4times  drugD  drugE
1time        0       0      0      0
2times       1       0      0      0
4times       0       1      0      0
```

```
drugD        0       0       1       0
drugE        0       0       0       1
```

If a patient is in the `drugD` condition, then the variable `drugD` equals 1, and the variables `2times`, `4times`, and `drugE` each equal zero. You don't need a variable for the first group because a zero on each of the four indicator variables uniquely determines that the patient is in the `1times` condition.

In listing 9.11, the variable `trt2times` represents a contrast between the levels `1time` and `2times`. Similarly, `trt4times` is a contrast between `1time` and `4times`, and so on. You can see from the probability values in the output that each drug condition is significantly different from the first (`1time`).

You can change the default contrasts used in `lm()` by specifying a `contrasts` option. For example, you can specify Helmert contrasts by using

```
fit.lm <- lm(response ~ trt, data=cholesterol, contrasts="contr.helmert")
```

You can change the default contrasts used during an R session via the `options()` function. For example,

```
options(contrasts = c("contr.SAS", "contr.helmert"))
```

would set the default contrast for unordered factors to `contr.SAS` and for ordered factors to `contr.helmert`. Although we've limited our discussion to the use of contrasts in linear models, note that they're applicable to other modeling functions in R. This includes the generalized linear models covered in chapter 13.

Summary

- Analysis of variance (ANOVA) is a set of statistical methods frequently used when analyzing data from experimental and quasi-experimental research.
- ANOVA methodologies are particularly helpful when investigating the relationship between a quantitative outcome variable and one or more categorical explanatory variables.
- If a quantitative outcome variable is related to a categorical explanatory variable with *more than* two levels, post hoc tests are conducted to identify which levels/groups differ on that outcome.
- When there are two or more categorical explanatory variables, a factorial ANOVA can be used to study their unique and joint effects on the outcome variable.
- When the effects of one or more quantitative nuisance variables are statistically controlled (removed), the design is called an analysis of covariance (ANCOVA).
- When there is more than one outcome variable, the design is called a multivariate analysis of variance or covariance.
- ANOVA and multiple regression are two equivalent expressions of the general linear model. The different terminologies, R functions, and output formats for these two approaches reflect their separate origins in different fields of research. When studies focus on group differences, ANOVA results are often easier to understand and communicate to others.

Power analysis

As a statistical consultant, I'm often asked, "How many subjects do I need for my study?" Sometimes the question is phrased this way: "I have *x* number of people available for this study. Is the study worth doing?" Questions like these can be answered through *power analysis*, an important set of techniques in experimental design.

Power analysis allows you to determine the sample size required to detect an effect of a given size with a given degree of confidence. Conversely, it allows you to determine the probability of detecting an effect of a given size with a given level of confidence under sample size constraints. If the probability is unacceptably low, you'd be wise to alter or abandon the experiment.

In this chapter, you'll learn how to conduct power analyses for various statistical tests, including tests of proportions, t-tests, chi-square tests, balanced one-way ANOVA, tests of correlations, and linear models. Because power analysis applies to hypothesis testing situations, we'll start with a brief review of null hypothesis significance testing (NHST). Then we'll review conducting power analyses within R, focusing primarily on the `pwr` package. Finally, we'll consider other approaches to power analysis available with R.

10.1   *A quick review of hypothesis testing*

To help you understand the steps in a power analysis, we'll briefly review statistical hypothesis testing in general. If you have a statistical background, feel free to skip to section 10.2.

In statistical hypothesis testing, you specify a hypothesis about a population parameter (your *null hypothesis*, or H_0). You then draw a sample from this population and calculate a statistic that's used to make inferences about the population parameter. Assuming that the null hypothesis is true, you calculate the probability of obtaining the observed sample statistic or one more extreme. If the probability is sufficiently small, you reject the null hypothesis in favor of its opposite (referred to as the *alternative* or *research hypothesis*, H_1).

An example will clarify the process. Say you're interested in evaluating the impact of cell phone use on drivers' reaction time. Your null hypothesis is $H_0: \mu_1 - \mu_2 = 0$, where μ_1 is the mean response time for drivers using a cell phone and μ_2 is the mean response time for drivers who are cell phone free (here, $\mu_1 - \mu_2$ is the population parameter of interest). If you reject this null hypothesis, you're left with the alternate or research hypothesis: $H_1: \mu_1 - \mu_2 \neq 0$. This is equivalent to $\mu_1 \neq \mu_2$, that the mean reaction times for the two conditions are not equal.

A sample of individuals is selected and randomly assigned to one of two conditions. In the first condition, participants react to a series of driving challenges in a simulator while talking on a cell phone. In the second condition, participants complete the same series of challenges without a cell phone. Overall reaction time is assessed for each individual.

Based on the sample data, you can calculate the statistic $(\bar{X}_1 - \bar{X}_2)/(s/\sqrt{n})$, where $\bar{X}_1$ and $\bar{X}_2$ are the sample reaction time means in the two conditions, s is the pooled sample standard deviation, and n is the number of participants in each condition. If the null hypothesis is true and you can assume reaction times are normally distributed, this sample statistic will follow a t-distribution with $2n - 2$ degrees of freedom. Using this fact, you can calculate the probability of obtaining a sample statistic this large or larger. If the probability (p) is smaller than some predetermined cutoff (say $p < .05$), you reject the null hypothesis in favor of the alternate hypothesis. This predetermined cutoff (0.05) is called the *significance level* of the test.

Note that you use *sample* data to make an inference about the *population* it's drawn from. Your null hypothesis is that the mean reaction time of *all* drivers talking on cell phones isn't different from the mean reaction time of *all* drivers who aren't talking on cell phones, not just those drivers in your sample. The four possible outcomes from your decision are as follows:

- If the null hypothesis is false and the statistical test leads you to reject it, you've made a correct decision. You've correctly determined that reaction time is affected by cell phone use.
- If the null hypothesis is true and you don't reject it, again, you've made a correct decision. Reaction time isn't affected by cell phone use.
- If the null hypothesis is true but you reject it, you've committed a Type I error. You've concluded that cell phone use affects reaction time when it doesn't.
- If the null hypothesis is false and you fail to reject it, you've committed a Type II error. Cell phone use affects reaction time, but you've failed to discern this.

Each of these outcomes is illustrated in table 10.1.

Table 10.1 Hypothesis testing

		Decision	
		Reject H_0	Fail to reject H_0
Actual	H_0 **true**	Type I error	Correct
	H_0 **false**	Correct	Type II error

Controversy surrounding null hypothesis significance testing

Null hypothesis significance testing isn't without controversy, and detractors have raised many concerns about it, particularly as it is practiced in the field of psychology. They point to a widespread misunderstanding of p values, reliance on statistical significance over practical significance, the fact that the null hypothesis is never exactly true and will always be rejected for sufficient sample sizes, and a number of logical inconsistencies in NHST practices.

An in-depth discussion of this topic is beyond the scope of this book. Interested readers are referred to Harlow, Mulaik, and Steiger (1997).

In planning research, the researcher typically pays special attention to four quantities (see figure 10.1):

- *Sample size* refers to the number of observations in each condition/group of the experimental design.
- The *significance level* (also referred to as *alpha*) is defined as the probability of making a Type I error. The significance level can also be thought of as the probability of finding an effect that is *not* there.

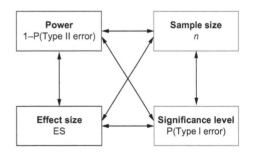

Figure 10.1 Four primary quantities considered in a study design power analysis. Given any three, you can calculate the fourth.

- *Power* is defined as one minus the probability of making a Type II error. Power can be thought of as the probability of finding an effect that *is* there.
- *Effect size* is the magnitude of the effect under the alternate or research hypothesis. The formula for effect size depends on the statistical methodology employed in the hypothesis testing.

Although the researcher directly controls the sample size and significance level, power and effect size are affected more indirectly. For example, as you relax the significance level (in other words, make it easier to reject the null hypothesis), power increases. Similarly, increasing the sample size increases power.

Your research goal is typically to maximize the power of your statistical tests while maintaining an acceptable significance level and employing as small a sample size as possible. That is, you want to maximize the chances of finding a real effect and minimize the chances of finding an effect that isn't really there, while keeping study costs within reason.

The four quantities (sample size, significance level, power, and effect size) have an intimate relationship. *Given any three, you can determine the fourth.* You'll use this fact to carry out various power analyses throughout the remainder of the chapter. In the next section, we'll look at ways to implement power analyses using the R package `pwr`. Later, we'll briefly look at some highly specialized power functions that are used in biology and genetics.

10.2 *Implementing power analysis with the pwr package*

The `pwr` package, developed by Stéphane Champely, implements power analysis as outlined by Cohen (1988). Table 10.2 lists some of the more important functions. For each function, the user can specify three of the four quantities (sample size, significance level, power, effect size), and the fourth will be calculated.

Table 10.2 `pwr` package functions

Function	Power calculations for ...
`pwr.2p.test`	Two proportions (equal n)
`pwr.2p2n.test`	Two proportions (unequal n)
`pwr.anova.test`	Balanced one-way ANOVA
`pwr.chisq.test`	Chi-square test
`pwr.f2.test`	General linear model
`pwr.p.test`	Proportion (one sample)
`pwr.r.test`	Correlation
`pwr.t.test`	T-tests (one sample, two samples, paired)
`pwr.t2n.test`	T-test (two samples with unequal n)

Of the four quantities, effect size is often the most difficult to specify. Calculating effect size typically requires some experience with the measures involved and knowledge of past research. But what can you do if you have no clue what effect size to expect in a given study? You'll look at this difficult question in section 10.2.7. In the remainder of this section, you'll look at the application of pwr functions to common statistical tests. Before invoking these functions, be sure to install and load the pwr package.

10.2.1 *T-tests*

When the statistical test you will use is a t-test, the pwr.t.test() function provides a number of useful power analysis options. The format is

```
pwr.t.test(n=, d=, sig.level=, power=, alternative=)
```

where

- n is the sample size.
- d is the effect size defined as the standardized mean difference.

$$d = \frac{|\mu_1 - \mu_2|}{\sigma} \quad \begin{array}{l} \mu_1 = \text{mean of group 1} \\ \mu_2 = \text{mean of group 2} \\ \sigma^2 = \text{common error variance} \end{array}$$

- sig.level is the significance level (0.05 is the default).
- power is the power level.
- type is two-sample t-test ("two.sample"), a one-sample t-test ("one.sample"), or a dependent sample t-test ("paired"). A two-sample test is the default.
- alternative indicates whether the statistical test is two-sided ("two.sided") or one-sided ("less" or "greater"). A two-sided test is the default.

Let's work through an example. Continuing the experiment from section 10.1 involving cell phone use and driving reaction time, assume that you'll be using a two-tailed independent sample t-test to compare the mean reaction time for participants in the cell phone condition with the mean reaction time for participants driving unencumbered.

Let's assume that you know from past experience that reaction time has a standard deviation of 1.25 seconds. Also suppose that a 1-second difference in reaction time is considered an important difference. You'd therefore like to conduct a study in which you're able to detect an effect size of d = 1/1.25 = 0.8 or larger. Additionally, you want to be 90% sure to detect such a difference if it exists and 95% sure that you won't declare a difference to be significant when it's actually due to random variability. How many participants will you need in your study?

Entering this information in the pwr.t.test() function, you have the following:

```
> library(pwr)
> pwr.t.test(d=.8, sig.level=.05, power=.9, type="two.sample",
            alternative="two.sided")
```

```
    Two-sample t test power calculation

                n = 34
                d = 0.8
        sig.level = 0.05
            power = 0.9
      alternative = two.sided

    NOTE: n is number in *each* group
```

The results suggest that you need 34 participants in each group (for a total of 68 participants) to detect an effect size of 0.8 with 90% certainty and no more than a 5% chance of erroneously concluding that a difference exists when, in fact, it doesn't.

Let's alter the question. Assume that in comparing the two conditions, you want to be able to detect a 0.5 standard deviation difference in population means. You want to limit the chances of falsely declaring the population means to be different to 1 out of 100. Additionally, you can only afford to include 40 participants in the study. What's the probability that you'll be able to detect a difference this large between the population means, given these constraints?

Assuming that an equal number of participants will be placed in each condition, you have

```
> pwr.t.test(n=20, d=.5, sig.level=.01, type="two.sample",
            alternative="two.sided")

    Two-sample t test power calculation

                n = 20
                d = 0.5
        sig.level = 0.01
            power = 0.14
      alternative = two.sided

    NOTE: n is number in *each* group
```

With 20 participants in each group, an a priori significance level of 0.01, and a dependent variable standard deviation of 1.25 seconds, you have less than a 14% chance of declaring a difference of 0.625 seconds or less significant (d = 0.5 = 0.625/1.25). Conversely, there's an 86% chance that you'll miss the effect that you're looking for. You may want to seriously rethink putting the time and effort into the study as it stands.

The previous examples assumed that there are equal sample sizes in the two groups. If the sample sizes for the two groups are unequal, the function

```
pwr.t2n.test(n1=, n2=, d=, sig.level=, power=, alternative=)
```

can be used. Here, n1 and n2 are the sample sizes, and the other parameters are the same as for pwer.t.test. Try varying the values input to the pwr.t2n.test function and see the effect on the output.

10.2.2 ANOVA

The `pwr.anova.test()` function provides power analysis options for a balanced one-way analysis of variance. The format is

```
pwr.anova.test(k=, n=, f=, sig.level=, power=)
```

where k is the number of groups and n is the common sample size in each group.

For a one-way ANOVA, effect size is measured by f, where

$$f = \sqrt{\frac{\sum_{i=1}^{k} p_i \times (\mu_1 - \mu_2)}{\sigma^2}}$$

$p_i = n_i / N$

n_i = number of observations in group i

N = total number of observations

μ_i = mean of group i

μ = grand mean

σ^2 = error variance within groups

Let's try an example. For a one-way ANOVA comparing five groups, calculate the sample size needed in each group to obtain a power of 0.80, when the effect size is 0.25 and a significance level of 0.05 is employed. The code looks like this:

```
> pwr.anova.test(k=5, f=.25, sig.level=.05, power=.8)

     Balanced one-way analysis of variance power calculation

              k = 5
              n = 39
              f = 0.25
      sig.level = 0.05
          power = 0.8

NOTE: n is number in each group
```

The total sample size is therefore 5 × 39, or 195. Note that this example requires you to estimate what the means of the five groups will be, along with the common variance. When you have no idea what to expect, the approaches described in section 10.2.7 may help.

10.2.3 Correlations

The `pwr.r.test()` function provides a power analysis for tests of correlation coefficients. The format is

```
pwr.r.test(n=, r=, sig.level=, power=, alternative=)
```

where n is the number of observations, r is the effect size (as measured by a linear correlation coefficient), `sig.level` is the significance level, `power` is the power level, and `alternative` specifies a two-sided ("two.sided") or a one-sided ("less" or "greater") significance test.

For example, let's assume that you're studying the relationship between depression and loneliness. Your null and research hypotheses are

$$H_0: \rho \leq 0.25 \text{ versus } H_1: \rho > 0.25$$

where ρ is the population correlation between these two psychological variables. You've set your significance level to 0.05, and you want to be 90% confident that you'll reject H_0 if it's false. How many observations will you need? This code provides the answer:

```
> pwr.r.test(r=.25, sig.level=.05, power=.90, alternative="greater")

     approximate correlation power calculation (arctangh transformation)

              n = 134
              r = 0.25
      sig.level = 0.05
          power = 0.9
    alternative = greater
```

Thus, you need to assess depression and loneliness in 134 participants to be 90% confident that you'll reject the null hypothesis if it's false.

10.2.4 *Linear models*

For linear models (such as multiple regression), the `pwr.f2.test()` function can be used to carry out a power analysis. The format is

```
pwr.f2.test(u=, v=, f2=, sig.level=, power=)
```

where u and v are the numerator and denominator degrees of freedom and f2 is the effect size.

$$f^2 = \frac{R^2}{1-R^2} \quad \text{where} \quad R^2 = \text{population multiple correlation}$$

$$f^2 = \frac{R_{AB}^2 - R_A^2}{1 - R_{AB}^2} \quad \text{where} \quad R_A^2 = \text{variance accounted for in the population by variable set } A$$

$$R_{AB}^2 = \text{variance accounted for in the population by variable set } A \text{ and } B \text{ together}$$

The first formula for f2 is appropriate when you're evaluating the impact of a set of predictors on an outcome. The second formula is appropriate when you're evaluating the impact of one set of predictors above and beyond a second set of predictors (or covariates).

Let's say you're interested in whether a boss' leadership style impacts workers' satisfaction above and beyond the salary and perks associated with the job. Leadership style is assessed by four variables, and salary and perks are associated with three variables. Past experience suggests that salary and perks account for roughly 30% of the variance in workers' satisfaction. From a practical standpoint, it would be interesting if leadership style accounted for at least 5% above this figure. Assuming a significance level of 0.05, how many subjects would be needed to identify such a contribution with 90% confidence?

Here, `sig.level=0.05`, `power=0.90`, `u=3` (the total number of predictors minus the number of predictors in set B), and the effect size is $f2 = (.35 - .30)/(1 - .35) = 0.0769$. Entering this into the function yields the following:

```
> pwr.f2.test(u=3, f2=0.0769, sig.level=0.05, power=0.90)

     Multiple regression power calculation

              u = 3
              v = 184.2426
             f2 = 0.0769
      sig.level = 0.05
          power = 0.9
```

In multiple regression, the denominator degrees of freedom equals $N - k - 1$, where N is the number of observations and k is the number of predictors. In this case, $N - 7 - 1 = 185$, which means the required sample size is $N = 185 + 7 + 1 = 193$.

10.2.5 *Tests of proportions*

The `pwr.2p.test()` function can be used to perform a power analysis for comparing two proportions. The format is

```
pwr.2p.test(h=, n=, sig.level=, power=)
```

where h is the effect size and n is the common sample size in each group. The effect size h is defined as

$$h = 2\arcsin\left(\sqrt{p_1}\right) - 2\arcsin\left(\sqrt{p_2}\right)$$

and can be calculated with the function `ES.h(p1, p2)`.

For unequal ns, the desired function is

```
pwr.2p2n.test(h =, n1 =, n2 =, sig.level=, power=)
```

The `alternative=` option can be used to specify a two-tailed (`"two.sided"`) or one-tailed (`"less"` or `"greater"`) test. A two-tailed test is the default.

Let's say you suspect that a popular medication relieves symptoms in 60% of users. A new (and more expensive) medication will be marketed if it improves symptoms in 65% of users. How many participants will you need to include in a study comparing these two medications if you want to detect a difference this large?

Assume that you want to be 90% confident in concluding that the new drug is better and 95% confident that you won't reach this conclusion erroneously. You'll use a one-tailed test because you're only interested in assessing whether the new drug is better than the standard. The code looks like this:

```
> pwr.2p.test(h=ES.h(.65, .6), sig.level=.05, power=.9,
            alternative="greater")

     Difference of proportion power calculation for binomial
     distribution (arcsine transformation)

              h = 0.1033347
              n = 1604.007
      sig.level = 0.05
          power = 0.9
    alternative = greater

NOTE: same sample sizes
```

Based on these results, you'll need to conduct a study with 1,605 individuals receiving the new drug and 1,605 receiving the existing drug to meet the criteria.

10.2.6 *Chi-square tests*

Chi-square tests are often used to assess the relationship between two categorical variables. The null hypothesis is typically that the variables are independent versus a research hypothesis that they aren't. The `pwr.chisq.test()` function can be used to evaluate the power, effect size, or requisite sample size when employing a chi-square test. The format is

```
pwr.chisq.test(w =, N = , df = , sig.level =, power = )
```

where w is the effect size, N is the total sample size, and df is the degrees of freedom. Here, effect size w is defined as

$$w = \sqrt{\sum_{i=1}^{m} \frac{(p0_i - p1_i)^2}{p0_i}} \qquad \text{where} \quad \begin{array}{l} p0_i = \text{cell probability in the ith cell under } H_0 \\ p1_i = \text{cell probability in the ith cell under } H_1 \end{array}$$

The summation goes from 1 to m, where m is the number of cells in the contingency table. The function `ES.w2(P)` can be used to calculate the effect size corresponding to the alternative hypothesis in a two-way contingency table. Here, `P` is a hypothesized two-way probability table.

As a simple example, let's assume that you're looking at the relationship between ethnicity and promotion. You anticipate that 70% of your sample will be Caucasian, 10% will be African American, and 20% will be Hispanic. Furthermore, you believe that 60% of Caucasians tend to be promoted, compared with 30% of African Americans and 50% of Hispanics. Your research hypothesis is that the probability of promotion follows the values in table 10.3.

Table 10.3   Proportion of individuals expected to be promoted based on the research hypothesis

Ethnicity	Promoted	Not promoted
Caucasian	0.42	0.28
African American	0.03	0.07
Hispanic	0.10	0.10

For example, you expect that 42% of the population will be promoted Caucasians (.42 = .70 × .60) and 7% of the population will be unpromoted African Americans (.07 = .10 × .70). Let's assume a significance level of 0.05 and that the desired power level is 0.90. The degrees of freedom in a two-way contingency table are $(r − 1) × (c − 1)$, where r is the number of rows and c is the number of columns. You can calculate the hypothesized effect size with the following code:

```
> prob <- matrix(c(.42, .28, .03, .07, .10, .10), byrow=TRUE, nrow=3)
> ES.w2(prob)

[1] 0.1853198
```

Using this information, you can calculate the necessary sample size like this:

```
> pwr.chisq.test(w=.1853, df=2, sig.level=.05, power=.9)

     Chi squared power calculation

              w = 0.1853
              N = 368.5317
             df = 2
      sig.level = 0.05
          power = 0.9

NOTE: N is the number of observations
```

The results suggest that a study with 369 participants will be adequate to detect a relationship between ethnicity and promotion given the effect size, power, and significance level specified.

10.2.7   *Choosing an appropriate effect size in novel situations*

In power analysis, the expected effect size is the most difficult parameter to determine. It typically requires that you have experience with the subject matter and the measures employed. For example, the data from past studies can be used to calculate effect sizes, which can then be used to plan future studies.

But what can you do when the research situation is completely novel and you have no experience to call upon? In the behavioral sciences, Cohen (1988) attempted to provide benchmarks for "small," "medium," and "large" effect sizes for various statistical tests. Table 10.4 provides these guidelines.

Table 10.4   Cohen's effect size benchmarks

Statistical method	Effect size measures	Suggested guidelines for effect size		
		Small	Medium	Large
T-test	d	0.20	0.50	0.80
ANOVA	f	0.10	0.25	0.40
Linear models	f2	0.02	0.15	0.35
Test of proportions	h	0.20	0.50	0.80
Chi-square	w	0.10	0.30	0.50

When you have no idea what effect size may be present, this table may provide some guidance. For example, what's the probability of rejecting a false null hypothesis (that is, finding a real effect) if you're using a one-way ANOVA with 5 groups, 25 subjects per group, and a significance level of 0.05?

Using the `pwr.anova.test()` function and the suggestions in the f row of table 10.3 gives the following results:

```
pwr.anova.test(k=5, n=25, sig.level=0.05, f=c(.10, .25, .40))

    Balanced one-way analysis of variance power calculation
          k = 5
          n = 25
          f = 0.10, 0.25, 0.40
    sig.level = 0.05
        power = 0.1180955, 0.5738000, 0.9569163

   NOTE: n is number in each group
```

The power would be 0.118 for detecting a small effect, 0.574 for detecting a moderate effect, and 0.957 for detecting a large effect. Given the sample size limitations, you're only likely to find an effect if it's large.

It's important to keep in mind that Cohen's benchmarks are just general suggestions derived from a range of social research studies and may not apply to your particular field of research. An alternative is to vary the study parameters and note the impact on such things as sample size and power. For example, again assume that you want to compare five groups using a one-way ANOVA and a 0.05 significance level. The following listing computes the sample sizes needed to detect a range of effect sizes and plots the results in figure 10.2.

Listing 10.1   Sample sizes for detecting significant effects in a one-way ANOVA

```
library(pwr)
es <- seq(.1, .5, .01)
nes <- length(es)
```

```
samsize <- NULL
for (i in 1:nes){
    result <- pwr.anova.test(k=5, f=es[i], sig.level=.05, power=.9)
    samsize[i] <- ceiling(result$n)
}

plotdata <- data.frame(es, samsize)
library(ggplot2)
ggplot(plotdata, aes(x=samsize, y=es)) +
  geom_line(color="red", size=1) +
  theme_bw() +
  labs(title="One Way ANOVA (5 groups)",
       subtitle="Power = 0.90,  Alpha = 0.05",
       x="Sample Size (per group)",
       y="Effect Size")
```

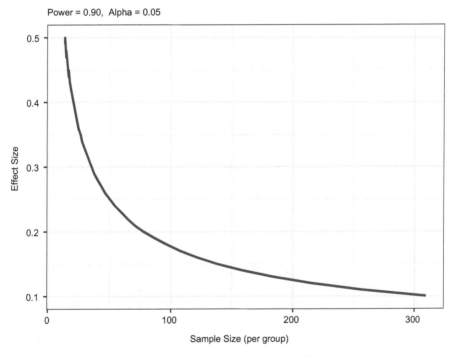

Figure 10.2   Sample size needed to detect various effect sizes in a one-way ANOVA with five groups (assuming a power of 0.90 and significance level of 0.05)

Graphs such as these can help you estimate the impact of various conditions on your experimental design. For example, there appears to be little bang for the buck in increasing the sample size above 200 observations per group. We'll look at another plotting example in the next section.

10.3   *Creating power analysis plots*

Before leaving the `pwr` package, let's look at a more involved graphing example. Suppose you'd like to see the sample size necessary to declare a correlation coefficient statistically significant for a range of effect sizes and power levels. You can use the `pwr.r.test()` function and `for` loops to accomplish this task, as shown in the following listing.

Listing 10.2   Sample size curves for detecting correlations of various sizes

```
library(pwr)
r <- seq(.1,.5,.01)       ❶ Sets the range of correlatio
p <- seq(.4,.9,.1)          and power values

df <- expand.grid(r, p)
colnames(df) <- c("r", "p")

for (i in 1:nrow(df)){
    result <- pwr.r.test(r = df$r[i],
                         sig.level = .05, power = df$p[i],      ❷ Obtains
                         alternative = "two.sided")               sample sizes
    df$n[i] <- ceiling(result$n)
}

library(ggplot2)
ggplot(data=df,
       aes(x=r, y=n, color=factor(p))) +
  geom_line(size=1) +
  theme_bw() +                                                  ❸ Plots power
  labs(title="Sample Size Estimation for Correlation Studies",    curves
       subtitle="Sig=0.05 (Two-tailed)",
       x="Correlation Coefficient (r)",
       y="Samsple Size (n)",
       color="Power")
```

Listing 10.2 uses the `seq()` function to generate a range of effect sizes r (correlation coefficients under H_1) and power levels p ❶. The `expand.grid()` function creates a data frame with every combination of these two variables. A `for` loop then cycles through rows of the data frame, calculating the sample size (n) for that row's correlation and power level and saving the result ❷. The `ggplot2` package plots a sample size versus a correlation curve for each power level ❸. Figure 10.3 shows the resulting graph. If you're reading this chapter in greyscale, the line colors can be difficult to distinguish. Starting at the bottom, the lines represent a power of 0.4, 0.5, 0.6, up to 0.9.

As the graph shows, you'd need a sample size of approximately 75 to detect a correlation of 0.20 with 40% confidence. You'd need approximately 185 additional observations ($n = 260$) to detect the same correlation with 90% confidence. With simple modifications, this approach can be used to create sample size and power curve graphs for a wide range of statistical tests.

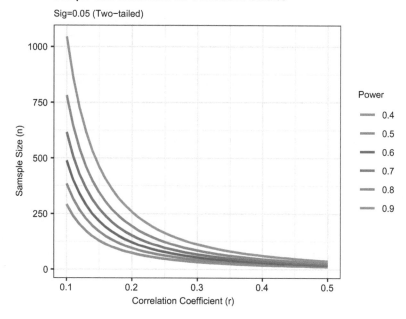

Figure 10.3   Sample size curves for detecting a significant correlation at various power levels

We'll close this chapter by briefly looking at other R functions that are useful for power analysis.

10.4   Other packages

Many other packages in R can be useful in the planning stages of studies. Table 10.5 lists several. Some contain general tools, whereas some are highly specialized. The last four in the table are particularly focused on power analysis in genetic studies. Genome-wide association studies (GWAS) are used to identify genetic associations with observable traits. For example, these studies would focus on why some people get a specific type of heart disease.

Table 10.5   Specialized power analysis packages

Package	Purpose
asypow	Power calculations via asymptotic likelihood ratio methods
longpower	Sample-size calculations for longitudinal data
PwrGSD	Power analysis for group sequential designs
pamm	Power analysis for random effects in mixed models
powerSurvEpi	Power and sample-size calculations for survival analysis in epidemiological studies

Table 10.5 Specialized power analysis packages (continued)

Package	Purpose
powerMediation	Power and sample-size calculations for mediation effects in linear, logistic, Poisson, and Cox regression
semPower	Power analyses for structural equation models (SEM)
powerpkg	Power analyses for the affected sib pair and the transmission disequilibrium test (TDT) design
powerGWASinteraction	Power calculations for interactions for GWAS
gap	Functions for power and sample-size calculations in case-cohort designs
ssize.fdr	Sample-size calculations for microarray experiments

Finally, the MBESS and `WebPower` packages contains a wide range of functions that can be used for various forms of power analysis and sample-size determination. The functions are particularly relevant for researchers in the behavioral, educational, and social sciences.

Summary

- Power analysis helps determine the sample sizes needed to discern an effect of a given size with a given degree of confidence. It can also tell you the probability of detecting such an effect for a given sample size. You can directly see the tradeoff between limiting the likelihood of wrongly declaring an effect significant (a Type I error) with the likelihood of rightly identifying a real effect (power).

- Functions provided by the `pwr` package can be used to carry out power and sample-size determinations for common statistical methods (including t-tests, chi-square tests, and tests of proportions, ANOVA, and regression). The final Section 10.4 points to more specialized methods.

- Power analysis is typically an interactive process. The investigator varies the parameters of sample size, effect size, desired significance level, and desired power to observe their impact on each other. The results are used to plan studies that are more likely to yield meaningful results. Information from past research (particularly regarding effect sizes) can be used to design more effective and efficient future research.

- An important side benefit of power analysis is the shift that it encourages away from a singular focus on binary hypothesis testing (that is, does an effect exists or not) toward an appreciation of the *size* of the effect under consideration. Journal editors are increasingly requiring authors to include effect sizes and p-values when reporting research results. This helps you determine both the practical implications of the research and provides you with information that can be used to plan future studies.

Intermediate graphs

This chapter covers

- Visualizing bivariate and multivariate relationships
- Working with scatter and line plots
- Understanding corrgrams
- Using mosaic plots

In chapter 6 (basic graphs), we considered a wide range of graph types for displaying the distribution of single categorical or continuous variables. Chapter 8 (regression) reviewed graphical methods that are useful when predicting a continuous outcome variable from a set of predictor variables. In chapter 9 (analysis of variance), we considered techniques that are particularly useful for visualizing how groups differ on a continuous outcome variable. In many ways, this chapter is a continuation and extension of the topics we've covered so far.

In this chapter, we'll focus on graphical methods for displaying relationships between two variables (bivariate relationships) and between many variables (multivariate relationships). For example:

- What's the relationship between automobile mileage and car weight? Does it vary by the number of cylinders the car has?
- How can you picture the relationships among an automobile's mileage, weight, displacement, and rear axle ratio in a single graph?
- When plotting the relationship between two variables drawn from a large dataset (say, 10,000 observations), how can you deal with the massive overlap of data points you're likely to see? In other words, what do you do when your graph is one big smudge?
- How can you visualize the multivariate relationships among three variables at once (given a 2D computer screen or sheet of paper, and a budget slightly less than the latest *Star Wars* movie)?
- How can you display the growth of several trees over time?
- How can you visualize the correlations among a dozen variables in a single graph? How does it help you to understand the structure of your data?
- How can you visualize the relationship of class, gender, and age with passenger survival on the *Titanic*? What can you learn from such a graph?

These are the types of questions that can be answered with the methods described in this chapter. The datasets we'll use are examples of what's possible. The general techniques are what's most important. If the topic of automobile characteristics or tree growth isn't interesting to you, plug in your own data.

We'll start with scatter plots and scatter plot matrices. Then we'll explore line charts of various types. These approaches are well known and widely used in research. Next, we'll review the use of corrgrams for visualizing correlations and mosaic plots for visualizing multivariate relationships among categorical variables. These approaches are also useful but much less known among researchers and data analysts. You'll see examples of how you can use each of these approaches to gain a better understanding of your data and communicate these findings to others.

11.1   *Scatter plots*

As you've seen, scatter plots describe the relationship between two continuous variables. In this section, we'll start with a depiction of a single bivariate relationship (*x* versus *y*). We'll then explore ways to enhance this plot by superimposing additional information. Next, you'll learn how to combine several scatter plots into a scatter plot matrix so you can view many bivariate relationships at once. We'll also review the special case where many data points overlap, limiting your ability to picture the data, and we'll discuss several ways around this difficulty. Finally, we'll extend the two-dimensional graph to three dimensions with the addition of a third continuous variable. This will include 3D scatter plots and bubble plots. Each can help you understand the multivariate relationship among three variables at once.

We'll start by visualizing the relationship between automobile weight and fuel efficiency. The following listing presents an example.

Listing 11.1   A scatter plot with best-fit lines

```
data(mtcars)                     ❶ Loads data
ggplot(mtcars, aes(x=wt, y=mpg)) + geom_point()      ❷ Creates scatter plot
  geom_smooth(method="lm", se=FALSE, color="red") +  ❸ Adds linear fit
  geom_smooth(method="loess", se=FALSE,              ❹ Adds loess fit
            color="blue", linetype="dashed") +
      labs(title = "Basic Scatter Plot of MPG vs. Weight",   Adds annotations
      x = "Car Weight (lbs/1000)",
      y = "Miles Per Gallon")
```

Figure 11.1 shows the resulting graph.

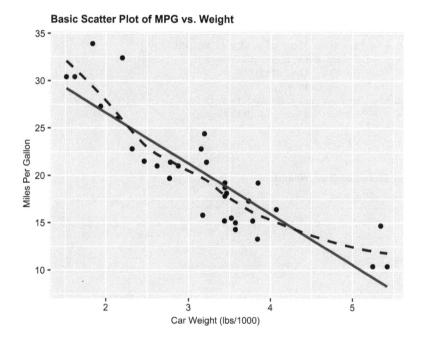

Figure 11.1   Scatter plot of car mileage vs. weight, with superimposed linear and loess fit lines

The code in listing 11.1 loads a fresh copy of the built-in data frame `mtcars` ❶ and creates a basic scatter plot using filled circles for the plotting symbol ❷. As expected, as car weight increases, miles per gallon decreases, although the relationship isn't perfectly linear. The first `geom_smooth()` function adds a linear fit line (solid red) ❸. The `se=FALSE` option suppresses the 95% confidence interval for the line. The second `geom_smooth()` function adds a *loess* fit (dashed blue line) ❹. The loess line is a nonparametric fit line based on locally weighted polynomial regression and provides a smoothed trend line for the data. See Cleveland (1981) for technical details on the algorithm. Josh Starmer provides a highly intuitive explanation of loess fit lines on YouTube (www.youtube.com/watch?v=Vf7oJ6z2LCc).

What if we want to look at the relationship between car weight and fuel efficiency separately for 4-, 6-, and 8-cylinder cars? This is easy to do with `ggplot2` and a few simple modifications of the previous code. Figure 11.2 provides the graph.

Listing 11.2　A scatter plot with separate best-fit lines

```
ggplot(mtcars,
       aes(x=wt, y=mpg,
           color=factor(cyl),
           shape=factor(cyl))) +
  geom_point(size=2) +
  geom_smooth(method="lm", se=FALSE) +
  geom_smooth(method="loess", se=FALSE, linetype="dashed") +
  labs(title = "Scatter Plot of MPG vs. Weight",
       subtitle = "By Number of Cylinders",
       x = "Car Weight (lbs/1000)",
       y = "Miles Per Gallon",
       color = "Number of \nCylinders",
       shape = "Number of \nCylinders") +
  theme_bw()
```

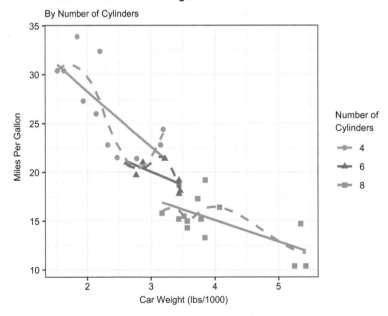

Figure 11.2　Scatter plot with subgroups and separately estimated fit lines

By mapping the number of cylinders to color and shape in the `aes()` function, the three groups (4, 6, or 8 cylinders) are differentiated by color and plotting symbol and separate linear and loess lines. Since the `cyl` variable is numeric, `factor(cyl)` is used to convert the variable into discrete categories.

You can control the smoothness of the loess lines using the `span` parameter. The default is `geom_smooth(method="loess", span=0.75)` Larger values lead to smoother fits. In this example, the loess lines overfit the data (follow the points too closely). A value of `span=4` (not shown) provides a much smoother fit.

Scatter plots help you visualize relationships between quantitative variables two at a time, but what if you wanted to look at the bivariate relationships between automobile mileage, weight, displacement (cubic inch), and rear axle ratio? When there are several quantitative variables, you can represent their relationships using a scatter plot matrix.

11.1.1 *Scatter plot matrices*

There are many useful functions for creating scatter plot matrices in R. Base R provides the `pairs()` function for creating simple scatter plot matrices. Section 8.2.4 (multiple linear regression) demonstrates the creation of scatter plot matrices using the `scatterplotMatrix` function from the `car` package.

In this section, we'll use the `ggpairs()` function in the `GGally` package to create a `ggplot2` version of a scatter plot matrix. As you'll see, this approach provides options for creating highly customized graphs. Be sure to install the `GGally` package (`install.packages("GGally")`) before proceeding.

First, let's create a default scatter plot matrix for the `mpg`, `disp`, `drat`, and `wt` variables in the `mtcars` data frame:

```
library(GGally)
ggpairs(mtcars[c("mpg","disp","drat", "wt")])
```

Figure 11.3 shows the resulting graph.

By default, the principal diagonal of the matrix contains the kernel density curve for each variable (see section 6.5 for details). Miles per gallon is right skewed (there are a few high values), and the rear axle ratio appears to be bimodal. The six scatter plots are placed below the principal diagonal. The scatter plot between miles per gallon and engine displace lies at the intersection of these two variables (second row, first column) and indicates a negative relationship. The Pearson correlation coefficients between each pair of variables is above the principal diagonal. The correlation between miles per gallon and engine displacement is –0.848 (first row, second column) and supports our conclusion that as engine displacement increases, gas mileage decreases.

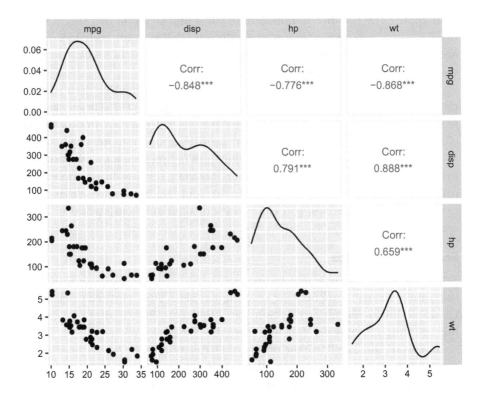

Figure 11.3 Scatter plot matrix created by the `ggpairs()` function

Next, we'll create a highly customized scatter plot matrix, adding fit lines, histograms, and a personalized theme. The `ggpairs()` function lets you specify separate functions for creating plots on, below, and above the principal diagonal. The following listing provides the code.

Listing 11.3 A scatter plot matrix with fit lines, histograms, and correlation coefficients

```
library(GGally)

diagplots <- function(data, mapping) {
  ggplot(data = data, mapping = mapping) +
    geom_histogram(fill="lightblue", color="black")
}

lowerplots <- function(data, mapping) {
  ggplot(data = data, mapping = mapping) +
    geom_point(color="darkgrey") +
    geom_smooth(method = "lm", color = "steelblue", se=FALSE) +
    geom_smooth(method="loess", color="red", se=FALSE, linetype="dashed")
}
```

❶ Function for plots on principal diagonal

Function for plots below diagonal ❷

```
upperplots <- function(data, mapping) {
    ggally_cor(data=data, mapping=mapping,
            display_grid=FALSE, size=3.5, color="black")
}
```

❸ **Function for plots above diagonal**

```
mytheme <-  theme(strip.background = element_blank(),
                  panel.grid       = element_blank(),
                  panel.background = element_blank(),
                  panel.border = element_rect(color="grey20", fill=NA))
```

❹ **Customized theme**

```
ggpairs(mtcars,
        columns=c("mpg","disp", "drat", "wt"),
        columnLabels=c("MPG", "Displacement",
                    "R Axle Ratio", "Weight"),
        title = "Scatterplot Matrix with Linear and Loess Fits",
        lower = list(continuous = lowerplots),
        diag =  list(continuous = diagplots),
        upper = list(continuous = upperplots)) +
        mytheme
```

❺ **Generates scatter plot matrix**

First, a function is defined for creating a histogram using light blue bars with black borders ❶. Next, a function is created for generating a scatter plot with dark grey points, a steel blue line of best fit, and a dashed red loess smoothed line. Confidence intervals are suppressed (se=FALSE) ❷. A third function is specified for displaying correlation coefficients ❸. This function uses the ggally_cor() function to obtain and print the coefficient, while the size and color option affect the appearance, and the displayGrid option suppresses grid lines. A customized theme has also been added ❹. This optional step eliminates facet strips and grid lines and surrounds each cell with a grey box.

Finally, the ggpairs() function ❺ uses these functions to create the customized graph in figure 11.4. The columns option specifies the variables, and the column-Labels option provides descriptive names. The lower, diag, and upper options specify the functions that will be used to create the cell plots in each portion of the matrix. This approach gives you a great deal of flexibility in designing the finished graph.

R provides many other ways to create scatter plot matrices. You may want to explore the splom() function in the lattice package, the pairs2() function in the TeachingDemos package, the xysplom() function in the HH package, the kdepairs() function in the ResourceSelection package, and pairs.mod() in the SMPracticals package. Each adds its own unique twist. Analysts must love scatter plot matrices!

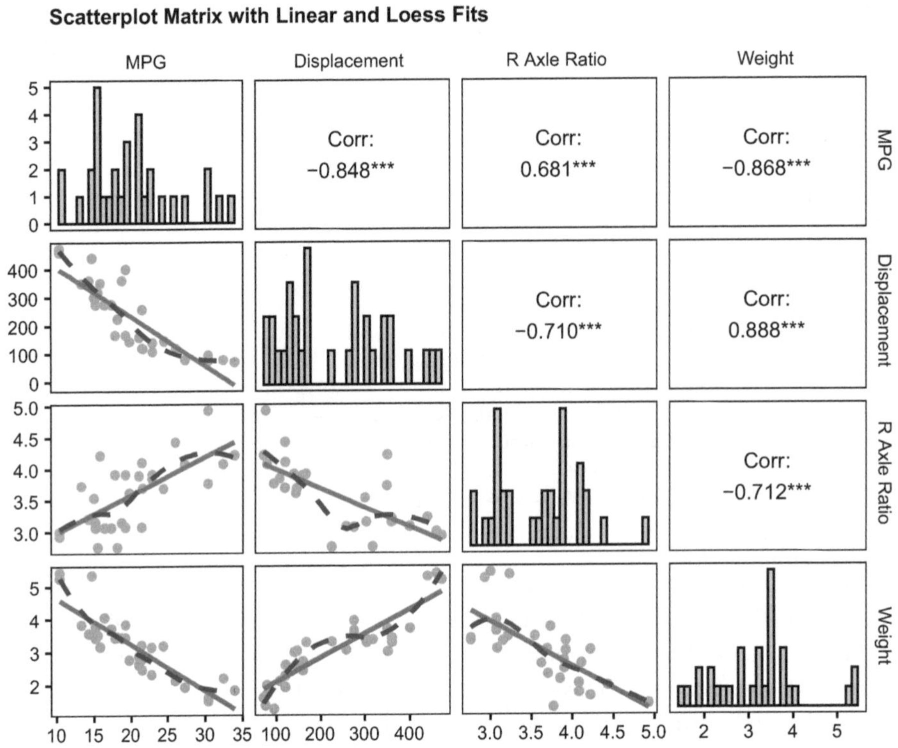

Scatterplot Matrix with Linear and Loess Fits

Figure 11.4   A scatter plot matrix created with the `ggpairs()` function and user-supplied functions for the scatter plots, histograms, and correlations

11.1.2   High-density scatter plots

When there's a significant overlap among data points, scatter plots become less useful for observing relationships. Consider the following contrived example with 10,000 observations falling into two overlapping clusters of data:

```
set.seed(1234)
n <- 10000
c1 <- matrix(rnorm(n, mean=0, sd=.5), ncol=2)
c2 <- matrix(rnorm(n, mean=3, sd=2), ncol=2)
mydata <- rbind(c1, c2)
mydata <- as.data.frame(mydata)
names(mydata) <- c("x", "y")
```

If you generate a standard scatter plot between these variables using the following code

```
ggplot(mydata, aes(x=x, y=y)) + geom_point() +
  ggtitle("Scatter Plot with 10,000 Observations")
```

you'll obtain a graph like the one in figure 11.5.

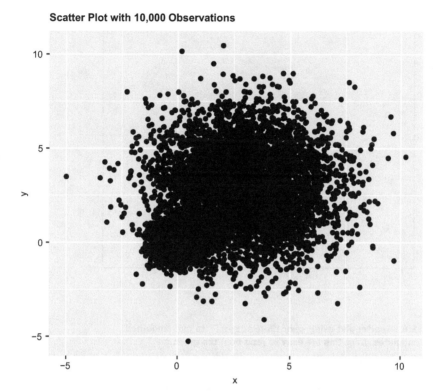

Scatter Plot with 10,000 Observations

Figure 11.5 Scatter plot with 10,000 observations and significant overlap of data points. Note that the overlap of data points makes it difficult to discern where the concentration of data is greatest.

The overlap of data points in figure 11.5 makes it difficult to discern the relationship between x and y. R provides several graphical approaches that can be used when this occurs, including binning, color, and transparency to indicate the number of over-printed data points at any point on the graph.

The `smoothScatter()` function uses a kernel density estimate to produce smoothed color density representations of the scatter plot. The code

```
with(mydata,
     smoothScatter(x, y,
                   main="Scatter Plot Colored by Smoothed Densities"))
```

produces the graph in figure 11.6.

Scatter Plot Colored by Smoothed Densities

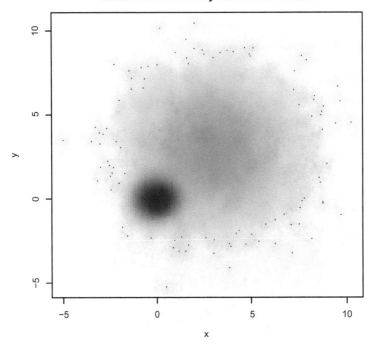

Figure 11.6 Scatter plot using `smoothScatter()` **to plot smoothed density estimates. Densities are easy to read from the graph.**

Using an alternative approach, the `geom_hex()` function in the `ggplot2` package provides bivariate binning into hexagonal cells (it looks better than it sounds). Basically, the plot area is divided into a grid of hexagonal cells, and the number of points in each cell is displayed using color or shading. Applying this function to the dataset

```
ggplot(mydata, aes(x=x, y=y)) +
  geom_hex(bins=50) +
  scale_fill_continuous(trans = 'reverse') +
  ggtitle("Scatter Plot with 10,000 Observations")
```

gives you the scatter plot in figure 11.7.

By default, `geom_hex()` uses lighter colors to indicate greater density. In your code, the function `scale_fill_continuous(trans = 'reverse')` ensures that darker colors are used to indicate areas of greater density. I think that this is more intuitive and matches the approach of other R functions used to visualize large datasets.

Note that the `hexbin()` function in the `hexbin` package, along with the `iplot()` function in the `IDPmisc` package, can be used to create readable scatter plot matrices for large datasets as well. See `?hexbin` and `?iplot` for examples.

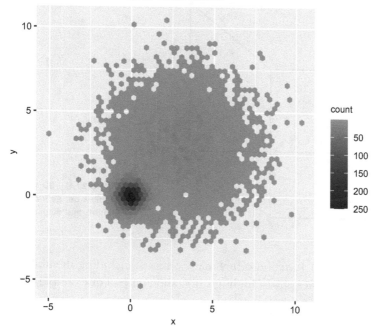

Figure 11.7 Scatter plot using hexagonal binning to display the number of observations at each point. Data concentrations are easy to see, and counts can be read from the legend.

11.1.3 3D scatter plots

Scatter plots and scatter plot matrices display bivariate relationships. What if you want to visualize the interaction of three quantitative variables at once? You can use a 3D scatter plot.

For example, say that you're interested in the relationship between automobile mileage, weight, and displacement. You can use the scatterplot3d() function in the scatterplot3d package to picture their relationship. The format is

```
scatterplot3d(x, y, z)
```

where x is plotted on the horizontal axis, y is plotted on the vertical axis, and z is plotted in perspective. Continuing the example,

```
library(scatterplot3d)
with(mtcars,
     scatterplot3d(wt, disp, mpg,
                   main="Basic 3D Scatter Plot"))
```

produces the 3D scatter plot in figure 11.8.

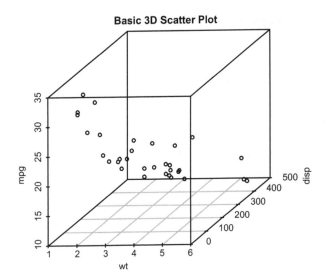

Figure 11.8   3D scatter plot of miles per gallon, auto weight, and displacement

The `scatterplot3d()` function offers many options, including the ability to specify symbols, axes, colors, lines, grids, highlighting, and angles. For example, the code

```
library(scatterplot3d)
with(mtcars,
     scatterplot3d(wt, disp, mpg,
                   pch=16,
                   highlight.3d=TRUE,
                   type="h",
                   main="3D Scatter Plot with Vertical Lines"))
```

produces a 3D scatter plot with highlighting that enhances the impression of depth and vertical lines connecting points to the horizontal plane (see figure 11.9).

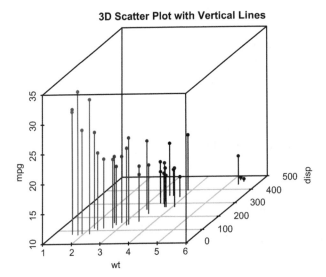

Figure 11.9   3D scatter plot with vertical lines and shading

As a final example, let's take the previous graph and add a regression plane. The code is

```
library(scatterplot3d)
s3d <-with(mtcars,
            scatterplot3d(wt, disp, mpg,
                          pch=16,
                          highlight.3d=TRUE,
                          type="h",
            main="3D Scatter Plot with Vertical Lines and Regression Plane"))
fit <- lm(mpg ~ wt+disp, data=mtcars)
s3d$plane3d(fit)
```

Figure 11.10 shows the resulting graph.

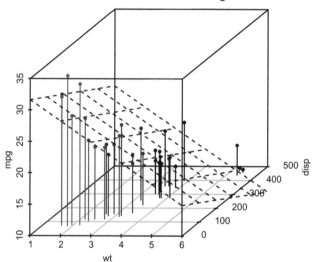

3D Scatter Plot with Vertical Lines and Regression Plane

Figure 11.10   3D scatter plot with vertical lines, shading, and overlaid regression plane

The graph allows you to visualize the prediction of miles per gallon from automobile weight and displacement using a multiple regression equation. The plane represents the predicted values, and the points are the actual values. The vertical distances from the plane to the points are the residuals. Points that lie above the plane are underpredicted, whereas points that lie below the line are overpredicted. Chapter 8 covers multiple regression.

11.1.4 *Spinning 3D scatter plots*

Three-dimensional scatter plots are much easier to interpret if you can interact with them. R provides several mechanisms for rotating graphs so you can see the plotted points from more than one angle.

For example, you can create an interactive 3D scatter plot using the `plot3d()` function in the `rgl` package. It creates a spinning 3D scatter plot that can be rotated with the mouse. The format is

```
plot3d(x, y, z)
```

where *x*, *y*, and *z* are numeric vectors representing points. You can also add options like `col` and `size` to control the color and size of the points, respectively. Continuing the example, try this code:

```
library(rgl)
with(mtcars,
     plot3d(wt, disp, mpg, col="red", size=5))
```

You should get a graph like the one depicted in figure 11.11. Use the mouse to rotate the axes. I think you'll find that being able to rotate the scatter plot in three dimensions makes the graph much easier to understand.

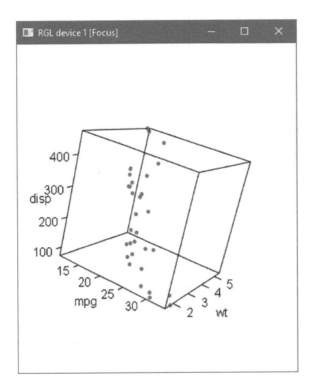

Figure 11.11 Rotating 3D scatter plot produced by the `plot3d()` function in the `rgl` package

You can perform a similar function with `scatter3d()` in the `car` package:

```
library(car)
with(mtcars,
     scatter3d(wt, disp, mpg))
```

Figure 11.12 displays the results.

The `scatter3d()` function can include a variety of regression surfaces, such as linear, quadratic, smooth, and additive. The linear surface is the default. Additionally, there are options for interactively identifying points. See `help(scatter3d)` for more details.

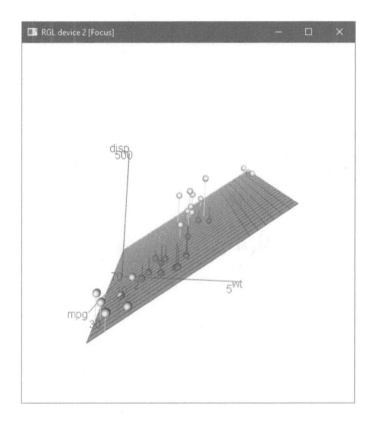

Figure 11.12
Spinning 3D scatter plot produced by the `scatter3d()` function in the `car` package

11.1.5 *Bubble plots*

In the previous section, we displayed the relationship between three quantitative variables using a 3D scatter plot. Another approach is to create a 2D scatter plot and use the size of the plotted point to represent the value of the third variable. This approach is called a *bubble plot*.

A simple example of a bubble plot is given here:

```
ggplot(mtcars,
    aes(x = wt, y = mpg, size = disp)) +
    geom_point() +
    labs(title="Bubble Plot with point size proportional to displacement",
        x="Weight of Car (lbs/1000)",
        y="Miles Per Gallon")
```

The resulting scatter plot shows the relationship between car weight and fuel efficiency, where point size is proportional to each car's engine displacement. Figure 11.13 shows the graph.

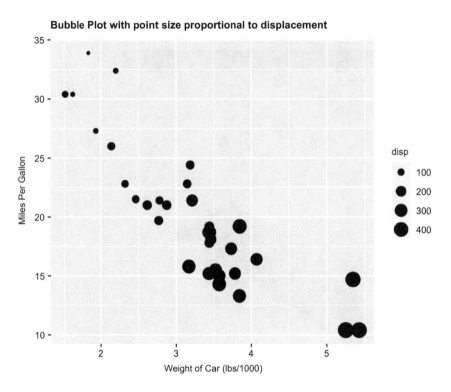

Figure 11.13   Bubble plot of car weight vs. mpg, where point size is proportional to engine displacement

We can improve the default appearance by choosing a different point shape and color and adding transparency to deal with point overlaps. We'll also increase the possible range of bubble sizes to make discrimination easier. Finally, we'll use color to add the number of cylinders as a fourth variable. The following listing gives the code, and figure 11.14 shows the graph. The colors are difficult to distinguish in greyscale, but readily apparent in color.

Listing 11.4   An enhanced bubble plot

```
ggplot(mtcars,
       aes(x = wt, y = mpg, size = disp, fill=factor(cyl))) +
    geom_point(alpha = .5,
               color = "black",
               shape = 21) +
```

```
scale_size_continuous(range = c(1, 10)) +
labs(title = "Auto mileage by weight and horsepower",
     subtitle = "Motor Trend US Magazine (1973-74 models)",
     x = "Weight (1000 lbs)",
     y = "Miles/(US) gallon",
     size = "Engine\ndisplacement",
     fill = "Cylinders") +
theme_minimal()
```

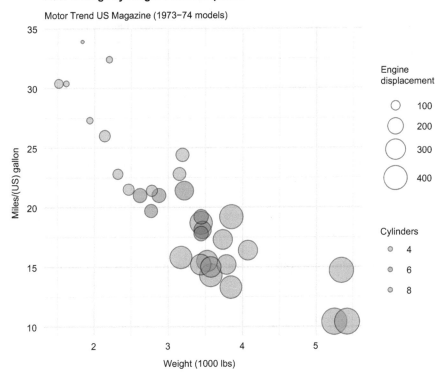

Figure 11.14 Enhanced bubble plot. Automobiles with more engine cylinders tend to have increased weight and engine displacement and poorer fuel efficiency.

In general, statisticians who use R tend to avoid bubble plots for the same reason they avoid pie charts: humans typically have a harder time making judgments about volume than distance. But bubble charts are popular in the business world, so I'm including them here.

I've certainly had a lot to say about scatter plots. This attention to detail is due, in part, to the central place that scatter plots hold in data analysis. Although simple, they can help you visualize your data in an immediate and straightforward manner, uncovering relationships that might otherwise be missed.

11.2 Line charts

If you connect the points in a scatter plot moving from left to right, you have a line plot. The dataset `Orange` that comes with the base installation contains age and circumference data for five orange trees. Consider the growth of the first orange tree, depicted in figure 11.15. The plot on the left is a scatter plot, and the plot on the right is a line chart. As you can see, line charts are particularly good vehicles for conveying change. The graphs in figure 11.15 were created with the code in the listing 11.5..

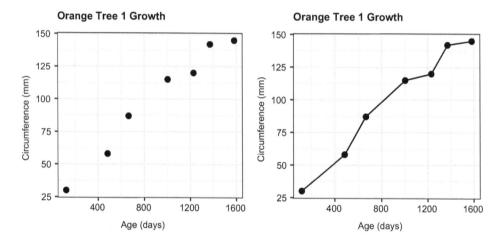

Figure 11.15 Comparison of a scatter plot and a line plot. A line chart helps the reader see growth and trends in the data.

Listing 11.5   Scatter plots vs. line plots

```
library(ggplot2)
tree1 <- subset(Orange, Tree == 1)
ggplot(data=tree1,
       aes(x=age, y=circumference)) +
  geom_point(size=2) +
  labs(title="Orange Tree 1 Growth",
       x = "Age (days)",
       y = "Circumference (mm)") +
  theme_bw()

ggplot(data=tree1,
       aes(x=age, y=circumference)) +
  geom_point(size=2) +
  geom_line() +
  labs(title="Orange Tree 1 Growth",
       x = "Age (days)",
       y = "Circumference (mm)") +
  theme_bw()
```

The only difference between the code for the two plots is the addition of the `geom_line()` function. Table 11.1 gives common options for this function. Each can be assigned a value or mapped to a categorical variable.

Table 11.1 `geom_line()` options

Option	Effect
`size`	Thickness of the line
`color`	Line color
`linetype`	Line pattern (e.g., dashed)

Figure 11.16 shows possible line types.

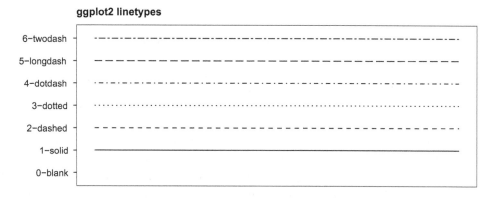

Figure 11.16 `ggplot2` line types. You can specify either the name or the number.

To demonstrate the creation of a more complex line chart, let's plot the growth of all five orange trees over time. Each tree will have its own distinctive line and color. The code is shown in the next listing, and the results in figure 11.17.

Listing 11.6 Line chart displaying the growth of five orange trees over time

```
library(ggplot2)
ggplot(data=Orange,
       aes(x=age, y=circumference, linetype=Tree, color=Tree)) +
  geom_point() +
  geom_line(size=1) +
  scale_color_brewer(palette="Set1") +
  labs(title="Orange Tree Growth",
       x = "Age (days)",
       y = "Circumference (mm)") +
  theme_bw()
```

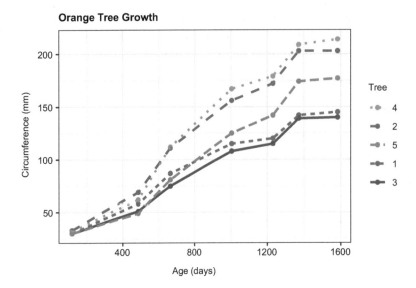

Figure 11.17 Line chart displaying the growth of five orange trees

In listing 11.6, the `aes()` function maps the tree number to both line type and color. The `scale_color_brewer()` function is used to select a color palette. Since I am chromatically challenged (i.e., I'm awful at choosing good colors), I rely heavily on predefined color palettes like those provided by the `RColorBrewer` package. Chapter 19 (advanced graphs) describes color palettes in great detail.

You can see in the figure that tree 4 and tree 2 demonstrated the greatest growth across the range of days measured and that tree 4 overtakes tree 2 at around 664 days. By default, the legend lists the lines in the opposite order that they appear on the chart (top to bottom in the legend is bottom to top in the graph). To make the orders match top to bottom, add

```
+ guides(color = guide_legend(reverse = TRUE),
        linetype = guide_legend(reverse = TRUE))
```

to the code in listing 11.6. In the next section, you'll explore ways of examining a number of correlation coefficients at once.

11.3 *Corrgrams*

Correlation matrices are a fundamental aspect of multivariate statistics. Which variables are strongly related to each other, and which aren't? Are some clusters of variables related in specific ways? As the number of variables grows, such questions can be harder to answer. *Corrgrams* are a relatively recent tool for visualizing the data in correlation matrices.

It's easier to explain a corrgram once you've seen one. Consider the correlations among the variables in the `mtcars` data frame. Here you have 11 variables, each measuring some aspect of 32 automobiles. You can get the correlations using the following code:

```
> round(cor(mtcars), 2)
       mpg   cyl  disp    hp  drat    wt  qsec    vs    am  gear  carb
mpg   1.00 -0.85 -0.85 -0.78  0.68 -0.87  0.42  0.66  0.60  0.48 -0.55
cyl  -0.85  1.00  0.90  0.83 -0.70  0.78 -0.59 -0.81 -0.52 -0.49  0.53
disp -0.85  0.90  1.00  0.79 -0.71  0.89 -0.43 -0.71 -0.59 -0.56  0.39
hp   -0.78  0.83  0.79  1.00 -0.45  0.66 -0.71 -0.72 -0.24 -0.13  0.75
drat  0.68 -0.70 -0.71 -0.45  1.00 -0.71  0.09  0.44  0.71  0.70 -0.09
wt   -0.87  0.78  0.89  0.66 -0.71  1.00 -0.17 -0.55 -0.69 -0.58  0.43
qsec  0.42 -0.59 -0.43 -0.71  0.09 -0.17  1.00  0.74 -0.23 -0.21 -0.66
vs    0.66 -0.81 -0.71 -0.72  0.44 -0.55  0.74  1.00  0.17  0.21 -0.57
am    0.60 -0.52 -0.59 -0.24  0.71 -0.69 -0.23  0.17  1.00  0.79  0.06
gear  0.48 -0.49 -0.56 -0.13  0.70 -0.58 -0.21  0.21  0.79  1.00  0.27
carb -0.55  0.53  0.39  0.75 -0.09  0.43 -0.66 -0.57  0.06  0.27  1.00
```

Which variables are most related? Which variables are relatively independent? Are there any patterns? It isn't that easy to tell from the correlation matrix without significant time and effort (and probably a set of colored pens to make notations).

You can display that same correlation matrix using the `corrgram()` function in the `corrgram` package (see figure 11.18). The code is

```
library(corrgram)
corrgram(mtcars, order=TRUE, lower.panel=panel.shade,
         upper.panel=panel.pie, text.panel=panel.txt,
         main="Corrgram of mtcars intercorrelations")
```

Corrgram of mtcars intercorrelations

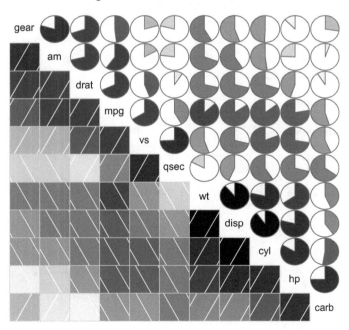

Figure 11.18 Corrgram of the correlations among the variables in the `mtcars` data frame. Rows and columns have been reordered using principal components analysis.

To interpret this graph, start with the lower triangle of cells (the cells below the principal diagonal). By default, a blue color and hashing that goes from lower left to upper right represent a positive correlation between the two variables that meet at that cell. Conversely, a red color and hashing that goes from the upper left to lower right represent a negative correlation. The darker and more saturated the color, the greater the magnitude of the correlation. Weak correlations, near zero, appear washed out. In the current graph, the rows and columns have been reordered (using principal components analysis that we'll discuss in chapter 14) to cluster variables together that have similar correlation patterns.

You can see from the shaded cells that gear, am, drat, and mpg are positively correlated with one another. You can also see that wt, disp, cyl, hp, and carb are positively correlated with one another. But the first group of variables is negatively correlated with the second group. You can also see that the correlation between carb and am is weak, as is the correlation between vs and gear, vs and am, and drat and qsec.

The upper triangle of cells displays the same information using pies. Here, color plays the same role, but the strength of the correlation is indicated by the size of the filled pie slice. Positive correlations fill the pie starting at 12 o'clock and moving clockwise. Negative correlations fill the pie by moving counterclockwise.

The format of the corrgram() function is

```
corrgram(x, order=, panel=, text.panel=, diag.panel=)
```

where x is a data frame with one observation per row. When order=TRUE, the variables are reordered using a principal component analysis of the correlation matrix. Reordering can help make patterns of bivariate relationships more obvious.

The option panel specifies the type of off-diagonal panels to use. Alternatively, you can use the options lower.panel and upper.panel to choose different options below and above the main diagonal. The text.panel and diag.panel options refer to the main diagonal. Table 11.2 describes allowable values.

Table 11.2 Panel options for the corrgram() function

Placement	Panel option	Description
Off diagonal	panel.pie	The filled portion of the pie indicates the magnitude of the correlation.
	panel.shade	The depth of the shading indicates the magnitude of the correlation.
	panel.ellipse	Plots a confidence ellipse and smoothed line
	panel.pts	Plots a scatter plot
	panel.conf	Prints correlations and their confidence intervals
	panel.cor	Prints correlations without their confidence intervals
Main diagonal	panel.txt	Prints the variable name

Table 11.2 Panel options for the `corrgram()` function *(continued)*

Placement	Panel option	Description
	`panel.minmax`	Prints the minimum and maximum value and variable name
	`panel.density`	Prints the kernel density plot and variable name

Let's try a second example. The code

```
library(corrgram)
corrgram(mtcars, order=TRUE, lower.panel=panel.ellipse,
        upper.panel=panel.pts, text.panel=panel.txt,
        diag.panel=panel.minmax,
        main="Corrgram of mtcars data using scatter plots
              and ellipses")
```

produces the graph in figure 11.19. Here, you're using smoothed fit lines and confidence ellipses in the lower triangle and scatter plots in the upper triangle.

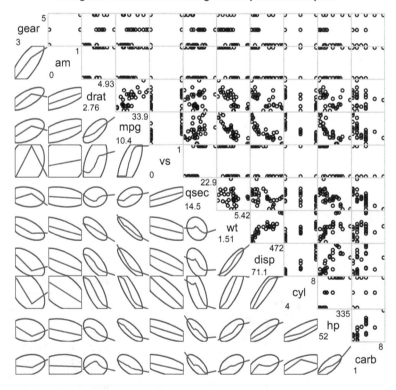

Corrgram of mtcars data using scatter plots and ellipses

Figure 11.19 Corrgram of the correlations among the variables in the `mtcars` data frame. The lower triangle contains smoothed best-fit lines and confidence ellipses, and the upper triangle contains scatter plots. The diagonal panel contains minimum and maximum values. Rows and columns have been reordered using principal components analysis.

Why do the scatter plots look odd?

Several of the variables plotted in figure 11.19 have limited allowable values. For example, the number of gears is 3, 4, or 5. The number of cylinders is 4, 6, or 8. Both am (transmission type) and vs (V/S) are dichotomous. This explains the odd-looking scatter plots in the upper diagonal.

Always be careful that the statistical methods you choose are appropriate to the form of the data. Specifying these variables as ordered or unordered factors can serve as a useful check. When R knows that a variable is categorical or ordinal, it attempts to apply statistical methods that are appropriate to that level of measurement.

We'll finish with one more example. The code

```
corrgram(mtcars, order=TRUE, lower.panel=panel.shade,
         upper.panel=panel.cor,
         main="Corrgram of mtcars data using shading and coefficients")
```

produces the graph in figure 11.20. Here you're using shading in the lower triangle and order variables to emphasize correlation patterns, and you're printing the correlation values in the upper triangle.

Corrgram of mtcars data using shading and coefficients

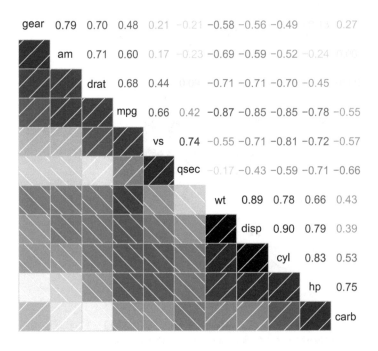

Figure 11.20 Corrgram of the correlations among the variables in the mtcars data frame. The lower triangle is shaded to represent the magnitude and direction of the correlations. Rows and columns have been reordered using principal components analysis. Correlation coefficients are printed in the upper triangle.

Before moving on, I should point out that you can control the colors used by the `corrgram()` function. To do so, specify four colors in the `colorRampPalette()` function and include the results using the `col.regions` option. Here's an example:

```
library(corrgram)
cols <- colorRampPalette(c("darkgoldenrod4", "burlywood1",
                           "darkkhaki", "darkgreen"))
corrgram(mtcars, order=TRUE, col.regions=cols,
         lower.panel=panel.shade,
         upper.panel=panel.conf, text.panel=panel.txt,
         main="A Corrgram (or Horse) of a Different Color")
```

Try it and see what you get.

Corrgrams can be useful for examining large numbers of bivariate relationships among quantitative variables. Because they're relatively new, the greatest challenge is to educate the recipient on how to interpret them. To learn more, see Michael Friendly, "Corrgrams: Exploratory Displays for Correlation Matrices," https://www.datavis.ca/papers/corrgram.pdf.

11.4 Mosaic plots

Up to this point, we've been exploring methods of visualizing relationships among quantitative/continuous variables. But what if your variables are categorical? When you're looking at a single categorical variable, you can use a bar or pie chart. If there are two categorical variables, you can use a stacked bar chart (section 6.1.2). But what do you do if there are more than two categorical variables?

One approach is to use *mosaic plots*, in which the frequencies in a multidimensional contingency table are represented by nested rectangular regions that are proportional to their cell frequency. Color and/or shading can be used to represent residuals from a fitted model. For details, see Meyer, Zeileis, and Hornick (2006) or Michael Friendly's excellent tutorial (http://mng.bz/3p0d).

Mosaic plots can be created with the `mosaic()` function from the vcd library (there's a `mosaicplot()` function in the basic installation of R, but I recommend you use the vcd package for its more extensive features). As an example, consider the `Titanic` dataset available in the base installation. It describes the number of passengers who survived or died, cross-classified by their class (1st, 2nd, 3rd, Crew), sex (Male, Female), and age (Child, Adult). This is a well-studied dataset. You can see the cross-classification using the following code:

```
> ftable(Titanic)
                    Survived  No Yes
Class Sex    Age
1st   Male   Child             0   5
             Adult           118  57
      Female Child             0   1
             Adult             4 140
2nd   Male   Child             0  11
             Adult           154  14
```

```
        Female Child              0   13
               Adult            13   80
3rd    Male   Child            35   13
               Adult           387   75
        Female Child            17   14
               Adult            89   76
Crew   Male   Child             0    0
               Adult           670  192
        Female Child             0    0
               Adult             3   20
```

The `mosaic()` function can be invoked as

`mosaic(table)`

where `table` is a contingency table in array form, or

`mosaic(formula, data=)`

where `formula` is a standard R formula and `data` specifies either a data frame or a table. Adding the option `shade=TRUE` colors the figure based on Pearson residuals from a fitted model (independence by default), and the option `legend=TRUE` displays a legend for these residuals.

For example, both

```
library(vcd)
mosaic(Titanic, shade=TRUE, legend=TRUE)
```

and

```
library(vcd)
mosaic(~Class+Sex+Age+Survived, data=Titanic, shade=TRUE, legend=TRUE)
```

will produce the graph shown in figure 11.21. The formula version gives you greater control over the selection and placement of variables in the graph.

A great deal of information is packed into this one picture. For example, as a person moves from crew to first class, the survival rate increases precipitously. Most children were in third and second class. Most females in first class survived, whereas only about half the females in third class survived. There were few females in the crew, causing the Survived labels (No, Yes at the bottom of the chart) to overlap for this group. Keep looking, and you'll see many more interesting facts. Remember to look at the relative widths and heights of the rectangles. What else can you learn about that night?

Extended mosaic plots add color and shading to represent the residuals from a fitted model. In this example, the blue shading indicates cross-classifications that occur more often than expected, assuming that survival is unrelated to class, gender, and age. Red shading indicates cross-classifications that occur less often than expected under the independence model. Be sure to run the example so that you can see the results in color. The graph indicates that more first-class women survived and more male crew members died than would be expected under an independence model. Fewer third-class men survived than would be expected if survival was independent of

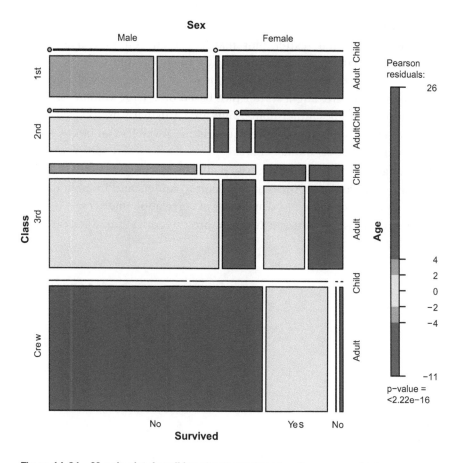

Figure 11.21 Mosaic plot describing *Titanic* survivors by class, sex, and age

class, gender, and age. If you'd like to explore mosaic plots in greater detail, try running `example(mosaic)`.

In this chapter, we considered a wide range of techniques for displaying relationships among two or more variables, including 2D and 3D scatter plots, scatter plot matrices, bubble plots, line plots, corrgrams, and mosaic plots. Some of these methods are standard techniques, where others are less well known.

Taken together with methods for displaying univariate distributions (chapter 6), exploring regression models (chapter 8), and visualizing group differences (chapter 9), you now have a comprehensive toolbox for visualizing and extracting meaning from your data (and fame and fortune is surely near at hand)! In later chapters, you'll expand your skills with additional specialized techniques, including graphics for latent variable models (chapter 14), time series (chapter 15), clustered data (chapter 16), missing data (chapter 18), and techniques for creating graphs that are conditioned on one or more variables (chapter 19).

Summary

- Scatter plots and scatter plot matrices allow you to visualize relationships between quantitative variables two at a time. The plots can be enhanced with linear and loess fit lines showing trends.

- When you're creating a scatter plot based on a large volume of data, methods that plot densities rather than points are particularly useful.

- The relationships among three quantitative variables can be explored using 3D scatter plots or 2D bubble charts.

- Change over time can be described effectively with line charts.

- Large correlation matrices are difficult to understand in table form, but easily explored via corrgrams—visual plots of correlation matrices.

- The relationships between two or more categorical variables can be visualized with mosaic charts.

Resampling statistics and bootstrapping

In chapters 7, 8, and 9, we reviewed statistical methods that test hypotheses and estimate confidence intervals for population parameters by assuming that the observed data is sampled from a normal distribution or some other well-known theoretical distribution. But in many cases, this assumption is unwarranted. Statistical approaches based on randomization and resampling can be used in cases where the data is sampled from unknown or mixed distributions, where sample sizes are small, where outliers are a problem, or where devising an appropriate test based on a theoretical distribution is too complex and mathematically intractable.

In this chapter, we'll explore two broad statistical approaches that use randomization: permutation tests and bootstrapping. Historically, these methods were only available to experienced programmers and expert statisticians. Contributed packages in R now make them readily available to a wider group of data analysts.

We'll also revisit problems that were initially analyzed using traditional methods (for example, t-tests, chi-square tests, ANOVA, and regression) and see how they can be approached using these robust, computer-intensive methods. To get the most out of section 12.2, be sure to read chapter 7 first. Chapters 8 and 9 serve as prerequisites for section 12.3.

12.1   Permutation tests

Permutation tests, also called *randomization* or *re-randomization* tests, have been around for decades, but it took the advent of high-speed computers to make them practically available. To understand the logic of a permutation test, consider a hypothetical problem: 10 subjects have been randomly assigned to one of two treatment conditions (A or B), and an outcome variable (score) has been recorded. The results of the experiment are presented in table 12.1.

Figure 12.1 also displays the data. Is there enough evidence to conclude that the impact of the treatments differs?

Table 12.1   Hypothetical two-group problem

Treatment A	Treatment B
40	57
57	64
45	55
55	62
58	65

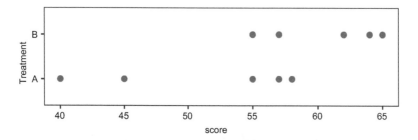

Figure 12.1   Strip chart of the hypothetical treatment data in table 12.1

In a parametric approach, you might assume that the data are sampled from normal populations with equal variances and apply a two-tailed independent-groups t-test. The null hypothesis is that the population mean for Treatment A is equal to the population mean for Treatment B. You'd calculate a t-statistic from the data and compare it to the theoretical distribution. If the observed t-statistic is sufficiently extreme, say outside the middle 95% of values in the theoretical distribution, you'd reject the null hypothesis and declare that the population means for the two groups are unequal at the 0.05 level of significance.

A permutation test takes a different approach. If the two treatments are truly equivalent, the label (Treatment A or Treatment B) assigned to an observed score is arbitrary. To test for differences between the two treatments, you could follow these steps:

1. Calculate the observed t-statistic, as in the parametric approach; call this t0.
2. Place all 10 scores in a single group.
3. Randomly assign 5 scores to Treatment A and 5 scores to Treatment B.
4. Calculate and record the new observed t-statistic.
5. Repeat steps 3–4 for every possible way of assigning 5 scores to Treatment A and 5 scores to Treatment B. There are 252 such possible arrangements.
6. Arrange the 252 t-statistics in ascending order. This is the empirical distribution, based on (or conditioned on) the sample data.
7. If t0 falls outside the middle 95% of the empirical distribution, reject the null hypothesis that the population means for the two treatment groups are equal at the 0.05 level of significance.

Notice that the same t-statistic is calculated in both the permutation and parametric approaches. But instead of comparing the statistic to a theoretical distribution to determine if it was extreme enough to reject the null hypothesis, it's compared to an empirical distribution created from permutations of the observed data. This logic can be extended to most classical statistical tests and linear models.

In the previous example, the empirical distribution was based on all possible permutations of the data. In such cases, the permutation test is called an *exact* test. As the sample sizes increase, the time required to form all possible permutations can become prohibitive. In such cases, you can use Monte Carlo simulation to sample from all possible permutations. Doing so provides an approximate test.

If you're uncomfortable assuming that the data is normally distributed, concerned about the impact of outliers, or feel that the dataset is too small for standard parametric approaches, a permutation test provides an excellent alternative. R has some of the most comprehensive and sophisticated packages currently available for performing permutation tests. The remainder of this section focuses on two contributed packages: the `coin` package and the `lmPerm` package. The `coin` package provides a comprehensive framework for permutation tests applied to independence problems, whereas the `lmPerm` package provides permutation tests for ANOVA and regression designs. We'll consider each package in turn. Be sure to install them (`install.packages(c("coin", "lmPerm"))`) before continuing.

Setting the random number seed

Before moving on, it's important to remember that permutation tests use pseudo-random numbers to sample from all possible permutations when performing an approximate test. Therefore, the results will change each time the test is performed. Setting the random number seed in R allows you to fix the random numbers generated. This is particularly useful when you want to share your examples with others because

> *(continued)*
> results will always be the same if the calls are made with the same seed. Setting the
> random number seed to `1234` (that is, `set.seed(1234)`) will allow you to replicate
> the results presented in this chapter.

12.2 *Permutation tests with the coin package*

The `coin` package provides a general framework for applying permutation tests to
independence problems. With this package, you can answer such questions these:

- Are responses independent of group assignment?
- Are two numeric variables independent?
- Are two categorical variables independent?

Using convenience functions provided in the package (see table 12.2), you can perform permutation test equivalents for most of the traditional statistical tests covered in
chapter 7.

Table 12.2   `coin` functions providing permutation test alternatives to traditional tests

Test	`coin` function
Two- and K-sample permutation test	`oneway_test( y ~ A)`
Wilcoxon–Mann–Whitney rank-sum test	`wilcox_test( y ~ A )`
Kruskal–Wallis test	`kruskal_test( y ~ A )`
Pearson's chi-square test	`chisq_test( A ~ B )`
Cochran–Mantel–Haenszel test	`cmh_test( A ~ B | C )`
Linear-by-linear association test	`lbl_test( D ~ E)`
Spearman's test	`spearman_test( y ~ x )`
Friedman test	`friedman_test( y ~ A | C )`
Wilcoxon signed-rank test	`wilcoxsign_test( y1 ~ y2 )`

In the `coin` function column, `y` and `x` are numeric variables, `A` and `B` are categorical
factors, `C` is a categorical blocking variable, `D` and `E` are ordered factors, and `y1` and
`y2` are matched numeric variables.

Each of the functions listed in table 12.2 takes the form

```
function_name( formula, data, distribution= )
```

where

- *formula* describes the relationship among variables to be tested. Examples are
  given in the table.

- *data* identifies a data frame.
- distribution specifies how the empirical distribution under the null hypothesis should be derived. Possible values are exact, asymptotic, and approximate.

If distribution="exact", the distribution under the null hypothesis is computed exactly (that is, from all possible permutations). The distribution can also be approximated by its asymptotic distribution (distribution="asymptotic") or via Monte Carlo resampling (distribution="approximate(nresample=n)"), where *n* indicates the number of random replications used to approximate the exact distribution. The default is 10,000 replications. At present, distribution="exact" is only available for two-sample problems.

NOTE In the coin package, categorical variables and ordinal variables must be coded as factors and ordered factors, respectively. Additionally, the data must be stored in a data frame.

In the remainder of this section, you'll apply several of the permutation tests described in table 12.2 to problems from previous chapters. This will allow you to compare the results to more traditional parametric and nonparametric approaches. We'll end this discussion of the coin package by considering advanced extensions.

12.2.1 Independent two-sample and k-sample tests

To begin, let's compare an independent samples t-test with a one-way exact test applied to the hypothetical data in table 12.2. The results are given in the following listing.

Listing 12.1 t-test vs. one-way permutation test for the hypothetical data

```
> library(coin)
> score <- c(40, 57, 45, 55, 58, 57, 64, 55, 62, 65)
> treatment <- factor(c(rep("A",5), rep("B",5)))
> mydata <- data.frame(treatment, score)
> t.test(score~treatment, data=mydata, var.equal=TRUE)

        Two Sample t-test

data:  score by treatment
t = -2.345, df = 8, p-value = 0.04705
alternative hypothesis: true difference in means is not equal to 0
95 percent confidence interval:
 -19.0405455  -0.1594545
sample estimates:
mean in group A mean in group B
         51.0             60.6

> oneway_test(score~treatment, data=mydata, distribution="exact")

        Exact Two-Sample Fisher-Pitman Permutation Test

data:  score by treatment (A, B)
Z = -1.9147, p-value = 0.07143
alternative hypothesis: true mu is not equal to 0
```

The traditional t-test indicates a significant group difference ($p < .05$), whereas the exact test doesn't ($p > 0.071$). With only 10 observations, I'd be more inclined to trust the results of the permutation test and attempt to collect more data before reaching a final conclusion.

Next, consider the Wilcoxon–Mann–Whitney U test. In chapter 7, we examined the difference in the probability of imprisonment in Southern versus non-Southern US states using the `wilcox.test()` function. Using an exact Wilcoxon rank-sum test, you'd get

```
> library(MASS)
> UScrime$So <- factor(UScrime$So)
> wilcox_test(Prob ~ So, data=UScrime, distribution="exact")

        Exact Wilcoxon Mann-Whitney Rank Sum Test

data:  Prob by So (0, 1)
Z = -3.7, p-value = 8.488e-05
alternative hypothesis: true mu is not equal to 0
```

suggesting that incarceration is more likely in Southern states. Note that in the previous code, the numeric variable `So` was transformed into a factor. This is because the `coin` package requires that all categorical variables be coded as factors. Additionally, you may have noted that these results agree exactly with the results of the `wilcox.test()` function in chapter 7. This is because `wilcox.test()` also computes an exact distribution by default.

Finally, consider a k-sample test. In chapter 9, you used a one-way ANOVA to evaluate the impact of five drug regimens on cholesterol reduction in a sample of 50 patients. An approximate k-sample permutation test can be performed instead, using this code:

```
> library(multcomp)
> set.seed(1234)
> oneway_test(response~trt, data=cholesterol,
    distribution=approximate(nresample=9999))

        Approximative K-Sample Fisher-Pitman Permutation Test

data:  response by trt (1time, 2times, 4times, drugD, drugE)
chi-squared = 36.381, p-value < 1e-04
```

Here, the reference distribution is based on 9,999 permutations of the data. The random-number seed is set so that your results will be the same as mine. There's clearly a difference in response among patients in the various groups.

12.2.2 *Independence in contingency tables*

You can use permutation tests to assess the independence of two categorical variables using either the `chisq_test()` or `cmh_test()` function. The latter function is used when data is stratified on a third categorical variable. If both variables are ordinal, you can use the `lbl_test()` function to test for a linear trend.

In chapter 7, you applied a chi-square test to assess the relationship between arthritis treatment and improvement. Treatment had two levels (Placebo and Treated), and Improved had three levels (None, Some, and Marked). The Improved variable was encoded as an ordered factor.

If you want to perform a permutation version of the chi-square test, you can use the following code:

```
> library(coin)
> library(vcd)
> Arthritis <- transform(Arthritis,
  Improved=as.factor(as.numeric(Improved)))
> set.seed(1234)
> chisq_test(Treatment~Improved, data=Arthritis,
             distribution=approximate(nresample=9999))

        Approximative Pearson Chi-Squared Test

data:  Treatment by Improved (1, 2, 3)
chi-squared = 13.055, p-value = 0.0018
```

This gives you an approximate chi-square test based on 9,999 replications. You might ask why you transformed the variable `Improved` from an ordered factor to a categorical factor. (Good question!) If you'd left it an ordered factor, `coin()` would have generated a linear × linear trend test instead of a chi-square test. Although a trend test would be a good choice in this situation, keeping it a chi-square test allows you to compare the results with those in chapter 7.

12.2.3 Independence between numeric variables

The `spearman_test()` function provides a permutation test of the independence of two numeric variables. In chapter 7, we examined the correlation between illiteracy and murder rates for US states. You can test the association via permutation using the following code:

```
> states <- as.data.frame(state.x77)
> set.seed(1234)
> spearman_test(Illiteracy~Murder, data=states,
               distribution=approximate(B=9999))

        Approximative Spearman Correlation Test

data:  Illiteracy by Murder
Z = 4.7065, p-value < 1e-04
alternative hypothesis: true rho is not equal to 0
```

Based on an approximate permutation test with 9,999 replications, the hypothesis of independence can be rejected. Note that `state.x77` is a matrix. It had to be converted into a data frame for use in the `coin` package.

12.2.4 *Dependent two-sample and k-sample tests*

Dependent sample tests are used when observations in different groups have been matched or when repeated measures are used. For permutation tests with two paired groups, the `wilcoxsign_test()` function can be used. For more than two groups, use the `friedman_test()` function.

In chapter 7, we compared the unemployment rate for urban males aged 14–24 (U1) with urban males aged 35–39 (U2). Because the two variables are reported for each of the 50 US states, you have a two-dependent groups design (`state` is the matching variable). You can use an exact Wilcoxon signed-rank test to see if unemployment rates for the two age groups are equal:

```
> library(coin)
> library(MASS)
> wilcoxsign_test(U1~U2, data=UScrime, distribution="exact")

        Exact Wilcoxon-Signed-Rank Test

data:  y by x (neg, pos)
        stratified by block
Z = 5.9691, p-value = 1.421e-14
alternative hypothesis: true mu is not equal to 0
```

Based on the results, you'd conclude that the unemployment rates differ.

12.2.5 *Going further*

The `coin` package provides a general framework for testing whether one group of variables is independent of a second group of variables (with optional stratification on a blocking variable) against arbitrary alternatives, via approximate permutation tests. In particular, the `independence_test()` function lets you approach most traditional tests from a permutation perspective and create new and novel statistical tests for situations not covered by traditional methods. This flexibility comes at a price: a high level of statistical knowledge is required to use the function appropriately. See the vignettes that accompany the package (accessed via `vignette("coin")`) for further details.

In the next section, you'll learn about the `lmPerm` package. This package provides a permutation approach to linear models, including regression and analysis of variance.

12.3 *Permutation tests with the lmPerm package*

The `lmPerm` package provides support for a permutation approach to linear models. In particular, the `lmp()` and `aovp()` functions are the `lm()` and `aov()` functions modified to perform permutation tests rather than normal theory tests.

The parameters in the `lmp()` and `aovp()` functions are similar to those in the `lm()` and `aov()` functions, with the addition of a `perm=` parameter. The `perm=` option can take the value `Exact`, `Prob`, or `SPR`. `Exact` produces an exact test, based on all possible permutations. `Prob` samples from all possible permutations. Sampling continues until the estimated standard deviation falls below 0.1 of the estimated

opping rule is controlled by an optional `Ca` parameter. Finally, `SPR` uses robability ratio test to decide when to stop sampling. Note that if the servations is greater than 10, `perm="Exact"` will automatically default ob". Exact tests are only available for small problems.

how this works, you'll apply a permutation approach to simple regression, nial regression, multiple regression, one-way analysis of variance, one-way analysis of covariance, and a two-way factorial design.

.1 Simple and polynomial regression

In chapter 8, you used linear regression to study the relationship between weight and height for a group of 15 women. Using `lmp()` instead of `lm()` generates the permutation test results shown in the following listing.

Listing 12.2 Permutation tests for simple linear regression

```
> library(lmPerm)
> set.seed(1234)
> fit <- lmp(weight~height, data=women, perm="Prob")
[1] "Settings:  unique SS : numeric variables centered"
> summary(fit)

Call:
lmp(formula = weight ~ height, data = women, perm = "Prob")

Residuals:
   Min    1Q Median    3Q    Max
-1.733 -1.133 -0.383  0.742  3.117

Coefficients:
       Estimate Iter Pr(Prob)
height     3.45 5000   <2e-16 ***
---
Signif. codes:  0 '***' 0.001 '**' 0.01 '*' 0.05 '.' 0.1 ' ' 1

Residual standard error: 1.5 on 13 degrees of freedom
Multiple R-Squared: 0.991,       Adjusted R-squared: 0.99
F-statistic: 1.43e+03 on 1 and 13 DF,  p-value: 1.09e-14
```

To fit a quadratic equation, you could use the code in this next listing.

Listing 12.3 Permutation tests for polynomial regression

```
> library(lmPerm)
> set.seed(1234)
> fit <- lmp(weight~height + I(height^2), data=women, perm="Prob")
[1] "Settings:  unique SS : numeric variables centered"
> summary(fit)

Call:
lmp(formula = weight ~ height + I(height^2), data = women, perm = "Prob")
```

```
Residuals:
    Min      1Q  Median      3Q      Max
-0.5094 -0.2961 -0.0094  0.2862  0.5971

Coefficients:
             Estimate Iter Pr(Prob)
height        -7.3483 5000    <2e-16 ***
I(height^2)    0.0831 5000    <2e-16 ***
---
Signif. codes:  0 '***' 0.001 '**' 0.01 '*' 0.05 '.' 0.1 ' ' 1

Residual standard error: 0.38 on 12 degrees of freedom
Multiple R-Squared: 0.999,      Adjusted R-squared: 0.999
F-statistic: 1.14e+04 on 2 and 12 DF,  p-value: <2e-16
```

As you can see, it's a simple matter to test these regressions using permutation tests and requires little change in the underlying code. The output is also similar to that produced by the lm() function. Note that an Iter column is added, indicating how many iterations were required to reach the stopping rule.

12.3.2 *Multiple regression*

In chapter 8, multiple regression was used to predict the murder rate based on population, illiteracy, income, and frost for 50 US states. Applying the lmp() function to this problem results in the following listing.

Listing 12.4   Permutation tests for multiple regression

```
> library(lmPerm)
> set.seed(1234)
> states <- as.data.frame(state.x77)
> fit <- lmp(Murder~Population + Illiteracy+Income+Frost,
             data=states, perm="Prob")
[1] "Settings:  unique SS : numeric variables centered"
> summary(fit)

Call:
lmp(formula = Murder ~ Population + Illiteracy + Income + Frost,
    data = states, perm = "Prob")

Residuals:
     Min      1Q   Median      3Q      Max
-4.79597 -1.64946 -0.08112  1.48150  7.62104

Coefficients:
           Estimate Iter Pr(Prob)
Population 2.237e-04   51   1.0000
Illiteracy 4.143e+00 5000   0.0004 ***
Income    6.442e-05   51   1.0000
Frost     5.813e-04   51   0.8627
---
Signif. codes:  0 '***' 0.001 '**' 0.01 '*' 0.05 '. ' 0.1 ' ' 1
```

```
Residual standard error: 2.535 on 45 degrees of freedom
Multiple R-Squared: 0.567,     Adjusted R-squared: 0.5285
F-statistic: 14.73 on 4 and 45 DF,  p-value: 9.133e-08
```

Looking back to chapter 8, both Population and Illiteracy are significant (p < 0.05) when normal theory is used. Based on the permutation tests, the Population variable is no longer significant. When the two approaches don't agree, you should look at your data more carefully. It may be that the assumption of normality is untenable or that outliers are present.

12.3.3 *One-way ANOVA and ANCOVA*

Each of the analysis of variance designs discussed in chapter 9 can be performed via permutation tests. First, let's look at the one-way ANOVA problem considered in section 9.1 on the impact of treatment regimens on cholesterol reduction. The code and results are given in the next listing.

Listing 12.5   Permutation test for one-way ANOVA

```
> library(lmPerm)
> library(multcomp)
> set.seed(1234)
> fit <- aovp(response~trt, data=cholesterol, perm="Prob")
[1] "Settings:  unique SS "
> anova(fit)
Component 1 :
           Df R Sum Sq R Mean Sq Iter  Pr(Prob)
trt         4  1351.37    337.84 5000 < 2.2e-16 ***
Residuals  45   468.75     10.42
---
Signif. codes:  0 '***' 0.001 '**' 0.01 '*' 0.05 '. ' 0.1 ' ' 1
```

The results suggest that the treatment effects are not all equal.

This second example in this section applies a permutation test to a one-way analysis of covariance. The problem is from chapter 9, where you investigated the impact of four drug doses on the litter weights of rats, controlling for gestation times. The next listing shows the permutation test and results.

Listing 12.6   Permutation test for one-way ANCOVA

```
> library(lmPerm)
> set.seed(1234)
> fit <- aovp(weight ~ gesttime + dose, data=litter, perm="Prob")
[1] "Settings:  unique SS : numeric variables centered"
> anova(fit)
Component 1 :
           Df R Sum Sq R Mean Sq Iter Pr(Prob)
gesttime    1   161.49   161.493 5000   0.0006 ***
dose        3   137.12    45.708 5000   0.0392 *
Residuals  69  1151.27    16.685
---
Signif. codes:  0 '***' 0.001 '**' 0.01 '*' 0.05 '.' 0.1 ' ' 1
```

Based on the p-values, the four drug doses don't equally impact litter weights, controlling for gestation time.

12.3.4 *Two-way ANOVA*

You'll end this section by applying permutation tests to a factorial design. In chapter 9, you examined the impact of vitamin C on the tooth growth in guinea pigs. The two manipulated factors were dose (three levels) and delivery method (two levels). Ten guinea pigs were placed in each treatment combination, resulting in a balanced 3×2 factorial design. The permutation tests are provided in the next listing.

Listing 12.7 Permutation test for two-way ANOVA

```
> library(lmPerm)
> set.seed(1234)
> fit <- aovp(len~supp*dose, data=ToothGrowth, perm="Prob")
[1] "Settings:  unique SS : numeric variables centered"
> anova(fit)
Component 1 :
            Df R Sum Sq R Mean Sq Iter Pr(Prob)
supp         1   205.35    205.35 5000  < 2e-16 ***
dose         1  2224.30   2224.30 5000  < 2e-16 ***
supp:dose    1    88.92     88.92 2032  0.04724 *
Residuals   56   933.63     16.67
---
Signif. codes:  0 '***' 0.001 '**' 0.01 '*' 0.05 '.' 0.1 ' ' 1
```

At the .05 level of significance, all three effects are statistically different from zero. At the .01 level, only the main effects are significant.

It's important to note that when aovp() is applied to ANOVA designs, it defaults to unique sums of squares (also called *SAS Type III sums of squares*). Each effect is adjusted for every other effect. The default for parametric ANOVA designs in R is sequential sums of squares (*SAS Type I sums of squares*). Each effect is adjusted for those that appear *earlier* in the model. For balanced designs, the two approaches will agree, but for unbalanced designs with unequal numbers of observations per cell, they won't. The greater the imbalance, the greater the disagreement. If desired, specifying seqs=TRUE in the aovp() function will produce sequential sums of squares. For more on Type I and Type III sums of squares, see section 9.2.

12.4 *Additional comments on permutation tests*

Permutation tests provide a powerful alternative to tests that rely on a knowledge of the underlying sampling distribution. In each of these permutation tests, you were able to test statistical hypotheses without recourse to the normal, t, F, or chi-square distributions.

You may have noticed how closely the results of the tests based on normal theory agreed with the results of the permutation approach in previous sections. The data in these problems were well behaved, and the agreement between methods is a testament to how well normal-theory methods work in such cases.

Permutation tests really shine in cases where the data are clearly non-normal (for example, highly skewed), outliers are present, samples sizes are small, or no parametric tests exist. But if the original sample is a poor representation of the population of interest, no test, including permutation tests, will improve the inferences generated.

Permutation tests are primarily useful for generating p-values that can be used to test null hypotheses. They can help answer the question, "Does an effect exist?" It's more difficult to use permutation methods to obtain confidence intervals and estimates of measurement precision. Fortunately, this is an area in which bootstrapping excels.

12.5 *Bootstrapping*

Bootstrapping generates an empirical distribution of a test statistic or set of test statistics by repeated random sampling with replacement from the original sample. It allows you to generate confidence intervals and test statistical hypotheses without having to assume a specific underlying theoretical distribution.

It's easiest to demonstrate the logic of bootstrapping with an example. Say that you want to calculate the 95% confidence interval for a sample mean. Your sample has 10 observations, a sample mean of 40, and a sample standard deviation of 5. If you're willing to assume that the sampling distribution of the mean is normally distributed, the $(1 - \alpha/2)\%$ confidence interval can be calculated using

$$\overline{X} - t\frac{s}{\sqrt{n}} < \mu < \overline{X} + t\frac{s}{\sqrt{n}}$$

where t is the upper $1 - \alpha/2$ critical value for a t distribution with $n - 1$ degrees of freedom. For a 95% confidence interval, you have $40 - 2.262(5/3.163) < \mu < 40 + 2.262 - (5/3.162)$ or $36.424 < \mu < 43.577$. You'd expect 95% of confidence intervals created in this way to surround the true population mean.

But what if you aren't willing to assume that the sampling distribution of the mean is normally distributed? You can use a bootstrapping approach instead:

1 Randomly select 10 observations from the sample, with replacement after each selection. Some observations may be selected more than once, and some may not be selected at all.
2 Calculate and record the sample mean.
3 Repeat the first two steps 1,000 times.
4 Order the 1,000 sample means from smallest to largest.
5 Find the sample means representing the 2.5th and 97.5th percentiles. In this case, it's the 25th number from the bottom and top. These are your 95% confidence limits.

In this case, where the sample mean is likely to be normally distributed, you gain little from the bootstrap approach. Yet in many cases, the bootstrap approach is advantageous. What if you wanted confidence intervals for the sample median or the difference between two sample medians? There are no simple normal-theory formulas here, and bootstrapping is the approach of choice. If the underlying distributions are unknown; if outliers are a problem; if sample sizes are small; or if parametric approaches don't exist, bootstrapping can often be a useful method of generating confidence intervals and testing hypotheses.

12.6 *Bootstrapping with the boot package*

The boot package provides extensive facilities for bootstrapping and related resampling methods. You can bootstrap a single statistic (for example, a median) or a vector of statistics (for example, a set of regression coefficients). Be sure to download and install the boot package before first use (install.packages("boot")).

The bootstrapping process will seem complicated, but once you review the examples it should make sense.

In general, bootstrapping involves three main steps:

1 Write a function that returns the statistic or statistics of interest. If there is a single statistic (for example, a median), the function should return a number. If there is a set of statistics (for example, a set of regression coefficients), the function should return a vector.
2 Process this function through the boot() function to generate R bootstrap replications of the statistic(s).
3 Use the boot.ci() function to obtain confidence intervals for the statistic(s) generated in step 2.

Now to the specifics. The main bootstrapping function is boot(). It has the format

```
bootobject <- boot(data=, statistic=, R=, ...)
```

Table 12.3 describes the parameters.

Table 12.3 Parameters of the boot() function

Parameter	Description
data	A vector, matrix, or data frame
statistic	A function that produces the k statistics to be bootstrapped ($k = 1$ if bootstrapping a single statistic). The function should include an indices parameter that the boot() function can use to select cases for each replication (see the examples in the text).
R	Number of bootstrap replicates
...	Additional parameters to be passed to the function that produces the statistic of interest

The boot() function calls the statistic function R times. Each time, it generates a set of random indices, with replacement, from the integers 1:nrow(data). These indices are used in the statistic function to select a sample. The statistics are calculated on the sample, and the results are accumulated in `bootobject`. Table 12.4 describes the `bootobject` structure.

Table 12.4   Elements of the object returned by the `boot()` function

Element	Description
t0	The observed values of *k* statistics applied to the original data
t	An *R* × k matrix, where each row is a bootstrap replicate of the *k* statistics

You can access these elements as `bootobject$t0` and `bootobject$t`.

Once you generate the bootstrap samples, you can use `print()` and `plot()` to examine the results. If the results look reasonable, you can use the `boot.ci()` function to obtain confidence intervals for the statistic(s). The format is

```
boot.ci(bootobject, conf=, type= )
```

Table 12.5 gives the parameters.

Table 12.5   Parameters of the `boot.ci()` function

Parameter	Description
bootobject	The object returned by the `boot()` function.
conf	The desired confidence interval (default: `conf=0.95`)
type	The type of confidence interval returned. Possible values are `norm`, `basic`, `stud`, `perc`, `bca`, and `all` (default: `type="all"`)

The `type` parameter specifies the method for obtaining the confidence limits. The `perc` method (percentile) was demonstrated in the sample mean example. `bca` provides an interval that makes simple adjustments for bias. I find `bca` preferable in most circumstances. See Mooney and Duval (1993) for an introduction to these methods.

In the remaining sections, we'll look at bootstrapping a single statistic and a vector of statistics.

12.6.1 *Bootstrapping a single statistic*

The `mtcars` dataset contains information on 32 automobiles reported in the 1974 *Motor Trend* magazine. Suppose you're using multiple regression to predict miles per gallon from a car's weight (lb/1,000) and engine displacement (cu. in.). In addition to the standard regression statistics, you'd like to obtain a 95% confidence interval for the R-squared value (the percent of variance in the response variable explained by the predictors). The confidence interval can be obtained using nonparametric bootstrapping.

The first task is to write a function for obtaining the R-squared value:

```
rsq <- function(formula, data, indices) {
        d <- data[indices,]
```

```
        fit <- lm(formula, data=d)
        return(summary(fit)$r.square)
}
```

The function returns the R-squared value from a regression. The d <- data[indi-ces,] statement is required for boot() to be able to select samples.

You can then draw a large number of bootstrap replications (say, 1,000) with the following code:

```
library(boot)
set.seed(1234)
results <- boot(data=mtcars, statistic=rsq,
                R=1000, formula=mpg~wt+disp)
```

The boot object can be printed using

```
> print(results)

ORDINARY NONPARAMETRIC BOOTSTRAP

Call:
boot(data = mtcars, statistic = rsq, R = 1000, formula = mpg ~
    wt + disp)

Bootstrap Statistics :
     original       bias      std. error
t1* 0.7809306  0.01333670   0.05068926
```

and plotted using plot(results). Figure 12.2 shows the resulting graph.

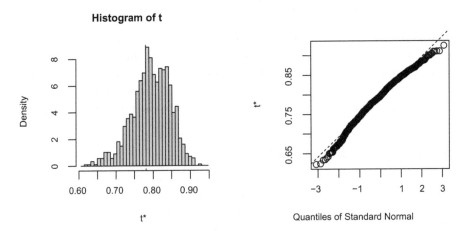

Figure 12.2   Distribution of bootstrapped R-squared values

In figure 12.2, you can see that the distribution of bootstrapped R-squared values isn't normally distributed. A 95% confidence interval for the R-squared values can be obtained using

```
> boot.ci(results, type=c("perc", "bca"))
BOOTSTRAP CONFIDENCE INTERVAL CALCULATIONS
Based on 1000 bootstrap replicates

CALL :
boot.ci(boot.out = results, type = c("perc", "bca"))

Intervals :
Level      Percentile            BCa
95%    ( 0.6753,  0.8835 )   ( 0.6344,  0.8561 )
Calculations and Intervals on Original Scale
Some BCa intervals may be unstable
```

You can see from this example that different approaches to generating the confidence intervals can lead to different intervals. In this case, the bias-adjusted interval is moderately different from the percentile method. In either case, the null hypothesis H_0: R-square = 0 would be rejected because zero is outside the confidence limits.

In this section, you estimated the confidence limits of a single statistic. In the next section, you'll estimate confidence intervals for several statistics.

12.6.2 *Bootstrapping several statistics*

In the previous example, bootstrapping was used to estimate the confidence interval for a single statistic (R-squared). Continuing the example, let's obtain the 95% confidence intervals for a vector of statistics. Specifically, let's get confidence intervals for the three model regression coefficients (intercept, car weight, and engine displacement).

First, create a function that returns the vector of regression coefficients:

```
bs <- function(formula, data, indices) {
    d <- data[indices,]
    fit <- lm(formula, data=d)
    return(coef(fit))
}
```

Then, use this function to bootstrap 1,000 replications:

```
library(boot)
set.seed(1234)
results <- boot(data=mtcars, statistic=bs,
                R=1000, formula=mpg~wt+disp)
> print(results)
ORDINARY NONPARAMETRIC BOOTSTRAP
Call:
boot(data = mtcars, statistic = bs, R = 1000, formula = mpg ~
    wt + disp)

Bootstrap Statistics :
    original    bias      std. error
t1*  34.9606   0.137873     2.48576
t2*  -3.3508  -0.053904     1.17043
t3*  -0.0177  -0.000121     0.00879
```

When bootstrapping multiple statistics, add an index parameter to the plot() and boot.ci() functions to indicate which column of bootobject$t to analyze. In this example, index 1 refers to the intercept, index 2 is car weight, and index 3 is the engine displacement. To plot the results for car weight, use

```
plot(results, index=2)
```

Figure 12.3 shows the graph.

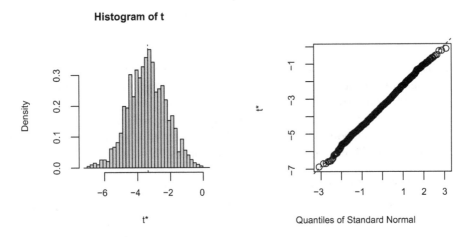

Figure 12.3 **Distribution of bootstrapping regression coefficients for car weight**

To get the 95% confidence intervals for car weight and engine displacement, use

```
> boot.ci(results, type="bca", index=2)
BOOTSTRAP CONFIDENCE INTERVAL CALCULATIONS
Based on 1000 bootstrap replicates

CALL :
boot.ci(boot.out = results, type = "bca", index = 2)

Intervals :
Level       Bca
95%    (-5.477, -0.937 )
Calculations and Intervals on Original Scale

> boot.ci(results, type="bca", index=3)

BOOTSTRAP CONFIDENCE INTERVAL CALCULATIONS
Based on 1000 bootstrap replicates

CALL :
boot.ci(boot.out = results, type = "bca", index = 3)

Intervals :
Level       BCa
95%    (-0.0334, -0.0011 )
Calculations and Intervals on Original Scale
```

NOTE The previous example resamples the entire sample of data each time. If you can assume that the predictor variables have fixed levels (typical in planned experiments), you'd do better to only resample residual terms. See Mooney and Duval (1993, pp. 16–17) for a simple explanation and algorithm.

Before we leave bootstrapping, it's worth addressing two questions that come up often:

- How large does the original sample need to be?
- How many replications are needed?

There's no simple answer to the first question. Some say that an original sample size of 20–30 is sufficient for good results as long as the sample is representative of the population. Random sampling from the population of interest is the most trusted method for assuring the original sample's representativeness. With regard to the second question, I find that 1,000 replications are more than adequate in most cases. Computer power is cheap, and you can always increase the number of replications if desired.

There are many helpful sources of information about permutation tests and bootstrapping. An excellent starting place is an online article by Yu (2003). Good (2006) provides a comprehensive overview of resampling in general and includes R code. Mooney and Duval (1993) provide a good, accessible introduction to bootstrapping. The definitive source on bootstrapping is Efron and Tibshirani (1998). Finally, there are a number of great online resources, including Simon (1997), Canty (2002), Shah (2005), and Fox (2002).

Summary

- Resampling statistics and bootstrapping are computer-intensive methods that allow you to test hypotheses and form confidence intervals without reference to a known theoretical distribution.
- They are particularly valuable when your data comes from unknown population distributions, when there are serious outliers, when your sample sizes are small, and when there are no existing parametric methods to answer the hypotheses of interest.
- They are particularly exciting because they provide an avenue for answering questions when your standard data assumptions are clearly untenable or when you have no other idea how to approach the problem.
- However, they aren't a panacea. They can't turn bad data into good data. If your original samples aren't representative of the population of interest or are too small to accurately reflect it, then these techniques won't help.

Part 4

Advanced methods

In this part of the book, we'll consider advanced methods of statistical analysis to round out your data analysis toolkit. The methods in this part play a key role in the growing field of data mining and predictive analytics.

Chapter 13 expands on the regression methods in chapter 8 to cover parametric approaches to data that are not normally distributed. The chapter starts with a discussion of the generalized linear model and then focuses on cases where you're trying to predict an outcome variable that is either categorical (logistic regression) or a count (Poisson regression).

Dealing with a large number of variables can be challenging because of the complexity inherent in multivariate data. Chapter 14 describes two popular methods for exploring and simplifying multivariate data. Principal components analysis can be used to combine many correlated variables into a smaller set of composite variables. Factor analysis consists of a set of techniques for uncovering the latent structure underlying a given set of variables. Chapter 14 provides step-by-step instructions for carrying out each.

Chapter 15 explores time-dependent data. Analysts are frequently faced with the need to understand trends and predict future events. Chapter 15 provides a thorough introduction to the analysis of time-series data and forecasting. After describing the general characteristics of time-series data, two of the most popular forecasting approaches (exponential and ARIMA) are illustrated.

Cluster analysis is the subject of chapter 16. While principal components and factor analysis simplify multivariate data by combining individual variables into composite variables, cluster analysis attempts to simplify multivariate data by combining individual observations into subgroups called *clusters*. Clusters contain cases that are similar to each other and different from the cases in other clusters. The chapter considers methods for determining the number of clusters present in a dataset and combining observations into these clusters.

Chapter 17 addresses the important topic of classification. In classification problems, the analyst attempts to develop a model for predicting the group membership of new cases (for example, good credit/bad credit risk, benign/malignant, pass/fail) from a (potentially large) set of predictor variables. Many methods are considered, including logistic regression, decision trees, random forests, and support-vector machines. Methods for assessing the efficacy of the resulting classification models are also described.

In practice, researchers must often deal with incomplete datasets. Chapter 18 considers modern approaches to the ubiquitous problem of missing data values. R supports a number of elegant approaches for analyzing datasets that are incomplete. Several of the best are described here, along with guidance about which ones to use and which ones to avoid.

After completing part 4, you'll have the tools to manage a wide range of complex data analysis problems. This includes modeling non-normal outcome variables, dealing with large numbers of correlated variables, reducing a large number of cases to a smaller number of homogeneous clusters, developing models to predict future values or categorical outcomes, and handling messy and incomplete data.

Generalized linear models

This chapter covers
- Formulating a generalized linear model
- Predicting categorical outcomes
- Modeling count data

In chapters 8 (regression) and 9 (ANOVA), we explored linear models that can be used to predict a normally distributed response variable from a set of continuous and/or categorical predictor variables. But in many situations, it's unreasonable to assume that the dependent variable is normally distributed (or even continuous). For example:

- The outcome variable may be categorical. Binary variables (for example, yes/no, passed/failed, lived/died) and polytomous variables (for example, poor/good/excellent, Republican/Democrat/independent) clearly aren't normally distributed.

- The outcome variable may be a count (for example, the number of traffic accidents in a week, the number of drinks per day). Such variables take on a limited number of values and are never negative. Additionally, their mean and variance are often related (which isn't true for normally distributed variables).

Generalized linear models extend the linear-model framework to include dependent variables that are decidedly non-normal.

In this chapter, we'll start with a brief overview of generalized linear models and the `glm()` function used to estimate them. Then we'll focus on two popular models in this framework: *logistic regression* (where the dependent variable is categorical) and *Poisson regression* (where the dependent variable is a count variable).

To motivate the discussion, you'll apply generalized linear models to two research questions that aren't easily addressed with standard linear models:

- What personal, demographic, and relationship variables predict marital infidelity? In this case, the outcome variable is binary (affair/no affair).
- What impact does a drug treatment for seizures have on the number of seizures experienced over an eight-week period? In this case, the outcome variable is a count (number of seizures).

You'll apply logistic regression to address the first question and Poison regression to address the second. Along the way, we'll consider extensions of each technique.

13.1 *Generalized linear models and the glm() function*

A wide range of popular data analytic methods are subsumed within the framework of the generalized linear model. In this section, we'll briefly explore some of the theory behind this approach. You can safely skip this section if you like and come back to it later.

Let's say that you want to model the relationship between a response variable Y and a set of p predictor variables $X_1 \ldots X_p$. In the standard linear model, you assume that Y is normally distributed and that the form of the relationship is

$$\mu_y = \beta_0 + \sum\nolimits_{j=1}^{p} \beta_j X_j$$

This equation states that the conditional mean of the response variable is a linear combination of the predictor variables. The β_j are the parameters specifying the expected change in Y for a unit change in X_j, and β_0 is the expected value of Y when all the predictor variables are 0. You're saying that you can predict the mean of the Y distribution for observations with a given set of X values by applying the proper weights to the X variables and adding them up.

Note that you've made no distributional assumptions about the predictor variables, X_j. Unlike Y, there's no requirement that they be normally distributed. In fact, they're often categorical (for example, ANOVA designs). Additionally, nonlinear functions of the predictors are allowed. You often include such predictors as X^2 or $X_1 \times X_2$. What is important is that the equation is linear in the parameters $(\beta_0, \beta_1, \ldots, \beta_p)$.

In generalized linear models, you fit models of the form

$$g\left(\mu_y\right) = \beta_0 + \sum\nolimits_{j=1}^{p} \beta_j X_j$$

where $g(\mu_Y)$ is a function of the conditional mean (called the *link function*). Additionally, you relax the assumption that Y is normally distributed. Instead, you assume that Y follows a distribution that's a member of the exponential family. You specify the link function and the probability distribution, and the parameters are derived through an iterative maximum-likelihood-estimation procedure.

13.1.1 The glm() function

Generalized linear models are typically fit in R through the `glm()` function (although other specialized functions are available). The form of the function is similar to `lm()` but includes additional parameters. The basic format of the function is

```
glm(formula, family=family(link=function), data=)
```

where the probability distribution (`family`) and corresponding default link function (`function`) are given in table 13.1.

Table 13.1 `glm()` parameters

Family	Default link function
binomial	(link = "logit")
gaussian	(link = "identity")
gamma	(link = "inverse")
inverse.gaussian	(link = "1/mu^2")
poisson	(link = "log")
quasi	(link = "identity", variance = "constant")
quasibinomial	(link = "logit")
quasipoisson	(link = "log")

The `glm()` function allows you to fit a number of popular models, including logistic regression, Poisson regression, and survival analysis (not considered here). You can demonstrate this for the first two models as follows. Assume that you have a single response variable (Y), three predictor variables (X1, X2, X3), and a data frame (mydata) containing the data.

Logistic regression is applied to situations in which the response variable is dichotomous (0 or 1). The model assumes that Y follows a binomial distribution and that you can fit a linear model of the form

$$\log_e\left(\frac{\pi}{1-\pi}\right) = \beta_0 + \sum_{j=1}^{p} \beta_j X_j$$

where $\pi = \mu_Y$ is the conditional mean of Y (that is, the probability that $Y = 1$ given a set of X values), $(\pi/1 - \pi)$ is the odds that $Y = 1$, and $\log(\pi/1 - \pi)$ is the log odds, or *logit*.

In this case, $\log(\pi/1-\pi)$ is the link function, the probability distribution is binomial, and the logistic regression model can be fit using

```
glm(Y~X1+X2+X3, family=binomial(link="logit"), data=mydata)
```

Logistic regression is described more fully in section 13.2.

Poisson regression is applied to situations in which the response variable is the number of events to occur in a given period of time. The Poisson regression model assumes that Y follows a Poisson distribution and that you can fit a linear model of the form

$$\log_e(\lambda) = \beta_0 + \sum\nolimits_{j=1}^{p} \beta_j X_j$$

where λ is the mean (and variance) of Y. In this case, the link function is $\log(\lambda)$, the probability distribution is Poisson, and the Poisson regression model can be fit using

```
glm(Y~X1+X2+X3, family=poisson(link="log"), data=mydata)
```

Poisson regression is described in section 13.3.

It's worth noting that the standard linear model is also a special case of the generalized linear model. If you let the link function $g(\mu_Y) = \mu_Y$ or the identity function and specify that the probability distribution is normal (Gaussian), then

```
glm(Y~X1+X2+X3, family=gaussian(link="identity"), data=mydata)
```

would produce the same results as

```
lm(Y~X1+X2+X3, data=mydata)
```

To summarize, generalized linear models extend the standard linear model by fitting a *function* of the conditional mean response (rather than the conditional mean response) and assuming that the response variable follows a member of the *exponential* family of distributions (rather than being limited to the normal distribution). The parameter estimates are derived via maximum likelihood rather than least squares.

13.1.2　*Supporting functions*

Many of the functions that you used in conjunction with `lm()` when analyzing standard linear models have corresponding versions for `glm()`. Table 13.2 gives some commonly used functions.

Table 13.2　Functions that support `glm()`

Function	Description
`summary()`	Displays detailed results for the fitted model
`coefficients()`, `coef()`	Lists the model parameters (intercept and slopes) for the fitted model
`confint()`	Provides confidence intervals for the model parameters (95% by default)

Table 13.2 Functions that support `glm()` *(continued)*

Function	Description
`residuals()`	Lists the residual values in a fitted model
`anova()`	Generates an ANOVA table comparing two fitted models
`plot()`	Generates diagnostic plots for evaluating the fit of a model
`predict()`	Uses a fitted model to predict response values for a new dataset
`deviance()`	Deviance for the fitted model
`df.residual()`	Residual degrees of freedom for the fitted model

We'll explore examples of these functions in later sections. In the next section, we'll briefly consider the assessment of model adequacy.

13.1.3 *Model fit and regression diagnostics*

The assessment of model adequacy is as important for generalized linear models as it is for standard (OLS) linear models. Unfortunately, there's less agreement in the statistical community regarding appropriate assessment procedures. In general, you can use the techniques described in chapter 8 with the following caveats.

When assessing model adequacy, you'll typically want to plot predicted values expressed in the metric of the original response variable against residuals of the deviance type. For example, a common diagnostic plot would be

```
plot(predict(model, type="response"),
    residuals(model, type= "deviance"))
```

where `model` is the object returned by the `glm()` function.

The hat values, studentized residuals, and Cook's D statistics that R provides will be approximate values. Additionally, there's no general consensus on cutoff values for identifying problematic observations. Values have to be judged relative to each other. One approach is to create index plots for each statistic and look for unusually large values. For example, you could use the following code to create three diagnostic plots:

```
plot(hatvalues(model))
plot(rstudent(model))
plot(cooks.distance(model))
```

Alternatively, you could use the code

```
library(car)
influencePlot(model)
```

to create one omnibus plot. In the latter graph, the horizontal axis is the leverage, the vertical axis is the studentized residual, and the plotted symbol is proportional to the Cook's distance.

Diagnostic plots tend to be most helpful when the response variable takes on many values. When the response variable can only take on a limited number of values (for example, logistic regression), the utility of these plots is decreased.

For more on regression diagnostics for generalized linear models, see Fox (2008) and Faraway (2006). In the rest of this chapter, we'll consider two of the most popular forms of the generalized linear model in detail: logistic regression and Poisson regression.

13.2 *Logistic regression*

Logistic regression is useful when you're predicting a binary outcome from a set of continuous and/or categorical predictor variables. To demonstrate this, let's explore the data on infidelity contained in the data frame `Affairs`, provided with the AER package. Be sure to download and install the package (using `install.pack-ages("AER")`) before first use.

The infidelity data, known as Fair's Affairs, is based on a cross-sectional survey conducted by *Psychology Today* in 1969 and is described in Greene (2003) and Fair (1978). It contains 9 variables collected on 601 participants and includes how often the respondent engaged in extramarital sexual intercourse during the past year, as well as their gender, age, years married, whether they had children, their religiousness (on a 5-point scale from 1 = anti to 5 = very), education, occupation (Hollingshead 7-point classification with reverse numbering), and a numeric self-rating of their marriage (from 1 = very unhappy to 5 = very happy).

Let's look at some descriptive statistics:

```
> data(Affairs, package="AER")
> summary(Affairs)
     affairs            gender          age         yearsmarried      children
 Min.   : 0.000   female:315   Min.   :17.50   Min.   : 0.125   no :171
 1st Qu.: 0.000   male  :286   1st Qu.:27.00   1st Qu.: 4.000   yes:430
 Median : 0.000                Median :32.00   Median : 7.000
 Mean   : 1.456                Mean   :32.49   Mean   : 8.178
 3rd Qu.: 0.000                3rd Qu.:37.00   3rd Qu.:15.000
 Max.   :12.000                Max.   :57.00   Max.   :15.000
  religiousness      education       occupation        rating
 Min.   :1.000   Min.   : 9.00   Min.   :1.000   Min.   :1.000
 1st Qu.:2.000   1st Qu.:14.00   1st Qu.:3.000   1st Qu.:3.000
 Median :3.000   Median :16.00   Median :5.000   Median :4.000
 Mean   :3.116   Mean   :16.17   Mean   :4.195   Mean   :3.932
 3rd Qu.:4.000   3rd Qu.:18.00   3rd Qu.:6.000   3rd Qu.:5.000
 Max.   :5.000   Max.   :20.00   Max.   :7.000   Max.   :5.000

> table(Affairs$affairs)
  0   1   2   3   7  12
451  34  17  19  42  38
```

From these statistics, you can see that that 52% of respondents were female, 72% had children, and the median age for the sample was 32 years. With regard to the response variable, 75% of respondents reported not engaging in an infidelity in the past year (451/601). The largest number of encounters reported was 12 (6%).

Although the *number* of indiscretions was recorded, your interest here is in the binary outcome (had an affair/didn't have an affair). You can transform affairs into a dichotomous factor called ynaffair with the following code:

```
> Affairs$ynaffair <- ifelse(Affairs$affairs > 0, 1, 0)
> Affairs$ynaffair <- factor(Affairs$ynaffair,
                        levels=c(0,1),
                        labels=c("No","Yes"))
> table(Affairs$ynaffair)
No Yes
451 150
```

This dichotomous factor can now be used as the outcome variable in a logistic regression model:

```
> fit.full <- glm(ynaffair ~ gender + age + yearsmarried + children +
                religiousness + education + occupation +rating,
                data=Affairs, family=binomial())
> summary(fit.full)

Call:
glm(formula = ynaffair ~ gender + age + yearsmarried + children +
    religiousness + education + occupation + rating, family = binomial(),
    data = Affairs)

Deviance Residuals:
   Min      1Q  Median      3Q     Max
-1.571  -0.750  -0.569  -0.254   2.519

Coefficients:
              Estimate Std. Error z value Pr(>|z|)
(Intercept)    1.3773     0.8878    1.55  0.12081
gendermale     0.2803     0.2391    1.17  0.24108
age           -0.0443     0.0182   -2.43  0.01530 *
yearsmarried   0.0948     0.0322    2.94  0.00326 **
childrenyes    0.3977     0.2915    1.36  0.17251
religiousness -0.3247     0.0898   -3.62  0.00030 ***
education      0.0211     0.0505    0.42  0.67685
occupation     0.0309     0.0718    0.43  0.66663
rating        -0.4685     0.0909   -5.15 2.6e-07 ***
---
Signif. codes:  0 '***' 0.001 '**' 0.01 '*' 0.05 '.' 0.1 ' ' 1

(Dispersion parameter for binomial family taken to be 1)

    Null deviance: 675.38  on 600  degrees of freedom
Residual deviance: 609.51  on 592  degrees of freedom
AIC: 627.5

Number of Fisher Scoring iterations: 4
```

From the p-values for the regression coefficients (the last column), you can see that gender, presence of children, education, and occupation may not make a significant contribution to the equation (you can't reject the hypothesis that the parameters are 0). Let's fit a second equation without them and test whether this reduced model fits the data as well:

```
> fit.reduced <- glm(ynaffair ~ age + yearsmarried + religiousness +
                  rating, data=Affairs, family=binomial())
> summary(fit.reduced)
Call:
glm(formula = ynaffair ~ age + yearsmarried + religiousness + rating,
    family = binomial(), data = Affairs)

Deviance Residuals:
   Min      1Q   Median      3Q      Max
-1.628   -0.755  -0.570  -0.262    2.400

Coefficients:
              Estimate Std. Error z value Pr(>|z|)
(Intercept)     1.9308     0.6103    3.16  0.00156 **
age            -0.0353     0.0174   -2.03  0.04213 *
yearsmarried    0.1006     0.0292    3.44  0.00057 ***
religiousness  -0.3290     0.0895   -3.68  0.00023 ***
rating         -0.4614     0.0888   -5.19  2.1e-07 ***
---
Signif. codes:  0 '***' 0.001 '**' 0.01 '*' 0.05 '.' 0.1 ' ' 1

(Dispersion parameter for binomial family taken to be 1)

    Null deviance: 675.38  on 600  degrees of freedom
Residual deviance: 615.36  on 596  degrees of freedom
AIC: 625.4

Number of Fisher Scoring iterations: 4
```

Each regression coefficient in the reduced model is statistically significant ($p < .05$). Because the two models are nested (`fit.reduced` is a subset of `fit.full`), you can use the `anova()` function to compare them. For generalized linear models, you'll want a chi-square version of this test:

```
> anova(fit.reduced, fit.full, test="Chisq")
Analysis of Deviance Table

Model 1: ynaffair ~ age + yearsmarried + religiousness + rating
Model 2: ynaffair ~ gender + age + yearsmarried + children +
    religiousness + education + occupation + rating
  Resid. Df Resid. Dev Df Deviance P(>|Chi|)
1       596        615
2       592        610  4     5.85      0.21
```

The nonsignificant chi-square value ($p = 0.21$) suggests that the reduced model with four predictors fits as well as the full model with nine predictors, reinforcing your belief that gender, children, education, and occupation don't add significantly to the prediction above and beyond the other variables in the equation. Therefore, you can base your interpretations on the simpler model.

13.2.1 Interpreting the model parameters

Let's look at the regression coefficients:

```
> coef(fit.reduced)
  (Intercept)         age yearsmarried religiousness       rating
        1.931      -0.035        0.101        -0.329       -0.461
```

In a logistic regression, the response being modeled is the log(odds) that $Y = 1$. The regression coefficients give the change in log(odds) in the response for a unit change in the predictor variable, holding all other predictor variables constant.

Because log(odds) are difficult to interpret, you can exponentiate them to put the results on an odds scale:

```
> exp(coef(fit.reduced))
  (Intercept)         age yearsmarried religiousness       rating
        6.895       0.965        1.106         0.720        0.630
```

Now you can see that the odds of an extramarital encounter are increased by a factor of 1.106 for a one-year increase in years married (holding age, religiousness, and marital rating constant). Conversely, the odds of an extramarital affair are multiplied by a factor of 0.965 for every year increase in age. The odds of an extramarital affair increase with years married and decrease with age, religiousness, and marital rating. Because the predictor variables can't equal 0, the intercept isn't meaningful in this case.

If desired, you can use the confint() function to obtain confidence intervals for the coefficients. For example, exp(confint(fit.reduced)) would print 95% confidence intervals for each of the coefficients on an odds scale.

Finally, a one-unit change in a predictor variable may not be inherently interesting. For binary logistic regression, the change in the odds of the higher value on the response variable for an n unit change in a predictor variable is $\exp(\beta_j)^n$. If a 1-year increase in years married multiplies the odds of an affair by 1.106, a 10-year increase would increase the odds by a factor of 1.106^10, or 2.7, holding the other predictor variables constant.

13.2.2 Assessing the impact of predictors on the probability of an outcome

For many of us, it's easier to think in terms of probabilities than odds. You can use the predict() function to observe the impact of varying the levels of a predictor variable on the probability of the outcome. The first step is to create an artificial dataset containing the values of the predictor variables you're interested in. Then you can use this artificial dataset with the predict() function to predict the probabilities of the outcome event occurring for these values.

Let's apply this strategy to assess the impact of marital ratings on the probability of having an extramarital affair. First, create an artificial dataset where age, years married, and religiousness are set to their means, and marital rating varies from 1 to 5:

```
> testdata <- data.frame(rating=c(1, 2, 3, 4, 5), age=mean(Affairs$age),
                 yearsmarried=mean(Affairs$yearsmarried),
                 religiousness=mean(Affairs$religiousness))
```

```
> testdata
  rating  age yearsmarried religiousness
1      1 32.5         8.18          3.12
2      2 32.5         8.18          3.12
3      3 32.5         8.18          3.12
4      4 32.5         8.18          3.12
5      5 32.5         8.18          3.12
```

Next, use the test dataset and prediction equation to obtain probabilities:

```
> testdata$prob <- predict(fit.reduced, newdata=testdata, type="response")
  testdata
  rating  age yearsmarried religiousness  prob
1      1 32.5         8.18          3.12 0.530
2      2 32.5         8.18          3.12 0.416
3      3 32.5         8.18          3.12 0.310
4      4 32.5         8.18          3.12 0.220
5      5 32.5         8.18          3.12 0.151
```

From these results, you see that the probability of an extramarital affair decreases from 0.53 when the marriage is rated 1 = very unhappy to 0.15 when the marriage is rated 5 = very happy (holding age, years married, and religiousness constant). Now look at the impact of age:

```
> testdata <- data.frame(rating=mean(Affairs$rating),
                         age=seq(17, 57, 10),
                         yearsmarried=mean(Affairs$yearsmarried),
                         religiousness=mean(Affairs$religiousness))
> testdata
  rating age yearsmarried religiousness
1   3.93  17         8.18          3.12
2   3.93  27         8.18          3.12
3   3.93  37         8.18          3.12
4   3.93  47         8.18          3.12
5   3.93  57         8.18          3.12
```

```
> testdata$prob <- predict(fit.reduced, newdata=testdata, type="response")
> testdata
  rating age yearsmarried religiousness   prob
1   3.93  17         8.18          3.12  0.335
2   3.93  27         8.18          3.12  0.262
3   3.93  37         8.18          3.12  0.199
4   3.93  47         8.18          3.12  0.149
5   3.93  57         8.18          3.12  0.109
```

Here, you see that as age increases from 17 to 57, the probability of an extramarital encounter decreases from 0.34 to 0.11, holding the other variables constant. Using this approach, you can explore the impact of each predictor variable on the outcome.

13.2.3 Overdispersion

The expected variance for data drawn from a binomial distribution is $\sigma^2 = n\pi(1 - \pi)$, where n is the number of observations and π is the probability of belonging to the $Y = 1$ group. *Overdispersion* occurs when the observed variance of the response variable is larger than what would be expected from a binomial distribution. Overdispersion can lead to distorted test standard errors and inaccurate tests of significance.

When overdispersion is present, you can still fit a logistic regression using the `glm()` function, but in this case, you should use the quasibinomial distribution rather than the binomial distribution.

One way to detect overdispersion is to compare the residual deviance with the residual degrees of freedom in your binomial model. If the ratio

$$\phi = \frac{\text{Residual deviance}}{\text{Residual df}}$$

is considerably larger than 1, you have evidence of overdispersion. Applying this to the `Affairs` example, you have

```
> deviance(fit.reduced)/df.residual(fit.reduced)
[1] 1.032
```

which is close to 1, suggesting no overdispersion.

You can also test for overdispersion. To do this, you fit the model twice, but in the first instance, you use `family="binomial"`, and in the second instance, you use `family="quasibinomial"`. If the `glm()` object returned in the first case is called `fit` and the object returned in the second case is called `fit.od`, then

```
pchisq(summary(fit.od)$dispersion * fit$df.residual,
       fit$df.residual, lower = F)
```

provides the p-value for testing the null hypothesis H_0: $\phi = 1$ versus the alternative hypothesis H_1: $\phi \neq 1$. If p is small (say, less than 0.05), you'd reject the null hypothesis.

Applying this to the `Affairs` dataset, you have

```
> fit <- glm(ynaffair ~ age + yearsmarried + religiousness +
             rating, family = binomial(), data = Affairs)
> fit.od <- glm(ynaffair ~ age + yearsmarried + religiousness +
                rating, family = quasibinomial(), data = Affairs)
> pchisq(summary(fit.od)$dispersion * fit$df.residual,
         fit$df.residual, lower = F)

[1] 0.34
```

The resulting p-value (0.34) is clearly not significant (p > 0.05), strengthening your belief that overdispersion isn't a problem. We'll return to the issue of overdispersion when we discuss Poisson regression.

13.2.4 Extensions

Several logistic regression extensions and variations are available in R:

- *Robust logistic regression*—The `glmRob()` function in the `robustbase` package can be used to fit a robust generalized linear model, including robust logistic regression. Robust logistic regression can be helpful when fitting logistic regression models to data containing outliers and influential observations.

- *Multinomial logistic regression*—If the response variable has more than two unordered categories (for example, married/widowed/divorced), you can fit a polytomous logistic regression using the `mlogit()` function in the `mlogit` package. Alternatively, you can use the `multinom()` function in the `nnet` package.
- *Ordinal logistic regression*—If the response variable is a set of ordered categories (for example, credit risk as poor/good/excellent), you can fit an ordinal logistic regression using the `polyr()` function in the `MASS` package.

The ability to model a response variable with multiple categories (both ordered and unordered) is an important extension, but it comes at the expense of greater interpretive complexity. Assessing model fit and regression diagnostics in these cases will also be more complex.

In the `Affairs` example, the number of extramarital contacts was dichotomized into a yes/no response variable because our interest centered on whether respondents had an affair in the past year. If our interest had been centered on magnitude—the number of encounters in the past year—we would have analyzed the count data directly. One popular approach to analyzing count data is Poisson regression, the next topic we'll address.

13.3 *Poisson regression*

Poisson regression is useful when you're predicting an outcome variable representing counts from a set of continuous and/or categorical predictor variables. Coxe, West, and Aiken (2009) provide a comprehensive, yet accessible, introduction to Poisson regression.

To illustrate the fitting of a Poisson regression model, along with some issues that can come up in the analysis, we'll use the Breslow seizure data (Breslow, 1993) provided in the `robustbase` package. Specifically, we'll consider the impact of an antiepileptic drug treatment on the number of seizures occurring over an eight-week period following the initiation of therapy. Be sure to install the `robustbase` package before continuing.

Data were collected on the age and number of seizures reported by patients suffering from simple or complex partial seizures during an eight-week period before, and an eight-week period after, randomization into a drug or placebo condition. `Ysum` (the number of seizures in the eight-week period post-randomization) is the response variable. Treatment condition (`Trt`), age in years (`Age`), and number of seizures reported in the baseline eight-week period (`Base`) are the predictor variables. The baseline number of seizures and age are included because of their potential effect on the response variable. We're interested in whether evidence exists that the drug treatment decreases the number of seizures after accounting for these covariates.

First, let's look at summary statistics for the dataset:

```
> data(epilepsy, package="robustbase")
> names(epilepsy)
 [1] "ID"    "Y1"    "Y2"    "Y3"    "Y4"    "Base"  "Age"   "Trt"   "Ysum"
[10] "Age10" "Base4"
```

```
> summary(breslow.dat[6:9])
      Base              Age              Trt              Ysum
 Min.   :  6.0    Min.   :18.0    placebo  :28    Min.   :  0.0
 1st Qu.: 12.0    1st Qu.:23.0    progabide:31    1st Qu.: 11.5
 Median : 22.0    Median :28.0                    Median : 16.0
 Mean   : 31.2    Mean   :28.3                    Mean   : 33.1
 3rd Qu.: 41.0    3rd Qu.:32.0                    3rd Qu.: 36.0
 Max.   :151.0    Max.   :42.0                    Max.   :302.0
```

Note that although there are 11 variables in the dataset, we're limiting our attention to the 4 described earlier. Both the baseline and post-randomization number of seizures are highly skewed. Let's look at the response variable in more detail. The following code produces the graphs in figure 13.1:

```
library(ggplot2)
  ggplot(epilepsy, aes(x=Ysum)) +
  geom_histogram(color="black", fill="white") +
  labs(title="Distribution of seizures",
       x="Seizure Count",
       y="Frequency") +
  theme_bw()
ggplot(epilepsy, aes(x=Trt, y=Ysum)) +
  geom_boxplot() +
  labs(title="Group comparisons", x="", y="") +
  theme_bw()
```

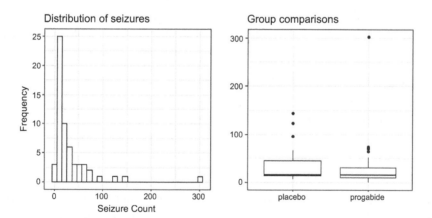

Figure 13.1   Distribution of post-treatment seizure counts (source: Breslow seizure data)

You can clearly see the skewed nature of the dependent variable and the possible presence of outliers. At first glance, the number of seizures in the drug condition appears to be smaller and has a smaller variance. (You'd expect a smaller variance to accompany a smaller mean with Poisson distributed data.) Unlike standard OLS regression, this heterogeneity of variance isn't a problem in Poisson regression.

The next step is to fit the Poisson regression:

```
> fit <- glm(Ysum ~ Base + Age + Trt, data=epilepsy, family=poisson())
> summary(fit)

Call:
glm(formula = Ysum ~ Base + Age + Trt, family = poisson(), data = epilepsy)

Deviance Residuals:
    Min       1Q   Median       3Q      Max
  -6.057   -2.043   -0.940    0.793   11.006

Coefficients:
               Estimate Std. Error z value Pr(>|z|)
(Intercept)    1.948826   0.135619   14.37  < 2e-16 ***
Base           0.022652   0.000509   44.48  < 2e-16 ***
Age            0.022740   0.004024    5.65  1.6e-08 ***
Trtprogabide  -0.152701   0.047805   -3.19   0.0014 **
---
Signif. codes:  0 '***' 0.001 '**' 0.01 '*' 0.05 '.' 0.1 ' ' 1

(Dispersion parameter for poisson family taken to be 1)

    Null deviance: 2122.73  on 58  degrees of freedom
Residual deviance:  559.44  on 55  degrees of freedom
AIC: 850.7

Number of Fisher Scoring iterations: 5
```

The output provides the deviances, regression parameters, standard errors, and tests that these parameters are 0. Note that each of the predictor variables is significant at the $p < 0.05$ level.

13.3.1 *Interpreting the model parameters*

The model coefficients are obtained using the coef() function or by examining the Coefficients table in the summary() function output:

```
> coef(fit)
 (Intercept)        Base         Age Trtprogabide
      1.9488      0.0227      0.0227      -0.1527
```

In a Poisson regression, the dependent variable being modeled is the log of the conditional mean $\log_e(\lambda)$. The regression parameter 0.0227 for Age indicates that a one-year increase in age is associated with a 0.02 increase in the log mean number of seizures, holding baseline seizures and treatment condition constant. The intercept is the log mean number of seizures when each of the predictors equals 0. Because you can't have a zero age and none of the participants had a zero number of baseline seizures, the intercept isn't meaningful in this case.

It's usually much easier to interpret the regression coefficients in the original scale of the dependent variable (number of seizures, rather than log number of seizures). To accomplish this, exponentiate the coefficients:

```
> exp(coef(fit))
(Intercept)        Base          Age Trtprogabide
      7.020       1.023        1.023        0.858
```

Now you see that a one-year increase in age *multiplies* the expected number of seizures by 1.023, holding the other variables constant. This means that increased age is associated with higher numbers of seizures. More important, a one-unit change in Trt (that is, moving from placebo to progabide) multiplies the expected number of seizures by 0.86. You'd expect a 14% (i.e., 1–0.86) decrease in the number of seizures for the drug group compared with the placebo group, holding the baseline number of seizures and age constant.

It's important to remember that, like the exponentiated parameters in logistic regression, the exponentiated parameters in the Poisson model have a multiplicative rather than an additive effect on the response variable. Also, as with logistic regression, you must evaluate your model for overdispersion.

13.3.2 Overdispersion

In a Poisson distribution, the variance and mean are equal. Overdispersion occurs in Poisson regression when the observed variance of the response variable is larger than would be predicted by the Poisson distribution. Because overdispersion is often encountered when dealing with count data and can have a negative impact on the interpretation of the results, we'll spend some time discussing it.

There are several reasons why overdispersion may occur (Coxe et al., 2009):

- The omission of an important predictor variable can lead to overdispersion.
- Overdispersion can also be caused by a phenomenon known as *state dependence*. Within observations, each event in a count is assumed to be independent. For the seizure data, this would imply that for any patient, the probability of a seizure is independent of each other seizure. But this assumption is often untenable. For a given individual, the probability of having a first seizure is unlikely to be the same as the probability of having a 40th seizure, given that they've already had 39.
- In longitudinal studies, overdispersion can be caused by the clustering inherent in repeated measures data. We won't discuss longitudinal Poisson models here.

If overdispersion is present and you don't account for it in your model, you'll get standard errors and confidence intervals that are too small and significance tests that are too liberal (that is, you'll find effects that aren't really there).

As with logistic regression, overdispersion is suggested if the ratio of the residual deviance to the residual degrees of freedom is much larger than 1. For the seizure data, the ratio is

```
> deviance(fit)/df.residual(fit)
[1] 10.17
```

which is clearly much larger than 1.

The qcc package provides a test for overdispersion in the Poisson case. (Be sure to download and install this package before first use.) You can test for overdispersion in the seizure data using the following code:

```
> library(qcc)
> qcc.overdispersion.test(breslow.dat$sumY, type="poisson")
Overdispersion test Obs.Var/Theor.Var Statistic p-value
        poisson data             62.9      3646       0
```

Not surprisingly, the significance test has a p-value less than 0.05, strongly suggesting the presence of overdispersion.

You can still fit a model to your data using the glm() function by replacing family="poisson" with family="quasipoisson". Doing so is analogous to the approach to logistic regression when overdispersion is present:

```
> fit.od <- glm(sumY ~ Base + Age + Trt, data=breslow.dat,
                family=quasipoisson())
> summary(fit.od)

Call:
glm(formula = sumY ~ Base + Age + Trt, family = quasipoisson(),
    data = breslow.dat)

Deviance Residuals:
   Min      1Q  Median      3Q     Max
-6.057  -2.043  -0.940   0.793  11.006

Coefficients:
              Estimate Std. Error t value Pr(>|t|)
(Intercept)    1.94883    0.46509    4.19  0.00010 ***
Base           0.02265    0.00175   12.97  < 2e-16 ***
Age            0.02274    0.01380    1.65  0.10509
Trtprogabide  -0.15270    0.16394   -0.93  0.35570
---
Signif. codes:  0 '***' 0.001 '**' 0.01 '*' 0.05 '.' 0.1 ' ' 1

(Dispersion parameter for quasipoisson family taken to be 11.8)

    Null deviance: 2122.73  on 58  degrees of freedom
Residual deviance:  559.44  on 55  degrees of freedom
AIC: NA

Number of Fisher Scoring iterations: 5
```

Notice that the parameter estimates in the quasi-Poisson approach are identical to those produced by the Poisson approach, but the standard errors are much larger. In this case, the larger standard errors have led to p-values for Trt (and Age) that are greater than 0.05. When you take overdispersion into account, there's insufficient evidence to declare that the drug regimen reduces seizure counts more than receiving a placebo, after controlling for baseline seizure rate and age.

Please remember that this example is used for demonstration purposes only. The results shouldn't be taken to imply anything about the efficacy of progabide in the real world. I'm not a doctor—at least not a medical doctor—and I don't even play one on TV.

We'll finish this exploration of Poisson regression with a discussion of some important variants and extensions.

13.3.3 *Extensions*

R provides several useful extensions to the basic Poisson regression model, including models that allow varying time periods, models that correct for too many zeros, and robust models that are useful when data includes outliers and influential observations. I'll describe each separately.

POISSON REGRESSION WITH VARYING TIME PERIODS

Our discussion of Poisson regression has been limited to response variables that measure a count over a fixed length of time (for example, number of seizures in an eight-week period, number of traffic accidents in the past year, or number of pro-social behaviors in a day). The length of time is constant across observations. But you can fit Poisson regression models that allow the time period to vary for each observation. In this case, the outcome variable is a rate.

To analyze rates, you must include a variable (for example, time) that records the length of time over which the count occurs for each observation. You then change the model from

$$\log_e(\lambda) = \beta_0 + \sum_{j=1}^{p} \beta_j X_j$$

to

$$\log_e\left(\frac{\lambda}{\text{time}}\right) = \beta_0 + \sum_{j=1}^{p} \beta_j X_j$$

or, equivalently,

$$\log_e(\lambda) = \log_e(\text{time}) + \beta_0 + \sum_{j=1}^{p} \beta_j X_j$$

To fit this new model, you use the `offset` option in the `glm()` function. For example, assume that the length of time that patients participated post-randomization in the Breslow study varied from 14 days to 60 days. You could use the rate of seizures as the dependent variable (assuming you had recorded time for each patient in days) and fit the model

```
fit <- glm(Ysum ~ Base + Age + Trt, data=epilepsy,
        offset= log(time), family=poisson)
```

where `Ysum` is the number of seizures that occurred post-randomization for a patient during the time the patient was studied. In this case, you're assuming that rate doesn't vary over time (for example, 2 seizures in 4 days is equivalent to 10 seizures in 20 days).

ZERO-INFLATED POISSON REGRESSION

Sometimes, the number of zero counts in a dataset is larger than would be predicted by the Poisson model. This can occur when there's a subgroup of the population that would never engage in the behavior being counted. For example, in the `Affairs` dataset described in the section on logistic regression, the original outcome variable (affairs) counted the number of extramarital sexual intercourse experiences participants had in the past year. It's likely that there's a subgroup of faithful marital partners who would never have an affair, no matter how long the period of time studied. These are called *structural zeros* (primarily by the swingers in the group).

In such cases, you can analyze the data using an approach called *zero-inflated Poisson regression*, which fits two models simultaneously—one that predicts who would or would not have an affair, and one that predicts how many affairs a participant would have if you excluded the permanently faithful. Think of this as a model that combines a logistic regression (for predicting structural zeros) and a Poisson regression model (that predicts counts for observations that aren't structural zeros). Zero-inflated Poisson regression can be fit using the `zeroinfl()` function in the `pscl` package.

ROBUST POISSON REGRESSION

Finally, the `glmRob()` function in the `robustbase` package can be used to fit a robust generalized linear model, including robust Poisson regression. As mentioned, this can be helpful in the presence of outliers and influential observations.

Going further

Generalized linear models are a complex and mathematically sophisticated subject, but many fine resources are available for learning about them. A good, short introduction to the topic is Dunteman and Ho (2006). The classic (and advanced) text on generalized linear models is provided by McCullagh and Nelder (1989). Comprehensive and accessible presentations are provided by Dobson and Barnett (2008) and Fox (2008). Faraway (2006) and Fox (2002) provide excellent introductions within the context of R.

Summary

- Generalized linear models allow you to analyze response variables that are decidedly non-normal, including categorical outcomes and discrete counts.
- Logistic regression can be used when analyzing studies with a dichotomous (yes/no) outcome.
- Poisson regression can be used to analyze studies when outcomes are measured as counts or rates.
- Regression diagnostics can be more difficult for generalized linear models than for the linear models described in chapter 8. In particular, you should evaluate logistic and Poisson regression models for overdispersion. If overdispersion is found, consider using an alternate error distribution such as quasi-binomial or quasi-Poisson when fitting the model.

Principal components and factor analysis

14

This chapter covers

- Principal components analysis
- Exploratory factor analysis
- Understanding other latent variable models

One of the most challenging aspects of multivariate data is the sheer complexity of the information. If you have a dataset with 100 variables, how do you make sense of all the interrelationships present? Even with 20 variables, there are 190 pairwise correlations to consider when you're trying to understand how the individual variables relate to one another. Two related but distinct methodologies for exploring and simplifying complex multivariate data are principal components and exploratory factor analysis.

Principal components analysis (PCA) is a data-reduction technique that transforms a larger number of correlated variables into a much smaller set of uncorrelated variables called *principal components*. For example, you might use PCA to transform

30 correlated (and possibly redundant) environmental variables into 5 uncorrelated composite variables that retain as much information from the original set of variables as possible.

In contrast, *exploratory factor analysis (EFA)* is a collection of methods designed to uncover the latent structure in a given set of variables. It looks for a smaller set of underlying or *latent* variables that can explain the relationships among the observed or *manifest* variables. For example, the dataset `Harman74.cor` contains the correlations among 24 psychological tests given to 145 seventh- and eighth-grade children. If you apply EFA to this data, the results suggest that the 276 test intercorrelations can be explained by the children's abilities on 4 underlying factors (verbal ability, processing speed, deduction, and memory). The 24 psychological tests are the observed or manifest variables, and the four underlying factors or latent variables are derived from the correlations among these observed variables.

Figure 14.1 shows the differences between the PCA and EFA models. Principal components (PC1 and PC2) are linear combinations of the observed variables (X1 to X5). The weights used to form the linear composites are chosen to maximize the variance each principal component accounts for, while keeping the components uncorrelated.

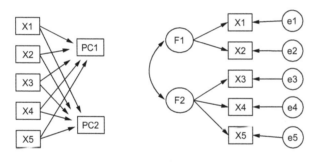

Figure 14.1   Comparing the principal components and factor analysis models. The diagrams show the observed variables (X1 to X5), the principal components (PC1, PC2), factors (F1, F2), and errors (e1 to e5).

Principal components   Factor analysis

In contrast, factors (F1 and F2) are assumed to underlie or "cause" the observed variables, rather than being linear combinations of them. The errors (e1 to e5) represent the variance in the observed variables that is unexplained by the factors. The circles indicate that the factors and errors aren't directly observable but are inferred from the correlations among the variables. In this example, the curved arrow between the factors indicates that they're correlated. Correlated factors are common, but not required, in the EFA model.

The methods described in this chapter require large samples to derive stable solutions. What constitutes an adequate sample size is somewhat complicated. Until recently, analysts used rules of thumb like "factor analysis requires 5–10 times as many subjects as variables." Recent studies suggest that the required sample size depends on the number of factors, the number of variables associated with each factor, and how well the set of factors explains the variance in the variables (Bandalos and Boehm-Kaufman, 2009). I'll go out on a limb and say that if you have several hundred observations, you're probably safe. In this chapter, we'll look at artificially small problems to keep the output (and page count) manageable.

We'll start by reviewing the functions in R that can be used to perform PCA or EFA and give a brief overview of the steps involved. Then we'll work carefully through two PCA examples, followed by an extended EFA example. A brief overview of other packages in R that can be used for fitting latent variable models is provided at the end of the chapter. This discussion includes packages for confirmatory factor analysis, structural equation modeling, correspondence analysis, and latent class analysis.

14.1 Principal components and factor analysis in R

In the base installation of R, the functions for PCA and EFA are `princomp()` and `factanal()`, respectively. In this chapter, we'll focus on functions provided in the `psych` package. They offer many more useful options than their base counterparts. Additionally, the results are reported in a metric that will be more familiar to social scientists and more likely to match the output provided by corresponding programs in other statistical packages such as SAS and IBM SPSS.

Table 14.1 lists the `psych` package functions that are most relevant. Be sure to install the package before trying the examples in this chapter.

Table 14.1　Useful factor analytic functions in the `psych` package

Function	Description
`principal()`	Principal components analysis with optional rotation
`fa()`	Factor analysis by principal axis, minimum residual, weighted least squares, or maximum likelihood
`fa.parallel()`	Scree plots with parallel analyses
`factor.plot()`	Plots the results of a factor or principal components analysis
`fa.diagram()`	Graphs factor or principal components loading matrices
`scree()`	Scree plot for factor and principal components analysis

EFA (and to a lesser degree PCA) are often confusing to new users because they describe a wide range of approaches, and each approach requires several steps (and decisions) to achieve a final result. The most common steps are as follows:

1　Prepare the data. Both PCA and EFA derive their solutions from the correlations among the observed variables. You can input either the raw data matrix or the correlation matrix to the `principal()` and `fa()` functions. If raw data is input, the correlation matrix is automatically calculated. Be sure to screen the data for missing values before proceeding. By default, the `psych` package uses pairwise deletion when calculating correlations.

2   Select a factor model. Decide whether PCA (data reduction) or EFA (uncovering latent structure) is a better fit for your research goals. If you select an EFA approach, you'll also need to choose a specific factoring method (for example, maximum likelihood).

3   Decide how many components/factors to extract.

4   Extract the components/factors.

5   Rotate the components/factors.

6   Interpret the results.

7   Compute component or factor scores.

In the remainder of this chapter, we'll carefully consider each step, starting with PCA. At the end of the chapter, you'll find a detailed flow chart of the possible steps in PCA/EFA (figure 14.7). The chart will make more sense once you've read through the intervening material.

14.2   *Principal components*

The goal of PCA is to replace a large number of correlated variables with a smaller number of uncorrelated variables while capturing as much information from the original variables as possible. These derived variables, called *principal components*, are linear combinations of the observed variables. Specifically, the first principal component

$$PC_1 = a_1 X_1 + a_2 X_2 + \dots + a_k X_k$$

is the weighted combination of the k observed variables that accounts for the most variance in the original set of variables. The second principal component is the linear combination that accounts for the most variance in the original variables, under the constraint that it's *orthogonal* (uncorrelated) to the first principal component. Each subsequent component maximizes the amount of variance accounted for, while at the same time remaining uncorrelated with all previous components. Theoretically, you can extract as many principal components as there are variables. But from a practical viewpoint, you hope that you can approximate the full set of variables with a much smaller set of components. Let's look at a simple example.

The dataset `USJudgeRatings` contains lawyers' ratings of state judges in the US Superior Court. The data frame contains 43 observations on 12 numeric variables. Table 14.2 lists the variables.

Table 14.2   Variables in the `USJudgeRatings` dataset

Variable	Description	Variable	Description
CONT	Number of contacts of lawyer with judge	PREP	Preparation for trial
INTG	Judicial integrity	FAMI	Familiarity with law
DMNR	Demeanor	ORAL	Sound oral rulings

Table 14.2 Variables in the `USJudgeRatings` dataset *(continued)*

Variable	Description	Variable	Description
DILG	Diligence	WRIT	Sound written rulings
CFMG	Case flow managing	PHYS	Physical ability
DECI	Prompt decisions	RTEN	Worthy of retention

From a practical point of view, can you summarize the 11 evaluative ratings (INTG to RTEN) with a smaller number of composite variables? If so, how many will you need, and how will they be defined? Because the goal is to simplify the data, you'll approach this problem using PCA. The data is in raw score format, and no values are missing. Therefore, your next step is deciding how many principal components you'll need.

14.2.1 Selecting the number of components to extract

Several criteria are available for deciding how many components to retain in a PCA. They include

- Basing the number of components on prior experience and theory
- Selecting the number of components needed to account for some threshold cumulative amount of variance in the variables (for example, 80%)
- Selecting the number of components to retain by examining the eigenvalues of the $k \times k$ correlation matrix among the variables

The most common approach is based on the eigenvalues. Each component is associated with an eigenvalue of the correlation matrix. The first PC is associated with the largest eigenvalue, the second PC with the second-largest eigenvalue, and so on. The *Kaiser–Harris criterion* suggests retaining components with eigenvalues greater than 1. Components with eigenvalues less than 1 explain less variance than that contained in a single variable. In *Cattell's Scree test*, the eigenvalues are plotted against their component numbers. Such plots typically demonstrate a bend or elbow, and the components above this sharp break are retained. Finally, you can run simulations, extracting eigenvalues from random data matrices of the same size as the original matrix. If an eigenvalue based on real data is larger than the average corresponding eigenvalues from a set of random data matrices, that component is retained. The approach is called *parallel analysis* (see Hayton, Allen, and Scarpello, 2004, for more details).

You can assess all three eigenvalue criteria at the same time via the `fa.parallel()` function. For the 11 ratings (dropping the CONT variable), the necessary code is as follows:

```
library(psych)
fa.parallel(USJudgeRatings[,-1], fa="pc", n.iter=100,
            show.legend=FALSE, main="Scree plot with parallel analysis")
abline(h=1)
```

This code produces the graph shown in figure 14.2. The plot displays the scree test based on the observed eigenvalues (as straight-line segments and x's), the mean eigenvalues derived from 100 random data matrices (as dashed lines), and the eigenvalues greater than 1 criterion (as a horizontal line at y = 1). The abline() function is used to add a horizontal line at y = 1.

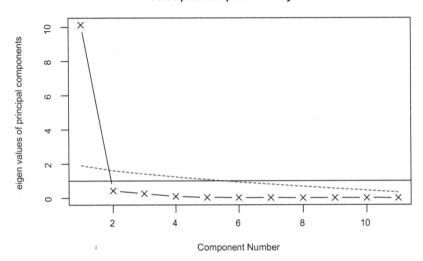

Scree plot with parallel analysis

Figure 14.2   Assessing the number of principal components to retain for the USJudgeRatings example. A scree plot (the line with x's), eigenvalues greater than 1 criterion (horizontal line), and parallel analysis with 100 simulations (dashed line) suggest retaining a single component.

All three criteria suggest that a single component is appropriate for summarizing this dataset. Your next step is to extract the principal component using the principal() function.

14.2.2 *Extracting principal components*

As indicated earlier, the principal() function performs a principal components analysis starting with either a raw data matrix or a correlation matrix. The format is

```
principal(r, nfactors=, rotate=, scores=)
```

where

- *r* is a correlation matrix or a raw data matrix.
- nfactors specifies the number of principal components to extract (1 by default).
- rotate indicates the rotation to be applied (varimax by default; see section 14.2.3).

- scores specifies whether to calculate principal-component scores (false by default).

To extract the first principal component, you can use the code in the following listing.

Listing 14.1 Principal components analysis of USJudgeRatings

```
> library(psych)
> pc <- principal(USJudgeRatings[,-1], nfactors=1)
> pc

Principal Components Analysis
Call: principal(r = USJudgeRatings[, -1], nfactors=1)
Standardized loadings based upon correlation matrix
      PC1   h2    u2
INTG 0.92 0.84 0.157
DMNR 0.91 0.83 0.166
DILG 0.97 0.94 0.061
CFMG 0.96 0.93 0.072
DECI 0.96 0.92 0.076
PREP 0.98 0.97 0.030
FAMI 0.98 0.95 0.047
ORAL 1.00 0.99 0.009
WRIT 0.99 0.98 0.020
PHYS 0.89 0.80 0.201
RTEN 0.99 0.97 0.028


                  PC1
SS loadings     10.13
Proportion Var   0.92
[... additional output omitted ...]
```

Here you're inputting the raw data without the CONT variable and specifying that one unrotated component should be extracted. (Rotation is explained in section 14.3.3.) Because PCA is performed on a correlation matrix, the raw data is automatically converted to a correlation matrix before the components are extracted.

The column labeled PC1 contains the component *loadings,* which are the correlations of the observed variables with the principal component(s). If you extracted more than one principal component, there would be columns for PC2, PC3, and so on. Component loadings are used to interpret the meaning of components. You can see that each variable correlates highly with the first component (PC1). It therefore appears to be a general evaluative dimension.

The column labeled h2 contains the component *communalities*—the amount of variance in each variable explained by the components. The u2 column contains the component *uniqueness*—the amount of variance not accounted for by the components (or 1 – h2). For example, 80% of the variance in physical ability (PHYS) ratings is accounted for by the first PC, and 20% isn't. PHYS is the variable least well represented by a one-component solution.

The row labeled SS Loadings contains the eigenvalues associated with the components. The eigenvalues are the standardized variances associated with a particular component (in this case, the value for the first component is 10). Finally, the row labeled Proportion Var represents the amount of variance accounted for by each component. Here you see that the first principal component accounts for 92% of the variance in the 11 variables.

Let's consider a second example, one that results in a solution with more than one principal component. The dataset `Harman23.cor` contains data on eight body measurements for 305 girls. In this case, the dataset consists of the correlations among the variables rather than the original data (see table 14.3).

Table 14.3   Correlations among body measurements for 305 girls (`Harman23.cor`)

	Height	Arm span	Forearm	Lower leg	Weight	Bitro diameter	Chest girth	Chest width
Height	1.00	0.85	0.80	0.86	0.47	0.40	0.30	0.38
Arm span	0.85	1.00	0.88	0.83	0.38	0.33	0.28	0.41
Forearm	0.80	0.88	1.00	0.80	0.38	0.32	0.24	0.34
Lower leg	0.86	0.83	0.8	1.00	0.44	0.33	0.33	0.36
Weight	0.47	0.38	0.38	0.44	1.00	0.76	0.73	0.63
Bitro diameter	0.40	0.33	0.32	0.33	0.76	1.00	0.58	0.58
Chest girth	0.30	0.28	0.24	0.33	0.73	0.58	1.00	0.54
Chest width	0.38	0.41	0.34	0.36	0.63	0.58	0.54	1.00

Source: H. H. Harman, *Modern Factor Analysis, Third Edition Revised* (University of Chicago Press, 1976), Table 2.3.

Again, you wish to replace the original physical measurements with a smaller number of derived variables. You can determine the number of components to extract using the following code. In this case, you need to identify the correlation matrix (the `cov` component of the `Harman23.cor` object) and specify the sample size (`n.obs`):

```
library(psych)
fa.parallel(Harman23.cor$cov, n.obs=302, fa="pc", n.iter=100,
            show.legend=FALSE, main="Scree plot with parallel analysis")
abline(h=1)
```

Figure 14.3 shows the resulting graph.

Scree plot with parallel analysis

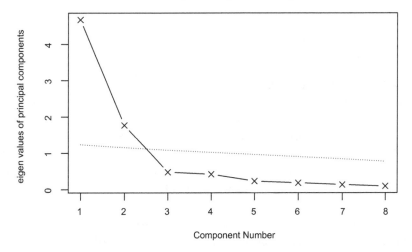

Figure 14.3 Assessing the number of principal components to retain for the body measurements example. The scree plot (line with x's), eigenvalues greater than 1 criterion (horizontal line), and parallel analysis with 100 simulations (dashed line) suggest retaining two components.

You can see from the plot that a two-component solution is suggested. As in the first example, the Kaiser–Harris criteria, scree test, and parallel analysis agree. This won't always be the case, and you may need to extract different numbers of components and select the solution that appears most useful. The next listing extracts the first two principal components from the correlation matrix.

Listing 14.2 Principal components analysis of body measurements

```
> library(psych)
> pc <- principal(Harman23.cor$cov, nfactors=2, rotate="none")
> pc

Principal Components Analysis
Call: principal(r = Harman23.cor$cov, nfactors = 2, rotate = "none")
Standardized loadings based upon correlation matrix
                 PC1   PC2   h2    u2
height          0.86 -0.37 0.88 0.123
arm.span        0.84 -0.44 0.90 0.097
forearm         0.81 -0.46 0.87 0.128
lower.leg       0.84 -0.40 0.86 0.139
weight          0.76  0.52 0.85 0.150
bitro.diameter  0.67  0.53 0.74 0.261
chest.girth     0.62  0.58 0.72 0.283
chest.width     0.67  0.42 0.62 0.375
```

```
                   PC1  PC2
SS loadings        4.67 1.77
Proportion Var 0.58 0.22
Cumulative Var 0.58 0.81
```

```
[... additional output omitted ...]
```

If you examine the PC1 and PC2 columns in listing 14.2, you see that the first component accounts for 58% of the variance in the physical measurements, whereas the second component accounts for 22%. Together, the two components account for 81% of the variance. The two components together account for 88% of the variance in the height variable.

Components and factors are interpreted by examining their loadings. The first component correlates positively with each physical measure and appears to be a general size factor. The second component contrasts the first four variables (height, arm span, forearm, and lower leg), with the second four variables (weight, bitro diameter, chest girth, and chest width). It therefore appears to be a length-versus-volume factor. Conceptually, this isn't an easy construct to work with. Whenever two or more components have been extracted, you can rotate the solution to make it more interpretable. This is the topic we'll turn to next.

14.2.3 *Rotating principal components*

Rotations are a set of mathematical techniques for transforming the component loading matrix into one that's more interpretable. They do this by *purifying* the components as much as possible. Rotation methods differ with regard to whether the resulting components remain uncorrelated (*orthogonal rotation*) or are allowed to correlate (*oblique rotation*). They also differ in their definition of purifying. The most popular orthogonal rotation is the *varimax* rotation, which attempts to purify the columns of the loading matrix so that each component is defined by a limited set of variables (that is, each column has a few large loadings and many very small loadings). Applying a varimax rotation to the body measurement data, you get the results provided in the next listing. You'll see an example of an oblique rotation in section 14.4.

Listing 14.3   Principal components analysis with varimax rotation

```
> rc <- principal(Harman23.cor$cov, nfactors=2, rotate="varimax")
> rc

Principal Components Analysis
Call: principal(r = Harman23.cor$cov, nfactors = 2, rotate = "varimax")
Standardized loadings based upon correlation matrix
           RC1  RC2   h2    u2
height     0.90 0.25 0.88 0.123
arm.span   0.93 0.19 0.90 0.097
forearm    0.92 0.16 0.87 0.128
lower.leg  0.90 0.22 0.86 0.139
weight     0.26 0.88 0.85 0.150
```

```
bitro.diameter 0.19 0.84 0.74 0.261
chest.girth    0.11 0.84 0.72 0.283
chest.width    0.26 0.75 0.62 0.375

               RC1  RC2
SS loadings    3.52 2.92
Proportion Var 0.44 0.37
Cumulative Var 0.44 0.81

[... additional output omitted ...]
```

The column names change from PC to RC to denote rotated components. Looking at the loadings in column RC1, you see that the first component is primarily defined by the first four variables (length variables). The loadings in the column RC2 indicate that the second component is primarily defined by variables 5 through 8 (volume variables). Note that the two components are still uncorrelated and that together, they still explain the variables equally well. You can see that the rotated solution explains the variables equally well because the variable communalities haven't changed. Additionally, the cumulative variance accounted for by the two-component rotated solution (81%) hasn't changed. But the proportion of variance accounted for by each individual component has changed (from 58% to 44% for component 1 and from 22% to 37% for component 2). This spreading out of the variance across components is common, and technically, you should now call them components rather than principal components (because the variance-maximizing properties of individual components haven't been retained).

The ultimate goal is to replace a larger set of correlated variables with a smaller set of derived variables. To do this, you need to obtain scores for each observation on the components.

14.2.4 *Obtaining principal component scores*

In the USJudgeRatings example, you extracted a single principal component from the raw data describing lawyers' ratings on 11 variables. The principal() function makes it easy to obtain scores for each participant on this derived variable (see the next listing).

Listing 14.4 Obtaining component scores from raw data

```
> library(psych)
> pc <- principal(USJudgeRatings[,-1], nfactors=1, score=TRUE)
> head(pc$scores)
                     PC1
AARONSON,L.H. -0.1857981
ALEXANDER,J.M. 0.7469865
ARMENTANO,A.J. 0.0704772
BERDON,R.I.    1.1358765
BRACKEN,J.J.  -2.1586211
BURNS,E.B.     0.7669406
```

The principal component scores are saved in the `scores` element of the object returned by the `principal()` function when the option `scores=TRUE`. If you wanted, you could now get the correlation between the number of contacts occurring between a lawyer and a judge and their evaluation of the judge using

```
> cor(USJudgeRatings$CONT, pc$score)
             PC1
[1,] -0.008815895
```

Apparently, there's no relationship between the lawyer's familiarity and their opinions!

When the principal components analysis is based on a correlation matrix and the raw data isn't available, getting principal component scores for each observation is clearly not possible. But you can get the coefficients used to calculate the principal components.

In the body measurement data, you have correlations among body measurements, but you don't have the individual measurements for these 305 girls. You can get the scoring coefficients using the code in the following listing.

Listing 14.5 Obtaining principal component scoring coefficients

```
> library(psych)
> rc <- principal(Harman23.cor$cov, nfactors=2, rotate="varimax")
> round(unclass(rc$weights), 2)
                  RC1    RC2
height           0.28  -0.05
arm.span         0.30  -0.08
forearm          0.30  -0.09
lower.leg        0.28  -0.06
weight          -0.06   0.33
bitro.diameter  -0.08   0.32
chest.girth     -0.10   0.34
chest.width     -0.04   0.27
```

The component scores are obtained using the formulas

```
PC1 = 0.28*height + 0.30*arm.span + 0.30*forearm + 0.29*lower.leg -
      0.06*weight - 0.08*bitro.diameter - 0.10*chest.girth -
      0.04*chest.width
```

and

```
PC2 = -0.05*height - 0.08*arm.span - 0.09*forearm - 0.06*lower.leg +
      0.33*weight + 0.32*bitro.diameter + 0.34*chest.girth +
      0.27*chest.width
```

These equations assume that the physical measurements have been standardized (mean = 0, sd = 1). Note that the weights for PC1 tend to be around 0.3 or 0. The same is true for PC2. As a practical matter, you could simplify your approach further by taking the first composite variable as the mean of the standardized scores for the first four variables. Similarly, you could define the second composite variable as the mean of the standardized scores for the second four variables. This is typically what I'd do in practice.

Little Jiffy conquers the world

There's quite a bit of confusion among data analysts regarding PCA and EFA. One reason for this is historical and can be traced back to a program called Little Jiffy (no kidding). Little Jiffy was one of the most popular early programs for factor analysis, and it defaulted to a principal components analysis, extracting components with eigenvalues greater than 1 and rotating them to a varimax solution. The program was so widely used that many social scientists came to think of this default behavior as synonymous with EFA. Many later statistical packages also incorporated these defaults in their EFA programs.

As I hope you'll see in the next section, there are important and fundamental differences between PCA and EFA. To learn more about the PCA/EFA confusion, see Hayton, Allen, and Scarpello (2004).

If your goal is to look for latent underlying variables that explain your observed variables, you can turn to factor analysis. This is the topic of the next section.

14.3   *Exploratory factor analysis*

The goal of EFA is to explain the correlations among a set of observed variables by uncovering a smaller set of more fundamental unobserved variables underlying the data. These hypothetical, unobserved variables are called *factors*. (Each factor is assumed to explain the variance shared among two or more observed variables, so technically, they're called *common factors*.)

The model can be represented as

$$X_i = a_1F_1 + a_2F_2 + ... + a_pF_p + U_i$$

where X_i is the *i*th observed variable ($i = 1...k$), F_j are the common factors ($j = 1...p$), and $p < k$. U_i is the portion of variable X_i that is unique to that variable (not explained by the common factors). a_i is the degree to which each factor contributes to the composition of an observed variable. If we go back to the `Harman74.cor` example at the beginning of this chapter, we'd say that an individual's scores on each of the 24 observed psychological tests is due to a weighted combination of their ability on 4 underlying psychological constructs.

Although the PCA and EFA models differ, many of the steps appear similar. To illustrate the process, you'll apply EFA to the correlations among six psychological tests. One hundred twelve individuals were given six tests, including a nonverbal measure of general intelligence (general), a picture-completion test (picture), a block design test (blocks), a maze test (maze), a reading comprehension test (reading), and a vocabulary test (vocab). Can you explain the participants' scores on these tests with a smaller number of underlying or latent psychological constructs?

The covariance matrix among the variables is provided in the dataset `ability.cov`. You can transform this into a correlation matrix using the `cov2cor()` function:

```
> options(digits=2)
> covariances <- ability.cov$cov
> correlations <- cov2cor(covariances)
> correlations
        general picture blocks maze reading vocab
general    1.00    0.47   0.55 0.34    0.58  0.51
picture    0.47    1.00   0.57 0.19    0.26  0.24
blocks     0.55    0.57   1.00 0.45    0.35  0.36
maze       0.34    0.19   0.45 1.00    0.18  0.22
reading    0.58    0.26   0.35 0.18    1.00  0.79
vocab      0.51    0.24   0.36 0.22    0.79  1.00
```

Because you're looking for hypothetical constructs that explain the data, you'll use an EFA approach. As in PCA, the next task is to decide how many factors to extract.

14.3.1 *Deciding how many common factors to extract*

To decide on the number of factors to extract, turn to the `fa.parallel()` function:

```
> library(psych)
> covariances <- ability.cov$cov
> correlations <- cov2cor(covariances)
> fa.parallel(correlations, n.obs=112, fa="both", n.iter=100,
            main="Scree plots with parallel analysis")
> abline(h=c(0, 1))
```

Figure 14.4 shows the resulting plot. Notice you've requested that the function display results for both a principal components and a common factor approach so you can compare them (fa = "both").

There are several things to notice in this graph. If you'd taken a PCA approach, you might have chosen one component (scree test, parallel analysis) or two components (eigenvalues greater than 1). When in doubt, it's usually better to overfactor than to underfactor because overfactoring tends to lead to less distortion of the "true" solution.

Looking at the EFA results, a two-factor solution is clearly indicated. The first two eigenvalues (triangles) are above the bend in the scree test and also above the mean eigenvalues based on 100 simulated data matrices. For EFA, the Kaiser–Harris criterion is number of eigenvalues above 0, rather than 1. (Most people don't realize this, so it's a good way to win bets at parties.) In this case, the Kaiser–Harris criteria also suggest two factors.

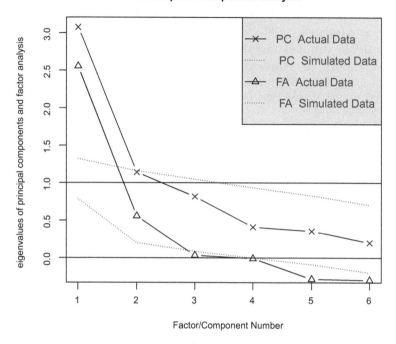

Scree plots with parallel analysis

Figure 14.4 **Assessing the number of factors to retain for the psychological tests example. Results for both PCA and EFA are present. The PCA results suggest one or two components. The EFA results suggest two factors.**

14.3.2 *Extracting common factors*

Now that you've decided to extract two factors, you can use the fa() function to obtain your solution. The format of the fa() function is

```
fa(r, nfactors=, n.obs=, rotate=, scores=, fm=)
```

where

- *r* is a correlation matrix or a raw data matrix.
- nfactors specifies the number of factors to extract (1 by default).
- n.obs is the number of observations (if a correlation matrix is input).
- rotate indicates the rotation to be applied (oblimin by default).
- scores specifies whether to calculate factor scores (false by default).
- fm specifies the factoring method (minres by default).

Unlike PCA, there are many methods of extracting common factors, including maximum likelihood (ml), iterated principal axis (pa), weighted least square (wls), generalized weighted least squares (gls), and minimum residual (minres). Statisticians tend to prefer the maximum likelihood approach because of its well-defined statistical model. Sometimes this approach fails to converge, in which case the iterated principal axis option often works well. To learn more about the different approaches, see Mulaik (2009) and Gorsuch (1983).

For this example, you'll extract the unrotated factors using the iterated principal axis (fm = "pa") approach. The next listing gives the results.

Listing 14.6 Principal axis factoring without rotation

```
> fa <- fa(correlations, nfactors=2, rotate="none", fm="pa")
> fa
Factor Analysis using method =  pa
Call: fa(r = correlations, nfactors = 2, rotate = "none", fm = "pa")
Standardized loadings based upon correlation matrix
          PA1   PA2   h2   u2
general 0.75  0.07 0.57 0.43
picture 0.52  0.32 0.38 0.62
blocks  0.75  0.52 0.83 0.17
maze    0.39  0.22 0.20 0.80
reading 0.81 -0.51 0.91 0.09
vocab   0.73 -0.39 0.69 0.31
                PA1  PA2
SS loadings    2.75 0.83
Proportion Var 0.46 0.14
Cumulative Var 0.46 0.60
[... additional output deleted ...]
```

You can see that the two factors account for 60% of the variance in the six psychological tests. When you examine the loadings, though, they aren't easy to interpret. Rotating them should help.

14.3.3 *Rotating factors*

You can rotate the two-factor solution from section 14.3.2 using either an orthogonal rotation or an oblique rotation. Let's try both so you can see how they differ. First, try an orthogonal rotation (in the next listing).

Listing 14.7 Factor extraction with orthogonal rotation

```
> fa.varimax <- fa(correlations, nfactors=2, rotate="varimax", fm="pa")
> fa.varimax
Factor Analysis using method =  pa
Call: fa(r = correlations, nfactors = 2, rotate = "varimax", fm = "pa")
Standardized loadings based upon correlation matrix
          PA1  PA2   h2   u2
general 0.49 0.57 0.57 0.43
picture 0.16 0.59 0.38 0.62
blocks  0.18 0.89 0.83 0.17
maze    0.13 0.43 0.20 0.80
reading 0.93 0.20 0.91 0.09
vocab   0.80 0.23 0.69 0.31
```

```
                  PA1  PA2
SS loadings       1.83 1.75
Proportion Var 0.30 0.29
Cumulative Var 0.30 0.60

[... additional output omitted ...]
```

Looking at the factor loadings, the factors are certainly easier to interpret. Reading and vocabulary load on the first factor, and picture completion, block design, and mazes load on the second factor. The general nonverbal intelligence measure loads on both factors. This suggests that the correlations among the six psychological tests (the manifest variables) may be explained by two underlying latent variables (a verbal intelligence factor and a nonverbal intelligence factor).

By using an orthogonal rotation, you artificially force the two factors to be uncorrelated. What would you find if you allowed the two factors to correlate? You can try an oblique rotation such as promax (see the next listing).

Listing 14.8 Factor extraction with oblique rotation

```
> fa.promax <- fa(correlations, nfactors=2, rotate="promax", fm="pa")
> fa.promax
Factor Analysis using method =   pa
Call: fa(r = correlations, nfactors = 2, rotate = "promax", fm = "pa")
Standardized loadings based upon correlation matrix
          PA1    PA2   h2   u2
general  0.36   0.49 0.57 0.43
picture -0.04   0.64 0.38 0.62
blocks  -0.12   0.98 0.83 0.17
maze    -0.01   0.45 0.20 0.80
reading  1.01 -0.11 0.91 0.09
vocab    0.84 -0.02 0.69 0.31

                  PA1  PA2
SS loadings       1.82 1.76
Proportion Var 0.30 0.29
Cumulative Var 0.30 0.60

 With factor correlations of
      PA1  PA2
PA1 1.00 0.57
PA2 0.57 1.00
[... additional output omitted ...]
```

Several differences exist between the orthogonal and oblique solutions. In an orthogonal solution, attention focuses on the *factor structure matrix* (the correlations of the variables with the factors). In an oblique solution, there are three matrices to consider: the factor structure matrix, the factor pattern matrix, and the factor intercorrelation matrix.

The *factor pattern matrix* is a matrix of standardized regression coefficients. They give the weights for predicting the variables from the factors. The *factor intercorrelation matrix* gives the correlations among the factors.

In listing 14.8, the values in the PA1 and PA2 columns constitute the factor pattern matrix. They're standardized regression coefficients rather than correlations. Examining the columns of this matrix is still used to name the factors (although there's some controversy here). Again, you'd find a verbal and nonverbal factor.

The factor intercorrelation matrix indicates that the correlation between the two factors is 0.57, which is hefty. If the factor intercorrelations had been low, you might have gone back to an orthogonal solution to keep things simple.

The *factor structure matrix* (or factor-loading matrix) isn't provided, but you can easily calculate it using the formula $F = P \times Phi$, where F is the factor-loading matrix, P is the factor pattern matrix, and Phi is the factor intercorrelation matrix. A simple function for carrying out the multiplication is as follows:

```
fsm <- function(oblique) {
if (class(oblique)[2]=="fa" & is.null(oblique$Phi)) {
    warning("Object doesn't look like oblique EFA")
} else {
    P <- unclass(oblique$loading)
    F <- P %*% oblique$Phi
    colnames(F) <- c("PA1", "PA2")
    return(F)
}
}
```

Applying this to the example, you get

```
> fsm(fa.promax)
        PA1  PA2
general 0.64 0.69
picture 0.33 0.61
blocks  0.44 0.91
maze    0.25 0.45
reading 0.95 0.47
vocab   0.83 0.46
```

Now you can review the correlations between the variables and the factors. Comparing them to the factor-loading matrix in the orthogonal solution, you see that these columns aren't as pure. This is because you've allowed the underlying factors to be correlated. Although the oblique approach is more complicated, it's often a more realistic model of the data.

You can graph an orthogonal or oblique solution using the factor.plot() or fa.diagram() function. The code

```
factor.plot(fa.promax, labels=rownames(fa.promax$loadings))
```

produces the graph in figure 14.5.

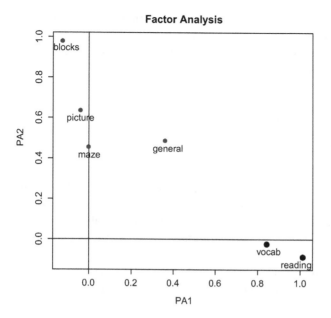

Figure 14.5 Two-factor plot for the psychological tests in `ability.cov.vocab` and `reading` load on the first factor (PA1), and `blocks`, `picture`, and `maze` load on the second factor (PA2). The general intelligence test loads on both.

The code

```
fa.diagram(fa.promax, simple=FALSE)
```

produces the diagram in figure 14.6. If you let `simple=TRUE`, only the largest loading per item is displayed. The figure shows the largest loadings for each factor as well as the correlations between the factors. This type of diagram is helpful when there are several factors.

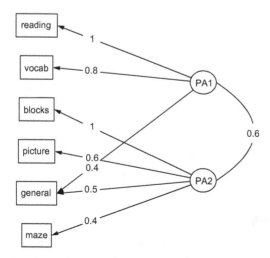

Figure 14.6 Diagram of the oblique two-factor solution for the psychological test data in `ability.cov`

When you're dealing with data in real life, it's unlikely that you'd apply factor analysis to a dataset with so few variables. We've done it here to keep things manageable. If you'd like to test your skills, try factor-analyzing the 24 psychological tests contained in Harman74.cor. The code

```
library(psych)
fa.24tests <- fa(Harman74.cor$cov, nfactors=4, rotate="promax")
```

should get you started.

14.3.4 *Factor scores*

Compared with PCA, the goal of EFA is much less likely to be the calculation of factor scores. But these scores are easily obtained from the fa() function by including the score=TRUE option (when raw data are available). Additionally, the scoring coefficients (standardized regression weights) are available in the weights element of the object returned.

For the ability.cov dataset, you can obtain the beta weights for calculating the factor score estimates for the two-factor oblique solution using

```
> fa.promax$weights
          [,1]   [,2]
general 0.080  0.210
picture 0.021  0.090
blocks  0.044  0.695
maze    0.027  0.035
reading 0.739  0.044
vocab   0.176  0.039
```

Unlike component scores, which are calculated exactly, factor scores can only be estimated. Several methods exist. The fa() function uses the regression approach. To learn more about factor scores, see DiStefano, Zhu, and Mîndrila (2009).

Before moving on, let's briefly review other R packages that are useful for exploratory factor analysis.

14.3.5 *Other EFA-related packages*

R contains several other contributed packages that are useful for conducting factor analyses. The FactoMineR package provides methods for PCA and EFA as well as other latent variable models. It offers many options that we haven't considered here, including the use of both numeric and categorical variables. The FAiR package estimates factor analysis models using a genetic algorithm that allows inequality restrictions on model parameters. The GPArotation package offers many additional factor rotation methods. Finally, the nFactors package offers sophisticated techniques for determining the number of factors underlying data.

14.4 *Other latent variable models*

EFA is only one of a wide range of latent variable models used in statistics. We'll end this chapter with a brief description of other models that can be fit within R. These include models that test a priori theories that can handle mixed data types (numeric and categorical), or that are based solely on categorical multiway tables.

In EFA, you allow the data to determine the number of factors to be extracted and their meaning. But you could start with a theory about how many factors underlie a set of variables, how the variables load on those factors, and how the factors correlate with one another. You could then test this theory against a set of collected data. The approach is called *confirmatory factor analysis (CFA)*.

CFA is a subset of a methodology called *structural equation modeling (SEM)*. SEM allows you to posit not only the number and composition of underlying factors, but also how these factors impact one another. You can think of SEM as a combination of confirmatory factor analyses (for the variables) and regression analyses (for the factors). The resulting output includes statistical tests and fit indices. There are several excellent packages for CFA and SEM in R, including `sem`, `OpenMx`, and `lavaan`.

The `ltm` package can be used to fit latent models to the items contained in tests and questionnaires. The methodology is often used to create large-scale standardized tests such as the Scholastic Aptitude Test (SAT) and the Graduate Record Exam (GRE).

Latent class models (in which the underlying factors are assumed to be categorical rather than continuous) can be fit with the `FlexMix`, `lcmm`, `randomLCA`, and `poLCA` packages. The `lcda` package performs latent class discriminant analysis, and the `lsa` package performs latent semantic analysis, a methodology used in natural language processing.

The `ca` package provides functions for simple and multiple correspondence analysis. These methods allow you to explore the structure of categorical variables in two-way and multiway tables, respectively.

Finally, R contains numerous methods for *multidimensional scaling (MDS)*. MDS is designed to detect underlying dimensions that explain the similarities and distances between a set of measured objects (for example, countries). The `cmdscale()` function in the base installation performs a classical MDS, whereas the `isoMDS()` function in the `MASS` package performs a nonmetric MDS. The `vegan` package also contains functions for classical and nonmetric MDS.

Summary

- Principal components analysis (PCA) is a useful data-reduction method that can replace many correlated variables with a smaller number of uncorrelated composite variables.

- Exploratory factor analysis (EFA) contains a broad range of methods for identifying latent or unobserved constructs (factors) that may underlie a set of observed or manifest variables.

- While the goal of PCA is typically to summarize data and reduce its dimensionality, EFA can be used as a hypothesis-generating tool that is useful when you're trying to understand the relationships among variables. It's often used in the social sciences for theory development.

- PCA and EFA are both multistep processes that require the data analyst to make choices at each step. Figure 14.7 shows these steps.

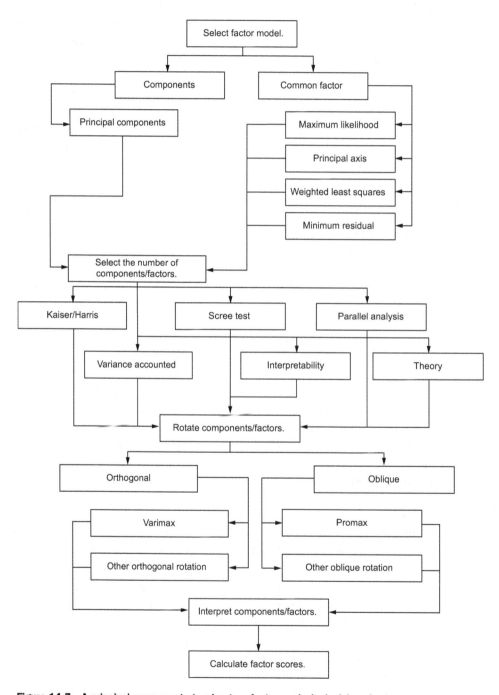

Figure 14.7   A principal components/exploratory factor analysis decision chart

Time series

How fast is global warming occurring, and what will the impact be in 10 years? With the exception of repeated measures ANOVA in section 9.6, each of the preceding chapters has focused on *cross-sectional* data. In a cross-sectional dataset, variables are measured at a single point in time. In contrast, *longitudinal* data involves measuring variables repeatedly over time. By following a phenomenon over time, it's possible to learn a great deal about it.

In this chapter, we'll examine observations that have been recorded at regularly spaced time intervals for a given span of time. We can arrange observations such as these into a *time series* of the form Y_1, Y_2, Y_3, ... , Y_t, ..., Y_T, where Y_t represents the value of Y at time t and T is the total number of observations in the series.

Consider two very different time series displayed in figure 15.1. The series on the left contains the quarterly earnings (dollars) per Johnson & Johnson share between 1960 and 1980. There are 84 observations: 1 for each quarter over 21 years. The series on the right describes the monthly mean relative sunspot numbers from 1749 to 1983 recorded by the Swiss Federal Observatory and the Tokyo Astronomical Observatory. The sunspots time series is much longer, with 2,820 observations—1 per month for 235 years.

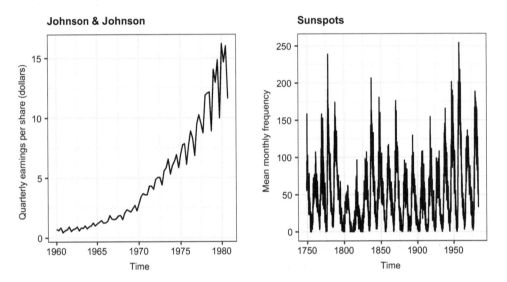

Figure 15.1   **Time-series plots for (left) Johnson & Johnson quarterly earnings per share (in dollars) from 1960 to 1980, and (right) the monthly mean relative sunspot numbers recorded from 1749 to 1983**

Studies of time-series data involve two fundamental questions: what happened (description), and what will happen next (forecasting)? For the Johnson & Johnson data, you might ask,

- Is the price of Johnson & Johnson shares changing over time?
- Are there quarterly effects, with share prices rising and falling in a regular fashion throughout the year?
- Can you forecast what future share prices will be and, if so, to what degree of accuracy?

For the sunspot data, you might ask,

- What statistical models best describe sunspot activity?
- Do some models fit the data better than others?
- Are the number of sunspots at a given time predictable, and, if so, to what degree?

The ability to accurately predict stock prices has relevance for my (hopefully) early retirement to a tropical island, whereas the ability to predict sunspot activity has relevance for my cell phone reception on said island.

Predicting future values of a time series, or *forecasting*, is a fundamental human activity, and studies of time-series data have important real-world applications. Economists use time-series data to understand and predict changes in financial markets. City planners use time-series data to predict future transportation demands. Climate scientists use time-series data to study global climate change. Corporations use time series to predict product demand and future sales. Health-care officials use time-series data to study the spread of disease and to predict the number of future cases in a given region. Seismologists study times-series data to predict earthquakes. In each case, the study of historical time series is an indispensable part of the process. Because different approaches may work best with different types of time series, we'll investigate many examples in this chapter.

There is a wide range of methods for describing time-series data and forecasting future values. If you work with time-series data, you'll find that R has some of the most comprehensive analytic capabilities available. This chapter explores some of the most common descriptive and forecasting approaches and the R functions used to perform them. Table 15.1 lists the time-series data that you'll analyze. They're available with the base installation of R. The datasets vary greatly in their characteristics and the models that fit them best.

Table 15.1   Datasets used in this chapter

Time series	Description
AirPassengers	Monthly airline passenger numbers from 1949–1960
JohnsonJohnson	Quarterly earnings per Johnson & Johnson share
nhtemp	Average yearly temperatures in New Haven, Connecticut, from 1912–1971
Nile	Flow of the river Nile
sunspots	Monthly sunspot numbers from 1749–1983

We'll start with methods for creating and manipulating time series, describing and plotting them, and decomposing them into level, trend, seasonal, and irregular (error) components. Then we'll turn to forecasting, starting with popular exponential modeling approaches that use weighted averages of time-series values to predict future values. Next, we'll consider a set of forecasting techniques called *autoregressive integrated moving averages (ARIMA) models* that use correlations among recent data points and among recent prediction errors to make future forecasts. Throughout, we'll consider methods of evaluating the fit of models and the accuracy of their predictions. The chapter ends with a description of resources for learning more about these topics.

To reproduce the analyses in this chapter, be sure to install the xts, forecast, tseries, and directlabels packages before continuing (install.packages (c("xts", "forecast", "tseries", "directlabels"))).

15.1 Creating a time-series object in R

To work with a time series in R, you have to place it in a *time-series object*—an R structure that contains the observations and date specifications for the observations. Once the data is in a time-series object, you can use numerous functions to manipulate, model, and plot it.

R packages offer a variety of structures for holding time series (see the sidebar "Time-series objects in R"). In this chapter, we'll use the xts class offered by the xts package. It supports both regularly and irregularly spaced time series and has many functions for manipulating time-series data.

Time-series objects in R

It's easy to get lost among the many objects R provides for holding time-series data. Base R comes with ts for holding a single time series with regularly spaced time intervals and mts for multiple time series with regularly spaced intervals. The zoo package offers a class that can hold time series with irregularly spaced intervals, and the xts package offers a superset of the zoo class with more supporting functions. Other popular formats include tsibble, timeSeries, irts, and tis. Luckily, the tsbox package provides functions to convert a data frame into any of these formats and can also convert one time-series format into another.

To create an xts time series, you'll use

```
library(xts)
myseries <- xts(data, index)
```

where *data* is a numeric vector at values and *index* is a date vector indicating when the values were observed. The following listing shows an example. The data consists of monthly sales figures for two years, starting in January 2018.

Listing 15.1   Creating a time-series object

```
library(xts)
sales <- c(18, 33, 41,  7, 34, 35, 24, 25, 24, 21, 25, 20,
           22, 31, 40, 29, 25, 21, 22, 54, 31, 25, 26, 35)
date   <- seq(from = as.Date("2018/1/1"),
              to = as.Date("2019/12/1"),
              by = "month")

sales.xts <- xts(sales, date)
```

Time-series objects in xts format can be subset using bracket [] notation. For example, sales.xts["2018"] will return all data from 2018. Specifying sales.xts ["2018-3/2019-5"] will return all data from March 2018 to May 2019.

There are also apply functions designed to execute a function on each distinct period of a time-series object. They are particularly useful for aggregating a time series into larger time periods. The format is

```
newseries <- apply.period(x, FUN, ...)
```

where *period* can be daily, weekly, monthly, quarterly, or yearly, *x* is an xts time-series object, *FUN* is the function to be applied, and ... are arguments passed to *FUN*.

For example, quarterlies <- apply.quarterly(sales.xts, sum) will return a time series with eight quarterly sales totals. The sum function could be replaced with mean, median, min, max, or any other function returning a single value.

The autoplot() function in the forecast package can be used for plotting time-series data as ggplot2 graphs. The following listing provides two examples.

Listing 15.2   Plotting time series

```
library(ggplot2)
library(forecast)
autoplot(sales.xts)                           ❶ Default graph

autoplot(sales.xts) +
    geom_line(color="blue") +                 ❷ Sets line color
    scale_x_date(date_breaks="1 months",      ❸ Specifies x-axis labels
                date_labels="%b %y") +
    labs(x="", y="Sales", title="Customized Time Series Plot") +
    theme_bw() +                              ❹ Adjusts theme
    theme(axis.text.x = element_text(angle = 90, vjust = 0.5, hjust=1),
        panel.grid.minor.x=element_blank())
```

In the first example, the autoplot() function is used to create ggplot2 graph ❶. Figure 15.2 shows the graph.

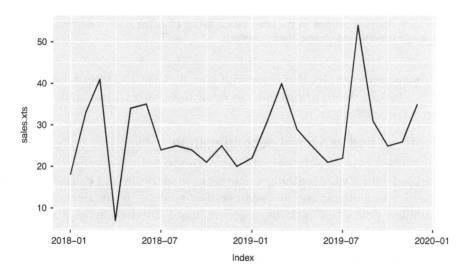

Figure 15.2   Time-series plot for the sales data in listing 15.1. This is the default format provided by the autoplot() function.

In the second example, the plot is modified to make it more appealing. The line color is changed to blue ❷. The `scale_x_date()` function is used to provide better labels for the *x*-axis ❸. The `data_breaks` option specifies the distance between tick marks and takes on values like `"1 day"`, `"2 weeks"`, `"5 years"`, or whatever is appropriate. The `date_labels` option specifies the format for the labels. Here `"%b %y"` specifies month (3 letters) and year (2 digits) with a space in between. See section 4.6 for a table of these codes. Finally, a black-and-white theme is chosen, the *x*-axis labels are rotated 90 degrees, and the vertical minor grid lines are suppressed ❹. Figure 15.3 displays the customized graph.

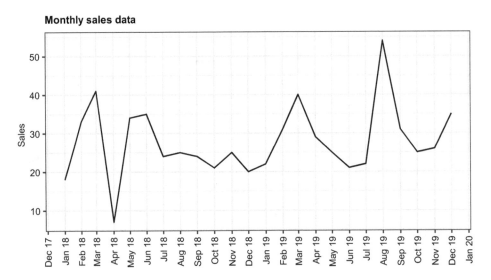

Figure 15.3   Times-series plot for the sales data in listing 15.1. The graph is customized with color, better labeling, and cleaner theme elements.

The time-series examples that come with base R (table 15.1) are actually in `ts` format, but luckily, the functions introduced in this chapter can handle time series in either `ts` or `xts` format.

15.2   Smoothing and seasonal decomposition

Just as analysts explore a dataset with descriptive statistics and graphs before attempting to model the data, describing a time series numerically and visually should be the first step before attempting to build complex models. In this section, we'll look at smoothing a time series to clarify its general trend and decomposing a time series to observe any seasonal effects.

15.2.1 Smoothing with simple moving averages

The first step when investigating a time series is to plot it, as in listing 15.1. Consider the `Nile` time series. It records the annual flow of the river Nile at Aswan from 1871–1970.

A plot of the series can be seen in the upper-left panel of figure 15.4. The time series appears to be decreasing, but there is a great deal of variation from year to year.

Time series typically have a significant irregular or error component. To discern any patterns in the data, you'll frequently want to plot a smoothed curve that damps down these fluctuations. One of the simplest methods of smoothing a time series is to use simple moving averages. For example, each data point can be replaced with the mean of that observation and one observation before and after it. This is called a *centered moving average*. A centered moving average is defined as

$$S_t = \left(Y_{t-q} + \ldots + Y_t + \ldots + Y_{t+q}\right) / \left(2q+1\right)$$

where S_t is the smoothed value at time t and $k = 2q + 1$ is the number of observations that are averaged. The k value is usually chosen to be an odd number (in this example, 3). By necessity, when using a centered moving average, you lose the $(k - 1) / 2$ observations at each end of the series.

Several functions in R can provide a simple moving average, including SMA() in the TTR package, rollmean() in the zoo package, and ma() in the forecast package. Here, you'll use the ma() function to smooth the Nile time series that comes with the base R installation.

The code in the next listing plots the raw time series and smoothed versions using k equal to 3, 7, and 15. Figure 15.3 shows the plots.

Listing 15.3 Simple moving averages

```
library(forecast)
library(ggplot2)

theme_set(theme_bw())
ylim <- c(min(Nile), max(Nile))

autoplot(Nile) +
  ggtitle("Raw time series") +
  scale_y_continuous(limits=ylim)

autoplot(ma(Nile, 3)) +
  ggtitle("Simple Moving Averages (k=3)") +
  scale_y_continuous(limits=ylim)

autoplot(ma(Nile, 7)) +
  ggtitle("Simple Moving Averages (k=7)") +
  scale_y_continuous(limits=ylim)

autoplot(ma(Nile, 15)) +
  ggtitle("Simple Moving Averages (k=15)") +
  scale_y_continuous(limits=ylim)
```

As k increases, the plot becomes increasingly smoothed. The challenge is to find the value of k that highlights the major patterns in the data without under- or over-smoothing. This is more art than science, and you'll probably want to try several values of k before settling on one. From the plots in figure 15.4, there certainly appears to have been a drop in river flow between 1892 and 1900. Other changes are open to interpretation. For example, there may have been a small increasing trend between 1941 and 1961, but this could also have been a random variation.

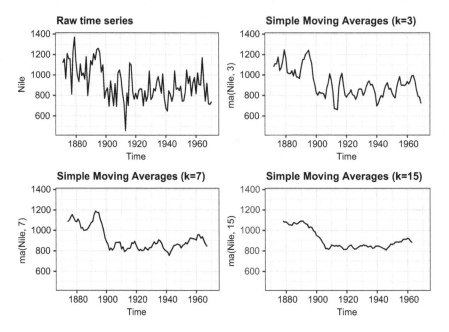

Figure 15.4   The Nile time series measuring annual river flow at Aswan from 1871–1970 (upper left). The other plots are smoothed versions using simple moving averages at three smoothing levels (k = 3, 7, and 15).

For time-series data with a periodicity greater than 1 (that is, with a seasonal component), you'll want to go beyond a description of the overall trend. You can use seasonal decomposition to examine both seasonal and general trends.

15.2.2 *Seasonal decomposition*

Time-series data that have a seasonal aspect (such as monthly or quarterly data) can be decomposed into a trend component, a seasonal component, and an irregular component. The *trend component* captures changes in level over time. The *seasonal component* captures cyclical effects due to the time of year. The *irregular* (or *error*) *component* captures those influences not described by the trend and seasonal effects.

The decomposition can be additive or multiplicative. In an additive model, the components sum to give the values of the time series. Specifically,

$$Y_t = \text{Trend}_t + \text{Seasonal}_t + \text{Irregular}_t$$

where the observation at time t is the sum of the contributions of the trend at time t, the seasonal effect at time t, and an irregular effect at time t.

In a multiplicative model, given by the equation

$$Y_t = \text{Trend}_t \times \text{Seasonal}_t \times \text{Irregular}_t$$

the trend, seasonal, and irregular influences are multiplied. Figure 15.5 shows examples.

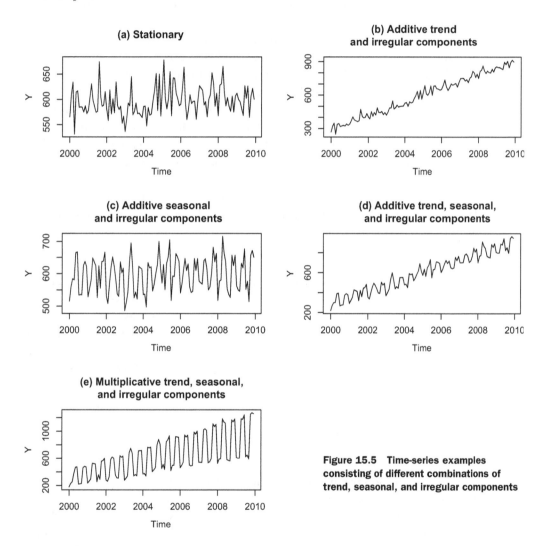

Figure 15.5 Time-series examples consisting of different combinations of trend, seasonal, and irregular components

In the first plot (a), there is neither a trend nor a seasonal component. The only influence is a random fluctuation around a given level. In the second plot (b), there is an upward trend over time as well as random fluctuations. In the third plot (c), there are seasonal effects and random fluctuations, but no overall trend away from a horizontal line. In the fourth plot (d), all three components are present: an upward trend, seasonal effects, and random fluctuations. You also see all three components in the final plot (e), but here, they combine in a multiplicative way. Notice how the variability is proportional to the level: as the level increases, so does the variability. This amplification (or possible damping) based on the current level of the series strongly suggests a multiplicative model.

An example may make the difference between additive and multiplicative models clearer. Consider a time series that records the monthly sales of motorcycles over a 10-year period. In a model with an additive seasonal effect, the number of motorcycles sold tends to increase by 500 in November and December (due to the Christmas rush) and decrease by 200 in January (when sales tend to slow down). The seasonal increase or decrease is independent of the current sales volume.

In a model with a multiplicative seasonal effect, motorcycle sales in November and December tend to increase by 20% and decrease in January by 10%. In the multiplicative case, the impact of the seasonal effect is proportional to the current sales volume, which isn't the case in an additive model. In many instances, the multiplicative model is more realistic.

A popular method for decomposing a time series into trend, seasonal, and irregular components is seasonal decomposition by loess smoothing. In R, this can be accomplished with the `stl()` function. The format is

```
stl(ts, s.window=, t.window=)
```

where *ts* is the time series to be decomposed, `s.window` controls how fast the seasonal effects can change over time, and `t.window` controls how fast the trend can change over time. Setting `s.window="periodic"` forces seasonal effects to be identical across years. Only the `ts` and `s.window` parameters are required. See `help(stl)` for details.

The `stl()` function can only handle additive models, but this isn't a serious limitation. Multiplicative models can be transformed into additive models using a log transformation:

$$\log(Y_t) = \log(Trend_t \times Seasonal_t \times Irregular_t)$$
$$= \log(Trend_t) + \log(Seasonal_t) + \log(Irregular_t)$$

After fitting the additive model to the log-transformed series, the results can be back-transformed to the original scale. Let's look at an example.

The time series `AirPassengers` comes with a base R installation and describes the monthly totals (in thousands) of international airline passengers between 1949 and 1960. The top of figure 15.6 shows a plot of the data. From the graph, it appears that variability of the series increases with the level, suggesting a multiplicative model.

The plot in the lower portion of figure 15.6 displays the time series created by taking the log of each observation. The variance has stabilized, and the logged series looks like an appropriate candidate for an additive decomposition. This is carried out using the `stl()` function listing 15.4.

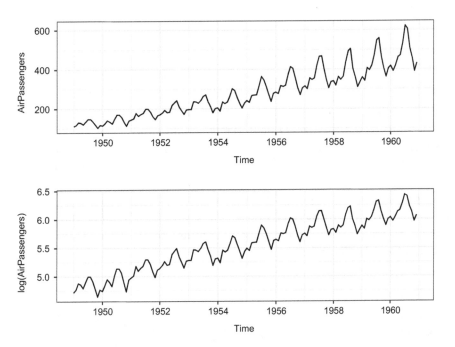

Figure 15.6 Plot of the `AirPassengers` time series (top). The time series contains the monthly totals (in thousands) of international airline passengers between 1949 and 1960. The log-transformed time series (bottom) stabilizes the variance and fits an additive seasonal decomposition model better.

Listing 15.4 Seasonal decomposition using `stl()`

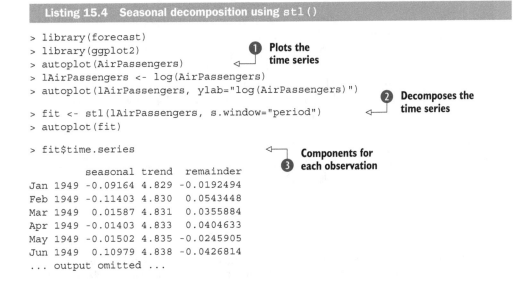

```
> library(forecast)
> library(ggplot2)
> autoplot(AirPassengers)                                    ❶ Plots the
                                                               time series
> lAirPassengers <- log(AirPassengers)
> autoplot(lAirPassengers, ylab="log(AirPassengers)")

> fit <- stl(lAirPassengers, s.window="period")             ❷ Decomposes the
> autoplot(fit)                                                time series

> fit$time.series                                           ❸ Components for
                                                               each observation
           seasonal trend   remainder
Jan 1949 -0.09164 4.829 -0.0192494
Feb 1949 -0.11403 4.830  0.0543448
Mar 1949  0.01587 4.831  0.0355884
Apr 1949 -0.01403 4.833  0.0404633
May 1949 -0.01502 4.835 -0.0245905
Jun 1949  0.10979 4.838 -0.0426814
... output omitted ...
```

```
> exp(fit$time.series)

         seasonal trend remainder
Jan 1949   0.9124 125.1   0.9809
Feb 1949   0.8922 125.3   1.0558
Mar 1949   1.0160 125.4   1.0362
Apr 1949   0.9861 125.6   1.0413
May 1949   0.9851 125.9   0.9757
Jun 1949   1.1160 126.2   0.9582

... output omitted ...
```

First, the time series is plotted and transformed ❶. A seasonal decomposition is performed and saved in an object called `fit` ❷. Plotting the results gives the graph in figure 15.7, which shows the time series, seasonal, trend, and irregular components from 1949 to 1960. Note that the seasonal components have been constrained to remain the same across each year (using the `s.window="period"` option). The trend is monotonically increasing, and the seasonal effect suggests more passengers in the summer (perhaps during vacations). The grey bars on the right are magnitude guides—each bar represents the same magnitude. This is useful because the y-axes are different for each graph.

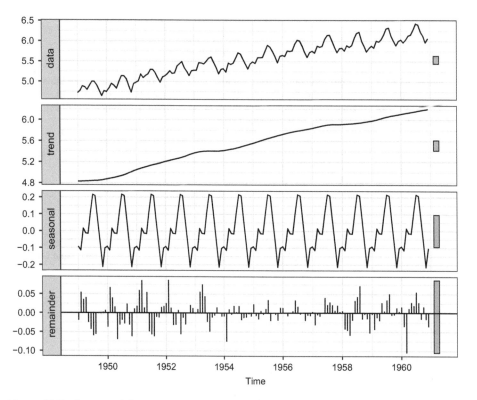

Figure 15.7 A seasonal decomposition of the logged `AirPassengers` time series using the `stl()` function. The time series (data) is decomposed into seasonal, trend, and irregular components.

The object returned by the `stl()` function includes a component called `time.series` that contains the trend, season, and irregular portion of each observation ❸. In this case, `fit$time.series` is based on the logged time series. `exp(fit$time.series)` converts the decomposition back to the original metric. Examining the seasonal effects suggests that the number of passengers increased by 24% in July (a multiplier of 1.24) and decreased by 20% in November (a multiplier of .80).

The `forecast` package provides additional tools for visualizing the seasonal decomposition. The following listing demonstrates the creation of a month plot and seasonal plot.

Listing 15.5 Month and season plots

```
library(forecast)
library(ggplot2)
library(directlabels)

ggmonthplot(AirPassengers)   +
  labs(title="Month plot: AirPassengers",       ❶ Month plot
       x="",
       y="Passengers (thousands)")

p <- ggseasonplot(AirPassengers) + geom_point() +
  labs(title="Seasonal plot: AirPassengers",      ❷ Season plot
       x="",
       y="Passengers (thousands)")
direct.label(p)
```

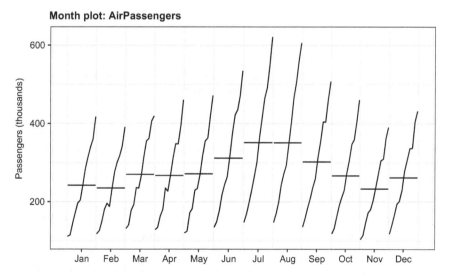

Figure 15.8   A month plot of `AirPassengers` time series. The month plot displays the subseries for each month (all January values from 1949 to 1960 connected, all February values connected, and so on), along with the average of each subseries. There is a uniform increasing trend for each month, and the most passengers tend to fly in July and August.

The month plot (figure 15.8) displays the subseries for each month (all January values connected, all February values connected, and so on), along with the average of each subseries. From this graph, it appears that the trend is increasing for each month in a roughly uniform way. Additionally, the greatest number of passengers occurs in July and August.

The season plot (figure 15.9) displays the subseries by year. Again, you see a similar pattern, with increases in passengers each year and the same seasonal pattern. By default, the `ggplot2` package would create a legend for the year variable. The `directlabels` package is used to place the year labels directly on the graph, next to each line in the time series.

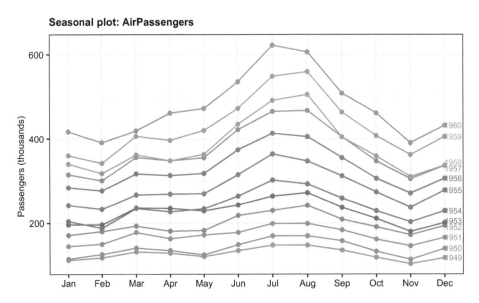

Figure 15.9   A season plot (bottom) for the `AirPassengers` time series. Each shows an increasing trend and similar seasonal pattern year to year.

Note that although you've described the time series, you haven't predicted any future values. In the next section, we'll consider the use of exponential models for forecasting beyond the available data.

15.3   *Exponential forecasting models*

Exponential models are some of the most popular approaches to forecasting the future values of a time series. They're simpler than many other types of models, but they can yield good short-term predictions in a wide range of applications. They differ from each other in the components of the time series that are modeled. A simple exponential model (also called a *single exponential model*) fits a time series that has a constant level and an irregular component at time i, but has neither a trend nor a seasonal component. A *double exponential model* (also called a *Holt exponential smoothing*) fits a time series with both a level and a trend. Finally, a *triple exponential model* (also called a *Holt–Winters exponential smoothing*) fits a time series with level, trend, and seasonal components.

Exponential models can be fit with the ets() function that comes with the fore-cast package. The format of the ets() function is

```
ets(ts, model="ZZZ")
```

where *ts* is a time series and the model is specified by three letters. The first letter denotes the error type, the second letter denotes the trend type, and the third letter denotes the seasonal type. Allowable letters are *A* for additive, *M* for multiplicative, *N* for none, and *Z* for automatically selected. Table 15.2 shows examples of common models.

Table 15.2 Functions for fitting simple, double, and triple exponential forecasting models

Type	Parameters fit	Functions
simple	level	ets(ts, model="ANN") ses(ts)
double	level, slope	ets(ts, model="AAN") holt(ts)
triple	level, slope, seasonal	ets(ts, model="AAA") hw(ts)

The ses(), holt(), and hw() functions are convenience wrappers to the ets() function with prespecified defaults. First, we'll look at the most basic exponential model: simple exponential smoothing.

15.3.1 *Simple exponential smoothing*

Simple exponential smoothing uses a weighted average of existing time-series values to make a short-term prediction of future values. The weights are chosen so that observations have an exponentially decreasing impact on the average as you go back in time.

The simple exponential smoothing model assumes that an observation in the time series can be described by

$$Y_t = \text{level} + \text{irregular}_t$$

The prediction at time Y_{t+1} (called the *1-step-ahead forecast*) is written as

$$Y_{t+1} = c_0 Y_t + c_1 Y_{t-1} + c_2 Y_{t-2} + \dots$$

where $c_i = \alpha(1-\alpha)^i$, t = 0,1,2, ... and $0 \le \alpha \le 1$. The c_i weights sum to one, and the 1-step-ahead forecast can be seen to be a weighted average of the current value and all past values of the time series. The alpha (α) parameter controls the rate of decay for the weights. The closer alpha is to 1, the more weight is given to recent observations.

The closer alpha is to 0, the more weight is given to past observations. The actual value of alpha is usually chosen by computer to optimize a fit criterion. A common fit criterion is the sum of squared errors between the actual and predicted values. An example will help clarify these ideas.

The nhtemp time series contains the mean annual temperature in degrees Fahrenheit in New Haven, Connecticut, from 1912 to 1971. Figure 15.10 shows a plot of the time series as a line.

There is no obvious trend, and the yearly data lack a seasonal component, so the simple exponential model is a reasonable place to start. The code for making a 1-step-ahead forecast using the ses() function is given in the following listing.

Listing 15.6 Simple exponential smoothing

```
> library(forecast)
> fit <- ets(nhtemp, model="ANN")        ❶ Fits the model
> fit

ETS(A,N,N)

Call:
 ets(y = nhtemp, model = "ANN")

  Smoothing parameters:
    alpha = 0.1819

  Initial states:
    l = 50.2762

  sigma:  1.1455

     AIC      AICc       BIC
265.9298 266.3584 272.2129

> forecast(fit, 1)        ❷ 1-step-ahead forecast

     Point Forecast  Lo 80  Hi 80   Lo 95   Hi 95
1972          51.87 50.402 53.338  49.625  54.115

> autoplot(forecast(fit, 1)) +
  labs(x = "Year",
       y = expression(paste("Temperature (", degree*F,")",)),
       title = "New Haven Annual Mean Temperature")

> accuracy(fit)        ❸ Prints accuracy measures

                ME  RMSE   MAE   MPE  MAPE   MASE
Training set 0.146 1.126 0.895 0.242 1.749 0.751
```

The ets(mode="ANN") statement fits the simple exponential model to the nhtemp time series ❶. The A indicates that the errors are additive, and the NN indicates that there is no trend and no seasonal component. The relatively low value of alpha (0.18) indicates that distant as well as recent observations are being considered in the forecast. This value is automatically chosen to maximize the fit of the model to the given dataset.

The forecast() function is used to predict the time series *k* steps into the future. The format is forecast(*fit, k*). The 1-step-ahead forecast for this series is 51.9°F with a 95% confidence interval (49.6°F to 54.1°F) ❷. Figure 15.10 shows plots of the time series, the forecast value, and the 80% and 95% confidence intervals.

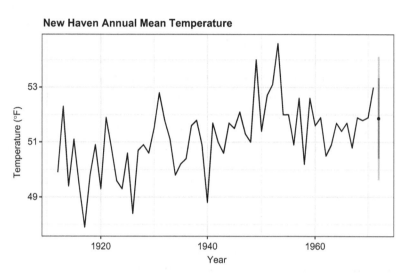

Figure 15.10 Average yearly temperatures in New Haven, Connecticut and a 1-step-ahead prediction from a simple exponential forecast using the ets() function

The forecast package also provides an accuracy() function that displays the most popular predictive accuracy measures for time-series forecasts ❸. Table 15.3 describes each one. The e_t represents the error or irregular component of each observation $(Y_i - \hat{Y}_i)$.

Table 15.3 Predictive accuracy measures

Measure	Abbreviation	Definition
Mean error	ME	mean(e_t)
Root mean squared error	RMSE	sqrt(mean(e_t^2))
Mean absolute error	MAE	mean($\lvert e_t \rvert$)
Mean percentage error	MPE	mean($100 \times e_t / Y_t$)
Mean absolute percentage error	MAPE	mean($\lvert 100 \times e_t / Y_t \rvert$)

Table 15.3   Predictive accuracy measures *(continued)*

Measure	Abbreviation	Definition
Mean absolute scaled error	MASE	mean($\lvert q_t \rvert$) where $q_t = e_t / (1/(T{-}1) * \text{sum}(\lvert y_t - y_{t-1} \rvert))$, T is the number of observations, and the sum goes from t = 2 to t = T

The mean error and mean percentage error may not be that useful because positive and negative errors can cancel out. The RMSE gives the square root of the mean square error, which in this case is 1.13°F. The mean absolute percentage error reports the error as a percentage of the time-series values. It's unitless and can be used to compare prediction accuracy across time series. But it assumes a measurement scale with a true zero point (for example, number of passengers per day). Because the Fahrenheit scale has no true zero, you can't use it here. The mean absolute scaled error is the most recent accuracy measure and is used to compare the forecast accuracy across time series on different scales. There is no one best measure of predictive accuracy. The RMSE is certainly the best known and most often cited.

Simple exponential smoothing assumes the absence of trend or seasonal components. The next section considers exponential models that can accommodate both.

15.3.2   *Holt and Holt–Winters exponential smoothing*

The Holt exponential smoothing approach can fit a time series that has an overall level and a trend (slope). The model for an observation at time *t* is

$$Y_t = \text{level} + \text{slope} \times t + \text{irregular}_t$$

An alpha smoothing parameter controls the exponential decay for the level, and a beta smoothing parameter controls the exponential decay for the slope. Again, each parameter ranges from 0 to 1, with larger values giving more weight to recent observations.

The Holt–Winters exponential smoothing approach can be used to fit a time series that has an overall level, a trend, and a seasonal component. Here, the model is

$$Y_t = \text{level} + \text{slope} \times t + s_t + \text{irregular}_t$$

where s_t represents the seasonal influence at time *t*. In addition to alpha and beta parameters, a gamma smoothing parameter controls the exponential decay of the seasonal component. Like the others, it ranges from 0 to 1, and larger values give more weight to recent observations in calculating the seasonal effect.

In section 15.2, you decomposed a time series describing the monthly totals (in log thousands) of international airline passengers into additive trend, seasonal, and irregular components. Let's use an exponential model to predict future travel. Again, you'll use log values so that an additive model fits the data. The code in the following listing applies the Holt–Winters exponential smoothing approach to predicting the next five values of the `AirPassengers` time series.

Listing 15.7 Exponential smoothing with level, slope, and seasonal components

```
> library(forecast)
> fit <- ets(log(AirPassengers), model="AAA")
> fit

ETS(A,A,A)

Call:
 ets(y = log(AirPassengers), model = "AAA")

    Smoothing parameters:          ❶ Smoothing parameters
    alpha = 0.6975
    beta  = 0.0031
    gamma = 1e-04

  Initial states:
    l = 4.7925
    b = 0.0111
    s = -0.1045 -0.2206 -0.0787 0.0562 0.2049 0.2149
          0.1146 -0.0081 -0.0059 0.0225 -0.1113 -0.0841

  sigma:  0.0383

    AIC    AICc    BIC
-207.17 -202.31 -156.68

>accuracy(fit)

                   ME    RMSE      MAE      MPE    MAPE    MASE
Training set -0.0018307 0.03607 0.027709 -0.034356 0.50791 0.22892
> pred <- forecast(fit, 5)                      ◁──┐
> pred                                             ❷ Future forecasts
          Point Forecast  Lo 80  Hi 80  Lo 95  Hi 95
Jan 1961          6.1093 6.0603 6.1584 6.0344 6.1843
Feb 1961          6.0925 6.0327 6.1524 6.0010 6.1841
Mar 1961          6.2366 6.1675 6.3057 6.1310 6.3423
Apr 1961          6.2185 6.1412 6.2958 6.1003 6.3367
May 1961          6.2267 6.1420 6.3115 6.0971 6.3564

> autoplot(pred) +
  labs(title = "Forecast for Air Travel",
       y = "Log(AirPassengers)",
       x ="Time")

> pred$mean <- exp(pred$mean)           ❸ Makes forecasts in
> pred$lower <- exp(pred$lower)            the original scale
> pred$upper <- exp(pred$upper)
> p <- cbind(pred$mean, pred$lower, pred$upper)
> dimnames(p)[[2]] <- c("mean", "Lo 80", "Lo 95", "Hi 80", "Hi 95")
> p

           mean  Lo 80  Lo 95  Hi 80  Hi 95
Jan 1961 450.04 428.51 417.53 472.65 485.08
Feb 1961 442.54 416.83 403.83 469.85 484.97
```

```
Mar 1961 511.13 477.01 459.88 547.69 568.10
Apr 1961 501.97 464.63 446.00 542.30 564.95
May 1961 506.10 464.97 444.57 550.87 576.15
```

The smoothing parameters for the level (.70), trend (.0004), and seasonal components (.003) are given in ❶. The low value for the trend (.0001) doesn't mean there is no slope; it indicates that the slope estimated from early observations didn't need to be updated.

The forecast() function produces forecasts for the next five months ❷ and is plotted in figure 15.11. Because the predictions are on a log scale, exponentiation is used to get the predictions in the original metric: numbers (in thousands) of passengers ❸. The matrix pred$mean contains the point forecasts, and the matrices pred$lower and pred$upper contain the 80% and 95% lower and upper confidence limits, respectively. The exp() function is used to return the predictions to the original scale, and cbind() creates a single table. Thus, the model predicts 509,200 passengers in March, with a 95% confidence band ranging from 454,900 to 570,000.

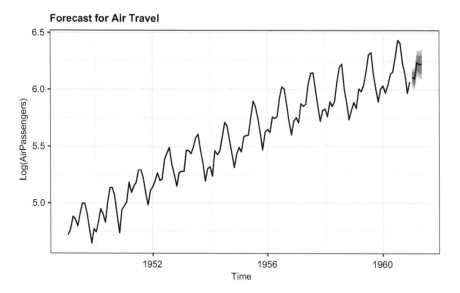

Figure 15.11   Five-year forecast of log(number of international airline passengers in thousands) based on a Holt-Winters exponential smoothing model. The data is from the AirPassengers time series.

15.3.3   *The ets() function and automated forecasting*

The ets() function has additional capabilities. You can use it to fit exponential models that have multiplicative components, add a dampening component, and perform automated forecasts. Let's consider each in turn.

In the previous section, you fit an additive exponential model to the log of the AirPassengers time series. Alternatively, you could fit a multiplicative model to the original data. The function call would be ets(AirPassengers, model="MAM"). The trend remains additive, but the seasonal and irregular components are assumed to be multiplicative. By using a multiplicative model in this case, the accuracy statistics and forecasted values are reported in the original metric (thousands of passengers)—a decided advantage.

The ets() function can also fit a damping component. Time-series predictions often assume that a trend will continue up forever (housing market, anyone?). A damping component forces the trend to a horizontal asymptote over a period of time. In many cases, a damped model makes more realistic predictions.

Finally, you can invoke the ets() function to automatically select a best-fitting model for the data. Let's fit an automated exponential model to the Johnson & Johnson data described in the introduction to this chapter. The code in the following listing allows the software to select a best-fitting model.

Listing 15.8 Automatic exponential forecasting with ets()

```
> library(forecast)
> fit <- ets(JohnsonJohnson)
> fit

ETS(M,M,M)

Call:
 ets(y = JohnsonJohnson)

    Smoothing parameters:
    alpha = 0.2776
    beta  = 0.0636
    gamma = 0.5867

  Initial states:
    l = 0.6276
    b = 0.0165
    s = -0.2293 0.1913 -0.0074 0.0454

  sigma:  0.0921

    AIC    AICc    BIC
163.64 166.07 185.52

> autoplot(forecast(fit)) +
  labs(x = "Time",
       y = "Quarterly Earnings (Dollars)",
       title="Johnson and Johnson Forecasts")
```

Because no model is specified, the software performs a search over a wide array of models to find one that minimizes the fit criterion (log-likelihood by default). The selected model has multiplicative trend, seasonal, and error components. Figure 15.12 gives the plot, along with forecasts for the next eight quarters (the default in this case).

Johnson & Johnson Forecasts

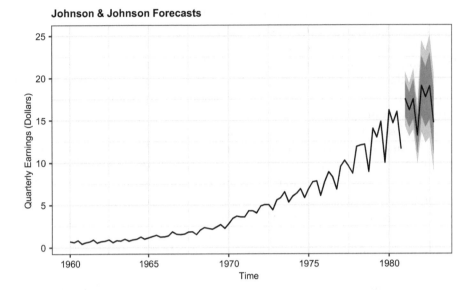

Figure 15.12   Multiplicative exponential smoothing forecast with trend and seasonal components. The forecasts are a dashed line, and the 80% and 95% confidence intervals are shown in light and dark blue, respectively.

As stated earlier, exponential time-series modeling is popular because it can give good short-term forecasts in many situations. A second popular approach is the Box–Jenkins methodology, commonly referred to as ARIMA models. These are described in the next section.

15.4   ARIMA forecasting models

In the *autoregressive integrated moving average (ARIMA)* approach to forecasting, predicted values are a linear function of recent actual values and recent errors of prediction (residuals). ARIMA is a complex approach to forecasting. In this section, we'll limit discussion to ARIMA models for nonseasonal time series.

Before describing ARIMA models, several terms need to be defined, including lags, autocorrelation, partial autocorrelation, differencing, and stationarity. Each is considered in the next section.

15.4.1   Prerequisite concepts

When you *lag* a time series, you shift it back by a given number of observations. Consider the first few observations from the Nile time series, displayed in table 15.4. Lag 0 is the unshifted time series. Lag 1 is the time series shifted one position to the left. Lag 2 shifts the time series two positions to the left, and so on. Time series can be lagged using the function lag(ts, k), where ts is the time series and k is the number of lags.

Table 15.4   The `Nile` time series at various lags

Lag	1869	1870	1871	1872	1873	1874	1875	...
0			1120	1160	963	1210	1160	...
1		1120	1160	963	1210	1160	1160	...
2	1120	1160	963	1210	1160	1160	813	...

Autocorrelation measures the way observations in a time series relate to each other. AC_k is the correlation between a set of observations (Y_t) and observations k periods earlier (Y_{t-k}). Thus, AC_1 is the correlation between the Lag 1 and Lag 0 time series, AC_2 is the correlation between the Lag 2 and Lag 0 time series, and so on. Plotting these correlations (AC_1, AC_2, ..., AC_k) produces an *autocorrelation function (ACF) plot*. The ACF plot is used to select appropriate parameters for the ARIMA model and to assess the fit of the final model.

An ACF plot can be produced with the `Acf()` function in the `forecast` package. The format is `Acf(ts)`, where *ts* is the original time series. The ACF plot for the `Nile` time series, with $k = 1$ to 18, is provided a little later in the top half of figure 15.13.

A *partial autocorrelation* is the correlation between Y_t and Y_{t-k} with the effects of all Y values between the two (Y_{t-1}, Y_{t-2}, ..., Y_{t-k+1}) removed. Partial autocorrelations can also be plotted for multiple values of k. The PACF plot can be generated with the `Pacf()` function in the `forecast` package. The function call is `Pacf(ts)`, where *ts* is the time series to be assessed. The PACF plot is also used to determine the most appropriate parameters for the ARIMA model. The bottom half of figure 15.13 gives the results for the `Nile` time series.

ARIMA models are designed to fit *stationary* time series (or time series that can be made stationary). In a stationary time series, the statistical properties of the series don't change over time. For example, the mean and variance of Y_t are constant. Additionally, the autocorrelations for any lag k don't change with time.

It may be necessary to transform the values of a time series to achieve constant variance before proceeding to fitting an ARIMA model. The log transformation is often useful here, as you saw in section 15.1.3. Other transformations, such as the Box–Cox transformation described in section 8.5.2, may also be helpful.

Because stationary time series are assumed to have constant means, they can't have a trend component. Many nonstationary time series can be made stationary through *differencing*. In differencing, each value of a time series Y_t is replaced with $Y_{t-1} - Y_t$. Differencing a time series once removes a linear trend. Differencing it a second time removes a quadratic trend. A third time removes a cubic trend. It's rarely necessary to difference more than twice.

You can difference a time series with the `diff()` function. The format is `diff(ts, differences=d)`, where *d* indicates the number of times the time series ts is differenced. The default is d=1. The ndiffs() function in the forecast package can be used to help determine the best value of d. The format is ndiffs(ts).

Stationarity is often evaluated with a visual inspection of a time-series plot. If the variance isn't constant, the data are transformed. If there are trends, the data are differenced. You can also use a statistical procedure called the *Augmented Dickey–Fuller (ADF) test* to evaluate the assumption of stationarity. In R, the function adf.test() in the tseries package performs the test. The format is adf.test(ts), where *ts* is the time series to be evaluated. A significant result suggests stationarity.

To summarize, ACF and PCF plots are used to determine the parameters of ARIMA models. Stationarity is an important assumption, and transformations and differencing are used to help achieve stationarity. With these concepts in hand, we can now turn to fitting models with an autoregressive (AR) component, a moving averages (MA) component, or both components (ARMA). Finally, we'll examine ARIMA models that include ARMA components and differencing to achieve stationarity (integration).

15.4.2 ARMA and ARIMA models

In an *autoregressive* model of order p, each value in a time series is predicted from a linear combination of the previous p-values

$$AR(p) : Y_t = \mu + \beta_1 Y_{t-1} + \beta_2 Y_{t-2} + \ldots + \beta_p Y_{t-p} + \varepsilon_t$$

where Y_t is a given value of the series, μ is the mean of the series, the βs are the weights, and ε_t is the irregular component. In a *moving average* model of order q, each value in the time series is predicted from a linear combination of q previous errors. In this case,

$$MA(q) : Y_t = \mu + \theta_1 \varepsilon_{t-1} + \theta_2 \varepsilon_{t-2} + \ldots + \theta_p \varepsilon_{t-q} + \varepsilon_t$$

where the εs are the errors of prediction and the θs are the weights. (It's important to note that the moving averages described here aren't the simple moving averages described in section 15.1.2.)

Combining the two approaches yields an ARMA(p, q) model of the form

$$Y_t = \mu + \beta_1 Y_{t-1} + \beta_2 Y_{t-2} + \ldots + \beta_p Y_{t-p} - \theta_1 \varepsilon_{t-1} - \theta_2 \varepsilon_{t-2} - \ldots - \theta_p \varepsilon_{t-q} + \varepsilon_t$$

that predicts each value of the time series from the past p values and q residuals.

An ARIMA(p, d, q) model is a model in which the time series has been differenced d times, and the resulting values are predicted from the previous p actual values and q previous errors. The predictions are *un-differenced* or *integrated* to achieve the final prediction.

The steps in ARIMA modeling are as follows:

1   Ensure that the time series is stationary.
2   Identify a reasonable model or models (possible values of p and q).
3   Fit the model.

4 Evaluate the model's fit, including statistical assumptions and predictive accuracy.

5 Make forecasts.

Let's apply each step in turn to fit an ARIMA model to the `Nile` time series.

ENSURING THAT THE TIME SERIES IS STATIONARY

First, you plot the time series and assess its stationarity (see listing 15.7 and the top half of figure 15.13). The variance appears to be stable across the years observed, so there's no need for a transformation. There may be a trend, which is supported by the results of the `ndiffs()` function.

Listing 15.9   Transforming the time series and assessing stationarity

```
> library(forecast)
> library(tseries)
> autoplot(Nile)
> ndiffs(Nile)

[1] 1

> dNile <- diff(Nile)
> autoplot(dNile)
> adf.test(dNile)

    Augmented Dickey-Fuller Test

data:  dNile
Dickey-Fuller = -6.5924, Lag order = 4, p-value = 0.01
alternative hypothesis: stationary
```

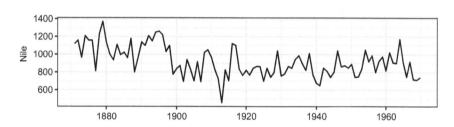

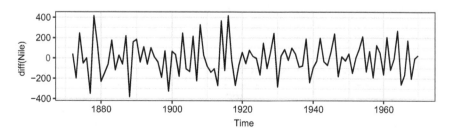

Figure 15.13   Time series displaying the annual flow of the river Nile at Aswan from 1871 to 1970 (top) along with the times series differenced once (bottom). The differencing removes the decreasing trend evident in the original plot.

The series is differenced once (lag = 1 is the default) and saved as dNile. The differenced time series is plotted in the bottom half of figure 15.13 and certainly looks more stationary. Applying the ADF test to the differenced series suggests that it's now stationary, so you can proceed to the next step.

IDENTIFYING ONE OR MORE REASONABLE MODELS

Possible models are selected based on the ACF and PACF plots:

```
autoplot(Acf(dNile))
autoplot(Pacf(dNile))
```

Figure 15.14 shows the resulting plots.

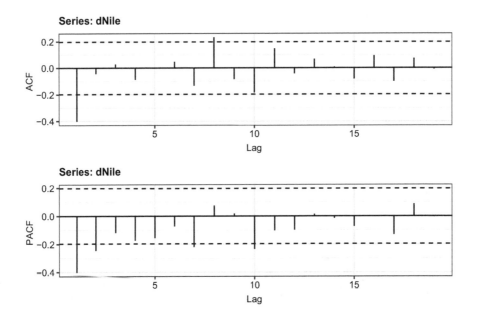

Figure 15.14   Autocorrelation and partial autocorrelation plots for the differenced Nile time series

The goal is to identify the parameters p, d, and q. You already know that d = 1 from the previous section. You get p and q by comparing the ACF and PACF plots with the guidelines given in table 15.5.

Table 15.5   Guidelines for selecting an ARIMA model

Model	ACF	PACF
ARIMA(p, d, 0)	Trails off to zero	Zero after lag p
ARIMA(0, d, q)	Zero after lag q	Trails off to zero
ARIMA(p, d, q)	Trails off to zero	Trails off to zero

The results in table 15.5 are theoretical, and the actual ACF and PACF may not match this exactly, but they can be used to give a rough guide of reasonable models to try. For the `Nile` time series in figure 15.13, there appears to be one large autocorrelation at Lag 1, and the partial autocorrelations trail off to zero as the lags get bigger. This suggests trying an ARIMA(0, 1, 1) model.

FITTING THE MODEL(S)

The ARIMA model is fit with the `Arima()` function. The format is `Arima(ts, order=c(q, d, q))`. The following listing gives the result of fitting an ARIMA(0, 1, 1) model to the `Nile` time series.

Listing 15.10 Fitting an ARIMA model

```
> library(forecast)
> fit <- arima(Nile, order=c(0,1,1))
> fit

Series: Nile
ARIMA(0,1,1)

Coefficients:
          ma1
      -0.7329
s.e.   0.1143

sigma^2 estimated as 20600:  log likelihood=-632.55
AIC=1269.09   AICc=1269.22   BIC=1274.28

> accuracy(fit)

                ME   RMSE   MAE    MPE   MAPE   MASE
Training set -11.94  142.8  112.2  -3.575  12.94  0.8089
```

Note that you apply the model to the original time series. By specifying d = 1, it calculates first differences for you. The coefficient for the moving averages (–0.73) is provided along with the AIC. If you fit other models, the AIC can help you choose which one is most reasonable. Smaller AIC values suggest better models. The accuracy measures can help you determine whether the model fits with sufficient accuracy. Here the mean absolute percent error is 13% of the river level.

EVALUATING MODEL FIT

If the model is appropriate, the residuals should be normally distributed with mean zero, and the autocorrelations should be zero for every possible lag. In other words, the residuals should be normally and independently distributed (no relationship between them). The assumptions can be evaluated with the code in the following listing.

Listing 15.11 Evaluating the model fit

```
> library(ggplot2)
> df <- data.frame(resid = as.numeric(fit$residuals))    ◁─┤ Extracts residuals
```

```
> ggplot(df, aes(sample = resid)) +          ⊲─┤ Creates Q-Q plot
    stat_qq() + stat_qq_line() +
    labs(title="Normal Q-Q Plot")

> Box.test(fit$residuals, type="Ljung-Box")  ⊲─┤ Tests autocorrelations
    Box-Ljung test                                are zero for all lags

data:  fit$residuals
X-squared = 1.3711, df = 1, p-value = 0.2416
```

First, the residuals are extracted from the `fit` object and saved in a data frame. Then `qq_*` functions are used to produce the Q-Q plot (figure 15.15). Normally distributed data should fall along the line. In this case, the results look good.

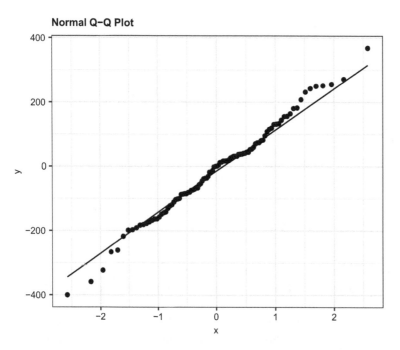

Figure 15.15 Normal Q-Q plot for determining the normality of the time-series residuals. Normally distributed values are expected to fall along the line.

The `Box.test()` function provides a test that the autocorrelations are all zero. The results aren't significant, suggesting that the autocorrelations don't differ from zero. This ARIMA model appears to fit the data well.

MAKING FORECASTS

If the model hadn't met the assumptions of normal residuals and zero autocorrelations, it would have been necessary to alter the model, add parameters, or try a different approach. Once a final model has been chosen, it can be used to make predictions of future values. In the next listing, the forecast() function from the forecast package is used to predict three years ahead.

> **Listing 15.12 Forecasting with an ARIMA model**

```
> forecast(fit, 3)

     Point Forecast      Lo 80      Hi 80      Lo 95      Hi 95
1971        798.3673  614.4307  982.3040  517.0605  1079.674
1972        798.3673  607.9845  988.7502  507.2019  1089.533
1973        798.3673  601.7495  994.9851  497.6663  1099.068

> autoplot(forecast(fit, 3)) + labs(x="Year", y="Annual Flow")
```

The autoplot() function is used to plot the forecast in figure 15.16. Point estimates are given by the black line, and 80% and 95% confidence bands are represented by dark and light blue bands, respectively.

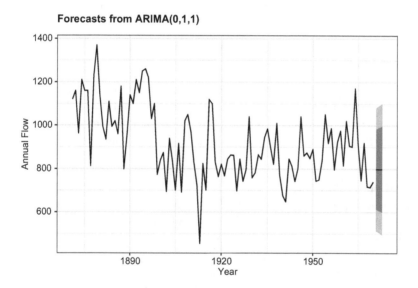

Figure 15.16   Three-year forecast for the Nile time series from a fitted ARIMA(0,1,1) model. The black line represents point estimates, and the light and dark blue bands represent the 80% and 95% confidence bands limits, respectively.

15.4.3   *Automated ARIMA forecasting*

In section 15.2.3, you used the ets() function in the forecast package to automate the selection of a best exponential model. The package also provides an auto.arima() function to select a best ARIMA model. The next listing applies this approach to the sunspots time series described in the chapter introduction.

Listing 15.13 Automated ARIMA forecasting

```
> library(forecast)
> fit <- auto.arima(sunspots)
> fit
Series: sunspots
ARIMA(2,1,2)
Coefficients:
         ar1      ar2      ma1      ma2
        1.35   -0.396    -1.77    0.810
s.e.    0.03    0.029     0.02    0.019

sigma^2 estimated as 243:  log likelihood=-11746
AIC=23501    AICc=23501    BIC=23531

> forecast(fit, 3)


         Point Forecast       Lo 80      Hi 80        Lo 95     Hi 95
Jan 1984      40.437722   20.4412613  60.43418     9.855774  71.01967
Feb 1984      41.352897   18.2795867  64.42621     6.065314  76.64048
Mar 1984      39.796425   15.2537785  64.33907     2.261686  77.33116

> accuracy(fit)
                     ME RMSE    MAE MPE MAPE MASE
Training set -0.02673 15.6  11.03 NaN  Inf 0.32
```

The function selects an ARIMA model with $p = 2$, $d = 1$, and $q = 2$. These are values that minimize the AIC criterion over a large number of possible models. The MPE and MAPE accuracy blow up because there are zero values in the series (a drawback of these two statistics). Plotting the results and evaluating the fit are left for you as an exercise.

A caveat on forecasting

Forecasting has a long and varied history, from early shamans predicting the weather to modern data scientists predicting the results of recent elections. Prediction is fundamental to both science and human nature.

Although these methodologies can be crucial in understanding and predicting a wide variety of phenomena, it's important to remember that they each entail extrapolation—going beyond the data. They assume that future conditions will mirror current conditions. Financial predictions made in 2007 assumed continued economic growth in 2008 and beyond. As we all know now, that isn't exactly how things turned out. Significant events can change the trend and pattern in a time series, and the farther out you try to predict, the greater the uncertainty.

15.5 *Going further*

There are many good books on time-series analysis and forecasting. *Forecasting: Principles and Practice* (http://otexts.com/fpp2, 2018) is a clear and concise online textbook by Rob Hyndman and George Athanasopoulos that includes R code throughout. I highly recommend it. Additionally, Cowpertwait and Metcalfe (2009) have written an excellent text on analyzing time series with R. A more advanced treatment that also includes R code can be found in Shumway and Stoffer (2010). Finally, you can consult the CRAN Task View on Time Series Analysis (http://cran.r-project.org/web/views/ TimeSeries.html), which contains a comprehensive summary of all of R's time-series capabilities.

Summary

- R provides a wide array of data structures for holding time-series data. Base R offers classes for holding one (`ts`) or more than one (`mts`) series of observations recorded at regular intervals. The `xts` and `zoo` packages extend this to include observations recorded at irregular intervals.

- Time-series data stored as `xts` objects can be easily subsetted using bracket `[]` notation and aggregated using `apply.`*`period`* functions.

- The `forecast` package provides several functions for visually exploring time-series data. The `autoplot()` function can be used to plot time-series data as `ggplot2` graphs. The `ma()` function can be used smooth irregularities in a time series to highlight trends. The `stl()` function can be used to decompose a time series into trend, seasonal, and irregular (residual) components.

- The `forecast` package can also be used to forecast future values of a time series. We covered two popular forecasting approaches: exponential models and autoregressive integrated moving average (ARIMA) models.

Cluster analysis

16

This chapter covers

- Identifying cohesive subgroups (clusters) of observations
- Determining the number of clusters present
- Obtaining a nested hierarchy of clusters
- Obtaining discrete clusters

Cluster analysis is a data-reduction technique designed to uncover subgroups of observations within a dataset. It allows you to reduce a large number of observations to a much smaller number of clusters or types. A *cluster* is defined as a group of observations that are more similar to each other than they are to the observations in other groups. This isn't a precise definition, and that fact has given rise to an enormous variety of clustering methods.

Cluster analysis is widely used in the biological and behavioral sciences, marketing, and medical research. For example, a psychological researcher might cluster data on the symptoms and demographics of depressed patients, seeking to uncover subtypes of depression. The hope would be that finding such subtypes might lead to more targeted and effective treatments and a better understanding of the disorder. Marketing researchers use cluster analysis as a customer-segmentation strategy. Customers are arranged into clusters based on the similarity of their demographics and buying behaviors. Marketing campaigns are then tailored to appeal to one or more of these subgroups. Medical researchers use cluster analysis to help catalog gene expression patterns obtained from DNA microarray data. This can help them understand normal growth and development and the underlying causes of many human diseases.

The two most popular clustering approaches are *hierarchical agglomerative clustering* and *partitioning clustering*. In agglomerative hierarchical clustering, each observation starts as its own cluster. Clusters are then combined, two at a time, until all clusters are merged into a single cluster. In the partitioning approach, you specify K: the number of clusters you're seeking. Observations are then randomly divided into K groups and reshuffled to form cohesive clusters.

Within each of these broad approaches, there are many clustering algorithms to choose from. For hierarchical clustering, the most popular are single linkage, complete linkage, average linkage, centroid, and Ward's method. For partitioning, the two most popular are k-means and partitioning around medoids (PAM). Each clustering method has advantages and disadvantages, which we'll discuss.

The examples in this chapter focus on food and wine (I suspect my friends aren't surprised). Hierarchical clustering is applied to the `nutrient` dataset contained in the `flexclust` package to answer the following questions:

- What are the similarities and differences among 27 types of fish, fowl, and meat, based on 5 nutrient measures?
- Can these foods be meaningfully clustered into a smaller number of groups?

Partitioning methods will be used to evaluate 13 chemical analyses of 178 Italian wine samples. The data are contained in the `wine` dataset available with the `rattle` package. Here, the questions are

- Are there subtypes of wine in the data?
- If so, how many subtypes are there, and what are their characteristics?

In fact, the wine samples represent three varietals (recorded as `Type`). This will allow you to evaluate how well the cluster analysis recovers the underlying structure.

Although there are many approaches to cluster analysis, they usually follow a similar set of steps. These common steps are described in section 16.1. Hierarchical agglomerative clustering is described in section 16.3, and partitioning methods are covered in section 16.4. Some final advice and cautionary statements are provided in section 16.6. To run the examples in this chapter, be sure to install the `cluster`, `NbClust`, `flexclust`, `fMultivar`, `ggplot2`, `ggdendro`, `factoextra`, `clusterability`, and `rattle` packages. The `rattle` package will also be used in chapter 17.

16.1   *Common steps in cluster analysis*

Like factor analysis (chapter 14), an effective cluster analysis is a multistep process with numerous decision points. Each decision can affect the quality and usefulness of the results. This section describes the 11 typical steps in a comprehensive cluster analysis:

1   *Choose appropriate attributes.* The first (and perhaps most important) step is to select variables that you feel may be important for identifying and understanding differences among groups of observations within the data. For example, in a study of depression, you might want to assess one or more of the following: psychological symptoms; physical symptoms; age at onset; the number, duration, and timing of episodes; the number of hospitalizations; functional status with regard to self-care; social and work history; current age; gender; ethnicity; socioeconomic status; marital status; family medical history; and response to previous treatments. A sophisticated cluster analysis can't compensate for a poor choice of variables.

2   *Scale the data.* If the variables in the analysis vary in range, the variables with the largest range will have the greatest impact on the results. This is often undesirable, so analysts scale the data before continuing. The most popular approach is to standardize each variable to a mean of 0 and a standard deviation of 1. Other alternatives include dividing each variable by its maximum value or subtracting the variable's mean and dividing by the variable's median absolute deviation. The three approaches are illustrated with the following code snippets:

```
df1 <- apply(mydata, 2, function(x){(x-mean(x))/sd(x)})
df2 <- apply(mydata, 2, function(x){x/max(x)})
df3 <- apply(mydata, 2, function(x){(x - mean(x))/mad(x)})
```

In this chapter, you'll use the `scale()` function to standardize the variables to a mean of 0 and a standard deviation of 1. This is equivalent to the first code snippet (`df1`).

3   *Screen for outliers.* Many clustering techniques are sensitive to outliers, which can distort the cluster solutions obtained. You can screen for (and remove) univariate outliers using functions from the `outliers` package. The `mvoutlier` package contains functions that can be used to identify multivariate outliers. An alternative is to use a clustering method that is robust to the presence of outliers. Partitioning around medoids (section 16.4.2) is an example of the latter approach.

4   *Calculate distances.* Although clustering algorithms vary widely, they typically require a measure of the distance among the entities to be clustered. The most popular measure of the distance between two observations is the Euclidean distance, but the Manhattan, Canberra, asymmetric binary, maximum, and Minkowski distance measures are also available (see `?dist` for details). In this chapter, the Euclidean distance is used throughout. Calculating Euclidean distances is covered in section 16.2.

5 *Select a clustering algorithm.* Next, you select a method of clustering the data. Hierarchical clustering is useful for smaller problems (say, 150 observations or less) and when a nested hierarchy of groupings is desired. The partitioning method can handle much larger problems but requires that the number of clusters be specified in advance.

Once you've chosen the hierarchical or partitioning approach, you must select a specific clustering algorithm. Again, each has advantages and disadvantages. Sections 16.3 and 16.4 describe the most popular. You may wish to try more than one algorithm to see how robust the results are to the choice of methods.

6 *Obtain one or more cluster solutions.* This step uses the method(s) selected in step 5.

7 *Determine the number of clusters present.* To obtain a final cluster solution, you must decide how many clusters are present in the data. This is a thorny problem, and many approaches have been proposed. It usually involves extracting various numbers of clusters (say, 2 to *K*) and comparing the quality of the solutions. The NbClust() function in the NbClust package provides 26 different indices to help you make this decision (which elegantly demonstrates how unresolved this issue is). NbClust is used throughout this chapter.

8 *Obtain a final clustering solution.* Once the number of clusters has been determined, a final clustering is performed to extract that number of subgroups.

9 *Visualize the results.* Visualization can help you determine the meaning and usefulness of the cluster solution. The results of a hierarchical clustering are usually presented as a dendrogram. Partitioning results are typically visualized using a bivariate cluster plot.

10 *Interpret the clusters.* Once a cluster solution has been obtained, you must interpret (and possibly name) the clusters. What do the observations in a cluster have in common? How do they differ from the observations in other clusters? This step is typically accomplished by obtaining summary statistics for each variable by cluster. For continuous data, the mean or median for each variable within each cluster is calculated. For mixed data (data that contains categorical variables), the summary statistics will also include modes or category distributions.

11 *Validate the results.* Validating the cluster solution involves asking the question, "Are these groupings in some sense real and not a manifestation of unique aspects of this dataset or statistical technique?" If a different cluster method or different sample is employed, would the same clusters be obtained? The fpc, clv, and clValid packages each contain functions for evaluating the stability of a clustering solution.

Because the calculations of distances between observations is such an integral part of cluster analysis, it's described next in some detail.

16.2 Calculating distances

Every cluster analysis begins with the calculation of a distance, dissimilarity, or proximity between each entity to be clustered. The Euclidean distance between two observations is given by

$$d_{ij} = \sqrt{\sum_{p=1}^{P} \left(x_{ip} - x_{jp} \right)^2}$$

where i and j are observations and P is the number of variables. In other words, the Euclidean distance between two observations is the square root of the sum of squared differences on each variable.

Consider the `nutrient` dataset provided with the `flexclust` package. The dataset contains measurements on the nutrients of 27 types of meat, fish, and fowl. The first few observations are given by

```
> data(nutrient, package="flexclust")
> head(nutrient, 4)

              energy protein fat calcium iron
BEEF BRAISED     340      20  28       9  2.6
HAMBURGER        245      21  17       9  2.7
BEEF ROAST       420      15  39       7  2.0
BEEF STEAK       375      19  32       9  2.6
```

and the Euclidean distance between the first two (beef braised and hamburger) is

$$d = \sqrt{(340 - 245)^2 + (20 - 21)^2 + (28 - 17)^2 + (9 - 9)^2 + (26 - 27)^2} = 95.64$$

The `dist()` function in the base R installation can be used to calculate the distances between all rows (observations) of a matrix or data frame. The format is `dist(x, method=)`, where `x` is the input data and `method="euclidean"` by default. The function returns a lower triangle matrix by default, but the `as.matrix()` function can be used to access the distances using standard bracket notation. For the `nutrient` data frame,

```
> d <- dist(nutrient)
> as.matrix(d)[1:4,1:4]

             BEEF BRAISED HAMBURGER BEEF ROAST BEEF STEAK
BEEF BRAISED          0.0      95.6       80.9       35.2
HAMBURGER            95.6       0.0      176.5      130.9
BEEF ROAST           80.9     176.5        0.0       45.8
BEEF STEAK           35.2     130.9       45.8        0.0
```

Larger distances indicate larger dissimilarities between observations. The distance between an observation and itself is 0. As expected, the `dist()` function provides the same distance between beef braised and hamburger as the hand calculations.

> ### Cluster analysis with mixed data types
>
> Euclidean distances are usually the distance measure of choice for continuous data. But if other variable types are present, alternative dissimilarity measures are required. You can use the `daisy()` function in the `cluster` package to obtain a dissimilarity matrix among observations that have any combination of binary, nominal, ordinal, and continuous attributes. Other functions in the `cluster` package can use these dissimilarities to carry out a cluster analysis. For example, `agnes()` offers agglomerative hierarchical clustering, and `pam()` provides partitioning around medoids.

Note that distances in the `nutrient` data frame are heavily dominated by the contribution of the `energy` variable, which has a much larger range. Scaling the data will help equalize the impact of each variable. In the next section, you'll apply hierarchical cluster analysis to this dataset.

16.3 *Hierarchical cluster analysis*

As stated, in agglomerative hierarchical clustering, each case or observation starts as its own cluster. Clusters are then combined two at a time until all clusters are merged into a single cluster. The algorithm is as follows:

1 Define each observation (row, case) as a cluster.

2 Calculate the distances between every cluster and every other cluster.

3 Combine the two clusters that have the smallest distance. This reduces the number of clusters by one.

4 Repeat steps 2 and 3 until all clusters have been merged into a single cluster containing all observations.

The primary difference among hierarchical clustering algorithms is their definitions of cluster distances (step 2). Table 16.1 lists five of the most common hierarchical clustering methods and their definitions of the distance between two clusters.

Table 16.1 Hierarchical clustering methods

Cluster method	Definition of the distance between two clusters
Single linkage	Shortest distance between a point in one cluster and a point in the other cluster
Complete linkage	Longest distance between a point in one cluster and a point in the other cluster
Average linkage	Average distance between each point in one cluster and each point in the other cluster (also called *UPGMA* [*unweighted pair group mean averaging*])
Centroid	Distance between the centroids (vector of variable means) of the two clusters. For a single observation, the centroid is the variable's values.
Ward	The ANOVA sum of squares between the two clusters added up over all the variables

Single-linkage clustering tends to find elongated, cigar-shaped clusters. It also commonly displays a phenomenon called *chaining*—dissimilar observations are joined in the same cluster because they're similar to intermediate observations between them. Complete-linkage clustering tends to find compact clusters of approximately equal diameter. It can also be sensitive to outliers. Average-linkage clustering offers a compromise between the two. It's less likely to chain and is less susceptible to outliers. It also has a tendency to join clusters with small variances.

Ward's method tends to join clusters with small numbers of observations and tends to produce clusters with roughly equal numbers of observations. It can also be sensitive to outliers. The centroid method offers an attractive alternative due to its simple and easily understood definition of cluster distances. It's also less sensitive to outliers than other hierarchical methods. But it may not perform as well as the average-linkage or Ward method.

Hierarchical clustering can be accomplished using the `hclust()` function. The format is `hclust(d, method=)`, where `d` is a distance matrix produced by the `dist()` function, and methods include `"single"`, `"complete"`, `"average"`, `"centroid"`, and `"ward"`.

In this section, you'll apply average-linkage clustering to the `nutrient` data introduced in section 16.2 to identify similarities, differences, and groupings among 27 food types based on nutritional information. The following listing provides the code for carrying out the clustering.

Listing 16.1   Average-linkage clustering of the nutrient data

```
data(nutrient, package="flexclust")
row.names(nutrient) <- tolower(row.names(nutrient))
nutrient.scaled <- scale(nutrient)

d <- dist(nutrient.scaled)

fit.average <- hclust(d, method="average")

library(ggplot2)
library(ggdendro)
ggdedgrogram(fit.average) + labs(title="Average Linkage Clustering")
```

First, the data are imported, and the row names are set to lowercase (because I hate UPPERCASE LABELS). Because the variables differ widely in range, they're standardized to a mean of 0 and a standard deviation of 1. Euclidean distances between each of the 27 food types are calculated, and an average-linkage clustering is performed. Finally, the results are plotted as a dendrogram using the `ggplot2` and `ggdendro` packages (see figure 16.1).

The dendrogram displays how items are combined into clusters and is read from the bottom up. Each observation starts as its own cluster. Then the two observations that are closest (beef braised and smoked ham) are combined. Next, pork roast and pork simmered are combined, followed by chicken canned and tuna canned. In the

Average-Linkage Clustering

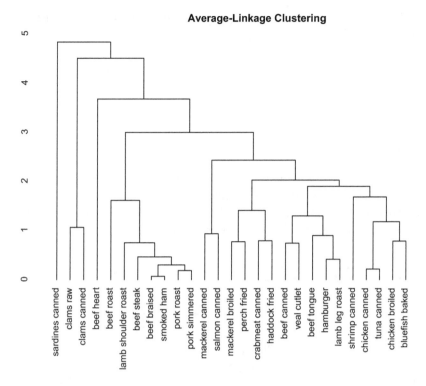

Figure 16.1 Average-linkage clustering of nutrient data

fourth step, the beef braised/smoked ham cluster and the pork roast/pork simmered clusters are combined (and the cluster now contains four food items). This continues until all observations are combined into a single cluster. The height dimension indicates the criterion value at which clusters are joined. For average-linkage clustering, this criterion is the average distance between each point in one cluster and each point in the other cluster.

If your goal is to understand how food types are similar or different in terms of their nutrients, then figure 16.1 may be sufficient. It creates a hierarchical view of the similarity/dissimilarity among the 27 items. Canned tuna and chicken are similar, and both differ greatly from canned clams. But if the end goal is to assign these foods to a smaller number of (hopefully meaningful) groups, additional analyses are required to select an appropriate number of clusters.

The NbClust package offers numerous indices for determining the best number of clusters in a cluster analysis. There is no guarantee that they will agree with each other. In fact, they probably won't. But the results can be used as a guide for selecting possible candidate values for *K*, the number of clusters. Input to the NbClust() function includes the matrix or data frame to be clustered, the distance measure and clustering method to employ, and the minimum and maximum number of clusters to consider. It returns each of the clustering indices along with the best number of clusters proposed by each. The next listing applies this approach to the average-linkage clustering of the nutrient data.

Listing 16.2   Selecting the number of clusters

```
> library(NbClust)
> library(factoextra)
> nc <- NbClust(nutrient.scaled, distance="euclidean",
                min.nc=2, max.nc=15, method="average")
> fviz_nbclust(nc)
```

Here, two criteria favor zero clusters, one criterion favors one cluster, four criteria favor two clusters, and so on. The results are plotted using the `fviz_nbclust()` function (figure 16.2). The optimal number of clusters has the most votes. In the case of a tie, the solution with fewer clusters is usually favored.

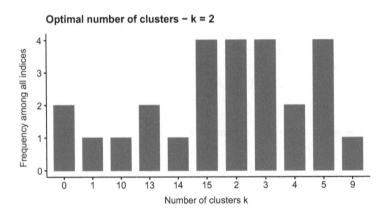

Figure 16.2   Recommended number of clusters using 26 criteria provided by the `NbClust` package

Although two clusters are suggested in the graph, you could also try 3-, 5-, and 15-cluster solutions and select the one that makes the most interpretive sense. The following listing explores the 5-cluster solution.

Listing 16.3   Obtaining the final cluster solution

```
> clusters <- cutree(fit.average, k=5)          ❶ Assigns
> table(clusters)                                   cases

clusters
 1  2  3  4  5
 7 16  1  2  1

> nutrient.scaled$clusters <- clusters

> library(dplyr)
> profiles <- nutrient.scaled %>%
      group_by(clusters) %>%                     ❷ Describes
      summarize_all(median)                          clusters
```

```
> profiles %>% round(3) %>% data.frame()

  cluster energy protein    fat calcium    iron
1       1  1.310   0.000  1.379  -0.448  0.0811
2       2 -0.370   0.235 -0.487  -0.397 -0.6374
3       3 -0.468   1.646 -0.753  -0.384  2.4078
4       4 -1.481  -2.352 -1.109   0.436  2.2709
5       5 -0.271   0.706 -0.398   4.140  0.0811

> library(colorhcplot)
> cl <-factor(clusters, levels=c(1:5),
          labels=paste("cluster", 1:5))
> colorhcplot(fit.average, cl, hang=-1, lab.cex=.8, lwd=2,
          main="Average-Linkage Clustering\n5 Cluster Solution")
```

❸ Plots results

The cutree() function is used to cut the tree into 5 clusters ❶. The first cluster has 7 observations, the second cluster has 16 observations, and so on. The dplyr functions are then used to obtain the median profile for each cluster ❷. Finally, the dendrogram is replotted, and the colorhcplot function is used to identify the 5 clusters ❸. Here, cl is a factor with the cluster labels, hang=-1 aligns the labels at the bottom of the graph, lab.cex controls the size of the labels (80% of default here), and lwd controls the width of the dendrogram lines. Figure 16.3 displays the results. If you are using the printed version of this text, be sure to run this code. In greyscale, the color distinctions are difficult to see.

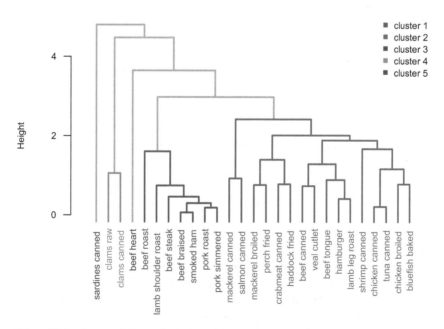

Figure 16.3   Average-linkage clustering of the nutrient data with a 5-cluster solution

Sardines form their own cluster and are much higher in calcium than the other food groups. Beef heart is also a singleton and is high in protein and iron. The clam cluster is low in protein and high in iron. The items in the cluster containing beef roast to pork simmered are high in energy and fat. Finally, the largest group (mackerel to bluefish) is relatively low in iron.

Hierarchical clustering can be particularly useful when you expect nested clustering and a meaningful hierarchy. This is often the case in the biological sciences. But the hierarchical algorithms are greedy in the sense that once an observation is assigned to a cluster, it can't be reassigned later. Additionally, hierarchical clustering is difficult to apply in large samples that may include hundreds or even thousands of observations. Partitioning methods can work well in these situations.

16.4 *Partitioning-cluster analysis*

In the partitioning approach, observations are divided into K groups and reshuffled to form the most cohesive clusters possible according to a given criterion. This section considers two methods: k-means and partitioning around medoids (PAM).

16.4.1 *K-means clustering*

The most common partitioning method is the k-means cluster analysis. Conceptually, the k-means algorithm is as follows:

1 Select K centroids (K rows chosen at random).
2 Assign each data point to its closest centroid.
3 Recalculate the centroids as the average of all data points in a cluster (that is, the centroids are p-length mean vectors where p is the number of variables).
4 Assign data points to their closest centroids.
5 Continue steps 3 and 4 until the observations aren't reassigned or the maximum number of iterations (R uses 10 as a default) is reached.

Implementation details for this approach can vary.

R uses an efficient algorithm by Hartigan and Wong (1979) that partitions the observations into k groups such that the sum of squares of the observations to their assigned cluster centers is a minimum. This means that in steps 2 and 4, each observation is assigned to the cluster with the smallest value of

$$ss(k) = \sum_{i=1}^{n} \sum_{j=0}^{p} \left(x_{ij} - \bar{x}_{kj} \right)^2$$

where k is the cluster, x_{ij} is the value of the jth variable for the ith observation, $\bar{x}_{kj}$ is the mean of the jth variable for the kth cluster, and p is the number of variables.

K-means clustering can handle larger datasets than hierarchical clustering approaches. Additionally, observations aren't permanently committed to a cluster— they're moved when doing so improves the overall solution. But the use of means implies that all variables must be continuous, and the approach can be severely affected by outliers. It also performs poorly in the presence of nonconvex (for example, U-shaped) clusters.

The format of the k-means function in R is kmeans(*x, centers*), where *x* is a numeric dataset (matrix or data frame) and *centers* is the number of clusters to extract. The function returns the cluster memberships, centroids, sums of squares (within, between, total), and cluster sizes.

Because k-means cluster analysis starts with *k* randomly chosen centroids, a different solution can be obtained each time the function is invoked. Use the set.seed() function to guarantee that the results are reproducible. Additionally, this clustering approach can be sensitive to the initial selection of centroids. The kmeans() function has an nstart option that attempts multiple initial configurations and reports on the best one. For example, adding nstart=25 generates 25 initial configurations. This approach is often recommended.

Unlike hierarchical clustering, k-means clustering requires that you specify in advance the number of clusters to extract. Again, the NbClust package can be used as a guide. Additionally, a plot of the total within-groups sums of squares against the number of clusters in a k-means solution can be helpful. A bend in the graph (similar to the bend in the Scree test described in section 14.2.1) can suggest the appropriate number of clusters.

The graph can be produced with the following function:

```
wssplot <- function(data, nc=15, seed=1234){
  require(ggplot2)
  wss <- numeric(nc)
  for (i in 1:nc){
    set.seed(seed)
    wss[i] <- sum(kmeans(data, centers=i)$withinss)
  }
  results <- data.frame(cluster=1:nc, wss=wss)
  ggplot(results, aes(x=cluster,y=wss)) +
    geom_point(color="steelblue", size=2) +
    geom_line(color="grey") +
    theme_bw() +
    labs(x="Number of Clusters",
         y="Within groups sum of squares")
}
```

The data parameter is the numeric dataset to be analyzed, nc is the maximum number of clusters to consider, and seed is a random number seed.

Let's apply k-means clustering to a dataset containing 13 chemical measurements on 178 Italian wine samples. The data originally comes from the UCI Machine Learning Repository (www.ics.uci.edu/~mlearn/MLRepository.html), but you'll access them here via the rattle package. In this dataset, the observations represent three wine varietals, as indicated by the first variable (Type). You'll drop this variable, perform the cluster analysis, and see if you can recover the known structure.

Listing 16.4   K-means clustering of wine data

```
> data(wine, package="rattle")
> library(NbClust)
> library(factoextra)
> head(wine)

  Type Alcohol Malic  Ash Alcalinity Magnesium Phenols Flavanoids
1    1   14.23  1.71 2.43       15.6       127    2.80       3.06
2    1   13.20  1.78 2.14       11.2       100    2.65       2.76
3    1   13.16  2.36 2.67       18.6       101    2.80       3.24
4    1   14.37  1.95 2.50       16.8       113    3.85       3.49
5    1   13.24  2.59 2.87       21.0       118    2.80       2.69
6    1   14.20  1.76 2.45       15.2       112    3.27       3.39
  Nonflavanoids Proanthocyanins Color  Hue Dilution Proline
1          0.28            2.29  5.64 1.04     3.92    1065
2          0.26            1.28  4.38 1.05     3.40    1050
3          0.30            2.81  5.68 1.03     3.17    1185
4          0.24            2.18  7.80 0.86     3.45    1480
5          0.39            1.82  4.32 1.04     2.93     735
6          0.34            1.97  6.75 1.05     2.85    1450
```

```
> df <- scale(wine[-1])      ◄─┐  ❶ Standardizes
> head(df)                        the data
```

```
  Alcohol Malic   Ash Alcalinity Magnesium Phenols Flavanoids
1    1.51 -0.56  0.23      -1.17      1.91    0.81       1.03
2    0.25 -0.50 -0.83      -2.48      0.02    0.57       0.73
3    0.20  0.02  1.11      -0.27      0.09    0.81       1.21
4    1.69 -0.35  0.49      -0.81      0.93    2.48       1.46
5    0.29  0.23  1.84       0.45      1.28    0.81       0.66
6    1.48 -0.52  0.30      -1.29      0.86    1.56       1.36
  Nonflavanoids Proanthocyanins Color   Hue Dilution Proline
1         -0.66            1.22  0.25  0.36     1.84    1.01
2         -0.82           -0.54 -0.29  0.40     1.11    0.96
3         -0.50            2.13  0.27  0.32     0.79    1.39
4         -0.98            1.03  1.18 -0.43     1.18    2.33
5          0.23            0.40 -0.32  0.36     0.45   -0.04
6         -0.18            0.66  0.73  0.40     0.34    2.23
```

```
> wssplot(df)
> set.seed(1234)                                                        ❷ Determines the
> nc <- NbClust(df, min.nc=2, max.nc=15, method="kmeans")                 number of clusters
> fviz_nbclust(nc)
```

```
> set.seed(1234)
> fit.km <- kmeans(df, 3, nstart=25)    ◄─┐  Performs the k-means
> fit.km$size                                ❸ cluster analysis
```

```
[1] 62 65 51
```

```
> fit.km$centers
```

```
  Alcohol Malic   Ash Alcalinity Magnesium Phenols Flavanoids Nonflavanoids
```

```
1    0.83 -0.30  0.36       -0.61    0.576   0.883      0.975        -0.561
2   -0.92 -0.39 -0.49        0.17   -0.490  -0.076      0.021        -0.033
3    0.16  0.87  0.19        0.52   -0.075  -0.977     -1.212         0.724
   Proanthocyanins Color   Hue Dilution Proline
1            0.579  0.17  0.47    0.78    1.12
2            0.058 -0.90  0.46    0.27   -0.75
3           -0.778  0.94 -1.16   -1.29   -0.41

> aggregate(wine[-1], by=list(cluster=fit.km$cluster), mean)

  cluster Alcohol Malic Ash Alcalinity Magnesium Phenols Flavanoids
1       1      14   1.8 2.4         17       106     2.8        3.0
2       2      12   1.6 2.2         20        88     2.2        2.0
3       3      13   3.3 2.4         21        97     1.6        0.7
  Nonflavanoids Proanthocyanins Color  Hue Dilution Proline
1          0.29             1.9   5.4 1.07      3.2    1072
2          0.35             1.6   2.9 1.04      2.8     495
3          0.47             1.1   7.3 0.67      1.7     620
```

Because the variables vary in range, they're standardized prior to clustering ❶. Next, the number of clusters is determined using the wssplot() and NbClust() functions ❷. Figure 16.4 indicates that there is a distinct drop in the within-groups sum of squares when moving from one to three clusters. After three clusters, this decrease drops off, suggesting that a three-cluster solution may be a good fit to the data. In figure 16.5, 19 of 23 criteria provided by the NbClust package suggest a three-cluster solution. Note that not all 30 criteria can be calculated for every dataset.

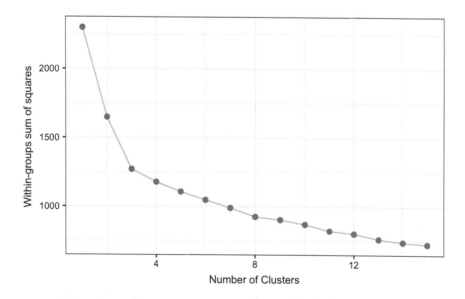

Figure 16.4 Plotting the within-groups sums of squares vs. the number of clusters extracted. The sharp decreases from one to three clusters (with little decrease thereafter) suggests a three-cluster solution.

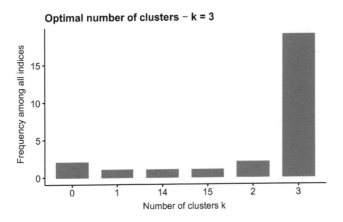

Figure 16.5   Recommended number of clusters using 26 criteria provided by the NbClust package

A final cluster solution is obtained with the kmeans() function, and the cluster centroids are printed ❸. Because the centroids provided by the function are based on standardized data, the aggregate() function is used along with the cluster memberships to determine variable means for each cluster in the original metric.

The easiest way to compare the clusters is with a cluster profile plot. The following listing continues the example from listing 16.4.

Listing 16.5   Cluster profile plots

```
library(ggplot2)
library(tidyr)
means <- as.data.frame(fit.km$centers)        ❶ Prepares mean profiles
means$cluster <- 1:nrow(means)

plotdata <- gather(means, key="variable", value="value", -cluster)
                                                            Converts data
ggplot(plotdata,                    Plots profiles as      to long format ❷
       aes(x=variable,          ❸  faceted bar charts
           y=value,
           fill=variable,
           group=cluster)) +
  geom_bar(stat="identity") +
  geom_hline(yintercept=0) +
  facet_wrap(~cluster) +
  theme_bw() +
  theme(axis.text.x=element_text(angle=90, vjust=0),
        legend.position="none") +
  labs(x="", y="Standardized scores",
       title = "Mean Cluster Profiles")
```

First, we get the cluster means on the standardized variables and add a variable representing cluster membership ❶. Then, we convert this wide-format data frame to long form (wide-to-long form conversion is described in section 5.5.2) ❷. Finally, we plot the profiles as faceted bar charts ❸. Figure 16.6 shows the results. The mean cluster profiles help you see what makes each cluster unique. For example, compared to clusters 2 and 4, cluster 1 has high mean scores on alcohol, phenols, proanthocyanins, and proline.

Mean Cluster Profiles

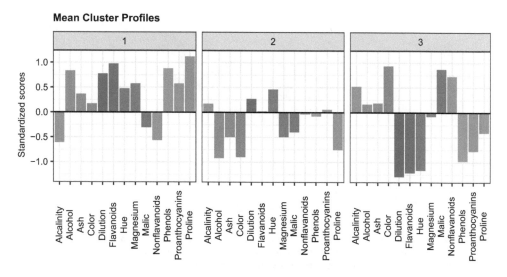

Figure 16.6 **Mean profiles for each cluster based on standardized data. This graph helps identify the distinctive features of each cluster.**

Another approach to visualizing the results of a cluster analysis is the *bivariate cluster plot*. The plot is created by plotting the coordinates of each observation (wine) on the first two principal components derived from the 13 assay variables. (Principal components are described chapter 14.) The color and shape of each point identifies its cluster membership. The point labels represent each wine's row number in the data. Additionally, each cluster is surrounded by the smallest ellipse that can contain all the points in that cluster.

A bivariate cluster plot can be created with the `fviz_cluster()` function from the `factoextra` package:

```
library(factoextra)
fviz_cluster(fit.km, data=df)
```

Figure 16.7 shows the graph. We can see that cluster 1 and cluster 3 are most dissimilar. Wines 4 and 19 are similar, while wines 4 and 171 are very different.

Cluster analysis is usually an unsupervised technique in that there is no outcome variable we are trying to predict. However, in the wine example, there are actually three wine varietals (`Type`) in the dataset.

Cluster plot

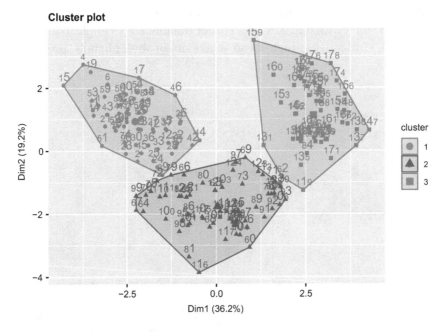

Figure 16.7   Cluster plot of 178 wines clustered into 3 groups. Each wine is plotted against the first two principal components of the data. The graphs can help us see the similarities/differences between wines and between clusters.

How well did k-means clustering uncover the actual structure of the data contained in the Type variable? A cross-tabulation of Type (wine varietal) and cluster membership is given by

```
> ct.km <- table(wine$Type, fit.km$cluster)
> ct.km

    1  2  3
  1 59  0  0
  2  3 65  3
  3  0  0 48
```

You can quantify the agreement between type and cluster using an adjusted Rand index, provided by the flexclust package:

```
> library(flexclust)
> randIndex(ct.km)
[1] 0.897
```

The adjusted Rand index provides a measure of the agreement between two partitions, adjusted for chance. It ranges from –1 (no agreement) to 1 (perfect agreement). Agreement between the wine varietal type and the cluster solution is 0.9. Not bad—shall we have some wine?

16.4.2 Partitioning around medoids

Because it's based on means, the k-means clustering approach can be sensitive to outliers. A more robust solution is provided by partitioning around medoids (PAM). Rather than representing each cluster using a centroid (a vector of variable means), each cluster is identified by its most representative observation (called a *medoid*). Whereas k-means uses Euclidean distances, PAM can be based on any distance measure. It can therefore accommodate mixed data types and isn't limited to continuous variables.

The PAM algorithm is as follows:

1. Randomly select *K* observations (call each a medoid).
2. Calculate the distance/dissimilarity of every observation to each medoid.
3. Assign each observation to its closest medoid.
4. Calculate the sum of the distances of each observation from its medoid (total cost).
5. Select a point that isn't a medoid and swap it with its medoid.
6. Reassign every point to its closest medoid.
7. Calculate the total cost.
8. If this total cost is smaller, keep the new point as a medoid.
9. Repeat steps 5-8 until the medoids don't change.

A good, worked example of the underlying math in the PAM approach can be found at http://en.wikipedia.org/wiki/k-medoids (I don't usually cite Wikipedia, but this is a great example).

You can use the pam() function in the cluster package to partition around medoids. The format is pam(*x, k*, metric="euclidean", stand=FALSE), where *x* is a data matrix or data frame, *k* is the number of clusters, metric is the type of distance/dissimilarity measure to use, and stand is a logical value indicating whether the variables should be standardized before calculating this metric. In the following listing, PAM is applied to the wine data.

> **Listing 16.6 Partitioning around medoids for the wine data**

```
> library(cluster)
> set.seed(1234)
> fit.pam <- pam(wine[-1], k=3, stand=TRUE)       <--|  Clusters standardized data
> fit.pam$medoids                                  <--|  Prints the medoids

      Alcohol Malic  Ash Alcalinity Magnesium Phenols Flavanoids
[1,]     13.5  1.81 2.41       20.5       100    2.70       2.98
[2,]     12.2  1.73 2.12       19.0        80    1.65       2.03
[3,]     13.4  3.91 2.48       23.0       102    1.80       0.75
      Nonflavanoids Proanthocyanins Color  Hue Dilution Proline
[1,]           0.26            1.86   5.1 1.04     3.47     920
[2,]           0.37            1.63   3.4 1.00     3.17     510
[3,]           0.43            1.41   7.3 0.70     1.56     750
```

Note that the medoids are actual observations contained in the wine dataset. In this case, they're observations 36, 107, and 175, and they have been chosen to represent the three clusters.

Also note that PAM didn't perform as well as k-means in this instance:

```
> ct.pam <- table(wine$Type, fit.pam$clustering)

    1  2  3
 1 59  0  0
 2 16 53  2
 3  0  1 47

> randIndex(ct.pam)
[1] 0.699
```

The adjusted Rand index has decreased from 0.9 (for k-means) to 0.7. Creation of the cluster profile plot and bivariate cluster plot is left as an exercise.

16.5 *Avoiding nonexistent clusters*

Before I finish this discussion, a word of caution is in order. Cluster analysis is a methodology designed to identify cohesive subgroups in a dataset. It's very good at doing this. In fact, it's so good, it can find clusters where none exist.

Consider the following code:

```
library(fMultivar)
library(ggplot2)
set.seed(1234)
df <- rnorm2d(1000, rho=.5)
df <- as.data.frame(df)
ggplot(df, aes(x=V1, y=V2)) +
  geom_point(alpha=.3) + theme_minimal() +
  labs(title="Bivariate Normal Distribution with rho=0.5")
```

The rnorm2d() function in the fMultivar package is used to sample 1,000 observations from a bivariate normal distribution with a correlation of 0.5. Figure 16.8 shows the resulting graph. Clearly, there are no clusters in this data.

The wssplot() and NbClust() functions are then used to determine the number of clusters present:

```
wssplot(df)
library(NbClust)
library(factoextra)
nc <- NbClust(df, min.nc=2, max.nc=15, method="kmeans")
fviz_nbclust(nc)
```

Figures 16.9 and 16.10 plot the results.

Bivariate Normal Distribution with rho=0.5

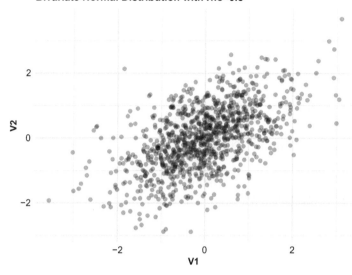

**Figure 16.8
Bivariate normal data
(*n* = 1000). There are
no clusters in this data.**

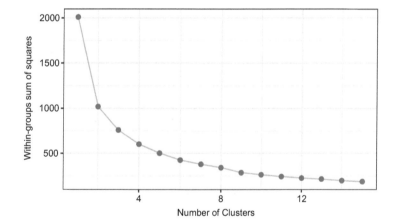

**Figure 16.9   Plot of within-
groups sums of squares vs.
number of k-means clusters
for bivariate normal data**

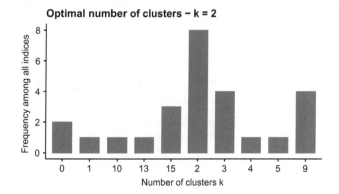

**Figure 16.10   Number of
clusters recommended for
bivariate normal data by criteria
in the NbClust package. Two
clusters are suggested.**

Both approaches suggest at least two clusters. If you carry out a two-cluster analysis with k-means,

```
library(ggplot2)
fit <- kmeans(df, 2)
df$cluster <- factor(fit$cluster)
ggplot(data=df, aes(x=V1, y=V2, color=cluster, shape=cluster)) +
      theme_minimal() +
      geom_point(alpha=.5) +
      ggtitle("Clustering of Bivariate Normal Data")
```

you get the two-cluster plot shown in figure 16.11.

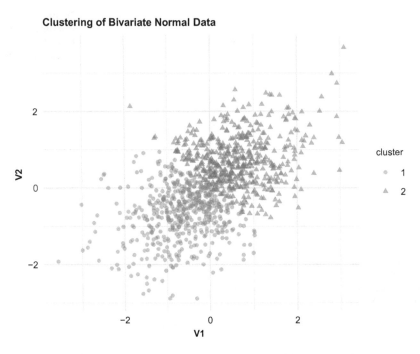

Figure 16.11   K-means cluster analysis of bivariate normal data, extracting two clusters. Note that the clusters are an arbitrary division of the data.

Clearly, the partitioning is artificial. There are no real clusters here. How can you avoid this mistake? Although it isn't foolproof, I have found two approaches to be helpful. The first is the DIP test provided by the `clusterability` package:

```
> library(clusterability)
> clusterabilitytest(df[-3], "dip")

Null Hypothesis: number of modes = 1
Alternative Hypothesis: number of modes > 1
```

```
p-value: 0.9655
Dip statistic: 0.00823
```

The df[-3] drops the factor variable (cluster membership) from the data. The null hypothesis is that there is a single cluster (mode). Since p > .05, we can't reject the hypothesis. The data do not support a cluster structure.

The other approach uses the Cubic Clustering Criteria (CCC) reported by NbClust. CCC can often help uncover situations where no structure exists. The code is

```
CCC = nc$All.index[, 4]
k <- length(CCC)
plotdata <- data.frame(CCC = CCC, k = seq_len(k))
ggplot(plotdata, aes(x=k, y=CCC)) +
  geom_point() + geom_line() +
  theme_minimal() +
  scale_x_continuous(breaks=seq_len(k)) +
  labs(x="Number of Clusters")
```

and the resulting graph is displayed in figure 16.12. When the CCC values are all negative and decreasing for two or more clusters, the distribution is typically unimodal.

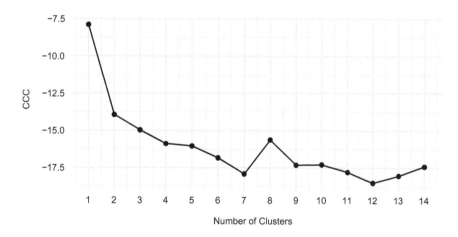

Figure 16.12 Cubic clustering criteria plot for bivariate normal data. It correctly suggests that no clusters are present.

The ability of cluster analysis (or your interpretation of it) to find erroneous clusters makes the validation step of cluster analysis important. If you're trying to identify clusters that are real in some sense (rather than a convenient partitioning), be sure the results are robust and repeatable. Try different clustering methods, and replicate the findings with new samples. If the same clusters are consistently recovered, you can be more confident in the results.

16.6   *Going further*

Cluster analysis is a broad topic, and R has some of the most comprehensive facilities currently available for applying this methodology. To learn more about these capabilities, see the CRAN Task View for Cluster Analysis & Finite Mixture Models (http://cran.r-project.org/web/views/Cluster.html). Additionally, Tan, Steinbach, and Kumar (2006) have an excellent book on data mining techniques that includes a lucid chapter on cluster analysis that you can downloaded freely (www-users.cs.umn.edu/~kumar/dmbook/ch8.pdf). Finally, Everitt, Landau, Leese, and Stahl (2011) have written a practical and highly regarded textbook on this subject.

Summary

- Cluster analysis is a common approach for arranging observations into cohesive groups.
- Since there is no single definition of what we mean by a "cluster," or by what we mean by the "distance between clusters," many clustering approaches have been developed.
- Two of the most popular categories of cluster analysis are hierarchical clustering and partitioning. There are many clustering approaches within each category. No single approach is best in all situations.
- There is also no one best approach for determining the number of clusters in a dataset. It may be valuable to try several different approaches and settle on the one that is most meaningful or practically useful.
- Cluster analysis can uncover clusters whether they exist are not! If your goal is to divide the data into convenient, cohesive groups (e.g., customer segmentation), this may be fine. However, if you are seeking to uncover naturally occurring groups with theoretically meaningful differences (e.g., subtypes of depression based on symptoms and history), it's important to validate your findings by replicating them with new data.

Classification 17

This chapter covers
- Classifying with decision trees
- Building a random forest classifier
- Creating a support vector machine
- Evaluating classification accuracy
- Understanding complex models

Data analysts frequently need to predict a categorical outcome from a set of predictor variables. Some examples include

- Predicting whether an individual will repay a loan, given their demographics and financial history
- Determining whether an ER patient is having a heart attack, based on their symptoms and vital signs
- Deciding whether an email is spam, given the presence of key words, images, hypertext, header information, and origin

Each of these cases involves the prediction of a binary categorical outcome (good credit risk/bad credit risk; heart attack/no heart attack; spam/not spam) from a set of predictors (also called *features*). The goal is to find an accurate method of classifying new cases into one of the two groups.

The field of supervised machine learning offers numerous classification methods for predicting categorical outcomes, including logistic regression, decision trees, random forests, support vector machines, and artificial neural networks. The first four are discussed in this chapter. Artificial neural networks are beyond the scope of this book. See Ciaburro and Venkateswaran (2017) and Chollet and Allaire (2018) to learn more about them.

Supervised learning starts with a set of observations containing values for both the predictor variables and the outcome. The dataset is then divided into a training sample and a test sample. A predictive model is developed using the data in the training sample and tested for accuracy using the data in the test sample. Both samples are needed because classification techniques maximize prediction for a given set of data. Estimates of their effectiveness will be overly optimistic if they're evaluated using the same data that generated the model. By applying the classification rules developed on a training sample to a separate test sample, you can obtain a more realistic accuracy estimate. Once you've created an effective predictive model, you can use it to predict outcomes in situations when only the predictor variables are known.

In this chapter, you'll use the `rpart`, `rattle`, and `partykit` packages to create and visualize decision trees; the `randomForest` package to fit random forests; and the `e1071` package to build support vector machines. Logistic regression will be fit with the `glm()` function in the base R installation. Before starting, be sure to install the necessary packages:

```
pkgs <- c("rpart", "rattle", "partykit",
          "randomForest", "e1071")
install.packages(pkgs, depend=TRUE)
```

The primary example used in this chapter comes from the Wisconsin Breast Cancer data originally posted to the UCI Machine Learning Repository. The goal will be to develop a model for predicting whether a patient has breast cancer from the characteristics of a fine-needle tissue aspiration (a tissue sample taken with a thin hollow needle from a lump or mass just under the skin).

17.1   *Preparing the data*

The Wisconsin Breast Cancer dataset is available as a comma-delimited text file on the UCI Machine Learning Server (http://archive.ics.uci.edu/ml). The dataset contains 699 fine-needle aspirate samples, where 458 (65.5%) are benign and 241 (34.5%) are malignant. The dataset contains 11 variables and doesn't include the variable names in the file. Sixteen samples have missing data and are coded in the text file with a question mark (?).

The variables are as follows:

- ID
- Clump thickness

- Uniformity of cell size
- Uniformity of cell shape
- Marginal adhesion
- Single epithelial cell size
- Bare nuclei
- Bland chromatin
- Normal nucleoli
- Mitoses
- Class

The first variable is an ID variable (which you'll drop), and the last variable (class) contains the outcome (coded 2=benign, 4=malignant). You'll also exclude the observations containing missing values.

For each sample, nine cytological characteristics previously found to correlate with malignancy are also recorded. Each of these variables is scored from 1 (closest to benign) to 10 (most anaplastic). But no one predictor alone can distinguish between benign and malignant samples. The challenge is to find a set of classification rules that can be used to accurately predict malignancy from some combination of these nine cell characteristics. See Mangasarian and Wolberg (1990) for details.

In the following listing, the comma-delimited text file containing the data is downloaded from the UCI repository and randomly divided into a training sample (70%) and a test sample (30%).

Listing 17.1 Preparing the breast cancer data

```
loc <- "http://archive.ics.uci.edu/ml/machine-learning-databases"
ds  <- "breast-cancer-wisconsin/breast-cancer-wisconsin.data"
url <- paste(loc, ds, sep="/")

breast <- read.table(url, sep=",", header=FALSE, na.strings="?")
names(breast) <- c("ID", "clumpThickness", "sizeUniformity",
                   "shapeUniformity", "maginalAdhesion",
                   "singleEpithelialCellSize", "bareNuclei",
                   "blandChromatin", "normalNucleoli", "mitosis", "class")

df <- breast[-1]
df$class <- factor(df$class, levels=c(2,4),
                   labels=c("benign", "malignant"))
df <- na.omit(df)

set.seed(1234)
index <- sample(nrow(df), 0.7*nrow(df))
train <- df[index,]
test <- df[-index,]
table(train$class)
table(test$class)
```

The training sample has 478 cases (302 benign, 176 malignant), and the test sample has 205 cases (142 benign, 63 malignant).

The training sample will be used to create classification schemes using logistic regression, a decision tree, a conditional decision tree, a random forest, and a support vector machine. The test sample will be used to evaluate the effectiveness of these schemes. By using the same example throughout the chapter, you can compare the results of each approach.

17.2   *Logistic regression*

Logistic regression is a type of generalized linear model that is often used to predict a binary outcome from a set of numeric variables (see section 13.2 for details). The glm() function in the base R installation is used for fitting the model. Categorical predictors (factors) are automatically replaced with a set of dummy coded variables. All the predictors in the Wisconsin Breast Cancer data are numeric, so dummy coding is unnecessary. The next listing provides a logistic regression analysis of the data.

Listing 17.2   Logistic regression with glm()

```
> fit.logit <- glm(class~., data=train, family=binomial())        Fits the logistic
> summary(fit.logit)                                           ❶ regression
                                                        ❷ Examines the model
Call:
glm(formula = class ~ ., family = binomial(), data = train)

Deviance Residuals:
    Min       1Q   Median       3Q      Max
-3.6141  -0.1204  -0.0744   0.0236   2.1845

Coefficients:
                          Estimate Std. Error z value Pr(>|z|)
(Intercept)               -9.68650    1.29722  -7.467 8.20e-14 ***
clumpThickness             0.48002    0.15244   3.149  0.00164 **
sizeUniformity             0.05643    0.29272   0.193  0.84714
shapeUniformity            0.13180    0.31643   0.417  0.67703
maginalAdhesion            0.40721    0.14038   2.901  0.00372 **
singleEpithelialCellSize  -0.03274    0.18095  -0.181  0.85643
bareNuclei                 0.44744    0.11176   4.004 6.24e-05 ***
blandChromatin             0.48257    0.19220   2.511  0.01205 *
normalNucleoli             0.23550    0.12903   1.825  0.06798 .
mitosis                    0.66184    0.28785   2.299  0.02149 *
---
Signif. codes:  0 '***' 0.001 '**' 0.01 '*' 0.05 '.' 0.1 ' ' 1

> prob <- predict(fit.logit, test, type="response")          ❸ Classifies
> logit.pred <- factor(prob > .5, levels=c(FALSE, TRUE),        new cases
                  labels=c("benign", "malignant"))
> logit.perf <- table(test$class, logit.pred,                ❹ Evaluates the
                  dnn=c("Actual", "Predicted"))                 predictive accuracy
> logit.perf

          Predicted
Actual     benign malignant
  benign      140         2
  malignant     3        60
```

First, a logistic regression model is fit using `class` as the dependent variable and the remaining variables as predictors ❶. The model is based on the cases in the train data frame. The coefficients for the model are displayed next ❷. Section 13.2 provides guidelines for interpreting logistic model coefficients.

Next, the prediction equation developed on the train dataset is used to classify cases in the test dataset. By default, the `predict()` function predicts the log odds of having a malignant outcome. By using the `type="response"` option, the probability of obtaining a malignant classification is returned instead ❸. In the next line, cases with probabilities greater than 0.5 are classified into the malignant group, and cases with probabilities less than or equal to 0.5 are classified as benign.

Finally, a cross-tabulation of actual status and predicted status (called a *confusion matrix*) is printed ❹. It shows that 140 cases that were benign were classified as benign, and 60 cases that were malignant were classified as malignant.

The total number of cases correctly classified (also called the accuracy) was (140 + 60) / 205 or 98% in the test sample. Statistics for evaluating the accuracy of a classification scheme are discussed more fully in section 17.6.

Before moving on, note that three of the predictor variables (`sizeUniformity`, `shapeUniformity`, and `singleEpithelialCellSize`) have coefficients that don't differ from zero at the $p < .10$ level. What, if anything, should you do with predictor variables that have nonsignificant coefficients?

In a prediction context, it's often useful to remove such variables from the final model. This is especially important when a large number of non-informative predictor variables are adding what is essentially noise to the system.

In this case, stepwise logistic regression can be used to generate a smaller model with fewer variables. Predictor variables are added or removed to obtain a model with a smaller AIC value. In the current context, you could use

```
logit.fit.reduced <- step(fit.logit)
```

to obtain a more parsimonious model. The reduced model excludes the three previously mentioned variables. When used to predict outcomes in the test dataset, this reduced model performs equally well. Try it out.

The next approach we'll consider involves the creation of decision or classification trees.

17.3 Decision trees

Decision trees are popular in data mining contexts. They involve creating a set of binary splits on the predictor variables in order to create a tree that can be used to classify new observations into one of two groups. In this section, we'll look at two types of decision trees: classical trees and conditional inference trees.

17.3.1 Classical decision trees

The process of building a *classical decision tree* starts with a binary outcome variable (in this case, benign/malignant) and a set of predictor variables (the nine cytology measurements). The algorithm is as follows:

1 Choose the predictor variable that best splits the data into two groups such that the purity (homogeneity) of the outcome in the two groups is maximized (that is, as many benign cases in one group and malignant cases in the other as possible). If the predictor is continuous, choose a cut-point that maximizes purity for the two groups. If the predictor variable is categorical (not applicable in this case), combine the categories to obtain two groups with maximum purity.

2 Separate the data into these two groups and continue the process for each subgroup.

3 Repeat steps 1 and 2 until a subgroup contains fewer than a minimum number of observations or no splits decrease the impurity beyond a specified threshold.

   The subgroups in the final set are called *terminal nodes*. Each terminal node is classified as one category of the outcome or the other, based on the most frequent value of the outcome for the sample in that node.

4 To classify a case, run it down the tree to a terminal node, and assign it the modal outcome value assigned in step 3.

Unfortunately, this process tends to produce a tree that is too large and suffers from overfitting. As a result, new cases aren't classified well. To compensate, you can prune the tree by choosing the tree with the lowest 10-fold cross-validated prediction error. This pruned tree is then used for future predictions.

In R, decision trees can be grown and pruned using the rpart() and prune() functions in the rpart package. The following listing creates a decision tree for classifying the cell data as benign or malignant.

Listing 17.3 Creating a classical decision tree with rpart()

```
> library(rpart)
> dtree <- rpart(class ~ ., data=train, method="class",      ① Grows the tree
            parms=list(split="information"))
> dtree$cptable

          CP nsplit  rel error   xerror      xstd
1 0.79545455      0 1.00000000 1.0000000 0.05991467
2 0.07954545      1 0.20454545 0.3068182 0.03932359
3 0.01704545      2 0.12500000 0.1590909 0.02917149
4 0.01000000      5 0.07386364 0.1704545 0.03012819

> plotcp(dtree)

> dtree.pruned <- prune(dtree, cp=.01705)
                                                   ② Prunes the tree
> library(rattle)
> fancyRpartPlot(dtree.pruned,   sub="Classification Tree")

> dtree.pred <- predict(dtree.pruned, test, type="class")     ③ Classifies
> dtree.perf <- table(test$class, dtree.pred,                    new cases
                dnn=c("Actual", "Predicted"))
> dtree.perf
```

```
                Predicted
Actual       benign malignant
  benign        136         6
  malignant       3        60
```

First, the tree is grown using the `rpart()` function ❶. You can use `print(dtree)` and `summary(dtree)` to examine the fitted model (not shown here). The tree may be too large and require pruning.

To choose a final tree size, examine the `cptable` component of the list returned by `rpart()`. It contains data about the prediction error for various tree sizes. The complexity parameter (cp) is used to penalize larger trees. Tree size is defined by the number of branch splits (`nsplit`). A tree with n splits has $n + 1$ terminal nodes. The `rel error` column contains the error rate for a tree of a given size in the training sample. The cross-validated error (`xerror`) is based on 10-fold cross-validation (also using the training sample). The `xstd` column contains the standard error of the cross-validation error.

The `plotcp()` function plots the cross-validated error against the complexity parameter (see figure 17.1). A good choice for the final tree size is the smallest tree with a cross-validated error within one standard error of the minimum cross-validated error value.

The minimum cross-validated error is 0.16 with a standard error of 0.03. In this case, the smallest tree with a cross-validated error within 0.16 ± 0.03 (that is, between 0.13 and 0.19) is selected. Looking at the `cptable` table in listing 17.3, a tree with two splits (cross-validated error = 0.16) fits this requirement. Equivalently, you can select

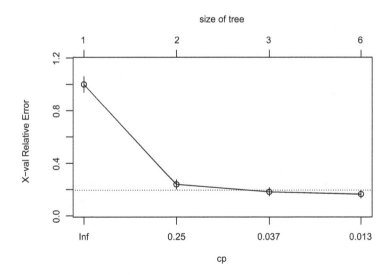

Figure 17.1 Complexity parameter vs. cross-validated error. The dotted line is the upper limit of the one standard deviation rule (0.16 + 0.03 = 0.19). The plot suggests selecting the tree with the leftmost cp value below the line.

the tree size associated with the largest complexity parameter below the line in figure 17.1. Results again suggest a tree with two splits (three terminal nodes).

The prune() function uses the complexity parameter to cut back a tree to the desired size. It takes the full tree and snips off the least important splits based on the desired complexity parameter. Based on the earlier discussion, we'll use prune (dtree, cp=0.01705), which returns a tree with the desired size ❷. The function returns the largest tree with a complexity parameter below the specified cp value.

The fancyRpartPlot() function in the rattle package is used to draw an attractive plot of the final decision tree (see figure 17.2). This function has several options (see ?fancyRpartPlot for details). The type=2 option (default) draws the split labels below each node. Additionally, the proportion of each class and the percentage of observations in each node are displayed. To classify an observation, start at the top of the tree, moving to the left branch if a condition is true or to the right otherwise. Continue moving down the tree until you hit a terminal node. Classify the observation using the label of the node.

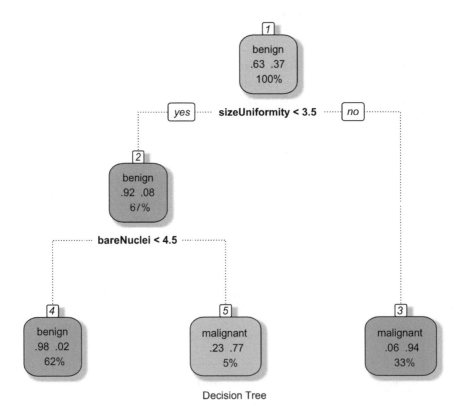

Decision Tree

Figure 17.2   Traditional (pruned) decision tree for predicting cancer status. Start at the top of the tree, moving left if a condition is true or right otherwise. When an observation hits a terminal node, it's classified. Each node contains the probability of the classes in that node, along with the percentage of the sample.

Finally, the `predict()` function is used to classify each observation in the test sample ❸. A cross-tabulation of the actual status against the predicted status is provided. The overall accuracy was 96% in the test sample. Note that decision trees can be biased toward selecting predictors that have many levels or many missing values.

17.3.2 Conditional inference trees

Before moving on to random forests, let's look at an important variant of the traditional decision tree called a *conditional inference tree*. Conditional inference trees are similar to traditional trees, but variables and splits are selected based on significance tests rather than purity/homogeneity measures. The significance tests are permutation tests (discussed in chapter 12).

In this case, the algorithm is as follows:

1 Calculate p-values for the relationship between each predictor and the outcome variable.
2 Select the predictor with the lowest p-value.
3 Explore all possible binary splits on the chosen predictor and dependent variable (using permutation tests) and pick the most significant split.
4 Separate the data into these two groups and continue the process for each subgroup.
5 Continue until splits are no longer significant or the minimum node size is reached.

Conditional inference trees are provided by the `ctree()` function in the `party` package. In the next listing, a conditional inference tree is grown for the breast cancer data.

Listing 17.4 Creating a conditional inference tree with `ctree()`

```
library(partykit)
fit.ctree <- ctree(class~., data=train)
plot(fit.ctree, main="Conditional Inference Tree",
     gp=gpar(fontsize=8))

> ctree.pred <- predict(fit.ctree, test, type="response")
> ctree.perf <- table(test$class, ctree.pred,
                       dnn=c("Actual", "Predicted"))
> ctree.perf

          Predicted
Actual     benign malignant
  benign      138         4
  malignant     2        61
```

Note that pruning isn't required for conditional inference trees, and the process is somewhat more automated. Additionally, the `partykit` package has attractive plotting options. Figure 17.3 plots the conditional inference tree. The shaded area of each node represents the proportion of malignant cases in that node.

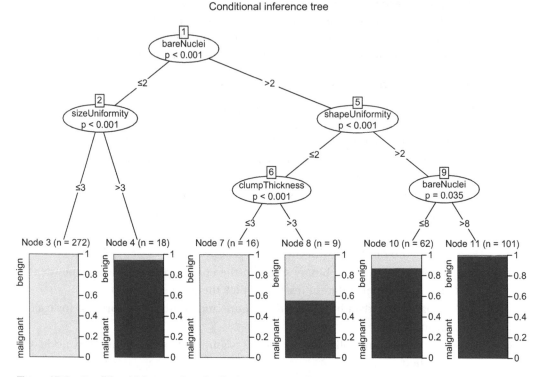

Figure 17.3   Conditional inference tree for the breast cancer data

Displaying an rpart() tree with a ctree()-like graph

If you create a classical decision tree using `rpart()`, but you'd like to display the resulting tree using a plot like the one in figure 17.3, the `partykit` package can help. You can use the statement `plot(as.party(an.rpart.tree))` to create the desired graph. For example, try creating a graph like figure 17.3 using the `dtree.pruned` object created in listing 17.3, and compare the results to the plot presented in figure 17.2.

The decision trees grown by the traditional and conditional methods can differ substantially. In the current example, the accuracy of each is similar (96% versus 97%), but the trees are quite different. In the next section, a large number of decision trees are grown and combined to classify cases into groups.

17.4   *Random forests*

A random forest is an ensemble learning approach to supervised learning. Multiple predictive models are developed, and the results are aggregated to improve classification rates. You can find a comprehensive introduction to random forests, written by Leo Breiman and Adele Cutler, at http://mng.bz/7Nul.

The algorithm for a random forest involves sampling cases and variables to create a large number of decision trees. Each case is classified by each decision tree. The most common classification for that case is then used as the outcome.

Assume that *N* is the number of cases in the training sample and *M* is the number of variables. Then the algorithm is as follows:

1 Grow a large number of decision trees by sampling *N* cases with replacement from the training set.
2 Sample *m* < *M* variables at each node. These variables are considered candidates for splitting in that node. The value *m* is the same for each node.
3 Grow each tree fully without pruning (the minimum node size is set to 1).
4 Terminal nodes are assigned to a class based on the mode of cases in that node.
5 Classify new cases by sending them down all the trees and taking a vote—majority rules.

An out-of-bag (OOB) error estimate is obtained by classifying the cases that aren't selected when building a tree, using that tree. This is an advantage when a test sample is unavailable. Random forests also provide a natural measure of variable importance, as you'll see.

Random forests are grown using the `randomForest()` function in the `random-Forest` package. The default number of trees is 500, the default number of variables sampled at each node is `sqrt(M)`, and the minimum node size is 1.

The following listing provides the code and results for predicting malignancy status in the breast cancer data.

Listing 17.5 Random forest

```
> library(randomForest)
> set.seed(1234)
> fit.forest <- randomForest(class~., data=train,      ❶ Grows the forest
                             importance=TRUE)
> fit.forest

Call:
 randomForest(formula = class ~ ., data = train, importance = TRUE)
               Type of random forest: classification
                     Number of trees: 500
No. of variables tried at each split: 3

        OOB estimate of  error rate: 2.93%
Confusion matrix:
          benign malignant class.error
benign       293         9  0.02980132
malignant      5       171  0.02840909

> randomForest::importance(fit.forest, type=2)      ❷ Determines variable importance

                  MeanDecreaseGini
clumpThickness            9.794852
sizeUniformity           58.635963
shapeUniformity          49.754466
```

```
maginalAdhesion                  8.373530
singleEpithelialCellSize        16.814313
bareNuclei                      36.621347
blandChromatin                  25.179804
normalNucleoli                  14.177153
mitosis                          2.015803
```

```
> forest.pred <- predict(fit.forest, test)
> forest.perf <- table(test$class, forest.pred,
                    dnn=c("Actual", "Predicted"))
> forest.perf
```

❸ Classifies new cases

```
             Predicted
Actual      benign malignant
   benign       140         2
   malignant      3        60
```

First, the `randomForest()` function is used to grow 500 traditional decision trees by sampling 489 observations with replacement from the training sample and sampling 3 variables at each node of each tree ❶.

Random forests can provide a natural measure of variable importance, requested with the `information=TRUE` option, and printed with the `importance()` function ❷. Both the `rattle` and `randomForest` packages have a function called `importance()`. Since we've loaded both packages in this chapter, `randomForest::importance()` is used in the code to assure that the correct function is called. The relative importance measure specified by the `type=2` option is the total decrease in node impurities (heterogeneity) from splitting on that variable, averaged over all trees. Node impurity is measured with the Gini coefficient. `sizeUniformity` is the most important variable and `mitosis` is the least important.

Finally, the test sample is classified using the random forest, and the predictive accuracy is calculated ❸. Note that cases with missing values in the test sample aren't classified. The prediction accuracy (98% overall) is excellent.

Whereas the `randomForest` package provides forests based on traditional decision trees, the `cforest()` function in the `party` package can be used to generate random forests based on conditional inference trees. If predictor variables are highly correlated, a random forest using conditional inference trees may provide better predictions.

Random forests tend to be very accurate compared with other classification methods. Additionally, they can handle large problems (many observations and variables), large amounts of missing data in the training set, and cases in which the number of variables is much greater than the number of observations. The provision of OOB error rates and measures of variable importance are also significant advantages.

A significant disadvantage is that it's difficult to understand the classification rules (there are 500 trees!) and communicate them to others. Additionally, you need to store the entire forest to classify new cases.

A random forests is a *black box* model. Predictor values go in and accurate predictions come out, but it is difficult to understand what's happening in the box (model). We'll address this issue in section 17.7.

The final classification model we'll consider is the support vector machine.

17.5 *Support vector machines*

Support vector machines (SVMs) are a group of supervised machine learning models that can be used for classification and regression. They're popular at present, in part because of their success in developing accurate prediction models and in part because of the elegant mathematics that underlie the approach. We'll focus on using SVMs for binary classification.

SVMs seek an optimal hyperplane for separating two classes in a multidimensional space. The hyperplane is chosen to maximize the *margin* between the two classes' closest points. The points on the boundary of the margin are called *support vectors* (they help define the margin), and the middle of the margin is the separating hyperplane.

For an N-dimensional space (that is, with N predictor variables), the optimal hyperplane (also called a *linear decision surface*) has $N - 1$ dimensions. If there are two variables, the surface is a line. For three variables, the surface is a plane. For 10 variables, the surface is a 9-dimensional hyperplane. Trying to picture it will give you headache.

Consider the two-dimensional example shown in figure 17.4. Circles and triangles represent the two groups. The *margin* is the gap, represented by the distance between the two dashed lines. The points on the dashed lines (filled circles and triangles) are the support vectors. In the two-dimensional case, the optimal hyperplane is the black line in the middle of the gap. In this idealized example, the two groups are linearly separable—the line can completely separate the two groups without errors.

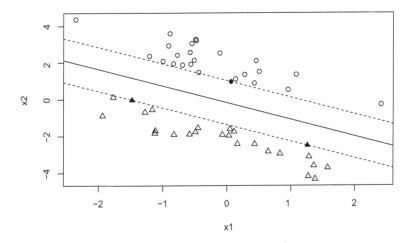

Figure 17.4 Two-group classification problem where the two groups are linearly separable. The separating hyperplane is indicated by the solid black line. The margin is the distance from the line to the dashed line on either side. The filled circles and triangles are the support vectors.

The optimal hyperplane is identified using quadratic programming to optimize the margin under the constraint that the data points on one side have an outcome value of +1 and the data on the other side has an outcome value of –1. If the data points are *almost* separable (not all the points are on one side or the other), a penalizing term is added to the optimization to account for errors, and *soft* margins are produced.

But the data may be fundamentally nonlinear. In the example in figure 17.5, no line can correctly separate the circles and triangles. SVMs use kernel functions to transform the data into higher dimensions in the hope that they will become more linearly separable. Imagine transforming the data in figure 17.5 in such a way that the circles lift off the page. One way to do this is to transform the two-dimensional data into three dimensions using

$$(X,Y) \rightarrow (X^2, \sqrt{XY}, Y^2) \rightarrow (Z_1, Z_2, Z_3)$$

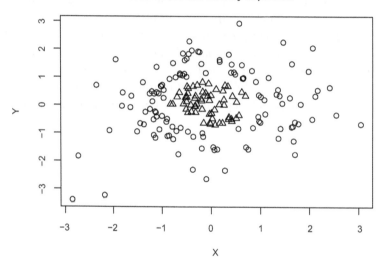

Features are not linearly separable

Figure 17.5　Two-group classification problem where the two groups aren't linearly separable. The groups can't be separated with a hyperplane (line).

Then you can separate the triangles from the circles using a rigid sheet of paper (that is, a two-dimensional plane in what is now a three-dimensional space).

The mathematics of SVMs is complex and well beyond the scope of this book. Statnikov, Aliferis, Hardin, and Guyon (2011) offer a lucid and intuitive presentation of SVMs that goes into quite a bit of conceptual detail without getting bogged down in higher math.

SVMs are available in R using the ksvm() function in the kernlab package and the svm() function in the e1071 package. The former is more powerful, but the latter is a bit easier to use. The example in the next listing uses the latter (easy is good) to develop an SVM for the Wisconsin breast cancer data.

Listing 17.6   A support vector machine

```
> library(e1071)
> set.seed(1234)
> fit.svm <- svm(class~., data=train)
> fit.svm

Call:
svm(formula = class ~ ., data = train)


Parameters:
   SVM-Type:  C-classification
 SVM-Kernel:  radial
       cost:  1

Number of Support Vectors:  84

> svm.pred <- predict(fit.svm, test)
> svm.perf <- table(test$class,
                    svm.pred, dnn=c("Actual", "Predicted"))
> svm.perf

          Predicted
Actual    benign malignant
  benign     138         4
  malignant    0        63
```

Because predictor variables with larger variances typically have a greater influence on the development of SVMs, the svm() function scales each variable to a mean of 0 and standard deviation of 1 before fitting the model by default. As you can see, the predictive accuracy (99%) is very good.

17.5.1   *Tuning an SVM*

By default, the svm() function uses a *radial basis function (RBF)* to map samples into a higher-dimensional space. The RBF kernel is often a good choice because it's a non-linear mapping that can handle relations between class labels and predictors that are nonlinear.

When fitting an SVM with the RBF kernel, two parameters can affect the results: *gamma* and *cost*. Gamma is a kernel parameter that controls the shape of the separating hyperplane. Larger values of gamma typically result in a larger number of support vectors. Gamma can also be thought of as a parameter that controls how widely a training sample *reaches*, with larger values meaning far and smaller values meaning close. Gamma must be greater than zero.

The cost parameter represents the cost of making errors. A large value severely penalizes errors and leads to a more complex classification boundary. There will be fewer misclassifications in the training sample, but overfitting may result in poor predictive ability in new samples. Smaller values lead to a flatter classification boundary but may result in underfitting. Like gamma, cost is always positive.

By default, the `svm()` function sets gamma to 1 / (number of predictors) and cost to 1. But a different combination of gamma and cost may lead to a more effective model. You can try fitting SVMs by varying parameter values one at a time, but a grid search is more efficient. You can specify a range of values for each parameter using the `tune.svm()` function. `tune.svm()` fits every combination of values and reports on the performance of each. An example is given in the next listing.

Listing 17.7   Tuning an RBF support vector machine

```
> set.seed(1234)
> tuned <- tune.svm(class~., data=train,
                    gamma=10^(-6:1),          ❶ Varies the
                    cost=10^(-10:10))             parameters

> tuned                              ←──┐  Prints the
                                      ❷ └─ best model
Parameter tuning of 'svm':

- sampling method: 10-fold cross validation

- best parameters:
 gamma cost
  0.01    1
                                              Fits the model with ❸
                                              these parameters
- best performance: 0.03355496

> fit.svm <- svm(class~., data=train, gamma=.01, cost=1)   ←──
> svm.pred <- predict(fit.svm, na.omit(test))
> svm.perf <- table(na.omit(test)$class,              ❹ Evaluates the
              svm.pred, dnn=c("Actual", "Predicted"))     cross-validation
> svm.perf                                                 performance

          Predicted
Actual     benign malignant
  benign      139         3
  malignant     1        62
```

First, an SVM model is fit with an RBF kernel and varying values of gamma and cost ❶. Eight values of gamma (ranging from 0.000001 to 10) and 21 values of cost (ranging from 0.0000000001 to 100000000) are specified. In all, 168 models (8 × 21) are fit and compared. The model with the fewest 10-fold cross-validated errors in the training sample has gamma = 0.01 and cost = 1.

Using these parameter values, a new SVM is fit to the training sample ❸. The model is then used to predict outcomes in the test sample ❹, and the number of errors is displayed. Tuning the model ❷ had virtually no effect on the number of errors. This is not surprising for this example. The default parameter values (cost = 1, gamma = 0.111) are very similar to the tuned values (cost = 1, gamma = 0.01). In many cases, tuning the SVM parameters will lead to greater gains.

As stated, SVMs are popular because they work well in many situations. They can also handle situations in which the number of variables is much larger than the number of observations. This has made them popular in the field of biomedicine, where the number of variables collected in a typical DNA microarray study of gene expressions may be one or two orders of magnitude larger than the number of cases available.

One drawback of SVMs is that, like random forests, the resulting classification rules are difficult to understand and communicate. Again, they're essentially a black box. Additionally, SVMs don't scale as well as random forests when building models from large training samples. But once a successful model is built, classifying new observations scales quite well.

17.6 *Choosing a best predictive solution*

In sections 17.4 through 17.5, fine-needle aspiration samples were classified as malignant or benign using several supervised machine learning techniques. Which approach was most accurate? To answer this question, we need to define the term *accurate* in a binary classification context:

- The most commonly reported statistic is the *accuracy*, or how often the classifier is correct. Although informative, accuracy is insufficient by itself. Additional information is needed to evaluate the utility of a classification scheme.

- Consider a set of rules for classifying individuals as schizophrenic or non-schizophrenic. Schizophrenia is a rare disorder, with a prevalence of roughly 1% in the general population. If you classify everyone as non-schizophrenic, you'll be right 99% of time. But this isn't a good classifier because it will also misclassify every schizophrenic as non-schizophrenic. In addition to the accuracy, you should ask these questions:

  - What percentage of schizophrenics are correctly identified?
  - What percentage of nonschizophrenics are correctly identified?
  - If a person is classified as schizophrenic, how likely is it that this classification will be correct?
  - If a person is classified as nonschizophrenic, how likely is it that this classification is correct?

These questions pertain to a classifier's sensitivity, specificity, positive predictive power, and negative predictive power. Each is defined in table 17.1.

Table 17.1 Measures of predictive accuracy

Statistic	Interpretation
Sensitivity	Probability of getting a positive classification when the true outcome is positive (also called true positive rate or recall)
Specificity	Probability of getting a negative classification when the true outcome is negative (also called true negative rate)

Table 17.1   Measures of predictive accuracy *(continued)*

Statistic	Interpretation
Positive predictive value	Probability that an observation with a positive classification is correctly identified as positive (also called precision)
Negative predictive value	Probability that an observation with a negative classification is correctly identified as negative
Accuracy	Proportion of observations correctly identified (also called ACC)

The following listing provides a function for calculating these statistics.

Listing 17.8   Function for assessing binary classification accuracy

```
performance <- function(table, n=2){
  if(!all(dim(table) == c(2,2)))
     stop("Must be a 2 x 2 table")
  tn = table[1,1]
  fp = table[1,2]              ❶ Extracts frequencies
  fn = table[2,1]
  tp = table[2,2]
  sensitivity = tp/(tp+fn)
  specificity = tn/(tn+fp)
  ppp = tp/(tp+fp)            ❷ Calculates statistics
  npp = tn/(tn+fn)
  hitrate = (tp+tn)/(tp+tn+fp+fn)
  result <- paste("Sensitivity = ", round(sensitivity, n) ,
     "\nSpecificity = ", round(specificity, n),
     "\nPositive Predictive Value = ", round(ppp, n),
     "\nNegative Predictive Value = ", round(npp, n),   ❸ Prints results
     "\nAccuracy = ", round(hitrate, n), "\n", sep="")
  cat(result)
}
```

The performance() function takes a table containing the true outcome (rows) and predicted outcome (columns) and returns the five accuracy measures. First, the number of *true negatives* (benign tissue identified as benign), *false positives* (benign tissue identified as malignant), *false negatives* (malignant tissue identified as benign), and *true positives* (malignant tissue identified as malignant) are extracted ❶. Next, these counts are used to calculate the sensitivity, specificity, positive and negative predictive values, and accuracy ❷. Finally, the results are formatted and printed ❸.

In the following listing, the performance() function is applied to each of the five classifiers developed in this chapter.

Listing 17.9   Performance of breast cancer data classifiers

```
> performance(logit.perf)
Sensitivity = 0.95
Specificity = 0.99
Positive Predictive Value = 0.97
```

```
Negative Predictive Value = 0.98
Accuracy = 0.98

> performance(dtree.perf)
Sensitivity = 0.95
Specificity = 0.96
Positive Predictive Value = 0.91
Negative Predictive Value = 0.98
Accuracy = 0.96

> performance(ctree.perf)
Sensitivity = 0.97
Specificity = 0.97
Positive Predictive Value = 0.94
Negative Predictive Value = 0.99
Accuracy = 0.97

> performance(forest.perf)
Sensitivity = 0.95
Specificity = 0.99
Positive Predictive Value = 0.97
Negative Predictive Value = 0.98
Accuracy = 0.98

> performance(svm.perf)
Sensitivity = 0.98
Specificity = 0.98
Positive Predictive Value = 0.95
Negative Predictive Value = 0.99
Accuracy = 0.98
```

Each of these classifiers (logistic regression, traditional decision tree, conditional inference tree, random forest, and support vector machine) performed exceedingly well on each of the accuracy measures. This won't always be the case!

In this particular instance, the award appears to go to the support vector machine model (although the differences are so small, they may be due to chance). For the SVM model, 98% of malignancies were correctly identified (sensitivity), 98% of benign samples were correctly identified (specificity), and the overall percent of correct classifications is 98% (accuracy). A diagnosis of malignancy was correct 95% of the time (positive predictive value), and a benign diagnosis was correct 99% of the time (negative predictive value). For diagnoses of cancer, the specificity (proportion of malignant samples correctly identified as malignant) is particularly important.

Although it's beyond the scope of this chapter, you can often improve a classification system by trading specificity for sensitivity and vice versa. In the logistic regression model, predict() was used to estimate the probability that a case belonged in the malignant group. If the probability was greater than 0.5, the case was assigned to that group. The 0.5 value is called the *threshold* or *cutoff value*. If you vary this threshold, you can increase the sensitivity of the classification model at the expense of its specificity. predict() can also generate probabilities for decision trees, random forests, and SVMs (although the syntax varies by method).

The impact of varying the threshold value is typically assessed using a *receiver operating characteristic (ROC)* curve. An ROC curve plots sensitivity versus specificity for a range of threshold values. You can then select a threshold with the best balance of sensitivity and specificity for a given problem. Many R packages generate ROC curves, including `ROCR` and `pROC`. Analytic functions in these packages can help you select the best threshold values for a given scenario or compare the ROC curves produced by different classification algorithms to choose the most useful approach. To learn more, see Kuhn and Johnson (2013). A more advanced discussion is offered by Fawcett (2005).

17.7 *Understanding black box predictions*

Classification models are used to make real work decisions that can have significant human consequences. Imagine that you've applied for and been turned down for a bank loan and you want to understand why. If the decision was based on a logistic regression or classification tree model, the reason can be determined by looking at the model coefficient in the former case or the decision tree in the latter case. But what if the classification was based on a random forest, support vector machine model, or artificial neural network model? Until recently, the answer was "because the computer said so," which is a very unsatisfactory answer!

In recent years, there has been a movement to understand black box models employing methods and techniques called *Explainable Artificial Intelligence* (XAI, http://ema.drwhy.ai). The goal of XAI is to better understand how black box models work in general (global understanding) and when making individual predictions (local understanding).

Consider a patient named Alex. Alex's biopsy produced the following lab values:

```
bareNuclei = 9,
sizeUniformity = 1,
shapeUniformity = 1,
blandChromatin = 7,
maginalAdhesion = 1,
mitosis = 3,
normalNucleoli = 3,
clumpThickness = 6,
singleEpithelialCellSize = 3
```

Running these values through the random forest model developed in section 17.4 yields a prediction of malignancy (with a probability of 0.658). In the remainder of this section, we'll use XAI techniques to explore how our random forest model produced this diagnosis. We'll be using the `DALEX` package, so be sure to install it (`install.packages("DALEX")`) before continuing.

17.7.1 *Break-down plots*

Our goal is to partition Alex's predictor scores into their unique contributions to the final classification (malignant with probability 0.658). To accomplish this, we'll use *break-down* values:

1 Using the training sample, calculate the average predicted response value (probability of malignancy in this case) across all observations (0.365). Call this the intercept.

2 For all observations where `bareNuclei` = 9, calculate the average predicted res-ponse (0.544). The contribution of `bareNuclei` in this case is 0.544 – 0365 = +0.179.

3 For all observations where `bareNuclei` = 9 *and* `sizeUniformity` = 1, calculate the average predicted response (0.476). The contribution of `sizeUniformity` 0.476 – 0.544 = –0.068.

4 For all observations where `bareNuclei` = 9, *and* `sizeUniformity` = 1, *and* `shapeUniformity` = 1, calculate the average predicted response (0.42). The contribution of `shapeUniformity` is –0.05.

5 Keep going until you have included all predictor values for the observation. The individual predictor contributions will add up the model's prediction for that case. Positive contributions increase the likelihood of a malignancy diagnosis. Negative contribution decreases this likelihood. The magnitude of the contribution assesses the variable's impact on the final prediction.

The following listing provides the code for calculating break-down values, and figure 17.6 displays a break-down plot.

Listing 17.10   Using a break-down plot to understand a black box prediction

```
> library(DALEX)

> alex <- data.frame(
      bareNuclei = 9,
      sizeUniformity = 1,
      shapeUniformity = 1,
      blandChromatin = 7,                    ❶ Observation
      maginalAdhesion = 1,                     to explore
      mitosis = 3,
      normalNucleoli = 3,
      clumpThickness = 6,
      singleEpithelialCellSize = 3
  )

> predict(fit.forest, alex, type="prob")    ❷ Predicts outcome for
                                               that observation
  benign malignant
1  0.278     0.722

set.seed(1234)
explainer_rf_malignant <-                          ❸ Builds an
  explain(fit.forest, data = train,  y = train$class == "malignant",   explainer
  predict_function = function(m, x) predict(m, x, type = "prob")[,2])    object

rf_pparts <- predict_parts(explainer=explainer_rf_malignant,
                   new_observation = alex,
                   type = "break_down")         ❹ Produces the
                                                   break-down plot
plot(rf_pparts)
```

After loading the `DALEX` package, the case of interest is input as a data frame ❶. The `predict()` function runs the case through the random forest and produces the prediction. Since `type="prob"`, the probabilities for a benign and malignant outcome are returned ❷. Next, a `DALEX explainer` object is created ❸. The object takes the random forest model, the training data, the outcome variable, and the function used to predict the outcome as parameters. Here we specify that we want to predict the malignant category. Using the `[,2]` in the prediction function returns just the probability of malignancy. Finally, we generate the break-down plot using the `explainer` object and observation to be explained ❹.

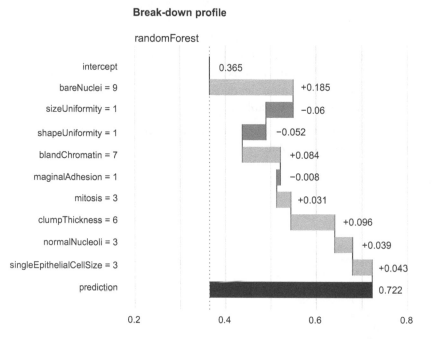

Break-down profile

randomForest

intercept	0.365
bareNuclei = 9	+0.185
sizeUniformity = 1	−0.06
shapeUniformity = 1	−0.052
blandChromatin = 7	+0.084
maginalAdhesion = 1	−0.008
mitosis = 3	+0.031
clumpThickness = 6	+0.096
normalNucleoli = 3	+0.039
singleEpithelialCellSize = 3	+0.043
prediction	0.722

0.2   0.4   0.6   0.8

Figure 17.6   A break-down plot for one individual's random forest prediction. The average predicted probability of a malignant biopsy is 0.365. Given this individual's scores, the predicted probability is 0.722. Since this probability is greater than 0.5, the prediction is that the biopsy represents malignancy. The individual contribution of each predictor value for this individual can also be seen. Green bars represent positive contributions to the predicted outcome, while red bars represent negative contributions.

Looking at figure 17.6, you can see that for Alex, `bareNuclei = 9` and `clump-Thickness = 6` had major contributions to the malignant diagnosis. The `size-Uniformity = 1` and `shapeUniformity = 1` scores reduced the probability of the cells being malignant. Taking all nine predictor values into account led to a malignant probability of 0.658. Since 0.658 > 0.50, the random forest model classified Alex's sample as malignant.

17.7.2 *Plotting Shapley values*

Break-down plots can be very helpful in understanding why an individual received a given prediction from a black box model. However, note that the break-down is order dependent. If there are interaction effects between two or more predictor variables, you will get different break-down results for different variable orders.

Shapley additive explanations or *SHAP* values get around this reliance on order by calculating break-down contributions for many predictor variable orders and averaging the results for each variable. Continuing the example in listing 17.10,

```
set.seed(1234)
rf_pparts = predict_parts(explainer = explainer_rf_malignant,
                          new_observation = alex,
                          type = "shap")
plot(rf_pparts)
```

produces the plot in figure 17.7.

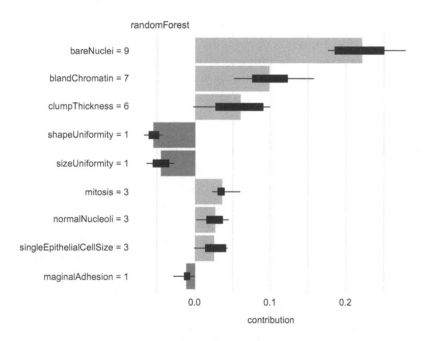

Figure 17.7 A SHAP values plot for one individual's random forest prediction

The box plots show the range of break-down contributions for a variable over different variable orderings. The bars represent the mean break-down value. Larger bars represent a greater impact on the prediction for this individual. Positive (green) bars indicate contributions to a malignant diagnosis, while negative (red) bars indicate contributions to a benign diagnosis.

The XAI methods discussed are model agnostic—they can be used with any machine learning approach, including those covered in this chapter. The DALEX package offers many other such statistics and is worth checking out. Besides, *WHO DOESN'T LIKE DALEX?* (pun intended!)

17.8 *Going further*

Building a predictive model using machine learning techniques is a complex, iterative process. Common steps include

1 *Data splitting*—Available data is segregated into training and testing datasets.
2 *Data preprocessing*—Predictor variables are selected and possibly transformed. For example, support vector machines often work best with standardized predictors. Highly correlated variables may be combined into composite variables or dropped. Missing values must be imputed or deleted.
3 *Model building*—Many possible candidate prediction models are developed. Most will have hyperparameters that have to be tuned. Hyperparameters are model parameters that control the learning process and are selected by trial and error. The complexity parameter in classification trees, the number of candidate variables for a split in random forests, and the cost and gamma parameters in support vector machines are all examples. You vary these parameters and select the values that result in the most predictive and robust models.
4 *Model comparisons*—After fitting a series of models, their performances are compared, and a final model is chosen.
5 *Model release*—Once the final model is chosen, it is used to make future predictions. Since the environment may change, it is important to continuously evaluate the model's effectiveness over time.

The task is further complicated by the fact that machine learning techniques exist in many different packages and use different syntaxes. To simplify the workflow, omnibus or meta packages have been developed. These packages serve as wrappers to other packages and provide a simplified and consistent interface for building predictive models. Learning one of these approaches can greatly simplify the task of building an effective predictive system.

Three of the most popular approaches are the caret package, the mlr3 framework, and the tidymodels framework (frameworks consist of several interrelated packages). The caret package (http://topepo.github.io/caret) is perhaps the most mature package and supports more than 230 machine learning algorithms. The mlr3 framework (https://mlr3.mlr-org.com/) is highly structured and will appeal to object-oriented programmers. The tidymodels framework (https://www.tidymodels.org/) is the newest and perhaps the most flexible. Since it was created by the same individuals responsible for the caret package, I suspect that it will supersede the caret package over time. If you are going to use R for machine learning, I suggest that you select one of these frameworks and study it in depth. Which one you choose is a matter of personal preference.

To learn more about the functions in R that support prediction and classification, look in the CRAN Task View for Machine Learning and Statistical Learning (http://mng.bz/I1Lm). Other good resources include books by Kuhn and Johnson (2013), Forte (2015), Lanz (2015), and Torgo (2017).

Summary

- A common task in data science is the prediction of a binary categorical outcome (pass/fail; succeed/fail; live/die; benign/malignant), and these predictions can have real-world consequences for individuals.
- Predictive models can range from relatively simple (logistic regression, classification trees) to exceeding complex (random forest, support vector machine, artificial neural network).
- Models often have hyperparameters (parameters that control the learning process) that must be tuned by trial and error.
- The effectiveness of predictive models is evaluated by using performance measures such as accuracy, sensitivity, specificity, positive predictive power, and negative predictive power.
- New techniques for exploring highly complex black box models have been developed.
- The process of developing a predictive model involves numerous iterative steps, which can be simplified by using an omnibus package or framework such as `caret`, `mlr2`, or `tidymodels`.

Advanced methods
for missing data

18

This chapter covers

- Identifying missing data
- Visualizing missing-data patterns
- Deleting missing values
- Imputing missing values

In previous chapters, we focused on analyzing complete datasets (that is, datasets without missing values). Although doing so helps simplify the presentation of statistical and graphical methods, in the real world, missing data are ubiquitous.

In some ways, the impact of missing data is a subject most of us want to avoid. Statistics books may not mention it or may limit discussion to a few paragraphs. Statistical packages offer automatic handling of missing data using methods that may not be optimal. Even though most data analyses (at least in the social sciences) involve missing data, this topic is rarely mentioned in the methods and results sections of journal articles. Given how often missing values occur and the degree to which their presence can invalidate study results, it's fair to say that the subject has received insufficient attention outside of specialized books and courses.

Data can be missing for many reasons. Survey participants may forget to answer one or more questions, refuse to answer sensitive questions, or grow fatigued and fail to complete a long questionnaire. Study participants may miss appointments or drop out of a study prematurely. Recording equipment may fail, internet connections may be lost, or data may be miscoded. Analysts may even plan for some data to be missing. For example, to increase study efficiency or reduce costs, you may choose not to collect all data from all participants. Finally, data may be lost for reasons that you're never able to ascertain.

Unfortunately, most statistical methods assume that you're working with complete matrices, vectors, and data frames. In most cases, you have to eliminate missing data before you address the substantive questions that led you to collect the data. You can eliminate missing data by either removing cases with missing data or replacing missing data with reasonable substitute values. In either case, the end result is a dataset without missing values.

In this chapter, we'll look at both traditional and modern approaches for dealing with missing data. We'll primarily use the `VIM`, `mice`, and `missForest` packages. The command `install.packages(c("VIM", "mice", "missForest"))` will download and install them.

To motivate the discussion, we'll look at the mammal sleep dataset (`sleep`) provided in the `VIM` package (not to be confused with the `sleep` dataset describing the impact of drugs on sleep, provided in the base installation). The data come from a study by Allison and Chichetti (1976) that examined the relationship between sleep and ecological and constitutional variables for 62 mammal species. The authors were interested in why animals' sleep requirements vary from species to species. The sleep variables served as the dependent variables, whereas the ecological and constitutional variables served as the independent or predictor variables.

Sleep variables included length of dreaming sleep (`Dream`), nondreaming sleep (`NonD`), and their sum (`Sleep`). The constitutional variables included body weight in kilograms (`BodyWgt`), brain weight in grams (`BrainWgt`), life span in years (`Span`), and gestation time in days (`Gest`). The ecological variables included the degree to which species were preyed upon (`Pred`), the degree of their exposure while sleeping (`Exp`), and overall danger (`Danger`) they faced. The ecological variables were measured on 5-point rating scales ranging from 1 (low) to 5 (high).

In their original article, Allison and Chichetti limited their analyses to the species that had complete data. We'll go further, analyzing all 62 cases with a multiple imputation approach.

18.1 Steps in dealing with missing data

If you're new to the study of missing data, you'll find a bewildering array of approaches, critiques, and methodologies. The classic text in this area is Little and Rubin (2002). Excellent, accessible reviews can be found in Allison (2001); Schafer and Graham (2002); Enders (2010); and Schlomer, Bauman, and Card (2010). A comprehensive approach usually includes the following steps:

1   Identify the missing data.
2   Examine the causes of the missing data.
3   Delete the cases containing missing data or replace (impute) the missing values with reasonable alternative data values.

Unfortunately, identifying missing data is usually the only unambiguous step. Learning why data are missing depends on your understanding of the processes that generated the data. Deciding how to treat missing values will depend on your estimation of which procedures will produce the most reliable and accurate results.

A classification system for missing data

Statisticians typically classify missing data into one of three types. These types are usually described in probabilistic terms, but the underlying ideas are straightforward. We'll use the measurement of dreaming in the sleep study (where 12 animals have missing values) to illustrate each type in turn:

- *Missing completely at random*—If the presence of missing data on a variable is unrelated to any other observed or unobserved variable, then the data are missing completely at random (MCAR). If there's no systematic reason why dream sleep is missing for these 12 animals, the data are said to be MCAR. Note that if every variable with missing data is MCAR, you can consider the complete cases to be a simple random sample from the larger dataset.
- *Missing at random*—If the presence of missing data on a variable is related to other observed variables but not to its own unobserved value, the data are missing at random (MAR). For example, if animals with smaller body weights are more likely to have missing values for dream sleep (perhaps because it's harder to observe smaller animals) and the "missingness" is unrelated to an animal's time spent dreaming, the data are considered MAR. In this case, the presence or absence of dream sleep data is random, once you control for body weight.
- *Not missing at random*—If the missing data for a variable are neither MCAR nor MAR, the data are not missing at random (NMAR). For example, if animals that spend less time dreaming are also more likely to have a missing dream value (perhaps because it's harder to measure shorter events), the data are considered NMAR.

Most approaches to missing data assume that the data are either MCAR or MAR. In this case, you can ignore the mechanism producing the missing data and (after replacing or deleting the missing data) model the relationships of interest directly.

Data that are NMAR can be difficult to analyze properly. When data are NMAR, you have to model the mechanisms that produced the missing values as well as the relationships of interest. (Current approaches to analyzing NMAR data include the use of selection models and pattern mixtures. The analysis of NMAR data can be complex and is beyond the scope of this book.)

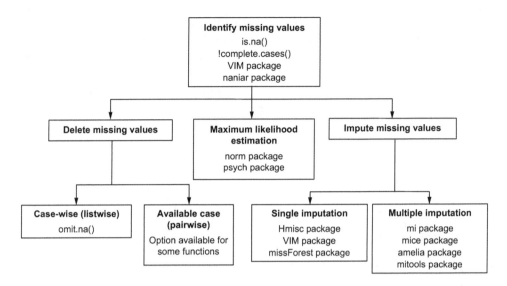

Figure 18.1 **Methods for handling incomplete data, along with the R packages that support them**

There are *many* methods for dealing with missing data—and no guarantee that they'll produce the same results. Figure 18.1 describes an array of methods used for handling incomplete data and the R packages that support them.

A complete review of missing-data methodologies would require a book in itself (Enders [2010] is a great example). In this chapter, we'll review methods for exploring missing-values patterns and focus on the four most popular methods for dealing with incomplete data: a rational approach, listwise deletion, single imputation, and multiple imputation. We'll end with a brief discussion of other methods, including those that are useful in special circumstances.

18.2 *Identifying missing values*

To begin, let's review the material introduced in section 3.5 and expand on it. R represents missing values using the symbol NA (not available) and impossible values using the symbol NaN (not a number). In addition, the symbols Inf and -Inf represent positive infinity and negative infinity, respectively. The functions `is.na()`, `is.nan()`, and `is.infinite()` can be used to identify missing, impossible, and infinite values, respectively. Each returns either TRUE or FALSE. Table 18.1 gives examples.

Table 18.1 **Examples of return values for the `is.na()`, `is.nan()`, and `is.infinite()` functions**

x	is.na(x)	is.nan(x)	is.infinite(x)
x <- NA	TRUE	FALSE	FALSE
x <- 0 / 0	TRUE	TRUE	FALSE
x <- 1 / 0	FALSE	FALSE	TRUE

These functions return an object that's the same size as its argument, with each element replaced by TRUE if the element is of the type being tested or FALSE otherwise. For example, let y <- c(1, 2, 3, NA). Then is.na(y) will return the vector c(FALSE, FALSE, FALSE, TRUE).

The function complete.cases() can be used to identify the rows in a matrix or data frame that don't contain missing data. It returns a logical vector with TRUE for every row that contains complete cases and FALSE for every row that has one or more missing values.

Let's apply this to the sleep dataset:

```
# load the dataset
data(sleep, package="VIM")

# list the rows that do not have missing values
sleep[complete.cases(sleep),]

# list the rows that have one or more missing values
sleep[!complete.cases(sleep),]
```

Examining the output reveals that 42 cases have complete data and 20 cases have one or more missing values.

Because the logical values TRUE and FALSE are equivalent to the numeric values 1 and 0, the sum() and mean() functions can be used to obtain useful information about missing data. Consider the following:

```
> sum(is.na(sleep$Dream))
[1] 12
> mean(is.na(sleep$Dream))
[1] 0.19
> mean(!complete.cases(sleep))
[1] 0.32
```

The results indicate that 12 values are missing for the variable Dream. Nineteen percent of the cases have a missing value on this variable. In addition, 32% of the cases in the dataset have one or more missing values.

There are two things to keep in mind when identifying missing values. First, the complete.cases() function only identifies NA and NaN as missing. Infinite values (Inf and -Inf) are treated as valid values. Second, you must use missing-values functions, like those in this section, to identify the missing values in R data objects. Logical comparisons such as myvar == NA are never true.

Now that you know how to identify missing values programmatically, let's look at tools that help you explore possible patterns in the occurrence of missing data.

18.3   *Exploring missing-values patterns*

Before deciding how to deal with missing data, you'll find it useful to determine which variables have missing values, in what amounts, and in what combinations. In this section, we'll review tabular, graphical, and correlational methods for exploring missing-values patterns. Ultimately, you want to understand why the data is missing. The answer will have implications for how you proceed with further analyses.

18.3.1 Visualizing missing values

The md.pattern() function in the mice package produces a tabulation of the missing-data patterns in a matrix or data frame. Additionally, it plots the tabulation as a graph. Applying this function to the sleep dataset produces the output in the following listing and the graph in figure 18.2.

Listing 18.1 Missing-values patterns with md.pattern()

```
> library(mice)
> data(sleep, package="VIM")
> md.pattern(sleep, rotate.names=TRUE)
   BodyWgt BrainWgt Pred Exp Danger Sleep Span Gest Dream NonD
42       1        1    1   1      1     1    1    1     1    1  0
2        1        1    1   1      1     1    0    1     1    1  1
3        1        1    1   1      1     1    1    0     1    1  1
9        1        1    1   1      1     1    1    1     0    0  2
2        1        1    1   1      1     0    1    1     1    0  2
1        1        1    1   1      1     1    0    0     1    1  2
2        1        1    1   1      1     0    1    1     0    0  3
1        1        1    1   1      1     1    0    1     0    0  3
         0        0    0   0      0     4    4    4    12   14 38
```

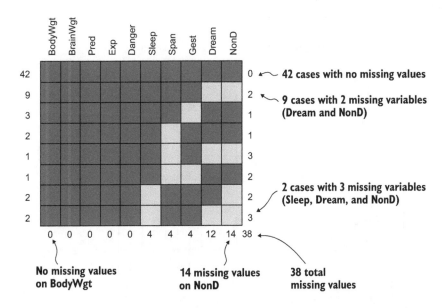

Figure 18.2 Missing-values patterns summarized by the md.pattern() function. Each row represents a pattern of missing (light red) and nonmissing (dark blue) data.

The 1s and 0s in the body of the table indicate the missing-values patterns, with a 0 indicating a missing value for a given column variable and a 1 indicating a nonmissing value. The first row describes the pattern of *no missing values* (all elements are 1). The second row describes the pattern *no missing values except for Span*. The first column indicates the number of cases in each missing-data pattern, and the last column indicates the number of variables with missing values present in each pattern. Here you can see that there are 42 cases without missing data and 2 cases that are missing Span alone. Nine cases are missing both NonD and Dream values. The dataset has a total of $(42 \times 0) + (2 \times 1) + \ldots + (1 \times 3) = 38$ missing values. The last row gives the total number of missing values on each variable.

Although the tabular output from the md.pattern() function is compact, I often find it easier to discern patterns visually. In figure 18.2, each row represents a pattern. Dark blue indicates values that are present, while light red indicates missing values. Numbers on the left indicate the number of cases in a pattern, the numbers on the right indicate the number of missing variables in a pattern, and the numbers on the bottom indicate the number of missing values for each variable.

The VIM package provides numerous functions for visualizing missing-values patterns in datasets. Here, we will look at three of the most useful: aggr(), matrixplot(), and marginplot().

The aggr() function plots the number of missing values for each variable alone and for each combination of variables. It provides a nice alternative to figure 18.2. For example, the code

```
library("VIM")
aggr(sleep, prop=FALSE, numbers=TRUE)
```

produces the graph in figure 18.3.

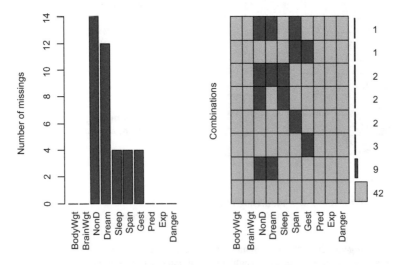

Figure 18.3   aggr()-produced plot of missing-values patterns for the sleep dataset

You can see that the variable NonD has the largest number of missing values (14), and that two mammals are missing NonD, Dream, and Sleep scores. Forty-two mammals have no missing data.

The statement `aggr(sleep, prop=TRUE, numbers=TRUE)` produces the same plot, but proportions are displayed instead of counts. The option `numbers=FALSE` (the default) suppresses the numeric labels. Note that as the number of variables in the dataset increases, the plot labels for this graph can become badly distorted. You can fix this by manually decreasing the size of plot labels. Including the parameters `cex.lab=`*n*, `cex.axis=`*n*, and `cex.number=`*n* (where *n* is a number less than 1) will shrink the size of the axis, variable, and number labels, respectively.

The `matrixplot()` function produces a plot displaying the data for each case. Figure 18.4 shows a graph created using `matrixplot(sleep, sort="BodyWgt")`. Here, the numeric data are rescaled to the interval [0, 1] and represented by gray-scale colors, with lighter colors representing lower values and darker colors representing larger values. By default, missing values are represented in red. Note that in figure 18.4, red has been replaced with crosshatching by hand, so that the missing values are viewable in grayscale. The rows in figure 18.4 are sorted by BodyWgt.

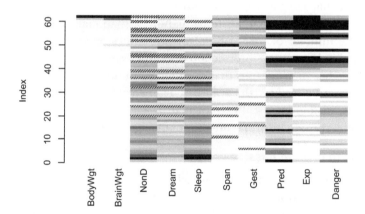

Figure 18.4 Matrix plot of actual and missing values by case (row) for the `sleep` dataset. The matrix is sorted by `BodyWgt`.

The `marginplot()` function produces a scatter plot between two variables with information about missing values shown in the plot's margins. Consider the relationship between the amount of dream sleep and the length of a mammal's gestation. The statement

```
marginplot(sleep[c("Gest","Dream")], pch=20,
           col=c("darkgray", "red", "blue"))
```

produces the graph in figure 18.5. The pch and col parameters are optional and provide control over the plotting symbols and colors.

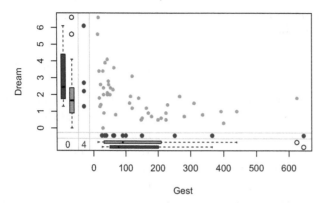

Figure 18.5 Scatter plot between amount of dream sleep and length of gestation, with information about missing data in the margins

The body of the graph displays the scatter plot between `Gest` and `Dream` (based on complete cases for the two variables). In the left margin, box plots display the distribution of `Dream` for mammals with (dark gray) and without (red) `Gest` values. (Note that in grayscale, red is the darker shade.) Four red dots represent the values of `Dream` for mammals missing `Gest` scores. In the bottom margin, the roles of `Gest` and `Dream` are reversed. You can see that a negative relationship exists between length of gestation and dream sleep and that dream sleep tends to be higher for mammals that are missing a gestation score. The number of observations missing values on both variables at the same time is printed in blue at the intersection of both margins (bottom left).

The `VIM` package has many graphs that can help you understand the role of missing data in a dataset and is well worth exploring. There are functions to produce scatter plots, box plots, histograms, scatter plot matrices, parallel plots, rug plots, and bubble plots that incorporate information about missing values.

18.3.2 *Using correlations to explore missing values*

Before we move on, there's one more approach worth noting. You can replace the data in a dataset with indicator variables coded 1 for missing and 0 for present. The resulting matrix is sometimes called a shadow matrix. Correlating these indicator variables with each other and with the original (observed) variables can help you see which variables tend to be missing together, as well as relationships between a variable's *missingness* and the values of the other variables.

Consider the following code:

```
x <- as.data.frame(abs(is.na(sleep)))
```

The elements of data frame x are 1 if the corresponding element of `sleep` is missing and 0 otherwise. You can see this by viewing the first few rows of each:

```
> head(sleep, n=5)
  BodyWgt BrainWgt NonD Dream Sleep Span Gest Pred Exp Danger
1 6654.000   5712.0   NA    NA   3.3 38.6  645    3   5      3
2    1.000      6.6  6.3   2.0   8.3  4.5   42    3   1      3
```

```
3     3.385      44.5   NA    NA   12.5 14.0   60    1   1      1
4     0.920       5.7   NA    NA   16.5  NA    25    5   2      3
5  2547.000    4603.0  2.1   1.8    3.9 69.0  624    3   5      4

> head(x, n=5)
  BodyWgt BrainWgt NonD Dream Sleep Span Gest Pred Exp Danger
1       0        0    1     1     0    0    0    0   0      0
2       0        0    0     0     0    0    0    0   0      0
3       0        0    1     1     0    0    0    0   0      0
4       0        0    1     1     0    1    0    0   0      0
5       0        0    0     0     0    0    0    0   0      0
```

The statement

```
y <- x[which(apply(x,2,sum)>0)]
```

extracts the variables that have some (but not all) missing values, and

```
cor(y)
```

gives you the correlations among these indicator variables:

```
        NonD   Dream   Sleep    Span    Gest
NonD   1.000   0.907   0.486   0.015  -0.142
Dream  0.907   1.000   0.204   0.038  -0.129
Sleep  0.486   0.204   1.000  -0.069  -0.069
Span   0.015   0.038  -0.069   1.000   0.198
Gest  -0.142  -0.129  -0.069   0.198   1.000
```

Here, you can see that Dream and NonD tend to be missing together ($r = 0.91$). To a lesser extent, Sleep and NonD tend to be missing together ($r = 0.49$), and Sleep and Dream tend to be missing together ($r = 0.20$).

Finally, you can look at the relationship between missing values in a variable and the observed values on other variables:

```
> cor(sleep, y, use="pairwise.complete.obs")
           NonD   Dream   Sleep    Span    Gest
BodyWgt   0.227   0.223  0.0017  -0.058  -0.054
BrainWgt  0.179   0.163  0.0079  -0.079  -0.073
NonD        NA      NA      NA   -0.043  -0.046
Dream    -0.189      NA -0.1890   0.117   0.228
Sleep    -0.080  -0.080      NA   0.096   0.040
Span      0.083   0.060  0.0052      NA  -0.065
Gest      0.202   0.051  0.1597  -0.175      NA
Pred      0.048  -0.068  0.2025   0.023  -0.201
Exp       0.245   0.127  0.2608  -0.193  -0.193
Danger    0.065  -0.067  0.2089  -0.067  -0.204
Warning message:
In cor(sleep, y, use = "pairwise.complete.obs") :
  the standard deviation is zero
```

In this correlation matrix, the rows are observed variables, and the columns are indicator variables representing missingness. You can ignore the warning message and NA values in the correlation matrix; they're artifacts of our approach.

From the first column of the correlation matrix, you can see that nondreaming sleep scores are more likely to be missing for mammals with higher body weight (r = 0.227), gestation period (r = 0.202), and sleeping exposure (r = 0.245). Other columns are read in a similar fashion. None of the correlations in this table are particularly large or striking, which suggests that the data deviate minimally from MCAR and may be MAR.

Note that you can never rule out the possibility that the data are NMAR because you don't know what the values would have been for data that are missing. For example, you don't know if there's a relationship between the amount of dreaming a mammal engages in and the probability of a value being missing on this variable. In the absence of strong external evidence to the contrary, we typically assume that data are either MCAR or MAR.

18.4   *Understanding the sources and impact of missing data*

You can identify the amount, distribution, and pattern of missing data to evaluate the potential mechanisms leading to the missing data and the impact of the missing data on your ability to answer substantive questions. In particular, you want to answer the following questions:

- What percentage of the data is missing?
- Are the missing data concentrated in a few variables or widely distributed?
- Do the missing values appear to be random?
- Does the covariation of missing data with each other or with observed data suggest a possible mechanism that's producing the missing values?

Answers to these questions help determine which statistical methods are most appropriate for analyzing your data. For example, if the missing data are concentrated in a few relatively unimportant variables, you may be able to delete these variables and continue your analyses normally. If a small amount of data (say, less than 10%) is randomly distributed throughout the dataset (MCAR), you may be able to limit your analyses to cases with complete data and still get reliable and valid results. If you can assume that the data are either MCAR or MAR, you may be able to apply multiple imputation methods to arrive at valid conclusions. If the data are NMAR, you can turn to specialized methods, collect new data, or go into an easier and more rewarding profession.

Here are some examples:

- In a recent survey employing paper questionnaires, I found that several items tended to be missing together. It became apparent that these items clustered together because participants didn't realize that the third page of the questionnaire had a reverse side—which contained the items. In this case, the data could be considered MCAR.
- In another study, an education variable was frequently missing in a global survey of leadership styles. Investigation revealed that European participants were

more likely to leave this item blank. It turned out that the categories didn't make sense for participants in certain countries. In this case, the data were most likely MAR.

- Finally, I was involved in a study of depression in which older patients were more likely to omit items describing depressed mood compared with younger patients. Interviews revealed that older patients were loath to admit to such symptoms because doing so violated their values about "keeping a stiff upper lip." Unfortunately, it was also determined that severely depressed patients were more likely to omit these items due to a sense of hopelessness and difficulties with concentration. In this case, the data had to be considered NMAR.

As you can see, identifying patterns is only the first step. You need to bring your understanding of the research subject matter and the data collection process to bear to determine the source of the missing values.

Now that we've considered the source and impact of missing data, let's see how standard statistical approaches can be altered to accommodate them. We'll focus on four popular approaches: a rational approach for recovering data, a traditional approach that involves deleting missing data, a modern approach that imputes individual missing values, and a modern approach that uses simulation to account for the impact of missing data on conclusions. Along the way, we'll briefly look at methods for specialized situations and methods that have become obsolete and should be retired. The goal will remain constant: to answer, as accurately as possible, the substantive questions that led you to collect the data, given the absence of complete information.

18.5 *Rational approaches for dealing with incomplete data*

In a rational approach, you use mathematical or logical relationships among variables to attempt to fill in or recover missing values. A few examples will help clarify this approach.

In the sleep dataset, the variable Sleep is the sum of the Dream and NonD variables. If you know a mammal's scores on any two, you can derive the third. Thus, if some observations were missing only one of the three variables, you could recover the missing information through addition or subtraction.

As a second example, consider research that focuses on work/life balance differences between generational cohorts (for example, Silents, Early Boomers, Late Boomers, Xers, Millennials), where cohorts are defined by their birth year. Participants are asked both their date of birth and their age. If date of birth is missing, you can recover their birth year (and therefore their generational cohort) by knowing their age and the date they completed the survey.

An example that uses logical relationships to recover missing data comes from a set of leadership studies in which participants were asked if they were a manager (yes/no) and the number of their direct reports (integer). If they left the manager question blank but indicated that they had one or more direct reports, it would be reasonable to infer that they were a manager.

As a final example, I frequently engage in gender research that compares the leadership styles and effectiveness of men and women. Participants complete surveys that include their name (first and last), their gender, and a detailed assessment of their leadership approach and impact. If participants leave the gender question blank, I have to impute the value to include them in the research. In one recent study of 66,000 managers, 11,000 (17%) were missing a value for gender.

To remedy the situation, I employed the following rational process. First, I cross-tabulated first name with gender. Some first names were associated with males, some with females, and some with both. For example, *William* appeared 417 times and was always a male. Conversely, the name *Chris* appeared 237 times but was sometimes a male (86%) and sometimes a female (14%). If a first name appeared more than 20 times in the dataset and was always associated with males or with females (but never both), I assumed that the name represented a single gender. I used this assumption to create a gender-lookup table for gender-specific first names. By using this lookup table for participants with missing gender values, I was able to recover 7,000 cases (63% of the missing responses).

A rational approach typically requires creativity and thoughtfulness, along with a degree of data management skill. Data recovery may be exact (as in the sleep example) or approximate (as in the gender example). In the next section, we'll explore approaches that create complete datasets by removing observations.

18.6 Deleting missing data

The most common approach to missing data is to simply delete them. This usually involves deleting variables (columns) with excessive amounts of missing data and then deleting observations (rows) containing missing data on any of the remaining variables (listwise deletion). A less common alternative is to only delete missing data involved in a particular analysis (e.g., pairwise deletion). Each is described next.

18.6.1 Complete-case analysis (listwise deletion)

In complete-case analysis, only observations containing valid data values on every variable are retained for further analysis. Practically, this involves deleting any row with one or more missing values and is also known as *listwise*, or *case-wise*, *deletion*. Most popular statistical packages employ listwise deletion as the default approach for handling missing data. In fact, it's so common that many analysts carrying out analyses like regression or ANOVA may not even realize that there's a *missing-values problem* to be dealt with!

The function `complete.cases()` can be used to save the cases (rows) of a matrix or data frame without missing data:

```
newdata <- mydata[complete.cases(mydata),]
```

The same result can be accomplished with the `na.omit` function:

```
newdata <- na.omit(mydata)
```

In both statements, any rows that are missing data are deleted from `mydata` before the results are saved to `newdata`.

Suppose you're interested in the correlations among the variables in the sleep study. Applying listwise deletion, you'd delete all mammals with missing data prior to calculating the correlations:

```
> options(digits=1)
> cor(na.omit(sleep))
         BodyWgt BrainWgt NonD Dream Sleep  Span  Gest  Pred  Exp Danger
BodyWgt     1.00     0.96 -0.4 -0.07  -0.3  0.47  0.71  0.10  0.4   0.26
BrainWgt    0.96     1.00 -0.4 -0.07  -0.3  0.63  0.73 -0.02  0.3   0.15
NonD       -0.39    -0.39  1.0  0.52   1.0 -0.37 -0.61 -0.35 -0.6  -0.53
Dream      -0.07    -0.07  0.5  1.00   0.7 -0.27 -0.41 -0.40 -0.5  -0.57
Sleep      -0.34    -0.34  1.0  0.72   1.0 -0.38 -0.61 -0.40 -0.6  -0.60
Span        0.47     0.63 -0.4 -0.27  -0.4  1.00  0.65 -0.17  0.3   0.01
Gest        0.71     0.73 -0.6 -0.41  -0.6  0.65  1.00  0.09  0.6   0.31
Pred        0.10    -0.02 -0.4 -0.40  -0.4 -0.17  0.09  1.00  0.6   0.93
Exp         0.41     0.32 -0.6 -0.50  -0.6  0.32  0.57  0.63  1.0   0.79
Danger      0.26     0.15 -0.5 -0.57  -0.6  0.01  0.31  0.93  0.8   1.00
```

The correlations in this table are based solely on the 42 mammals that have complete data on all variables. (Note that the statement `cor(sleep, use="complete.obs")` would have produced the same results.)

If you wanted to study the impact of life span and length of gestation on the amount of dream sleep, you could employ linear regression with listwise deletion:

```
> fit <- lm(Dream ~ Span + Gest, data=na.omit(sleep))
> summary(fit)

Call:
lm(formula = Dream ~ Span + Gest, data = na.omit(sleep))

Residuals:
   Min     1Q Median     3Q    Max
-2.333 -0.915 -0.221  0.382  4.183

Coefficients:
             Estimate Std. Error t value Pr(>|t|)
(Intercept)  2.480122   0.298476    8.31  3.7e-10 ***
Span        -0.000472   0.013130   -0.04    0.971
Gest        -0.004394   0.002081   -2.11    0.041 *
---
Signif. codes:  0 '***' 0.001 '**' 0.01 '*' 0.05 '.' 0.1 ' ' 1

Residual standard error: 1 on 39 degrees of freedom
Multiple R-squared: 0.167,      Adjusted R-squared: 0.125
F-statistic: 3.92 on 2 and 39 DF,  p-value: 0.0282
```

Here, you see that mammals with shorter gestation periods have more dream sleep (controlling for life span) and that life span is unrelated to dream sleep when controlling for gestation period. The analysis is based on 42 cases with complete data.

In the previous example, what would have happened if `data=na.omit(sleep)` had been replaced with `data=sleep`? Like many R functions, `lm()` uses a limited definition of listwise deletion. Cases with any missing data on the variables fitted by the function (Dream, Span, and Gest in this case) would have been deleted. The analysis would have been based on 42 cases.

Listwise deletion assumes that the data are MCAR (that is, the complete observations are a random subsample of the full dataset). In the current example, we've assumed that the 42 mammals used are a random subsample of the 62 mammals collected. To the degree that the MCAR assumption is violated, the resulting regression parameters will be biased. Deleting all observations with missing data can also reduce statistical power by reducing the available sample size. In the current example, listwise deletion reduced the sample size by 32%.

18.6.2 Available case analysis (pairwise deletion)

Pairwise deletion is often considered an alternative to listwise deletion when you're working with datasets that have missing values. In pairwise deletion, observations are deleted only if they're missing data for the variables involved in a specific analysis. Consider the following code:

```
> cor(sleep, use="pairwise.complete.obs")
          BodyWgt BrainWgt NonD Dream Sleep  Span Gest   Pred  Exp Danger
BodyWgt    1.00     0.93  -0.4  -0.1  -0.3   0.30  0.7   0.06  0.3   0.13
BrainWgt   0.93     1.00  -0.4  -0.1  -0.4   0.51  0.7   0.03  0.4   0.15
NonD      -0.38    -0.37   1.0   0.5   1.0  -0.38 -0.6  -0.32 -0.5  -0.48
Dream     -0.11    -0.11   0.5   1.0   0.7  -0.30 -0.5  -0.45 -0.5  -0.58
Sleep     -0.31    -0.36   1.0   0.7   1.0  -0.41 -0.6  -0.40 -0.6  -0.59
Span       0.30     0.51  -0.4  -0.3  -0.4   1.00  0.6  -0.10  0.4   0.06
Gest       0.65     0.75  -0.6  -0.5  -0.6   0.61  1.0   0.20  0.6   0.38
Pred       0.06     0.03  -0.3  -0.4  -0.4  -0.10  0.2   1.00  0.6   0.92
Exp        0.34     0.37  -0.5  -0.5  -0.6   0.36  0.6   0.62  1.0   0.79
Danger     0.13     0.15  -0.5  -0.6  -0.6   0.06  0.4   0.92  0.8   1.00
```

In this example, correlations between any two variables use all available observations for those two variables (ignoring the other variables). The correlation between Body-Wgt and BrainWgt is based on all 62 mammals (the number of mammals with data on both variables). The correlation between Dream and BodyWgt is based on 50 mammals, and the correlation between Dream and NonD is based on 48 mammals.

Although pairwise deletion appears to use all available data, each calculation is in fact based on a different subset of the data. This can lead to distorted and difficult-to-interpret results. I recommend staying away from this approach.

Next, we'll consider an approach that employs the entire dataset (including cases with missing data).

18.7   Single imputation

In *single imputation*, each missing value is replaced by a reasonable alternative value (i.e., a plausible guess). In this section, we'll cover three approaches and describe when to use (or not use) each.

18.7.1 Simple imputation

In *simple imputation*, the missing values in a variable are replaced with a single value (for example, the mean, median, or mode). Using mean substitution, you could replace each missing value on the Dream variable with 1.972 (the mean of the non-missing values).

An advantage of simple imputation is that it solves the missing-values problem without reducing the sample size available for analyses. Because simple imputation is, well, simple, it has become quite popular. However, it produces biased results for data that aren't MCAR. If moderate-to-large amounts of data are missing, simple imputation is likely to underestimate standard errors, distort correlations among variables, and produce incorrect p-values in statistical tests. I recommend avoiding this approach for most missing-data problems.

18.7.2 K-nearest neighbor imputation

The idea behind *k-nearest neighbor imputation* is simple. For an observation with one or more missing values, find the observations that are most similar but have the values, and use these cases to make the imputation.

For example, consider the following observation from the sleep data frame:

```
BodyWgt BrainWgt NonD Dream Sleep Span Gest Pred Exp Danger
   1.41     17.5  4.8   1.3   6.1   34   NA    1   2      1
```

This observation has a missing value on the gestation variable (Gest). To impute this missing value, you could

1 Find the *k* observations in the data frame that are nearest (most similar) to this case, based on the other nine variables.
2 Aggregate the Gest values over these *k* observations. For example, take the mean of the *k* Gest values.
3 Replace the missing value with this aggregated value.

The steps would be repeated for each observation containing missing values.

To use this approach, three questions must be answered. How should we define a nearest neighbor? How many nearest neighbors should we use? How should we aggregate the values?

The kNN() function in the VIM package performs k-nearest neighbor imputation. The defaults follow:

- Nearest neighbors are defined as those cases with the smallest Gower distance (Kowarik and Templ, 2016) to the target observation. Unlike the Euclidean distances described in chapter 16, the Gower distance can be computed for data that contains both quantitative and categorical variables. All available variables are used when defining a nearest neighbor.
- For each observation with missing values, five nearest neighbors are identified.

- The aggregated value for a quantitative missing value is the median of the *k* nearest-neighbor values. For categorical missing values, the mode (most frequently occurring category) is used.

Each of these defaults can be modified by the user. See help(kNN) for details.

An application of kNN imputation for the sleep data frame is provided in the following listing.

Listing 18.2   K-nearest neighbor Imputation for the sleep data frame

```
> library(VIM)
> head(sleep)

  BodyWgt BrainWgt NonD Dream Sleep Span Gest Pred Exp Danger
1 6654.000   5712.0   NA    NA   3.3 38.6  645    3   5      3
2    1.000      6.6  6.3   2.0   8.3  4.5   42    3   1      3
3    3.385     44.5   NA    NA  12.5 14.0   60    1   1      1
4    0.920      5.7   NA    NA  16.5   NA   25    5   2      3
5 2547.000   4603.0  2.1   1.8   3.9 69.0  624    3   5      4
6   10.550    179.5  9.1   0.7   9.8 27.0  180    4   4      4

> sleep_imp <- kNN(sleep, imp_var=FALSE)

> head(sleep_imp)

  BodyWgt BrainWgt NonD Dream Sleep Span Gest Pred Exp Danger
1 6654.000   5712.0  3.2   0.8   3.3 38.6  645    3   5      3
2    1.000      6.6  6.3   2.0   8.3  4.5   42    3   1      3
3    3.385     44.5 12.8   2.4  12.5 14.0   60    1   1      1
4    0.920      5.7 10.4   2.4  16.5  3.2   25    5   2      3
5 2547.000   4603.0  2.1   1.8   3.9 69.0  624    3   5      4
6   10.550    179.5  9.1   0.7   9.8 27.0  180    4   4      4
```

In the sleep_imp data frame, all missing values have been replaced with imputed values. By default, the kNN() function would add 10 new variables to the data frame (BodyWgt_imp, BrainWgt_imp, ... , Danger_imp), coded TRUE/FALSE to indicate which values have been imputed. Setting var_imp=FALSE suppresses these additional variables.

kNN imputation is an excellent option for small-to-moderately sized datasets (say, < 1000 observations). Since a distance is calculated between each observation with missing data and all other observations in the data frame, it does not scale well to larger problems. In that case, the approach described next can be very effective.

18.7.3   *missForest*

For larger data sets, random forests (chapter 17) can be used to impute missing values. If you have p variables $X_1, X_2, ..., X_p$) the steps would be as follows:

1 Replace missing values in each quantitative variable using mean substitution. Replace missing values for each categorical variable using the mode. Keep track of the location of missing values.

2 Return the missing data for variable X_1. Create a training dataset of cases that don't have missing values on this variable. Using the training set, build a random forest model (chapter 17) to predict X_1. Use the model to impute X_1 for the cases with missing X_1 values.

3 Repeat step 2 for variables X_2 through X_p.

4 Repeat steps 2 and 3 until imputed values do not change more than a specified amount.

It's actually easier to perform these operations than to describe them! The `missForest()` function in the `missForest` package can be used. Using the `sleep` data frame, the code is provided in the following listing.

Listing 18.3 Random forest imputation for the `sleep` data frame

```
> library(missForest)
> set.seed(1234)
> sleep_imp <- missForest(sleep)$ximp

  missForest iteration 1 in progress...done!
  missForest iteration 2 in progress...done!
  missForest iteration 3 in progress...done!
  missForest iteration 4 in progress...done!
  missForest iteration 5 in progress...done!
  missForest iteration 6 in progress...done!

> head(sleep_imp)
     BodyWgt BrainWgt      NonD  Dream Sleep    Span Gest Pred Exp Danger
1   6654.000   5712.0  3.391857 1.1825   3.3  38.600  645    3   5      3
2      1.000      6.6  6.300000 2.0000   8.3   4.500   42    3   1      3
3      3.385     44.5 10.758000 2.4300  12.5  14.000   60    1   1      1
4      0.920      5.7 11.572000 2.7020  16.5   7.843   25    5   2      3
5   2547.000   4603.0  2.100000 1.8000   3.9  69.000  624    3   5      4
6     10.550    179.5  9.100000 0.7000   9.8  27.000  180    4   4      4
```

A random number seed is set so that the results are reproducible. In this case, it takes six iterations over the data frame before the imputed values stabilize.

Like the `kNN()` function, the `missForest()` function can work with data that is both quantitative and categorical. The random forest approach requires a moderate-to-large dataset (say, 500+ cases) to avoid issues of overfitting. For smaller datasets, the kNN approach tends to be more effective.

If hypothesis testing is the focus of the analyses, it's a good idea to use an imputation method that takes into account the uncertainty introduced by missing values. Multiple imputation is such an approach.

18.8 *Multiple imputation*

Multiple imputation (MI) provides an approach to missing values that's based on repeated simulations. MI is frequently the method of choice for complex missing-values problems. In MI, a set of complete datasets (typically 3 to 10) is generated from an existing dataset that has missing values. Monte Carlo methods are used to fill in the missing data in each simulated dataset. Standard statistical methods are applied to each simulated dataset, and the outcomes are combined to provide estimated results and confidence intervals that take into account the uncertainty introduced by the missing values. Good implementations are available in R through the `Amelia`, `mice`, and `mi` packages.

In this section, we'll focus on the approach provided by the `mice` (multivariate imputation by chained equations) package. To understand how the `mice` package operates, consider the diagram in figure 18.6.

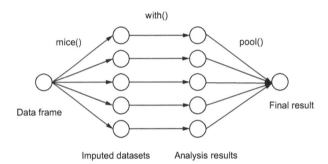

Figure 18.6   Steps in applying multiple imputation to missing data via the `mice` approach

The function `mice()` starts with a data frame that's missing data and returns an object containing several complete datasets (the default is five). Each complete dataset is created by imputing values for the missing data in the original data frame. There's a random component to the imputations, so each complete dataset is slightly different. The `with()` function is then used to apply a statistical model (for example, a linear or generalized linear model) to each complete dataset in turn. Finally, the `pool()` function combines the results of these separate analyses into a single set of results. The standard errors and p-values in this final model correctly reflect the uncertainty produced by both the missing values and the multiple imputations.

How does the mice() function impute missing values?

Missing values are imputed by *Gibbs sampling*. By default, each variable with missing values is predicted from all other variables in the dataset. These prediction equations are used to impute plausible values for the missing data. The process iterates until convergence over the missing values is achieved. For each variable, you can choose the form of the prediction model (called an *elementary imputation method*) and the variables entered into it.

By default, predictive mean matching is used to replace missing data on continuous variables, whereas logistic or polytomous logistic regression is used for target variables that are *dichotomous* (factors with two levels) or *polytomous* (factors with more

> than two levels), respectively. Other elementary imputation methods include Bayesian linear regression, discriminant function analysis, two-level normal imputation, and random sampling from observed values. You can supply your own methods as well.

An analysis based on the `mice` package typically conforms to the following structure:

```
library(mice)
imp <- mice(data, m)
fit <- with(imp, analysis)
pooled <- pool(fit)
summary(pooled)
```

where

- *data* is a matrix or data frame containing missing values.
- `imp` is a list object containing the *m* imputed datasets, along with information on how the imputations were accomplished. By default, *m* = 5.
- *analysis* is a formula object specifying the statistical analysis to be applied to each of the *m* imputed datasets. Examples include `lm()` for linear regression models, `glm()` for generalized linear models, and `gam()` for generalized additive models. Formulas within the parentheses give the response variables on the left of the ~ and the predictor variables (separated by + signs) on the right.
- `fit` is a list object containing the results of the *m* separate statistical analyses.
- `pooled` is a list object containing the averaged results of these *m* statistical analyses.

Let's apply multiple imputation to the `sleep` dataset. You'll repeat the analysis from section 18.6, but this time use all 62 mammals. Set the seed value for the random number generator to 1,234 so that your results will match the following:

```
> library(mice)
> data(sleep, package="VIM")
> imp <- mice(sleep, seed=1234)

 [...output deleted to save space...]

> fit <- with(imp, lm(Dream ~ Span + Gest))
> pooled <- pool(fit)
> summary(pooled)
        term estimate std.error statistic   df  p.value
1 (Intercept)  2.59669   0.24861    10.445 52.0 2.29e-14
2        Span -0.00399   0.01169    -0.342 55.6 7.34e-01
3        Gest -0.00432   0.00146    -2.961 55.2 4.52e-03
```

Here, you see that the regression coefficient for `Span` isn't significant ($p \cong 0.07$), and the coefficient for `Gest` is significant at the $p < 0.01$ level. If you compare these results with those produced by a complete case analysis (section 18.6), you see that you'd come to the same conclusions in this instance. Length of gestation has a (statistically) significant, negative relationship with amount of dream sleep, controlling for life span. Although the complete-case analysis was based on the 42 mammals with complete data, the current analysis is based on information gathered from the full set of 62 mammals.

You can view the imputations by looking at subcomponents of the `imp` object. For example,

```
> imp$imp$Dream
      1   2   3   4   5
1   0.0 0.5 0.5 0.5 0.3
3   0.5 1.4 1.5 1.5 1.3
4   3.6 4.1 3.1 4.1 2.7
14  0.3 1.0 0.5 0.0 0.0
24  3.6 0.8 1.4 1.4 0.9
26  2.4 0.5 3.9 3.4 1.2
30  2.6 0.8 2.4 2.2 3.1
31  0.6 1.3 1.2 1.8 2.1
47  1.3 1.8 1.8 1.8 3.9
53  0.5 0.5 0.6 0.5 0.3
55  2.6 3.6 2.4 1.8 0.5
62  1.5 3.4 3.9 3.4 2.2
```

displays the 5 imputed values for each of the 12 mammals with missing data on the `Dream` variable. A review of these matrices helps you determine whether the imputed values are reasonable. A negative value for length of sleep might give you pause (or nightmares).

You can view each of the *m* imputed datasets via the `complete()` function. The format is

```
complete(imp, action=#)
```

where *#* specifies one of the *m* synthetically complete datasets. For example,

```
> dataset3 <- complete(imp, action=3)
> dataset3
    BodyWgt BrainWgt NonD Dream Sleep  Span  Gest Pred Exp Danger
1  6654.000  5712.00  3.2   0.5   3.3  38.6 645.0    3   5      3
2     1.000     6.60  6.3   2.0   8.3   4.5  42.0    3   1      3
3     3.385    44.50 11.0   1.5  12.5  14.0  60.0    1   1      1
4     0.920     5.70 13.2   3.1  16.5   7.0  25.0    5   2      3
5  2547.000  4603.00  2.1   1.8   3.9  69.0 624.0    3   5      4
6    10.550   179.50  9.1   0.7   9.8  27.0 180.0    4   4      4
[...output deleted to save space...]
```

displays the third (out of five) complete dataset created by the multiple imputation process.

Due to space limitations, we've only briefly considered the MI implementation provided in the `mice` package. The `mi` and `Amelia` packages also contain valuable approaches. If you're interested in the multiple imputation approach to missing data, I recommend the following resources:

- An online book titled *Applied Missing Data Analysis with SPSS and (R)Studio* by Martijn W. Heymans and Iris Eekhout (https://bookdown.org/mwheymans/bookmi/)
- Articles by van Buuren and Groothuis-Oudshoorn (2010) and Yu-Sung, Gelman, Hill, and Yajima (2010)
- "Amelia II: A Program for Missing Data" (http://gking.harvard.edu/amelia)

Each can help reinforce and extend your understanding of this important, but underutilized, methodology.

18.9 Other approaches to missing data

R supports several other approaches for dealing with missing data. Although not as broadly applicable as the methods described thus far, the packages described in table 18.2 offer functions that can be useful in specialized circumstances.

Table 18.2 Specialized methods for dealing with missing data

Package	Description
norm	Maximum-likelihood estimation for multivariate normal data with missing values
cat	Analysis of categorical variable datasets with missing values
longitudinalData	Utility functions, including interpolation routines for imputing missing time-series values
kmi	Kaplan-Meier multiple imputation for survival analysis with missing data
mix	Multiple imputation for mixed categorical and continuous data
pan	Multiple imputation for multivariate panel or clustered data

See the CRAN Task View on Missing Data (https://cran.r-project.org/web/views/MissingData.html) for a review of all the approaches R provides.

Summary

- Statistical methods require complete datasets, but most real-world data contains missing values.
- Function in the VIM and mice packages can be used to explore the distribution of missing values in a dataset.
- Listwise deletion is the most popular method for dealing with missing values and is the default approach for many statistical routines. It can result in loss of power if significant amounts of data are deleted.
- kNN and missForest are excellent methods of imputing missing values. The former works well with small-to-medium-sized datasets, while the latter works well with large datasets.

- Multiple imputation uses simulation to account for the uncertainty that missing values add to statistical inference problems.
- Unless the amount of missing data is very small, simple imputation (e.g., mean substitution) and pairwise deletion should usually be avoided.

Part 5

Expanding your skills

In this final section, we consider advanced topics that will enhance your skills as an R programmer. Chapter 19 completes our discussion of graphics with detailed information on how to customize graphs created with the ggplot2 package. You'll learn to modify a graph's titles, labels, axes, colors, fonts, legends, and more. You'll also learn to combine several graphs into one overall image and turn a static graph into an interactive web graphic.

Chapter 20 reviews the R language at a deeper level. This includes a discussion of R's object-oriented programming features, working with environments, and advanced function writing. Tips for writing efficient code and debugging programs are also given. Although chapter 20 is more technical than the other chapters in this book, it provides extensive practical advice for developing more useful programs.

Chapter 21 is all about report writing. R provides compressive facilities for generating attractive reports dynamically from data. In this chapter, you'll learn how to create reports as web pages, PDF documents, and word processor documents (including Microsoft Word documents).

Throughout this book, you've used packages to get work done. In chapter 22, you'll learn to write your *own* packages. This can help you organize and document your work, create more complex and comprehensive software solutions, and share your creations with others. Sharing a useful package of functions with others can also be a wonderful way to give back to the R community (while spreading your fame far and wide).

After completing part 5, you'll have a much deeper appreciation of how R works and the tools it offers for creating more sophisticated graphics, software, and reports.

Advanced graphs

19

This chapter covers

- Customizing `ggplot2` graphs
- Adding annotations
- Combining multiple graphs into a single plot
- Creating interactive graphs

There are many ways to create a graph in R. We've focused on the use of `ggplot2` because of its coherent grammar, flexibility, and comprehensiveness. The `ggplot2` package was introduced in chapter 4, with coverage of geoms, scales, facets, and titles. In chapter 6, we created bar charts, pie charts, tree maps, histograms, kernel density plots, box and violin plots, and dot plots. Chapters 8 and 9 covered graphics for regression and ANOVA models. Chapter 11 discussed scatter plots, scatter plot matrices, bubble plots, line charts, corrgrams, and mosaic charts. Other chapters have covered graphs to visualize the topics at hand.

This chapter will continue the coverage of `ggplot2`, but with a focus on customization—creating a graph that precisely meet your needs. Graphs help you uncover patterns and describe trends, relationships, differences, compositions, and distributions in data. The primary reason to customize a `ggplot2` graph is to enhance your ability to explore the data or communicate your findings to others. A secondary goal is to meet the look-and-feel requirements of an organization or publisher.

In this chapter, we'll explore the use `ggplot2` scale functions to customize axes and colors. We will use the `theme()` function to customize a graph's overall look and feel, including the appearance of text, legends, grid lines, and plot background. Geoms will be used to add annotations such as reference lines and labels. Additionally, the `patchwork` package will be used to combine several plots into one complete graph. Finally, the `plotly` package will be used to convert static `ggplot2` graphs into interactive web graphics that let you explore the data more fully.

The `ggplot2` package has an enormous number of options for customizing graph elements. The `theme()` function alone has over 90 arguments! Here, we'll focus on the most frequently used functions and arguments. If you're reading this chapter in greyscale, I encourage you to run the code so you can see the graphs in color. Simple datasets are used so that you can focus on the code itself.

At this point, you should already have the `ggplot2` and `dplyr` packages installed. Before continuing, you'll need several additional packages, including `ISLR` and `gapminder` for data, and `ggrepel`, `showtext`, `patchwork`, and `plotly` for enhanced graphing. You can install them all using `install.packages(c("ISLR", "gapminder", "scales", "showtext", "ggrepel", "patchwork", "plotly"))`.

19.1 *Modifying scales*

The scale functions in `ggplot2` control the mapping of variable values to specific plot characteristics. For example, the `scale_x_continuous()` function creates a mapping of the values of a quantitative variable to positions along the *x*-axis. The `scale_color_discrete()` function creates a mapping between the values of a categorical variable and a color value. In this section, you'll use scale functions to customize a graph's axes and plot colors.

19.1.1 *Customizing axes*

In `ggplot2`, the *x*- and *y*-axes in a graph are controlled with the `scale_x_*` and `scale_y_*` functions, where `*` specifies the type of scale. Table 19.1 lists the most common functions. The primary reason for customizing these axes is to make the data easier to read or make trends more obvious.

Table 19.1 Functions that specify axis scales

Function	Description
`scale_x_continuous`, `scale_y_continuous`	Scales for continuous data
`scale_x_binned`, `scale_y_binned`	Scales for binning continuous data

Table 19.1 Functions that specify axis scales *(continued)*

Function	Description
`scale_x_discrete,` `scale_y_discrete`	Scales for discrete (categorical) data
`scale_x_log10, scale_y_log10`	Scales for continuous data on a logarithmic scale (base 10)
`scale_x_date, scale_y_date`	Scales for date data. Other variants include datetime and time.

CUSTOMIZING AXES FOR CONTINUOUS VARIABLES

In the first example, we'll use the `mtcars` data frame, a dataset with car characteristics for 32 automobiles. The `mtcars` data frame is included in base R. Let's plot fuel efficiency (mpg) by automobile weight (wt) in 1000 pounds:

```
library(ggplot2)
ggplot(data = mtcars, aes(x = wt, y = mpg)) +
  geom_point() +
  labs(title = "Fuel efficiency by car weight")
```

Figure 19.1 shows the graph. By default, major breaks are labeled. For mpg, these occur at positions 10 to 35 in 5-point intervals. Minor breaks occur evenly between major breaks and are not labeled.

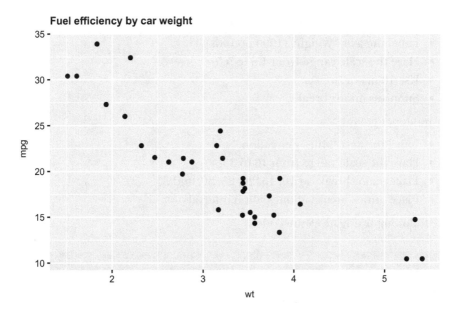

Figure 19.1 Default `ggplot2` scatter plot of miles per gallon by car weight (1000 pounds) for the 32 automobiles in the `mtcars` dataset

What's the weight of the heaviest car in this plot? What's the `mpg` for the third-lightest car? It takes some work to determine the values from these axes. We may want to tweak the *x*- and *y*-axes to make reading the values off the plot easier.

Since `wt` and `mpg` are continuous variables, we'll use the `scale_x_continuous()` and `scale_y_continuous()` functions to modify the axes. Table 19.2 lists common options for these functions.

Table 19.2   Some common `scale_*_continuous` options

Argument	Description
name	Name of the scale. Same as using the `labs(x = , y = )` function.
breaks	Numeric vector of positions for major breaks. Major breaks are labeled automatically unless overridden by the `labels` option. Use `NULL` to suppress breaks.
minor_breaks	Numeric vector of positions for minor tick marks. Minor breaks are not labeled. Use `NULL` to suppress minor breaks.
n.breaks	Integer guiding the number of major breaks. The number is taken as a suggestion. The function may vary this number to ensure attractive break labels.
labels	Character vector giving alternative break labels (must be same length as breaks)
limits	Numeric vector of length 2 giving minimum and maximum value
position	Axis placement (left/right for *y*-axis, top/bottom for *x*-axis)

Let's make the following changes. For weight,

- Label the axis "Weight (1000 pounds)."
- Have the scale range from 1.5 to 5.5.
- Use 10 major breaks.
- Suppress minor breaks.

For miles per gallon,

- Label the axis "Miles per gallon."
- Have the scale range from 10 to 35.
- Place major breaks at 10, 15, 20, 25, 30, and 35.
- Place minor breaks at one-gallon intervals.

The following listing gives the code.

Listing 19.1   Plot of fuel efficiency by car weight with customized axes

```
library(ggplot2)
ggplot(mtcars, aes(x = wt, y = mpg)) +
  geom_point() +
  scale_x_continuous(name = "Weight (1000 lbs.)",
                     n.breaks = 10,
                     minor_breaks = NULL,
                     limits = c(1.5, 5.5)) +
```

Modifies *x*-axis

```
scale_y_continuous(name = "Miles per gallon",
                   breaks = seq(10, 35, 5),
                   minor_breaks = seq(10, 35, 1),
                   limits = c(10, 35)) +
labs(title = "Fuel efficiency by car weight")
```

Modifies *y*-axis

Figure 19.2 shows the new graph. We can see that the heaviest car is almost 5.5 tons, and that the third-lightest car gets 34 miles per gallon. Notice that you specified 10 major breaks for wt, but the plot only has 9. The n.breaks argument is taken as a suggestion. The argument may be replaced with a close number if it gives nicer labels. We'll continue to work with this graph later.

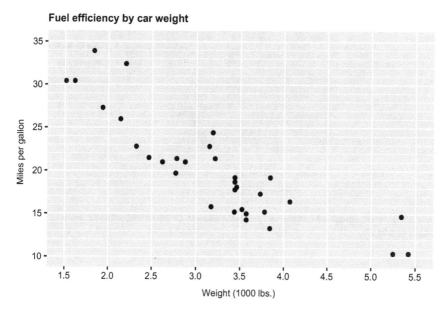

Figure 19.2 ggplot2 scatter plot of miles per gallon by car weight (1000 pounds) with modified x- and y-axes. It is now easier to read off the values of the points.

CUSTOMIZING AXES FOR CATEGORICAL VARIABLES

The previous example involved customizing axes for continuous variables. In the next example, you'll customize the axes for categorical variables. The data comes from the Wage data frame in the ISLR package. The data frame contains wage and demographic information on 3000 male workers in the mid Atlantic region of the United States collected in 2011. Let's plot the relationship between race and education in this sample. The code is

```
library(ISLR)
library(ggplot2)
ggplot(Wage, aes(race, fill = education)) +
```

```
geom_bar(position = "fill") +
labs(title = "Participant Education by Race")
```

and figure 19.3 shows the graph.

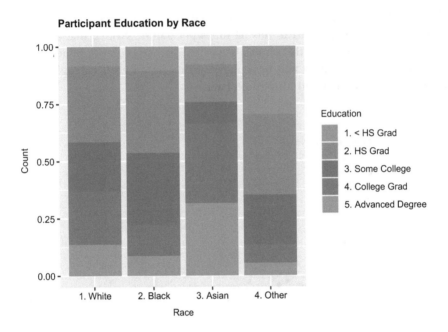

Figure 19.3 Participant education by race for a sample of 3000 mid Atlantic male workers in 2011

Note that the numbering on the race and education labels is actually coded in the data:

```
> head(Wage[c("race", "education")], 4)
           race         education
231655 1. White    1. < HS Grad
86582  1. White 4. College Grad
161300 1. White 3. Some College
155159 3. Asian 4. College Grad
```

We can improve the graph by removing the numbers from the race category labels (they aren't ordinal categories), using percent formatting on the *y*-axis, using better scale labels, and reordering the race categories by percent with higher degrees. You may also want to drop the Race: Other category since the composition of this group is unknown.

Modifying scales for categorical variables involve using `scale_*_discrete()` functions. Table 19.3 lists common options. You can order (and/or omit) the discrete values using the `limits` argument and change their labels using the `labels` argument.

Table 19.3 Some common `scale_*_discrete` **options**

Argument	Description
name	Name of the scale. Same as using the `labs(x = , y = )` function.
breaks	A character vector of breaks
limits	A character vector that defines the values of the scale and their order
labels	A character vector giving the labels (must be same length as breaks). Using `labels=abbreviate` will shorten long labels.
position	Axis placement (left/right for *y*-axis, top/bottom for *x*-axis)

The following listing gives the revised code, and figure 19.4 presents the graph.

Listing 19.2 Plot of education by race with customized axes

```
library(ISLR)
library(ggplot2)
library(scales)
ggplot(Wage, aes(race, fill=education)) +
  geom_bar(position="fill") +
  scale_x_discrete(name = "",
                   limits = c("3. Asian", "1. White", "2. Black"),    Modifies x-axis
                   labels = c("Asian", "White", "Black")) +
  scale_y_continuous(name = "Percent",
                     label = percent_format(accuracy=2),    Modifies y-axis
                     n.breaks=10) +
  labs(title="Participant Education by Race")
```

The horizontal axis represents a categorical variable, so it's customized using the `scale_x_discrete()` function. The race categories are reordered using `limits` and relabeled using `labels`. The Other category is omitted from the graph by leaving it out of these specifications. The axis title is dropped by setting the name to "".

The vertical axis represents a numeric variable, so it's customized using the `scale_y_continuous()` function. The function is used to modify the axis title and change the axis labels. The `percent_format()` function from the `scales` package reformats the axis labels to percents. The argument `accuracy=2` specifies the number of significant digits to print for each percent.

The `scales` package can be very useful for formatting axes. There are options for formatting monetary values, dates, percents, commas, scientific notation, and more. See https://scales.r-lib.org/ for details. The `ggh4x` and `ggprism` packages provide additional capabilities for customizing axes, including greater customization of major and minor tick marks.

In the previous example, education was represented on a discrete color scale. We'll consider customizing colors next.

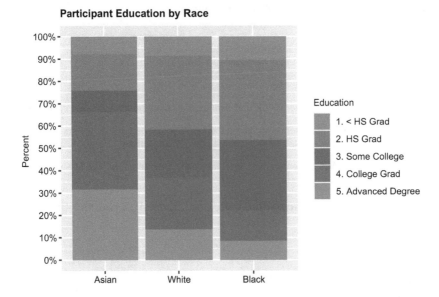

Figure 19.4   Participant education by race for a sample of 3000 mid Atlantic male workers in 2011. The race categories have been rearranged and relabeled. The Other category has been omitted. The x-axis label has been omitted, and the y-axis is now formatted as percentages.

19.1.2 *Customizing colors*

The ggplot2 package provides functions for mapping both categorical and numeric variables to color schemes. Table 19.4 describes the functions. The scale_color_*() functions are used for points, lines, borders, and text. The scale_fill_*() functions are used for objects that have area, such as rectangles, and ovals.

Color palettes can be *sequential, diverging,* or *qualitative.* Sequential palettes are used to map colors to a monotonic numeric variable. A diverging palette is used for numeric variables that have a meaningful middle or zero point. It's two sequential palettes that share an endpoint at the central value. For example, a diverging palette is often used to represent the values of correlation coefficients (see section 11.3). A qualitative color scale maps the values of a categorical variable to discrete colors.

Table 19.4   Functions for specifying color scales

Function	Description
scale_color_gradient() scale_fill_gradient()	Gradient color scale for a continuous variable. Specify the low color and the high color. Use the *_gradient2() versions to specify low, mid, and high colors.
scale_color_steps() scale_fill_steps()	Binned gradient color scale for a continuous variable. Specify the low color and the high color. Use the *_steps2() versions to specify low, mid, and high colors.

Table 19.4 Functions for specifying color scales *(continued)*

Function	Description
`scale_color_brewer()` `scale_fill_brewer()`	Sequential, diverging, and qualitative color schemes from ColorBrewer (https://colorbrewer2.org). Primary argument is `palette=`. See `?scale_color_brewer` for a list of palettes.
`scale_color_grey()` `scale_fill_gray()`	Sequential grey color scale. Optional arguments are `start` (grey value at the low end) and `end` (grey value at the high end). The defaults are 0.2 and 0.8, respectively.
`scale_color_manual()` `scale_fill_manual()`	Create your own color scale for a discrete variable by specifying a vector of colors in the values argument.
`scale_color_virdis_*` `scale_fill_virdis_*`	Viridis color scales from `viridisLite` package. Designed to be perceived by viewers with common forms of color blindness and prints well in black and white. Use `*_d` for discrete, `*_c` for continuous, and `*_b` for binned scales. For example, `scale_fill_viridis_d()` would provide safe color fills for a discrete variable. The argument `option` provides four color scheme variations (`"inferno"`, `"plasma"`, `"viridis"` (the default), and `"cividis"`).

CONTINUOUS COLOR PALETTES

Let's look at examples of mapping a continuous quantitative variable to a color palette. In figure 19.1, fuel efficiency was plotted against car weight. We'll add a third variable to the plot by mapping engine displacement to point color. Since engine displacement is a numeric variable, you create a color gradient to represent its values. The following listing demonstrates several possibilities.

Listing 19.3 Color gradients for continuous variables

```
library(ggplot2)
p <- ggplot(mtcars, aes(x=wt, y=mpg, color=disp)) +
  geom_point(shape=19, size=3) +
  scale_x_continuous(name = "Weight (1000 lbs.)",
                     n.breaks = 10,
                     minor_breaks = NULL,
                     limits=c(1.5, 5.5)) +
  scale_y_continuous(name = "Miles per gallon",
                     breaks = seq(10, 35, 5),
                     minor_breaks = seq(10, 35, 1),
                     limits = c(10, 35))

p + ggtitle("A. Default color gradient")

p + scale_color_gradient(low="grey", high="black") +
  ggtitle("B. Greyscale gradient")

p + scale_color_gradient(low="red", high="blue") +
  ggtitle("C. Red-blue color gradient")

p + scale_color_steps(low="red", high="blue") +
  ggtitle("D. Red-blue binned color Gradient")
```

```
p + scale_color_steps2(low="red", mid="white", high="blue",
                                  midpoint=median(mtcars$disp)) +
  ggtitle("E. Red-white-blue binned gradient")

p + scale_color_viridis_c(direction = -1) +
  ggtitle("F. Viridis color gradient")
```

The code creates the plots in figure 19.5. The `ggtitle()` function is equivalent to
the `labs(title=)` used elsewhere in this book. If you are reading a greyscale version
of this book, be sure to run the code yourself so that you can appreciate the color
variations.

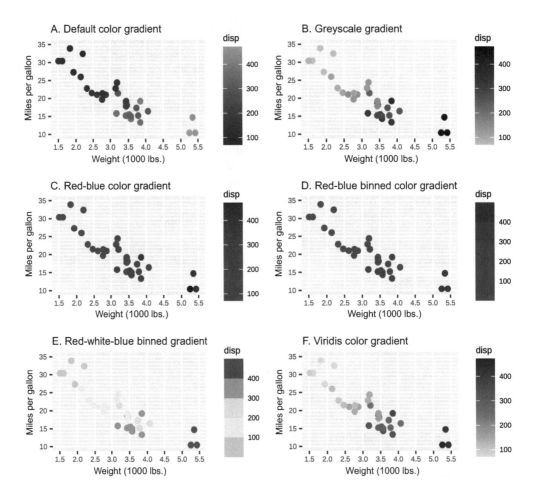

Figure 19.5   **Plot of fuel efficiency by car weight. Color is used to represent engine displacement. Six
color schemes are presented. A is the default. B is greyscale. Both C and D go from red to blue, but D is
binned into five discrete colors. E goes from red to white (at the median) to blue. F uses a Viridis color
scheme. In each graph, engine displacement increases with car weight and lower gas mileage.**

Plot A uses the `ggplot2` default. Plot B shows the plot in greyscale. Plots C and D use a red to blue gradient. A binned color gradient takes a continuous gradient and divides it up into discrete values (usually five). Plot E demonstrates a divergent color gradient, moving from red (low) to white (midpoint) to blue (high). Finally, Plot F shows a Viridis color gradient. The option `direction = -1` in Plot F reverses the color anchors, leading to darker colors for greater engine displacement.

QUALITATIVE COLOR PALETTES

The following listing demonstrates qualitative color schemes. Here `education` is the categorical variable mapped to discrete colors. Figure 19.6 provides the resulting graphs.

> **Listing 19.4 Color schemes for categorical variables**

```
library(ISLR)
library(ggplot2)
p <- ggplot(Wage, aes(race, fill=education)) +
  geom_bar(position="fill") +
  scale_y_continuous("Percent", label=scales::percent_format(accuracy=2),
                     n.breaks=10) +
  scale_x_discrete("",
                   limits=c("3. Asian", "1. White", "2. Black"),
                   labels=c("Asian", "White", "Black"))

p + ggtitle("A. Default colors")

p + scale_fill_brewer(palette="Set2") +
    ggtitle("B. ColorBrewer Set2 palette")

p + scale_fill_viridis_d() +
  ggtitle("C. Viridis color scheme")

p + scale_fill_manual(values=c("gold4", "orange2", "deepskyblue3",
                               "brown2", "yellowgreen")) +
  ggtitle("D. Manual color selection")
```

Plot A uses the `ggplot2` default colors. Plot B uses the ColorBrewer qualitative palette Set2. Other qualitative ColorBrewer palettes include Accent, Dark2, Paired, Pastel1, Pastel2, Set1, and Set3. Plot C demonstrates the default Viridis discrete scheme. Finally, plot D demonstrates a manual scheme, proving that I have no business picking colors on my own.

R packages provide a wide variety of color palettes for use in `ggplot2` graphs. Emil Hvitfeldt has created a comprehensive repository at https://github.com/Emil Hvitfeldt/r-color-palettes (almost 600 at last count!). Choose the scheme that you find appealing and helps communicate the information most effectively. Can the reader easily see the relationships, differences, trends, composition, or outliers that you are trying to highlight?

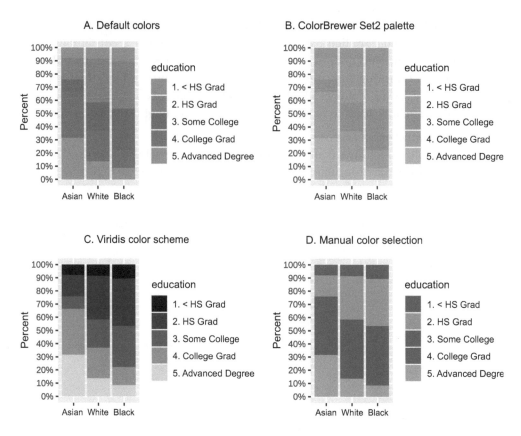

Figure 19.6   Participant education by race for a sample of 3000 mid Atlantic male workers in 2011. Four different color schemes are displayed. A is the default. B and C are preset color schemes. In D, the colors are specified by the user.

19.2   *Modifying themes*

The ggplot2 theme() function allows you to customize the nondata components of your plot. The help for the function (?theme) describes arguments for modifying a graph's titles, labels, fonts, background, gridlines, and legends.

For example, in the code

```
ggplot(mtcars, aes(x = wt, y = mpg)) +
  geom_point()+
  theme(axis.title = element_text(size = 14, color = "blue"))
```

the theme() function renders the *x*- and *y*-axis titles in a 14-point blue font. Functions are typically used to provide the values for theme arguments (see table 19.5).

Table 19.5 Theme elements

Function	Description
element_blank()	Blank-out element (useful for removing text, lines, etc.).
element_rect()	Specify rectangle characteristics. Arguments include fill, color, size, and linetype. The last three refer to the border.
element_line()	Specify line characteristics. Arguments include color, size, linetype, lineend ("round", "butt", "square"), and arrow (created with the grid::arrow() function).
element_text()	Specify text characteristics. Arguments include family (font family), face ("plain", "italic", "bold", "bold.italic"), size (text size in pts.), hjust (horizontal justification in [0,1]), vjust (vertical justification in [0,1]), angle (in degrees), and color.

First, we'll look at some preconfigured themes that change numerous elements at once to provide a cohesive look and feel. Then we'll dive into customizing individual theme elements.

19.2.1 *Prepackaged themes*

The ggplot2 package comes with eight preconfigured themes that can be applied to ggplot2 graphs via theme_*() functions. Listing 19.5 and figure 19.7 show four of

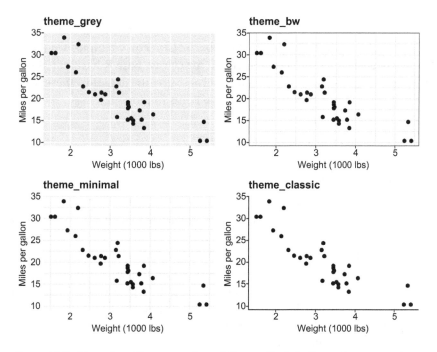

Figure 19.7 Examples of four preconfigured themes. By default, ggplot2 uses theme_grey().

the most popular. The theme_grey() function is the default theme, while theme_void() creates a completely empty theme.

Listing 19.5   Demonstration of four preconfigured ggplot2 themes

```
library(ggplot2)
p <- ggplot(data = mtcars, aes(x = wt, y = mpg)) +
  geom_point() +
  labs(x = "Weight (1000 lbs)",
       y = "Miles per gallon")

p + theme_grey() + labs(title = "theme_grey")
p + theme_bw() + labs(title = "theme_bw")
p + theme_minimal() + labs(title = "theme_minimal")
p + theme_classic() + labs(title = "theme_classic")
```

Additional themes are provided by the ggthemes, hbrthemes, xaringanthemer, tgamtheme, cowplot, tvthemes, and ggdark packages. Each is available from CRAN. Additionally, some organizations provide preconfigured themes to their employees to assure a consistent appearance in reports and presentations.

In addition to preconfigured themes, you can modify individual theme elements. In the following sections, you'll use theme arguments to customize fonts, legends, and other graph elements.

19.2.2 *Customizing fonts*

It is important to use typography to help communicate meaning without distracting or confusing the reader (see http://mng.bz/5Z1q). For example, Google's Roboto and Lora typefaces are often recommended for clarity. Base R has limited native font-handling capabilities. The showtext package greatly expands these capabilities, allowing you to add system fonts and Google Fonts to plots.

The steps are

1 Load local and/or Google fonts.
2 Set showtext as the output graphics device.
3 Specify fonts in the ggplot2 theme() function.

When considering local fonts, the location, number, and type of fonts vary greatly from computer to computer. To use local fonts other than R's defaults, you need to know the names and locations of the font files on your system. Currently supported formats include TrueType fonts (*.ttf, *.ttc) and OpenType fonts (*.otf).

The font_paths() function lists the location of font files, while font_files() list the font files and their characteristics. Listing 19.6 provides a short function for locating font files on your local system. Here the function is used to locate the font files for the Comic Sans MS font. Since the results depend on your system (I'm using a Windows PC), your results are likely to vary.

Listing 19.6   Locating local font files

```
> findfont <- function(x){
    suppressMessages(require(showtext))
    suppressMessages(require(dplyr))
    filter(font_files(), grepl(x, family, ignore.case=TRUE)) %>%
      select(path, file, family, face)
  }

> findfont("comic")

              path         file       family         face
1 C:/Windows/Fonts   comic.ttf Comic Sans MS      Regular
2 C:/Windows/Fonts comicbd.ttf Comic Sans MS         Bold
3 C:/Windows/Fonts  comici.ttf Comic Sans MS       Italic
4 C:/Windows/Fonts  comicz.ttf Comic Sans MS  Bold Italic
```

Once you've located local font files, use `font_add()` to load them. For example, on my machine

```
font_add("comic", regular = "comic.ttf",
         bold = "comicbd.ttf", italic="comici.ttf")
```

makes the Comic Sans MS font available in R under the arbitrary name "comic."

To load Google Fonts (https://fonts.google.com/), use the statement

```
font_add_google(name, family)
```

where *name* is the name of the Google font, and *family* is the arbitrary name you'll use to refer to the font in later code. For example,

```
font_add_google("Schoolbell", "bell")
```

loads the Schoolbell Google Font under the name *bell*.

Once you've loaded the fonts, the statement `showtext_auto()` will set `showtext` as the output device for new graphics.

Finally, use the `theme()` function to indicate which elements of the graph will use which fonts. Table 19.6 lists the theme arguments related to text. You can specify font family, face, size, color, and orientation using `element_text()`.

Table 19.6   `theme()` arguments related to the text

Argument	Description
`axis.title`, `axis.title.x`, `axis.title.y`	Axis titles
`axis.text` with the same variations as `axis.title`	Tick labels along axes
`legend.text`, `legend.title`	Legend item labels and legend title
`plot.title`, `plot.subtitle`, `plot.caption`	Plot title, subtitle, and caption
`strip.text`, `strip.text.x`, `strip.text.y`	Facet labels

The following listing demonstrates customizing a ggplot2 graph with two local fonts from my machine (Comic Sans MS and Caveat) and two Google Fonts (Schoolbell and Gochi Hand). Figure 19.8 displays the graph.

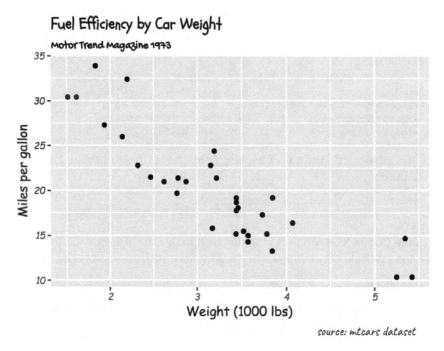

Figure 19.8 Graph using several fonts (Schoolbell for title, Gochi Hand for the subtitle, Caveat for the source, and Comic Sans MS for the axis titles and text)

Listing 19.7   Customizing fonts in a `ggplot2` graph

```
library(ggplot2)
library(showtext)

font_add("comic", regular = "comic.ttf",
         bold = "comicbd.ttf", italic="comici.ttf")       ❶ Loads local
font_add("caveat", regular = "caveat-regular.ttf",           fonts
         bold = "caveat-bold.ttf")

font_add_google("Schoolbell", "bell")        ❷ Loads Google
font_add_google("Gochi Hand", "gochi")          fonts

showtext_auto()                              ⟵┐  Uses showtext as
                                             ❸   the graphic device
ggplot(data = mtcars, aes(x = wt, y = mpg)) +
  geom_point() +
  labs(title = "Fuel Efficiency by Car Weight",
       subtitle = "Motor Trend Magazine 1973",
```

```
       caption = "source: mtcars dataset",
       x = "Weight (1000 lbs)",
       y = "Miles per gallon") +

theme(plot.title    = element_text(family = "bell", size=14),
      plot.subtitle = element_text(family = "gochi"),
      plot.caption  = element_text(family = "caveat", size=15),
      axis.title    = element_text(family = "comic"),
      axis.text     = element_text(family = "comic",
                                   face="italic", size=8))
```

④ **Specifies plot fonts**

Figure 19.8 presents the resulting graph, which is used for demonstrations purposes only. Using several fonts in a single plot is often distracting and takes away from the message the graph was designed to convey. Pick the one or two fonts that best high-light the information and stick with them. A useful starting guide is Tiffany France's *Choosing Fonts for Your Data Visualization* (http://mng.bz/nrY5).

19.2.3 Customizing legends

The ggplot2 package creates legends whenever variables are mapped to color, fill, shape, line type, or size (basically any scaling the does not involve positional scales). You can modify the appearance of a legend using the theme() arguments in table 19.7.

The most frequently used argument is legend.position. Setting the argument to top, right (default), bottom, or left allows you to position the legend on any side of the graph. Alternatively, a two-element numeric vector (*x, y*) positions the leg-end on the *x*- and *y*-axis, with the *x*-coordinate ranging from 0-left to 1-right and the *y*-coordinate ranging from 0-bottom to 1-top.

Table 19.7 theme() arguments related to the plot legend

Argument	Description
legend.background, legend.key	Background of the legend and the legend key (symbols). Specify with element_rect().
legend.title, legend.text	Text characteristics for the legend title and text. Specify values with element_text().
legend.position	Position of the legend. Values are "none", "left", "right", "bottom", "top", or two-element numeric vector (each between 0-left/bottom and 1-right/top).
legend.justification	If legend.postion is set with a two-element numeric vector, legend.justification gives the *anchor point within the legend*, as a two-element vector. For example, if legend.position = c(1, 1) and legend.justification = c(1, 1), the anchor point is the right cor-ner of the legend. This anchor point is placed in the top-right corner of the plot.
legend.direction	Legend direction as "horizontal" or "vertical"
legend.title.align, legend.text.align	Alignment of legend title and text (number from 0-left to 1-right).

Let's create a scatterplot for the mtcars data frame. Place wt on the *x*-axis, mpg on the *y*-axis, and color the points by the number of engine cylinders. Using table 19.7, customize the graph by

- Placing the legend in the upper-right-hand corner of the plot
- Titling the legend "Cylinders"
- Listing the legend categories horizontally rather than vertically
- Setting the legend background to light gray and removing the background around the key elements (the colored symbols)
- Placing a white border around the legend

The following listing provides the code, and figure 19.9 shows the resulting plot.

Listing 19.8   Customizing a plot legend

```
library(ggplot2)
ggplot(mtcars, aes(wt, mpg, color = factor(cyl))) +
        geom_point(size=3) +
  scale_color_discrete(name="Cylinders") +
  labs(title = "Fuel Efficiency for 32 Automobiles",
       x = "Weight (1000 lbs)",
       y = "Miles per gallon") +
  theme(legend.position = c(.95, .95),
        legend.justification = c(1, 1),
        legend.background = element_rect(fill = "lightgrey",
                                         color = "white",
                                         size = 1),
        legend.key = element_blank(),
        legend.direction = "horizontal")
```

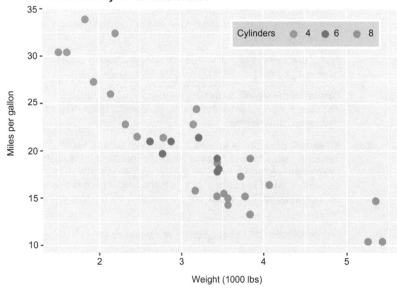

Figure 19.9   Plot with a customized legend. The upper-right corner of the legend is placed in the upper-left corner of the plot. The legend is printed horizontally, with a grey background, a solid white border, and a title.

Again, this graph is provided for demonstration purposes. It's actually easier to relate the legend to the graph if it's placed on the right side and vertical (the default in this case). See *Data Visualization Standards* (http://mng.bz/6m15) for recommendations regarding legend formatting.

19.2.4 Customizing the plot area

The theme() arguments in table 19.8 allow you to customize the plot area. The most common changes are the background color and major and minor grid lines. Listing 19.9 demonstrates customizing many features of the plot area for a faceted scatterplot. Figure 19.10 presents the resulting graph.

Table 19.8 theme() **arguments related to plot area**

Argument	Description
plot.background	Background of the entire plot. Specify with element_rect().
plot.margin	Margin around entire plot. Use units() function with sizes for top, right, bottom, and left margins.
panel.background	Background for plotting area. Specify with element_rect().
strip.background	Background of the facet strip label
panel.grid, panel.grid.major, panel.grid.minor, panel.grid.major.x panel.grid.major.y panel.grid.minor.x panel.grid.minor.y	Grid lines, major grid lines, minor grid lines, or specific major or minor grid lines. Specify with element_line().
axis.line, axis.line.x, axis.line.y, axis.line.x.top, axis.line.x.bottom, axis.line.y.left, axis.line.y.right	Lines along the axes (axis.line), the lines for each plane (axis.line.x, axis.line.y), or individual lines for each axis (axis.line.x.bottom, etc.). Specify with element_line().

Listing 19.9 Customizing the plot area

```
library(ggplot2)
mtcars$am <- factor(mtcars$am, labels = c("Automatic", "Manual"))
ggplot(data=mtcars, aes(x = disp, y = mpg)) +            ❶ Grouped
  geom_point(aes(color=factor(cyl)), size=2) +               scatterplot
  geom_smooth(method="lm", formula = y ~ x + I(x^2),
              linetype="dotted", se=FALSE) +          ❷ Fits line    ❸ Faceting
  scale_color_discrete("Number of cylinders") +
  facet_wrap(~am, ncol=2) +
  labs(title = "Mileage, transmission type, and number of cylinders",
       x = "Engine displacement (cu. in.)",
       y = "Miles per gallon") +                ❹ Sets black-white
  theme_bw() +                                       theme      ❺ Modify
  theme(strip.background = element_rect(fill = "white"),          theme
        panel.grid.major = element_line(color="lightgrey"),
```

```
panel.grid.minor = element_line(color="lightgrey",
                                linetype="dashed"),
axis.ticks = element_blank(),
legend.position = "top",
legend.key = element_blank())
```

The code creates a graph with engine displacement (disp) on the *x*-axis and miles per gallon (mpg) on the *y*-axis. The number of cylinders (cyl) and transmission type (am) are originally coded as numeric but are converted to factors for plotting. For cyl, converting to a factor assures a single color for each number of cylinders. For am, this provides better labels than 0 and 1.

A scatterplot is created with enlarged points, colored by number of cylinders ❶. A quadratic line of best fit is then added ❷. A quadratic fit line allows for a line with one bend (see section 8.2.3). A faceted plot for each transmission type is then added ❸.

To modify the theme, we started with theme_bw() ❹ and then modified it with the theme() function ❺. The strip background color is set to white. Major grid lines are set to solid light grey, and minor grid lines are set to dashed light grey. Axis tick marks are removed. Finally, the legend is placed at the top of the graph and the legend keys (symbols) are given a blank background.

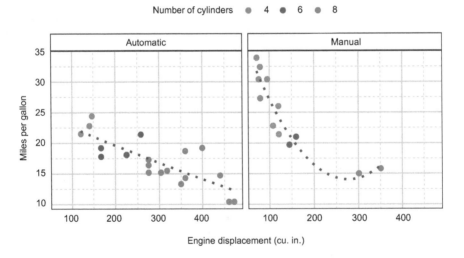

Figure 19.10   Faceted scatter plot with fit lines. The final theme is based on a modified version of the black-and-white theme.

19.3   *Adding annotations*

Annotations allow you to add additional information to a graph, making it easier for the reader to discern relationships, distributions, or unusual observations. The most common annotations are reference lines and text labels. The functions for adding these annotations are listed in table 19.9.

Table 19.9 Functions for adding annotations

Function	Description
`geom_text, geom_label`	`geom_text()` adds text to a plot. `geom_label()` is similar, but draws a rectangle around the text.
`geom_text_repel, geom_label_repel`	These are functions from the `ggrepel` package. They are similar to `geom_text()` and `geom_label()`, but avoid overlapping text.
`geom_hline, geom_vline, geom_abline`	Adds horizontal, vertical, and diagonal reference lines
`geom_rect`	Adds rectangles to the graph. Useful for highlighting areas of the plot.

LABELING POINTS

In figure 19.1, we plotted the relationship between car weight (`wt`) and fuel efficiency (`mpg`). However, the reader can't determine which cars are represented by which points without reference to the original dataset. The following listing adds this information to the plot. Figure 19.11 displays the graph.

Listing 19.10 Scatter plot with labeled points

```
library(ggplot2)
ggplot(data = mtcars, aes(x = wt, y = mpg)) +
  geom_point(color = "steelblue") +
  geom_text(label = row.names(mtcars)) +
  labs(title = "Fuel efficiency by car weight",
       x = "Weight (1000 lbs)",
       y = "Miles per gallon")
```

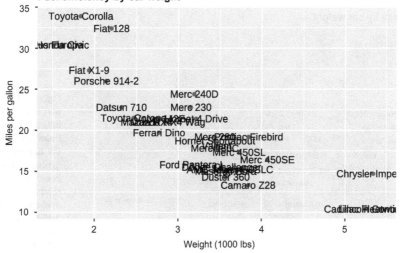

Figure 19.11 Scatterplot of car weight by miles per gallon. Points are labeled with car names.

The resulting graph is difficult to read due to overlapping text. The `ggrepel` package addresses this limitation by repositioning text labels to avoid overlaps. We'll recreate the graph using this package to label the points. Additionally, we'll add a reference line and label indicating the median MPG. The following listing gives the code, and figure 19.12 shows the graph.

Listing 19.11   Scatter plot with labeled points using `ggrepel`

```
library(ggplot2)
library(ggrepel)
ggplot(data = mtcars, aes(x= wt, y = mpg)) +
  geom_point(color = "steelblue") +
  geom_hline(yintercept = median(mtcars$mpg),
             linetype = "dashed",
             color = "steelblue") +
  geom_label(x = 5.2, y = 20.5,
             label = "median MPG",
             color = "white",
             fill = "steelblue",
             size = 3) +
  geom_text_repel(label = row.names(mtcars), size = 3) +
  labs(title = "Fuel efficiency by car weight",
       x = "Weight (1000 lbs)",
       y = "Miles per gallon")
```

❶ Reference line

❷ Reference line label

❸ Point labels

The reference line indicates which cars are above or below the median miles per gallon ❶. The line is labeled using `geom_label` ❷. The proper placement of the line label (*x*, *y*) takes some experimentation. Finally, the `geom_text_repel()` function is used to label the points ❸. The size of the labels is also decreased from a default of 4 to 3. This graph is much easier to read and interpret.

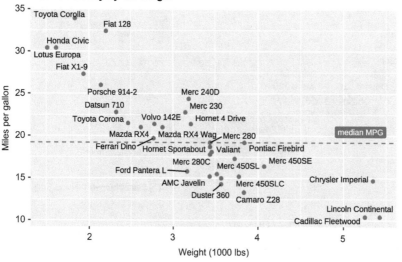

Fuel efficiency by car weight

Figure 19.12   Scatter plot of car weight by miles per gallon. Points are labeled with car names. The `ggrepel` package has been used to reposition labels to avoid overlapping text. Additionally, a reference line and label have been added.

LABELING BARS

Labels can be added to bar charts to clarify the distribution of a categorical variable or the composition of a stacked bar chart. Adding percentage labels to each bar is a two-step process. First, calculate the percentages for each bar. Then create the bar chart using these percentages directly, adding the labels via the geom_text() function. The following listing shows the process. Figure 19.13 displays the graph.

> **Listing 19.12 Adding percent labels to a bar chart**

```
library(ggplot2)
library(dplyr)
library(ISLR)

plotdata <- Wage %>%
  group_by(race) %>%
  summarize(n = n()) %>%
  mutate(pct = n / sum(n),                          ❶ Calculates
         lbls = scales::percent(pct),                  percentages
         race = factor(race, labels = c("White", "Black",
                                        "Asian", "Other")))

plotdata

## # A tibble: 4 x 4
##   race         n     pct lbl
##   <fct>    <int>   <dbl> <chr>
## 1 1. White  2480 0.827   82.7%
## 2 2. Black   293 0.0977  9.8%
## 3 3. Asian   190 0.0633  6.3%
## 4 4. Other    37 0.0123  1.2%

ggplot(data=plotdata, aes(x=race, y=pct)) +           ❷ Adds bars
  geom_bar(stat = "identity", fill="steelblue") +   ◄┐
  geom_text(aes(label = lbls),                        ❸ Adds bar
            vjust = -0.5,                                labels
            size = 3) +
  labs(title = "Participants by Race",
       x = "",
       y="Percent") +
  theme_minimal()
```

The percentages for each race category are calculated ❶, and formatted labels (lbls) are created using the percent() function in the scales package. A bar chart is then created using this summary data ❷. The option stat = "identity" in the geom_bar() function tells ggplot2 to use the *y*-values (bar heights) provided, rather than calculating them. The geom_text() function is then used to print the bar labels ❸. The vjust = -0.5 parameter raises the text slightly above the bar.

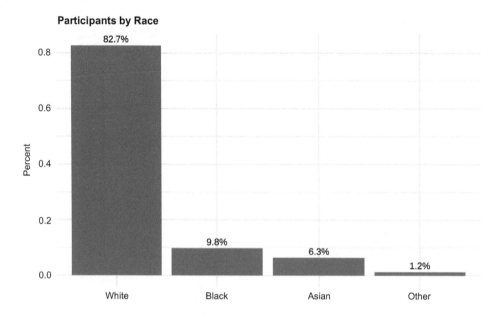

Figure 19.13   Simple bar chart with percent labels

You can also add percentage labels to stacked bar charts. In the following listing, the filled bar chart from figure 19.4 is reproduced with added percent labels. Figure 19.14 shows the final plot.

Listing 19.13   Adding percent labels to a stacked (filled) bar chart

```
library(ggplot2)
library(dplyr)
library(ISLR)

plotdata <- Wage %>%
  group_by(race, education) %>%          ❶ Calculates
  summarize(n = n()) %>%                     percentages
  mutate(pct = n/sum(n),
         lbl = scales::percent(pct))

ggplot(plotdata, aes(x=race, y=pct, fill=education)) +
  geom_bar(stat = "identity",
           position="fill",
           color="lightgrey") +
  scale_y_continuous("Percent",
                     label=scales::percent_format(accuracy=2),
                     n.breaks=10) +                                    ❷ Customizes
  scale_x_discrete("",                                                   y- and x-axes
                   limits=c("3. Asian", "1. White", "2. Black"),
                   labels=c("Asian", "White", "Black")) +
```

```
geom_text(aes(label = lbl),
          size=3,
          position = position_stack(vjust = 0.5)) +
labs(title="Participant Education by Race",
     fill = "Education") +
theme_minimal() +
theme(panel.grid.major.x=element_blank())
```

❸ **Adds percent labels**

❹ **Customizes theme**

This code is similar to the previous code. The percentages for each race by education combination are calculated ❶, and the bar charts are produced using these percentages. The *x*- and *y*-axes are customized to match listing 19.2 ❷. Next, the geom_text() function is used to add the percent labels ❸. The position_stack() function assures that the percentages for each stack segment are placed properly. Finally, the plot and fill titles are specified, and a minimal theme ❹ is chosen without *x*-axis grid lines (they aren't needed).

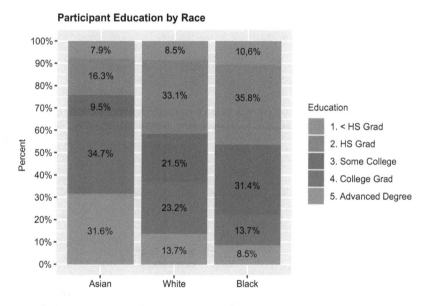

Figure 19.14 Stacked (filled) bar chart with percent labels

HIGHLIGHTING DETAILS

A final example demonstrates the use of annotation to highlight information in a complex graph. The gapminder data frame in the gapminder package contains the average annual life expectancy for 142 countries recorded every 5 years from 1952 to 2002. Life expectancy in Cambodia differs greatly from other Asian countries in this dataset. Let's create a graph that highlights these differences. Listing 19.14 gives the code, and figure 19.15 shows the results.

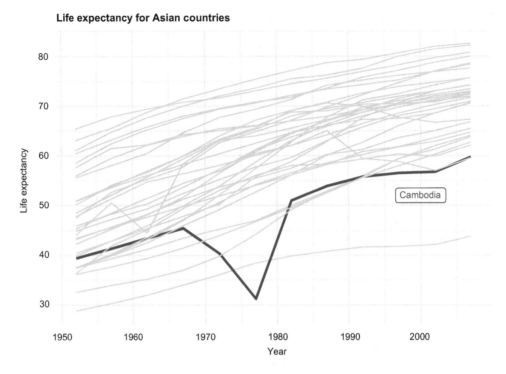

Figure 19.15 Average life expectancy trends for 33 Asian countries. The trend for Cambodia is highlighted. Although the trend is positive for each country, Cambodia had a sharp decline from 1967 to 1977.

Listing 19.14   Highlighting one trend among many

```
library(ggplot2)
library(dplyr)
library(gapminder)
plotdata <- gapminder %>%                    ❶ Subsets Asian
  filter(continent == "Asia")                   countries

plotdata$highlight <- ifelse(plotdata$country %in%      ❷ Creates indicator
                      c("Cambodia"), "y", "n")             variable for Cambodia

ggplot(plotdata, aes(x = year, y = lifeExp,
                     group = country,
                     size = highlight,
                     color = highlight)) +          ❸ Visually highlights
  scale_color_manual(values=c("lightgrey", "red")) +    Cambodia
  scale_size_manual(values=c(.5, 1)) +
  geom_line() +
  geom_label(x=2000, y= 52, label="Cambodia",      ❹ Adds an annotation
          color="red", size=3) +                       label
  labs(title="Life expectancy for Asian countries",
     x="Year",
```

```
        y="Life expectancy") +
    theme_minimal() +
    theme(legend.position="none",
        text=element_text(size=10))
```

First, the data is subset to include only Asian countries **❶**. Next, a binary variable is created to indicate Cambodia versus other countries **❷**. Life expectancy is plotted against year, and a separate line is plotted for each country **❸**. The Cambodian line is thicker than those of other countries and is colored red. All other country lines are colored light grey. A label for the Cambodian line is added **❹**. Finally, plot and axis labels are specified, and a minimal theme is added. The legends (size, color) are suppressed (they aren't needed), and the base text size is decreased.

Looking at the graph, it is clear that average life expectancy has increased for each country. But the trend for Cambodia is quite different, with a major decline between 1967 and 1977. This is likely due to the genocide Pol Pot and the Khmer Rouge carried out during that period.

19.4 Combining graphs

Combining related `ggplot2` graphs into a single overall graph can often help emphasize relationships and differences. I used this when creating several plots in the text (see figure 19.7, for an example). The `patchwork` package provides a simple yet powerful language for combining plots. To use it, save each `ggplot2` graph as an object. Then use the vertical bar (|) operator to combine graphs horizontally and the forward slash (/) operator to combine graphs vertically. You can use parentheses () to create subgroups of graphs. Figure 19.16 demonstrates various plot arrangements.

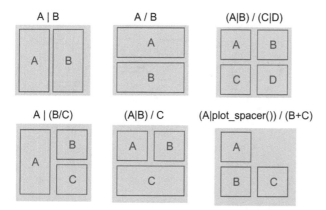

Figure 19.16 The `patchwork` package provides a simple set of arithmetic symbols for arranging multiple graphs in a single plot.

Let's create several `mpg`-related plots from the `mtcars` data frame and combine them into a single graph. The following listing gives the code, and figure 19.17 displays the graph.

Listing 19.15   Combining graphs using the `patchwork` package

```
library(ggplot2)
library(patchwork)

p1 <- ggplot(mtcars, aes(disp, mpg)) +
  geom_point() +
  labs(x="Engine displacement",
       y="Miles per gallon")

p2 <- ggplot(mtcars, aes(factor(cyl), mpg)) +
  geom_boxplot() +
  labs(x="Number of cylinders",
       y="Miles per gallon")

p3 <- ggplot(mtcars, aes(mpg)) +
  geom_histogram(bins=8, fill="darkgrey", color="white") +
  labs(x = "Miles per gallon",
       y = "Frequency")

(p1 | p2) / p3 +
  plot_annotation(title = 'Fuel Efficiency Data') &
  theme_minimal() +
  theme(axis.title = element_text(síze=8),
        axis.text = element_text(size=8))
```

❶ Three graphs are created.

❷ The graphs are combined into one plot.

Three separate graphs are created and saved as p1, p2, and p3 ❶. The code `(p1 | p2)/p3` indicates that the first two plots should be placed in the first row and the third plot should take up the entire second row ❷.

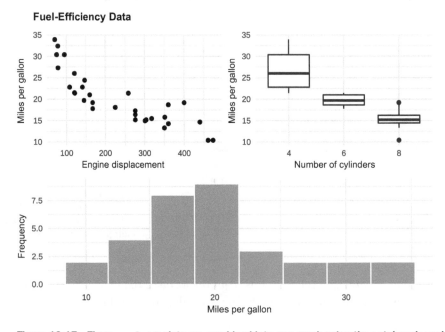

Figure 19.17   Three `ggplot2` plots are combined into one graph using the patchwork package.

The resulting graph is also a `ggplot2` graph and can be edited. The `plot_annota-tion()` function adds a title to the combined graph (rather than to one of the sub-plots). Finally, the theme is modified. Note the use of the ampersand (`&`) to add theme elements. If you had used a plus (`+`) sign, the changes would only apply to the *last* subplot (`p3`). The `&` sign indicates that the theme functions should apply to each subplot (`p1`, `p2`, and `p3`).

The `patchwork` package has many additional options. To learn more, see the package reference site (https://patchwork.data-imaginist.com/).

19.5 *Making graphs interactive*

With few exceptions, the graphs in this book have been static images. There are several reasons for creating *interactive graphs*. They allow you to focus on interesting results and call up additional information to understand patterns, trends, and unusual observations. Additionally, they're often more engaging than static graphs.

Several packages in R can be used to create interactive visualizations, including `leaflet`, `rbokeh`, `rCharts`, `highlighter`, and `plotly`. In this section, we'll focus on `plotly`.

The *Plotly R Open Source Graphing Library* (https://plotly.com/r/) can be used to create high-end interactive visualizations. A key advantage is its ability to convert a static `ggplot2` graph into an interactive web graphic.

Creating an interactive graph using the `plotly` package is an easy two-step process. First, save a `ggplot2` graph as an object. Then pass the object to the `ggplotly()` function.

In listing 19.16, a scatterplot between miles per gallon and engine displacement is created using `ggplot2`. The points are colored to represent the number of engine cylinders. The plot is then passed to the `ggplotly()` function in the `plotly` package, producing an interactive web-based visualization. Figure 19.18 provides a screenshot.

> **Listing 19.16 Converting a `ggplot2` graph to an interactive `plotly` graph**

```
library(ggplot2)
library(plotly)
mtcars$cyl <- factor(mtcars$cyl)
mtcars$name <- row.names(mtcars)

p <- ggplot(mtcars, aes(x = disp, y= mpg, color = cyl)) +
  geom_point()
ggplotly(p)
```

When you mouse over the graph, a toolbar will appear on the top right-hand side of the plot that allows you to zoom, pan, select areas, download an image, and more (see figure 19.19). Additionally, tooltips will pop up when the mouse cursor move over the plot area. By default, the tooltip displays the variable values use to create the graph (`disp`, `mpg`, and `cyl` in this example). Additionally, clicking on a key (symbol) in the legend will toggle that data on and off. This allows you to easily focus on subsets of the data.

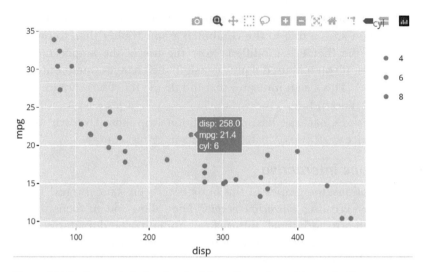

Figure 19.18 Screenshot of a `plotly` interactive web graphic created from a static `ggplot2` graph

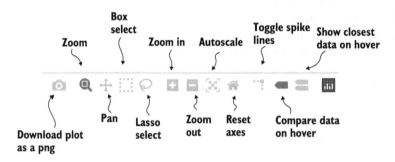

Figure 19.19 The `plotly` graph toolbar. The easiest way to understand these tools is to try them out one at a time.

There are two simple ways to customize the tooltip. You can add additional variables to the tooltip by including `label1 = var1`, `label2 = var2`, etc., in the `ggplot` `aes()` function. For example,

```
p <- ggplot(mtcars, aes(x = disp, y= mpg, color = cyl,
                        label1 = gear, label2 = am))) +
  geom_point()
ggplotly(p)
```

will create a tooltip with `disp`, `mpg`, `cyl`, `gear`, and `am`.

Alternatively, you can use an undocumented `text` argument in the `aes()` function to build the tooltip from an arbitrary text string. The following listing gives an example, and figure 19.20 provides a screenshot of the result.

Listing 19.17 Customizing the `plotly` tooltip

```
library(ggplot2)
library(plotly)
mtcars$cyl <- factor(mtcars$cyl)
mtcars$name <- row.names(mtcars)

p <- ggplot(mtcars,
            aes(x = disp, y=mpg, color=cyl,
                text = paste(name, "\n",
                            "mpg:", mpg, "\n",
                            "disp:", disp, "\n",
                            "cyl:", cyl, "\n",
                            "gear:", gear))) +
  geom_point()
ggplotly(p, tooltip=c("text"))
```

The `text` approach gives you great control over the tooltip. You can even include HTML markup in the text string, allowing you customize the text output further.

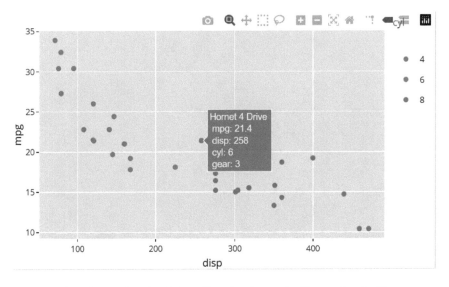

Figure 19.20 Screenshot of an interactive `plotly` graph with a custom tooltip created from within the `ggplot2` code

This chapter has covered various methods for customizing `ggplot2` graphs. Remember that the goal of customization is to enhance your insight into the data and improve communication of those insights to others. Anything added to a graph that detracts from these goals is mere decoration (also known as chart junk). Always try to avoid chart junk! See *Data Visualization Standards* (https://xdgov.github.io/data-design-standards/) for additional recommendations.

Summary

- The `ggplot2` scale functions map variable values to visual aspects of a graph. They are particularly useful for customizing the axes and color palette.
- The `ggplot2 theme()` function controls nondata elements of the graph. It is useful for customizing the appearance of fonts, legends, grid lines, and the plot background.
- The `ggplot2 geom` functions are useful for annotating a graph by adding useful information, such as reference lines and labels.
- Two or more graphs can be combined into a single graph using the `patchwork` package.
- Almost any `ggplot2` graph can be converted from a static image to an interactive web graphic using the `plotly` package.

Advanced programming

This chapter covers

- Diving deeper into the R language
- Using R's OOP features to create generic functions
- Tweaking code to run more efficiently
- Finding and correcting programming errors

Previous chapters introduced various topics that are important for application development, including data types (section 2.2), control flow (section 5.4), and function creation (section 5.5). This chapter will review these aspects of R as a programming language from a more advanced and detailed perspective. By the end of this chapter, you'll have a better idea of how the R language works, which will help you create your own functions, and ultimately, your own packages.

We'll start with a review of objects, data types, and control flow before moving on to details of function creation, including the role of scope and environments. The chapter introduces R's approach to object-oriented programming and discusses the creation of generic functions. Finally, we'll go over tips for writing efficient code-generating and debugging applications. Mastery of these topics will help you understand the code in other people's applications and aid you in creating new applications. In chapter 22, you'll have an opportunity to put these skills into practice by creating a useful package from start to finish.

20.1 A review of the language

R is an object-oriented, functional, array-oriented programming language in which objects are specialized data structures, stored in RAM, and accessed via names or symbols. Names of objects consist of uppercase and lowercase letters, the digits 0–9, the period, and the underscore. Names are case sensitive and can't start with a digit, and a period is treated as a simple character without special meaning.

Unlike in languages such as C and C++, you can't access memory locations directly. Data, functions, and just about everything else that can be stored and named are objects. Additionally, the names and symbols themselves are objects that can be manipulated. All objects are stored in RAM during program execution, which has significant implications for the analysis of massive datasets.

Every object has attributes: meta-information that describes the characteristics of the object. Attributes can be listed with the `attributes()` function and set with the `attr()` function. A key attribute is an object's class. R functions use information about an object's class to determine how the object should be handled. The class of an object can be read and set with the `class()` function. Examples will be given throughout this chapter and the next.

20.1.1 Data types

There are two fundamental data types: atomic vectors and generic vectors. Atomic vectors are arrays that contain a single data type. Generic vectors, also called lists, are collections of atomic vectors. Lists are recursive in that they can also contain other lists. This section considers both types in some detail.

Unlike many other programming languages, you don't have to declare an object's data type or allocate space for it. The type is determined implicitly from the object's contents, and the size grows or shrinks automatically depending on the type and number of elements the object contains.

ATOMIC VECTORS

Atomic vectors are arrays that contain a single data type (logical, real, complex, character, or raw). For example, each of the following is a one-dimensional atomic vector:

```
passed <- c(TRUE, TRUE, FALSE, TRUE)
ages <- c(15, 18, 25, 14, 19)
cmplxNums <- c(1+2i, 0+1i, 39+3i, 12+2i)
names <- c("Bob", "Ted", "Carol", "Alice")
```

Vectors of type *raw* hold raw bytes and aren't discussed here.

Many R data types are atomic vectors with special attributes. For example, R doesn't have a scalar type. A scalar is an atomic vector with a single element. So, `k <- 2` is a shortcut for `k <- c(2)`.

A matrix is an atomic vector that has a dimension attribute, dim, containing two elements (number of rows and number of columns). For example, start with a one-dimensional numeric vector x:

```
> x <- c(1,2,3,4,5,6,7,8)
> class(x)
[1] "numeric"
> print(x)
{1] 1 2 3 4 5 6 7 8
```

Then add a dim attribute:

```
> attr(x, "dim") <- c(2,4)
```

The object x is now a 2 × 3 matrix of class matrix:

```
> print(x)
     [,1] [,2] [,3] [,4]
[1,]    1    3    5    7
[2,]    2    4    6    8
> class(x)
[1] "matrix" "array"
> attributes(x)
$dim
[1] 2 2
```

Row and column names can be attached by adding a dimnames attribute:

```
> attr(x, "dimnames") <- list(c("A1", "A2"),
                                c("B1", "B2", "B3", "B4"))
> print(x)
   B1 B2 B3 B4
A1  1  3  5  7
A2  2  4  6  8
```

Finally, the matrix can be returned to a one-dimensional vector by removing the dim attribute:

```
> attr(x, "dim") <- NULL
> class(x)
[1] "numeric"
> print(x)
[1] 1 2 3 4 5 6 7 8
```

An array is an atomic vector with a dim attribute that has three or more elements. Again, you set the dimensions with the dim attribute, and you can attach labels with the dimnames attribute. Like one-dimensional vectors, matrices and arrays can be logical, numeric, character, complex, or raw types. But you can't mix types in a single matrix or array.

The attr() function allows you to create arbitrary attributes and associate them with an object. Attributes store additional information about an object and can be used by functions to determine how they're processed.

There are a number of special functions for setting attributes, including `dim()`, `dimnames()`, `names()`, `row.names()`, `class()`, and `tsp()`. The latter is used to create time series objects. These special functions have restrictions on the values that can be set. Unless you're creating custom attributes, it's always a good idea to use these special functions. Their restrictions and the error messages they produce make coding errors less likely and more obvious.

GENERIC VECTORS OR LISTS

Lists are collections of atomic vectors and/or other lists. Data frames are a special type of list in which each atomic vector in the collection has the same length. Consider the `iris` data frame that comes with the base R installation. It describes four physical measures taken on each of 150 plants, along with their species (setosa, versicolor, or virginica):

```
> head(iris)
  Sepal.Length Sepal.Width Petal.Length Petal.Width Species
1          5.1         3.5          1.4         0.2  setosa
2          4.9         3.0          1.4         0.2  setosa
3          4.7         3.2          1.3         0.2  setosa
4          4.6         3.1          1.5         0.2  setosa
5          5.0         3.6          1.4         0.2  setosa
6          5.4         3.9          1.7         0.4  setosa
```

This data frame is actually a list containing five atomic vectors. It has a `names` attribute (a character vector of variable names), a `row.names` attribute (a numeric vector identifying individual plants), and a `class` attribute with the value `"data.frame"`. Each vector represents a column (variable) in the data frame. This can be easily seen by printing the data frame with the `unclass()` function and obtaining the attributes with the `attributes()` function:

```
unclass(iris)
attributes(iris)
```

The output is omitted here to save space.

It's important to understand lists because R functions frequently return them as values. Let's look at an example using a cluster analysis technique from chapter 16. Cluster analysis uses a family of methods to identify naturally occurring groupings of observations.

Let's apply k-means cluster analysis (section 16.4.1) to the `iris` data. Assume that there are three clusters present in the data, and observe how the observations (rows) become grouped. We'll ignore the species variable and use only the physical measures of each plant to form the clusters. The required code is

```
set.seed(1234)
fit <- kmeans(iris[1:4], 3)
```

What information is contained in the object `fit`? The help page for `kmeans()` indicates that the function returns a list with seven components. The `str()` function displays the object's structure, and the `unclass()` function can be used to examine the object's contents directly. The `length()` function indicates how many components the object contains, and the `names()` function provides the names of these components. You can use the `attributes()` function to examine the attributes of the object. The contents of the object returned by `kmeans()` are explored here:

```
> names(fit)
[1] "cluster"      "centers"      "totss"        "withinss"
[5] "tot.withinss" "betweenss"    "size"         "iter"
[9] "ifault"

> unclass(fit)
$cluster
  [1] 1 1 1 1 1 1 1 1 1 1 1 1 1 1 1 1 1 1 1 1 1 1 1 1 1 1 1 1
 [29] 1 1 1 1 1 1 1 1 1 1 1 1 1 1 1 1 1 1 1 1 1 1 2 2 3 2 2 2
 [57] 2 2 2 2 2 2 2 2 2 2 2 2 2 2 2 2 2 2 2 2 3 2 2 2 2 2 2 2
 [85] 2 2 2 2 2 2 2 2 2 2 2 2 2 2 3 2 3 3 3 3 2 3 3 3 3 3 3 3
[113] 3 2 2 3 3 3 3 2 3 2 3 2 3 3 3 2 2 3 3 3 3 3 2 3 3 3 3 2 3
[141] 3 3 2 3 3 3 2 3 3 2

$centers
  Sepal.Length Sepal.Width Petal.Length Petal.Width
1        5.006       3.428        1.462       0.246
2        5.902       2.748        4.394       1.434
3        6.850       3.074        5.742       2.071

$totss
[1] 681.4

$withinss
[1] 15.15 39.82 23.88

$tot.withinss
[1] 78.85

$betweenss
[1] 602.5

$size
[1] 50 62 38

$iter
[1] 2

$ifault
[1] 0
```

Executing `sapply(fit, class)` returns the class of each component in the object:

```
> sapply(fit, class)
      cluster       centers         totss      withinss  tot.withinss
    "integer"      "matrix"     "numeric"     "numeric"     "numeric"
    betweenss          size          iter        ifault
    "numeric"     "integer"     "integer"     "integer"
```

In this example, `cluster` is an integer vector containing the cluster memberships, and `centers` is a matrix containing the cluster centroids (means on each variable for each cluster). The `size` component is an integer vector containing the number of plants in each of the three clusters. To learn about the other components, see the Value section of `help(kmeans)`.

INDEXING

Learning to unpack the information in a list is a critical R programming skill. The elements of any data object can be extracted via indexing. Before diving into a list, let's look at extracting elements from an atomic vector.

Elements are extracted using *object*[*index*], where *object* is the vector and *index* is an integer vector. If the elements of the atomic vector have been named, *index* can also be a character vector with these names. Note that in R, indices start with 1, not 0 as in many other languages.

Here is an example, using this approach for an atomic vector without named elements:

```
> x <- c(20, 30, 40)
> x[3]
[1] 40
> x[c(2,3)]
[1] 30 40
```

For an atomic vector with named elements, you could use

```
> x <- c(A=20, B=30, C=40)
> x[c(2,3)]
 B  C
30 40
> x[c("B", "C")]
 B  C
30 40
```

For lists, components (atomic vectors or other lists) can be extracted using *object*[*index*], where *index* is an integer vector. If the components are named, you can use a character vector of names.

Continuing the k-means example,

```
>fit[c(2, 7)]
$centers
  Sepal.Length Sepal.Width Petal.Length Petal.Width
1     5.006000    3.428000     1.462000    0.246000
2     5.901613    2.748387     4.393548    1.433871
3     6.850000    3.073684     5.742105    2.071053

$size
[1] 50 62 38
```

returns a two-component list (cluster means and cluster sizes). Each component contains a matrix.

It is important to note that using single brackets to subset a list always returns a list. For example,

```
>fit[2]
$centers
  Sepal.Length Sepal.Width Petal.Length Petal.Width
1     5.006000    3.428000     1.462000    0.246000
2     5.901613    2.748387     4.393548    1.433871
3     6.850000    3.073684     5.742105    2.071053
```

returns a one-component list, not a matrix. To extract the *contents* of a component, use *object*[[*index*]]. For example,

```
> fit[[2]]
  Sepal.Length Sepal.Width Petal.Length Petal.Width
1        5.006       3.428        1.462       0.246
2        5.902       2.748        4.394       1.434
3        6.850       3.074        5.742       2.071
```

returns a matrix. The difference can be important, depending on what you do with the results. If you want to pass the results to a function that requires a matrix as input, you want to use the double-bracket notation.

To extract the contents of a single named component, you can use the $ notation. In this case, `object[["name"]]` and `object$name` are equivalent:

```
> fit$centers
  Sepal.Length Sepal.Width Petal.Length Petal.Width
1        5.006       3.428        1.462       0.246
2        5.902       2.748        4.394       1.434
3        6.850       3.074        5.742       2.071
```

This also explains why the $ notation works with data frames. Consider the `iris` data frame. The data frame is a special case of a list, where each variable is represented as a component. For example, `iris$Sepal.Length` is equivalent to `iris[["Sepal.Length"]]`, and returns the 150-element vector of sepal lengths.

Notations can be combined to obtain the elements within components. For example,

```
> fit[[2]][1, ]
Sepal.Length  Sepal.Width Petal.Length  Petal.Width
       5.006        3.428        1.462        0.246
```

extracts the second component of `fit` (a matrix of means) and returns the first row (the means for the first cluster on each of the four variables). The blank after the comma in the final square brackets indicates that all four columns are to be returned.

By extracting the components and elements of lists returned by functions, you can take the results and go further. For example, to plot the cluster centroids with a line graph, you can use the code in the following listing.

Listing 20.1   Plotting the centroids from a k-means cluster analysis

```
> set.seed(1234)
> fit <- kmeans(iris[1:4], 3)
> means <- fit$center                        ❶ Obtains the
> means <- as.data.frame(means)                 cluster means
> means$cluster <- row.names(means)

> library(tidyr)
> plotdata <- gather(means,
                  key="variable",            ❷ Reshapes
                  value="value",                the data to
                  -cluster)                     long form
> names(plotdata) <- c("Cluster", "Measurement", "Centimeters")
> head(plotdata)

  Cluster  Measurement Centimeters
1       1 Sepal.Length       5.006
2       2 Sepal.Length       5.902
3       3 Sepal.Length       6.850
4       1  Sepal.Width       3.428
5       2  Sepal.Width       2.748
6       3  Sepal.Width       3.074

library(ggplot2)
ggplot(data=plotdata,
       aes(x=Measurement, y=Centimeters, group=Cluster)) +
       geom_point(size=3, aes(shape=Cluster, color=Cluster)) +   ❸ Plots a line
       geom_line(size=1, aes(color=Cluster)) +                      graph
       labs(title="Mean Profiles for Iris Clusters") +
       theme_minimal()
```

First, the matrix of cluster centroids is extracted (rows are clusters, and columns are variable means) and converted to a data frame. Cluster number is added as an additional variable ❶. The data frame is then reshaped into long format using the `tidyr` package (see section 5.5.2) ❷. Finally, the data is plotted using the `ggplot2` package ❸. Figure 20.1 displays the resulting graph.

This type of graph is possible because all the plotted variables have the same units of measurement (centimeters). If the cluster analysis involved variables on different scales, you must standardize the data before plotting and label the *y*-axis something like standardized scores. See section 16.1 for details.

Now that you can represent data in structures and unpack the results, let's look at flow control.

20.1.2   *Control structures*

When the R interpreter processes code, it reads sequentially, line by line. If a line isn't a complete statement, it reads additional lines until a fully formed statement can be constructed. For example, if you wanted to add 3 + 2 + 5,

```
> 3 + 2 + 5
[1] 10
```

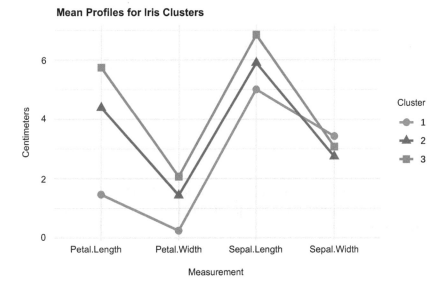

Mean Profiles for Iris Clusters

Figure 20.1   A plot of the centroids (means) for three clusters extracted from the iris dataset using k-means clustering

will work. So will

```
> 3 + 2 +
  5
[1] 10
```

The + sign at the end of the first line indicates that the statement isn't complete. But

```
> 3 + 2
[1] 5
> + 5
[1] 5
```

obviously doesn't work, because 3 + 2 is interpreted as a complete statement.

Sometimes, you need to process code nonsequentially. You may want to execute code conditionally or repeat one or more statements multiple times. This section describes three control-flow functions that are particularly useful in writing functions: `for()`, `if()`, and `ifelse()`.

FOR LOOPS

The `for()` function allows you to execute a statement repeatedly. The syntax is

```
for(var in seq){
    statements
}
```

where `var` is a variable name and `seq` is an expression that evaluates to a vector. If there is only one statement, the curly braces are optional:

```
> for(i in 1:5) print(1:i)
[1] 1
[1] 1 2
[1] 1 2 3
[1] 1 2 3 4
[1] 1 2 3 4 5

> for(i in 5:1)print(1:i)
[1] 1 2 3 4 5
[1] 1 2 3 4
[1] 1 2 3
[1] 1 2
[1] 1
```

Note that var continues to exist after the function exits. Here, i equals 1.

In the previous examples, the seq parameter was a numeric vector. It can also be a character vector. For example,

```
> vars <- c("mpg", "disp", "hp", "wt")
> for(i in vars) hist(mtcars[[i]])
```

would create four histograms.

IF() AND ELSE

The if() function allows you to execute statements conditionally. The syntax for the if() construct is

```
if(condition){
    statements
} else {
    statements
}
```

The condition should be a one-element logical vector (TRUE or FALSE) and can't be missing (NA). The else portion is optional. If there is only one statement, the curly braces are also optional.

As an example, consider the following code fragment:

```
if(interactive()){
    plot(x, y)
} else {
    png("myplot.png")
    plot(x, y)
    dev.off()
}
```

If the code is being run interactively, the interactive() function returns TRUE and a plot is sent to the screen. Otherwise, the plot is saved to disk. You'll use the if() function extensively in chapter 22.

IFELSE()

The ifelse() function is a vectorized version of if(). Vectorization allows a function to process objects without explicit looping. The format of ifelse() is

```
ifelse(test, yes, no)
```

where `test` is an object that has been coerced to logical mode, `yes` returns values for true elements of `test`, and `no` returns values for false elements of `test`.

Let's say that you have a vector of p-values that you have extracted from a statistical analysis that involved six statistical tests, and you want to flag the tests that are significant at the $p < .05$ level. This can be accomplished with the following code:

```
> pvalues <- c(.0867, .0018, .0054, .1572, .0183, .5386)
> results <- ifelse(pvalues <.05, "Significant", "Not Significant")
> results

[1] "Not Significant" "Significant"     "Significant"
[4] "Not Significant" "Significant"     "Not Significant"
```

The `ifelse()` function loops through the vector `pvalues` and returns a character vector containing the value `"Significant"` or `"Not Significant"` depending on whether the corresponding element of `pvalues` is greater than .05.

The same result can be accomplished with explicit loops using

```
pvalues <- c(.0867, .0018, .0054, .1572, .0183, .5386)
results <- vector(mode="character", length=length(pvalues))
for(i in 1:length(pvalues)){
  if (pvalues[i] < .05) results[i] <- "Significant"
  else results[i] <- "Not Significant"
}
```

The vectorized version is faster and more efficient.

There are other control structures, including `while()`, `repeat()`, and `switch()`, but the ones presented here are the most commonly used. Now that you have data structures and control structures, we can talk about creating functions.

20.1.3 Creating functions

Almost everything in R is a function. Even arithmetic operators like +, -, /, and * are actually functions. For example, `2 + 2` is equivalent to `"+"(2, 2)`. This section describes function syntax. Section 20.2 examines scope.

FUNCTION SYNTAX

The syntax of a function is

```
functionname <- function(parameters){
                    statements
                    return(value)
}
```

If there is more than one parameter, they are separated by commas.

Parameters can be passed by keyword, position, or both. Additionally, parameters can have default values. Consider the following function:

```
f <- function(x, y, z=1){
    result <- x + (2*y) + (3*z)
```

```
    return(result)
}

> f(2,3,4)
[1] 20
> f(2,3)
[1] 11
> f(x=2, y=3)
[1] 11
> f(z=4, y=2, 3)
[1] 19
```

In the first case, the parameters are passed by position (x = 2, y = 3, z = 4). In the second case, the parameters are passed by position, and z defaults to 1. In the third case, the parameters are passed by keyword, and z again defaults to 1. In the final case, y and z are passed by keyword, and x is assumed to be the first parameter not explicitly specified (x=3). This also demonstrates that parameters passed by keyword can appear in any order.

Parameters are optional, but you must include the parentheses even if no values are being passed. The return() function returns the object produced by the function. It's also optional, and if it's missing, the results of the last statement in the function are returned.

You can use the args() function to view the parameter names and default values:

```
> args(f)
  function (x, y, z = 1)
  NULL
```

The args() function is designed for interactive viewing. If you need to obtain the parameter names and default values programmatically, use the formals() function, which returns a list with the necessary information.

Parameters are passed by value, not by reference. Consider this function statement:

```
result <- lm(height ~ weight, data=women)
```

The dataset women isn't accessed directly. A copy is made and passed to the function. If the women dataset was very large, RAM could be used up quickly. This can become an issue when you're dealing with *big* data problems, and you may need to use special techniques (see appendix F).

OBJECT SCOPE

The scope of the objects in R (how names are resolved to produce contents) is complex. In the typical case,

- Objects created outside of any function are global (can be resolved within any function). Objects created within a function are local (available only within the function).
- Local objects are discarded at the end of function execution. Only objects passed back via the return() function (or assigned using an operator like <<-) are accessible after the function finishes executing.

- Global objects can be accessed (read) from within a function but not altered (again, unless the << - operator is used).
- Objects passed to a function through parameters aren't altered by the function. Copies of the objects are passed, not the objects themselves.

Here is a simple example:

```
> x <- 2
> y <- 3
> z <- 4
> f <- function(w){
        z <- 2
        x <- w*y*z
        return(x)
  }
> f(x)
[1] 12
> x
[1] 2
> y
[1] 3
> z
[1] 4
```

In this example, a copy of x is passed to the function f(), but the original isn't altered. The value of y is obtained from the environment. Even though z exists in the environment, the value set in the function is used and doesn't alter the value in the environment.

To understand scoping rules better, we need to discuss environments.

20.2 *Working with environments*

An *environment* in R consists of a frame and enclosure. A *frame* is set of symbol-value pairs (object names and their contents), and an *enclosure* is a pointer to an enclosing environment. The enclosing environment is also called the *parent environment*. R allows you to manipulate environments from within the language, resulting in fine-grained control over scope and the segregation of functions and data.

In an interactive session, when you first see the R prompt, you're in the global environment. You can create a new environment with the new.env() function and create assignments in that environment with the assign() function. Object values can be retrieved from an environment using the get() function. Environments are data structures that allow you to control object scope (you can also think of them as places to store objects). Here's an example:

```
> x <- 5
> myenv <- new.env()
> assign("x", "Homer", env=myenv)
> ls()
[1] "myenv" "x"
> ls(myenv)
[1] "x"
```

```
> x
[1] 5
> get("x", env=myenv)
[1] "Homer"
```

An object called x exists in the global environment and has the value 5. An object also called x exists in the environment myenv and has the value "Homer". Using separate environments keep the two objects from being confused.

In addition to using the assign() and get() functions, you can use the $ notation. For example,

```
> myenv <- new.env()
> myenv$x <- "Homer"
> myenv$x
[1] "Homer"
```

produces the same results.

The parent.env() function displays the parent environment. Continuing the example, the parent environment for myenv is the global environment:

```
> parent.env(myenv)
<environment: R_GlobalEnv>
```

The parent environment for the global environment is the empty environment. See help(environment) for details.

Because functions are objects, they also have environments. This is important when considering *function closures* (functions that are packaged with the state that existed when they were created). Consider a function that is created by another function:

```
trim <- function(p){
    trimit <- function(x){
      n <- length(x)
      lo <- floor(n*p) + 1
      hi <- n + 1 - lo
      x <- sort.int(x, partial = unique(c(lo, hi)))[lo:hi]
    }
    trimit
}
```

The trim(p) function returns a function that trims p percent of the high and low values from a vector:

```
> x <- 1:10
> trim10pct <- trim(.1)
> y <- trim10pct(x)
> y
[1] 2 3 4 5 6 7 8 9
> trim20pct <- trim(.2)
> y <- trim20pct(x)
> y
  [1] 3 4 5 6 7 8
```

This works because the value of *p* is in the environment of the `trimit()` function and is saved with the function:

```
> ls(environment(trim10pct))
[1] "p"      "trimit"
> get("p", env=environment(trim10pct))
[1] 0.1
```

The lesson here is that, in R, functions include the objects that existed in their environment when they were created. This fact helps to explain the following behavior:

```
> makeFunction <- function(k){
    f <- function(x){
      print(x + k)
    }
  }

> g <- makeFunction(10)
> g(4)
[1] 14
> k <- 2
> g(5)
[1] 15
```

The `g()` function uses `k=10` no matter what value k has in the global environment, because k equaled 10 when the function was created. Again, you can see this with

```
> ls(environment(g))
[1] "f" "k"
> environment(g)$k
[1] 10
```

In general, the value of an object is obtained from its local environment. If the object isn't found in its local environment, R searches in the parent environment, then the parent's parent environment, and so on, until the object is found. If R reaches the empty environment and still hasn't found the object, it throws an error. This is called *lexical scoping*.

To learn more about environments and lexical scoping, see "Environments in R" by Christopher Bare (http://mng.bz/uPYM) and "Lexical Scope and Function Closures in R" by Darren Wilkinson (http://mng.bz/R286).

20.3 *Non-standard evaluation*

R has a default method for when and how to evaluate expressions. Consider the following example. Create a function named `mystats`:

```
mystats <- function(data, x){
    x <- data[[x]]
    c(n=length(x), mean=mean(x), sd=sd(x))
  }
```

Next, call the function without quoting the value passed to x:

```
> mystats(mtcars, mpg)

 Error in (function(x, i, exact) if (is.matrix(i)) as.matrix(x)[[i]] else
     .subset2(x,   : object 'mpg' not found
```

R is greedy. As soon as you use an expression (name or function) as an argument to a function, R tries to evaluate it. You get the error because R attempts to look up the name mpg and doesn't find it in the workspace (the global environment in this case).

If you quote the value passed to x, the function runs successfully. String literals are simply passed as is (no lookup necessary):

```
> mystats(mtcars, "mpg")
        n       mean         sd
32.000000 20.090625  6.026948
```

This is R's default behavior and is called *standard evaluation (SE)*.

But what if you really like the first way of calling the function? In this case, you could modify the function as follows:

```
mystats <- function(data, x){
   x <- as.character(substitute(x))
   x <- data[[x]]
   c(n=length(x), mean=mean(x), sd=sd(x))
   }
```

The substitute() function passes the object name without evaluating it. The name is then converted to a string by as.character(). Now both

```
> mystats(mtcars, mpg)
        n       mean         sd
32.000000 20.090625  6.026948
```

and

```
> mystats(mtcars, "mpg")
        n       mean         sd
32.000000 20.090625  6.026948
```

work! This is called *non-standard evaluation (NSE)*. The library() function uses NSE, which is why both library(ggplot2) and library("ggplot2") work.

Why use NSE rather than SE? It basically comes down to ease of use. The following two statements are equivalent.

```
df <- mtcars[mtcars$mpg < 20 & mtcars$carb==4,
             c("disp", "hp", "drat", "wt")]

df <- subset(mtcars, mpg < 20 & carb == 4, disp:wt)
```

The first statement uses SE, while the second statement uses NSE. The second statement is easier to type and possibly easier to read. But to make things easier for the user, the programmer must work harder when creating the functions.

Base R has several functions for controlling how and when expressions are evaluated. Tidyverse packages such as `dplyr`, `tidyr`, and `ggplot2` use their own version of NSE called *tidy evaluation*. If you want to include functions from tidyverse in your own functions, you'll have to use the tools automatically provided by the `rlang` package for that purpose.

In particular, you can use the `enquo()` and `!!` to quote and unquote arguments. For example,

```
myscatterplot <- function(data, x, y){
  require(ggplot2)
  x <- enquo(x)
  y <- enquo(y)
  ggplot(data, aes(!!x, !!y)) + geom_point() + geom_smooth()
}

  myscatterplot(mtcars, wt, mpg)
```

works fine. Try it out.

For multiple arguments, use `enquos()` and `!!!` to quote and unquote the values passed to `...`. The 3 dots are a placeholder for one or more arguments (names or expressions) passed to a function:

```
mycorr <- function(data, ..., digits=2){
  require(dplyr)
  vars <- enquos(...)
  data %>% select(!!!vars) %>% cor() %>% round(digits)
}

mycorr(mtcars, mpg, wt, disp, hp)
```

Recent versions of `rlang` provide shortcuts. The previous functions can also be written as

```
myscatterplot <- function(data, x, y){
  require(ggplot2)
  ggplot(data, aes({{x}}, {{y}})) + geom_point() + geom_smooth()
}
mycorr <- function(data, ..., digits=2){
  require(dplyr)
  data %>% select(...) %>% cor() %>% round(digits)
}
```

The two pairs of curly braces and three-dot notation eliminate the need to explicitly use `enquo()` and `enquos()`, but they won't work with versions of `rlang` older than 0.4.0.

R gives the programmer considerable control over how and when code is evaluated. But with great power comes great responsibility (and a dull ache behind the eyes). NSE is a very complex topic, and this section has only touched on elements frequently encountered when writing your own functions. To learn more, see the discussions by Brodie Gaslam (www.brodieg.com/2020/05/05/on-nse/) and Hadley Wickham (http://adv-r.hadley.nz).

20.4   *Object-oriented programming*

R is an *object-oriented programming (OOP)* language that's based on the use of generic functions. Each object has a class attribute that is used to determine what code to run when a copy of the object is passed to a generic function such as `print()`, `plot()`, or `summary()`.

R has several OOP models, including S3, S4, RC, and R6. The S3 model is older, simpler, and less structured. The S4 model is newer and more structured. Both come with base R. The S3 approach is easier to use, and most applications in R use this model. In this section, we'll focus on the S3 model and end with a brief discussion of its limitations and how the S4 attempts to address them. RC and R6 are less widely used and not covered here.

20.4.1 *Generic functions*

R uses the class of an object to determine what action to take when a generic function is called. Consider the following code:

```
summary(women)
fit <- lm(weight ~ height, data=women)
summary(fit)
```

In the first instance, the `summary()` function produces descriptive statistics for each variable in the data frame women. In the second instance, `summary()` produces a description of a linear regression model. How does this happen?

Let's look at the code for `summary()`:

```
> summary
function (object, ...) UseMethod("summary")
```

Now let's look at the class for the women data frame and the `fit` object:

```
> class(women)
[1] "data.frame"
> class(fit)
[1] "lm"
```

The function call `summary(women)` executes the function `summary.data.frame(women)` if it exists, or `summary.default(women)` otherwise. Similarly, `summary(fit)` executes the function `summary.lm(fit)` if it exists, or `summary.default(fit)` otherwise. The `UseMethod()` function dispatches the object to the generic function that has an extension matching the object's class.

To list all S3 generic functions available, use the `methods()` function:

```
> methods(summary)
  [1] summary.aov              summary.aovlist
  [3] summary.aspell*          summary.connection
  [5] summary.data.frame       summary.Date
  [7] summary.default          summary.ecdf*
                 ...output omitted...
 [31] summary.table            summary.tukeysmooth*
 [33] summary.wmc*

   Non-visible functions are asterisked
```

The number of functions returned depends on the packages you have installed on your machine. On my computer, separate summary() functions have been defined for 33 classes!

You can view the code for the functions in the previous example by typing their names without the parentheses (summary.data.frame, summary.lm, and summary .default). Nonvisible functions (functions in the methods list followed by asterisks) can't be viewed this way. In these cases, you can use the getAnywhere() function to view their code. To see the code for summary.ecdf(), type getAnywhere(summary.ecdf). Viewing existing code is a great way to get ideas for your own functions.

You've seen classes such as numeric, matrix, data.frame, array, lm, glm, and table, but the class of an object can be any arbitrary string. Additionally, a generic function doesn't have to be print(), plot(), or summary(). Any function can be generic. The following listing defines a generic function called mymethod().

Listing 20.2   An example of an arbitrary generic function

```
> mymethod <- function(x, ...) UseMethod("mymethod")
> mymethod.a <- function(x) print("Using A")
> mymethod.b <- function(x) print("Using B")
> mymethod.default <- function(x) print("Using Default")

> x <- 1:5
> y <- 6:10
> z <- 10:15
> class(x) <- "a"
> class(y) <- "b"

> mymethod(x)
[1] "Using A"
> mymethod(y)
[1] "Using B"
> mymethod(z)
[1] "Using Default"

> class(z) <- c("a", "b")
> mymethod(z)
[1] "Using A"

> class(z) <- c("c", "a", "b")
> mymethod(z)
[1] "Using A"
```

❶ Defines a generic function

❷ Assigns classes to objects

❸ Applies the generic function to the objects

❹ Applies the generic function to an object with two classes

❺ Generic function has no default for class "c"

In this example, mymethod() generic functions are defined for objects of classes a and b. A default() function is also defined ❶. The objects x, y, and z are then defined, and a class is assigned to x and y ❷. Next, mymethod() is applied to each object, and the appropriate function is called ❸. The default method is used for object z because the object has class integer, and no mymethod.integer() function has been defined.

An object can be assigned to more than one class (for example, building, residential, and commercial). How does R determine which generic function to call in such a case? When z is assigned two classes ❹, the first class is used to determine which generic function to call. In the final example ❺, there is no mymethod.c() function, so the next class in line (a) is used. R searches the class list from left to right, looking for the first available generic function.

20.4.2 *Limitations of the S3 model*

The primary limitation of the S3 object model is the fact that any class can be assigned to any object. There are no integrity checks. In the next example, the data frame women is assigned class lm, which is nonsensical and leads to errors:

```
> class(women) <- "lm"
> summary(women)
Error in if (p == 0) { : argument is of length zero
```

The S4 OOP model is more formal and rigorous and designed to avoid the difficulties raised by the S3 method's less structured approach. In the S4 approach, classes are defined as abstract objects that have slots containing specific types of information (that is, typed variables). Object and method constructions are formally defined, with rules that are enforced. But programming using the S4 model is more complex and restrictive. To learn more about the S4 OOP model, see "A (Not So) Short Introduction to S4" by Chistophe Genolini (http://mng.bz/1VkD).

20.5 *Writing efficient code*

There is a saying among programmers: "A power user is someone who spends an hour tweaking their code so that it runs a second faster." R is a spritely language, and most R users don't have to worry about writing efficient code. The easiest way to make your code run faster is to beef up your hardware (RAM, processor speed, and so on). As a general rule, it's more important to write code that is understandable and easy to maintain than to optimize its speed. But when you're working with large datasets or highly repetitive tasks, speed can become an issue.

Several coding techniques can help to make your programs more efficient:

- Read in only the data you need.
- Use vectorization rather than loops whenever possible.
- Create objects of the correct size rather than resizing repeatedly.
- Use parallelization for repetitive, independent tasks.

Let's look at each one in turn.

20.5.1 *Efficient data input*

When importing data, read only the data you need and provide as much information to the importing function as possible. Additionally, choose an optimized function whenever possible.

Suppose you want to access three numeric variables (age, height, weight), two character variables (race, sex), and one date variable (dob) from a comma-delimited text file containing a large number of variables and rows. The read.csv (base R), fread (data.table package) and read_csv (readr package) functions will all do the job, but the latter two are significantly faster when you're working with large files.

Additionally, you can speed up your code by selecting only the variables necessary and indicating their types (so the function does not have to spend time guessing). For example,

```
library(readr)
mydata <- read_csv(mytextfile,
                col_types=cols_only(age="i", height="d", weight="d",
                                    race="c", sex="c", dob="D"))
```

will run faster than

```
mydata <- read_csv(mytextfile)
```

alone. Here i=integer, d=double, c=character, and D=Date. See ?read_csv for additional variable types.

20.5.2 *Vectorization*

Use vectorization rather than loops whenever possible. Here, *vectorization* means using R functions that are designed to process vectors in a highly optimized manner. Examples in the base installation include ifelse(), colSums(), colMeans(), rowSums(), and rowMeans(). The matrixStats package offers optimized functions for many additional calculations, including counts, sums, products, measures of central tendency and dispersion, quantiles, ranks, and binning. Packages such as dplyr and data.table also provide functions that are highly optimized.

Consider a matrix with 1 million rows and 10 columns. Let's calculate the column sums using loops and again using the colSums() function. First, create the matrix:

```
set.seed(1234)
mymatrix <- matrix(rnorm(10000000), ncol=10)
```

Next, create a function called accum() that uses for loops to obtain the column sums:

```
accum <- function(x){
    sums <- numeric(ncol(x))
    for (i in 1:ncol(x)){
        for(j in 1:nrow(x)){
            sums[i] <- sums[i] + x[j,i]
        }
    }
}
```

The system.time() function can be used to determine the amount of CPU and real time needed to run the function:

```
> system.time(accum(mymatrix))
   user  system elapsed
  25.67    0.01   25.75
```

Calculating the same sums using the `colSums()` function produces

```
> system.time(colSums(mymatrix))
   user  system elapsed
   0.02    0.00    0.02
```

On my machine, the vectorized function ran more than 1,200 times faster. Your mileage may vary.

20.5.3 *Correctly sizing objects*

It's more efficient to initialize objects to their required final size and fill in the values than it is to start with a smaller object and grow it by appending values. Let's say you have a vector x with 100,000 numeric values. You want to obtain a vector y with the squares of these values:

```
> set.seed(1234)
> k <- 100000
 > x <- rnorm(k)
```

One approach is as follows:

```
>  y <- 0
>  system.time(for (i in 1:length(x)) y[i] <- x[i]^2)
   user  system elapsed
   10.03    0.00    10.03
```

y starts as a one-element vector and grows to be a 100,000-element vector containing the squared values of x. It takes about 10 seconds on my machine.

If you first initialize y to be a vector with 100,000 elements,

```
>  y <- numeric(length=k)
>  system.time(for (i in 1:k) y[i] <- x[i]^2)
   user  system elapsed
   0.23    0.00    0.24
```

the same calculations take less than a second. You avoid the considerable time it takes R to continually resize the object.

If you use vectorization,

```
> y <- numeric(length=k)
> system.time(y <- x^2)
   user  system elapsed
      0       0       0
```

the process is even faster. Note that operations like exponentiation, addition, multiplication, and the like are all vectorized functions.

20.5.4 *Parallelization*

Parallelization involves chunking up a task, running the chunks simultaneously on two or more cores, and combining the results. The cores might be on the same computer or on different machines in a cluster. Tasks that require the repeated independent execution of a numerically intensive function are likely to benefit from parallelization. This includes many Monte Carlo methods, including bootstrapping.

Many packages in R support parallelization (see "CRAN Task View: High Performance and Parallel Computing with R" by Dirk Eddelbuettel, http://mng.bz/65sT). In this section, you'll use the foreach and doParallel packages to see parallelization on a single computer. The foreach package supports the foreach looping construct (iterating over the elements in a collection) and facilitates executing loops in parallel. The doParallel package provides a parallel back end for the foreach package.

In principal components and factor analysis, a critical step is identifying the appropriate number of components or factors to extract from the data (see section 14.2.1). One approach involves repeatedly performing an *eigenanalysis* of correlation matrices derived from random data that have the same number of rows and columns as the original data. The following listing shows the analysis, which compares parallel and nonparallel versions. To execute this code, you'll need to install both packages.

Listing 20.3   Parallelization with `foreach` and `doParallel`

```
> library(foreach)                              ❶ Loads packages and registers
> library(doParallel)                              the number of cores
> registerDoParallel(cores=detectCores())

> eig <- function(n, p){
          x <- matrix(rnorm(100000), ncol=100)
          r <- cor(x)                           ❷ Defines the function
          eigen(r)$values
  }

> n <- 1000000
> p <- 100
> k <- 500


> system.time(
    x <- foreach(i=1:k, .combine=rbind) %do% eig(n, p)   ❸ Executes
  )                                                          normally

   user  system elapsed
  10.97    0.14   11.11

> system.time(
    x <- foreach(i=1:k, .combine=rbind) %dopar% eig(n, p)  ❹ Executes
  )                                                           in parallel

   user  system elapsed
   0.22    0.05    4.24
```

First, the packages are loaded, and the number of cores (four on my machine) is registered ❶. Next, the function for the eigenanalysis is defined ❷. Here, $100{,}000 \times 100$ random data matrices are analyzed. The eig() function is executed 500 times using

foreach and %do% ❸. The %do% operator runs the function sequentially, and the
.combine=rbind option appends the results to object x as rows. Finally, the function
is run in parallel using the %dopar% operator ❹. In this case, parallel execution was
about 2.5 times faster than sequential execution.

In this example, each iteration of the eig() function was numerically intensive,
didn't require access to other iterations, and didn't involve disk I/0. This is the type of
situation that benefits most from parallelization. The downside of parallelization is
that it can make the code less portable—there is no guarantee that others will have
the same hardware configuration you do.

The four efficiency measures described in this section can help with everyday coding problems. But they only go so far in helping you to process really large datasets
(for example, those in the terabyte range). When you're working with *big* datasets,
methods like those described in appendix F are required.

Locating bottlenecks

"Why is my code taking so long?" R provides tools for profiling programs to identify
the most time-consuming functions. Place the code to be profiled between Rprof()
and Rprof(NULL). Then execute summaryRprof() to get a summary of the time
spent executing each function. See ?Rprof and ?summaryRprof for details.

Rstudio can also profile your code. Select *Start Profiling* from the RStudio Profile
menu, run your code, and click the red *Stop Profiling* button when finished. The
results are presented in a table and a graph.

Efficiency is little comfort when a program won't execute or gives nonsensical results.
Methods for uncovering programming errors are considered next.

20.6   *Debugging*

Debugging is the process of finding and reducing the number of errors or defects in a
program. It would be wonderful if programs worked the first time. It would also be
wonderful if unicorns lived in my neighborhood. In all but the simplest programs,
errors occur. Determining the cause of these errors and fixing them is time consuming. In this section, we'll look at common sources of errors and tools that can help to
uncover errors.

20.6.1 *Common sources of errors*

The following are some common reasons functions fail in R:

- An object name is misspelled, or the object doesn't exist.
- One or more parameters in the function call are misspecified. This can happen
  if parameter names are misspelled, required parameters are omitted, parameter
  values are the wrong type (e.g., a vector when a list is required), or parameter values are entered in the wrong order (when parameter names are omitted).

- The contents of an object aren't what the user expects. In particular, errors are often caused by passing objects that are NULL or contain NaN or NA values to a function that can't handle them.

The third reason is more common than you may think. It results from R's terse approach to errors and warnings.

Consider the following example. For the mtcars dataset in the base installation, you want to provide the variable am (transmission type) with a more informative title and labels. Next, you want to compare the gas mileage of cars with automatic transmissions to those with manual transmissions:

```
> mtcars$Transmission <- factor(mtcars$a,
                                 levels=c(1,2),
                                 labels=c("Automatic", "Manual"))
> aov(mpg ~ Transmission, data=mtcars)
Error in `contrasts<-`(`*tmp*`, value = contr.funs[1 + isOF[nn]]) :
  contrasts can be applied only to factors with 2 or more levels
```

Yikes! (Embarrassing, but this is actually what I said.) What happened?

You didn't get an "Object xxx not found" error, so you probably didn't misspell a function, data frame, or variable name. Let's look at the data that was passed to the aov() function:

```
> head(mtcars[c("mpg", "Transmission")])
                   mpg Transmission
Mazda RX4          21.0    Automatic
Mazda RX4 Wag      21.0    Automatic
Datsun 710         22.8    Automatic
Hornet 4 Drive     21.4         <NA>
Hornet Sportabout  18.7         <NA>
Valiant            18.1         <NA>

> table(mtcars$Transmission)

Automatic    Manual
       13         0
```

There are no cars with a manual transmission. Looking back at the original dataset, the variable am is coded 0=automatic, 1=manual (not 1=automatic, 2=manual).

The factor() function happily did what you asked without warnings or errors. It set all cars with manual transmissions to automatic and all cars with automatic transmissions to missing. With only one group available, the analysis of variance failed. Confirming that each input to a function contains the expected data can save you hours of frustrating detective work.

20.6.2 *Debugging tools*

Although examining object names, function parameters, and function inputs will uncover many sources of error, sometimes you must delve into the inner workings of functions and functions that call functions. In these cases, the internal debugger that comes with R can be useful. Table 20.1 lists some helpful debugging functions.

Table 20.1   Built-in debugging functions

Function	Action
debug()	Marks a function for debugging
undebug()	Unmarks a function for debugging
browser()	Allows single-stepping through the execution of a function. While you're debugging, typing n or pressing the Enter key executes the current statement and moves on to the next. Typing c continues execution to the end of the function without single-stepping. Typing where displays the call stack, and Q halts execution and jumps to the top level immediately. Other R commands like ls(), print(), and assignment statements can also be submitted at the debugger prompt.
trace()	Modifies a function to allow debug code to be temporarily inserted
untrace()	Cancels tracing and removes the temporary code
traceback()	Prints the sequence of function calls that led to the last uncaught error

The debug() function marks a function for debugging. When the function is executed, the browser() function is called and allows you to step through the function's execution one line at a time. The undebug() function turns this off, allowing the function to execute normally. You can temporarily insert debugging code into a function with the trace() function. This is particularly useful when you're debugging base functions and CRAN-contributed functions that can't be edited directly.

If a function calls other functions, it can be hard to determine where an error has occurred. In this case, executing the traceback() function immediately after an error will list the sequence of function calls that led to the error. The last call is the one that produced the error.

Let's look at an example. The mad() function calculates the median absolute deviation for a numeric vector. You'll use debug() to explore how this function works. The following listing displays the debugging session.

Listing 20.4   A sample debugging session

```
> args(mad)                                              ◁───┐   Views the
function (x, center = median(x), constant = 1.4826,         ❶  formal arguments
    na.rm = FALSE, low = FALSE, high = FALSE)
NULL

> debug(mad)        ◁───┐   Sets the function
> mad(1:10)           ❷  to debug

debugging in: mad(x)
debug: {
    if (na.rm)
        x <- x[!is.na(x)]
    n <- length(x)
    constant * if ((low || high) && n%%2 == 0) {
        if (low && high)
```

```
            stop("'low' and 'high' cannot be both TRUE")
        n2 <- n%/%2 + as.integer(high)
        sort(abs(x - center), partial = n2)[n2]
    }
    else median(abs(x - center))
}
```

❸ Lists objects

```
Browse[2]> ls()
[1] "center"   "constant" "high"     "low"     "na.rm"    "x"

Browse[2]> center
[1] 5.5

Browse[2]> constant
[1] 1.4826

Browse[2]> na.rm
[1] FALSE

Browse[2]> x
 [1]  1  2  3  4  5  6  7  8  9 10
```

❹ Single-steps through the code

```
Browse[2]> n
debug: if (na.rm) x <- x[!is.na(x)]

Browse[2]> n
debug: n <- length(x)

Browse[2]> n
debug: constant * if ((low || high) && n%%2 == 0) {
    if (low && high)
        stop("'low' and 'high' cannot be both TRUE")
    n2 <- n%/%2 + as.integer(high)
    sort(abs(x - center), partial = n2)[n2]
} else median(abs(x - center))

Browse[2]> print(n)
[1] 10

Browse[2]> where
where 1: mad(x)

Browse[2]> c
exiting from: mad(x)
[1] 3.7065
```

❺ Resumes continuous execution

```
> undebug(mad)
```

First, the arg() function is used to display the argument names and default values for the mad() function ❶. The debug flag is then set using debug(mad) ❷. Now, whenever mad() is called, the browser() function is executed, allowing you to step through the function a line at a time.

When mad() is called, the session goes into browser() mode. The code for the function is listed but not executed. Additionally, the prompt changes to Browse[n] >, where n indicates the *browser level*. The number increments with each recursive call.

In `browser()` mode, other R commands can be executed. For example, `ls()` lists the objects in existence at a given point during the function's execution ❸. Typing an object's name displays its contents. If an object is named n, c, or Q, you must use `print(n)`, `print(c)`, or `print(Q)` to view its contents. You can change the values of objects by typing assignment statements.

You step through the function and execute the statements one at a time by entering the letter n or pressing the Return or Enter key ❹. The `where` statement indicates where you are in the stack of function calls being executed. With a single function, this isn't very interesting, but if you have functions that call other functions, it can be helpful.

Typing c moves out of single-step mode and executes the remainder of the current function ❺. Typing Q exits the function and returns you to the R prompt.

The `debug()` function is useful when you have loops and want to see how values are changing. You can also embed the `browser()` function directly in code to help locate a problem. Let's say that you have a variable X that should never be negative. Adding the code

```
if (X < 0) browser()
```

allows you to explore the current state of the function when the problem occurs. You can take out the extra code when the function is sufficiently debugged. (I originally wrote "fully debugged," but this almost never happens, so I changed it to "sufficiently debugged" to reflect a programmer's reality.)

20.6.3 *Session options that support debugging*

When you have functions that call functions, two session options can help in debugging. Normally, when R encounters an error, it prints an error message and exits the function. Setting `options(error=traceback)` prints the call stack (the sequence of function calls that led to the error) as soon as an error occurs. This can help you determine which function generated the error.

Setting `options(error=recover)` also prints the call stack when an error occurs. In addition, it prompts you to select one of the functions on the list and then invokes `browser()` in the corresponding environment. Typing c returns you to the list, and typing 0 quits back to the R prompt.

Using this `recover()` mode lets you explore the contents of any object in any function chosen from the sequence of functions called. By selectively viewing the contents of objects, you can frequently determine the origin of the problem. To return to R's default state, set `options(error=NULL)`. The next listing shows a toy example.

Listing 20.5 Sample debugging session with `recover()`

```
f <- function(x, y){
    z <- x + y
    g(z)
}
g <- function(x){
    z <- round(x)
    h(z)
```

Creates
functions

```
}
h <- function(x){
      set.seed(1234)
      z <- rnorm(x)
      print(z)
}
> options(error=recover)
> f(2,3)
[1] -1.207  0.277  1.084 -2.346  0.429
> f(2, -3)
Error in rnorm(x) : invalid arguments

Enter a frame number, or 0 to exit

1: f(2, -3)
2: #3: g(z)
3: #3: h(z)
4: #3: rnorm(x)

Selection: 4
Called from: rnorm(x)

Browse[1]> ls()
[1] "mean" "n"     "sd"

Browse[1]> mean
[1] 0

Browse[1]> print(n)
[1] -1

Browse[1]> c

Enter a frame number, or 0 to exit
1: f(2, -3)
2: #3: g(z)
3: #3: h(z)
4: #3: rnorm(x)

Selection: 3
Called from: h(z)

Browse[1]> ls()
[1] "x"

Browse[1]> x
[1] -1
Browse[1]> c

Enter a frame number, or 0 to exit

1: f(2, -3)
2: #3: g(z)
3: #3: h(z)
4: #3: rnorm(x)

Selection: 2
Called from: g(z)
```

Creates functions

Enters values that cause an error

Examines rnorm()

Examines h(z)

Examines g(z)

```
Browse[1]> ls()
[1] "x" "z"

Browse[1]> x
[1] -1

Browse[1]> z
[1] -1

Browse[1]> c

Enter a frame number, or 0 to exit

1: f(2, -3)
2: #3: g(z)
3: #3: h(z)
4: #3: rnorm(x)

Selection: 1                    ⟵┐  Examines
Called from: f(2, -3)            │  f(2, -3)

Browse[1]> ls()
[1] "x" "y" "z"

Browse[1]> x
[1] 2

Browse[1]> y
[1] -3

Browse[1]> z
[1] -1

Browse[1]> print(f)
function(x, y){
    z <- x + y
    g(z)
}
Browse[1]> c

Enter a frame number, or 0 to exit

1: f(2, -3)
2: #3: g(z)
3: #3: h(z)
4: #3: rnorm(x)

Selection: 0

> options(error=NULL)
```

The code first creates a series of functions. Function f() calls function g(). Function g() calls function h(). Executing f(2, 3) works fine, but f(2, -3) throws an error. Because of options(error=recover), the interactive session is immediately moved into recover mode. The function call stack is listed, and you can choose which function to examine in browser() mode.

Typing 4 moves you into the `rnorm()` function, where `ls()` lists the objects; you can see that n = -1, which isn't allowed in `rnorm()`. This is clearly the problem, but to see how n became -1, you move up the stack.

Typing c returns you to the menu, and typing 3 moves you into the `h(z)` function, where x = -1. Typing c and 2 moves you into the `g(z)` function. Here, both x and z are –1. Finally, moving up to the `f(2, -3)` function reveals that z is –1 because x = 2 and y = -3.

Note the use of `print()` to view the function code. This is useful when you're debugging code that you didn't write. Normally, you can type the function name to view the code. In this example, f is a reserved word in browser mode that means "finish execution of the current loop or function"; the `print()` function is used explicitly to escape this special meaning.

Finally, c takes you back to the menu, and 0 returns you to the normal R prompt. Alternatively, typing Q at any time returns you to the R prompt.

To learn more debugging in general and recover mode in particular, see Roger Peng's excellent "An Introduction to the Interactive Debugging Tools in R" (http://mng.bz/GPR6).

20.6.4 Using RStudio's visual debugger

In addition to the tools described so far, RStudio offers visual support for debugging that parallels the material in the previous sections.

First, let's debug the `mad()` function in base R.

```
> debug(mad)
> mad(1:10)
```

The RStudio interface changes (see figure 20.2).

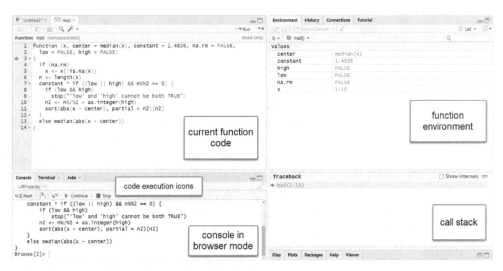

Figure 20.2 Visually debugging the `mad()` function in RStudio

The upper-left pane shows the current function. A green arrow indicates the current line. The upper-right pane shows the objects in the function's environment and their values at the current line. As you execute each line of the function, these values will change. The lower-right pane shows the call stack. Since there is only one function, this is uninteresting. Finally, the lower-left pane displays the console in browser mode. This is where you will spend most of your time.

You can enter each of the commands from the previous two sections at the browser prompt in the console window. Alternatively, you can click on the code execution icons at the top of this pane (see figure 20.2). From left to right, they will

- Execute the next line of code
- Step into the current function call
- Execute the remainder of the current function or loop
- Continue execution until the next breakpoint (not covered here)
- Exit debug mode

In this way, you can step through your function and observe what happens after each line of code in executed.

Next, let's debug the code in listing 20.5.

```
f <- function(x, y) {
        z <- x + y
        g(z)
}
g <- function(x) {
        z <- round(x)
        h(z)
}
h <- function(x) {
        set.seed(1234)
        z <- rnorm(x)
        print(z)
}
> options(error=recover)
> f(2,-3)
```

The interface changes to look like figure 20.3.

The function displayed in the upper-left pane is the function that threw the error. Since functions call other functions, the call stack is now interesting. By clicking on a function's call stack window (lower-right pane), you can view the code in each function, the order they are called, and the values that they pass. When a function is highlighted in the traceback list, the values of its objects will be displayed in the environment window in the upper-right pane. In this way, you can watch what happens as functions are called and values are passed until the error occurs.

To learn more about RStudio's visual debugger, see the article "Debugging with RStudio IDE" (http://mng.bz/4M65) and the video "Introduction to debugging in R" (http://mng.bz/Q2R1).

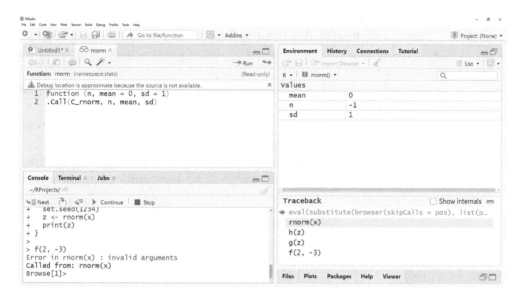

Figure 20.3 Visually reviewing the call stack in RStudio. The function `f(2,-3)` calls `g(z)`, which calls `h(z)`, which calls `rnorm(x)`, which is where the error occurs. You can see each function and its values by clicking on the appropriate line in the Traceback panel.

20.7 Going further

There are several excellent sources of information on advanced programming in R. The R Language Definition (http://mng.bz/U4Cm) is a good place to start. "Frames, environments, and scope in R and S-PLUS" by John Fox (http://mng.bz/gxw8) is a great article for gaining a better understanding of scope. "How R searches and finds stuff" by Suraj Gupta (http://mng.bz/2o5B) is a blog article that can help you understand just what the title implies. To learn more about efficient coding, see "FasteR! HigheR! StrongeR!—A Guide to Speeding Up R Code for Busy People" by Noam Ross (http://mng.bz/Iq3i). Finally, two books are very helpful. *Advanced R* by Hadley Wickham (https://adv-r.hadley.nz/) and *R Programming for Bioinformatics* (Chapman & Hall, 2009) by Robert Gentleman are comprehensive, yet highly accessible texts for programmers who want to look under the hood. I highly recommend them for anyone who wants to become a more effective R programmer.

Summary

- R has a rich variety of data structures, including atomic and generic vectors. Learning how to extract information from them is a key skill for effective R programming.
- Every R object has a class and optional attributes.
- Control structures such as `for()` and `if()`/`else()` allow you execute code conditionally and nonsequentially.

- Environments provide a mechanism for looking up object names and their contents. They provide fine control of the scope of names and functions.
- R has several systems for object-oriented programming. The S3 system is the most common by far.
- Nonstandard evaluation allows the programmer to customize how and when expressions are evaluated.
- Two ways to speed up your code are vectorization and parallel processing. Profiling your code can help you find speed bottlenecks.
- R has a rich variety of debugging tools. RStudio provides graphic interfaces to these tools. Together, they make finding logic and coding errors easier (but rarely easy!).

Creating dynamic reports

21

This chapter covers

- Publishing results to the web
- Incorporating R results into Microsoft Word or Open Document reports
- Creating dynamic reports in which changing the data changes the report
- Creating publication-quality documents with R, Markdown, and LaTeX
- Avoiding common R Markdown errors

In previous chapters you've accessed your data, cleaned it up, described its characteristics, modeled the relationships, and visualized the results. The next step is to

- **A** Relax and perhaps go to Disney World.
- **B** Communicate the results to others.

If you chose A, please take me with you. If you chose B, welcome to the real world.

Research doesn't end when the last statistical analysis or graph is finished. You'll almost always have to communicate the results to others. This means incorporating the analyses into a report of some kind.

There are three common report scenarios. In the first, you create a report that includes your code and the results so you can remember what you did six months from now. It's easier to reconstruct what was done from a single comprehensive document than from a set of related files.

In the second scenario, you have to generate a report for a teacher, a supervisor, a client, a government agency, an internet audience, or a journal editor. Clarity and attractiveness matter, and the report may only need to be created once.

In the third scenario, you need to generate a specific type of report on a regular basis. It may be a monthly report on product or resource usage, a weekly financial analysis, or a report on web traffic that's updated hourly. In any case, the data changes, but the analyses and the structure of the report remain the same.

One approach to incorporating R output into a report involves running the analyses, cutting and pasting each graph and text table into a word processing document, and reformatting the results. This approach is usually time consuming, inefficient, and frustrating. Although R creates state-of-the-art graphics, its text output is woefully retro—tables of monospaced text with columns lined up using spaces. Reformatting them is no easy task. And if the data changes, you'll have to go through the entire process again!

Given these limitations, you may feel that R won't work for you. Have no fear. (OK, have a little fear—it's an important survival mechanism.) R offers an elegant solution for incorporating R code and results into reports using a markup language called *R Markdown* (https://rmarkdown.rstudio.com). Additionally, the data can be tied to the report so that changing the data changes the report. These dynamic reports can be saved as

- Web pages
- Microsoft Word documents
- Open Document files
- Beamer, HTML5, and PowerPoint slides
- Publication-ready PDF or PostScript documents

For example, say you're using regression analysis to study the relationship between weight and height in a sample of women. R Markdown allows you to take the monospaced output generated by the `lm()` function:

```
> lm(weight ~ height, data=women)

Call:
lm(formula = weight ~ height, data = women)

Residuals:
    Min      1Q  Median      3Q     Max
-1.7333 -1.1333 -0.3833  0.7417  3.1167

Coefficients:
            Estimate Std. Error t value Pr(>|t|)
```

```
(Intercept) -87.51667    5.93694   -14.74 1.71e-09 ***
height       3.45000     0.09114    37.85 1.09e-14 ***
---
Signif. codes:  0 '***' 0.001 '**' 0.01 '*' 0.05 '.' 0.1 ' ' 1
Residual standard error: 1.525 on 13 degrees of freedom
Multiple R-squared:  0.991,    Adjusted R-squared:  0.9903
F-statistic:  1433 on 1 and 13 DF,  p-value: 1.091e-14
```

and turn it into a web page like that in figure 21.1. In this chapter, you'll learn how.

Regression report

RobK

7/8/2021

Heights and weights

Linear regression was used to model the relationship between weights and height in a sample of 15 women. The equation **weight = -87.517 + 3.45 * height** accounted for 0.99% of the variance in weights. The ANOVA table is given below.

term	estimate	std.error	statistic	p.value
(Intercept)	-87.52	5.937	-14.7	0
height	3.45	0.091	37.9	0

The regression is plotted in the following figure.

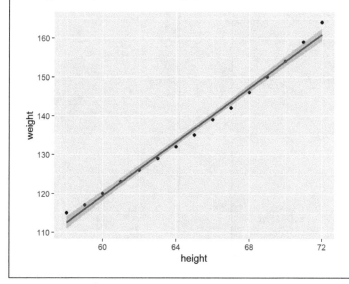

Figure 21.1 Regression analysis saved to a web page

Dynamic documents and reproducible research

There is a powerful movement growing within the academic community in support of *reproducible research*. The goal of reproducible research is to facilitate the replication of scientific findings by including the data and software code necessary to reproduce findings in the publications that report them. This allows readers to verify the findings for themselves and gives them an opportunity to build on the results more directly in their own work. The techniques described in this chapter, including the embedding of data and source code with documents, directly support this effort.

21.1   A template approach to reports

This chapter employs a template approach to report generation. A report starts with a template file that contains the report text, formatting syntax, and R code chunks.

The template file is processed, the R code is run, the formatting syntax is applied, and a report is generated. Different options control how R output is included in the report. Figure 21.2 shows a simple example using an R Markdown template to create a web page.

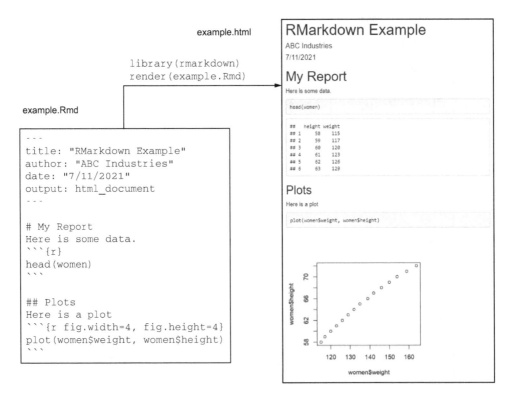

Figure 21.2   Creating a web page from a text file that includes Markdown syntax, report text, and R code chunks

The template file (example.Rmd) is a plain text file containing four components:

- *Metadata*—The metadata (called a YAML header) is bracketed by a pair of three dashes (—) and contains information on the document and the desired output.

- *Report text*—Any explanatory phrases and text. Here, the report text is "My Report," "Here is some data," "Plots," and "Here is a plot."

- *Formatting syntax*—The tags that control report formatting. In this file, Markdown tags are used to format the results. Markdown is a simple markup language that can be used to convert plain text files to structurally valid HTML or XHTML. The pound symbol # in the first line isn't a comment. It produces a level-1 header. ## produces a level-2 header, and so on.

- *R code*—R statements to be executed. In R Markdown documents, R code chunks are surrounded by ``` `{r}` and ``` ```. The first code chunk lists the first six rows of the dataset, and the second code chunk produces a scatter plot. In this example, both the code and the results are output to the report, but options allow you to control what's printed on a chunk-by-chunk basis.

The template file is passed to the `render()` function in the `rmarkdown` package, and a web page named example.html is created. The web page contains both the report text and R results.

The examples in this chapter are based on descriptive statistics, regression, and ANOVA problems. None of them represent full analyses of the data. The goal in this chapter is to learn how to incorporate the R results into various types of reports.

Depending on the template file you start with and the functions used to process it, different report formats (HTML web pages, Microsoft Word documents, OpenOffice Writer documents, PDF reports, articles, slides, and books) are created. The reports are dynamic in the sense that changing the data and reprocessing the template file will produce a new report.

21.2 Creating a report with R and R Markdown

In this section, you'll use the `rmarkdown` package to create documents generated from Markdown syntax and R code. When the document is processed, the R code is executed, and the output is formatted and embedded in the finished document. You can use this approach to generate reports in a wide variety of formats. Here are the steps:

1 Install the `rmarkdown` package (`install.packages("rmarkdown")`). This will install several other packages, including `knitr`. If you're using a recent version of RStudio, you can skip this step because you already have the necessary packages.

2 Install Pandoc (http://johnmacfarlane.net/pandoc/), which is a free application available for Windows, macOS, and Linux. It converts files from one markup format to another. Again, RStudio users can skip this step.

3 If you want to create PDF documents, install a LaTeX compiler, which converts a LaTeX document into a high-quality typeset PDF document. Comprehensive

installations include MiKTeX (www.miktex.org) for Windows, MacTeX for Macs (http://tug.org/mactex), and TeX Live for Linux (www.tug.org/texlive). I recommend a lightweight cross-platform installation called TinyTex (http://yihui.org/tinytex). To install it, run

```
install.packages("tinytex")
tinytex::install_tinytex()
```

4 While not strictly necessary, it's a good idea to install the `broom` package (`install.packages("broom")`). The `tidy()` function in this package can export the results from over 135 R statistical functions into data frames for inclusion in reports. See `methods(tidy)` to view a comprehensive list of the objects it can output.

5 Finally, install `kableExtra` (`install.packages("kableExtra")`). The `kable` function in the `knitr` package converts a matrix or data frame into a LaTeX or HTML table for inclusion in reports. The `kableExtra` package includes functions to style the table output.

With the software set up, you're ready to go.

To incorporate R output (values, tables, graphs) in a document using Markdown syntax, first create a text document that contains

- A YAML header
- Report text
- Markdown syntax
- R code chunks (R code surrounded by delimiters)

The text file should have the file extension .Rmd.

Listing 22.1 shows a sample file (named women.Rmd). To generate an HTML document, process this file using

```
library(rmarkdown)
render("women.Rmd")
```

or click on the RStudio Knit button. Figure 21.1 displays the results.

Listing 21.1   women.Rmd: an R Markdown template with embedded R code

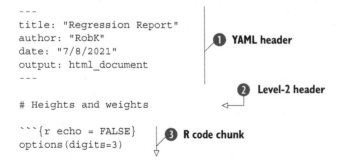

```
---
title: "Regression Report"
author: "RobK"
date: "7/8/2021"
output: html_document
---

# Heights and weights

```{r echo = FALSE}
options(digits=3)
```

❶ YAML header

❷ Level-2 header

❸ R code chunk
```

```
n    <- nrow(women)
fit  <- lm(weight ~ height, data=women)        ③ R code chunk
sfit <- summary(fit)
b    <- coefficients(fit)
```

```
Linear regression was used to model the relationship between
weights and height in a sample of `r n` women. The equation
**weight = `r b[1]` +  `r b[2]` * height**          ④ R inline code
accounted for `r round(sfit$r.squared,2)`% of the variance
in weights. The ANOVA table is given below.
```

```{r echo=FALSE}
library(broom)
library(knitr)
library(kableExtra)                              ⑤ Formatted
                                                    results table
results <- tidy(fit)
tbl <- kable(results)
kable_styling(tbl, "striped", full_width=FALSE, position="left")
```

The regression is plotted in the following figure.

```{r fig.width=5, fig.height=4}
library(ggplot2)
ggplot(data=women, aes(x=height, y=weight)) +
      geom_point() + geom_smooth(method="lm", formula=y~x)
```

The report starts with a YAML header ❶ indicating title, author, date, and output format. The date is hardcoded. To dynamically insert the current date, replace "7/8/2021" with "`r Sys.Date()`" (including the double quote marks). In a YAML header, only the output field is required. Table 21.1 lists the most common of the output options. A complete listing is available from RStudio (https://rmarkdown.rstudio.com/lesson-9.html).

Table 21.1   R Markdown document output options

Output options	Description
html_document	HTML document
pdf_document	PDF document
word_document	Microsoft Word document
odt_document	Open Document Text document
rtf_document	Rich Text document

Next is first-level header ❷. It indicates that "Heights and Weights" should be printed in a large, bold font. Table 21.2 shows examples of other Markdown syntax.

Table 21.2   Markdown code and the resulting output

Markdown syntax	Resulting HTML output

`# Heading 1`
`## Heading 2`
`. . .`
`###### Heading 6`
	`<h1>Heading 1</h1>`
	`<h2>Heading 2</h2>`
	`. . .`
	`<h6>Heading 6</h6>`

One or more blank lines between text	Separates text into paragraphs
Two or more spaces at the end of a line	Adds a line break
`*I mean it*`	`<em>I mean it</em>`
`**I really mean it**`	`<strong>I really mean it</strong>`

`* item 1`
`* item 2`
	`<ul>`
	`<li> item 1 </li>`
	`<li> item 2 </li>`
	`</ul>`

`1. item 1`
`2. item 2`
	`<ol>`
	`<li> item 1 </li>`
	`<li> item 2 </li>`
	`</ol>`

`[Google](http://google.com)`	`<a href="http://google.com">Google</a>`
`![My text](path to image)`	`<img src="path to image", alt="My text">`
`\newpage`	Page break—starts a new page. (This is a LaTeX command recognized by `rmarkdown`.)

Next comes an R code chunk ❸. R code in Markdown documents is delimited by
` ```{r options} ` and ` ``` `. When the file is processed, the R code is executed, and
the results are inserted. The option `echo=FALSE` omits the code from the output.
Table 21.3 lists code chunk options.

Table 21.3   Code chunk options

Option	Description
`echo`	Whether to include the R source code in the output (`TRUE`) or not (`FALSE`)
`results`	Whether to output raw results (`asis`) or hide the results (`hide`)
`warning`	Whether to include warnings in the output (`TRUE`) or not (`FALSE`)
`message`	Whether to include informational messages in the output (`TRUE`) or not (`FALSE`)
`error`	Whether to include error messages in the output (`TRUE`) or not (`FALSE`)
`cache`	Save results and only rerun the code chunk if the code has changed
`fig.width`	Figure width for plots (inches)
`fig.height`	Figure height for plots (inches)

Simple R output (a number or string) can also be placed directly within report text. Inline R code allows you to customize the text in individual sentences. Inline code is placed between `` `r `` and `` ` `` tags. In the regression example, the sample size, prediction equation, and R-squared value are embedded in the first paragraph **❹**.

The next R code chunk creates a nicely formatted ANOVA table **❺**. The `tidy()` function from the `broom` package exports the regression results as a data frame (tibble). The `kable()` function from the `knitr` package converts this data frame into HTML code, and the `kable_styling()` function from the `kableExtra` package sets the table width and table alignment, and adds color striping. See `help(kable_styling)` for additional formatting options.

The `kable()` and `kable_styling()` functions are simple and easy to use. Several packages in R can create more complex tables and offer a larger number of styling options. These include `xtable`, `expss`, `gt`, `huxtable`, `flextable`, `pixiedust`, and `stargazer`. Each has its pros and cons (see http://mng.bz/aKy9 and http://mng.bz/gxO8 for discussion). Use the package(s) that best meet your needs.

The final portion of the R Markdown file prints a `ggplot2` graph of the results. The figure size is set to 5 inches wide and 4 inches tall. The default is 7 by 5 inches.

Using RStudio to create and process R Markdown documents

RStudio makes it particularly easy to render reports from Markdown documents.

If you choose File > New File > R Markdown from the GUI menu, you'll see the dialog box shown next.

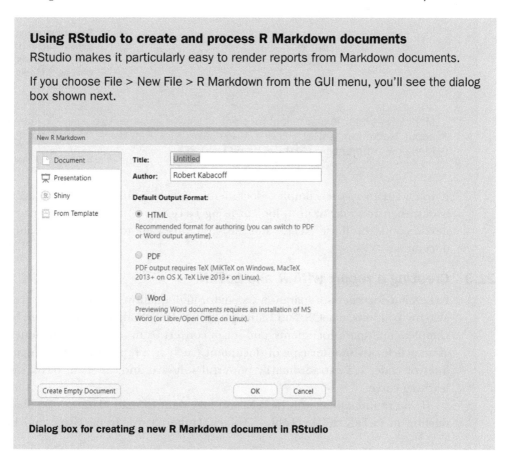

Dialog box for creating a new R Markdown document in RStudio

(continued)

Choose the type of report you want to generate, and RStudio will create a skeleton file for you. Edit it with your text and code, and then select the rendering option from the Knit drop-down list. That's it!

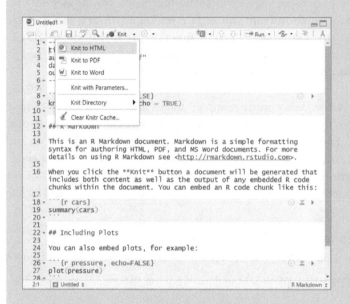

Drop-down menu for generating an HTML, PDF, or Word report from an R Markdown document

Markdown syntax is convenient for creating simple documents quickly. To learn more about Markdown, select HELP > Markdown Quick Reference, or visit the Pandoc Markdown reference page (http://mng.bz/0r8E).

If you want to create complex documents such as publication-quality articles and books, then you may want to look at using LaTeX as your markup language. In the next section, you'll use LaTeX and the `knitr` package to create high-quality typeset documents.

21.3 *Creating a report with R and LaTeX*

LaTeX is a document-preparation system for high-quality typesetting that's freely available for Windows, macOS, and Linux platforms. LaTeX allows you to create beautiful, complex, multipart documents, and it can convert from one type of document (such as an article) to another type of document (such as a report) by changing just a few lines of code. It's extraordinarily powerful software and, as such, has a significant learning curve.

If you're unfamiliar with LaTeX, you may want to read "The Not So Short Introduction to LaTeX 2e" by Tobias Oetiker, Hubert Partl, Irene Hyna, and Elisabeth

Schlegl (https://tobi.oetiker.ch/lshort/lshort.pdf) or *LaTeX Tutorials: A Primer by the Indian TEX Users Group* (http://mng.bz/2c0O) before continuing. The language is definitely worth learning, but it will take some time and patience to master. Once you're familiar with LaTeX, creating a dynamic report is a straightforward process.

The `knitr` package allows you to embed R code within the LaTeX document using techniques that are analogous to the ones used previously for creating web pages. If you installed `rmarkdown` or are using RStudio, you already have `knitr`. If not, install it now (`install.packages("knitr")`). Additionally, you'll need a LaTeX compiler; see section 21.2 for details.

In this section, you'll create a report describing patients' reactions to various drugs, using data from the `multcomp` package. If you didn't install it in chapter 9, be sure to run `install.packages("multcomp")` before continuing.

To generate a report using R and LaTeX, you first create a text file with the file extension .Rnw containing the report text, LaTeX markup code, and R code chunks. Listing 21.2 gives an example. Each R code chunk starts with the delimiter `<<options>>=` and ends with the delimiter `@`. Table 21.3 lists the code chunk options. Inline R code is included using the `\Sexpr{R code}` syntax. When the R code is evaluated, the number or string is inserted at that point in the text.

The file is then processed by the `knit2pdf()` function:

```
library(knitr)
knit2pdf("drugs.Rnw")
```

or by pressing the Compile PDF button in RStudio. During this step, the R code chunks are processed and, depending on the options, replaced with LaTeX-formatted R code and output. By default, `knit("drugs.Rnw")` inputs the file drugs.Rnw and outputs the file drugs.tex. The .tex file is then run through a LaTeX compiler, creating a PDF file. Figure 21.3 displays the resulting PDF document.

> **Listing 21.2 drugs.Rnw: a LaTeX template with embedded R code**

```
\documentclass[11pt]{article}
\title{Sample Report}
\author{Robert I. Kabacoff, Ph.D.}
\usepackage{float}
\usepackage[top=.5in, bottom=.5in, left=1in, right=1in]{geometry}
\begin{document}
\maketitle
<<echo=FALSE, results='hide', message=FALSE>>=
library(multcomp)
library(dplyr)
library(xtable)
library(ggplot2)
df <- cholesterol
@

\section{Results}
```

```
Cholesterol reduction was assessed in a study
that randomized \Sexpr{nrow(df)} patients
to one of \Sexpr{length(unique(df$trt))} treatments.
Summary statistics are provided in
Table \ref{table:descriptives}.

<<echo=FALSE, results='asis'>>=
descTable <- df %>%
  group_by(trt) %>%
  summarize(N = n(),
            Mean = mean(response, na.rm=TRUE),
            SD = sd(response, na.rm=TRUE)) %>%
  rename(Treatment = trt)
print(xtable(descTable, caption = "Descriptive statistics
for each treatment group", label = "table:descriptives"),
caption.placement = "top", include.rownames = FALSE)
@

The analysis of variance is provided in Table \ref{table:anova}.

<<echo=FALSE, results='asis'>>=
fit <- aov(response ~ trt, data=df)
print(xtable(fit, caption = "Analysis of variance",
             label = "table:anova"), caption.placement = "top")
@

\noindent and group distributions are plotted in Figure \ref{figure:tukey}.

\begin{figure}[H]\label{figure:tukey}
\begin{center}

<<echo=FALSE, fig.width=4, fig.height=3>>=
  ggplot(df, aes(x=trt, y=response )) +
    geom_boxplot() +
    labs(y = "Response", x="Treatment") +
    theme_bw()
@

\caption{Distribution of response times by treatment.}
\end{center}
\end{figure}
\end{document}
```

The knitr package is documented at http://yihui.name/knitr and in Yihui Xie's book *Dynamic Documents with R and knitr* (Chapman & Hall, 2013). To learn more about LaTeX, check out the tutorials mentioned earlier and visit www.latex-project.org.

21.3.1 *Creating a parameterized report*

You can pass parameters to a report at run time, allowing you to customize the output without having to change the R Markdown template. Parameters are defined in the YAML header in a section denoted with the params keyword. You access the values of the parameters in the body of your code using $ notation.

Sample report

Robert I. Kabacoff, Ph.D.

July11,2021

1 Results

Cholesterol reduction was assessed in a study that randomized 50 patients to one of 5 treatments. Summary statistics are provided in Table 1.

Table 1: Descriptive statistics for each treatment group

Treatment	N	Mean	SD
1tim	10	5.78	2.88
2time	10	9.22	3.48
4times	10	12.37	2.92
drugD	10	15.36	3.45
drugE	10	20.95	3.35

The analysis of variance is provided in Table 2.

Table 2: Analysis of variance

	Df	Sum Sq	Mean Sq	F value	Pr(>F)
trt	4	1351.37	337.84	32.43	0.0000
Residuals	45	468.75	10.42		

and group distributions are plotted in Figure 1.

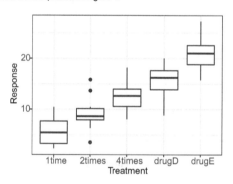

Figure 1: Distribution of response times by treatment.

1

Figure 21.3　The text file drugs.Rnw is processed through the `knit2pdf()` function, resulting in a typeset PDF document (drugs.pdf).

Consider the parameterized report in the following listing. This R Markdown document downloads stock prices for four large tech stocks (Apple, Amazon, Google, and Microsoft) from Yahoo Finance (https://finance.yahoo.com/) and plots them using `ggplot2` (see figure 21.4).

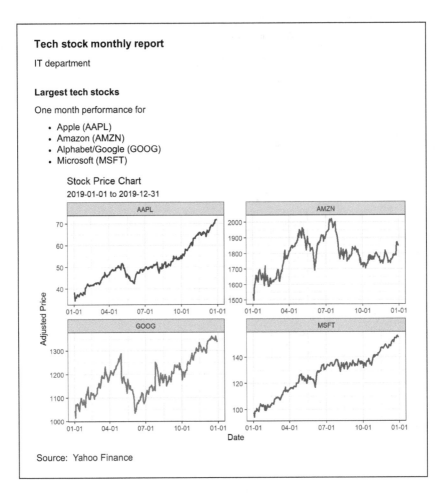

Figure 21.4   Dynamic report produced from the parameterized R Markdown file in listing 21.3

By default, the code reports stock performance for the past 30 days from the time the file is knitted. The report uses the `tidyquant` package to obtain stock prices, so install it before knitting the document (`install.packages("tidyquant")`).

Listing 21.3   R Markdown report with parameters (techstocks.Rmd)

```
---
title: "Tech Stock Monthly Report"
author: "IT Department"
output: html_document
params:
  enddate: !r Sys.Date()                    ❶ Defines parameter
  startdate: !r Sys.Date() - 30                values
```

```
---
## Largest tech stocks

One month performance for

- Apple (AAPL)
- Amazon (AMZN)
- Alphabet/Google (GOOG)
- Microsoft (MSFT)

```{r, echo=FALSE, message=FALSE}

library(tidyquant)
library(ggplot2)

tickers = c("AAPL", "MSFT", "AMZN", "GOOG")

prices <- tq_get(tickers,
                 from = params$startdate,
                 to = params$enddate,
                 get = "stock.prices")

ggplot(prices, aes(x=date, y=adjusted, color=symbol)) +
  geom_line(size=1) + facet_wrap(~symbol, scale="free") +
  theme_bw() +
  theme(legend.position="none") +
  scale_x_date(date_labels="%m-%d") +
  scale_color_brewer(palette="Set1") +
  labs(title="Stock Price Chart",
       subtitle = paste(params$startdate, "to", params$enddate),
       x = "Date",
       y="Adjusted Price")
```
Source: [Yahoo Finance](https://finance.yahoo.com/)
```

❷ Obtains stock quotes using parameter values

The parameters `enddate` and `startdate` are defined in the YAML header ❶. You can hardcode these values, or use `!r` to include R code that evaluates to the desired values. Here, `enddate` is set to the current date and `startdate` is set to 30 days prior.

When the code is run, the `tq_get()` function in the `tidyquant` package downloads the daily stock prices (symbol, date, open, high, low, close, volume, adjusted) for the date range defined by `params$startdate` and `params$enddate` ❷. The values are then plotted with `ggplot2`.

You can override the parameter values at run time by providing a list of values to the `render` function. For example,

```
render("techstocks.Rmd", params=list(startdate="2021-01-01",
                                      enddate="2019-01-31"))
```

would plot the daily stock performance for January 2019. Alternatively, if you run `render("techstocks.Rmd", params="ask")` (or click Knit > Knit with parameters... in RStudio), you will be prompted for the `startdate` and `enddate` values. The values you provide will override the defaults. Including parameter values give your reports an added degree of interactivity. To learn more, see section 15.3 of Yihui Xie, J.J Allaire, and Garret Grolemund's book *R Markdown: The Definitive Guide* (Chapman & Hall, 2019). An online version is available at https://bookdown.org/yihui/rmarkdown/.

21.4 *Avoiding common R Markdown problems*

R Markdown is a powerful vehicle for creating dynamic and attractive reports in R. But there are a few simple, common errors to avoid (table 21.4).

Table 21.4   Correcting common R Markdown errors

Rule	Correct	Incorrect

The indentation in YAML headers matters. Only indent subfields.	```---```
	```title: "Tech Stock```
	```Monthly Report"```
	```author: "IT Department"```
	```output: html_document```
	```params:```
	``` enddate: 2019-01-31```
	``` startdate: 2019-01-01```
	```---```
		```---```
		```title: "Tech Stock```
		```Monthly Report"```
		```author: "IT Department"```
		```output: html_document```
		```params:```
		```enddate: 2019-01-31```
		```startdate: 2019-01-01```
		```---```

Place a space after heading tags.	`# This is a level one heading.`	`#This is a level one heading.`

Lists should be preceded and followed by a blank line, and the asterisk tag should have a space after it.	```Here is a list```
	
	```* item one```
	```* item two```
		```Here is a list```
		```*item one```
		```*item two```

Optionally, R code chunks can be labeled, but each label must be unique.	```` ```{r anova1} ````
	```R code```
	```` ``` ````
	```` ```{r anova2} ````
	```R code```
	```` ``` ````
		```` ```{r anova} ````
		```R code```
		```` ``` ````
		```` ```{r anova} ````
		```R code```
		```` ``` ````

You can't install packages in R code chunks.	Install `ggplot2` outside of the R Markdown document. Then use
	```` ```r{} ````
	```library(ggplot2)```
	```` ``` ````
		```` ```r{} ````
		```install.packages(ggplot2)```
		```library(ggplot2)```
		```` ``` ````

Errors that occur when rendering R Markdown documents can be more difficult to debug than errors in simple R code. If you make sure that each R code chunk runs on its own, and you are careful to avoid the errors listed above, things should go more smoothly.

There is one more topic to mention before moving on. This is more about an inefficiency than an actual error. Let's say that you create an R Markdown document that has introductory text and an R code chunk that performs time-consuming analyses. If you edit your text and reknit the document, you will end up rerunning the R code, even though the results haven't changed.

To avoid this, you can cache the results of your R code chunks. Adding the R code chunk option `cache = TRUE` will save the results to a folder, and the code will only be rerun in the future if the R code itself has changed. If the code has not changed, the saved results will be inserted. Be careful here—caching will not catch changes in the underlying data, just in the code itself. If you change the data but not the data file-name, the code will not be rerun. In this case, you could add the chunk option `cache.extra = file.mtime(`*mydatafile*`)`, where *mydatafile* is the path to the dataset. If the data file timestamp has changed, the code chunk will be rerun.

21.5 *Going further*

In this chapter, you've seen several ways that R results can be incorporated into reports. The reports are dynamic in the sense that changing the data and reprocessing the code results in an updated report. Additionally, the report can be modified by passing parameters. You learned methods for creating web pages, typeset documents, Open Document Format reports, and Microsoft Word documents.

There are several advantages to the template approach described in this chapter. By embedding the code needed to perform statistical analyses directly into the report template, you can see exactly how the results were calculated. Six months from now, you can easily see what was done. You can also modify the statistical analyses or add new data and immediately regenerate the report with minimum effort. Additionally, you avoid the need to cut and paste and reformat the results. This in itself is worth the price of admission.

The templates in this chapter are static in the sense that their structure is fixed. Although not covered here, you can also use these methods to create a variety of expert reporting systems. For example, the output of an R code chunk can depend on the data submitted. If numeric variables are submitted, a scatterplot matrix can be produced. Alternatively, if categorical variables are submitted, a mosaic plot can be produced. In a similar fashion, the explanatory text that is generated can depend on the results of the analyses. Using R's `if/then` construct and text editing functions such as `grep` and `substr` makes the possibilities for customization endless. Basically, you write out the template to a temporary location and edit it via code before knitting. You can use this approach to create a sophisticated expert system.

To learn more about R Markdown, see Yihui Xie, Christophe Dervieux, and Emily Riederer's *R Markdown Cookbook* (https://bookdown.org/yihui/rmarkdown-cookbook/), Yihui Xie, J.J Allaire, and Garret Grolemund's *R Markdown: The Definitive Guide* (https://bookdown.org/yihui/rmarkdown/), and RStudio's *R Markdown* website (https://rmarkdown.rstudio.com/).

Summary

- R Markdown can be used to create attractive reports that combine text, code, and output.
- Reports can be output in HTML, Word, Open Document, RTF, and PDF formats.
- R Markdown documents can be parameterized, allowing you to pass parameters to the code at run time and thus create more dynamic reports.
- LaTeX markup language can be used to produce complex reports that are highly customized. The learning curve can be steep.
- The R Markdown (and LaTeX) template approach can be used promote research reproducibility, support documentation, and enhance the communication of results.

Creating a package

This chapter covers

- Creating the functions for a package
- Adding package documentation
- Building the package and sharing it with others

In previous chapters, you completed most tasks by using functions that were provided by others. The functions came from packages in the base R installation or from contributed packages downloaded from CRAN.

Installing a new package extends R's functionality. For example, installing the mice package provides you with new ways of dealing with missing data. Installing the ggplot2 packages provides you with new ways of visualizing data. Many of R's most powerful capabilities come from contributed packages.

Technically, a package is simply a set of functions, documentation, and data saved in a standardized format. A package allows you to organize your functions in a well-defined and fully documented manner and facilitates sharing your programs with others.

There are several reasons why you might want to create a package:

- To make a set of frequently used functions easily accessible, along with the documentation on how to use them.
- To create a set of examples and datasets that can be distributed to students in a classroom.
- To create a program (a set of interrelated functions) that can be used to solve a significant analytic problem (such as imputing missing values).
- To promote research reproducibility by organizing study data, analysis code, and documentation into a portable and standardized format.

Creating a useful package is also a great way of introducing yourself to others and giving back to the R community. Packages can be shared directly or through online repositories such as CRAN and GitHub.

In this chapter, you'll have an opportunity to develop a package from start to finish. By the end of the chapter, you'll be able to build your own R packages (and enjoy the smug self-satisfaction and bragging rights that attend such a feat).

The package you'll develop is called `edatools`. It provides functions for describing the contents of a data frame. The functions are purposely simple so you can focus on the process of creating a package without getting bogged down in code details. In section 22.1, you'll take the `edatools` package for a test drive. Then in section 22.2, you'll build your own copy of the package from scratch.

22.1   *The edatools package*

Exploratory data analysis (EDA) is an approach to understanding data by describing its characteristics through statistical summaries and visualizations. The `edatools` package is a small subset of a comprehensive EDA package called qacBase (http://rkabacoff.github.io/qacBase).

The `edatools` package contains functions that describe and visualize the contents of a data frame. The package also contains a dataset called `happiness` that contains the responses of 460 individuals to a survey about life satisfaction. The survey describes individuals' ratings of agreement with the statement "I am happy most of the time," along with demographic variables such as income, education, sex, race, and number of children. Ratings occur on a 6-point scale from *strongly disagree* to *strongly agree*. The data are fictitious and included to allow users to experiment with a data frame containing several types of variables and varying levels of missing data per variable.

You can install the `edatools` package with the following code:

```
if(!require(remotes)) install.packages("remotes")
remotes::install_github("rkabacoff/edatools")
```

This downloads the package from `GitHub` and installs it in your default R library.

The `edatools` package has one main function called `contents()` that collects information about a data frame, and `print()` and `plot()` functions to display the results. The following listing demonstrates the functions, and figure 22.1 provides the resulting graph.

Listing 22.1   Describing a data frame with the `edatools` package

```
> library(edatools)
> help(contents)
> df_info <- contents(happiness)
> df_info

Data frame: happiness
460 observations and 11 variables
size: 0.1 Mb
  pos    varname       type n_unique n_miss pct_miss
    1        ID* character      460      0    0.000
    2       Date       Date       12      0    0.000
    3        Sex     factor        2      0    0.000
    4       Race     factor        8     92    0.200
    5        Age    integer       73     46    0.100
  6 Education    factor       13     23    0.050
    7     Income    numeric      415     46    0.100
    8         IQ    numeric       45    322    0.700
    9        Zip  character       10      0    0.000
   10   Children    integer       11      0    0.000
   11      Happy    ordered        6     18    0.039

> plot(df_info)
```

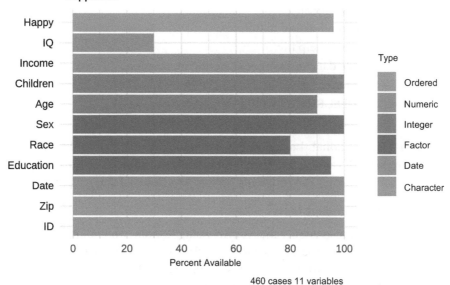

**Figure 22.1   Graph describing the contents of the `happiness` data frame. There are
11 variables, with 70% missing data on the `IQ` variable and 20% missing on the `Race`
variable. The data frame contains 6 different types of data (ordered factor, numeric,
integer, etc.).**

The printed output lists the number of variables and observations and the size of the data frame in megabytes. Each variable's position in the data frame, name, type, number of unique values, and number and percent of missing values are displayed. Variables that can serve as unique identifiers (where each row has a unique value) are starred. The graph arranges and color-codes the variables by type, and the length of the bars indicates the percentage of cases available for analysis.

From the table and graph, you can see that the data frame has 11 variables and 460 observations. It takes up 0.1 megabytes in RAM. ID is a unique identifier, there are 10 zip codes in the data, and 70% of the IQ data is missing. As expected, the happiness rating (happy) is an ordered factor with six levels. What else can you see?

The next section describes the general steps in building an R package. In the following sections, you'll go through the steps sequentially to build the edatools package from scratch.

22.2 *Creating a package*

Creating an R package was once an arduous task meant only for a select group of highly trained R professionals (secret handshake included). With the advent of user-friendly development tools, the process is much more straightforward. However, it's still a detailed, multistep process. The steps are

1 Install development tools.
2 Create a package project.
3 Add the functions.
4 Add function documentation.
5 Add a general help file.
6 Add sample data and sample data documentation.
7 Add a vignette.
8 Edit the DESCRIPTION file.
9 Build and install the package.

Steps 5–7 are optional, but good development practice. The following sections will take you through each step in turn. You can also download the finished product from http://rkabacoff.com/RiA/edatools.zip and save yourself some typing.

22.2.1 *Installing development tools*

In this chapter, I'm assuming that you are using RStudio when building the package. In addition, there are support packages you will want to install. First, install the devtools, usethis, and roxygen2 packages using install.packages(c("devtools", "usethis", "roxygen2"), depend=TRUE). The devtools and usethis packages contain functions that simplify and automate package development. The roxygen2 package streamlines the creation of package documentation.

The remaining software is situation-specific:

- Package documentation is normally in HTML format. If you want to create documentation (e.g., a manual and/or vignettes) in PDF format, you'll need to install LaTeX, a high-quality typesetting system. Several software distributions are available. I recommend TinyTex (https://yihui.org/tinytex/), a lightweight, cross-platform distribution. You can install it with the following code:

```
install.packages("tinytex")
tinytex::install_tinytex()
```

- The pkgdown package will help you create a website for your package. This is an optional step described in section 22.3.4.

- Finally, if you're on a Windows platform and you're going to build R packages that include C, C++, or Fortran code, you'll want to install Rtools.exe (http://cran.r-project.org/bin/windows/Rtools). Installation instructions are provided on the download page. macOS and Linux users already have the necessary tools. While I briefly describe use of external compiled code in section 22.4, we won't be using it in this book.

22.2.2 Creating a package project

Once you have the necessary tools, the next step is to create a package project. When you run the following code

```
library(usethis)
create_package("edatools")
```

an RStudio project is created with the folder structure given in figure 22.2. You are automatically placed into the project, with the current working directory set to the edatools folder.

Function code will go in the R folder. The other important files are the DESCRIPTION and NAMESPACE files. We will discuss them in later sections. The .gitignore, .Rbuildignore, and edatools.Rproj are support files that allow you to customize aspects of the package creation process. You can leave them as is.

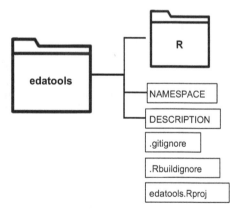

Figure 22.2 Contents of the edatools project folder created by the create_project() function

22.2.3 Writing the package functions

The edatools package consists of three functions: contents(), print.contents(), and plot.contents(). The first is the primary function that gathers information about the data frame, and the others are S3 object-oriented generic functions (see section 20.4.1) used to print and plot the results.

Function code files are placed in the R folder created in section 22.2.2. It's a good idea to place each function in a separate text file with a .R extension. This isn't strictly necessary, but it makes organizing the work easier. Additionally, it isn't necessary for the names of the functions and the names of the files to match, but again, it's good coding practice. Each file has a header consisting of a set of comments that start with the characters #'. The R interpreter ignores these lines, but you'll use the roxygen2 package to turn the comments into your package documentation. These header comments will be discussed in section 22.2.4.

Listings 22.2 through 22.4 provide the files.

GATHERING DATA FRAME INFORMATION

The contents() function in the contents.R text file describes a data frame and saves the results in a list. The function call is contents(*data*) where *data* is the name of a data frame in the working environment.

Listing 22.2 Contents of the contents.R file

```
#' @title Description of a data frame
#' @description
#' \code{contents} provides describes the contents
#' of a data frame.
#'
#' @param data a data frame.
#'
#' @importFrom utils object.size
#'
#' @return a list with 4 components:
#' \describe{
#' \item{dfname}{name of data frame}
#' \item{nrow}{number of rows}
#' \item{ncol}{number of columns}
#' \item{size}{size of the data frame in bytes}
#' \item{varinfo}{data frame of overall dataset characteristics}
#' }
#'
#' @details
#' For each variable in a data frame, \code{contents} describes
#' the position, type, number of unique values, number of missing
#' values, and percent of missing values.
#'
#' @seealso \link{print.contents}, \link{plot.contents}
#'
#' @export
#'
#' @examples
#' df_info <- contents(happiness)
#' df_info
#' plot(df_info)

contents <- function(data){
```

```
if(!(is.data.frame(data))){
  stop("You need to input a data frame")        ❶ Checks input
}

                                                 ❷ Saves the data
dataname <- deparse(substitute(data))              frame name

size <- object.size(data)        ←┐   Obtains the data
                                  ❸   frame size
varnames <- colnames(data)
colnames <- c("pos", "variable", "type", "n_unique",
              "n_miss", "pct_miss")
pos = seq_along(data)
varname <- colnames(data)
type = sapply(data, function(x)class(x)[1])          ❹ Collects variable
n_unique = sapply(data, function(x)length(unique(x)))   information
n_miss = sapply(data, function(x)sum(is.na(x)))
pct_miss = n_miss/nrow(data)
varinfo <- data.frame(
  pos, varname, type, n_unique, n_miss, pct_miss
)

results <- list(dfname=dataname, size=size,
                nrow=nrow(data), ncol=ncol(data),
                varinfo=varinfo)                    ❺ Returns results
class(results) <- c("contents", "list")
return(results)
}
```

When the function is called, it checks to see if the input is a data frame. If not, an error is generated ❶. Next, the name of the data frame is recorded as text ❷ and the size of the data frame is recorded in bytes ❸. For each variable, the position, name, type, number of unique values, and number and percent of missing values are recorded and saved into a data frame called `varinfo` ❹. Finally, the results are bundled up and returned as a list ❺. The list contains five components that are summarized in table 22.1. Additionally, the class of the list is set to `c("contents", "list")`. This is a critical step in creating generic functions for handling the results.

Table 22.1 List object returned by the `contents()` function

Component	Description
dfname	Name of the data frame
size	Size of the data frame
nrow	Number of rows
ncol	Number of columns
varinfo	A data frame containing variable information (position, name, type, number of unique values, and number and percent of missing values)

Although the list provides all the information required, you'd rarely access the components directly. Instead, you'll create generic `print()` and `plot()` functions to present this information in more concise and meaningful ways. We consider these generic functions next.

PRINT AND PLOT FUNCTIONS

Most analytic functions of any breadth come with generic `print()` and `summary()` functions. `print()` provides basic or raw information about an object, and `summary()` provides more detailed or processed (summarized) information. A `plot()` function is frequently included when a plot makes sense in the given context. You'll only need `print` and `plot` functions for this package.

Following the S3 OOP guidelines described in section 20.4.1, if an object has the class attribute `"foo"`, then `print(x)` executes `print.foo(x)` if it exists or `print.default(x)` otherwise. The same goes for `plot()`. Because the `contents()` function returns an object of class `"contents"`, you need to define the `print.contents()` and `plot.contents()` functions. The following listing gives the `print.contents()` function.

Listing 22.3 Contents of the print.R file

```
#' @title Description of a data frame
#'
#' @description
#' \code{print.contents} prints a concise description of a data frame.
#'
#' @param x an object of class \code{contents}.
#' @param digits number of significant digits to use for percentages.
#' @param ... additional arguments passed to the print function.
#'
#' @return NULL
#' @method print contents
#' @export
#'
#' @examples
#' df_info <- contents(happiness)
#' print(df_info, digits=4)

print.contents <- function(x, digits=2, ...){

    if (!inherits(x, "contents"))                          ❶ Checks input
      stop("Object must be of class 'contents'")
                                                           ❷ Prints a header
    cat("Data frame:", x$dfname, "\n")
    cat(x$nrow, "observations and", x$ncol, "variables\n")
    x$varinfo$varname <- ifelse(x$varinfo$n_unique == x$nrow,
                              paste0(x$varinfo$varname, "*"),   ❸ Identifies unique
                              x$varinfo$varname)                   identifiers
    cat("size:",  format(x$size, units="Mb"), "\n")
    print(x$varinfo, digits=digits, row.names=FALSE, ...)   ❺ Prints variable
}                                                              information
```

❹ Prints data frame size

First, the function checks that the input has class `"contents"` ❶. Next, a header with the data frame name and number of variables and observations is printed ❷. If the number of unique values in a column is equal to the number of observations, that variable uniquely identifies each case. Such variables are listed with a star (*) after their name ❸. Next, the size of the data frame is printed in megabytes ❹. Finally, a table of variable information is printed ❺.

The final function, `plot()`, visualizes the results returned by the `contents()` function. This is accomplished via a horizontal `ggplot2` bar chart. The following listing displays the code.

Listing 22.4 Contents of the plot.R file

```
#' @title Visualize a data frame
#'
#' @description
#' \code{plot.contents} visualizes the variables in a data frame.
#'
#' @details
#' For each variable, the plot displays
#' \itemize{
#'    \item{type (\code{numeric},
#'                \code{integer},
#'                \code{factor},
#'                \code{ordered factor},
#'                \code{logical}, or \code{date})}
#'    \item{percent of available (and missing) cases}
#' }
#' Variables are sorted by type and the total number of variables
#' and cases are printed in the caption.
#'
#' @param x an object of class \code{contents}.
#' @param ... additional arguments (not currently used).
#'
#' @import ggplot2
#' @importFrom stats reorder
#' @method plot contents
#' @export
#' @return a \code{ggplot2} graph
#' @seealso See \link{contents}.
#' @examples
#' df_info <- contents(happiness)
#' plot(df_info)

plot.contents <- function(x, ...){
  if (!inherits(x, "contents"))
    stop("Object must be of class 'contents'")          ❶ Checks input

  classes <- x$varinfo$type

  pct_n <-  100 *(1 - x$varinfo$pct_miss)
                                                         ❷ Generates data
  df <- data.frame(var = x$varinfo$varname,                to be plotted
                   classes = classes,
                   pct_n = pct_n,
                   classes_n = as.numeric(as.factor(classes)))
```

```
ggplot(df,
       aes(x=reorder(var, classes_n),
           y=pct_n,
           fill=classes)) +
    geom_bar(stat="identity") +
    labs(x="", y="Percent Available",
        title=x$dfname,
        caption=paste(x$nrow, "cases",
                       x$ncol, "variables"),
        fill="Type") +
    guides(fill = guide_legend(reverse=TRUE)) +
    scale_y_continuous(breaks=seq(0, 100, 20)) +
    coord_flip() +
    theme_minimal()
}
```

❸ Plots the bar chart

❹ Reverses order of the legend

❺ Reverses the x- and y-axes

Again, you check the class of the object passed to the function ❶. Next, the variable names, classes, and percent of nonmissing data are arranged into a data frame. The class of each variable is appended as a number that is used to sort the variables by type when the graph is plotted ❷. The data is plotted as a bar chart ❸, and the order of the legend is reversed so the colors line up vertically with the bars ❹. Finally, the *x*- and *y*-axes are flipped so that you get a horizontal bar chart ❺. When you have many variables or variables with long names, a horizontal bar chart can help avoid overlapping labels.

22.2.4 *Adding function documentation*

Every R package follows the same set of enforced guidelines for documentation. Each function in a package must be documented in the same fashion using LaTeX. Each function is placed in a separate .R file, and the documentation for that function (written in LaTeX) is placed in a .Rd file. Both the .R and .Rd files are text files.

There are two limitations to this approach. First, the documentation is stored separately from the functions it describes. If you change the function code, you have to search out the documentation and change it as well. Second, the user has to learn LaTeX. If you thought R has a steep learning curve, wait until you start working with LaTeX!

The roxygen2 package can dramatically simplify the creation of documentation. You place comments in the head of each .R file that will serve as the function's documentation. These comments start with the characters #' and use a simple set of markup tags (called *roclets*). Table 22.2 lists common tags. The R interpreter sees these lines as comments and ignores them. But when the file is processed by roxygen2, lines that start with #' are used to generate the LaTeX (.Rd) documentation files automatically.

Table 22.2 Tags for use with roxygen2

Tag	Description
@title	Function title
@description	One-line function description

Table 22.2 Tags for use with `roxygen2` *(continued)*

Tag	Description
`@details`	Multiline function description (indent after the first line)
`@parm`	Function parameter
`@export`	Makes this function available to users of your package
`@import`	Imports all functions from a package for use in your own package's functions
`@importFrom`	Selectively imports functions from a package for use in your own package's functions
`@return`	Value returned by the function
`@author`	Author(s) and contact address(es)
`@examples`	Examples using the function
`@note`	Any notes about the operation of the function
`@references`	References concerning the methodology employed by function
`@seealso`	Link to related functions

In addition to the tags in table 22.2, a few markup elements are useful to know as you create documentation:

- `\code{`*text*`}` prints text in `code font`.
- `\link{`*function*`}` generates a hypertext link to help on another R function.
- `\href{`*URL*`}{`*text*`}` adds a hyperlink.
- `\item{`*text*`}` can be used to generate an itemized list.

The `roxygen2` comments from the `contents()` function in listing 22.2 are reproduced in listing 22.5. First, the title and description of the function are specified ❶. Next, the parameters are described ❷. Tags can appear in any order.

Listing 22.5 `roxygen2` comments for the `contents()` function

```
#' @title Description of a data frame
#'
#' @description
#' \code{contents} provides describes the contents
#' of a data frame.
#'
#' @param data a data frame.
#'
#' @importFrom utils object.size
#'
#' @return a list with 4 components:
#' \describe{
#' \item{dfname}{name of data frame}
#' \item{nrow}{number of rows}
#' \item{ncol}{number of columns}
```

❶ Title and description

❷ Parameters

❸ Imports functions

❹ Returns value

```
#' \item{size}{size of the data frame in bytes}
#' \item{varinfo}{data frame of overall dataset characteristics}
#' }
#'
#' @details
#' For each variable in a data frame, \code{contents} describes
#' the position, type, number of unique values, number of missing
#' values, and percent of missing values.
#'
#' @seealso \link{print.contents}, \link{plot.contents}
#'
#' @export
#'
#' @examples
#' df_info <- contents(happiness)
#' df_info
#' plot(df_info)
```

④ Returns value

⑤ Exports function

The @importFrom tag indicates that this function uses the object.size() function from the utils package ❸. Use @importFrom when you want to make a limited set of functions available from a given package. Use the @import function to make *all* the functions of a package available. For example, the plot.contents() function uses the @import ggplot2 tag to make all ggplot2 functions available to that function.

The @return tag indicates what the function returns (a list in this case) ❹. It will appear in the help under the heading Value. Use @details to provide more information about the function. The @seealso tag provides hyperlinks to other functions of interest. The @export tag makes the function available to the user ❺. If you omit it, the function is still accessible to other functions in your package but cannot be called directly from the command line. You would omit the @export tag for functions that shouldn't be called directly by the user.

Finally, the @examples tag lets you include one or more examples demonstrating the function. Note that these examples are expected to work! Otherwise, surround the example code with the \dontrun{} markup code. For example, use

```
@examples
\dontrun{
contents(prettyflowers)
}
```

if there is no data frame called prettyflowers. Since the code is surrounded by \dontrun{}, it won't throw an error. The \dontrun{} markup is often used when an example would take a long time to run.

22.2.5 *Adding a general help file (optional)*

By adding roxygen2 comments to each function, help files are generated during the document and build steps (section 22.3) When the package is installed and loaded, typing ?contents or help(contents) will bring up the help file for that function. But there is no help available for the package name itself. In other words, help (edatools) will fail.

How is the user to know what package functions are available? One way would be to type `help(package="edatools")`, but you can make it easier for them by adding another file to the documentation. Add the file edatools.R (listing 22.6) to the R folder.

Listing 22.6   Contents of the edatools.R file

```
#' @title Functions for exploring the contents of a data frame.
#'
#' @details
#' edatools provides tools for exploring the variables in
#' a data frame.
#'
#' @docType package
#' @name edatools-package
#' @aliases edatools
NULL
... this file must end with a blank line after the NULL...
```

Note that the last line of this file must be blank. When the package is built, a call to `help(edatools)` will now produce a description of the package with a clickable link to an index of functions.

22.2.6 *Adding sample data to the package (optional)*

When you're creating a package, it's a good idea to include one or more datasets that can be used to demonstrate its functions. For the `edatools` package, you'll add the `happiness` data frame. It contains six types of variables and differing amounts of missing data per variable.

To add a data frame to a package, first place it in memory. The following code loads the `happiness` data frame into the global environment:

```
load(url("http://rkabacoff.com/RiA/happiness.rdata"))
```

Next, run

```
library(usethis)
use_data(happiness)
```

This creates a folder called data (if it doesn't exist) and places the happiness data frame into it as a compressed .rda file named happiness.rda.

You also need to create a .R file that documents the data frame. The following listing gives the code.

Listing 22.7   Contents of the happiness.R file

```
#' @title Happiness Dataset
#'
#' @description
#' A data frame containing a happiness survey and demographic data.
```

```
#' This data are fictitious.
#'
#' @source
#' The data were randomly generated using functions from the
#' \href{https://cran.r-project.org/web/packages/wakefield/
     index.html}{wakefield}
#' package.
#'
#' @format A data frame with 460 rows and 11 variables:
#' \describe{
#'   \item{\code{ID}}{character. A unique identifier.}
#'   \item{\code{Date}}{date. Date of the interview.}
#'   \item{\code{Sex}}{factor. Sex coded as \code{Male} or \code{Female}.}
#'   \item{\code{Race}}{factor. Race coded as an 8-level factor.}
#'   \item{\code{Age}}{integer. Age in years.}
#'   \item{\code{Education}}{factor. Education coded as a 13-level factor.}
#'   \item{\code{Income}}{double. Annual income in US dollars.}
#'   \item{\code{IQ}}{double. Adult intelligence quotient. This
#'   variable has a large amount of missing data.}
#'   \item{\code{Zip}}{character. USPS Zip code.}
#'   \item{\code{Children}}{integer. Number of children.}
#'   \item{\code{Happy}}{factor. Agreement with the statement
#'   "I am happy most of the time", coded as \code{Strongly Disagree} ,
#'   \code{Disagree}, \code{Neutral}, \code{Agree}, or
#'   \code{Strongly Agree}.}
#' }
"happiness"
```

Note that the code in listing 22.7 consists entirely of comments. Place it in the R folder with the function code files.

22.2.7 *Adding a vignette (optional)*

People are more likely to use your package if you include a brief article describing its features and use. To create a vignette, run

```
library(usethis)
use_vignette("edatools", "Introduction to edatools")
```

This will create a folder called vignettes (if it doesn't exist) and place an RMarkdown template file called edatools.Rmd in it. It will also open the file for editing in RStudio. Section 21.2 describes editing RMarkdown documents. The following listing shows the completed vignette.

Listing 22.8   `edatools` **vignette**

```
---
title: "Introduction to edatools"
output: rmarkdown::html_vignette
vignette: >
  %\VignetteIndexEntry{Introduction to edatools}
  %\VignetteEngine{knitr::rmarkdown}
  %\VignetteEncoding{UTF-8}
```

```
---

```{r, include = FALSE}
knitr::opts_chunk$set(
  collapse = TRUE,
  comment = "#>"
)
```
```

The `edatools` package is a demonstration project for learning how to
build an R package. It comes from chapter 22 of [R in Action (3rd
    ed.)](https://www.manning.com/books/r-in-action-third-edition).

The package has one main function for describing a data frame, and two
    generic functions.

```{r example}
library(edatools)
df_info <- contents(happiness)
print(df_info, digits=3)
plot(df_info)
```

When the package is installed, users can access the vignette using `vignette`
`("edatools")`.

22.2.8 *Editing the DESCRIPTION file*

Every package has a DESCRIPTION file that contains metadata such as package title,
version, author(s), license, and package dependencies. The file was created automatically when you invoked `build_package("edatools")` in section 22.2.2. Other
functions from the `usethis` package will add additional information to the
DESCRIPTION file.

First, indicate which contributed packages your package will require to run. The
edatools package depends on the `ggplot2` package to run. Executing

```
library(usethis)
use_package("ggplot2")
```

will add this requirement to the DESCRIPTION file. You can invoke the command
numerous times if you have multiple dependencies. You needn't specify any base R
packages. When `edtools` is installed, required contributed packages will also be
installed if they are missing.

Next, indicate the license under which the package is being released. Common
license types include MIT, GPL-2, and GPL-3. See www.r-project.org/Licenses for
license descriptions. We'll use the MIT license that basically says you can do anything
you want with this AS IS software as long as you retain the copyright notice. Type

```
use_mit_license("your name here")
```

in the console to add the license to your package.

Finally, edit the DESCRIPTION file manually. Since it is a simple text file, you can edit it in RStudio or via any text editor. The following listing gives the final version of the DESCRIPTION file.

Listing 22.9 Contents of the DESCRIPTION file

```
Package: edatools
Title: Functions for Exploratory Data Analysis
Version: 0.0.0.9000
Authors@R:
    person(given = "Robert",
           family = "Kabacoff",
           role = c("aut", "cre"),
           email = "rkabacoff@wesleyan.edu")
Description: This package contains functions for
    exploratory data analysis. It is a demonstration
    package for the book R in Action (3rd ed.).
License: MIT + file LICENSE
Encoding: UTF-8
LazyData: true
Roxygen: list(markdown = TRUE)
RoxygenNote: 7.1.1
Depends:
    R (>= 2.10)
Imports:
    ggplot2
Suggests:
    rmarkdown,
    knitr
VignetteBuilder: knitr
```

The only fields you will need to edit are `Title`, `Version`, `Authors@R`, and `Description`. The `Title` should be a single line in sentence case. The `Version` number is up to you. The convention is *major.minor.patch.dev*. See https://r-pkgs.org/release.html for details.

In the `Authors@R`: section, specify each contributor and their roles. Here I entered my name and indicated that I am a full author (`"auth"`) and package maintainer (`"cre"`). Of course, when creating your own package, don't use my name (unless the package is really good!). See http://mng.bz/eMlP to learn about participant roles.

The `Description`: section can span several lines but must be indented after the first line. The `LazyData: yes` statement indicates that the datasets in the package (happiness, in this case) should be available as soon as the package is loaded. If this was set to no, the user would have to use `data(happiness)` to access the dataset.

22.2.9 *Building and installing the package*

It's finally time to build the package. (Really, I promise.) At this point, your package should have the structure described in figure 22.3. The italicized folders and files are optional. (Note that the plot.R and print.R files are only required because the edatools package includes specialized print and plot functions.)

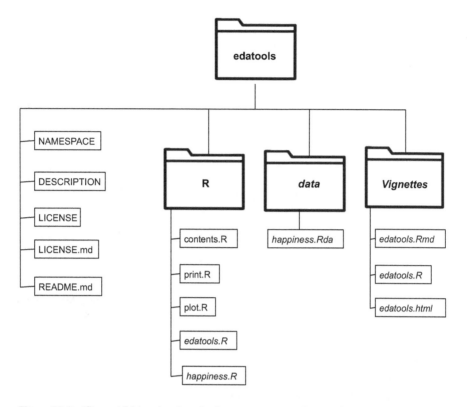

Figure 22.3 File and folder structure for the `edatools` package prior to the building step. Italicized folders and files are optional.

RStudio has a Build tab for building a package (see figure 22.4). Click the More drop-down menu and select Configure Build Tools. This will bring up the dialog in figure 22.5. Make sure that both options are checked. Then click the Configure button to bring up the Roxygen Options dialog. Make sure the first six options are checked (see figure 22.6).

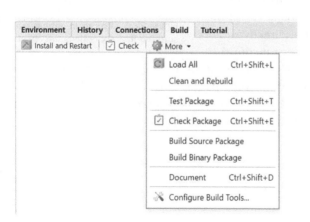

Figure 22.4 RStudio Build Tab. Use the options on this tab to create package documentation, build, and install the finished package.

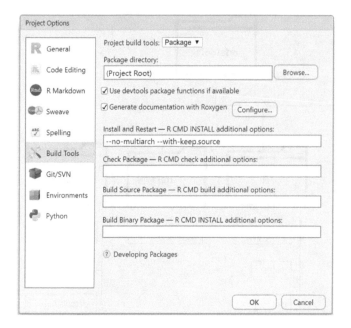

Figure 22.5   Project options dialog. Make sure both check boxes are checked.

Now there are two simple steps. First, build the documentation by selecting More > Document (or Ctrl+Shift+D). This will convert the `roxygen2` comments in the .R files into LaTeX help files (ending in .Rd). The .Rd files are placed in a folder called man (short for manual). The document command will also add information to the DESCRIPTION file and NAMESPACE file.

The following listing gives the resulting NAMESPACE file, which controls the visibility of your functions. Are all functions available to the package user directly, or are some used internally by other functions? In

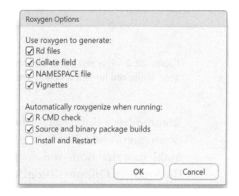

Figure 22.6   Roxygen options dialog. Make sure the first six options are checked.

the current case, all functions are available to the user. It also makes functions from contributed packages available to your package. In this case, the `object.size()`, `reorder()` and all `ggplot2` functions can be called. To learn more about namespaces, see http://adv-r.had.co.nz/Namespaces.html.

Listing 22.10   Contents of the NAMESPACE file

```
# Generated by roxygen2: do not edit by hand

S3method(plot,contents)
S3method(print,contents)
```

```
export(contents)
import(ggplot2)
importFrom(stats,reorder)
importFrom(utils,object.size)
```

Next, click the Install and Restart button. This will build the package, install it in your R local library, and load it into the session. At this point, your package will have the file structure depicted in figure 22.7. Congratulations, your package is ready to use!

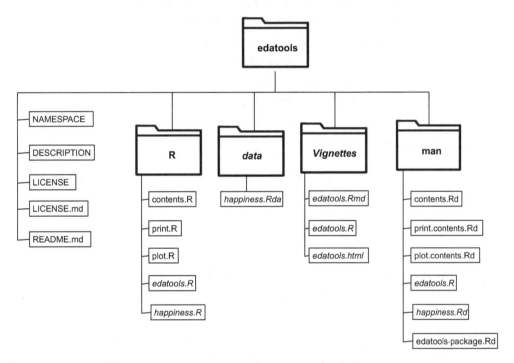

Figure 22.7 Package structure after running Document and Install and Restart. Again, optional files and folders are italicized.

Where is my vignette?

If you added a vignette to your package and followed the instructions in this section, you won't see the vignette. Why not?! The Install and Restart button does not build the vignette by default. Since this can be a time-consuming process, it's assumed that the developer will not want to do this each time the package is rebuilt. When you build a *source package* (section 22.2.9), the vignette *will* be built and added to it. To see it on your system, install the package from this source package (Packages Tab > Install > Install from Package Archive File). Alternatively, you can run the following code:

```
library(devtools)
build_vignettes()
install(build_vignettes=TRUE)
```

Before moving on, you should check the package for potential problems. Clicking the Check button on the Build tab runs extensive consistency checks on the package. It is a good idea to run these checks before sharing your package with others. If you find any errors, correct them, redocument (if documentation has changed), and rebuild the package.

22.3 Sharing your package

Once you've created a useful package, you'll probably want to share it with others. There are several common methods for distributing an R package, including these:

- Distributing a source or binary package file
- Submitting the package to CRAN
- Hosting the package on GitHub
- Creating a package website

In this section, we'll look at each in turn.

22.3.1 Distributing a source package file

You can bundle your package into a single compressed file that can be sent to others via email or cloud services. On the Build tab, click More > Build Source Package. This will create a source package file in your project's parent directory. In this case, edatools_0.0.0.90000.tar.gz will appear one level above the edatools folder. The version number in the name is taken from the DESCRIPTION file. The package is now in a format that can be sent to others or submitted to CRAN.

Recipients can install the package via the Packages tab by selecting Install and specifying Install from Package Archive File. Alternatively, they can use the code

```
install.packages(choose.files(), repos = NULL, type="source")
```

This will bring up a dialog box allowing them to select to the source package.

If you have a LaTeX distribution installed (section 22.2.1), you can also create a PDF manual for your package. Run

```
library(devtools)
build_manual()
```

in the console, and a PDF manual will be created in the parent directory.

22.3.2 Submitting to CRAN

The Comprehensive R Archive Network (CRAN) is the primary service for distributing contributed packages. This morning, the count was 17,788, but that number is already woefully out of date. To contribute your package to CRAN, follow these four steps:

1 Read the CRAN Repository Policy (http://cran.r-project.org/web/packages/policies.html).

2 Make sure the package passes all checks without errors or warnings (Build tab > Check). Otherwise, the package will be rejected.

3 Create a source package file (see section 22.3.1).

4 Submit the package. To do so via web form, use the submission form at http:// cran.r-project.org/submit.html. You'll receive an automated confirmation email that needs to be accepted.

But please don't upload the `edatools` package you just created to CRAN. You now have the tools to create your own packages.

22.3.3 *Hosting on GitHub*

Many package developers host their packages on GitHub (http://www.github.com) even if they're also posted on CRAN. GitHub is a popular Git repository-hosting service with many additional features. There are several good reasons to host a package on GitHub:

- Your package may not be ready for prime time (i.e., it's not fully developed yet).
- You want to allow others to work on the package with you or give you feedback and suggestions.
- You want to host the production version on CRAN and the current development version on GitHub.
- You want to use Git version control in the development process. (Nice, but not necessary.)

Hosting your packages on GitHub is free for both individuals and organizations.

To host a package on GitHub, first add a REAME.md file to your package. At the console, enter

```
library(usethis)
use_readme_md()
```

This will place a text file called README.md in the editor. The file uses a simple markdown language like RMarkdown. In RStudio, you can go to Help > Markdown Quick Reference for details. The following listing displays the README.md file for the `edatools` package.

> **Listing 22.11   Contents of the README.md file**

```
# edatools

This is a demonstration package for the book [R in Action (3rd ed.)]
(https://www.manning.com/books/r-in-action-third-edition).
It contains functions for exploratory data analysis.

## Installation

You can install this package with the following code:

``` r
if(!require(remotes)){
   install.packages("remotes")
```
```

```
}
remotes::install_github("rkabacoff/edatools")
```

```
## Example
```

```
This is a basic example which shows you how to describe a data frame:
```

```
``` r
library(edatools)
df_info<- contents(happiness)
df_info
plot(df_info)
```
```

Save the file, and you are ready to host the package on GitHub.

To host the package,

1 Sign up for an account and log in.
2 Click New to create a new repository. On the next page, give it the same name as your package (see figure 22.8). Use with the default options and click Create Repository.

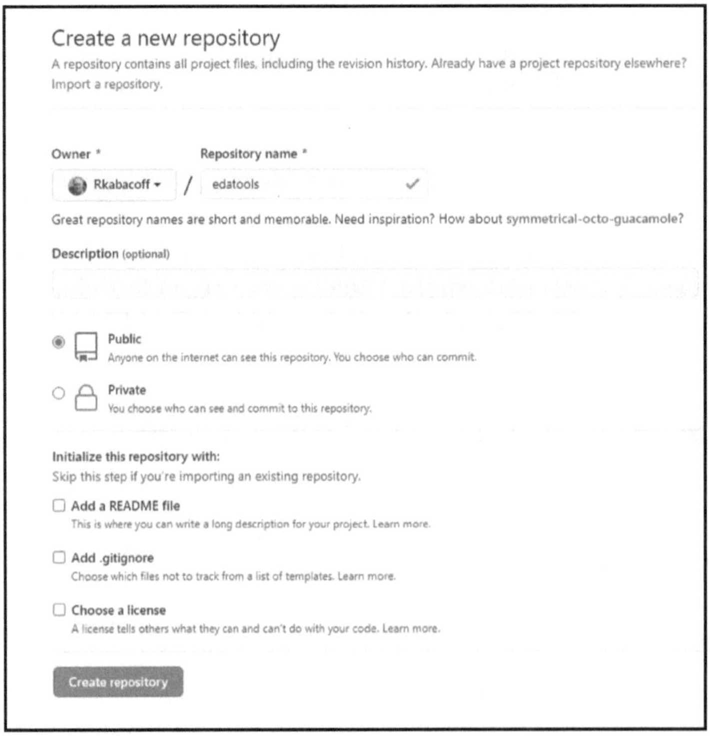

Figure 22.8 GitHub Create a new repository page. Enter the name of the package and click Create Repository.

3 On the next page, select Uploading an Existing File. The option can be hard to see (figure 22.9). Note that this assumes you want to upload the package files directly. If you are using Git version control, the process would be different. See Happy Git and GitHub for the user (https://happygitwithr.com/) for details.

4 On the next page, upload the contents of your package folder (the files and folders *in* your package, not the package folder itself). Click the Commit Changes button at the bottom of the page. Don't forget this last step or the files will not appear.

5 Give everyone the URL (https://github.com/*youraccountname*/*packagename*).

Figure 22.9   GitHub Quick Setup or new repository page. Select Uploading an Existing file.

You can see the GitHub repository for the `edatools` package at https://github.com/Rkabacoff/edatools.

22.3.4 *Creating a package website*

A dedicated website can be a great way to promote and support your package. You can create such website with the `pkgdown` package (https://pkgdown.r-lib.org/). From within the package project, type

```
library(pkgdown)
build_site()
```

in the console. This will add a folder to your project called docs, containing the HTML, cascading style sheets, and JavaScript files needed for a website. Simply put these files on a web server to make you package site available.

GitHub Pages gives you free websites for your projects. Simply upload the docs folder to your GitHub package repository (section 22.3.3). Go to the repository Settings and click the GitHub Pages link. For source, select main, /docs, and Save (see figure 22.10). Your website is now available at https://*youraccountname*.github.io/*packagename*.

Figure 22.10   Setup page for GitHub Pages

The edatools package website is https://rkabacoff.github.io/edatools (figure 22.11).

Note that the contents of the REAME.md file provide the text for the home page. The edatools vignette is linked to the Get Started tab. Each function is described and demonstrated in the Reference tab.

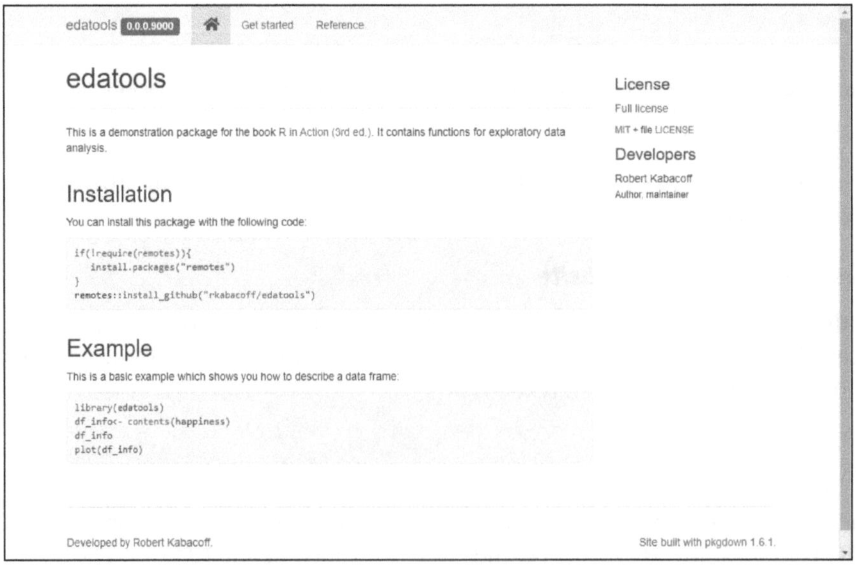

Figure 22.11   edatools website hosted on GitHub Pages

It is easy to customize your site by editing the _pkgdown.yml file in the docs folder before building the site. See "Customise Your Site" (http://mng.bz/pJw2) for details.

22.4 Going further

In this chapter, all the code used to create the edtools package was R code. In fact, most packages contain code that is written entirely in R. But you can also call compiled C, C++, Fortran, and Java code from R. External code is typically included when doing so will improve execution speed or when the author wants to use existing external libraries from within their R code.

There are several methods for including compiled external code. Useful base R functions include .C(), .Fortran(), .External(), and .Call(). Several packages have also been written to facilitate the process, including inline (C, C++, Fortran), Rcpp (C++), and rJava (Java). Adding external compiled code to an R package is beyond the scope of this book. See https://r-pkgs.org/src.html to learn more.

There are many excellent resources for learning more about developing R packages. "Writing R Extensions" by the R Core Team (https://cran.r-project.org/doc/manuals/r-release/R-exts.html) is the original text on the subject. Hadley Wickham and Jenny Bryan's R Packages (https://r-pkgs.org/) contains a wealth of information and is freely available online. Cosima Meyer and Dennis Hammershmidt offer a comprehensive blog article on "How to Write Your Own R Package and Publish it on CRAN" (http://mng.bz/O14o).

R packages are a great way to organize your frequently used functions, develop complete applications, and share your results with others. In this era of reproducible research, it can also be a great way of bundling all the data and code for an extensive project. In this chapter, you created a complete R package from start to finish. Although packages seem complicated at first, they're pretty easy to create once you have the process down. Now, get to work! And remember, have fun out there!

Summary

- An R package is a set of functions, documentation, and data saved in a standardized format.
- R packages can be used to simplify access to frequently used functions, solve complex analytic problems, share code and data with others, and give back to the R community.
- Developing a package is a multistep process. Packages such as devtools, usethis, and roxygen2 can streamline this process.
- Steps include creating a package project, writing functions and documentation, building and installing the package, and distributing the package to others.
- Packages can be shared with others by distributing source or binary package files, submitting to packages to CRAN, and/or hosting packages on GitHub.
- You can use the pkgdown package and GitHub pages to easily create a website that supports your package. It can also become part of your data science portfolio.

afterword
Into the rabbit hole

We've covered a broad range of topics in the book, including major ones like the R development environment, data management, traditional statistical models, and statistical graphics. We've also examined hidden gems like resampling statistics, missing values imputation, and interactive graphics. The great (or perhaps infuriating) thing about R is that there's always more to learn.

R is a large, robust, and evolving statistical platform and programming language. With so many new packages, frequent updates, and new directions, how can you stay current? Happily, many websites support this active community and provide coverage of platform and package changes, new methodologies, and a wealth of tutorials. I've listed some of my favorite sites:

- The R Project for Statistical Computing (www.r-project.org)

    The official R website and your first stop for all things R. The site includes extensive documentation, including "An Introduction to R," "The R Language Definition," "Writing R Extensions," "R Data Import/Export," "R Installation and Administration," and "The R FAQ."

- The R Journal (http://journal.r-project.org)

    A freely accessible, refereed journal containing articles on the R project and contributed packages.

- *R Bloggers* (www.r-bloggers.com)

    A central hub (blog aggregator) that collects content from bloggers writing about R. It contains new articles daily. I'm addicted to it.

- CRANberries (http://dirk.eddelbuettel.com/cranberries)

    A site that aggregates information about new and updated packages and contains links to CRAN for each.

- Journal of Statistical Software (www.jstatsoft.org)

    A freely accessible, refereed journal containing articles, book reviews, and code snippets on statistical computing. Contains frequent articles about R.

- CRAN Task Views (http://cran.r-project.org/web/views)

    Task views are guides to the use of R in different academic and research fields. They include a description of the packages and methods available for a given area. Currently, 41 task views are available (see the following table).

CRAN task views	
Bayesian Inference	Model Deployment with R
Chemometrics and Computational Physics	Multivariate Statistics
Clinical Trial Design, Monitoring, and Analysis	Natural Language Processing
Cluster Analysis and Finite Mixture Models	Numerical Mathematics
Databases with R	Official Statistics and Survey Methodology
Differential Equations	Optimization and Mathematical Programming
Probability Distributions	Analysis of Pharmacokinetic Data
Econometrics	Phylogenetics, Especially Comparative Methods
Analysis of Ecological and Environmental Data	Psychometric Models and Methods
Design of Experiments (DoE) and Analysis of Experimental Data	Reproducible Research
Extreme Value Analysis	Robust Statistical Methods
Empirical Finance	Statistics for the Social Sciences
Functional Data Analysis	Spatial
Statistical Genetics	Handling and Analyzing Spatio-Temporal Data
Graphics and Graphic Devices and Visualization	Survival Analysis
High-Performance and Parallel Computing with R	Teaching Statistics
Hydrological Data and Modeling	Time Series Analysis
Machine Learning and Statistical Learning	Processing and Analysis of Tracking Data
Medical Image Analysis	Web Technologies and Services
Meta-Analysis	gRaphical Models in R
Missing Data	

- B Book of R (https://www.bigbookofr.com/)

    This website contains an archive list of free R-related eBooks.

- R mailing list (https://www.r-project.org/mail.html)

    This electronic mailing list is the best place to ask questions about R. The archives are also searchable. Be sure to read the FAQ before posting questions.

- Cross Validated (http://stats.stackexchange.com)

  A question and answer site for people interested in statistics and data science. This is a good place to post questions about R and see what other people are asking. It's a great place to go if you're stuck.

- Quick-R (www.statmethods.net)

  This is my R website. It's stocked with more than 80 brief tutorials on R topics. False modesty forbids me from saying more.

- Data Visualization with R (http://rkabacoff.github.io/datavis)

  This is my R graphics website. Same disclaimer as above.

The R community is a helpful, vibrant, and exciting lot. Welcome to Wonderland.

appendix A
Graphical user interfaces

You turned here first, didn't you? By default, R provides a simple *command-line interface* (CLI). The user enters statements at a command-line prompt (> by default), and each command is executed one at a time. For many data analysts, the CLI is one of R's most significant limitations.

Several attempts have been made to create more graphical interfaces, ranging from code editors that interact with R (such as RStudio) to GUIs for specific functions or packages (such as BiplotGUI) to full-blown GUIs that allow you to construct analyses through interactions with menus and dialog boxes (such as R Commander).

Table A.1 lists several of the more useful code editors that let you edit and execute R code and include syntax highlighting, statement completion, object exploration, project organization, and online help. RStudio is the most popular *integrated development environment* (IDE) for R programmers by far, but it's nice to have a choice.

Table A.1   Integrated development environments and syntax editors

Name	URL
RStudio Desktop	https://www.rstudio.com/products/rstudio/
R Tools for Visual Studio	http://mng.bz/VGjr
Eclipse with StatET plug-in	https://projects.eclipse.org/projects/science.statet
Architect	https://www.getarchitect.io/
ESS (Emacs Speaks Statistics)	http://ess.r-project.org
Atom Editor with Rbox	https://atom.io/ and https://atom.io/packages/rbox
Notepad++ with NppToR (Windows only)	http://notepad-plus-plus.org and http://sourceforge.net/projects/npptor

Table A.2 lists several promising, full-blown GUIs for R. The GUIs available for R are less comprehensive and mature than those offered by SAS or IBM SPSS, but they're developing rapidly.

Table A.2   Comprehensive GUIs for R

Name	URL
JGR/Deducer	http://rforge.net/JGR/ and http://www.deducer.org
R AnalyticFlow	http://r.analyticflow.com/en/
jamovi	https://www.jamovi.org/jmv/
JASP	https://jasp-stats.org/
Rattle (for data mining)	http://rattle.togaware.com
R Commander	https://socialsciences.mcmaster.ca/jfox/Misc/Rcmdr/
RkWard	https://rkward.kde.org/
Radiant	https://radiant-rstats.github.io/docs/install.html

My favorite GUI for introductory statistics courses is R Commander (shown in figure A.1).

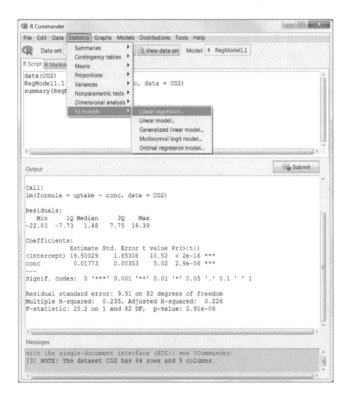

Figure A.1
R Commander GUI

Finally, several applications allow you to create GUI wrappers for R functions (including user-written functions). These include the R GUI Generator (RGG) (http://rgg.r-forge.r-project.org) and the `fgui` and `twiddler` packages available from CRAN. The most comprehensive approach is currently `Shiny` (https://shiny.rstudio.com/), which lets you easily create web applications and dashboards with interactive access to R functions.

appendix B
Customizing
the startup environment

One of the first things that programmers like to do is customize their startup environment to conform to their preferred way of working. Customizing the startup environment allows you to set R options, specify a working directory, load commonly used packages, load user-written functions, set a default CRAN download site, and perform any number of housekeeping tasks.

You can customize the R environment through either a site-initialization file (Rprofile.site) or a directory-initialization file (.Rprofile). These are text files containing R code to be executed at startup.

At startup, R will source the file Rprofile.site from the R_HOME/etc directory, where R_HOME is an environment value. It will then look for an .Rprofile file to source in the current working directory. If R doesn't find this file, it will look for it in the user's home directory. You can use Sys.getenv("R_HOME"), Sys.getenv("HOME"), and getwd() to identify the location of R_HOME, HOME, and the current working directory, respectively.

You can place two special functions in these files. The .First() function is executed at the start of each R session, and the .Last() function is executed at the end of each session. An example of an Rprofile.site file is shown in listing B.1.

Listing B.1   Sample .Rprofile

```
options(digits=4)
options(show.signif.stars=FALSE)    Sets common options
options(scipen=999)
options
```

```
options(prompt="> ")                                          Sets R interactive prompt
options(continue="  ")
                                                                      Sets CRAN
options(repos = c(CRAN = "https://cran.rstudio.com/"))    ◄──┘   mirror default

.libPaths("C:/my_R_library")                      ◄─────────────── Sets path for
                                                                   local library
.env <- new.env()
.env$h <- utils::head
.env$t <- utils::tail
.env$s <- base::summary
.env$ht <- function(x){
  base::rbind(utils::head(x), utils::tail(x))          Creates shortcuts
}
.env$phelp <- function(pckg){
  utils::help(package = deparse(substitute(pckg)))
}
attach(.env)

.First <- function(){
  v <- R.Version()
  msg1 <- paste0(v$version.string, ' -- ', ' "', v$nickname, '"')
  msg2 <- paste0("Platform: ", v$platform)
  cat("\f")
  cat(msg1, "\n", msg2, "\n\n", sep="")               Startup
                                                       function
  if(interactive()){
    suppressMessages(require(tidyverse))
  }

}

.Last <- function(){
  cat("\nGoodbye at ", date(), "\n")       Session end function
}
```

Let's look at what this .Rprofile accomplishes:

- Printed output is customized. The number of significant digits is set to 4 (the default is 7), stars are not printed on summary tables of coefficients, and scientific notation is suppressed.
- The prompt is set to ">" for the first line, and a space for continuation lines (rather than the "+" sign).
- The default CRAN mirror site for install.packages() commands is set to cran.rstudio.com.
- A personal directory is defined for installed packages. Setting a .libPaths value allows you to create a local library for packages outside of the R directory tree. This can be useful for retaining packages during an upgrade.

- One-letter shortcuts are defined for the `tail()`, `head()` and `summary()` functions. The new functions `ht()` and `phelp()` are defined. `ht()` combines the output of head and tail. `phelp()` lists the functions in a package (with linked help).
- The `.First()` function
  - Replaces the standard welcome message with a shorter customized welcome. On my machine, the new welcome message is simply this:

    R version 4.1.0 (2021-05-18)—"Camp Pontanezen"
    Platform: x86_64-w64-mingw32/x64 (64-bit)

  - Loads the `tidyverse` packages into interactive sessions. The `tidyverse` start-up message is suppressed.
- The `.Last()` function prints a customized goodbye message. This is also an excellent place to execute any cleanup activities, including archiving command histories, program output, and data files.

WARNING!   If you define functions or load packages in your .Rprofile file rather than in your scripts, they'll be less portable. Your code now depends on your startup file to run correctly. They'll fail on other machines that lack this file.

If you want to supercharge your .Rprofile, take a look at Jumping Rivers' `rprofile` package (https://www.jumpingrivers.com/blog/customising-your-rprofile/). There are other ways to customize the startup environment, including the use of command-line options and environment variables. See `help(Startup)` and appendix B in the "Introduction to R" manual (http://cran.r-project.org/doc/manuals/R-intro.pdf) for more details.

appendix C
Exporting data from R

In chapter 2, we review a wide range of methods for importing data into R. But sometimes, you'll want to go the other way—exporting data from R—so data can be archived or imported into external applications. In this appendix, you'll learn how to output an R object to a delimited text file, an Excel spreadsheet, or a statistical application (such as SPSS, SAS, or Stata).

C.1 Delimited text file

You can use the `write.table()` function to output an R object to a delimited text file. The format is

```
write.table(x, outfile, sep=delimiter, quote=TRUE, na="NA")
```

where *x* is the object and *outfile* is the target file. For example, the statement

```
write.table(mydata, "mydata.txt", sep=",")
```

saves the dataset `mydata` to a comma-delimited file named mydata.txt in the current working directory. Include a path (for example, `"c:/myprojects/mydata.txt"`) to save the output file elsewhere. Replacing `sep=","` with `sep="\t"` saves the data in a tab-delimited file. By default, strings are enclosed in quotes (`""`), and missing values are written as `NA`.

C.2 Excel spreadsheet

The `write.xlsx()` function in the `xlsx` package can be used to save an R data frame to an Excel 2007 workbook. The format is

```
library(xlsx)
write.xlsx(x, outfile, col.Names=TRUE, row.names=TRUE,
           sheetName="Sheet 1", append=FALSE)
```

For example, the statements

```
library(xlsx)
write.xlsx(mydata, "mydata.xlsx")
```

export the data frame `mydata` to a worksheet (Sheet 1 by default) in an Excel workbook named mydata.xlsx in the current working directory. By default, the variable names in the dataset are used to create column headings in the spreadsheet, and row names are placed in the first column of the spreadsheet. If mydata.xlsx already exists, it's overwritten.

The `xlsx` package is a powerful tool for manipulating Excel workbooks. See the package documentation for more details.

C.3   *Statistical applications*

The `write.foreign()` function in the `foreign` package can be used to export a data frame to an external statistical application. Two files are created: a free-format text file containing the data and a code file containing instructions for reading the data into the external statistical application. The format is

```
write.foreign(dataframe, datafile, codefile, package=package)
```

For example, the code

```
library(foreign)
write.foreign(mydata, "mydata.txt", "mycode.sps", package="SPSS")
```

exports the data frame `mydata` into a free-format text file named mydata.txt in the current working directory and an SPSS program named mycode.sps that can be used to read the text file. Other values of `package` include `"SAS"` and `"Stata"`.

To learn more about exporting data from R, see the "R Data Import/Export" documentation, available from http://cran.r-project.org/doc/manuals/R-data.pdf.

appendix D
Matrix algebra in R

Many of the functions described in this book operate on matrices. The manipulation of matrices is built deeply into the R language. Table D.1 describes operators and functions that are particularly important for solving linear algebra problems. In the table, A and B are matrices, x and b are vectors, and k is a scalar.

Table D.1 Functions and operators for matrix algebra

Operator or function	Description
+ - * / ^	Element-wise addition, subtraction, multiplication, division, and exponentiation, respectively
A %*% B	Matrix multiplication
A %o% B	Outer product: AB'
cbind(A, B, …)	Combines matrices or vectors horizontally. Returns a matrix.
chol(A)	Cholesky factorization of A. If R <- chol(A), then chol(A) contains the upper triangular factor, such that R'R = A.
colMeans(A)	Returns a vector containing the column means of A
crossprod(A)	Returns A'A
crossprod(A,B)	Returns A'B
colSums(A)	Returns a vector containing the column sums of A
diag(A)	Returns a vector containing the elements of the principal diagonal
diag(x)	Creates a diagonal matrix with elements of x in the principal diagonal
diag(k)	If k is a scalar, this creates a $k \times k$ identity matrix. Go figure.

Table D.1 Functions and operators for matrix algebra *(continued)*

Operator or function	Description
eigen(A)	Eigenvalues and eigenvectors of A. If y <- eigen(A), then • y$val are the eigenvalues of A. • y$vec are the eigenvectors of A.
ginv(A)	Moore-Penrose Generalized Inverse of A. (Requires the MASS package.)
qr(A)	QR decomposition of A. If y <- qr(A), then • y$qr has an upper triangle that contains the decomposition and a lower triangle that contains information on the decomposition. • y$rank is the rank of A. • y$qraux is a vector that contains additional information on Q. • y$pivot contains information on the pivoting strategy used.
rbind(A, B, …)	Combines matrices or vectors vertically. Returns a matrix.
rowMeans(A)	Returns a vector containing the row means of A
rowSums(A)	Returns a vector containing the row sums of A
solve(A)	Inverse of A where A is a square matrix
solve(A, b)	Solves for vector x in the equation b = Ax
svd(A)	Single-value decomposition of A. If y <- svd(A), then • y$d is a vector containing the singular values of A. • y$u is a matrix with columns containing the left singular vectors of A. • y$v is a matrix with columns containing the right singular vectors of A.
t(A)	Transpose of A

Several user-contributed packages are particularly useful for matrix algebra. The matlab package contains wrapper functions and variables used to replicate MATLAB function calls as closely as possible. These functions can help you port MATLAB applications and code to R. There's also a useful cheat sheet for converting MATLAB statements to R statements at http://mathesaurus.sourceforge.net/octave-r.html.

The Matrix package contains functions that extend R to support highly dense or sparse matrices. It provides efficient access to BLAS (Basic Linear Algebra Subroutines), LAPACK (dense matrix), TAUCS (sparse matrix), and UMFPACK (sparse matrix) routines.

Finally, the matrixStats package provides methods for operating on the rows and columns of matrices, including functions that calculate counts, sums, products, central tendency, dispersion, and more. Each is optimized for speed and efficient memory use.

appendix E
Packages used in this book

R derives much of its breadth and power from the contributions of selfless authors. Table E.1 lists the user-contributed packages described in this book, along with the chapter(s) in which they appear. Some packages have too many authors to list here. Additionally, many packages have been enhanced by contributors. See the package documentation for details.

Table E.1 Contributed packages used in this book

Package	Authors	Description	Chapter(s)
AER	Christian Kleiber and Achim Zeileis	Functions, datasets, examples, demos, and vignettes from the book *Applied Econometrics with R* by Christian Kleiber and Achim Zeileis (Springer, 2008)	13
boot	S original by Angelo Canty. R port by Brian Ripley.	Bootstrap functions	12
bootstrap	S original from StatLib by Rob Tibshirani. R port by Friedrich Leisch.	Software (bootstrap, cross-validation, jackknife) and data from *An Introduction to the Bootstrap* by B. Efron and R. Tibshirani (Chapman and Hall, 1993)	8
broom	David Robinson, Alex Hayes, and Simon Couch	Summarizes key information about statistical objects in tidy tibbles	21
car	John Fox, Sanford Weisberg, and Brad Price	Functions for *Companion to Applied Regression*	8, 9, 11
carData	John Fox, Sanford Weisberg, and Brad Price	Datasets to accompany *Companion to Applied Regression*	7

Table E.2   Contributed packages used in this book *(continued)*

Package	Authors	Description	Chapter(s)
cluster	Martin Maechler, Peter Rousseeuw (Fortran original), Anja Struyf (S original), and Mia Hubert (S original)	Methods for cluster analysis	16
clusterability	Zachariah Neville, Naomi Brownstein, Maya Ackerman, and Andreas Adolfsson	Performs tests for cluster tendency of a dataset	16
coin	Torsten Hothorn, Kurt Hornik, Mark A. van de Wiel, and Achim Zeileis	Conditional inference procedures in a permutation test framework	12
colorhcplot	Damiano Fantini	Build dendrograms with color highlighted groups	16
corrgram	Kevin Wright	Plots a corrgram	11
DALEX	Przemyslaw Biecek, Szymon Maksymiuk, and Hubert Baniecki	Model-agnostic language for exploration and explanation	17
devtools	Hadley Wickham, Jim Hester, and Winston Chang	Tools to make developing R packages easier	22
directlabels	Toby Dylan Hocking	Direct labels for multicolor plots	15
doParallel	Michelle Wallig, Microsoft Corporation, and Steve Weston	`foreach` parallel adaptor for the `parallel` package	20
dplyr	Hadley Wickham, Romain François, Lionel Henry, and Kirill Müller	A grammar of data manipulation	3, 5, 6, 7, 9, 16, 19, 21
e1071	David Meyer, Evgenia Dimitriadou, Kurt Hornik, Andreas Weingessel, and Friedrich Leisch	Miscellaneous functions of the Department of Statistics, Probability Theory Group, TU Wien	17
effects	John Fox and Jangman Hong	Effect displays for linear, generalized linear, multinomial-logit, and proportional-odds logit models	8, 9
factoextra	Alboukadel Kassambara	Extract and visualize the results of multivariate data analyses	16
flexclust	Friedrich Leish and Evgenia Dimnitriadou	Flexible cluster algorithms	16
foreach	Michelle Wallig, Microsoft Corporation, and Steve Weston	Provides R with the foreach looping construct	20
forecast	Rob J. Hyndman and many other authors	Forecasting functions for time series and linear models	15

Table E.2 Contributed packages used in this book *(continued)*

Package	Authors	Description	Chapter(s)
gapminder	Jennifer Bryan	An excerpt of the data available at Gapminder.org	19
Ggally	Barret Schloerke and many other authors	Extends the functionality of ggplot2	11
ggdendro	Andrie de Vries and Brian D. Ripley	Create dendrograms and tree plots using ggplot2	16
ggm	Giovanni M. Marchetti, Mathias Drton, and Kayvan Sadeghi	Tools for marginalization, conditioning, and fitting by maximum likelihood	7
ggplot2	Hadley Wickam and many other authors	An implementation of the Grammar of Graphics	4, 6, 9, 10, 11, 12, 15, 16, 18, 19, 20, 21
ggrepel	Kamil Slowikowski	Automatically position non-overlapping text labels with ggplot2	19
gmodels	Gregory R. Warnes; includes R source code and/or documentation contributed by Ben Bolker, Thomas Lumley, and Randall C. Johnson. Contributions from Randall C. Johnson are copyrighted (SAIC-Frederick, Inc., 2005).	Various R programming tools for model fitting	7
haven	Hadley Wickham and Evan Miller	Import and export SPSS, Stata, and SAS files	2
Hmisc	Frank E. Harrell, Jr.	Miscellaneous functions for data analysis, high-level graphics, utility operations, and more	7
ISLR	Gareth James, Daniela Witten, Trevor Hastie and Rob Tibshirani	Data for an *Introduction to Statistical Learning with Applications in R*	19
kableExtra	Hao Zhu	Construct complex HTML and LaTeX tables	21
knitr	Yihui Xie	A general-purpose package for dynamic report generation in R	21
leaps	Thomas Lumley, using Fortran code by Alan Miller	Regression subset selection, including exhaustive search	8
lmPerm	Bob Wheeler	Permutation tests for linear models	12

Table E.2 Contributed packages used in this book (*continued*)

Package	Authors	Description	Chapter(s)
MASS	S original by Venables and Ripley; R port by Brian Ripley, following earlier work by Kurt Hornik and Albrecht Gebhardt	Functions and datasets to support Venables and Ripley's *Modern Applied Statistics with S,* 4th edition (Springer, 2003)	7, 9, 12, 13, 14, appendix D
mice	Stef van Buuren, and Karin Groothuis-Oudshoorn	Multivariate imputation by chained equations	18
mosaicData	Randall Pruim, Daniel Kaplan, and Nicholas Horton	Datasets from Project MOSAIC	4
multcomp	Torsten Hothorn, Frank Bretz Peter Westfall, Richard M. Heiberger, and Andre Schuetzenmeister	Simultaneous tests and confidence intervals for general linear hypotheses in parametric models, including linear, generalized linear, linear mixed effects, and survival models	9, 12, 21
MultiRNG	Hakan Demirtas, Rawan Allozi, and Ran Gao	Pseudo-random number generation for 11 multivariate distributions	5
mvoutlier	Moritz Gschwandtner and Peter Filzmoser	Multivariate outlier detection based on robust methods	9
naniar	Nicholas Tierney, Di Cook, Miles McBain, and Colin Fay	Data structures, summaries, and visualizations for missing data	18
NbClust	Malika Charrad, Nadia Ghazzali, Veronique Boiteau, and Azam Niknafs	An examination of indices for determining the number of clusters	16
partykit	Torsten Hothorn, Heidi Seibold, and Achim Zeileis	A toolkit for recursive partitioning	17
pastecs	Frederic Ibanez, Philippe Grosjean, and Michele Etienne	Package for the analysis of space-time ecological series	7
patchwork	Thomas Lin Pedersen	Composes a composition consisting of multiple plots	19
pkgdown	Hadley Wickham and Jay Hesselberth	Creates attractive HTML documentation and website for a package	22
plotly	Carson Sievert and many other authors	Create interactive web graphics via plotly.js	19
psych	William Revelle	Procedures for psychological, psychometric, and personality research	7, 14
pwr	Stephane Champely	Basic functions for power analysis	10
qcc	Luca Scrucca	Quality-control charts	13

Table E.2 Contributed packages used in this book *(continued)*

Package	Authors	Description	Chapter(s)
randomForest	Fortran original by Leo Breiman and Adele Cutler; R port by Andy Liaw and Matthew Wiener	Breiman and Cutler's random forests for classification and regression	17
rattle	Graham Williams, Mark Vere Culp, Ed Cox, Anthony Nolan, Denis White, Daniele Medri, Akbar Waljee (OOB AUC for Random Forest), and Brian Ripley (original author of print.summary.nnet)	Graphical user interface for data mining in R	16, 17
readr	Hadley Wickham and Jim Hester	Flexibly import rectangular text data	2
readxl	Hadley Wickham and Jennifer Bryan	Import Excel files	2
rgl	Daniel Adler and Duncan Murdoch	3D visualization device system (OpenGL)	11
rmarkdown	JJ Allaire, Yihui Xie, and many other authors	Convert R Markdown documents into a variety of documents	21
robustbase	Martin Maechler and many other authors	Tools for analyzing data with robust methods	13
rpart	Terry Therneau, Beth Atkinson, and Brian Ripley (author of the initial R port)	Recursive partitioning and regression trees	17
rrcov	Valentin Todorov	Robust location and scatter estimation and robust multivariate analysis with a high breakdown point	9
scales	Hadley Wickham and Dana Seidel	Scale functions for data visualization	6, 19
scatterplot3d	Uwe Ligges	Plots a three-dimensional (3D) point cloud	11
showtext	Yixuan Qiu and many other authors	Use various types of fonts in R graphs	19
sqldf	G. Grothendieck	Manipulate R data frames using SQL	3
tidyquant	Matt Dancho and Davis Vaughan	Tidy tools for quantitative financial analysis	21
tidyr	Hadley Wickham	Tools for tidying messy data, including pivoting, nesting, and unnesting data	5, 16, 20

586 APPENDIX E *Packages used in this book*

Table E.2 Contributed packages used in this book *(continued)*

Package	Authors	Description	Chapter(s)
treemapify	David Wilkins	Provides ggplot2 geoms for drawing treemaps	6
tseries	Adrian Trapletti and Kurt Hornik	Time series analysis and computational finance	15
usethis	Hadley Wickham and Jennifer Bryan	Automate package and project setup tasks	22
vcd	David Meyer, Achim Zeileis, and Kurt Hornik	Functions for visualizing categorical data	1, 6, 7, 11, 12
VIM	Matthias Templ, Andreas Alfons, and Alexander Kowarik	Visualization and imputation of missing values	18
xtable	David B. Dahl and many other authors	Export tables to LaTeX or HTML	21
xts	Jeffrey A. Ryan and Joshua M. Ulrich	Uniform handling of different time-based data classes	15

appendix F
Working with
large datasets

R holds all of its objects in virtual memory. For most of us, this design decision has led to a zippy interactive experience, but for analysts working with large datasets, it can lead to slow program execution and memory-related errors.

Memory limits depend primarily on the R build (32- versus 64-bit) and the OS version involved. Error messages starting with "cannot allocate vector of size" typically indicate a failure to obtain sufficient contiguous memory, whereas error messages starting with "cannot allocate vector of length" indicate that an address limit has been exceeded. When working with large datasets, try to use a 64-bit build if at all possible. See `help(Memory)` for more information.

There are three issues to consider when working with large datasets: efficient programming to speed execution, storing data externally to limit memory issues, and using specialized statistical routines designed to efficiently analyze massive amounts of data. First, we'll consider simple solutions for each. Then we'll turn to more comprehensive (and complex) solutions for working with *big* data.

F.1   Efficient programming

Several programming tips can help you improve performance when working with large datasets:

- Vectorize calculations when possible. Use R's built-in functions for manipulating vectors, matrices, and lists (for example, `ifelse`, `colMeans`, and `rowSums`), and avoid loops (`for` and `while`) when feasible.
- Use matrices rather than data frames (they have less overhead).
- When importing delimited text files, use an optimized function like `fread()` from the `data.table` package or `vroom()` from the `vroom` package. They are *considerably* faster than base R's `read.table()` function.

587

- Correctly size objects initially, rather than growing them from smaller objects by appending values.
- Use parallelization for repetitive, independent, and numerically intensive tasks.
- Test programs on a sample of the data to optimize code and remove bugs before attempting a run on the full dataset.
- Delete temporary objects and objects that are no longer needed. The call `rm(list=ls())` removes all objects from memory, providing a clean slate. Specific objects can be removed with `rm(object)`. After removing large objects, a call to `gc()` will initiate garbage collection, ensuring that the objects are removed from memory.
- Use the function `.ls.objects()` described in Jeromy Anglim's blog entry "Memory Management in R: A Few Tips and Tricks" (http://mng.bz/xGpq) to list all workspace objects sorted by size (MB). This function will help you find and deal with memory hogs.
- Profile your programs to see how much time is being spent in each function. You can accomplish this with the `Rprof()` and `summaryRprof()` functions. The `system.time()` function can also help. The `profr` and `prooftools` packages provide functions that can help you analyze profiling output.
- Use compiled external routines to speed up program execution. You can use the `Rcpp` package to transfer R objects to C++ functions and back when more optimized subroutines are needed.

Section 20.5 offers examples of vectorization, efficient data input, correctly sizing objects, and parallelization.

With large datasets, increasing code efficiency will only get you so far. When you bump up against memory limits or slow code execution, consider upgrading your hardware. You can also store your data externally and use specialized analysis routines.

F.2   *Storing data outside of RAM*

Several packages are available for storing data outside of R's main memory. The strategy involves storing data in external databases or in binary flat files on disk and then accessing portions as needed. Table F.1 lists several useful packages.

Table F.1   R packages for accessing large datasets

Package	Description
bigmemory	Supports the creation, storage, access, and manipulation of massive matrices. Matrices are allocated to shared memory and memory-mapped files.
disk.frame	A disk-based data manipulation framework for working with larger-than-RAM datasets
ff	Provides data structures that are stored on disk but behave as if they're in RAM

Table F.1   R packages for accessing large datasets *(continued)*

Package	Description
`filehash`	Implements a simple key-value database where character string keys are associated with data values stored on disk
`ncdf, ncdf4`	Provide an interface to Unidata NetCDF data files
`RODBC, RMySQL, ROracle, RPostgreSQL, RSQLite`	Each provides access to external relational database management systems.

These packages help overcome R's memory limits on data storage. But you also need specialized methods when you attempt to analyze large datasets in a reasonable length of time. Some of the most useful are described next.

F.3   *Analytic packages for out-of-memory data*

R provides several packages for the analysis of large datasets:

- The `biglm` and `speedglm` packages fit linear and generalized linear models to large datasets in a memory-efficient manner. This offers `lm()` and `glm()` type functionality when dealing with massive datasets.

- Several packages offer analytic functions for working with the massive matrices produced by the `bigmemory` package. The `biganalytics` package offers k-means clustering, column statistics, and a wrapper to `biglm`. The `bigrf` package can be used to fit classification and regression forests. The `bigtabulate` package provides `table()`, `split()`, and `tapply()` functionality, and the `bigalgebra` package provides advanced linear algebra functions.

- The `biglars` package offers least-angle regression, lasso, and stepwise regression for datasets that are too large to be held in memory, when used in conjunction with the `ff` package.

- The `data.table` package provides an enhanced version of `data.frame` that includes faster aggregation; faster ordered and overlapping range joins; and faster column addition, modification, and deletion by reference by group (without copies). You can use the `data.table` structure with large datasets (for example, 100 GB in RAM), and it's compatible with any R function expecting a data frame.

Each of these packages accommodates large datasets for specific purposes and is relatively easy to use. More comprehensive solutions for analyzing data in the terabyte range are described next.

F.4   *Comprehensive solutions for working with enormous datasets*

When I wrote the first edition of this book, the most I could say in this section was, "Well, we're trying." Since that time, there has been an explosion of projects that combine *high-performance computing* (HPC) and the R language. This section provides pointers to some of the more popular approaches to using R with terabyte-class datasets. Each requires some familiarity with HPC and the use of other software platforms such as Hadoop (a free Java-based software framework for processing large datasets in a distributed computing environment).

Table F.2 describes open source approaches for using R with massive datasets. The most popular approaches are RHadoop and sparklyr.

Table F.2   R open source platforms for big data

Approach	Description
RHadoop	Software for managing and analyzing data with Hadoop in an R environment. Consists of five interconnected packages: `rhbase`, `ravro`, `rhdfs`, `plyrmr`, and `rmr2`. See https://github.com/RevolutionAnalytics/RHadoop/wiki for details.
RHIPE	*R and Hadoop Integrated Programming Environment.* An R package that allows users to run Hadoop MapReduce jobs from within R. See https://github.com/delta-rho/RHIPE.
Hadoop Streaming	Hadoop streaming (https://hadoop.apache.org/docs/r1.2.1/streaming.html) is a utility for creating and running Map/Reduce jobs with any language as the mapper and/or the reducer. The `HadoopStreaming` package supports writing these scripts in R. See https://cran.rstudio.com/web/packages/HadoopStreaming/.
RHIVE	An R extension facilitating distributed computing via HIVE query. RHIVE supports easy use of HIVE SQL in R and the use of R objects and R functions in Hive. See https://github.com/nexr/RHive for information.
pbdR	"Programming with Big Data in R." Packages enabling data parallelism in R through a simple interface to scalable, high-performance libraries (such as MPI, ZeroMQ, ScaLAPACK, and netCDF4, and PAPI). The pbdR software also supports the single program, multiple data (SPMD) model on large-scale computing clusters. See http://r-pbd.org or details.
sparklyr	A package providing an R interface for Apache Spark. Supports connecting to local and remote Apache Spark clusters, provides a `'dplyr'`-compatible back end and an interface to Spark's machine learning algorithms. See https://cran.r-project.org/web/packages/sparklyr for details.

Cloud services offer a ready-made, scalable infrastructure with potentially enormous memory and storage resources. The most popular cloud services for R users are provided by Amazon, Microsoft, and Google. While not a cloud solution, per se, Oracle also offers big data computing for R users (see table F.3).

Table F.3   Commercial platforms for big data projects

Approach	Description
Amazon Web Services (AWS)	There are several approaches to using R with AWS. The R package `paws` (package for Amazon Web Services in R) provides a full suite of AWS services from within R (see https://paws-r.github.io/). The `aws.ec2` package is a simple client package for the AWS EC2 REST API (https://github.com/cloudyr/aws.ec2). Louis Aslett maintains Amazon Machine Images that make deploying an RStudio Server into the Amazon EC2 service relatively easy (https://www.louisaslett.com/RStudio_AMI/).

Table F.3   Commercial platforms for big data projects *(continued)*

Approach	Description
Microsoft Azure	Data Science Virtual Machines are VM images on the Azure cloud platform, built for data science. They include Microsoft R Open, Microsoft Machine Learning Server, RStudio Desktop, and RStudio Server. See https://azure.microsoft.com/en-us/services/virtual-machines/data-science-virtual-machines/ for details. Also see `AzureR`, a family of packages for working with Azure from R (https://github.com/Azure/AzureR).
Google Cloud Services	The `bigrquery` package provides an interface to Google's BigQuery API (https://github.com/r-dbi/bigrquery). The `googleComputeEngineR` package provides an R interface to the Google Cloud Compute Engine API. It makes the deployment of cloud resources for R (including RStudio and Shiny) as simple as possible (https://cloudyr.github.io/googleComputeEngineR/).
Oracle R Advanced Analytics for Hadoop	This is a collection of R packages that provide interfaces to HIVE tables, Hadoop infrastructure, Oracle database tables, and the local R environment. It also includes a wide range of predictive analytic techniques. See the Oracle help files (http://mng.bz/K4jn).

In addition to the resources in table F.3, consider the cloudyr project (https://cloudyr.github.io/), an initiative designed to make cloud computing with R easier. It contains a wide range of packages for melding the advantages of R and cloud services.

Working with datasets in the gigabyte-to-terabyte range can be challenging in any language. Each of these approaches comes with a significant learning curve. The book *Big Data Analytics with R and Hadoop* (Prajapati, 2013) is a useful resource for using R with Hadoop. For Spark, Mastering Spark with R (https://therinspark.com/) and Using Spark from R for Performance with Arbitrary Code (https://sparkfromr.com/) are very helpful. Finally, see the CRAN Task View: *"High-Performance and Parallel Computing with R"* (https://cran.r-project.org/web/views/HighPerformanceComputing.html). This is an area of rapid change and development, so be sure to check the task view often.

appendix G
Updating
an R installation

As consumers, we take for granted that we can update a piece of software via a "Check for Updates" option. In chapter 1, I noted that the update.packages() function can be used to download and install the most recent version of a contributed package. Unfortunately, updating the R installation itself can be more complicated.

If you want to update an R installation from version 5.1.0 to 6.1.1, you must get creative. (As I write this, the current version is actually 4.1.1, but I want this book to appear hip and current for years to come.) Two methods are described here: an automated method using the installr package and a manual method that works on all platforms.

G.1   *Automated installation (Windows only)*

If you're a Windows user, you can use the installr package to update an R installation. First install the package and load it:

```
install.packages("installr")
library(installr)
```

This adds an Update menu to the RGui (see figure G.1).

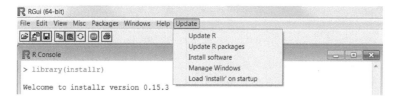

Figure G.1   Update menu added to Windows RGui by the installr package

The menu allows you to install a new version of R, update existing packages, and install other useful software produces (such as RStudio). Currently, the `installr` package is only available for Windows platforms. For macOS users or Windows users who don't want to use `installr`, updating R is usually a manual process.

G.2 *Manual installation (Windows and macOS)*

Downloading and installing the latest version of R from CRAN (http://cran.r-project .org/bin) is relatively straightforward. The complicating factor is that customizations (including previously installed contributed packages) aren't included in the new installation. In my current setup, I have more than 500 contributed packages installed. I really don't want to have to write down their names and reinstall them by hand the next time I upgrade my R installation!

There has been much discussion on the web concerning the most elegant and efficient way to update an R installation. The method described here is neither elegant nor efficient, but I find that it works well on both Windows and macOS platforms.

In this approach, you use the `installed.packages()` function to save a list of packages to a location outside of the R directory tree, and then you use the list with the `install.packages()` function to download and install the latest contributed packages into the new R installation. Here are the steps:

1 If you have a customized Rprofile.site file (see appendix B), save a copy outside of R.

2 Launch your current version of R, and issue the following statements:

```
oldip <- installed.packages()[,1]
save(oldip, file="path/installedPackages.Rdata")
```

where `path` is a directory outside of R.

3 Download and install the newer version of R.

4 If you saved a customized version of the Rprofile.site file in step 1, copy it into the new installation.

5 Launch the new version of R, and issue the following statements:

```
load("path/installedPackages.Rdata")
newip <- installed.packages()[,1]
for(i in setdiff(oldip, newip)){
  install.packages(i)
}
```

where `path` is the location specified in step 2.

6 Delete the old installation (optional).

This approach will install only packages that are available from CRAN. It won't find packages obtained from other locations. You'll have to find and download these separately. Luckily, the process displays a list of packages that can't be installed. During my last installation, `globaltest` and `Biobase` couldn't be found. Because I got them from the Bioconductor site, I was able to install them via this code:

```
source("http://bioconductor.org/biocLite.R")
biocLite("globaltest")
biocLite("Biobase")
```

Step 6 involves the optional deletion of the old installation. On a Windows machine, more than one version of R can be installed at a time. If desired, uninstall the older version via Start > Control Panel > Uninstall a Program. On macOS platforms, the new version of R will overwrite the older version. To delete any remnants on a macOS, use the Finder to go to the /Library/Frameworks/R.frameworks/versions/ directory, and delete the folder representing the older version.

Clearly, manually updating an existing version of R is more involved than is desirable for such a sophisticated piece of software. I'm hopeful that someday this appendix will simply say "Select the Check for Updates Option" to update an R installation.

G.3   *Updating an R installation (Linux)*

The process of updating an R installation on a Linux platform is quite different from the process used on Windows and macOS machines. Additionally, it varies by Linux distribution (Debian, Red Hat, SUSE, or Ubuntu). See http://cran.r-project.org/bin/linux for details.

references

Allison, T. and D. Chichetti. 1976. "Sleep in Mammals: Ecological and Constitutional Correlates." *Science* 194 (4266): 732–734.

Anderson, M. J. 2006. "Distance-based Tests for Homogeneity of Multivariate Dispersions." *Biometrics* 62: 245–253.

Baade, R. and R. Dye. 1990. "The Impact of Stadiums and Professional Sports on Metropolitan Area Development." *Growth and Change* 21: 1–14.

Bandalos, D. L. and M. R. Boehm-Kaufman. 2009. "Four Common Misconceptions in Exploratory Factor Analysis." In *Statistical and Methodological Myths and Urban Legends*, edited by C. E. Lance and R. J. Vandenberg, 61–87. New York: Routledge.

Bates, D. 2005. "Fitting Linear Mixed Models in R." *R News* 5 (1): 27–30. www.r-project.org/doc/Rnews/Rnews_2005-1.pdf.

Breslow, N. and D. Clayton. 1993. "Approximate Inference in Generalized Linear Mixed Models." *Journal of the American Statistical Association* 88:9–25.

Bretz, F., T. Hothorn, and P. Westfall. 2010. *Multiple Comparisons Using R.* Boca Raton, FL: Chapman & Hall.

Canty, A. J. 2002. "Resampling Methods in R: The boot Package." *R News* 2 (3): 2–7. www.r-project.org/doc/Rnews/Rnews_2002-3.pdf.

Chambers, J. M. 2008. *Software for Data Analysis: Programming with R.* New York: Springer.

Chambers, J., W. Cleveland, B. Kleiner, and P. Tukey. 1983. *Graphical Methods for Data Analysis.* Wadsworth & Brooks/Cole Statistics/Probability Series. Boston: Duxbury Press.

Chollet, F., and J. Allaire. 2018. *Deep Learning with R.* NY: Manning.

Ciaburro, G. and B. Venkateswaran. 2017. *Neural networks with R.* Birmingham: Packt.

Cleveland, W. 1981. "LOWESS: A Program for Smoothing Scatter Plots by Robust Locally Weighted Regression." *The American Statistician* 35:54.

_____. 1993. *Visualizing Data.* Summit, NJ: Hobart Press.

Cohen, J. 1988. *Statistical Power Analysis for the Behavioral Sciences*, 2nd ed. Hillsdale, NJ: Lawrence Erlbaum.

Cowpertwait, P. S. and A. V. Metcalfe. 2009. *Introductory Time Series with R.* Auckland, New Zealand: Springer.

Coxe, S., S. West, and L. Aiken. 2009. "The Analysis of Count Data: A Gentle Introduction to Poisson Regression and Its Alternatives." *Journal of Personality Assessment* 91: 121–136.

Culbertson, W. and D. Bradford. 1991. "The Price of Beer: Some Evidence for Interstate Comparisons." *International Journal of Industrial Organization* 9: 275–289.

DiStefano, C., M. Zhu, and D. Mîndrila. 2009. "Understanding and Using Factor Scores: Considerations for the Applied Researcher." *Practical Assessment, Research & Evaluation* 14 (20). http://pareonline.net/pdf/v14n20.pdf.

Dobson, A. and A. Barnett. 2008. *An Introduction to Generalized Linear Models*, 3rd ed. Boca Raton, FL: Chapman & Hall.

Dunteman, G. and M-H Ho. 2006. *An Introduction to Generalized Linear Models*. Thousand Oaks, CA: Sage.

Efron, B. and R. Tibshirani. 1998. *An Introduction to the Bootstrap*. New York: Chapman & Hall.

Enders, C. K. 2010. *Applied Missing Data Analysis*. New York: Guilford Press.

Everitt, B. S., S. Landau, M. Leese, and D. Stahl. 2011. *Cluster Analysis*, 5th ed. London: Wiley.

Fair, R. C. 1978. "A Theory of Extramarital Affairs." *Journal of Political Economy* 86: 45–61.

Faraway, J. 2006. *Extending the Linear Model with R: Generalized Linear, Mixed Effects and Nonparametric Regression Models*. Boca Raton, FL: Chapman & Hall.

Fawcett, T. 2005. "An Introduction to ROC Analysis." *Pattern Recognition Letters* 27: 861–874.

Forte, R. M. 2015. *Mastering Predictive Analytics with R*. Birmingham: Packt.

Fox, J. 2002. *An R and S-Plus Companion to Applied Regression*. Thousand Oaks, CA: Sage.

_____. 2002. "Bootstrapping Regression Models." http://mng.bz/pY9m.

_____. 2008. *Applied Regression Analysis and Generalized Linear Models*. Thousand Oaks, CA: Sage.

Fwa, T., ed. 2006. *The Handbook of Highway Engineering*, 2nd ed. Boca Raton, FL: CRC Press.

Gentleman, R. 2009. *R Programming for Bioinformatics*. Boca Raton, FL: Chapman &Hall/CRC.

Good, P. 2006. *Resampling Methods: A Practical Guide to Data Analysis*, 3rd ed. Boston: Birkhäuser.

Gorsuch, R. L. 1983. *Factor Analysis*, 2nd ed. Hillsdale, NJ: Lawrence Erlbaum.

Greene, W. H. 2003. *Econometric Analysis*, 5th ed. Upper Saddle River, NJ: Prentice Hall.

Hand, D. J. and C. C. Taylor. 1987. *Multivariate Analysis of Variance and Repeated Measures*. London: Chapman & Hall.

Harlow, L., S. Mulaik, and J. Steiger. 1997. *What If There Were No Significance Tests?* Mahwah, NJ: Lawrence Erlbaum.

Hartigan, J. A. and M. A. Wong. 1979. "A K-Means Clustering Algorithm." *Applied Statistics* 28: 100–108.

Hayton, J. C., D. G. Allen, and V. Scarpello. 2004. "Factor Retention Decisions in Exploratory Factor Analysis: A Tutorial on Parallel Analysis." *Organizational Research Methods* 7: 191–204.

Hsu, S., M. Wen, and M. Wu. 2009. "Exploring User Experiences as Predictors of MMORPG Addiction." *Computers and Education* 53: 990–999.

Johnson, J. 2000. "Multivariate Behavioral Research." 35: 1–19. ResearchGate.

_____. 2004. "Factors Affecting Relative Weights: The Influence of Sample and Measurement Error." *Organizational Research Methods* 7: 283–299.

Johnson, J. and J. LeBreton. 2004. "History and Use of Relative Importance Indices in Organizational Research." *Organizational Research Methods* 7: 238–257.

Kirk, R. 2008. *Statistics: An Introduction*, 5TH ed. California: Wadworth.

Kowarik, A. and M. Templ. 2016. "Imputation with R Package VIM." *Journal of Statistical Software*, 74: 1-16.

Koch, G. and S. Edwards. 1988. "Clinical Efficiency Trials with Categorical Data." In *Statistical Analysis with Missing Data*, 2nd ed., by R. J. A. Little and D. Rubin. Hoboken, NJ: John Wiley & Sons, 2002.

Kuhn, M. and K. Johnson. 2013. *Applied Predictive Modeling*. New York: Springer.

LeBreton, J. M and S. Tonidandel. 2008. "Multivariate Relative Importance: Extending Relative Weight Analysis to Multivariate Criterion Spaces." *Journal of Applied Psychology* 93: 329–345.

Lanz, B. 2015. *Machine Learning with R*, 2nd ed. Birmingham: Packt.

Licht, M. 1995. "Multiple Regression and Correlation." In *Reading and Understanding Multivariate Statistics*, edited by L. Grimm and P. Yarnold. Washington, DC: American Psychological Association, 19–64.

Little, R. J. A., and D. B. Rubin. (2002). *Statistical Analysis with Missing Data* (2nd ed.). New Jersey: John Wiley.

Mangasarian, O. L. and W. H. Wolberg. 1990. "Cancer Diagnosis via Linear Programming." *SIAM News*, 23: 1–18.

McCall, R. B. 2000. *Fundamental Statistics for the Behavioral Sciences*, 8th ed. New York: Wadsworth.

McCullagh, P. and J. Nelder. 1989. *Generalized Linear Models*, 2nd ed. Boca Raton, FL: Chapman & Hall.

Meyer, D., A. Zeileis, and K. Hornick. 2006. "The Strucplot Framework: Visualizing Multi-way Contingency Tables with vcd." *Journal of Statistical Software* 17 (3): 1–48. www.jstatsoft.org/v17/i03/paper.

Montgomery, D. C. 2007. *Engineering Statistics*. Hoboken, NJ: John Wiley & Sons.

Mooney, C. and R. Duval. 1993. *Bootstrapping: A Nonparametric Approach to Statistical Inference*. Monterey, CA: Sage.

Mulaik, S. 2009. *Foundations of Factor Analysis*, 2nd ed. Boca Raton, FL: Chapman & Hall.

Nenadic´, O. and M. Greenacre. 2007. "Correspondence Analysis in R, with Two- and Three-Dimensional Graphics: The ca Package." *Journal of Statistical Software* 20 (3). www.jstatsoft.org/v20/i03/paper.

Pinheiro, J. C. and D. M. Bates. 2000. *Mixed-Effects Models in S and S-PLUS*. New York: Springer.

Potvin, C., M. J. Lechowicz, and S. Tardif. 1990. "The Statistical Analysis of Ecophysiological Response Curves Obtained from Experiments Involving Repeated Measures." *Ecology* 71: 1389–1400.

Schafer, J. and J. Graham. 2002. "Missing Data: Our View of the State of the Art." *Psychological Methods* 7: 147–177.

Schlomer, G., S. Bauman, and N. Card. 2010. "Best Practices for Missing Data Management in Counseling Psychology." *Journal of Counseling Psychology* 57: 1–10.

Shah, A. 2005. "Getting Started with the boot Package in R for Statistical Inference." www.mayin.org/ajayshah/KB/R/documents/boot.html.

Shumway, R. H. and D. S. Stoffer. 2010. *Time Series Analysis and Its Applications*. New York: Springer.

Silva, R. B., D. F. Ferreirra, and D. A. Nogueira. 2008. "Robustness of Asymptotic and Bootstrap Tests for Multivariate Homogeneity of Covariance Matrices." *Ciênc. agrotec.* 32: 157–166.

Simon, J. 1997. "Resampling: The New Statistics." www.resample.com/intro-text-online/.

Snedecor, G. W. and W. G. Cochran. 1988. *Statistical Methods*, 8th ed. Ames, IA: Iowa State University Press.

Statnikov, A., C. F. Aliferis, D. P. Hardin, and I. Guyon. 2011. *A Gentle Introduction to Support Vector Machines in Biomedicine* (vol. 1: *Theory and Methods*). Hackensack, NJ: World Scientific Publishing.

Torgo, L. 2017. *Data Mining with R: Learning with Case Studies (2nd ed.)*. Boca Raton, Florida: Chapman & Hall/CRC.

UCLA: Academic Technology Services, Statistical Consulting Group. 2009. "Repeated Measures Analysis with R." http://mng.bz/a9c7.

van Buuren, S. and K. Groothuis-Oudshoorn. 2011. "MICE: Multivariate Imputation by Chained Equations in R." *Journal of Statistical Software*, 45(3), 1-67. http://mng.bz/3EH5.

Venables, W. N. and B. D. Ripley. 1999. *Modern Applied Statistics with S-PLUS*, 3rd ed. New York: Springer.

_____. 2000. *S Programming*. New York: Springer.

Westfall, P. H., Y. Hochberg, D. Rom, R. Wolfinger, and R. Tobias. 1999. *Multiple Comparisons and Multiple Tests Using the SAS System*. Cary, NC: SAS Institute.

Wickham, H. 2009a. *ggplot2: Elegant Graphics for Data Analysis*. New York: Springer.

_____. 2009b. "A Layered Grammar of Graphics." *Journal of Computational and Graphical Statistics* 19: 3–28.

_____. 2019. *Advanced R, 2nd ed.* Boca Raton, Florida: Chapman & Hall/CRC.

Wilkinson, L. 2005. *The Grammar of Graphics*. New York: Springer-Verlag.

Yu, C. H. 2003. "Resampling Methods: Concepts, Applications, and Justification." *Practical Assessment, Research & Evaluation* 8 (19). http://pareonline.net/getvn.asp?v=8&n=19.

Yu-Sung, S., A. Gelman, J. Hill, and M. Yajima. 2011. "Multiple Imputation with Diagnostics (mi) in R: Opening Windows into the Black Box." *Journal of Statistical Software* 45 (2). www.jstatsoft.org/v45/i02/paper.

Zuur, A. F., E. Ieno, N. Walker, A. A. Saveliev, and G. M. Smith. 2009. *Mixed Effects Models and Extensions in Ecology with R.* New York: Springer.

index

Get the eBook FREE!

(PDF, ePub, Kindle, and liveBook all included)

We believe that once you buy a book from us, you should be able to read it in any format we have available. To get electronic versions of this book at no additional cost to you, purchase and then register this book at the Manning website.

Go to https://www.manning.com/freebook and follow the instructions to complete your pBook registration.

That's it!
Thanks from Manning!